The JURISPRUDENCE
of the INSANITY DEFENSE

The JURISPRUDENCE of the INSANITY DEFENSE

Michael L. Perlin

Carolina Academic Press
Durham, North Carolina

Carolina Academic Press
700 Kent Street
Durham, North Carolina 27701
(919) 489-7486
FAX (919) 493-5668

Printed in the United States of America

Contents

Preface   vii

Chapter 1 Introduction   1

Chapter 2 Mental Illness, Crime, and the Culture
of Punishment   13
  A. The Current Debate: Medievalism, Myths
     and Superstitions   13
  B. Development of Psychiatry and Psychology   37
  C. The Role of Punishment   49
  D. Conclusion   70

Chapter 3 A History of Myths   73
  A. The Development of Insanity Defense Doctrine   73
  B. The Role of Externalities 100
  C. The Abolitionist Movement 133
  D. The Hinckley Verdict "Fit" 138

Chapter 4 The Law and Psychodynamic Principles 143
  A. Introduction 143
  B. The Law's Ambivalence About Psychiatry 144
  C. The Law's Ambivalence About the Psychiatric
     Method 161
  D. The Specific Rejection of Psychodynamic
     Principles: The Insanity Defense as Case Study 171
  E. The Law's Ambivalence About Punishing the
     Mentally Disabled 187
  F. Conclusion 227

Chapter 5 The Roots of Insanity Defense Myths 229
  A. Why Do Myths Persist? 229
  B. The Myths in "Real Life" 235

C. Unpacking the Myths 236
D. Conclusion 262

Chapter 6 Piercing the Veil of Consciousness 263
A. Introduction 263
B. The Significance of "Wrong" Verdicts 264
C. The Behavioral Roots of Insanity Defense
   Decision Making: The Power of Heuristic Reasoning . . 269
D. "Ordinary Common Sense" (OCS):
   The Unconsciousness of Legal Decision Making 287

Chapter 7 Authoritarianism and the Insanity Defense 331
A. Introduction 331
B. Reagan as Hinckley's Victim/Hinckley as
   Reagan's Victim. 333
C. The Roots of "Willful Deafness:" The Insanity
   Defense as Victim 348
D. Personality Theory: A Brief Overview 351

Chapter 8 New Jurisprudential Explanations 377
A. Is This Too Much for Our System to Bear?
   Of Hydraulic Pressure and Tensile Strength. 377
B. Why Do We Feel the Way We Do?
   The Meaning of Sanism. 383
C. How Do We Rationalize What We Do?
   The Role of Pretextuality. 393
D. Why Do Courts Decide Cases the Way They Do?
   The Power of Teleology and the Curious Role
   of Social Science 406
E. Conclusion. 415

Chapter 9 (How) Can We Make the Incoherent Coherent? 417
A. Introduction 417
B. The Promise of Therapeutic Jurisprudence. 417
C. Toward a Reconstruction of Insanity Defense
   Jurisprudence 438
D. Conclusion 444

Index. 447

Preface

I was a third year law student in the fall of 1968 and had signed up for an experimental seminar in Psychoanalysis and the Law (taught by Professors Martin Levine and Fritz Kinzel). The course was a breathtaking synthesis of law, psychiatry, psychoanalytic theory, psychology and politics; it remains one of the most important experiences of my professional and intellectual life. About midway through the semester, we were assigned an excerpt from Joseph Goldstein and Jay Katz's well-known article, "Abolish the 'Insanity Defense'—Why Not?"[1] I found the article to be provocative (but ultimately unconvincing, as the rest of this book should make clear), but was especially riveted by a footnote to J.C. Flugel's masterpiece, *Man, Morals, and Society*,[2] that sought to explain the roots of our deep, complex, internal needs to punish lawbreakers.

For the first time, I began to understand why criminal justice systems operate the way they do. I remember sitting with my friend and classmate Hank Wallace, and discussing what we called "the Flugel footnote" for hours. From that point on, Flugel's insights became a kind of benchmark against which I measured rationales for punishment, especially when the defendant was mentally disabled.

Many different experiences motivated me to write this book. Several years later, when I was a public defender in Trenton, New Jersey, specializing in cases of mentally disabled criminal defendants, I began to understand the way that the insanity defense served as a symbol for all that the public feared about individuals who committed seemingly inexplicable acts that, on their face, violated criminal statutes. Several years after that, when I became Director of the New Jersey Division of Mental Health Advocacy, I began to understand the significance of the attributions made about *all* mentally disabled persons based on the dominating fears that so many have about the

---

1. 72 YALE L.J. 855 (1963).
2. *See infra* chapter 2, text accompanying notes 241-42.

mentally disabled criminal defendant. Several years after that, I began to understand how one act—the shooting of President Reagan by John Hinckley—could serve as a screen upon which the public could project all of its fears about such individuals.

After I became a full-time law professor, I began to write extensively about all aspects of mental disability law, but I always returned to the question of mentally disabled defendants and the insanity defense. I was frustrated that the debate on these questions seemed so fruitless, and that we were frittering away our moral and intellectual capital on distinctions that truly made little difference in our overall social policy. I became convinced we did this because we never got to the roots of the single question that I believe is the most critical to any inquiry: why do we feel the way we do about "those people?"

I decided to write this book, in large part, to answer that question. I had been in the midst of publishing a series of articles that confronts this question as it applies to all of mental disability law, and that argues that many of the answers can be found in our "sanist" behavior that leads to "pretextual" court decisions.[3] I had also begun to consider the way that David Wexler's and Bruce Winick's trailblazing insights into therapeutic jurisprudence[4] apply to a whole variety of mental disability law areas.[5] In this book, I look at the insanity defense from these various perspectives, always keeping in mind the way ours truly is a "culture of punishment."

I have many people to thank for their help, starting with Professors Levine and Kinzel for leading me to this path nearly a quarter of a century ago. Tony Alfieri,[6] Peter Margulies, Rudy Peritz, B. James George, Richard Sherwin and Robert Blecker (all current or former colleagues at New York Law School), and Doug Mossman, Hank

---

3. See e.g., Perlin, *Morality and Pretextuality, Morality and Law: Of "Ordinary Common Sense," Heuristic Reasoning, and Cognitive Dissonance*, 19 BULL. AM. ACAD. PSYCHIATRY & L. 131 (1991); Perlin, *On "Sanism,"* 46 SMU L. REV. 373 (1992); Perlin & Dorfman, *Sanism, Social Science, and the Development of Mental Disability Law Jurisprudence*, 11 BEHAV. SCI. & L. 47 (1993); Perlin, *Pretexts and Mental Disability Law: The Case of Competency*, 47 U. MIAMI L. REV. (1993) (in press).
4. See e.g., THERAPEUTIC JURISPRUDENCE: THE LAW AS A THERAPEUTIC AGENT (D. Wexler ed. 1990); ESSAYS IN THERAPEUTIC JURISPRUDENCE (D. Wexler & B. Winick eds. 1991).
5. See 1 M.L. PERLIN, MENTAL DISABILITY LAW: CIVIL AND CRIMINAL (1989), §1.05A, at 5-8 (1992 pocket part).
6. Tony gets a special thanks for the "culture of punishment" phrase which he "gave me" during a day of fishing in southern Louisiana.

Wallace, Norman Finkel, Alex Brooks, and Jacques Quen all made helpful suggestions and comments on earlier drafts of several chapters and on the articles from which much of chapters 3–6 are adapted.[7] A remarkable team of student assistants—Susan Sheppard, Johanna Roth, Alex Widell, Cindy Dokas, Tom Ryan, Mark Dennison, Michael Bressler, Ilene Sacco and Monica Studdert—provided timely and invaluable research help,[8] and Karen Cooper of the New York Law School library staff and Roberta Tasley of the School's Media Law Center were exceptional in their support. I also wish to thank Mayapriya Long of Carolina Academic Press for her faith in this project, the New York Law School Research Fund for its generous financial support, and Deans James Simon and Harry Wellington for their support and encouragement. Finally, I wish to thank Janet Abisch for her flawless help in editing, proofreading and preparing the index to this book.

Special thanks, though, are reserved for Bob Sadoff, Joel Dvoskin, Keri Gould and Debbie Dorfman. Bob, director of the Center for Legal–Social–Medical Studies at the University of Pennsylvania, was the expert witness in the first insanity defense case I tried as a public defender in the winter of 1971–72, and has remained a close and valued friend to this day (and continues to teach me about all of the underlying issues). Joel, associate commissioner for forensic services of the New York State Office of Mental Health, has been a friend, co-author and co-presenter for over a decade, and continues to be the best and most rigorous editor I have ever had. Keri is my one colleague at New York Law School with a similar practice background to mine, and is also—perhaps not coincidentally—the one

---

7. See Perlin, *Unpacking the Myths: The Symbolism Mythology of Insanity Defense Jurisprudence*, 40 CASE W. RES. L. REV. 599 (1989-90); Perlin, *Psychodynamics and the Insanity Defense: "Ordinary Common Sense" and Heuristic Reasoning*, 69 NEB. L. REV. 3 (1990). I also wish to gratefully acknowledge both law reviews for their permission in allowing me to reprint portions of these articles, in modified form, in this book.

8. Other students helped in other ways. My courses in Criminal Law and Procedure: The Mentally Disabled Defendant and in Therapeutic Jurisprudence have always attracted a special group of bright, inquisitive and challenging minds: Daren Margolin, Lynn Mourey, Henry Dlugacz, Genie Moody, Cristina Cobb, Susan Perepeluk, Kathy Yates and the late Stephen Peduto are but a few of those who have forced me to think harder about many of the questions I try to answer in this book. I am also especially indebted to Ron Musselwhite for showing me the newspaper clipping about the Josee McNally case that forms the centerpiece of chapter 5 B.

person on whom I can always rely for a "reality check" on my writing. Our many lunchtime conversations were a major inspiration for this book. Debbie was my research assistant for two years, and now serves as a patients' rights advocate in the San Jose, California Mental Health Advocacy Project. She has been a sounding board for each section of this book, and her encouragement, support and insights have truly been extraordinary.

Finally, of course, I thank my wife Linda, my daughter Julie, and my son Alex for their love, their patience, and their constant faith in me and in this project. It is to them, to my mother, Mrs. Sophie Perlin, and to the memory of my father, the late Jacob W. Perlin, that I dedicate this book.

April 14, 1993

CHAPTER

· · ·

1

Introduction

Our insanity defense jurisprudence is incoherent. It reflects the public's episodic outrage at apparently inexplicable exculpations of obviously "guilty" acts,[1] the legislatures' pandering, pre-reflective responses to constituency cries,[2] and the judiciary's desperate ambivalence about having to decide hard cases involving mentally disabled criminal defendants.[3] Although paradoxically, we are beginning to come to grips with some of the scientific, biological, neurological and psychological reasons that play a role in the commission of some "crazy" crimes,[4] we simultaneously narrow and limit the substance of the insanity defense and the procedures used in such

---

1. The most recent obvious and important example is the response to John W. Hinckley's insanity acquittal. *See generally*, L. CAPLAN, THE INSANITY DEFENSE AND THE TRIAL OF JOHN W. HINCKLEY, JR. (1984); 3 M.L. PERLIN, MENTAL DISABILITY LAW: CIVIL AND CRIMINAL §§15.35-15.42 (1989).
2. *See, e.g.*, English, *The Light Between Twilight and Dusk: Federal Criminal Law and the Volitional Insanity Defense*, 40 HASTINGS L.J. 1, 46 (1988) (criticizing the Insanity Defense Reform Act of 1988, 18 U.S.C. §20 (1988), enacted in the wake of the Hinckley acquittal).
3. *See generally*, Perlin, *On "Sanism,"* 46 SMU L. REV. 373 (1992) (Perlin, *Sanism*); Perlin, *Pretexts and Mental Disability Law: The Case of Competency*, 47 U. MIAMI L. REV. (1993) (in press) (Perlin, *Pretexts*).
4. On the use of "crazy" in this context, *see* Morse, *Excusing the Crazy: The Insanity Defense Reconsidered*, 58 SO. CAL. L. REV. 777 (1985).

cases (and in post-acquittal commitment hearings).[5] We do this narrowing ostensibly both to lessen the possibility of a "moral mistake" (i.e., the entry of an insanity acquittal where we cannot be "sure" of the defendant's non-responsibility), and to make the choice of an insanity defense—never a high card in any criminal defense lawyer's hand—an even less attractive option.[6]

The jurisprudence's incoherence is important[7] because of the full scope of its social impact. First, through a series of legislative "reform" measures, it sanctions the criminal punishment of a significant number of individuals who—by any substantive standard—are not "responsible" for their "criminal acts." In addition to its evident punitive and damaging impact on these defendants, this outcome also makes prisons more chaotic and dangerous places for other inmates and for correctional staff. Second, it allows us—perhaps forces us—to deplete our intellectual and emotional resources and our creative energies by debating endlessly issues that are fundamentally irrelevant to the "real life" impact of the defense (e.g., whether there should be a volitional as well as a cognitive standard employed), and that lead to, at the best, illusory change. At the same time, it allows us—perhaps encourages us—to ignore empirical evidence, scientific study and moral reasoning that seek to shed light on the underlying issues.

Third, it leads us to spend money in counterproductive ways. Recent reforms will lead to more individuals being institutionalized for longer periods of time in more punitive facilities at precisely the same time that community resources are becoming scarcer. If the insanity defense is successful only in a fraction of one percent of all cases,[8] *why* do we devote such time and capital to this question, and why do we dramatically and egregiously exaggerate the impact that

---

5. For a full survey, *see* Callahan, Mayer & Steadman, *Insanity Defense in the United States—Post-Hinckley*, 11 MENT. & PHYS. DIS. L. REP. 54 (1987) (Table 2).

6. The notion of "moral mistake" is discussed in Bonnie, *The Moral Basis of the Insanity Defense*, 69 A.B.A. J. 194 (1983), and in Bonnie, *Morality, Equality and Expertise: Renegotiating the Relationship Between Psychiatry and Law*, 12 BULL. AM. ACAD. PSYCHIATRY & L. 5 (1984). *Compare* English, *supra* note 2, at 20-52 (criticizing arguments underlying Bonnie's position).

7. *See generally,* H. STEADMAN ET AL., REFORMING THE INSANITY DEFENSE: AN EVALUATION OF PRE- AND POST-HINCKLEY REFORMS (1993) (in press), manuscript at 8-10 (H. STEADMAN, REFORMING).

8. *See generally infra* chapter 3 B 1 b (1).

these cases have on the operation of our criminal justice system?[9]

Fourth, it leads us to avoid consideration of the single most important issue in mental disability law (one that is magnified many times in insanity defense analysis): why do we feel the way we do about "these people," and how do these feelings control our legislative, judicial and administrative policies? As I will subsequently explore, it is the answer to *this* question that is the "wild card" here, and it is essential that we see its role in the incoherence of the policies I am discussing.

No aspect of the criminal justice system is more controversial than is the insanity defense. Nowhere else does the successful employment of a defense regularly bring about cries for its abolition; no other aspect of the criminal law inspires position papers from trade associations spanning the full range of professions and political entities.[10] When the defense is successful in a high-level publicity case, (especially when it involves a defendant whose "factual guilt" is clear), the acquittal triggers public outrage and serves vividly as a screen upon which each relevant interest group can project its fears and concerns.

Although, on one hand, the defense is a reflection of the "fundamental moral principles of our criminal law"[11] and serves as a bulwark of the law's "moorings of condemnation for moral failure,"[12] we remain fixated on it as a symbol of all that is "wrong" with the criminal justice system and as a source of social and political anger. It is thus attacked by the nation's Attorney General as a major stumbling block in the restoration of the "effectiveness of Federal law enforcement" and as tilting the balance "between the forces of law and the forces of lawlessness."[13]

Our fixation on the insanity defense has evolved into a familiar story. The insanity defense, so common wisdom goes, encourages the factually (and morally) guilty to seek refuge in an excuse premised upon pseudoscience, shaky rehabilitation theory, and faintly duplici-

---

9.   *See generally* chapter 2 A.
10. *E.g.*, after the Hinckley acquittal, the National Association of Counties formed a committee to study the question of whether the insanity defense should be abolished. *See* L. CAPLAN, *supra* note 1, at 116.
11. United States v. Lyons, 739 F. 2d 994 (5th Cir. 1984) (Rubin, J., dissenting).
12. Livermore & Meehl, *The Virtues of* M'Naghten, 51 MINN. L. REV. 789, 797 (1967).
13. *The Insanity Defense Hearings Before the Senate Comm. on the Judiciary*, 97th Cong., 2d Sess. 27 (1982).

tous legal *légèrdemain*. The defense, allegedly, is used frequently (mostly in abusive ways), is generally successful, and often results in brief slap-on-the-wrist periods of confinement in loosely supervised settings; since it is basically a no-risk maneuver, the story continues, even when it fails, the defendant will suffer no harm. Purportedly, the defense is used disproportionately in death penalty cases (often involving garish multiple homicides), and inevitably results in trials in which high-priced experts do battle in front of befuddled jurors who are inevitably unable to make sense of contradictory, highly abstract and speculative testimony. Finally, the defense is seen as being subject to the worst sort of malingering or feigning, and it is assumed that, through this gambit, clever defendants can "con" gullible, "soft" experts into accepting a fraudulent defense.[14]

The largely unseen counterworlds of empirical reality, behavioral advance, scientific discovery and philosophical inquiry paint quite a different picture. Empirically, the insanity defense is rarely used, is less frequently successful, and generally results in lengthy stays in maximum security facilities (often far more restrictive than many prisons or reformatories) for far longer periods of time than the defendants would have been subject to had they been sentenced criminally.

It is also a risky plea; where it fails, penal terms are generally significantly longer than in like cases where the defense was not raised. The defense is most frequently pled in cases *not* involving a victim's death, and is often raised in cases involving minor property crimes. The vast majority of cases are so-called "walkthroughs" (that is, where both state and defense experts agree to the severity of the defendant's mental illness and his lack of responsibility). Feigned insanity is rare; successfully feigned insanity even rarer.[15] It is far more likely for a jury to convict in a case in which the defendant meets the relevant substantive insanity criteria than to acquit where he does not.[16]

---

14. *See generally*, Perlin, *After Hinckley: Old Myths, New Realities, and the Future of the Insanity Defense*, 5 DIRECTIONS IN PSYCHIATRY Lesson 22, at 4 (1985).
15. There is some startling evidence, however, that certain legitimately non-responsible criminal defendants feign *sanity. See e.g.*, Lewis et al., *Psychiatric and Psychoeducational Characteristics of 15 Death Row Inmates in the United States*, 143 AM. J. PSYCHIATRY 838, 841 (1986) (all but one of a sample of death row inmates studied attempted to minimize rather than exaggerate their degree of psychiatric disorder).
16. *See e.g.*, Rogers, Wasyliw & Cavanaugh, *Evaluating Insanity: A Study of*

As a result of these myths, we demand legislative "reform." This reform leads to a variety of changes in insanity defense statutes—in substantive standards, in burdens of proof, in standards of proof, in the creation of "hybrid" verdicts such as "guilty but mentally ill," even, in a few instances, in supposed "abolition" of the defense itself. No matter what their final form, these reforms stem from one primary source: "the public's overwhelming fear of the future acts of [released insanity] acquittees."[17]

Behaviorally, researchers are beginning to develop sophisticated assessment tools that can translate insanity concepts into quantifiable variables that appear to easily meet the traditional legal standard of "reasonable scientific certainty."[18] Scientifically, the development of "hard science" diagnostic tools (such as CT scanning or Magnetic Resonance Imaging) has helped determine the presence and severity of certain neurological illnesses that may be causally related to some forms of criminal behavior.[19] Finally, moral philosophers are increasingly trying—with some measure of success—to clarify such difficult underlying issues as the contextual meaning of terms such as "causation," "responsibility," and "rationality."[20]

Yet, these discoveries and developments have had virtually no impact on the basic debate. They are ignored, trivialized, denied and distinguished. The gap between myth and reality is a vast one that widens exponentially with the passage of time. Although the gap is acknowledged by virtually every empirical researcher who has studied any of these issues,[21] it continues to grow. We continue to honor and reify these myths through legislative action and judicial decisions

---

Construct Validity, 8 LAW & HUM. BEHAV. 293 (1984).

17. H. STEADMAN, REFORMING, *supra* note 7, manuscript at 69, quoting Mayer, "Insanity Defense Reforms: Pre- and Post-Hinckley," (paper presented at the annual meeting of the Law & Society Association, June 1987), manuscript at 28.

18. *See generally*, Rodriguez, LeWinn & Perlin, *The Insanity Defense Under Siege: Legislative Assaults and Legal Rejoinders*, 14 RUTGERS L.J. 397, 401-02 (1983); 3 M.L. PERLIN, *supra* note 1, §15.37, at 391-95.

19. *See e.g.*, Garber, *Use of Magnetic Resonance Imaging in Psychiatry*, 145 AM. J. PSYCHIATRY 164 (1988).

20. *See e.g.*, Morse, *supra* note 3; M. MOORE, LAW AND PSYCHIATRY: RETHINKING THE RELATIONSHIP (1984).

21. For the most recent confirmatory studies, *see* Callahan, Steadman, McGreevy & Robbins, *The Volume and Characteristics of Insanity Defense Pleas: An Eight State Study*, 19 BULL. AM. ACAD. PSYCHIATRY & L. 331, 332-36 (1991) (Callahan); H. STEADMAN, REFORMING, *supra* note 7.

and in public forums. The public continues to endorse a substantive standard for insanity that approximates the "wild beast" test of 1724,[22] and legislators look to the potential abolition of the insanity defense as a palliative for rampant crime problems in spite of incontrovertible statistics that show that the defense is raised in a fraction of one percent of felony prosecutions (and is successful only about one quarter of the time).[23] Our response to the most celebrated insanity acquittal of the twentieth century—that of John W. Hinckley—was to shrink the insanity defense in federal jurisdictions to a more narrow and restrictive version of an 1843 test that was seen as biologically, scientifically and morally outdated at the very time of its creation.[24]

Why is this? What is there about the insanity defense that allows for (perhaps encourages), such a discontinuity between firmly-held belief and statistical reality? Why is our insanity defense jurisprudence so irrational? Why do we continue to obsess about questions that are fundamentally irrelevant to the core jurisprudential inquiry of who should be exculpated because of lack of mental responsibility?[25] Why do we allow ourselves to be immobilized by an irresoluble debate? Why does our willful blindness allow us—lead us?—to ignore scientific and empirical developments and, instead, force us to

---

22. *See* Rex v. Arnold, 16 How. St. Tr. 695 (1724), in 16 T.B. HOWELL, A COMPLETE COLLECTION OF STATE TRIALS 695 (1812) (insanity acquittal proper where defendant is "totally deprived of his understanding and memory, and doth not know what he is doing, no more than a brute or wild beast, such a one is never the object of punishment"); Roberts, Golding & Fincham, *Implicit Theories of Criminial Responsibility Decision Making and the Insanity Defense*, 11 LAW & HUM. BEHAV. 207 (1987).
23. *See* Callahan, *supra* note 21, at 334, 336.
24. *See* 1 M.L. PERLIN, *supra* note 1, §15.04, at 292-94.
25. I recognize that this phraseology accepts as a given that there must be some sort of an insanity defense. Others disagree. *See e.g.*, Halpern, *The Fiction of Legal Insanity and the Misuse of Psychiatry*, 2 J. L. & MED. 18 (1980); Halpern, *Elimination of the Exculpatory Insanity Rule: A Modern Societal Need*, 6 PSYCHIATRIC CLINICS OF N. AMER. 611 (1983); Halpern, *The Insanity Defense in the 21st Century*, 35 INT'L J. OFFENDER THERAPY & COMP. CRIMINOL. 187 (1992). As I will make clear subsequently, I distinguish between Dr. Halpern's thoughtful and principled opposition and other opposition inspired by what I see as the cynical political opportunism of the Nixon and Reagan Administrations. On the lack of empirical data supporting Nixon's allegations, *see e.g.*, Pasewark & Pasewark, *Insanity Revised: Once More Over the Cuckoo's Nest*, 6 J. PSYCHIATRY & L. 481 (1978); on Reagan's targeting of the insanity defense as a criminal justice priority, *see* Keilitz, *Researching and Reforming the Insanity Defense*, 39 RUTGERS L. REV. 289, 306 n. 97 (1987).

waste time, energy and passion on a series of fruitless inquiries that will have negligible impact on any of the underlying social problems? Why, most importantly, do we continue to ignore the most fundamental and core question: why do we feel the way we do about "these people," and why, when we engage in our endless debates and incessant retinkering with insanity defense doctrine, do we not seriously consider our answer to this question?

Commentators have alternative, complementary explanations. Professor Bandes has suggested that the evolution of the insanity defense is "a continuing struggle to incorporate expanding knowledge into our system of laws."[26] Professor Spring has hinted that the controversy continues "because the subject combines all the high dramatic elements of good fiction."[27] Professor Hermann has focused upon the underlying issues that go to "the core philosophical premise of the criminal law."[28] In an earlier article I argued, perhaps a trifle over-dramatically, that the issue remained "the raw nerve at the cutting edge of law and psychiatry."[29]

My thesis now is that our insanity defense jurisprudence is a prisoner of a combination of these empirical myths and related social meta-myths.[30] Born of a medievalist and fundamentalist religious vision of the roots of mental illness and the relationships between mental illness, crime and punishment, the myths continue to dominate the landscape in spite of (and utterly independently of) the impressive scientific and behavioral evidence to the contrary.[31]

The legal system is a prisoner of these myths and of the concomitant powerful symbols that permeate any criminal trial (especially any *highly visible* criminal trial) at which a non-responsibility defense is raised.[32] It rejects psychodynamic explanations of human

---

26. Bandes, *Developments in the Insanity Defense*, 10 BARRISTER 45 (1983).

27. Spring, *The End of Insanity*, 19 WASHBURN L.J. 23, 23 (1979).

28. D. HERMANN, THE INSANITY DEFENSE: PHILOSOPHICAL, HISTORICAL AND LEGAL PERSPECTIVES 3 (1983).

29. Perlin, *"The Things We Do For Love:" John Hinckley's Trial and the Future of the Insanity Defense in the Federal Courts* (book review of L. CAPLAN, *supra* note 1), 30 N.Y. L. SCH. L. REV. 857, 863 (1985).

30. By this I mean myths that have developed *about* and *around* the empirical myths. For a partial explanation, *see* V. FOLEY, AN INTRODUCTION TO FAMILY THERAPY 74-75 (1974) (explaining metacommunication theory).

31. *See e.g.*, Rogers, Seaman & Clark, *Assessment of Criminal Responsibility: Initial Validation of the R-CRAS with the M'Naghten and GBMI Standards*, 9 INT'L J. L. & PSYCHIATRY 67 (1986).

32. *See e.g.*, Keilitz, *supra* note 25; Monahan, *Abolish the Insanity Defense—Not*

motivation and behavior,[33] and remains intensely suspicious of concepts of mental health and disability, of mental health professionals, and of the ability of such professionals to assess or ameliorate mental disability.[34] As a result, it remains most comfortable with all-or-nothing tests of mental illness,[35] and demands that non-responsible defendants match visual images of "deranged madmen" who, indisputably, "look crazy."[36] Again, it does this in utter disregard of the past 150 years of scientific and behavioral learning.

As will be clear from the remainder of the book, I am an unapologetic insanity defense retentionist, and, at heart, an expansionist, and am most comfortable with the positions taken by Judge David Bazelon.[37] Yet, I believe that, even had Judge Bazelon been able to convince his colleagues on the judiciary that a broader insanity defense would have "illuminate[d] and strengthen[ed] the moral authority of the criminal law,"[38] the defense, operationally, would still be incoherent. I write this book to argue that, until we turn our attention to the reasons *why* our jurisprudence in this area has developed as it has, arguments over, say, the relationship of the volitional prong of the ALI/Model Penal Code test[39] to the notion of "moral mistake"[40] will have little ultimate impact on the way we think about the insanity defense plea and those who plead it.

There have been many efforts to explain insanity defense jurisprudence, but almost all of those treat the question in the way that

---

Yet, 26 RUTGERS L. REV. 719 (1973).
33. *See e.g.*, for the classic explanation, State v. Sikora, 44 N.J. 453, 210 A. 2d 193, 204 (1965) (Weintraub, C.J., concurring).
34. *See e.g.*, Perlin, *The Supreme Court, the Mentally Disabled Criminal Defendant, and Symbolic Values: Random Decisions, Hidden Rationales, or "Doctrinal Abyss?"* 29 ARIZ. L. REV. 1 (1987). For a recent opinion expressing this suspicion, *see* Foucha v. Louisiana, 112 S. Ct. 1780, 1796-1802 (1992) (Thomas, J., dissenting), discussed in this context in Perlin & Dorfman, *Sanism, Social Science, and the Development of Mental Disability Law Jurisprudence*, 11 BEHAV. SCI. & L. 47, 60-61 (1993).
35. *See e.g.*, Johnson v. State, 292 Md. 405, 439 A. 2d 542, 552 (1982) ("For the purposes of guilt determination, an offender is either wholly sane or wholly insane").
36. For a classic statement, *see* Battalino v. People, 118 Colo. 587, 199 P. 2d 897, 901 (1948) (finding no evidence of defendant exhibiting "paleness, wild eyes and trembling" in affirming jury's rejection of insanity defense).
37. *See generally*, D. BAZELON, QUESTIONING AUTHORITY: JUSTICE AND CRIMINAL LAW 1-85 (1988).
38. *Id.* at 2.
39. *See infra* chapter 3 A 1 c (3).
40. *See infra* chapter 5, text accompanying note 55.

the Martians in the parable view the elephant—by focusing on one isolated aspect of the problem and then attempting to extrapolate a systemic theory based upon that partial observation. In this book, I argue that our efforts to understand the insanity defense and insanity-pleading defendants are doomed to eternal intellectual, political and moral gridlock unless we are willing to take a fresh look at the underlying doctrine through a series of filters: empirical research, scientific discovery, moral philosophy, cognitive and moral psychology, sociology, communications theory and political science. Only in this manner can we attempt to articulate the sort of coherent and integrated perspective that is necessary if we are to truly unpack the myths from the defense's facade and reconstruct a meaningful insanity defense jurisprudence.

I will approach these questions in the following manner. In chapter 2, I will demonstrate how the Hinckley trial served as a paradigm through which to understand the motivation animating the public's fury in response to the successful use of the insanity defense in a celebrated case, and how the legislative "reform" action undertaken in its aftermath perfectly reflected the contrast between insanity defense myth and reality. Then, I will trace the parallel development of psychiatry and substantive insanity defense doctrines, show how the tensions between the two emerged from the legal system's ambivalence about psychiatry and mental disability concepts, discuss how these tensions are exacerbated in famous cases (such as Hinckley's), and link these developments to our "culture of punishment" that flows from the medievalist conceptions of sin that have traditionally animated our beliefs in this area.

In chapter 3, I will trace the development of substantive insanity defense doctrine and argue that the lack of interest in such "externalities" as empirical research, behavioral instruments, scientific discovery and philosophical inquiry is largely a reflection of the legal system's persistent rejection of psychodynamic principles and our overwhelming ambivalence about psychiatry and mental disability. In chapter 4, I will then demonstrate that we reject psychodynamic principles because we see psychiatry as soft, exculpatory, confusing, "unseeable" or "imprecise," and view psychiatrists (especially forensic psychiatrists) as "wizards" or "charlatans." Even in those few areas where we appear to be inappropriately sympathetic to insanity pleaders—in cases of matricides or apparently unmotivated shootings by police officers—our judgments are informed by the same rejection of psychodynamic principles. These attitudes result in legal ambivalence about punishing mentally disabled offenders: defendants who unsuccessfully raise the insanity defense, defendants who seek to raise mental illness as a mitigating factor in a death penalty trial, and defendants who claim mental illness short of an actual insanity defense.

In an effort to understand why this is, I argue further in chapter 5 that these empirical myths are informed by social meta-myths. When *these* myths are unpacked, there are at least four core governing principles that society is unwilling to abandon: the "fear of faking" (that mental illness is easily feigned for duplicitous purposes), the sense that mental illness is critically "different" from other illnesses, the need for a successful insanity defendant to "look crazy" (in a way that is consonant with popular mass media depictions), and, ultimately, the idea that it is generally inappropriate to allow mental illness to excuse criminal punishment in all but the grossest cases.

In chapter 6, I then recast the question to ask *why* these myths persist in spite of all of the contrary behavioral and scientific evidence. Here, I identify two villains: the pernicious effect of heuristic reasoning and thinking (the use of implicit cognitive devices to over-simplify complex information processing tasks which often lead to distorted and systematically erroneous decisions),[41] and the way we use non-reflective, self-referential, allegedly "common sensical" thinking in our assumptions about mentally disabled criminal defendants.[42] Until we come to grips with the power of these thought processes, we cannot begin to understand (1) why the insanity myths have persisted, (2) what values retention of these myths reinforce, (3) why these myths become even more powerful in a case such as Hinckley's in which the victim, Ronald Reagan, appeared to so many to be an archetypal patriarch, and (4) why these myths continue to hold the legal system in thrall. I argue that this *faux* "ordinary

---

41. *See e.g.*, Saks & Kidd, *Human Information Processing and Adjudication: Trial by Heuristics*, 15 Law & Soc'y Rev. 123 (1980-81); Bersoff, *Judicial Deference to Nonlegal Decisionmakers: Imposing Simplistic Solutions on Problems of Cognitive Complexity in Mental Disability Law*, 46 SMU L. Rev 329 (1992); Perlin, *Are Courts Competent to Decide Competency Questions? Stripping the Facade from* United States v. Charters, 38 U. Kan. L. Rev. 957 (1990).

42. *See generally*, Sherwin, *Dialects and Dominance: A Study of Rhetorical Fields in the Law of Confessions*, 136 U. Pa. L. Rev. 729 (1988) (discussing "ordinary common sense" (OCS)); Perlin, *Morality and Pretextuality, Psychiatry and Law: Of "Ordinary Common Sense," Heuristic Reasoning, and Cognitive Dissonance*, 19 Bull. Am. Acad. Psychiatry & L. 131 (1991).

common sense" (OCS) and heuristic reasoning are major factors in the shaping of our insanity defense jurisprudence, and that these influences help explain and illuminate the extent to which this jurisprudence has developed irrationally and incoherently. In chapter 7, I look further at the impact of personality theory on insanity defense developments, focusing on the meaning of the "authoritarian personality," consider the influence of authoritarianism in the shaping of our insanity defense policies, and conclude that an understanding of this construct will help better illuminate the way that the insanity defense serves as an unwitting litmus test for our political, legal and social structures.

In chapter 8, I search for new jurisprudential explanations. First, I question whether the underlying problems are ever soluble, asking whether our legal system has enough "tensile strength" to withstand public fury over "wrong" insanity defense verdicts, and suggest that the concepts of cognitive dissonance and psychological reactance be employed in formulating a tentative answer.[43]

Next, I turn to the core question of why we feel the way we do about these matters and argue that we cannot formulate a response until we acknowledge the domination of what I call "sanism" over all aspects of mental disability law.[44] By this, I mean that insanity defense decision making—like all other mental disability law decision making—is inspired by (and reflects) the same kinds of irrational, unconscious, bias-driven stereotypes and prejudices that are exhibited in racist, sexist, homophobic and religiously- and ethnically-bigoted decision making.

Then, I argue that we rationalize our sanist attitudes and behavior through what I call "pretextuality,"[45] that is, that the legal system regularly accepts (either implicitly or explicitly) dishonest testimony in all mental disability cases, (but perhaps *especially* in insanity defense cases), and countenances liberty deprivations in disingenuous ways that bear little or no relationship to caselaw or statutes.

Next, I assess why courts decide these cases the way that they do

---

43. *See generally*, Perlin, *supra* note 42.
44. *See generally*, Perlin, *Sanism, supra* note 3; Perlin & Dorfman, *supra* note 34; M. Perlin, "The Americans With Disabilities Act and Mentally Disabled Persons: Can Sanist Myths Be Undone?" (paper presented at Hofstra Law School Disability Rights Conference, November 1992).
45. *See* Perlin, *supra* note 42; Perlin, *Pretexts, supra* note 3; Perlin & Dorfman, *supra* note 34.

and conclude that one answer is the judicial system's teleological use of social science data.[46] Courts, in short, generally dislike and distrust such data; as a result of this attitude, social science literature and studies that allow courts to meet predetermined sanist ends are frequently privileged while data that would require judges to question such ends are frequently rejected. Insanity defense decision making is, I argue, a perfect reflector of judicial teleology.

In chapter 9, I search for alternative jurisprudential methodologies that might make coherent our insanity defense's incoherence. Here, I examine the doctrine of therapeutic jurisprudence—the study of the role of the law as a therapeutic or antitherapeutic agent.[47] I conclude that the employment of a therapeutic jurisprudence methodology can illuminate a series of "pressure points" in insanity defense decision making and help us in a reconstruction of insanity defense doctrine, and that, when coupled with an understanding of sanism, pretextuality and judicial teleology, therapeutic jurisprudence can best answer the hard questions raised in insanity defense cases.

Finally, I conclude by offering a series of prescriptions for legal system policymakers, the media, behavioral researchers, lawyers representing mentally disabled criminal defendants or state officials charged with the prosecutions of such cases,[48] forensic witnesses who testify in such cases,[49] scholars writing about these issues,[50] and political figures who will—inevitably—again be faced with "outrageous" cases that consume the hearts and minds of the American public. My hope is that, if these recommendations are thoughtfully evaluated and considered, the insanity defense will no longer develop as it has for at least the past 150 years—out of consciousness.

---

46. Perlin, *supra* note 42; Perlin & Dorfman, *supra* note 34; Appelbaum, *The Empirical Jurisprudence of the United States Supreme Court*, 13 AM. J. L. & MED. 335, 341-42 (1987).
47. *See e.g.,* THERAPEUTIC JURISPRUDENCE: THE LAW AS A THERAPEUTIC AGENT (D. Wexler ed. 1990); ESSAYS IN THERAPEUTIC JURISPRUDENCE (D. Wexler & B. Winick eds. 1991).
48. *See* Perlin, *Fatal Assumption: A Critical Evaluation of the Role of Counsel in Mental Disability Cases*, 16 LAW & HUM. BEHAV. 39 (1992).
49. *See* Perlin, *Power Imbalances in Therapeutic and Forensic Relationships*, 9 BEHAV. SCI. & L. 111 (1991).
50. *See* M. Perlin and D. Dorfman, "The Invisible Renaissance of Mental Disability Law Scholarship: A Case Study in Subordination" (manuscript in progress).

CHAPTER

. . .

2

Mental Illness, Crime, and the Culture of Punishment

A. The Current Debate: Medievalism, Myths, and Superstitions

1. Introduction

The acquittal of John W. Hinckley galvanized the American public in a way that led directly to the reversal of 150 years of study and understanding of the complexities of psychological behavior and the relationship between mental illness and certain violent acts.[1] The public's outrage over a jurisprudential system that could allow a defendant who shot an American president on national television to plead "not guilty" (for *any* reason) became a "river of fury" after the jury's verdict was announced.[2]

In retrospect, this firestorm should have been entirely predictable. To the public, the defense strategy, the trial and the subsequent

---

1. *See* Callahan, Meyer & Steadman, *Insanity Defense in the United States—Post-Hinckley*, 11 MENT. & PHYS. DIS. L. REP. 54, 55 (1987); Wexler, *Redefining the Insanity Problem*, 53 GEO. WASH. L. REV. 528, 529-30 (1985); *see generally*, L. CAPLAN, THE INSANITY DEFENSE AND THE TRIAL OF JOHN W. HINCKLEY, JR. (1984).
2. *See* Perlin, *"The Things We Do For Love:" John Hinckley's Trial and the Future of the Insanity Defense in the Federal Courts* (Book Review), 30 N.Y.L. SCH. L. REV. 857, 859 (1985) (review of L. CAPLAN, *supra* note 1).

verdict were vivid reifications of many of the most powerful insanity defense myths—an intelligent (albeit troubled) defendant who plans a fiendish crime (not coincidentally, against one of the nation's most beloved and patriarchal political leaders), hires a top-dollar Washington, D.C. law firm, retains a panel of heavily-credentialed forensic mental health witnesses, and proceeds to successfully bamboozle a well-meaning (but evidently out of their depths) lay jury so as to avoid severe punishment.[3] The public, to no one's surprise, reacted with swift outrage.[4]

2. The Hinckley Case as Paradigm

a. The public furor.   Just as "[c]onstitutional law tends to define itself through reaction to great cases,"[5] insanity defense jurisprudence tends to define itself through reaction to scandalous, sensational, hysteria-creating or outrageous cases.[6] The development of the insanity defense

---

3.   *See generally,* P. Low, J. Jeffries & R. Bonnie, The Trial of John W. Hinckley, Jr.: Studying the Insanity Defense (1986). There may be some dispute over my characterization of the public's evaluation of the jury as "well-meaning." On the night that the verdict was announced, I was a guest on a national radio call-in show; several callers took the position that the all-black jury intentionally acquitted Hinckley because of their negative political feelings about President Reagan. I have no way of knowing if these calls reflected public opinion or were merely the type of "outliers" that frequently call such shows to make their views known. Apparently, Judge Barrington Parker—the trial judge and a black man—received similar correspondence. *See* L. Caplan, *supra* note 1, at 117.

4.   Eighty-three percent of respondents to an ABC overnight poll thought that justice was not done; seventy-five percent of those questioned in another poll stated that they did not did not favor exculpation for criminal acts based upon insanity. *See* 3 M. L. Perlin, Mental Disability Law: Civil and Criminal (1989), §15.36 at 390 (citing sources). Other polls placed the percentage of the public favoring abolition at as high as ninety percent. *See* Farabee & Spearly, *The New Insanity Law in Texas: Reliable Testimony and Judicial Review of Release,* 24 S. Tex. L.J. 671, 671 (1983).

5.   Sunstein, Lochner's *Legacy,* 87 Colum. L. Rev. 873, 873 (1987).

6.   This type of reactionary response to the Hinckley case has been described as exhibiting the "vividness" effect—the statistically undue prominence given to the characteristics of a phenomenon because of the concreteness and immediacy of a present example. *See* Finer, *Should the Insanity Defense Be Abolished? An Introduction to the Debate,* 1 J. L. & Health 113, 113 n. 2 (1986-87), *citing* Rosenhan, *Psychological Realities and Judicial Policy,* 19 Stan. Law 10 (1984). *See generally infra* chapter 6 C. On the way mechanisms that govern the release of hospitalized insanity acquittees may operate differentially in cases involving patients well known to the public, *see* Scott, Zonana & Getz, *Monitoring Insanity Acquittees: Connecticut's Psychiatry Review Board,* 41 Hosp. & Com-

in the last century and a half has been marked by the idiosyncratic, episodic and distorted responses of an angry public,[7] a frenzied media,[8] reactive legislatures,[9] and ultimately, "sanist" courts[10] to the use of the defense in such cases as the trials of Hinckley or Daniel M'Naghten.[11]

Both cases involved an attack on an authority figure and resulted in an acquittal that stunned the public and shocked its conscience.[12] When the defense is successful in such a case, it becomes

---

MUN. PSYCHIATRY 980, 980 (1989).

7. See e.g., I. KEILITZ & H. FULTON, THE INSANITY DEFENSE AND ITS ALTERNATIVES: A GUIDE FOR POLICYMAKERS 3 (1984).

8. On the role of the media, see e.g., Surette, *Media Trials*, 17 J. CRIM. JUST. 293 (1989).

9. On the response of legislatures to public opinion in responding to sensational insanity defense cases, see Mickenberg, *A Pleasant Surprise: The Guilty But Mentally Ill Verdict Has Both Succeeded On Its Own Right and Successfully Preserved the Traditional Role of the Insanity Defense*, 55 U. CIN. L. REV. 943, 972-74 (1987). The impetus for the passage of the federal Insanity Defense Reform Act of 1984, see 18 U.S.C. §17 (1988), was undoubtedly Hinckley's acquittal. See People v. Serravo, 823 P. 2d 128, 134 n. 8 (Colo. 1992); see generally infra chapter 2 A 2 c. Compare Brooks, *The Constitutionality and Morality of Civilly Committing Violent Sexual Predators*, 15 U. PUGET SOUND L. REV. 709, 712 (1992) ("Shocking events can generate beneficial responses, not only hysterical, ill thought-out ones").

10. See Perlin, On "Sanism," 46 SMU L. REV. 373 (1992); see generally infra chapter 8 B.

11. M'Naghten shot Edward Drummond, the secretary of the man he mistook for his intended victim, England's Prime Minister Robert Peel. His trial, "the most significant case in the history of the insanity defense in England," Hermann & Sor, *Convicting or Confining? Alternative Directions in Insanity Defense Reform: Guilty But Mentally Ill Versus New Rules for Release of Insanity Acquittees*, B.Y.U. L. REV. 499, 508 (1983), led to the creation of what has come to be known as the *M'Naghten* test, see M'Naghten's Case, 8 Eng. Rep. 718 (1843); see generally 3 M.L. PERLIN, supra note 4, §15.04 at 289-94; DANIEL McNAUGHTON: HIS TRIAL AND THE AFTERMATH (D.J. West & A. Walk eds. 1977); R. MORAN, KNOWING RIGHT FROM WRONG: THE INSANITY-DEFENSE OF DANIEL McNAUGHTAN (1981). It has been asserted that, had M'Naghten's victim been a person of "no importance," the event would have "scarcely troubled the waters of medico-legal history." See Rollin, *Crime and Mental Disorder: Daniel McNaughton, a Case in Point*, 50 MEDICO-LEGAL J. 102, 102 (1982).

12. For parallels between the *M'Naghten* and *Hinckley* cases, see e.g., English, *The Light Between Twilight and Dusk: Federal Criminal Law and the Volitional Insanity Defense*, 40 HASTINGS L.J. 1, 4-8 (1989); Golding, Eaves & Kowaz, *The Assessment, Treatment and Community Outcome of Insanity Acquittees*, 12 INT'L J. L. & PSYCHIATRY 149 (1989); Mickenberg, supra note 9, at 946-59; Sadoff, *Insanity: Evaluation of a Medicolegal Concept*, 9 TRANSACTIONS & STUD. COLL. PHYSICIANS PHILADELPHIA 237, 246 n. 47 (1987). Researchers

society's handy scapegoat; as Dr. Loren Roth has suggested, when a "wrong verdict" is entered in a sensational trial, the American public may simply be nothing more than a "bad loser."[13]

Sensational trials such as Hinckley's consume the hearts and minds of the American public.[14] They reflect our basic dissatisfaction with the perceived incompatibility of the due process and crime control models of criminal law[15] and with the notion that psychiatric "excuses" can allow a "guilty" defendant to "beat a rap" and escape punishment. Such dissatisfaction leads to a predictable response, *especially* when the defendant—like Hinckley—is perceived as one *not* sufficiently "like us" to warrant empathy or sympathy.[16] As John Hinckley was obsessed with Jodie Foster, so were we obsessed with John Hinckley.[17]

---

have begun to study profiles of individuals who have threatened the President in an effort to compare them to "average" patients who are seriously mentally disabled. *See e.g.,* Shore, Filson & Rae, *Violent Crime Arrest Rates of White House Case Subjects and Matched Control Subjects,* 147 AM. J. PSYCHIATRY 746 (1990).

Not all such changes in mental disability law follow in the wake of attacks on famous persons, though. *See e.g.,* Prins, *"How Dangerous Is It That This Man Goes Loose!"* 32 MED., SCI. & LAW 93, 93 (1992) (guidelines governing the release of mentally disordered offenders changed in Great Britain "in the wake of the killing of a social worker...by a former mental patient").

13. Roth, *Preserve but Limit the Insanity Defense,* 58 PSYCHIATRIC Q. 91, 91 (1986-87). Contrarily, the decision by a Milwaukee jury to reject the insanity defense in the case of Jeffrey Dahmer led a panel of experts to conclude that the defense was "alive and well." *See* De Benedictis, *Sane Serial Killer; Experts Say Insanity Plea Alive and Well, Thanks Partly to Dahmer Verdict,* 72 A.B.A. J. 22 (April 1992); *compare Crossfire* (Jan. 31, 1992) (Transcript #499) (experts debate "whether the insanity defense should be disallowed *in light of the Jeffrey Dahmer* case") (emphasis added) (full next available on NEXIS).

On the significance of "wrong" (or politically unpopular) verdicts, *see generally infra* chapter 6 A.

14. *See* Perlin, *supra* note 2, at 857. On our general "societal preoccupation with sensational jury trials," *see* Thomas & Pollack, *Rethinking Guilt, Juries, and Jeopardy,* 91 MICH. L. REV. 1, 8 (1992).

15. In this context, *see* Fentiman, *"Guilty But Mentally Ill:" The Real Verdict Is Guilty,* 26 B.C. L. REV. 601, 603 (1985); *see generally,* Miller, *Ideology and Criminal Justice Policy: Some Current Issues,* 64 J. CRIM. L. & CRIMINOLOGY 141, 143-46 (1973); Viano, *Victims' Rights and the Constitution: Reflections on a Bicentennial,* 33 CRIME & DELINQ. 438, 441-42 (1987); *see generally,* H. PACKER, THE LIMITS OF THE CRIMINAL SANCTION (1968).

16. *See e.g.,* Sendor, *Crimes as Communication: An Interpretive Theory of the Insanity Defense and the Mental Elements of Crime,* 74 GEO. L.J. 1371, 1396 (1986). On the role of empathy and sympathy in certain limited insanity defense decision making, *see generally infra* chapter 4 D 2-3.

17. *See* Braswell, *Resurrection of the Ultimate Issue Rule: Federal Rule of Evidence*

b. The Congressional debate. Members of Congress responded quickly to the public's outpouring of outrage by introducing twenty-six separate pieces of legislation designed to limit, modify, severely shrink or abolish the insanity defense;[18] the debate on these bills illuminates with clarity the character of the legislative decision making process. Statements by legislators introducing these bills or by Reagan Administration spokespersons supporting them reflected the fears and superstitions that have traditionally animated the insanity debate and the power of the behavioral and empirical myths about the defense's use, as well as the public's core ambivalence about mentally disabled criminal defendants.[19] Hyperbolically, "reform" of the insanity defense became the Maginot line at which "nothing less than the credibility of our Federal justice system [was] at stake."[20]

(1) Fears and superstitions. Former Attorney General Meese argued that eliminating the insanity defense would "rid...the streets of some of the most dangerous people that are out there, that are

---

    704(b) and the Insanity Defense, 72 CORNELL L. REV. 620, 626 (1987) (discussing the nation's "obsession" with Hinckley).

18. At the time of the Hinckley acquittal, the Model Penal Code-American Law Institute test was operative in all but one federal circuit. Under the volitional prong of the ALI test, a defendant was not responsible if he lacked substantial capacity "to conform his conduct to the requirements of law." *See* MODEL PENAL CODE §4.01(1). *See generally*, 3 M.L. PERLIN, *supra* note 4, §15.07 at 300-03; English, *supra* note 12, at 3-5; United States v. Pohlot, 827 F. 2d 889 (3d Cir. 1987), *cert. den.*, 484 U.S. 1011 (1988); R. SIMON & D. AARONSON, THE INSANITY DEFENSE: A CRITICAL ASSESSMENT OF LAW AND POLICY IN THE POST-HINCKLEY ERA 47 (1988) (Congress saw presence of volitional test as one of major factors contributing to Hinckley "getting off"); *see generally infra* chapter 3 A 1 c (5).

19. Besides the arguments discussed *infra* in text accompanying notes 20-56, *see also*, Mickenberg, *supra* note 9, at 970-72 (1987) (citing statements and testimony). Note, *Punishment Versus Treatment of the Guilty But Mentally Ill*, 74 J. CRIM. L. & CRIMINOL. 428, 434 n. 30 (1983) (same).

    These myths are repeated to the present day, and members of the Supreme Court are often the guiltiest parties. *See* Perlin & Dorfman, *Sanism, Social Science, and Mental Disability Law Jurisprudence*, 11 BEHAV. SCI. & L. 47, 57-61 (1993), critiquing Justice Thomas's dissenting opinions in Foucha v. Louisiana, 112 S. Ct. 1780, 1797-1806 (1992) (declaring unconstitutional a state statute that had allowed for the continued institutionalization of a non-mentally ill insanity acquittee), and in Riggins v. Nevada, 112 S. Ct. 1810, 1822-24 (1992) (reversing a death penalty conviction where defendant alleged that the involuntary imposition of antipsychotic medication at trial interfered with the presentation of his insanity defense).

20. *Reform of the Federal Insanity Defense*, Hearings before the Subcommittee on Criminal Justice of the Committee on the Judiciary, House of Representatives, 98th Cong., 1st Sess. 552, 553 (1983) (statement of Rep. Coughlin).

committing a disproportionate number of crimes."[21] Senator Strom Thurmond criticized the insanity defense for "exonerat[ing] a defendant who obviously planned and knew exactly what he was doing."[22] Senator Dan Quayle endorsed constituents' views that asserted the insanity defense "pampered criminals," and that the defense was "decadent," giving defendants the right to kill "with impunity."[23] Nearly as dramatically, Senator Steve Symms argued that the insanity defense reflected a criminal justice system "no longer representative of the interests of a civilized society."[24]

These positions parrot medieval views of the mentally disabled criminal defendant: mentally ill individuals are disproportionately dangerous; responsibility-based exculpation is somehow immoral and thwarts the public's right to vengeance; planfulness implies responsibility; the health of our civilization depends on our ability to punish the mentally ill criminal.

(2) Empirical and behavioral myths. Senators Larry Pressler and Orrin Hatch called the defense "a rich man's defense."[25] Congressman Myers alleged that it provided a "'safe harbor' for criminals who bamboozle a jury" into thinking they should not be held responsible.[26] Congressman Sensenbrenner portrayed the insanity trial as "protracted testimonial extravaganzas pitting high-priced prosecution experts against equally high-priced defense experts."[27] In perhaps the most bizarre statement, Congressman Lagomarsino—in testimony characterized by Congressman John Conyers as "thoughtful"—asserted that the controlling insanity defense test was that of *Durham*

---

21. *Reagan Advisor Edwin Meese Enunciates Administration's Crime Control Goals*, 12 CRIM. JUST. NEWSLETTER 4 (1981).
22. Roberts, *High U.S. Officials Express Outrage, Asking for New Laws on Insanity Plea*, N.Y. Times (June 23, 1982), at B6, col. 1.
23. *The Insanity Defense*, Hearings Before the Committee on the Judiciary, U.S. Senate, 97th Cong., 2d Sess. 18 (1982) (statement of Sen. Quayle).
24. *Id.* at 25 (testimony of Sen. Symms).
25. Roberts, *supra* note 22, at B6; *The Insanity Defense*, *supra* note 23, at 3, 9-10 (statement of Sen. Hatch).
26. *Insanity Defense in Federal Courts*, Hearings before the Subcommittee on Criminal Justice of the Committee on the Judiciary, House of Representatives, 97th Cong., 2d Sess. 19 (1982) (statement of Rep. Myers).
27. *Id.* at 143 (statement of Cong. Sensenbrenner). *See also*, Halpern, *The Politics of the Insanity Defense*, 14 AM. J. FORENS. PSYCHIATRY 3, 4 (1993), quoting Congressman John Ashbrook (insanity defense was "successfully employed in large numbers by dangerous criminals who thereby avoid punishment").

v. United States "that broadened the insanity defense to include everything from alcoholism and drug addiction to heartburn and itching."[28]

Former Attorney General William French Smith charged, "There must be an end to the doctrine that allows *so many persons* to commit crimes of violence, to use confusing procedures to their own advantage and then have the door opened for them to return to the society they victimized."[29] Ironically, when Smith made this statement, he apparently did not know that one of his top officials had candidly conceded that "we all know that the number of cases where the insanity defense becomes a factor is really probably statistically insignificant,"[30] and that another high-level prosecutor had informed Senator Thurmond that, in 1981, there were only *four* successful insanity acquittals in all federal jurisdictions.[31]

Each of these mythic statements is a textbook parody of empirical and behavioral reality. The insanity defense is disproportionately used in cases involving indigent defendants; jurors are rarely deceived

---

28. *Insanity Defense in Federal Courts*, *supra* note 26, at 151 (testimony of Cong. Lagomarsino), and *see id.* at 153 (comment by Cong. Conyers). On *Durham*, 214 F. 2d 862 (D.C. Cir. 1954) (establishing "product" test for insanity), *overruled*, United States v. Brawner, 471 F. 2d 969, 981 (D.C. Cir. 1972), *see generally*, 3 M.L. PERLIN, *supra* note 4, §15.06 at 296-99. On the way that this misreading of *Durham* reflects sanist behavior, *see* Perlin, *supra* note 10, at 373 n. 1.

29. Mickenberg, *supra* note 9, at 980, quoting Roberts, *supra* note 22 (emphasis added).

30. *Proceedings of the Forty-Sixth Judicial Conference of the District of Columbia Circuit*, 111 F.R.D. 91, 225 (1985) (remarks of Stephen Trott, Assistant Attorney General). These statistics should have been no surprise to Smith or any other law enforcement official since they simply replicated all earlier data, *see e.g.*, Perlin, *Overview of Rights in the Criminal Process*, in 3 LEGAL RIGHTS OF MENTALLY DISABLED PERSONS 1879, 1890 (P. Friedman ed. 1979) (citing Pollack, *The Insanity Defense as Defined by the Proposed Federal Criminal Code*, 4 BULL. AM. ACAD. PSYCHIATRY & L. 11, 21 (1976)) (fewer than 100 insanity acquittals—under the ALI test—in *all* federal jurisdictions per year), and were even well known to Congress, *see* H.R. REP. No. 577, 98th Cong., 1st Sess., 9 (1983) ("abuses of the insanity defense are few and have an insignificant direct impact on the criminal justice system").

  As to Smith's assertion regarding insanity acquittees' return to society, *see* Rodriguez, LeWinn & Perlin, *The Insanity Defense Under Siege: Legislative Assaults and Legal Rejoinders*, 14 RUTGERS L.J. 397, 403 (1983) (NGRI defendants spend "considerably more time in custody than do other criminal defendants").

31. Simon & Aaronson, *The Defense of Insanity*, in CONTROVERSIAL ISSUES IN CRIME AND JUSTICE 115, 126 (J. Scott & T. Hirschi eds. 1988).

by simulated pleas; the "battle of the experts" takes place in a small fraction of insanity cases; the number of defendants who even plead insanity is minute.[32] Congressman Lagomarsino's embarrassing misstatement of the law suggests an even graver truth: our thinking in this area is so distorted and irrational[33] that a mischaracterization of the law (that is at least a decade out of date)—compounded by a bizarre exaggeration of the overruled case's holding[34]—passes by unnoticed, save for a compliment that it was "thoughtful."

Perhaps even more bizarre, embarrassing, and ominous is the concession made in the House Report that accompanied the Insanity Defense Reform Act.[35] The drafters conceded that the basic beliefs about the insanity defense were "myths," but justified the new legislation because the *myths* "undermined public faith in the criminal justice system."[36] This concession—that Congress must assuage sentiment it knows to be false—reflects the myths' lasting power.[37]

---

32. *Compare Insanity Defense in Federal Courts, supra* note 26, at 80 (testimony of Dr. Henry Steadman) (ten year study revealed that over seventy-five percent of insanity pleaders were unemployed at time of crime); for the most comprehensive statistical research available, *see* H. STEADMAN ET AL., REFORMING THE INSANITY DEFENSE: AN EVALUATION OF PRE- AND POST-HINCKLEY REFORMS (1993) (in press) (H. STEADMAN, REFORMING). *See generally infra* chapter 3 B 1 b (1).

33. An explanation of *why* we are so irrational in our dealing with such matters is offered in Shindell, *The Public and the Criminal: Observations on the Tail of the Curve,* 50 A.B.A. J. 545, 549 (1964) (while public will be rational in dealing with aspects of the criminal procedure system about which they have little anxiety, public will remain "completely at the mercy of their emotions in dealing with the more extreme forms of aberrant behavior").

34. *Durham* had held that a defendant would not be criminally responsible if his "unlawful act was the product of mental disease or mental defect," 214 F. 2d at 874-75; *see generally infra* chapter 3 A 1 c (2). Although initially hailed as "the zenith of psychological optimism," *see* Bennett & Sullwold, *Qualifying the Psychiatrist as a Lay Witness: A Reaction to the American Psychiatric Association's Petition in* Barefoot v. Estelle, 20 J. FORENS. SCI. 462 (1985), its holding was eventually rejected by the courts in over twenty states, *see* Krash, *The Durham Rule and Judicial Administration of the Insanity Defense in the District of Columbia,* 70 YALE L.J. 905, 906 n.8 (1961). Significantly, it appears that, even in the District of Columbia, *Durham* was often honored only in the breach. *See* Arens & Susman, *Judges, Jury Charges, and Insanity,* 12 HOWARD L.J. 1, 6 (1966) (26 of 27 criminal defense lawyers surveyed reported that District of Columbia trial judges responded to the *Durham* rule "with suspicion and at times hostility").

35. 18 U.S.C. §17 (1988); *see generally infra* chapter 2 A 2 c.

36. H.R. REP. No. 577, *supra* note 30, at 10.

37. For instance, notwithstanding clinical evaluations or behavioral realities, St. Elizabeth's Hospital's Forensic Division staff "can be counted upon" to oppose any conditional release recommendation in cases of "controversial" patients. *See*

(3) U.S. Attorney Giuliani's testimony. Former United States Attorney Giuliani's testimony is especially disturbing, given his position and his public reputation.[38]

U.S. Attorney Giuliani's testimony reflects either a profound ignorance of the nature of the insanity defense or a complete disregard of the niceties of legal terminology. He uses the terms "insanity defense," "temporary insanity," "irresistible impulse," and *"mens rea"* almost interchangeably, seemingly without recognizing that they represent very different legal concepts. First, he focused the Senate's attention on a statement by the American Psychiatric Association that "the line between an irresistible impulse and an impulse not resisted is probably no shorter than that between twilight and dusk."[39] This was, of course, an ultimate red herring—the "irresistible impulse" test is operative as a modification of the M'Naghten test in only a handful of jurisdictions and is simply not relevant to any contemporaneous insanity defense policy debate.[40] Next, he asserted that defendants are found not guilty by reason of insanity (NGRI) "quite frequently," and that "experts themselves [have] recognized a virtual impossibility of determining whether the defendant can or cannot control his conduct."[41] By the time of his testimony it was clear that, in a typical urban state, the insanity defense was

---

Final Report of the National Institute of Mental Health (NIMH) Ad Hoc Forensic Advisory Panel, 12 MENT. & PHYS. DIS. L. REP. 77, 96 (1988) (*Ad Hoc Panel*); *see also,* Goldstein, *The Psychiatrist's Guide to Right and Wrong: Part IV: The Insanity Defense and the Ultimate Issue Rule,* 17 BULL. AM. ACAD. PSYCHIATRY & L. 269, 279 (1989) (American Psychiatric Association supported limitations on federal evidentiary rules as to scope of expert testimony in insanity cases because of its concern about negative public attitudes toward "unfavorable" forensic participation in "controversial" cases); Scott, Zonana & Getz, *supra* note 6, at 983 (any proposal to move insanity acquittees from maximum security facility "evokes public outrage;" treatment review board characterized as "the gatekeeper for political prisoners").

38.   *See* Mickenberg, *supra* note 9, at 980 n. 161.

39.   *Comprehensive Crime Control Act of 1983,* Hearings Before the Subcommittee on Criminal Law of the Committee on the Judiciary, U.S. Senate, 98th Cong., 1st Sess. 15 (1983) (*Comprehensive Act*). The quotation is paraphrased from *American Psychiatric Association Statement on the Insanity Defense,* 140 AM. J. PSYCHIATRY 681, 685 (1983) (which, in its original, states "...probably no *sharper...*") (emphasis added).

40.   *See* State v. White, 58 N.M. 324, 270 P. 2d 727 (1954), discussed in Committee Commentary to N.M. UNIFORM JY. INSTR. 14-5102 (1986), at 251-52; Caldwell v. State, 257 Ga. 10, 354 S.E. 2d 124 (1987); COLO. REV. STAT. §16-8-101 (1986); *see generally,* 3 M.L. PERLIN, *supra* note 4, §15.05 at 294-96.

41.   *Comprehensive Act, supra* note 39, at 15.

successful in one-twentieth of one percent of all cases;[42] also, the development of sophisticated assessment tools has revealed that evaluations of the defendant's responsibility may be *more* reliable in volitional than in cognitive determinations.[43]

In a separate prepared statement to a House of Representatives subcommittee, Giuliani stated, "Ordinarily, under our law, the reason or motivation for a criminal act is irrelevant, and produces no basis for exculpation," and complained about the "massive amounts of conflicting and irrelevant testimony by psychiatric experts" as a result of which there is "rarely medical agreement" as to responsibility, resulting in insanity defense trials that "are usually arduous, expensive, and, much worse, confusing for the jury."[44] When this statement is unpacked, it collapses of its own dead weight.

First, "motive" is certainly relevant in any so-called "specific intent" crime, especially in a significant number of homicide prosecutions.[45] Second, the availability of the whole range of justification and excuse defenses—self-defense, duress, entrapment, defense of another, lesser evil—belies his assertion that inquiries into the reason behind an act are ordinarily irrelevant.[46] Third, the uncontroverted empirical reality is that over eighty percent of all insanity defense cases are, and always have been, uncontested, and that there is medical disagreement in only a handful of cases per year.[47]

---

42. *See* Rodriguez, LeWinn & Perlin, *supra* note 30, at 401. More recent statistics found success in one quarter of one percent of all felony cases. *See* Callahan, Steadman, McGreevy & Robbins, *The Volume and Characteristics of Insanity Defense Pleas: An Eight State Study*, 19 BULL. AM. ACAD. PSYCHIATRY & L. 331 (1991) (Callahan); H. STEADMAN, REFORMING, *supra* note 32, manuscript at 46.

43. On the development of tools, *see e.g.*, Rogers, Dolmetsch & Cavanaugh, *An Empirical Approach to Insanity Evaluations*, 37 J. CLIN. PSYCHOLOGY 683 (1981); Rogers, Seman & Wasyliw, *The R-CRAS and Legal Insanity: A Cross-Validation Study*, 39 J. CLIN. PSYCHOLOGY 554 (1983); Rogers & Cavanaugh, *Application of the SADS Diagnostic Interview to Forensic Psychiatry*, 9 J. PSYCHIATRY & L. 329 (1981); *see generally infra* chapter 3 B 2. On the assessment of volition, *see* Rogers, *Assessment of Criminal Responsibility: Empirical Advances and Unanswered Questions*, 15 J. PSYCHIATRY & L. 73, 78 (1987) (arguments that volitional non-responsibility cannot be measured are "an intellectual charade played for the benefit of an uninformed public").

44. *Insanity Defense in Federal Courts, supra* note 26, at 39.

45. *See* W. LAFAVE & A. SCOTT, CRIMINAL LAW §3.6 (2d ed. 1986); Pillsbury, *Evil and the Law of Murder*, 24 U.C. DAVIS L. REV. 437, 447 (1990).

46. *See* W. LAFAVE & A. SCOTT, *supra* note 45, chapter 5.

47. *See e.g.*, Rogers, Bloom & Manson, *Insanity Defense: Contested or Conceded?*

Elsewhere, referring to commentary by Senator Strom Thurmond—"It doesn't make sense to me that a person can go to court
and plead insanity and be found not guilty, as in the Hinckley case,
and then be sent to an institution for examination and maybe stay
several weeks or several months"—Giuliani concurred, "We agree in
concept with everything you said."[48] Again, the empirical data—
which certainly should have been accessible to Giuliani[49]—belied
Thurmond's assertion.[50]

Next, Giuliani promised Thurmond a set of statistics that would
purportedly have revealed examples of individuals who "have been
acquitted in the Federal courts by reason of insanity and then left to
roam the streets for periods of time while state courts could gear up
to begin a civil commitment against them."[51] There is no evidence
either that this phantom set of statistics exists or that Giuliani ever
supplied further information on this point to Thurmond.[52]

---

141 AM. J. PSYCHIATRY 885, 887 (1984) (no psychiatric disagreement as to lack
of responsibility in over eighty percent of all cases in which insanity pleas are
entered); Fukunaga, Pasewark, Hawkins & Gudeman, *Insanity Plea: Interexaminer Agreement in Concordance of Psychiatric Opinion and Court Verdict*,
5 LAW & HUM. BEHAV. 325 (1981) (93 percent concordance). Over a quarter of
a century ago, a study of the impact of the *Durham* decision in Washington,
D.C. reported that between two-thirds and three-fourths of all insanity defenses
were uncontested. Acheson, McDonald v. U.S.: *The* Durham *Rule Revisited*, 51
GEO. L.J. 580, 589 (1963).

48. *The Insanity Defense, supra* note 23, at 39-40.

49. State governments have traditionally demonstrated a curious lack of interest in
the relevant underlying empirical data. As of 1985, directors of forensic services
in twenty states could give researchers no information whatsoever about the use
of the insanity plea; in only ten states could they give even baseline data about
the plea's frequency and success. Pasewark & McGinley, *Insanity Plea: National
Survey of Frequency and Success*, 13 J. PSYCHIATRY & L. 101, 106 (1985). *But
compare*, Way, Dvoskin & Steadman, *Forensic Inpatients Served in the United
States: Regional and System Differences*, 19 BULL. AM. ACAD. PSYCHIATRY & L.
405 (1991) (discussing recently compiled data).

50. *See e.g.*, Rodriguez, LeWinn & Perlin, *supra* note 30, at 403 (of entire universe
of individuals found NGRI over eight year period in one jurisdiction, only 15
percent had been relieved from all restraints, 35 percent remained in full custody,
and 47 percent were under partial court restraint after court-ordered conditional
release); *see also*, Golding, Eaves & Kowaz, *supra* note 12, at 153 (in British
Columbia, average insanity acquittee spent more than nine and a half years in
secure hospitalization); United States v. Wright, 511 F. 2d 1311, 1313 n. 11
(D.C. Cir. 1975) (despite Congressional charges that insanity acquittees enjoyed
a "revolving door" policy, between 1968 and 1975 *every* such acquittee was
committed unless *hospital* recommended release).

51. *The Insanity Defense, supra* note 23, at 38.

52. The Insanity Defense Reform Act established, for the first time, a comprehensive

Finally, in his testimony before the National Commission on the Insanity Defense, Giuliani charged that the insanity defense allowed defendants to "get away with murder" in "many, many...cases."[53] Again, Giuliani was wrong: first, NGRI acquittees frequently spend almost *double* the amount of time institutionalized that defendants convicted of similar charges spend in penal settings;[54] second, most statistical studies have found that sixty to seventy percent of all insanity pleas are entered in non-murder cases;[55] third, defendants who plead insanity in murder cases are no more successful than those raising it who are charged with lesser crimes.[56]

---

post-acquittal dispositional scheme for individuals found NGRI of federal offenses. *See* 18 *U.S.C.* §§4243, 4247 (1988), discussed extensively in 3 M.L. PERLIN, *supra* note 4, §15.39 at 400-01 n. 748. While the prior omission has been the result of "sporadic criticism," see Ellis, *The Consequences of the Insanity Defense: Proposals to Reform Post-Acquittal Commitment Laws,* 35 CATH. U. L. REV. 961, 991 n. 140 (1986) (previously, federal courts depended upon state courts to commit individuals found NGRI of federal offenses; *see e.g.,* United States v. McCracken, 488 F. 2d 406, 415-18 (5th Cir. 1974)), there is no evidence that the street-roaming scenario posited by Giuliani has any basis in reality. *Compare* English, *supra* note 12, at 50 n. 288 (in response to author's Freedom of Information Act request, the Executive Office of the U.S. Attorney said that "no records were kept regarding the number of insanity pleas entered"). On October 23, 1991, one of my student research assistants wrote to Giuliani asking for a copy of the statistics that had been referred to; Giuliani never answered his letter.

53. *Myths and Realities: Hearing Transcript of the National Commission on the Insanity Defense,* 36 (1983).

54. Rodriguez, LeWinn & Perlin, *supra* note 30, at 403-4; *see also,* Pogrebin, Regoli & Perry, *Not Guilty By Reason of Insanity: A Research Note,* 8 INT'L J. L. & PSYCHIATRY 237, 240 (1986). *Compare* H. STEADMAN, REFORMING, *supra* note 32, at 94 (in California, although defendants acquitted by reason of insanity spend less time in confinement than those found guilty of that crime, defendants found NGRI of other violent offenses spend twice as long in confinement as those convicted, and defendants convicted of non-violent crimes spend nine times as long in confinement).

55. Rodriguez, LeWinn & Perlin, *supra* note 30, at 402 (more than two-thirds); Golding, Eaves & Kowaz, *supra* note 12, at 161 (over sixty percent). For the most recent statistical reviews, *see* Callahan, *supra* note 42, at 337 (fewer than fifteen percent entered in murder cases; approximately half involved "violent or potentially violent" crimes); H. STEADMAN, REFORMING, *supra* note 32, at 48 (fewer than one quarter involved murder; slightly less than one third involved physical assault).

56. Steadman, Keitner, Braff & Arvanites, *Factors Associated With a Successful Insanity Plea,* 140 AM. J. PSYCHIATRY 401, 402-03 (1983).

c. Ultimate Congressional action. The Reagan Administration originally had called loudly for the abolition of the insanity defense.[57] However, in the face of a nearly unified front presented by most of the relevant professional organizations and trade associations, it eventually quietly dropped its loud public call for abolition and supported the IDRA as a "reform compromise."[58] The legislation ultimately enacted by Congress—legislation that closely comported with the public's moral feelings—returned the insanity defense to *"status quo ante* 1843: the year of...*M'Naghten.*[59] Besides relocating the burden of proof in insanity trials to defendants,[60] establishing strict procedures for the hospitalization and release of defendants found NGRI,[61] and severely limiting the scope of expert testimony in insanity cases,[62] it discarded the ALI-Model Penal Code test, and adopted a more restrictive version of M'*Naghten* by specifying that the level of mental disease or defect must be shown to qualify be "severe."[63]

---

57. Perlin, *supra* note 2, at 860 n. 9.
58. 3 M.L. PERLIN, *supra* note 4, §15.39 at 398-99 n. 743. On the various recommendations of the professional associations, *see id.,* § 15.38, at 395-97.
59. Perlin, *supra* note 2, at 862; *see also,* Mickenberg, *supra* note 9, at 954; English, *supra* note 12, at 46. On the M'*Naghten* test generally, *see* 3 M.L. PERLIN, *supra* note 4, §15.04 at 286-94. The new act implicitly also overruled Davis v. United States, 160 U.S. 469. 488 (1895), that had placed the burden of proof on the state to prove sanity beyond a reasonable doubt; *see generally,* McHugh, Greenfield v. Wainwright: *The Use of Post-*Miranda *Silence to Rebut the Insanity Defense,* 35 AM. U. L. REV. 221, 228 n. 26 (1985). On the significance of the "political realignment" that led to this legislation, *see* Johnson, *Book Review of* N. MORRIS, MADNESS AND THE CRIMINAL LAW (1982), 50 U. CHI. L. REV. 1534, 1549 (1983).

   See e.g., United States v. West, 962 F. 2d 1243, 1249 (7th Cir. 1992) (after the Hinckley trial, "one overall goal of Congress in passing the [IDRA] was to lessen the availability of and narrow the scope of the insanity defense").
60. 18 U.S.C. §17 (1988). The placement of the burden of proof upon the prosecution (to disprove insanity claims beyond a reasonable doubt) had been one of Congress's main focal points in the insanity defense debate. *See* R. SIMON & D. AARONSON, *supra* note 18, at 47. *See generally infra* chapter 3 A 2.
61. *See* 18 U.S.C. §4243 *et seq.* (1988), discussed in 3 M.L. PERLIN, *supra* note 14, §15.39 at 400-01 n. 748.
62. *See* FED. R. EVID. 704 (b); *see e.g.,* Rogers & Ewing, *Ultimate Opinion Proscription: A Cosmetic Fix and a Plea for Empiricism,* 13 LAW & HUM. BEHAV. 357, 372 (1989) (limitation "nothing more than a cosmetic suggestion, a shopworn restatement of concerns raised...following [M'Naghten's] acquittal"). This amendment is specifically criticized in Braswell, *supra* note 16, and in Cohen, *Punishing the Insane: Restriction of Expert Psychiatric Testimony by Federal Rule of Evidence 704(b),* 40 U. FLA. L. REV. 541 (1988).
63. 18 U.S.C. §17(a) (1988). This standard was adopted "to ensure that relatively

All of this had the ultimate effect of returning to a test that compelled the law to "do its punitive worst,"[64] that had "the rigidity of an army cot and the flexibility of a Procrustean bed,"[65] that retained the flavor "of the celebrated concepts of Hale and Coke of the seventeenth century,"[66] and that was, simply, "bad psychiatry and bad law."[67]

Importantly, Congress abolished the volitional prong without any consideration of the empirical studies then widely available as to the impact or wisdom of such a change. Those studies revealed that the amendment might likely systematically exclude those defendants "whose illness is clearest in symptomatology, most likely biologic in origin, most eminently treatable, and [who are] potentially most disruptive in penal detention."[68] There is thus now significant doubt that "morally correct" answers are more likely to be achieved under the narrower test than had been achieved under the ALI construction.[69]

At the time of the federal debate, Professor David Wexler suggested that it was "tiring—even embarrassing" to be discussing returning to *M'Naghten* in 1984.[70] Wexler's scorn is understated. Given the intense pressure mounted by abolitionists, the return to *M'Naghten* was eventually seen as a major tactical *victory* by the

---

minor disorders such as nonpsychotic behavior disorders or personality defects would not provide the basis for an insanity defense." HANDBOOK ON THE COMPREHENSIVE CRIME CONTROL ACT OF 1984 AND OTHER CRIMINAL STATUTES ENACTED BY THE 98TH CONGRESS 59 (1984).

64. A. GOLDSTEIN, THE INSANITY DEFENSE 47 (1967).
65. S. GLUECK, LAW AND PSYCHIATRY: COLD WAR OR ENTENTE CORDIALE? 43-48 (1966).
66. R. Sadoff, "Insanity: Evolution of a Medicolegal Concept" (paper presented at College Night, The College of Physicians of Philadelphia, Sept. 10, 1986), manuscript at 20.
67. English, *supra* note 12, at 47.
68. Silver & Spodak, *Dissection of the Prongs of ALI: Retrospective Assessment of Criminal Responsibility by the Psychiatric Staff of the Clifton T. Perkins Hospital Center,* 11 BULL. AM. ACAD. PSYCHIATRY & L. 383, 390 (1983) (describing patients with manic disorders); *see also,* English, *supra* note 12, at 20-52 (critiquing volitional prong criticisms on both constitutional and social policy grounds), and especially at 50 ("the empirical record is virtually nonexistent"); Rogers, *supra* note 43 (same).
69. *See* Keilitz, *Researching and Reforming the Insanity Defense,* 39 RUTGERS L. REV. 289, 297 (1987); R. SIMON & D. AARONSON, *supra* note 18, at 49-53.
70. Wexler, *An Offense-Victim Approach to Insanity Defense Reform,* 26 ARIZ. L. REV. 17, 25 (1984).

defense's *supporters*.[71] In light of the history that I will subsequently explore, the evisceration of the defense should have been seen—even at the start of the debate—as virtually inevitable.

d. Parallel state debates.   The states quickly followed the lead of the federal government. Two-thirds of all states reevaluated the defense; as a result, twelve states adopted the guilty but mentally ill (GBMI) test, seven narrowed the substantive test, sixteen shifted the burden of proof, and twenty-five tightened release provisions in the cases of those defendants found to be NGRI. Three states adopted legislation that purported to abolish the defense, but actually retained a mens rea exception.[72]

The debates in the states—explicitly spurred by the Hinckley acquittal[73]—tracked the federal discourse. Thus, in Pennsylvania, a member of the House of Representatives suggested that "the less mentally afflicted" might attempt to use the insanity defense to "confuse the jury," and urged the GBMI substitute to "discourag[e] the use of the insanity defense."[74] Delaware similarly adopted GBMI "to assure the public that a criminally responsible and mentally ill defendant will not be returned to the states to unleash further violence

---

71. Perlin, *supra* note 2, at 862; *see generally*, Milner, *What's Old and New About the Insanity Plea*, 67 JUDICATURE 499, 505 (1984).
72. *See* UTAH CODE ANN. §76-2-305 (1986); IDAHO CODE §18-207 (1986); MONT. CODE ANN. §§46-14-101 to -401 (1985). For a judicial explanation, *see* State v. Young, 1993 WL 79648, at **47-49 (Utah 1993). On the legislative changes in general, *see* Callahan, Mayer & Steadman, *supra* note 1, at 55-57, and *id.* at 57 (Table 2); Fentiman, *supra* note 15, at 603-4; H. STEADMAN, REFORMING, *supra note 32, at 64-65. The GBMI defense is discussed infra chapter 3 A 1 c (4).*
73. Commonwealth v. Trill, 374 Pa. Super. 549, 543 A. 2d 1106, 1119 (1988), appeal den., 523 Pa. 603, 562 A. 2d 826 (1989) (legislative reform in Pennsylvania "was clearly promulgated in response to the events surrounding the presidential assassination attempt and subsequent acquittal"); Bass v. State, 585 So. 2d 225, 232 (Ala. Cr. App. 1991), *cert. den.* (Ala. 1991) (new state law virtually identical to IDRA that was passed "in the wake of John Hinckley's acquittal," *quoting* United States v. Cameron, 907 F. 2d 1051, 1061 (11th Cir. 1990)); Ware v. State, 584 So. 2d 939, 942 (Ala. Cr. App. 1991), *cert. den.* (Ala. 1991)· (same).
74. Trill, 543 A. 2d at 1118, 1119 (statements by Rep. Piccola). *Compare id.* at 1118 (testimony by Rep. Levin, arguing that GBMI legislation was "fatally flawed"); 3 M.L. PERLIN, *supra* note 4, §15.09 at 311 (evidence suggests that GBMI increased psychiatric involvement in legal decision making; evidence mixed on question of whether GBMI reduces numbers of insanity acquittals), and *see id.* at nn. 215, 217 (discussing studies).

without having received psychiatric care after sentencing."[75] The same myths, the same ambivalences, the same focus on ensuring that any nonresponsibility defense be available only to the *totally* non-blameworthy were repeated in virtually every state legislative debate.[76]

e. Conclusion. The debate over the future of the insanity defense that followed John Hinckley's insanity acquittal was utterly predictable. State and federal legislators and federal prosecutors repeated discredited and outdated myths based on ancient superstitions and then *conceded* that their actions were driven by myth, not reality. Their statements went unchallenged; the empirical evidence refuting them went unnoticed. Had a mid-nineteenth century Member of Parliament stumbled into one of the legislative arenas during this debate, he would have felt—correctly—that we had learned nothing in the 140 years that had passed since the *M'Naghten* rules were articulated.

Congress responded directly and swiftly to public perceptions of a system run amok—one that, purportedly, allowed uncountable numbers of dangerous defendants to escape punishment through the meretricious loophole of the insanity defense.[77] Even though Congress knew full well that this perception was a myth, it responded as it did so as to assuage these fears and in an effort to persuade the

---

75. Daniels v. State, 538 A. 2d 1104, 1108 (Del. 1988). *But compare* empirical research reported in Steadman, Keitner, Braff & Arvanites, *supra* note 56, at 403:

   [T]here is virtually no empirical basis for this pattern of legislation-in-response-to-horror-story. In 1983, for example, researchers could point to only one person acquitted by reason of insanity in New York state—ever—who subsequently killed someone after being released.

76. *See also,* Mitchell v. Commonwealth, 781 S.W. 2d 510 (Ky. 1989); People v. Kohl, 72 N.Y. 2d 191, 527 N.E. 2d 1182, 532 N.Y.S. 2d 45 (1988); State v. Korell, 213 Mont. 316, 690 P. 2d 992 (1984) (all discussing revisions to state insanity defense laws).

   Not every state made such changes. *See Report of NJ Insanity Defense Study Commission* (1985) (noting New Jersey's retention of insanity defense and rejection of GBMI alternative). Perhaps significantly, during the legislative debate in New Jersey, statistics were presented to the Study Commission on the rarity of the plea and its subsequent general lack of success. *See id.* at 7; Rodriguez, LeWinn & Perlin, *supra* note 30, at 397, note ‡ (discussing empirical refutation of insanity myths at Study Commission hearing).

77. *See* Comment, *Insanity Defense: Should the Shock of the* Hayes *Verdict Compel North Carolina to Fix What "Ain't Broke?"* 25 WAKE FOREST L. REV. 547, 574 (1990).

voters that it was "doing something" by laudably enhancing public protection values. In short, it participated knowingly and openly in a massive legislative charade.

This should not surprise us. As I will demonstrate, our jurisprudence of mentally disabled criminal defendants has been historically driven by linking mental illness to sin, mental illness to demonic possession, and mental illness to social taboos. The law of criminal responsibility has been anchored by fundamentalist theology, feudal concepts and medieval folklore.[78] This jurisprudence is colored further by our punitive spirit and moralized aggression, our desperate desire to ensure that no individual threatens our fragile social order by improperly "getting away with it" or "beating the rap," our view of "soft" psychiatrists "getting defendants off," and our "fear of faking" that translates into pretextual rejections of insanity defenses in cases involving severely mentally disordered criminal defendants.[79] The stakes here are higher when the defendant seeks exculpation through the insanity plea, where he admits the underlying factual act[80] but denies legal and/or moral "guilt."[81]

While we have grudgingly allowed a few defendants to seek exculpation through the insanity defense,[82] we usually[83] limit it to defendants "utterly and obviously" beyond the reach of the criminal

---

78. *See generally infra* chapter 2 B 1.
79. *See generally infra* chapter 2 C, chapters 4 & 5.
80. *E.g.*, Jones v. United States, 463 U.S. 354, 376 (1983) (entry of not guilty by reason of insanity plea is admission of factual commission of underlying acts). On the relationship between *Jones* and the government's desire to deter "spurious claims of insanity," *see* Appel, *The Constitutionality of Automatic Commitment Procedures Applied to persons Found Not Guilty By Reason of Insanity*: Jones v. United States, 21 Hous. L. Rev. 421, 434 (1984).
81. On the difference between "factual" guilt and "legal" guilt, *see* Seidman, *Factual Guilt and the Burger Court: An Examination of Continuity and Change in Criminal procedure*, 80 Colum. L. Rev. 436 (1980). There is a jurisdictional split between those states that allow for the insanity defense in cases where the defendant did not know the act was "morally" wrong and those where he did not know it was "legally" wrong. *See* 3 M.L. Perlin, *supra* note 4, §15.04 at 121-22 n. 90 (1992 pocket part) (citing cases); for a recent helpful discussion, *see* Note, *The Immutable Command Meets the Unknowable Mind: Deific Decree Claims and the Insanity Defense After* People v. Serravo, 70 Denver U. L. Rev. 161 (1992).
82. That exculpation carries a heavy price tag. Insanity acquittees are usually incarcerated longer and in worse facilities than had they been convicted of the underlying criminal charges. *See generally infra* chapter 3 B 1 b (1).
83. On the "empathy outlier" exceptions, *see generally infra* chapter 4 D 2.

law.[84] If a defendant's behavior appears at all "planful," we categorically reject the notion that he is not responsible.[85] The "wild beast" test of the mid-eighteenth century most closely conforms with the public's view of the level of mental disability required for a successful insanity plea.[86] The ambivalence that comes from this tension between our punitive culture and our lip service to the concept of mental disability as an exculpatory factor infects doctrinal developments in a variety of criminal law, procedure and justice policy areas beyond the simple question of criminal responsibility.

The debate in both state and federal legislatures that followed John Hinckley's insanity acquittal illuminates the roots of our feelings, reflects the thrall in which medieval concepts still grip so much of the public, and demonstrates the futility of attempting to explain insanity defense jurisprudential developments through traditional doctrinal means. It also reveals the way that the law's "tensile strength" is tested severely when legal doctrine conflicts with the public's "common sense."[87]

3. The Insanity Defense as Symbol

Before any analysis of the underlying issues is undertaken, we must consider the significance of symbolism in insanity defense jurisprudence.[88] The insanity defense is, in many ways, "the acid test of

---

84. Kadish, *The Decline of Innocence*, 26 CAMB. L.J. 273, 284 (1968). We continue to mouth the shibboleth that "the insanity defense goes to the very root of our criminal justice system." State v. Curry, 45 Ohio St. 3d 109, 543 N.E. 2d 1228, 1230 (1989).

85. *See e.g.*, Roberts, Golding & Fincham, *Implicit Theories of Criminal Responsibility Decision Making and the Insanity Defense*, 11 LAW & HUM. BEHAV. 207, 226 (1987); Roberts & Golding, *The Social Construction of Criminal Responsibility and Insanity*, 15 LAW & HUM. BEHAV. 349, 351 (1991).

   Although there is some important jury research that suggests that simulated jurors *will* acquit in cases with some measure of planfulness, closer examination of these cases reveals the presence of other "override" factors. *See generally infra* chapter 4 D 2-3.

86. *See* Roberts, Golding & Fincham, *supra* note 85, at 226. Although there is some research that suggests that simulated jurors' verdicts do not vary significantly depending on the test used (including the "wild beast" test), *see e.g.*, Finkel, Shaw, Bercaw & Koch, *Insanity Defenses: From the Jurors' Perspective*, 9 LAW & PSYCHOLOGY REV. 77 (1985), jurors' willingness to use a specific substantive test in a simulation should not necessarily be read to reflect *endorsement* by those jurors of the test in question.

87. *See generally infra* chapter 8 A.

88. *See* Perlin, *The Supreme Court, the Mentally Disabled Criminal Defendant,*

our attitudes toward the insane and toward the criminal law itself."[89]
A "convenient symbolic target in [the] war of words [over the crisis
in crime]"[90] and "a scapegoat for the entire criminal justice system,"[91]
the insanity defense—like the death penalty[92]—has consistently reflected a "symbolic perspective" of citizens' basic values.[93] On such a

---

*Psychiatric Testimony in Death Penalty Cases, and the Power of Symbolism:
Dulling the Ake in* Barefoot's *Achilles Heel*, 3 N.Y.L.S. HUM. RTS. ANN. 91 n.
1 (1985) (discussing the relationship between Jungian symbolism and the
insanity defense); R. SMITH, TRIAL BY MEDICINE: INSANITY AND RESPONSIBIL-
ITY IN VICTORIAN TRIALS 3 (1981) ("Deciding between guilt and insanity has a
symbolism transcending an individual's fate"); *see also*, Sendor, *supra* note 16,
at 1397-1407. On the relationship between symbols and myths, *see* R. STIVERS,
EVIL IN MODERN MYTH AND RITUAL 115 (1982). On law as a "psychic
experience," see Snowden, Living With Ghosts, 70 NEB. L. REV. 446, 450
(1991).

For political overviews, see Edelman, *Law and Psychiatry as Political
Symbolism*, 3 INT'L J. L. & PSYCHIATRY 235 (1980); Lasswell, *What Psychiatrists
and Political Scientists Can Learn From One Another*, 1 PSYCHIATRY 33 (1938);
for an anthropological analysis, *see* M. DOUGLAS, IMPLICIT MEANINGS (1975).
On the general role of symbolism in the designation of deviant behavior, *see*
Gusfield, *On Legislating Morals: The Symbolic Process of Designating Deviance*, 56 CALIF. L. REV. 54 (1968); Gusfield, *Moral Passage: Symbolic Process
in Public Designations of Deviance*, 14 SOC'L PROBS. 175 (1967).

89. Herman, *The Insanity Defense in Fact and Fiction: On Norval Morris's* MAD-
NESS AND THE CRIMINAL LAW, AM. B. FOUND. RES. J. 385 (1985).
90. Bazelon, The Dilemma of Criminal Responsibility, 72 KY. L.J. 263, 277 (1982-
83).
91. Id. at 263. This symbolic role is not new. See e.g., Platt & Diamond, *The Origins
and Development of the 'Wild Beast' Concept of Mental Illness and Its Relation
to Theories of Criminal Responsibility*, 1 J. HIST. BEHAV. SCI. 355, 365 (1965)
("wild beast" test a "significant archetype in the history of law and medicine,"
see generally infra chapter 3 1 a (2)).
92. *See* White, *Patterns in Capital Punishment*, 75 CALIF. L. REV. 2165, 2174
(1987), *quoting* F. ZIMRING & G. HAWKINS, CAPITAL PUNISHMENT AND THE
AMERICAN AGENDA 45 (1987) ("The death penalty was precisely the type of
politically charged, symbolic policy issue to which judicial invalidation has
always provoked anger and resentment"). On the way that the death penalty
symbolizes an "avenging God," *see* Radin, *Proportionality, Subjectivity, and
Tragedy*, 18 U. C. DAVIS L. REV. 1165, 1175 (1985). On the relationship
between death penalty views and insanity defense views, *see infra* chapter 7 D 4
b.
93. R. SMITH, *supra* note 88, at 3 ("The [*M'Naghten*] Rules symbolised and
exacerbated an endemic conflict [between law and psychiatry]"); *see also*, Tyler
& Weber, *Support for the Death Penalty: Instrumental Response to Crime or
Symbolic Attitude?* 17 LAW & SOC'Y REV. 21, 43 (1982).

Any true understanding of the public's reaction to symbolism must be
premised, at least in part, on how public officials perceive their audience,
understand the relationship between symbolism and law, and manipulate symbols. Stolz, *Congress and Capital Punishment: An Exercise in Symbolic Politics*,

landscape, the actual insanity defense pleaders are often little more than "bit players in a larger social struggle."[94]

The insanity defense symbolizes the gap between the aspirations of a theoretically positivist, objective, common law legal system (in which behavior is allegedly animated by free will and is judged and assessed on a conscious level), and the reality of an indeterminate, subjective, psychosocial universe (in which behavior is determined by a host of biological, psychological, physiological, environmental and sociological factors, and is frequently driven by unconscious forces).[95] Contrarily, insanity defense *retentionists* also rely on symbolism in their opposition to the abolition movement; they see the defense as a symbol of the free will model of criminal responsibility.[96]

The dissonance caused by the gap between the operation of the insanity defense and the public's perception of how a criminal justice system should operate[97] must be considered in light of yet another layer of symbolism: the symbolic role of psychiatry in the determination of insanity defense cases[98] where the defense is seen as "a crucial

---

5 LAW & SOC'Y REV. 157, 162 (1983); *see generally* M. EDELMAN, POLITICS AS SYMBOLIC ACTION: MASS AROUSAL AND QUIESCENCE (1971); M. EDELMAN, THE SYMBOLIC USES OF POLITICS (1964).

94. Seidman, *supra* note 81, at 437.

95. "Because there is no correspondence between the ideal constructions we project and the actual practices that go on in the world, we create legal rituals and popular symbols which keep us unconscious of the discrepancy between illusion and reality, and facilitate a rough adjustment to an imperfect world." Hill, *The Psychological Realism of Thurman Arnold,* 22 U. CHI. L. REV. 377, 379-80 (1955).

96. *See* Northrup, *Guilty But Mentally Ill: Broadening the Scope of Criminal Responsibility,* 44 OHIO ST. L.J. 797, 807 n. 140 (1983).

97. The critical importance of this dissonance is examined in Wexler, *supra* note 70, at 20, discussing Meehl, *The Insanity Defense,* MINN. PSYCHOL. 11 (Summer 1983) (emphasis added):

...if either the philosophical justification or the statutory formulation or the administration of the insanity defense is *gravely disharmonious with the community sense of justice,* it is bad for the [mental health] profession, it is bad for the public attitude toward the criminal justice system, and, more to the point, it won't be carried out.

98. *See e.g.,* Dession, *Psychiatry and the Conditioning of Criminal Justice,* 47 YALE L.J. 319, 336 (1938): "The psychiatrist, representing as he does in the popular mind a symbol of the more exacting new penal expectationism and of current dissatisfaction, must take care less he find himself unwittingly sponsoring a psychopathic culture pattern." *See also, id.* at 328: "In a sense...what we have traditionally sought of criminal justice has not been so much actual as *symbolic performance*" (emphasis added).

prop in a 'public morality play,'"[99] a "surrogate for the resolution of the most profound issues in social and criminal justice,"[100] and a symbol of "the distribution of value and power between the individual and society."[101] In short, as Holmes pointed out almost seventy years ago, "We live by symbols, and what shall be symbolized by any image of the sight depends on the mind of who sees it."[102] The insanity defense discourse of lawyers, judges and witnesses is largely dependent on visual, demonic stereotypes of a nonresponsible defendant as "an insane, crazy monster;"[103] these sanist depictions reflect how pernicious these symbols may be.[104]

The purported abuse of the insanity defense symbolizes the alleged breakdown of law-and-order,[105] the failure of the crime control model,[106] and the ascendancy of a "liberal," exculpatory, excuse-rid-

---

99. Monahan, *Abolish the Insanity Defense? Not Yet*, 26 RUTGERS L. REV. 719, 721 (1973); *see also*, Heinbecker, *Two Year's Experience Under Utah's* Mens Rea *Insanity Law*, 14 BULL. AM. ACAD. PSYCHIATRY & L. 185, 190 (1986) (insanity defense serves "ritual function whereby lawyers can move clients from the legal system to the mental health system").

100. Keilitz, *supra* note 69, at 322.

101. R. SMITH, *supra* note 88, at 172.

102. Kurland, *The Religious Clauses and the Burger Court*, 34 CATH. U. L. REV. 1, 6 (1984), *quoting* O.W. HOLMES, COLLECTED LEGAL PAPERS 270 (1920). On the positive role of symbols in a related context, see Lovell & Stojkovic, Symbols, and Policymaking in Corrections, 2 CRIM. JUST. POL. REV. 225, 226 (1987), *citing* Conley, *Beyond Legislative Acts: Penal Reform, Public Policy and Symbolic Justice*, 1 PUB. HISTORIAN 26, 39 (1981):

   Myths and symbols, in effect, are useful to the long-term stability of correctional policy development; they protect the correctional organization from the charge that both decision making and policymaking are fundamentally politically driven and represent the interests of those who control and administer correctional systems.

103. *See* Kennedy v. Shillinger, 759 F. Supp. 1554, 1563 (D. Wyo. 1991) (no violation of effectiveness of counsel standard where defense counsel asked victim if she believed this phrase described defendant).

104. *See* Perlin, *supra* note 10; *see generally infra* chapter 7 B.

105. *See* Herman, *supra* note 89, at 398: "The debate on the insanity defense is one more battle on the field that includes preventive detention and good faith exceptions to the exclusionary rule." *See also*, Seidman, *supra* note 81, at 442-43 n. 35: "As soon as a criminal trial becomes a symbolic confrontation over issues of social policy, the actual facts of the criminal episode assume secondary importance."

106. *See* Ellsworth, Bukaty, Cowan & Thompson, *The Death Qualified Jury and the Defense of Insanity*, 8 LAW & HUM. BEHAV. 81, 92 (1984) ("a crime control ideology has underlain objections to the insanity defense at least since *M'Naghten*'s case").

den jurisprudence[107] in the context of the trial of a mentally disabled criminal defendant caught in the "pandemonium between the mad and the bad"[108] in our punitive legal culture.[109] The successful use of the defense in the *Hinckley* case thwarted punishment and robbed the community of the ability to exact a penalty that would have expressed a shared litany of the community's condemnation.[110] In a psychodynamic reading, it seemed to tolerate the aberrant behavior of an errant sibling who committed the perfect Oedipal crime against the perfect father figure;[111] under this reading, the subsequent furor was entirely explicable and inevitable.[112]

---

107. On the public's view of the Warren and Burger Courts' criminal procedure decision making (and the courts' responses to those views), *see generally*, Seidman, *supra* note 81; Arenella, *Rethinking the Functions of Criminal Procedure: The Warren and Burger Courts' Competing Ideologies*, 72 GEO. L.J. 185 (1983); *see also*, Amsterdam, *The Supreme Court and the Rights of Suspects in Criminal Cases*, 45 N.Y.U. L. REV. 785, 793 (1970) (discussing "vast mystical significance" of United States Supreme Court decisions).

108. Benham v. Edwards, 501 F. Supp. 1050, 1076 (N.D. Ga. 1980), *aff'd*, 678 F. 2d 511 (5th Cir. 1982), *vacated sub. nom.* Ledbetter v. Benham, 463 U.S. 1222 (1983), *on remand*, 609 F. Supp. 125 (N.D. Ga. 1985), *aff'd*, 785 F. 2d 1480 (11th Cir. 1986).

109. *See* Sarat, *Studying American Legal Culture: An Assessment of Survey Evidence*, 11 LAW & SOC'Y REV. 427, 447 (1977).

   In addition, the operation of the insanity defense inevitably triggers other value-laden symbols: the symbol of the criminal defendant, *see* Seidman, *supra* note 81, at 501; the symbol of the legislature in responding to social pressure, *see* Sherman, *Guilty But Mentally Ill: A Retreat From the Insanity Defense*, 7 AM. J. L. & MED. 237, 256 (1981); the ritualistic symbol of the criminal trial process, *see* Boldt, *Restitution, Criminal Law, and the Ideology of Individuality*, 77 J. CRIM. L. & CRIMINOLOGY 969, 1004-5 (1986); the symbol of mental health experts, *see e.g.*, Bonnie & Slobogin, *The Role of Mental Health Professionals in the Criminal Process: The Case for Informed Speculation*, 66 VA. L. REV. 427, 448-49 (1980); the symbol of the jury, *see generally*, Saks & Kidd, *Human Information Processing and Adjudication: Trial by Heuristics*, 15 LAW & SOC'Y REV. 123 (1980-81), and—in some cases—the symbol of the death penalty, *see supra* note 92; *see also*, Perlin, *The Supreme Court, the Mentally Disabled Criminal Defendant, and Symbolic Values: Random Decisions, Hidden Rationales, or "Doctrinal Abyss?"* 289 ARIZ. L. REV. 1, 89-92 (1987).

110. *See* J. FEINBERG, DOING AND DESERVING: ESSAYS IN THE THEORY OF RESPONSIBILITY 98, 100 (1970): "Punishment, in short, has a symbolic significance largely missing from other kinds of penalties; [it] generally expresses more than judgments of disapproval; it also is a symbolic way of getting back at the criminal, of expressing a kind of vindictive resentment...[T]he criminal's punishment bears the aspect of legitimatized vengefulness."

111. On the unique role of President Reagan as a father-figure, see e.g., L. DEMAUSE, REAGAN'S AMERICA (1984), and see generally infra chapter 7 B.

112. The New Jersey Supreme Court has explicitly articulated that the "controversy" surrounding the Hinckley acquittal "fueled a debate about the very idea of

As in the post-M'Naghten era, "The insanity defense symbolised a loss of social control in the eyes of the public."[113] The final report of the National Institute of Mental Health's Ad Hoc Forensic Advisory Panel's review of policies at St. Elizabeth's Hospital (the facility where John Hinckley is housed) makes explicit, in discussing the controversy that followed the proposal that Hinckley be given an unescorted holiday pass to visit his parents, the continuation and domination of symbolic values in Hinckley's post-acquittal institutionalization:

> Release or progressive relaxation of restrictions placed upon insanity acquittees reawakens public, even professional uncertainties about forensic psychiatry, and the viability of the insanity defense—whether it is fair or just...Therapeutic passes are, of course, *symbolic* of a forensic hospital's legitimate mission to rehabilitate its patients as well as provide the security necessary to protect the public.[114]

I do not mean to be facetious when I characterize the defense as "punishment *interruptus*."[115]

---

mental responsibility." State v. Breakiron, 108 N.J. 591, 599, 532 A. 2d 199 (1987).

113. R. SMITH, supra note 88, at 31 (emphasis in original).

Dr. Richard Rogers has criticized the public's response to the Hinckley verdict as reflecting the "tenuous logic," Rogers, *APA's Position on the Insanity Defense: Empiricism Versus Emotionalism*, 42 AM. PSYCHOLOGIST 840, 840 (1987), that "if the verdict was wrong, then the standard was wrong," Rogers, *supra* note 43, at 78. *Compare* De Benedictis, *supra* note 13 (guilty verdict in Dahmer case may have kept insanity defense alive).

114. *Ad Hoc Report, supra* note 37, at 81 (emphasis added).

115. In her analysis of the "rhetorical phenomenon" that followed the Hinckley acquittal, Professor Barbara Sharf employed "symbolic convergence theory" (*see* Bormann, *Fantasy and Rhetorical Vision: Ten Years Later*, 68 Q.J. SPEECH 288, 292 (1982)), to explain the trial's ultimate significance:

[T]he societal order received a severe blow due to the attempted assassination that endangered the life of the president...The "not guilty by reason of insanity" verdict further emphasized the descent into chaos, for surely something or someone had to be held responsible for the damages. Since the obvious choice, Hinckley, was now ruled out, guilt had to be assigned elsewhere. Psychiatry became a perfect scapegoat. Through the formulation, propagation, and sharing of the alien, rhetorical vision "that clearly distinguishe[d] the 'we' of the [public] from the 'they' of the [psychiatrists]," the public was able to feel cleansed and have a sense that the social order was restored.

Sharf, *Send in the Clowns: The Image of Psychiatry During the Hinckley Trial*, 36 J. COMMUNICATION 80, 91 (1986).

In addition, the insanity defense process is indeterminate. Unlike criminal trials, which generally end in a conviction or an acquittal—a system "unique in its ability to pit forces against each other in stark, primitively satisfying fashion and to provide clearcut winners and losers"[116]—the seemingly-endless disposition phase of the insanity defense case[117] simply does not "fit" with the extant criminal trial-process symbolism.[118] This dissonance helps explain public discomfort with the use of the insanity defense—especially with its successful use—and further helps explain the staying power of insanity defense myths.[119]

The growth and development of insanity defense jurisprudence must be read specifically against this symbolic backdrop. Only then can the mythology basic to the development of the insanity plea by realistically understood.

4. Conclusion

It is impossible to understand either the way these symbolic values have captured the insanity defense debate or the depths of the

---

116. Seidman, *supra* note 81, at 442.
117. *See e.g.,* Rodriguez, LeWinn & Perlin, *supra* note 30, at 403 (after eight years, 116 of 138 defendants in cases involving insanity defense acquittals in New Jersey were still under the trial court's jurisdiction and subject to its supervision, in accordance with the mandates of State v. Krol, 68 N.J. 236, 344 A. 2d 289 (1975)).
118. *See e.g.,* Perlin & Sadoff, *Ethical Issues in the Representation of Individuals in the Commitment Process,* 45 LAW & CONTEMP. PROBS. 161, 166-67 (Summer 1982) (footnotes omitted):

Unlike a typical criminal trial in which a defendant is either found 'not guilty' or 'guilty,'…a civil commitment matter does not fit into a discrete paradigm. This void causes ambivalence, as the lawyer may be incapable of perceiving the characteristics of a 'victory' or a 'loss.'
***   ***   ***   ***
[T]he dispositional phase of a commitment case is ambiguous and almost always open for modification (as a partial reflection of the frequent changes in mental condition and symptomatology of many persons who are subject to commitment proceedings). This ambiguity is inconsistent with the concept of 'finite resolution,' a hallmark of legal decision making.

---

119. The Supreme Court's decision in Jones v. United States, 463 U.S. 354 (1983), for example, accepts, honors and perpetuates these myths in a way that predictably refueled political fires. *See* Perlin, *supra* note 109, at 12-16; *see generally infra* chapter 4 E 2 d.

public's feelings about insanity defense cases such as Hinckley's unless we understand the way that mental illness, crime and punishment are inevitably entwined in the American *psyche*. I will thus next consider, sequentially, how modern psychiatry developed, the role of punishment in ancient and modern society, and the ways in which our ambivalence about mentally disabled criminal defendants has shaped our jurisprudence here.

B. Development of Psychiatry and Psychology

1. Pre-dynamic Psychiatry

Ever since Prince Ptah-hotep attempted the first classification of mental illness almost five thousand years ago,[120] conceptions of such illness have been inextricably linked to the notion of sin.[121] It was commonly believed in the pre-Common Era that, "[i]f a man sinned, he put himself into the power of a demon,"[122] or that sickness was "a punishment sent by God."[123] Notwithstanding the subsequent efforts

---

120. K. MENNINGER, M. MAYMAN & P. PRUYSER, THE VITAL BALANCE 420 (1963) (3000 B.C.); *see also, id.* at 420-489 (history of psychiatric classification since 2600 B.C.); *see also,* Mora, *Historical and Theoretical Trends in Psychiatry,* in 1 COMPREHENSIVE TEXTBOOK OF PSYCHIATRY: CHAPTER 2 1, 8-19 (Freedman, Kaplan & Sadock eds., 2d ed. 1975); Spitzer & Wilson, *Nosology and the Official Psychiatric Nomenclature,* in 1 *id.,* at 826, 831-833; Gurland, *Classification, Nosology, and Taxonomy of Mental Disorders,* in 3 INTERNATIONAL ENCYCLOPEDIA OF PSYCHIATRY, PSYCHOLOGY, PSYCHOANALYSIS, AND NEUROLOGY 156 (Wolman ed. 1977).

121. Michael Moore suggests that the excuse basis of the insanity defense that emerged from the rationale in support of the exculpation of children under the age of seven (who "knoweth not of good and evil") tracks the biblical language of Genesis. M. MOORE, LAW AND PSYCHIATRY: RETHINKING THE RELATIONSHIP 64-65 (1984). *See also,* Platt & Diamond, *The Origins of the "Right and Wrong" Test of Criminal Responsibility and Its Subsequent Development in the United States: An Historical Survey,* 54 CALIF. L. REV. 1227, 1227 (1966) ("One of the earliest sources of the 'right and wrong' test of responsibility, the core of the *M'Naghten* rules, is *Genesis*"). On the similar ways that mental retardation has historically also been seen as God's means of punishing sin, *see* W. WOLFENSBERGER, NORMALIZATION: THE PRINCIPLE OF NORMALIZATION IN HUMAN SERVICES 12-25 (1972).

122. *See* J. BIGGS, THE GUILTY MIND 26 (1955) (discussing Egyptian Papyrus of 1559 B.C.).

123. Id. at 38-39. *But see,* Musto, *A Historical Perspective,* in PSYCHIATRIC ETHICS 13, 15 (S. Bloch & P. Chodoff eds. 1981) (Jewish Talmudic tradition portrayed the insane as victims of disease, not possession). For a fascinating account of then-contemporary popular stereotypes of madness, *see* S. GILMAN, SEEING

of such physicians as Hippocrates,[124] "demonic possession remains the simplest, the most dramatic and, secretly, the most attractive of all explanations of insanity in the Middle Ages."[125]

At that time, the predominant view of the cause of mental disease "was that it was God's punishment for sin."[126] The madman was, "like the possessed, no longer a man."[127] By the middle of the eighteenth century, medical attitudes were "fixed in relation to mental illness, caused by demons."[128] Physicians collected case studies of

---

THE INSANE (1982). On the ways that these stereotypes still affect judicial and legislative decisions, *see generally*, Perlin, *supra* note 10.

124. See J. BIGGS, *supra* note 122, at 43 (Hippocrates responsible for the introduction of a scientific approach to medicine); *see generally*, G. ZILBOORG, A HISTORY OF MEDICAL PSYCHOLOGY (1941). For critiques of Zilboorg's reading of history, *see e.g.*, Neugebauer, *Medieval and Early Modern Theories of Mental Illness*, 36 ARCH. GEN. PSYCHIATRY 477 (1979); Kroll, *A Reappraisal of Psychiatry in the Middle Ages*, 29 ARCH. GEN. PSYCHIATRY 276 (1973).

On the question as to whether the Hippocratic Oath represented then-prevalent Greek of Roman medical practice, *see* Musto, *supra* note 123, at 14. For post-Hippocratic, pre-Middle Age developments, *see* J. BIGGS, *supra* note 122, at 48-62.

125. J. NEAMAN, SUGGESTION OF THE DEVIL: THE ORIGINS OF MADNESS 31 (Anchor ed. 1975). *See e.g.*, Society for Good Will to Retarded Children, Inc. v. Cuomo, 572 F. Supp. 1300, 1304 (E.D.N.Y. 1983) ("In post-medieval times the retarded, together...with the insane, from whom they were not generally distinguished, were viewed as the progeny of the supernatural, and in the last several centuries as agents of the devil").

On the insanity defense's "genesis" in a "homogeneous, religious and moralistic society," *see* Fentiman, *supra* note 15, at 651; *see generally*, G. ROSEN, MADNESS IN SOCIETY: CHAPTERS IN THE HISTORICAL SOCIOLOGY OF MENTAL ILLNESS 71-137 (1969 ed.)(views of mental illness in ancient Greece and Rome), and especially *id.* at 80-83 (attribution of madness to supernatural causes).

126. J. NEAMAN, *supra* note 125, at 50. *See also*, Midelfort, *Madness and Civilization in Early Modern Europe: A Reappraisal of Michel Foucault*, in AFTER THE REFORMATION: ESSAYS IN HONOR OF J.H. HEXTER 247, 254 (B. Malamut ed. 1980) ("madness was considered either a consequence of sin, or purgation, or a test of one's virtue") (*quoting* Penelope Doob).

127. J. NEAMAN, *supra* note 125, at 144. *See generally*, J. EHRENWALD, THE HISTORY OF PSYCHOTHERAPY: FROM HEALING MAGIC TO ENCOUNTER (1976). On the ways that plagues were traditionally seen as "God's punishment," *see* C. HARDING & R. IRELAND, PUNISHMENT: RHETORIC, RULE, AND PRACTICE 115-16 (1989) (PUNISHMENT). Compare E.F. TORREY, THE DEATH OF PSYCHIATRY 91-92 (1975) (task of explaining unknown behavior, once the job of the clergy, has been inherited by psychiatrists, "as they have inherited other aspects of the clerical role").

128. W. BROMBERG, FROM SHAMAN TO PSYCHOTHERAPIST: A HISTORY OF THE TREATMENT OF MENTAL ILLNESS 63 (1975 ed.). See *id.* at 64: "The cosmology of Satanism contained a satisfactory explanation for the manifestations of evil and 'sin' in a man: a screen upon which to visualize cause and effect in human

"demonaics" and began to study pathology and physiology in this context; their data was used by contemporaneous philosophers and theologians to explain such beliefs in terms of mental illness.[129] Such beliefs in evil spirits were "world wide" and were commonly relied upon as an explanation for abnormal behavior.[130] Society saw madness as a condition in which a person was "possessed, controlled, or affected by some supernatural power or being."[131] It is no wonder that Michael Foucault suggested that this "face of madness" has "haunted" Western man's imagination for at least five thousand years.[132]

Religious attitudes exerted the greatest influence on the medical "treatment" of the mentally ill.[133] To a significant extent, our characterization of "sickness" tracks precisely what medieval theologians called "sin."[134] Thus, the law of criminal responsibility has traditionally and historically "followed in theology's wake,"[135] and has re-

---

behavior."

129. G. ROSEN, *supra note 125, at 12; see generally,* F. MANUEL, THE EIGHTEENTH CENTURY: CONFRONTING THE GODS 70-81 (1959).

130. G. ROSEN, supra note 125, at 33; *see also,* E. NORBECK, RELIGION IN PRIMITIVE SOCIETY 215 (1961). On the relationship between evil and social control of deviant behavior, see R. STIVERS, supra note 88, at 101-62.

131. G. ROSEN, *supra note 125, at 82.*

132. M. FOUCAULT, MADNESS AND CIVILIZATION 15 (1965).

133. Musto, supra note 123, at 15. See also, Halleck, *A Critique of Current Psychiatric Roles in the Legal Process,* 1966 WIS. L. REV. 379, 383 ("In eras where mental illness was approached from a more theological standpoint, efforts were made to place the responsibility for sick behavior on external 'devils' such as incubi or succubi").

134. J. NEAMAN, *supra* note 125, at 55. Notes Dr. Jerome Kroll:

There are severe practical implications of a Christian fundamentalist philosophy [such as was prevalent in the Middle Ages]. The first is that the devil is powerful, operative, and hungry for human souls.

Kroll, *supra* note 124, at 277.

See also, Midelfort, *supra* note 126, at 254 ("the connection between sin and sickness has been extremely resilient in western culture") (drawing on the work of Pedrolain Entralgo, a Spanish medical historian).

135. Louisell & Diamond, *Law and Psychiatry: Détente, Entente, or Concomitance?* 50 CORNELL. L.Q. 217, 219 (1965). *See also,* Guttmacher, *The Psychiatrist as an Expert Witness,* 22 U. CHI. L. REV. 325, 329 (1955) (predicting that the psychiatrist "will be thinking and talking as a medical psychologist, rather than as a theologian or a metaphysician" after decision of D.C. Circuit in *Durham v. United States,* 214 F. 2d 862, 870-71 (D.C. Cir. 1954), expanding test for criminal responsibility to include evidence that defendant's act was the "product" of his mental illness); Weihofen, *The Metaphysical Jargon of the Criminal Law,*

mained "anchored to feudal concepts of responsibility."[136] Concomitantly, legal definitions have rested all too often on "medieval folklore."[137]

Anthropologists, philosophers and psychiatrists have all concluded that taboo violation,[138] "a social sanction in highly atomistic or disintegrating social groups," has been a universal explanation for mental illness.[139] It is precisely the ambivalent attitudes that we bring to taboo subjects—seeing them as simultaneously sacred and profane[140]—that are reconstructed in our insanity defense policies: "the socialized expressions of conflicts [that] are in their very nature ambivalent and imply a double attitude of desire and fear, of attraction and repulsion."[141]

This medievalist linking of the mentally disabled and the supernatural world, "viewed with the awe inspired by the mysterious and the inexplicable,"[142] sets the tone for the debate on the question that remains unresolved today: whether we can bring coherence to a

---

22 A.B.A.J. 267 (1936) (examination of traditional responsibility formulations "shows their theological origin"). The metaphor continues today. *See e.g.*, Thomas & Edelman, *An Evaluation of Conservative Crime Control Theology*, 63 Notre Dame L. Rev. 127 (1988).

136. Roche, *Criminal Responsibility*, in Psychiatry and the Law 107 (Hoch & Zubin eds. 1955).

137. Haney, *Psychology and Legal Change: On the Limits of a Factual Jurisprudence*, 4 L. & Hum. Behav. 147 (1980), *quoting* Cantor, *Law and the Social Sciences*, 16 A.B.A. J. 387 (1930).

138. A taboo is a prohibition that carries a supernatural or social sanction, and was historically the characteristic method of ensuring conformity and obedience to social custom in primitive societies. J.C. Flugel, Man, Morals and Society 123 (1961); *see generally*, H. Webster, Taboo: A Sociological Study (1973). On the relationship between taboo and "supernatural punishment," *see* Punishment, *supra* note 127, at 153-55.

139. A. Kiev, Transcultural Psychiatry 121 (1972). *See id.* at 78-108 (discussing culture-bound psychiatric disorders that stem from taboo violations).

140. S. Freud, Totem and Taboo 18 (1950). On the relationship among taboo, totem, magic, science, religion and psychology, *see* B. Malinowski, Magic, Science And Religion And Other Essays (1949).

141. J.C. Flugel, supra note 138, at 125. See also, Punishment, supra note 127, at 142 (social treatment of mentally disabled individuals product of "fear, superstition and religious beliefs"); Golding, *Mental Health Professionals and the Courts: The Ethics of Expertise*, 13 Int'l J. L. & Psychiatry 281, 287 (1990) (key to understanding the level of emotionality surrounding the insanity defense is in the "deeply rooted moral and religious tension which surrounds the attribution of individual responsibility for 'good' and 'evil'"); on the significance and function of our myths of evil, *see generally*, R. Stivers, *supra* note 88, at 52-53.

142. G. Rosen, *supra* note 125, at 83.

jurisprudence that is informed by "ambiguous and ambivalent feelings [toward the mentally disabled criminal defendant] in need of self-realization: unconscious feelings of awe, of fear, of revulsion and of wonder."[143] Only when we seriously and consciously confront *this* issue, will we be able to resolve the underlying questions of substantive and procedural law.

2. Dynamic Psychiatry[144]

The turning point in the development of modern, dynamic psychiatry[145] as a reaction against and rejection of medieval scholasticism and superstition[146] is generally seen in Mesmer's explanation in 1775 of his theory of "animal magnetism."[147] Over the next century, other theorists (Puységur, Liébeault, Charcot, Bernheim)[148] "undertook with great audacity the exploration and the therapeutic utiliza-

---

143. Perlin, *supra* note 88, at 168. For the most eloquent articulation of this problem, *see* Goldstein & Katz, *Abolish the "Insanity Defense"—Why Not?* 72 YALE L. J. 853, 868-69 (1963):

> The problem of 'whether there would be an insanity defense' or 'how to formulate it' must continue unresolved as long as largely unconscious feelings of apprehension, awe and anger toward the 'sick,' particularly if associated with 'criminality,' are hidden by the more acceptable conscious desire to protect the 'sick from criminal liability.' What must be recognized is the enormous ambivalence toward the 'sick' reflected in conflicting wishes to exculpate and to blame, to sanction and not to sanction; to degrade and to elevate; to stigmatize and not to stigmatize; to care and to reject; to treat and to mistreat; to protect and to destroy.

144. "Dynamic" psychiatry is the study of emotional processes, their origins and mental mechanisms, which seeks to analyze the active, energy-filled, and constantly changing factors in human behavior and motivation, and thus conveys the concepts of progress or regression. BLAKISTON'S GOULD MEDICAL DICTIONARY 416 (4th ed. 1979). *Cf.* Goldsmith & Mandell, *The Dynamic Formulation—A Critique of Psychiatric Ritual*, 125 AM. J. PSYCHIATRY 152 (1969).

145. *See* Loevinger, *Law and Science as Rival Systems*, 8 JURIMETRICS J. 63, 65 (1966) ("Science as an organized discipline with recognized tactics and strategy involving rigorous modes of observation and experiment has been developed only since the early seventeenth century") (footnote omitted). *See also,* Menninger, *Medicolegal Proposals of the American Psychiatric Association*, 19 J. CRIM. L., CRIMINOL. & POL. SCI. 367, 369 (1928-29) ("About 150 years ago...the scientific method began to be applied to the matter of human sickness").

146. Loevinger, *supra* note 145, at 66.

147. H. ELLENBERGER, THE DISCOVERY OF THE UNCONSCIOUS: THE HISTORY AND EVOLUTION OF DYNAMIC PSYCHIATRY 53-69 (1970). *See also, id.* at 3-52 (tracing ancient and "primitive" roots of psychotherapy).

148. *See id.* at 70-109.

tion of unconscious psychological energies[,] elaborat[ing] new theories about the human mind and the psychogenesis of illness."[149]

Two main trends emerged. One school of thought attributed mental disease to physical causes and brain conditions;[150] the other emphasized the emotional causes of such disease.[151] For the first time it was accepted that a person could be "insane" if his faculties of *emotion* and *will* were unbalanced, "even if his reason remained intact."[152] James Prichard, an English doctor, coined the phrase "moral insanity"[153] to describe the condition of persons who lacked a "moral sense, or rather, possessed only a warped one, despite their intellectual awareness of conventional moral values."[154] Insanity was

---

149. *Id.* at 110. On the social and cultural background of the first school of dynamic psychiatry, *see id.* at 182-253; on the then-prevailing conceptualizations of psychogenesis and illness, *see id.* at 148-150.

   See also, W. Overholser, The Psychiatrist and the Law 9 (1953) (crediting Pinel with setting forth psychiatry as "belonging in the field of medicine, rather than in that of theology or philosophy"). The "legend" of Pinel's heroic and "mythical" role is sharply criticized in M. Foucault, *supra* note 132, at 243; *see generally id.* at 241-78; *but see* Midelfort, *supra* note 126, at 258-59 (reevaluating Foucault's assessment of Pinel); J. Goldstein, Console and Classify: The French Psychiatric Profession in the Nineteenth Century (1987) (same). For a recent contextual evaluation of Pinel, *see* Weiner, *Philippe Pinel's "Memoir on Madness" of December 11, 1794: A Fundamental Text of Modern Psychiatry,* 149 Am. J. Psychiatry 725 (1992).

150. *See e.g.,* F. Alexander & S. Selesnick, The History of Psychiatry 151-52 (1966), discussing writings of Wilhelm Griesinger (1817-68), who argued that mental diseases were due to "direct or indirect action upon cerebral cells." Zilboorg called Griesinger's work "psychiatry without psychology." G. Zilboorg, *supra* note 124, at 437.

151. H. Ellenberger, *supra* note 147, at 284.

152. Dain & Carlson, *Moral Insanity in the United States 1835-1866,* 117 Am. J. Psychiatry 795 (1960).

153. J. Prichard, A Treatise on Insanity and Other Disorders Affecting the Mind (1835). For a survey of the literature on moral insanity, *see* A. Fink, Causes of Crime: Biological Theories in the United States, 1800-1915 48-76 (1938); for a helpful historical perspective, *see* Tighe, *Francis Wharton and the Nineteenth Century Insanity Defense: The Origins of a Reform Tradition,* 27 Am. J. Leg. Hist. 223 (1983); *see generally,* Tuke, *Mental Experts and Criminal Responsibility,* 28 J. Ment. Sci. 35 (1883); Laycock, *On the Legal Doctrines of the Responsibility of the Insane and Its Consequences,* 10 J. Ment. Sci. 350 (1865).
   On the significance of "moral insanity" in the development of American insanity defense jurisprudence, *see* Tighe, *supra,* at 231 n. 16 (citing sources). *See generally,* Ray, *Criminal Law of Insanity,* 28 Am. Jurist 253 (1835).

154. Dain & Carlson, *supra* note 152, at 795. *See* Tighe, *supra* note 153, at 232: "The key dynamic in nineteenth century discussions of mental illness and criminality was the movement away from theories stressing volition and absolute moral

linked to vice—especially sexual vice—and it was believed that im-moral acts could cause insanity.[155]

The influence of those schools of dynamic psychiatry and of "moral insanity" began to fade by the late nineteenth century.[156] The concept of "moral insanity" was under attack by somatically-oriented American psychiatrists like John P. Gray, editor of the *American Journal of Insanity* (forerunner of the *American Journal of Psychiatry*, the official journal of the American Psychiatric Association) from 1855 to 1885.[157] Gray argued that acceptance of such a construct would harm American "religious beliefs, moral standards, and legal practices."[158] Wrote Gray, using language remarkably like that adopted by insanity defense opponents in the 1970s and 1980s:

> The general tendency of the doctrine of moral insanity is bad, whatever show or real feeling of humanity there may be in it. It is bad, in a religious view, because it tempts men to indulge their strongest passions, under the false impression that God has so constituted them that their false

---

responsibility to theories which emphasized some form of 'scientific' determinism."

155. On the way sexual vices are historically linked with concepts of madness, *see e.g.*, McCandless, *Liberty and Lunacy: The Victorians and Wrongful Confinement*, in MADHOUSES, MAD-DOCTORS, AND MADMEN: THE SOCIAL HISTORY OF PSYCHIATRY IN THE VICTORIAN ERA 339, 354 (A. Scull ed. 1981) (masturbation and other "immoral acts" seen as causes of insanity); *see generally*, V. SKULTANS, ENGLISH MADNESS: IDEAS ON INSANITY, 1580-1890 69-97 (1979) (discussing "masturbational insanity" and "femininity and [mental] illness"). *Compare* M. FOUCAULT, *supra* note 132, at 24 ("The middle ages had given madness a place in the hierarchy of vices"); C. MERCIER, CRIMINAL RESPONSIBILITY 222 (1926) ("When pushed to extreme, vice becomes evidence of insanity").

156. H. ELLENBERGER, *supra* note 147, at 171-74. Both schools also exerted a profound influence on philosophy, literature and the arts. *See id.* at 158-70.

157. On the interplay between the development of psychiatry and the construction of institutions built to house the mentally disabled, *see generally*, M. FOUCAULT, *supra* note 132; 1 M.L. PERLIN, *supra* note 4, §§ 2.02-2.03; Morrissey & Goldman, *Care and Treatment of the Mentally Ill in the United States: Historical Developments and Reforms*, 484 ANNALS 12 (1986). On this interplay in the particular context of the criminally insane, *see* H. BARNES, THE REPRESSION OF CRIME 248-59 (1926). On institutions' role as a "religious domain,...an instrument of moral uniformity and of social denunciation," *see* M. FOUCAULT, *supra* note 132, at 257-59. *On the relationship between the creation of institutions and early civil commitment law, see* Dwyer, *Civil Commitment Laws in Nineteenth-Century New York*, 6 BEHAV. SCI. & L. 79 (1988); Appelbaum & Kemp, *The Evolution of Commitment Laws in the Nineteenth Century: A Reinterpretation*, 6 LAW & HUM. BEHAV. 343 (1982).

158. Dain & Carlson, *supra* note 152, at 797.

passions or impulses are not generally governable by their will or their reason, and that, therefore, there is no punishable guilt in indulging them. This is fatalism. It is bad in the legal view, because it protects from due punishment offenses which, with the self-denial and self-control that men rightly trained are quite capable of exercising, might be avoided. It tends to give to bad education, loose habits, vicious indulgence, neglected parental control and disobedience to God, an immunity...not warranted by the Scriptures, the law of reason, or any codes of human law that assume to be founded on the law of reason or the law of God.[159]

At that time, Emil Kraepelin's construction of the first rational modern classification and nosology of mental illness, and Eugen Bleuler's development of a theory of schizophrenia,[160] restructured the meaning of psychodynamics, culminating in Hughlings Jackson's neurological model.[161] This conception, along with rapidly-developing investigations into sexual psychology and psychopathology, the study of dreams, and the role of the unconscious in human behavior,[162] most likely had a great impact on the teachings and writings of Sigmund Freud, with whom the modern era of psychiatry began.[163]

Writing over sixty years ago, the historian Harry Elmer Barnes stated, "[T]here is no more notable chapter in the history of medical and social science than the progress of psychiatry from Pinel to

---

159. *Id., quoting* Gray, *Moral Insanity*, 14 AM. J. INSAN. 321 (1858). For a similar characterization, *see* E.F. TORREY, *supra* note 127, at 92 (quoting the sixteenth century writer, Bodin).

   For a blistering attack on the moral insanity doctrine, *see* Workman, *Moral Insanity—What Is It?* 39 AM. J. INSAN. 334 (1883); *see generally*, Tighe, *supra* note 153, at 231 ("No other doctrine of disease stimulated so much medico-legal interest and bitter conflict as did the notion of a mental disorder confined primarily to the non-intellectual faculties of the mind"), and *see also, id.* at 238 ("One of the most important forces shaping [Francis] Wharton's legal argument against moral insanity was his retributive penal philosophy").

160. H. ELLENBERGER, *supra* note 147, at 284-89.

161. *Id.* at 290-91: "It designated the physiological aspect in contrast to the anatomic, the functional in contrast to the organic, and it expressed at the same time the energetic aspect, even including at times the connotation of conflict and resistance."

162. *Id.* at 291-318.

163. *Id.* at 291; *see* W. OVERHOLSER, *supra* note 149, at 10-11. The story of the life, teachings, influence and importance of Sigmund Freud has been told sufficient times so as to require little elaboration here. *See e.g.*, E. JONES, THE LIFE AND WORK OF SIGMUND FREUD (1955); N. HALE, FREUD AND THE AMERICANS: THE BEGINNINGS OF PSYCHOANALYSIS IN THE UNITED STATES, 1876-1917 (1971); AMERICAN PSYCHOANALYSIS: ORIGINS AND DEVELOPMENT (J. Quen & E. Carlson eds. 1978).

Charcot, Janet and Freud."[164] There is no disputing Dr. Walter Bromberg's claim that the 1916 English-publication of Freud's *Introductory Lectures* "literally overturned the psychiatric world,"[165] and that, still, nearly a half century after Freud's death, the word "psychiatry" still meant "modern psychiatry as Freud has left it."[166]

Dynamic psychiatry rigorously criticized and rejected the pre-existing theological models of behavior.[167] This criticism, in turn, greatly influenced criminologists and criminal law theoreticians on such issues as punishment, rehabilitation, and responsibility.[168] In their influential text of the 1930s,[169] Alexander and Staub illuminate the significance of Freudian thought on the development of criminal law and criminology:

> Psychoanalysis was the first branch of human knowledge which undertook to investigate the psychology of the real individual, i.e., of the deeper motive powers of human actions. Psychoanalysis, therefore, claims a right to speak when the matter of the judging of the criminal is considered;

---

164. H. BARNES, *supra* note 157, at 249.
165. W. BROMBERG, *supra* note 128, at 229. A group of social science researchers have characterized the development of psychoanalytic theory as one of the four most significant achievements in the social sciences in the twentieth century. *See* Deutsch, Platt & Senghaas, *Conditions Favoring Major Advances in Social Science*, 171 SCIENCE 450, 451 (1971).
166. J. ROBITSCHER, PURSUIT OF AGREEMENT: PSYCHIATRY AND THE LAW 12 (1966). For a convenient and helpful summary, *see* Weisberg, *The "Discovery" of Sexual Abuse: Experts' Role in Legal Policy Formulation*, 18 U.C. DAVIS L. REV. 1, 10-13 (1984). *See also*, Forer, *Law and the Unreasonable Person*, 36 EMORY L.J. 181, 187 (1987) ("By the twentieth century, a host of new ideas [—including Freud's discovery of the role of the unconscious on human behavior—] combined to reshape attitudes that had prevailed for centuries"). On the impact of Freudian psychology on anthropology, *see e.g.*, Hartmann & Loewenstein, *Some Psychoanalytic Comments on "Culture and Personality,"* in PSYCHOANALYSIS AND CULTURE 3 (G. Wilbur & W. Muensterberger eds. 1953).
167. *See e.g.*, Weihofen, *supra* note 135, at 270: "We can never hope to reach any agreement of understanding upon the very fundamentals of our substantive criminal law until we realize first, that these fundamental propositions are man-made and not God-given, that they are made to serve human ends, and are not ends in themselves divinely imposed on human beings, and second, that in order to serve human ends, they must rest upon a clear knowledge of the actual human needs they undertake to serve."
168. *See e.g.*, Halleck, *The Historical and Ethical Antecedents of Psychiatric Criminology*, in PSYCHIATRIC ASPECTS OF CRIMINOLOGY 8, 8 (S. Halleck & W. Bromberg eds. 1968): "Criminology has been a field of special interest to psychiatrists almost from the time that psychiatry became an organized profession."
169. *See* Pollack, *Franz Alexander's Observations On Psychiatry and Law*, 121 AM. J. PSYCHIATRY 458 (1964).

it believes that it could, by means of its special methods, lead to a complete understanding of the criminal and his acts.

...Real psychology...was uncovered by Freud.[170]

This should not be read to imply that "psychiatry" has ever spoken with a unified voice on the underlying political and social issues. To an important extent, the split between somatically-oriented and psychologically-oriented psychiatrists still tracks the division between organic and analytic psychiatrists still present today.[171] Freud's teachings are no longer uncritically accepted.[172] Competing schools of psychiatry and psychology have emerged,[173] and the prophylactic value of psychodynamic psychiatry has been questioned closely.[174] However, Freudian psychodynamic psychiatry remains the

---

170. F. ALEXANDER & H. STAUB, THE CRIMINAL, THE JUDGE, AND THE PUBLIC 24-25 (1931). *See also*, F. ALEXANDER, OUR AGE OF UNREASON: A STUDY OF THE IRRATIONAL FORCES IN SOCIAL LIFE (rev. ed. 1971); *see also generally*, PSYCHO-ANALYSIS, SCIENTIFIC METHOD AND PHILOSOPHY (S. Hook ed. 1959); R. WEST, CONSCIENCE AND SOCIETY (2d ed. 1950).

171. *See e.g.*, Dain & Carlson, *supra* note 152, at 797-99 (conflict in nineteenth century psychiatric positions on "moral insanity"); A. HOLLINGSHEAD & F. REDLICH, SOCIAL CLASS AND MENTAL ILLNESS (1958); Kreitman, *Psychiatric Orientation: A Study of Attitudes Among Psychiatrists*, 108 J. MENT. SCI. 317 (1962); Bulmash, *The Irony of the Insanity Defense: A Theory of Relativity*, 10 J. L. & PSYCHIATRY 285, 290-94 (1982) (contrasting "psychological-cognitive, psychiatric-somatic, and psychoanalytic-social" models of human behavior). On the role of psychological individualism in the development of criminal justice policy, *see* Haney, *Criminal Justice and the Nineteenth-Century Paradigm: The Triumph of Psychological Individualism in the "Formative Era,"* 6 LAW & HUM. BEHAV. 191 (1982).

172. *See e.g.*, H. KOHUT, THE RESTORATION OF THE SELF (1977); Morse, *Failed Explanations and Criminal Responsibility: Experts and the Unconscious*, 68 VA. L. REV. 971, 1026 (1982) (characterizing psychodynamic formulations as "inherently unreliable"). For an account of contemporary resistance to Freud, *see* V. BROME, FREUD AND HIS EARLY CIRCLE 31-38 (1968).

173. *See e.g.*, *Treatments of Psychiatric Disorders: A Task Force of the American Psychiatric Association* (T.B. Karasu ed. 1989); J. BISCHOF, INTERPRETING PERSONALITY THEORIES (2d ed. 1970); HANDBOOK OF INNOVATIVE PSYCHO-THERAPIES (R. Corsini ed. 1981).

174. *See e.g.*, Schmideberg, *The Promise of Psychiatry: Hopes and Disillusionment*, 57 Nw. U. L. REV. 19, 20 (1962) ("In the last twenty years, we have been subjected to...a barrage of indiscriminate and often irresponsible glorification of psychiatry..."); *see also*, Hakeem, *A Critique of the Psychiatric Approach to Crime and Correction*, 23 L. & CONTEMP. PROBS. 650 (1958) (discussing psychiatry's influence on correctional policies); Shah, *Therapeutic Sanctions and Fundamental Notions of Justice: A Basic Dilemma in Law and Mental Health Interactions*, in HARMONIEEN TEGENSPRAAK 317, 318-19 (C. Kelk, F. Koenraadt & A. Mooij eds. 1990); J. ROBITSCHER, THE POWERS OF PSYCHIATRY 29-46

benchmark against which the questions under consideration in this paper—the relationship among mental illness, crime, punishment, evil, religiosity, sin, and legal insanity—are regularly assessed.

The most trenchant criticisms of psychiatry arose in response to the glorification of psychoanalysis's "right to speak" in responsibility assessments that dramatically "upped the ante" for organized psychiatry. Views like those expressed by Benjamin Karpman—"I belong to the small group of psychiatrists who hold the thesis that criminality is *without exception* symptomatic of abnormal mental states and is an expression of them"[175]—were heuristically attributed to all psychiatrists, leading to public derision,[176] and ultimately contributing significantly to the law's rejection of the psychodynamic model.[177]

Also, it became clear that mental illness could not be conceptualized statically.[178] Freudianism has thus been criticized sharply on a variety of empirical, political, philosophical, cultural, gender-based, sexual orientation-based and scientific grounds.[179] Specifically, in its

---

(1980) (on the broadening of psychoanalytically-oriented psychiatric power). On the relationship between the development of the "medical model" of mental disease and the growth of the insanity defense, *see generally*, Wales, *The Rise, The Fall, and the Resurrection of the Medical Model*, 63 GEO. L.J. 87 (1974).

See also, Commonwealth v. Carroll, 412 Pa. 525, 194 A. 2d 911, 918 (1963) (emphasis in original): *"The Courts of Justice should not abdicate their function and duty of determining criminal responsibility to the psychiatrist."*

175. Karpman, *Criminality, Insanity and the Law*, 39 J. CRIM. L., CRIMINOL. & POL. SCI. 584, 584-85 (1949) (emphasis added). *See also*, C. HIBBERT, THE ROOTS OF EVIL: A SOCIAL HISTORY OF CRIME AND PUNISHMENT 219 (1968 ed.) (*quoting* Karpman: "You can't have mental illness and criminal responsibility in the same person at the same time"); Pillsbury, *Understanding Penal Reform: The Dynamics of Change*, 80 J. CRIM. L. & CRIMINOL. 726, 742 (1989) ("crime was described as a disease").

176. *See* C. HIBBERT, *supra* note 175, at 219.

177. *See generally infra* chapter 4 B-D.

178. *See e.g.*, Slovenko, *The Meaning of Mental Illness in Criminal Responsibility*, 5 J. LEG. MED. 1, 5 (1984).

179. *See generally*, Morse, *supra* note 172; *see e.g.*, State v. Schantz, 98 Ariz. 200, 403 P. 2d 521, 527-528 n.7 (1965), *quoting* Hall, *Mental Disease and Criminal Responsibility*, 45 COLUM. L. REV. 677, 682 (1945):

"The best psychiatry is still more of an art than of science," writes a recognized expert…[A] forthright investigator concludes that "no critically minded person practiced in scientific research or in disciplined speculation can accept psychoanalysis on the basis of the writings of Freud or of any of his followers. The presentation of facts is inadequate; the speculation is irresponsible; verifications are lacking; conclusions are hastily arrived at, and concepts are hypostatized." Finally, it is admitted that, with some exceptions, "there has been no

application to the criminal law, Freudian psychiatry has been perceived as "deterministic and amoral, and therefore, incompatible
with traditional ideas of responsibility and punishment for voluntary
harm-doing."[180] It should not be surprising then that, for the most
part,[181] "rigorous psychoanalytic analyses of law are...notoriously
absent from American legal scholarship."[182]

---

real psychiatric insight into criminalistic behavior.

This attitude is still reflected in some contemporaneous United States Supreme Court opinions. *See e.g.*, Perlin & Dorfman, *supra* note 10, at 57-61,
discussing Justice Thomas's dissents in Riggins v. Nevada, 112 S. Ct. 1810
(1992), and Foucha v. Louisiana, 112 S. Ct. 1780 (1992).

180. J. Hall, Law, Social Science and Criminal Theory 87 (1982). *Cf.* Swartz,
"Mental Disease:" The Groundwork for Legal Analysis and Legislative Action,
111 U. Pa. L. Rev. 389, 390 (1963), *quoting*, in part, Wootton, *Sickness or Sin?*
159 Twentieth Century 433, 434 (1956) ("the modern trend [is] that 'the
concept of an illness expands continually at the expense of the concept of moral
failure'"). The decline in emphasis on psychoanalysis in criminal justice is
discussed extensively in Tigar, *Crime Talk, Rights Talk, and Double-Talk:
Thoughts on Reading Encyclopedia of Crime and Justice*, 65 Tex. L. Rev. 101,
148-50 (1986).
    On the other hand, it is fairly clear that Freud believed in the importance of
the criminal law, *id.* at 106-7, stating that "culture must be defended against the
individual, and its organizations, its institutions and its laws, are all directed to
this end," *id.* at 107, *quoting* S. Freud, The Future of an Illusion 9-10 (Jones
ed. 1928). On Freud's concept of the community's "cultural super-ego," *see* S.
Freud, Civilization and Its Discontents 88-89 (J. Strachey ed. 1962).
181. *But see e.g.*, Ehrenzweig, *A Psychoanalysis of the Insanity Plea—Clues to the
Problems of Criminal Responsibility and Insanity in the Death Cell*, 73 Yale
L.J. 425 (1964); A. Ehrenzweig, Psychoanalytic Jurisprudence 207-41
(1971); J.C. Smith, Law, Myth and the Oedipal Complex: Toward a
Psychoanalytic Jurisprudence (1988); Lawrence, *The Id, the Ego and Equal
Protection: Reckoning With Unconscious Racism*, 39 Stan. L. Rev. 317 (1987);
Wilson, *Vengeance and Mercy: Implications of Psychoanalytic Theory for the
Retributive Theory of Punishment*, 60 Neb. L. Rev. 276 (1981); Duncan, *"A
Strong Liking:" Our Admiration for Criminals*, 1991 U. Ill. L. Rev. 1; Stark,
Divorce Law, Feminism, and Psychoanalysis: In Dreams Begin Responsibilities,
38 U.C.L.A. L. Rev. 1483 (1991); Comment, *Corroborating Confessions: An
Empirical Analysis of Legal Safeguards Against False Confessions*, 1984 Wis.
L. Rev. 1121; Goreta, *The Psychoanalytical Approach as a Contribution to the
Assessment of Criminal Responsibility*, 18 J. Psychiatry & L. 329 (1990);
Bloom & Awad, *Unconscious Fantasies: From the Couch to the Court*, 19 Bull.
Am. Acad. Psychiatry & L. 119 (1991). On the way that legal scholarship in
this area is ignored and/or devalued, *see* M. Perlin & D. Dorfman, "The Invisible
Renaissance of Mental Disability Law Scholarship: A Case Study of Subordina-
tion" (manuscript in progress).
182. Chase, *Who Needs Information When You're Working Underground? Legal
Education, Social Context, and the Public Interest*, 12 Nova L. Rev. 55, 65
(1987); Bienenfeld, *Justice, Aggression and Eros*, 38 Int'l J. Psychoanalysis

Yet, a recent retrospective appraisal of the past four decades of psychotherapy concluded that "no real breakthroughs have occurred during the past forty years and that despite claims to the contrary, the innovations and modifications developed have not produced truly remarkable results."[183] Thus, a recent exhaustive study has "affirmed the basic soundness of Freud's thinking" about at least seven of the most important underpinnings of his theoretical thinking.[184] Professors Louisell and Diamond formulated the issue this way over thirty-five years ago:

> [T]here is ample evidence from psychoanalysis, psychiatry, and the other behavioral sciences that the more free the individual is from the internal pressures of psychopathology and the less he is burdened with the detrimental forces of adverse social, economic and cultural conditions, the more he is able to make choices and decisions, to select among alternative patterns of behavior, in a manner which appears to approximate our traditional notion of free will.[185]

C. The Role of Punishment

1. Introduction

Courts and legislators have traditionally feared that acceptance of psychodynamic principles, allegedly characterized by the psychia-

---

419 (1957). *See also*, Chase, *supra*, at 65 n. 32 (discussing Ehrenzweig's work as a "masterful exception which has failed to gain a formidable psychoanalytic following within American scholarship"). For a rare case example, *see* Miller v. United States, 320 F. 2d 767, 772-74 (D.C. Cir. 1963) (psychodynamic roots of guilt feelings); *see also*, Hamman v. County of Maricopa, 161 Ariz. 58, 775 P. 2d 1122, 1123 n. 3 & n. 4 (1989) (discussing meanings of "denial" and "projection").

183. Garfield, *Psychotherapy: A 40-Year Appraisal*, 36 AM. PSYCHOLOGIST 174, 182 (1981). On the efficacy of psychotherapy, *see* M. SMITH, G. GLASS & T. MILLER, THE BENEFITS OF PSYCHOTHERAPY 183 (1980); contra, Eysenck, An Exercise in Mega-Silliness, 33 AM. PSYCHOLOGIST 517 (1978) (letter to the editor) ("there is still no acceptable evidence for the efficacy of psychotherapy"). For recent comprehensive surveys of all studies, *see* Durham & LaFond, *A Search For the Missing Premise of Involuntary Therapeutic Commitment: Effective Treatment of the Mentally Ill*, 40 RUTGERS L. REV. 303, 330-43 (1988); Otto & Schmidt, *Malpractice in Verbal Psychotherapy: Problems and Potential Solutions*, 4 FORENS. REPORTS 309, 324 (1991); Smith, *A Crazy System: Mental Health Care Delivery in America*, 5 J. CONTEMP. HEALTH L. & POL. 75, 81-83 (1989).

184. S. FISHER & R. GREENBERG, THE SCIENTIFIC CREDIBILITY OF FREUD'S THEORIES AND THERAPY 414 (1985).

185. Louisell & Diamond, *supra* note 135, at 221 (footnote omitted).

trist's perceived "peculiar tolerant attitude toward criminal behavior"[186] and perceived urge to "replace the negative pattern of fear and repression which has dominated penology," would wrongly undermine the powerful force of punishment in the criminal justice process.[187] This fear is mirrored in President Reagan's campaign rhetoric on behalf of conservative Republican Senate candidates whom he could count on to support his efforts to appoint "tough" federal judges ("We don't need a bunch of sociology majors on the bench") or in Attorney General Thornburgh's declaration at a National Crime Summit, "We are not here...to discuss sociological theory."[188] While we know that these fears are inaccurate—perhaps even irrational[189] —they help explain, as much as any other source, the incoherence of our insanity defense jurisprudence.

---

186. Guttmacher, *The Psychiatric Approach to Crime and Correction*, 23 L. & CONTEMP. PROBS. 633, 633 (1958).

　　Again, psychiatry has never spoken in a unitary way on this issue. The debate over "moral insanity" reflected a deep split in psychiatric attitudes toward mentally ill persons charged with crime. *See e.g.*, Grissom, *True and False Experts*, 34 AM. J. INSAN. 1 (1878). Also, the deep rift between what have been characterized as the "directive/organic" and "psychotherapeutic/analytic" schools, *see, e.g.*, A. HOLLINGSHEAD & F. REDLICH, *supra* note 171, demonstrates the disunity of twentieth century psychiatry.

187. Guttmacher, *supra* note 186, at 642. For helpful overviews, *see* Zimring & Hawkins, *Dangerousness and Criminal Justice*, 85 MICH. L. REV. 481 (1986); Williams & Hawkins, *Perceptual Research on General Deterrence: A Critical Review*, 20 LAW & SOC'Y REV. 545 (1986). For an important critical reading of the underlying criminological issues, *see* Henry & Milovanovic, *Constitutive Criminology: The Maturation of Critical Theory*, 29 CRIMINOL. 293 (1991).

188. Rowland, Songer & Carp, *Presidential Effects on Criminal Justice Policy in the Lower Federal Courts: The Reagan Judges*, 22 LAW & SOC'Y REV. 191, 194 (1988); Krisberg, *Are You Now or Have You Ever Been a Sociologist?* 82 J. CRIM. L. & CRIMINOL. 141, 141 (1991). *But compare*, Andrews, Bonta & Hoge, *Classification for Effective Rehabilitation: Rediscovering Psychology*, 17 CRIM. JUST. & BEHAV. 19, 22 (1990) (psychological understanding of criminal conduct prerequisite for effective correctional programs).

189. Even a cursory reading of recent United States Supreme Court decisions in this area, *see generally* Perlin, *supra* note 109; Perlin, *supra* note 88; Perlin & Dorfman, *supra* note 10, quickly illuminates the difference in positions between what Guttmacher might call "tolerators" and psychiatrists such as Dr. James P. Grigson, known colloquially as "Dr. Death," *see* Ewing, *"Dr. Death" and the Case for An Ethical Ban on Psychiatric and Psychological Predictions of Dangerousness in Capital Sentencing Proceedings*, 8 AM. J. L. & MED. 407, 410 (1983). For a sampling of cases involving Dr. Grigson's testimony, *see e.g.,* Barefoot v. Estelle, 463 U.S. 880 (1983); Estelle v. White, 451 U.S. 454 (1981); Satterwhite v. Texas, 486 U.S. 249 (1988). For more recent commentary on Dr. Grigson, *see* R. ROSENBAUM, TRAVELS WITH DR. DEATH 206-37 (1990); Zaitchik, *Burying Dr. Death*, Boston Phoenix (Dec. 21, 1990).

2. The Social Role of Punishment

Punishment is a coercive, symbolic, judgmental, state-inflicted, condemnatory, normative, proportional deprivation[190] that "has been the main device for enforcing laws ever since the mists of prehistory lifted."[191] At least five major aims of punishment have been identified by criminologists and philosophers: restraint, general deterrence,[192] individual deterrence, rehabilitation[193] and desert.[194]

On the prosecution-bias of many psychiatrists, see J. ROBITSCHER, supra note 174, at 24, 262; on the authoritarianism of such psychiatrists, see id. at 389-404.

190. See generally, J. HALL, GENERAL PRINCIPLES OF CRIMINAL LAW 310-12 (2d ed. 1960); S. BARNES, EVOLUTIONARY IMPLICATIONS OF LEGALIZED PUNISHMENT (1974). For a recent thoughtful analysis of punishment from a moral philosophy perspective, see Lipkin, The Moral Good Theory of Punishment, 40 U. FLA. L. REV. 17 (1988). For other recent searching inquiries, see Dresser, Personal Identity and Punishment, 70 B.U.L. REV. 395 (1990); Sadurski, Theory of Punishment, Social Justice, and Liberal Neutrality, 7 LAW & PHILOS. 351 (1989); Pillsbury, supra note 44. On punishment's limitations, see e.g., Crocker, The Upper Limits of Just Punishment, 41 EMORY L.J. 1059 (1992); Campos, The Paradox of Punishment, 1992 WIS. L. REV. 1931.

191. E. VAN DEN HAAG, PUNISHING CRIMINALS 4 (1975). The religious roots of punishment theory have never been far from the surface. See W. BROMBERG, supra note 128, at 220, citing Moore v. Stickling, 33 S.E. 274 (W. Va. Ct. App. 1899): "The morality of our laws is the morality of the Mosaic interpretation of the Ten Commandments, modified only as to the degree and kind of punishment."

See also, Tighe, supra note 153, at 239, quoting Francis Wharton ("Sin is to be punished because it is Sin"); see generally, Grasmick, Davenport, Chamlin & Bursik, Protestant Fundamentalism and the Retributive Doctrine of Punishment, 30 CRIMINOL. 21 (1992).

192. See e.g., Andenaes, The Moral or Educative Influence of Criminal Law, 27 J. SOC. ISS. 17, 19; Andenaes, Determinism and Criminal Law, 47 J. CRIM. L., CRIMINOL. & POL. SCI. 406 (1956). On deterrence theory's assumption of rational behavior, see Rychlak, Society's Right to Punish: A Further Exploration of the Denunciation Theory of Punishment, 65 TULANE L. REV. 299, 209-10 (1990); Rychlak & Rychlak, The Insanity Defense and the Question of Human Agency, 8 NEW IDEAS IN PSYCHOLOGY 3 (1990).

193. For an excellent analysis of the "exciting and troubling" aspects of the therapeutic orientation implicit in the rehabilitative ideal in punishment, see Wexler, Therapeutic Justice, 57 MINN. L. REV. 289, 337 (1972); on the link between punishment and treatment of the mentally disabled criminal defendant, see Devlin, Mental Abnormality and the Criminal Law, in CHANGING LEGAL OBJECTIVES 71, 76 (R. St.J. MacDonald ed. 1963); on the relationship between the retributive model and the medical model of criminal justice, see Beahrs, Volition, Deception, and the Evolution of Justice, 19 BULL. AM. ACAD. PSYCHIATRY & L. 81 (1991).

194. Gaylin & Rothman, Introduction, in A. VON HIRSCH, DOING JUSTICE: THE CHOICE OF PUNISHMENTS xxi, xxviii-xxix (1976). On the question of whether

As recently as 1974, Professor Schulhofer noted that most American jurisdictions exclude retaliation from the legitimate goals of the criminal law, that legal theorists "[we]re virtually unanimous in applauding the judgment,"[195]and that the idea of punishment was "giving way" to the idea of treatment.[196] Yet, the notion of *desert*[197]

---

all of these theories are "anything other than [an] intricate *ex post facto* rationalization of an unarticulated social practice," *see* PUNISHMENT, *supra* note 127, at 20.

On the special issues involved in cases involving *mentally retarded* defendants, *see* Hermann, Singer & Roberts, *Sentencing of the Mentally Retarded Criminal Defendant*, 41 ARK. L. REV. 765 (1988).

195. Schulhofer, *Harm and Punishment: A Critique of Emphasis on the Results of Conduct in the Criminal Law*, 122 U. PA. L. REV. 1497, 1510-1511 (1974) (footnote omitted). *See e.g.*, Williams v. New York, 337 U.S. 241, 248 (1949) ("Retribution is no longer the dominant objective of the criminal law. Reformation and rehabilitation of offenders have become important goals of criminal jurisprudence"); Regina v. Sargent, 60 Crim. App. 74, 77 (1974) ("The Old Testament concept of an eye for an eye and tooth for tooth no longer plays any part in our criminal law"); *compare* Winter, *The Cognitive Dimension of the Agon Between Legal Power and Narrative Meaning*, 87 MICH. L. REV. 2225, 2246 (1989) ("eye for eye" interpreted by rabbis as requiring only monetary compensation for physical damage, *see* BABYLONIAN TALMUD, Tractate Baba Kamma 83b)). *But see* Waldron, *Lex Talionis*, 34 ARIZ. L. REV. 25, 25 (1992) (no incompatibility between "eye for eye" principle and "the more humane doctrine that punishment should be adjusted to reflect the degree of the offender's responsibility for his crime").

On the renaissance of retribution, *see e.g.*, Vitiello, *Reconsidering Rehabilitation*, 65 TULANE L. REV. 1011, 1012-13 (1991). On the renewed interest in criminal law doctrine from the victim's perspective, *see* Lamborn, *The Impact of Victimology on the Criminal Law in the United States*, 8 CANAD. COMMUN. L.J. 23 (1985).

196. Devlin, *supra* note 193, at 75-76. Lord Devlin made it clear that he was *not* referring solely to cases involving mentally disabled prisoners (*Id.* (emphasis added)):

No doubt there are still judges who think of psychiatrists as persons who invent long names for simple sins; and no doubt there are psychiatrists who think of the criminal calendar as a list of mental disorders with antiquated names, taken from the Ten Commandments. But both these extreme schools of thought are dying out. The idea of punishment is giving way—*and here I am not concerned solely with mental abnormality*—with the idea of treatment.

197. A term preferred to the more traditional "retribution," "vengeance," or "retaliation." *See* Gaylin & Rothman, *supra* note 194, at xxix, 45-46. There is important philosophical support for this position in the work of Hegel and Kant. *See e.g.*, HEGEL, PHILOSOPHY OF RIGHT §§ 90-103 (Knox trans. 1952); I. KANT, PHILOSOPHY OF LAW 194-204 (Hastie trans. 1887); *see also*, J. STEPHEN, GENERAL VIEW OF THE CRIMINAL LAW OF ENGLAND 99 (1863) ("The criminal law stands to the passion of revenge in much the same relation as marriage to

has since regained prominence as the most important contemporary justification for and aim of punishment.[198] The Supreme Court's recent decision upholding a first offender's sentence of life imprisonment without parole for a cocaine possession conviction specifically invokes retribution as one of the acceptable rationales for such a penalty.[199]

Increasingly punitive attitudes toward criminals have since appeared throughout the criminal justice system.[200] The movement from indeterminate to determinate sentencing is now premised philosophically on "the rejection of rehabilitation as a justification for punishment and the acceptance instead of retribution, deterrence or incapacitation to justify punishment."[201]

---

the sexual appetite"). On the distinction between vengeance (seen as rooted in anger) and retribution (seen as rooted in righteousness), see J. FEINBERG, supra note 110, at 69 n.16. On the differing kinds of retribution, see id. at 216 n. 20. On the role of denunciation as an aspect of retribution, see PUNISHMENT, supra note 127, at 106-7.

For the interplay between punishment-as-retribution and punishment-as-moral-education, see Hampton, The Moral Education Theory of Punishment, 13 PHIL. & PUB. AFFS. 208 (1984); see also, Pillsbury, Emotional Justice: Moralizing the Passions of Criminal Punishment, 74 CORNELL L. REV. 655 (1989) (formulating a "moral-emotive" theory of retribution).

198. See e.g., Goodell, Preface, in W. WHITE, INSANITY AND THE CRIMINAL LAW (1923), at xv, xvi-xvii (Da Capo ed. 1981) ("We conclude that the severity of the sentence should depend on the seriousness of the defendant's crime or crimes—on what he did rather than on what the sentencer expects he will do if treated in a certain fashion"); see generally, M. MOORE, supra note 121, at 235-45.

199. See Harmelin v. Michigan, 111 S. Ct. 2680, 2706 (1991) (Kennedy, J., concurring in part & concurring in judgment) ("The Michigan Legislature could with reason conclude that the threat posed to the individual and society by possession of this large an amount of cocaine [more than 650 grams]—in terms of violence, crime, and social displacement—is momentous enough to warrant the deterrence and retribution of a life sentence without parole").

200. I speak here primarily of public attitudes as reflected in changes in legislation and judicial opinions that appear to respond to opinion polls, popular surveys and the like. See e.g., Fox, Radelet & Bonsteel, Death Penalty Opinion in the Post-Furman Years, 18 N.Y.U. REV. L. & SOC'L CHANGE 499 (1990-91); Roberts & Doob, Sentencing and Public Opinion: Taking False Shadows for True Substances, 27 OSGOODE HALL L.J. 491 (1989); Doob & Roberts, Social Psychology, Social Attitudes, and Attitudes Toward Sentencing, 16 CANAD. J. BEHAV. SCI. 269 (1984).

201. See e.g., Harris, Constitutional Limits on Criminal Presumptions as an Expression of Changing Concepts of Fundamental Fairness, 77 J. CRIM. L. & CRIMINOL. 308, 353 (1986) (footnote omitted); see also, sources cited, id. at 353-54 n. 222. On the related question of when punishment is deserved, see Pillsbury, The Meaning of Deserved Punishment: An Essay on Choice, Character, and

While some commentators bravely suggest that the recent turn to retribution is a "false renaissance" and that the data reflects the "tenacity of rehabilitation" in correctional ideology,[202] and while we know that penal theories are cyclical,[203] the dominant trends in current social and criminal philosophy emphasize retribution and containment of the criminal, and society's right to protection.[204] The roots of this philosophical switch are complex, and public *perceptions* of rising crime rates and unpunished criminals are probably the major cause.[205] Whether or not we adopt Professor Singer's charac-

---

Responsibility, 67 IND. L.J. 718 (1992).

202. Seidman, *supra* note 81, at 483 (characterizing new developments as a "false renaissance of retribution"); Cullen, Skovron, Scott & Burton, *Public Support for Correctional Treatment: The Tenacity of the Rehabilitative Ideal*, 17 CRIM. JUST. & BEHAV. 6, 15 (1990) (data revealing "tenacity of rehabilitation as a correctional ideology"). For the most recent debate on the question of whether rehabilitation "works" as a correctional ideology, *compare* Andrews, Zinger, Hoge et al., *Does Correctional Treatment Work? A Critically Relevant and Psychologically Informed Meta-Analysis*, 28 CRIMINOL. 369 (1990); Lab & Whitehead, *From "Nothing Works" To "The Appropriate Works:" The Latest Stop on the Search for the Secular Grail*, 28 CRIMINOL. 405 (1990); Andrews, Zinger, Hoge et al., *A Human Sciences Approach or More Punishment and Pessimism: A Rejoinder to Lab and Whitehead*, 28 CRIMINOL. 419 (1990). On the gap between the "rhetoric of rehabilitation" and the "punitive reality" in juvenile corrections policies, *see* Feld, *The Punitive Juvenile Court and the Quality of Procedural Justice: Disjuncts Between Rhetoric and Reality*, 36 CRIME & DELINQ. 443, 453 (1990).

203. *See* J. ROBITSCHER, *supra* note 174, at 43 (discussing examples).

204. Stokman & Heiber, *The Insanity Defense Reform Act in New York State, 1980-1983*, 7 INT'L J. L. & PSYCHIATRY 367, 367 (1984). *See also*, Bonnie, *Morality, Equality, and Expertise: Renegotiating the Relationship Between Psychiatry and Law*, 12 BULL. AM. ACAD. PSYCHIATRY & L. 5, 6 (1984) (discussing the recent "reinvigoration of the moral basis of punishment"); Pillsbury, *supra* note 175, at 756 n. 139 (length of time that legal system embraced the rehabilitative ideal "remarkable"). *See generally*, Thomas & Edelman, *supra* note 135, at 127 (footnotes omitted):

Effectuating conservative theology demands consequences to crime that are certain, swift and terrible...The more certain, swift and terrible are these consequences, the less likely humans are to risk them.

205. *See generally*, Cullen, Clark, Cullen & Mathers, *Attribution, Salience, and Attitude Toward Criminal Sentencing*, 12 CRIM. JUST. & BEHAV. 305 (1985). Ours is not the first generation to have come to this conclusion. *See e.g.*, Miller, *Ideology and Criminal Justice Policy: Some Current Issues*, 64 J. CRIM. L. & CRIMINOL. 141, 141 (1973) ("Few generations have been free from the conviction that the nation was in the throes of 'the crisis of our times,' and such perceptions have not always corresponded with judgments of later historians").

For contemporaneous research on the role of perceptions in criminal justice

terization of this new direction as "neo-retributivism,"[206] our punitive spirit echoes William White's[207] forceful arguments that punishment is "both a sublimated form of vengeance and a rationalization
which permits it."[208]

3. Punishment as Ritual

Punishment also leads to suffering. The celebration of "punishment as *punishment*" thus legitimatized the institutional "infliction
of suffering" in much the same way as disease was seen as having to
be "completely suffered" as a way of ensuring that one's soul would
find purification.[209] Such punishment has been seen for centuries as
serving to express profound feelings of social disapproval and repro-
bation,[210] as well as being a corrective, educative and socializing

---

policy, see e.g., Baba & Austin, *Neighborhood Environmental Satisfaction,
Victimization, and Social Participation as Determinants of Perceived Neighborhood Safety*, 21 ENVIRON. BEHAV. 763 (1989); LaGrange & Ferraro, *Assessing
Age and Gender Differences in Perceived Risk and Fear of Crime*, 27 CRIMINOL.
697 (1989); Warr, *What Is the Perceived Seriousness of Crimes?* 27 CRIMINOL.
795 (1989); van der Wurff & Stringer, *Postvictimization Fear of Crime: Differences in the Perceptions of People and Places*, 4 J. INTERPERS. VIOL. 469 (1989);
Waller, *Victims, Safer Communities and Sentencing*, 32 CANAD. J. CRIMINOL.
461 (1991).

206. Singer, *The Resurgence of Mens Rea: I—Provocation, Emotional Disturbance,
and the Model Penal Code*, 27 B.C. L. REV. 243, 247 (1986).

207. White has been referred to as "perhaps the most distinguished of American
psychiatrists." DeGrazia, *Crime Without Punishment: A Psychiatric Conundrum*, 52 COLUM. L. REV. 746, 748 (1952).

208. W. WHITE, *supra* note 198, at 16 n. 4; *see* H. WEIHOFEN, THE URGE TO PUNISH
130-41 (1956). On the role of contrasting views of the bases of human nature
in the formulation of modern criminology, *see* J.Q. WILSON & R. HERRNSTEIN,
CRIME AND HUMAN NATURE 514-22 (1985). On the "unforgiving jury's potential for meting out community vengeance" in insanity acquittee release cases, *see*
Wexler, *Criminal Commitment Contingency Structures*, in THERAPEUTIC JU-
RISPRUDENCE: THE LAW AS A THERAPEUTIC AGENT 23, 30 (D. Wexler ed. 1990),
quoting Wexler & Scoville, *The Administration of Psychiatric Justice: Theory
and Practice in Arizona*, 13 ARIZ. L. REV. 1, 157 (1971).

209. Pillsbury, *supra* note 175, at 773 and *id.* n. 223; H. SIGERIST, SOCIOLOGY OF
MEDICINE 15 (1960). *See also*, Blecker, *Haven or Hell? Inside Lorton Central
Prison: Experiences of Punishment Justified*, 42 STAN. L. REV. 1149, 1167
(1990) (emphasis in original) ("We impose pain and suffering for *[the criminal's]*
sake. Through punishment, we make him whole"), and *id.*, *quoting* H. PACKER,
THE LIMITS OF THE CRIMINAL SANCTION 38 (1968) ("only through suffering
punishment can the criminal expiate his sin").

210. *See* Boldt, *supra* note 109, at 1004, discussing Andenaes, *The General Preventive
Effects of Punishment*, 114 U. PA. L. REV. 949 (1966); Hawkins, *Punishment
and Deterrence: The Educative, Moralizing and Habituative Effects*, 1969 WIS.

deterrent, necessary for the public welfare.[211]

Punishment was originally needed to "remove the evil spirit thought to cause an individual to transgress against society."[212] It is also a "ritualistic device" conveying "moral condemnation,"[213] inflicting humiliation,[214] and dramatizing evil through a public "degradation ceremony."[215] As many forms of crime were identified with sin,[216] they were thus believed to challenge "God and organized religion."[217]

L. REV. 550. *See also*, DeGrazia, *supra* note 207, at 756 ("The retributive aspect of punishment has its roots deep in the psyche of man").

211. J. HALL, *supra* note 191, at 312, discussing writings of St. Thomas Aquinas. On the way punishment "evens out" the transgressor's wrongs, *see* PUNISHMENT, *supra* note 125, at 115.

212. Note, *The Modern Day Scarlet Letter: A Critical Analysis of Modern Probation Conditions,* 1989 DUKE L.J. 1357, 1360, *citing* H. BARNES, THE STORY OF PUNISHMENT: A RECORD OF MAN'S INHUMANITY TO MAN 39 (1930); D. DRESSLER, PRACTICE AND THEORY OF PROBATION AND PAROLE 3 (2d ed. 1969).

213. Boldt, *supra* note 109, *quoting* Hawkins, *supra* note 210, at 553-60; *see also* Hawkins, *supra* note 210, at 555: "Punishment is a ritualistic device designed to influence by intimating symbolically social disapproval and society's moral condemnation." On the role of social disapproval as an animator of law-abiding behavior, *see* Massaro, *Shame, Culture, and American Criminal Law,* 89 MICH. L. REV. 1880, 1895-99 (1991).

214. C. HIBBERT, *supra* note 175, at 32 (discussing use of sticks, pillory, branding iron, ducking stool and "scarlet letters"); Note, *supra* note 212, at 1360 (discussing public humiliation as the focus of early punishments).

215. Boldt, *supra* note 109, at 1004, *quoting* Garfinkel, *Conditions of Successful Degradation Ceremonies,* 61 AM. J. SOC. 420, 421-23 (1956). *See also*, Note, *supra* note 212, at 1361 (role of degradation in punishment theories); Ingber, *A Dialectic: The Fulfillment and Decrease of Passion in Criminal Law,* 28 RUTGERS L. REV. 861, 911 (1975) ("The criminal process is...a pageant which dramatizes the differences between 'we' and 'they' by portraying a symbolic encounter between the two"); Brakel, *Presumption, Bias and Incompetency in the Criminal Process,* 1974 WIS. L. REV. 1105, 1116 (criminal trial as "morality play").

216. On the biblical roots of the link between crime, punishment and sin, *see* Lasky, *The Paradigm of Religion, Medicine, and Capital Punishment,* 16 MED., SCI. & L. 26, 27 (1974) (discussing symbols of Adam and Eve, and Cain and Abel, and concluding, "Crime and punishment are coeval in the history of the world, and it is difficult to say which had priority.") *Compare* Schedler, *Retributive Punishment and the Fall of Satan,* 30 AM. J. JURIS. 137 (1985).

   These opinions have not entirely disappeared. *See e.g.,* Burkett & Ward, *A Note on Perceptual Deterrence, Religiously Based Moral Condemnation, and Social Control,* 31 CRIMINOL. 119, 122 (1993), reporting on research in Warr, *supra* note 205 (many people rate all offenses, regardless of seriousness, as "equally morally wrong," and "equate crime with sin").

217. H. BARNES, *supra* note 157, at 25. *See also*, D. ROTHMAN, THE DISCOVERY OF THE ASYLUM: SOCIAL ORDER AND DISORDER IN THE NEW REPUBLIC 15 (1971)

Such punishment ceremonies stimulated socialization through a process which involves the internalization of normative social behavior rules.[218] The relinquishment of personal retaliation to the social institution was thus seen as a kind of mutual agreement whereby all parties would suppress their own, *personal* retaliative impulses by turning the problem of punishment over to the sovereign.[219] This would avoid "the greater evil of mob violence."[220] By nurturing emotions of vengeance, the punishment of criminals "furthers social solidarity and protects against the terrifying anxiety that the forces of good might not triumph against the forces of evil after all."[221] It does this through the context of a trial process that is a "moral parable [with] a religious meaning essential as a public exercise in which the prevailing moral ideals are dramatized and reaffirmed."[222]

(early American colonists equated crime with sin). *See* Radin, *supra* note 92, at 1175:

> Maybe the death penalty symbolizes the arbitrary, alien power of government over life and death; the government as avenging God run amok; our relinquishment of social responsibility to the government to fix things for us by conveniently getting rid of some bad actors. Maybe by attacking this symbol we play a part in the struggle for a more humane political order.

218. Boldt, *supra* note 109, at 1004-5, *quoting* Garfinkel, *supra* note 215, at 421, and Hawkins, *supra* note 210, at 557-60.
219. Watson, *A Critique of the Legal Approach to Crime and Correction*, 23 LAW & CONTEMP. PROBS. 611 (1958).
220. Schulhofer, *supra* note 195, at 1511; Ingber, *supra* note 215, at 956 ("the more the insane person is perceived as different, the less need there is to fear the passion of the mob"); *see* Furman v. Georgia, 408 U.S. 238, 303 (1982) (Brennan, J.) (capital punishment supporters argue that penalty "satisfies the popular demand for grievous condemnation of abhorrent crimes and thus prevents disorder, lynching, and attempts by private citizens to take the law into their own hands"); *cf.* Eacret v. Holmes, 215 Ore. 121, 333 P. 2d 741, 743 (1958) ("Punishment for crime is not a matter of private vengeance but of public policy").
221. Diamond, *From* Durham *to* Brawner, *A Futile Journey*, 1973 WASH. U. L.Q. 109, 110. *See generally*, G. ZILBOORG, THE PSYCHOLOGY OF THE CRIMINAL ACT AND PUNISHMENT 69-88 (1954) (roots of the urge to punish); H. WEIHOFEN, *supra* note 208, at 130-41 (same); H. BARNES, *supra* note 157, at 25 ("Society felt outraged at...an act of voluntary perversity and indignantly retaliated by a savage manifestation of group vengeance"). *Compare* Stake, *Status and Incentive Aspects of Judicial Decisions*, 79 GEO. L.J. 1447, 1453 n. 13 (1991) ("Whether the law ought to count one's pleasure in witnessing or knowing the pain of others is an intriguing question to some")
222. P. ROCHE, THE CRIMINAL MIND 245 (1958).

Punishment thus is clearly a socially-sanctioned "safety valve"[223] through which law-abiders express community condemnation of wrong-doers,[224] *especially* the wrongdoers whom we fear the most.[225] In this way, it is imbued with an important *symbolic* significance:[226] more than mere disapproval, it expresses "a kind of vindictive resentment" as a "way of getting back at the criminal."[227] If we identify those among us who are criminals, we can "keep straight who is good and who is bad."[228] This may be the reason that "the moment...rehabilitative impulses emerge into expressions, the legal system is doomed to encounter contradiction, confusion and frequent public criticism."[229]

This symbolic function explains "why even those sophisticated persons who abjure resentment of criminals and look with small favor generally on the penal law are likely to demand that certain kinds of conduct be punished when or if the law lets them go by."[230]

---

223. *See* Schulhofer, *supra* note 195, at 1512: "Even if popular resentment would not lead to mob violence, it can be argued that giving an outlet to this resentment will contribute to the psychological health of the community"); Watson, *supra* note 219, at 611-12 ("the [early] relinquishment of personal retaliation to the social institution of the law was a mutual agreement whereby all parties agreed to suppress their own retaliative impulses in exchange for similar suppression on the part of others, turning the function of punishment over to the sovereign"); *see also*, O.W. HOLMES, THE COMMON LAW 40 (1923) (individuals will resort to private vengeance if the law will not punish), as discussed in Rychlak, *supra* note 192, at 319-20 n. 71.

224. "[V]engeance is exercised against those who offend custom, who transgress tradition, and who attack the constituted order of things, and those who tend by their conduct to break down the structure of society." W. WHITE, *supra* note 198, at 16.

225. Davis, *Setting Penalties: What Does Rape Deserve?* 3 LAW & PHILOS. 61, 81 (1984).

226. *See generally,* Tyler & Weber, *supra* note 93, at 26-27 (discussing punitiveness as a symbolic attitude); Lovell & Stojkovic, *supra* note 102, at 226 (on role of myths and symbols in helping provide "long-term stability" to correctional policy development).

227. *See generally,* J. FEINBERG, *supra* note 110, at 98-100.

228. DeGrazia, *supra* note 207, at 764.

229. Watson, *supra* note 219, at 226.

230. J. FEINBERG, *supra* note 110, at 102. *See also,* 3 J. FEINBERG, HARM TO SELF: THE MORAL LIMITS OF THE CRIMINAL LAW (1986). It is precisely this attitude that surfaces in the charge that the insanity acquittee somehow "beats the rap."

Herbert Morris has focused attention explicitly on the symbolism of punishment: "As a response to guilt, punishment must be seen, then, as freighted with rich symbolic significance, and in considering what might justify punishment we risk, I believe, incompleteness in our theories if we neglect the symbolic baggage." Morris, *The Decline of Guilt*, 99 ETHICS 62, 65 (1988).

Punishment furthers "the mythology of justice, [by] creating the illusion that the world is fair.[231] As Professor Elyn Saks has astutely noted, "Society's *perception* that the person is being punished is perhaps the most important consideration."[232]

The standards enforced by such punishment transcend the "rock-bottom prohibitions of the criminal law;" they include "the affirmative standards and ideals of the group with which we wish to identify."[233] Punishment expresses to other members of the community "its self-image as a society" that places great value on the "preservation of designated interests."[234] This expression is all the more pointed when the defendant is enough unlike "us" so that we neither empathize nor sympathize.[235]

4. Our Culture of Punishment

This reading, however, does not fully inform us of punishment's *roots*: *Why* do we have the feelings that make us need to express this "vindictive resentment?" Also, why do we choose to punish some offenders more harshly than others who commit like crimes?[236] To

---

231. Diamond, *supra* note 221, at 110. On the role of the Supreme Court as "manager" of the "symbolic legality" that represents our core legal value, *see* Haney, *The Fourteenth Amendment and Symbolic Legality: Let Them Eat Due Process*, 15 LAW & HUM. BEHAV. 183 (1991).

232. Saks, *Multiple Personality Disorder and Criminal Responsibility*, 25 U.C. DAVIS L. REV. 383, 416 (1992) (emphasis in original). *Compare e.g.*, G. ZILBOORG, THE PSYCHOLOGY OF THE CRIMINAL ACT 77 (1954) (criminal law "represents more hostility against the criminal than concern about the body social").

233. Weihofen, *Capacity to Appreciate "Wrongfulness" or "Criminality" Under the A.L.I.-Model Penal Code Test of Mental Responsibility*, 58 J. CRIM. L., CRIMINOL. & POL. SCI. 27, 30 (1967). On the "scientific" basis of such punishment, *see* Pillsbury, *supra* note 175, at 741-46. On our identification with the victims of crime, and the part that identification plays in the formulation of our punishment policies, *see* PUNISHMENT, *supra* note 127, at 104.

234. Sendor, *supra* note 16, at 1428-29 n. 208.

235. *See generally infra* chapter 4 D 2-3.

236. On the existence of a "community tolerance threshold" in insanity cases, *see generally infra* chapter 4 D 4; *see e.g.*, Boehnert, *Psychological and Demographic Factors Associated With Individuals Using the Insanity Defense*, 13 J. PSYCHIATRY & L. 9, 27-28 (1985); Wexler, *supra* note 70, at 20-23 (we disproportionately tolerate the use of the insanity defense in cases where the victim is a non-stranger, and where the level of community outrage is thus comparatively lower); Schwartz, *The Proper Use of a Psychiatric Expert*, in SCIENTIFIC AND EXPERT EVIDENCE IN CRIMINAL ADVOCACY 97, 111 (1975) (success of insanity plea frequently hinges on defendant's "likeability").

what extent are variables such as gender relevant to our decisions?[237] Why do we so badly misperceive the empirical realities of criminal sentencing systems?[238] And, finally, why are our perceptions the most erroneous in cases involving mentally disabled criminal defendants?[239]

To understand the matter at hand—the roots of our rejection of psychodynamic principles in criminal justice decision making (as exemplified by our attitudes toward the insanity defense plea)—we need to consider the psychoanalytic explanation[240] offered by J.C. Flugel:

---

237. The most recent research suggests that women are more likely to be acquitted by reason of insanity than are men. *See* H. STEADMAN, REFORMING, *supra* note 32, at 49. For other recent empirical research, *see* Heilbrun, Heilbrun & Griffin, *Comparing Females Acquitted by Reason of Insanity, Convicted, and Civilly Committed in Florida, 1977-1984*, 12 LAW & HUM. BEHAV. 295 (1988). *See also*, L. WALKER, TERRIFYING LOVE 188-89 (1990) (insanity defense successful where defendant fits stereotype of "crazy woman" based upon cultural myths of women being biologically predestined to greater emotional instability). On the question of "judicial chivalry" in sentencing, *see* Crew, *Sex Differences in Criminal Sentencing: Chivalry or Patriarchy*, 8 JUST. Q. 59 (1991) (sex differences in sentencing reflect influence of patriarchal values); *but see* Streib, *Death Penalty for Female Offenders*, 58 CIN. L. REV. 845, 876-78 (1990) (gender bias in death penalty cases leads fact-finders to disproportionately apply death penalty to those defendants whose murders most reflect "unladylike" behavior); for other related inquiries, *see e.g.*, Jenkins & Davidson, *Battered Women in the Criminal Justice System: An Analysis of Gender Stereotypes*, 8 BEHAV. SCI. & L. 161 (1990); Jurik & Winn, *Gender and Homicide: A Comparison of Men and Women Who Kill*, 5 VIOLENCE & VICTIMS 227 (1990); Simpson, *Caste, Class, and Violent Crime: Explaining Difference in Female Offending*, 29 CRIMINOL. 115 (1991).

   For a historical perspective, *see* R. HARRIS, MURDERS AND MADNESS: MEDICINE, LAW, AND SOCIETY IN THE FIN DE SIÈCLE (1989).

238. *See e.g.*, Fox, Radelet & Bonstell, *supra* note 200; Roberts & Doob, *supra* note 200; Doob & Roberts, *supra* note 200.

239. *See* H. STEADMAN, BEATING A RAP? DEFENDANTS FOUND INCOMPETENT TO STAND TRIAL 17 (1979); Steadman & Cocozza, *Selective Reporting and the Public's Misconception of the Criminally Insane*, 41 PUB. OPIN. 523, 531 (1977-78) (random sample of general public incorrectly identified such notorious defendants as Patty Hearst and Charles Manson as being criminally insane; every person cited as being criminally insane by poll respondents was individual who had been charged with murder, kidnapping or bombing); *compare* State v. Watson, 686 P. 2d 879, 890 (Mont. 1984) (expert witness characterized defendant as having the "capacity to carry out a 'Manson' type homicide").

240. This should not be read to suggest that psychodynamic psychiatry rejects punishment as a necessary end of the criminal law. Freud, for instance, saw it as "the decisive step toward civilization" and the "first requisite of culture." Hall, *Psychiatric Criminology: Is It a Valid Marriage?: The Legal View*, 16 BUFF. L. REV. 349, 351 (1966-67), *quoting* S. FREUD, CIVILIZATION AND ITS DISCON-

In the first place, the criminal provides an outlet for our (moralized) aggression. In this respect he plays the same role as do our enemies in war and our political scapegoats in time of peace.[241]...In the second place, the criminal by his flouting of law and moral rule constitutes a temptation to the id; it is as though we said to ourselves, "if he does it, why should not we?" This stirring of criminal impulses within ourselves calls for an answering effort on the part of the super-ego, which can best achieve its object by showing that "crime doesn't pay."...By punishing [the criminal] we are not only showing that he can't "get away with it" but holding him up as a terrifying example to our own tempted and rebellious selves. Thirdly, and closely connected with this...is the danger with which our whole notion of justice is threatened when we observe that a criminal goes unpunished. The primitive foundation of this notion...lies in an equilibrium of pleasures and pains, of indulgence and punishment. This equilibrium is disturbed, either if the moral rewards of good conduct are not forthcoming...or if the normal punishments of crime are absent or uncertain....It is to prevent disturbance of the latter kind that we insist that those who have broken the law shall be duly punished. Through their punishment the equilibrium is re-established; without it (so we dimly feel) the whole psychological and social structure on which morality depends is imperiled.[242]

In other words, our sense of justice is disturbed if we see another go unpunished for antisocial or asocial behavior;[243] if society fails to

---

TENTS 59 (Riviere trans. 1930).

241. *Compare* K. MENNINGER, THE CRIME OF PUNISHMENT 153-54 (rev. ed. 1986):

> We need criminals to identify ourselves with, to secretly envy, and to stoutly punish. Criminals represent our alter egos—our "bad" selves—rejected and protected. They do for us the forbidden, illegal things we wish to do, and like scapegoats of old, they bear the burden of our displaced guilt and punishment....Our submerged hates and suppressed aggressions, our fantasized crimes, our feelings of need for punishment—all these can be managed in part by the scapegoat device.

The role of the scapegoat in this context is also discussed in PUNISHMENT, *supra* note 127, at 175-76, and in De Grazia, *supra* note 207, at 764.

242. J.C. FLUGEL, *supra* note 138, at 169-70. *See also*, F. ALEXANDER & H. STAUB, *supra* note 170, at 215 ("[T]he louder man calls for the punishment of the lawbreaker, the less he has to fight against his own repressed impulses"); *see generally*, P. RIEWALD, SOCIETY AND ITS CRIMINALS (T. James trans. 1950). Flugel's work is discussed carefully in Bienenfeld, *supra* note 182; *see also*, Duncan, *supra* note 181, at 8 n.29.

243. F. ALEXANDER & S. SELESNICK, *supra* note 150, at 352. *See also*, Hans, *An Analysis of Public Attitudes Toward the Insanity Defense*, 24 CRIMINOL. 393, 396 (1986) ("The failure to define a transgression as legally and morally wrong may disturb many law-abiding members of society").

punish, those who wish to violate the law may feel more free to do so, and those who are law-abiding may lose confidence in the legal system's ability to enforce the criminal law.[244]

The importance of punishing offenders is underscored: law-abiding society has its anti-aggression safety-valve;[245] we project our guilt, blame, shame, and fear[246] express our collective anger and hostility,[247] and show the criminal he cannot succumb to temptation

---

244. Rychlak, *supra* note 192, at 314.
245. *But see* Mickenberg, *supra* note 9, at 960-61 n. 66, suggesting that "law and order" sentiments are a pretext, covering retributive personal antipathy toward criminals, and *see id., quoting* H. PACKER, *supra* note 209, at 38 (emphasis in Mickenberg):

> We are somehow not content to say that criminals should be punished because *we* hate them and want to hurt them. It has to be because others hate them and would, were it not for our prudence in providing them with this spectacle, stage a far worse one of their own. This kind of hypocrisy is endemic in arguments about the death penalty, but it does not seem to be empirically verified. Lynchings do not, as this theory would lead us to conclude, seem to increase in places that have abolished capital punishment.

> *See also* Pillsbury, *supra* note 175, at 759 ("The crime control model gave emotional and substantive content to the revival of penal retaliation"). On the ways that judges are becoming increasingly more punitive, *see* Wald, *The Conscience of a Judge*, 25 SUFFOLK U. L. REV. 619, 626 (1991). On the role of pretextuality in insanity defense decision making, *see generally infra* chapter 8 C.

246. On the relationship between punishment and guilt, *see* Lasky, *supra* note 216, at 27, *quoting* W. BROMBERG, CRIME AND THE MIND: A PSYCHIATRIC ANALYSIS OF CRIME AND PUNISHMENT (1939) ("Crime stories constitute the foliage of our collective unconscious, which are the tendrils of our inner guilt concerning crime"). On blame, *see generally*, Boldt, *The Construction of Responsibility in the Criminal Law*, 140 U. PA. L. REV. 2245 (1992). On shame, *see* Grasmick & Bursik, *Conscience, Significant Others, and Rational Choice: Extending the Deterrence Model*, 24 LAW & SOC'Y REV. 837, 854 (1990) (impact of shame as crime deterrent); Massaro, *supra* note 213 (role of shame). On fear, *see e.g.,* Ouimet & Coyle, *Fear of Crime and Sentencing Punitiveness: Comparing the General Public and Court Practitioners*, 32 CANAD. J. CRIMINOL. 149 (1991).

247. *See* Sendor, *supra* note 16, at 1428; J.C. FLUGEL, *supra* note 138, at 150; G. ZILBOORG, *supra* note 221, at 77; *see also*, Sendor, *supra* note 16, at n. 208 ("Punishment is a form of communication to other people as well as to an offender"). Each week's press accounts of criminal trials inevitably includes a quotation from a prosecutor asking for a stiff sentence to "send a message to the community that such behavior will not be tolerated." *See e.g.,* Collins v. State, 1991 WL 119182 (Tex. App.—Hous. 1991), slip op. at 6; State v. Landry, 1991 WL 119727 (La. App. 1991), slip op. at 3; State v. Milashoski, 163 Wis. 2d 72, 471 N.W. 2d 42, 49 (1991); State v. Broadhead, 1991 WL 89835 (Idaho 1991), slip op. at 14; State v. Middlebrook, 1991 WL 76816 (Ohio App. 1991); Shoup v. State, 570 N.E. 2d 1298, 1306 (Ind. Ct. App. 1991); People v. Coppula, 212

(as *we* do not so succumb),[248] and the notion of an even-handed justice system is preserved.[249] As Weihofen suggests:

> When a reprehensible crime is committed, strong emotional reactions take place in all of us. Some people will be impelled to go out at once and work off their tensions in a lynching orgy. Even the calmest, most law-abiding of us is likely to be deeply stirred. All our ingrained concepts of morality and "justice" come into play, all our ancient tribal fears of anything that threatens the security of the group.[250]

Perhaps when we become too zealous in our demands for the punishment of one who has violated the law, we give off "a definite sign that the given individual failed to assimilate his own anti-social tendencies."[251] Jonathan Willens' study of the development of American prison law focuses on this key issue:

> [P]risons do not simply punish criminals for their crimes. They do not simply detain people who must be temporarily removed from the community. Instead they discipline delinquency. They adopt or inherit the pre-colonial view that custody is a moral act, part of the fight to the death between

---

Ill. App. 3d 52, 570 N.E. 2d 879, 880 (1991) (all employing "send a message" language).

248. On the way that parental values are more influential in determining their children's conservative (rather than liberal) ideology on criminal justice issues, see Dunaway & Cullen, *Explaining Crime Ideology: An Exploration of the Parental Socialization Perspective*, 37 CRIME & DELINQ. 536 (1991). On the way that death penalty opinions are shaped in childhood, see Tyler & Weber, *Support for the Death Penalty: Instrumental Response to Crime or Symbolic Attitude*, 17 LAW & SOC'Y REV. 121 (1982); see infra chapter 7, note 178.

249. See generally, Weihofen, *supra* note 233; J. BIGGS, *supra* note 122, at 174-77; Livermore & Meehl, *The Virtues of M'Naghten*, 51 MINN. L. REV. 789, 792 (1967); see also, Pillsbury, *supra* note 175, at 736 (penitentiary satisfied public's emotional need for "tough and dramatic retaliation against criminals"); Balkin, *The Rhetoric of Responsibility*, 76 VA. L. REV. 197, 238 (1990) (prosecutor implicitly suggested to jurors that, "if Hinckley had emotional problems, they were largely his own fault").

250. H. WEIHOFEN, *supra* note 208, at 130-31.

251. F. ALEXANDER & H. STAUB, *supra* note 170, at 215. *Cf.* Weihofen, *supra* note 233, at 29 (discussing strong religious convictions of certain mentally ill persons).
    On the other hand, the same unconscious motivating factors might well go to explain why the prospect of punishment does not keep the criminal within the law. See e.g., E. BERGHLER & A. MEERLOO, JUSTICE AND INJUSTICE 36 (1963), and see id. at 118: ("criminosis is not characterized by the ability or inability to distinguish between 'right and wrong' but by a tendency to commit acts, punishable by the specific society, under the influence of an unconscious defense mechanism").

good and evil, between us and them.[252]

The acceptance of psychodynamic principles is seen as a device that might temper our societal need for punishment, thus threatening our core social values.[253] That is because we cannot (or, at least, we *say* we cannot) punish where we cannot morally blame.[254] Such punishment is gratuitous, serving "no social purpose."[255]

This need for a mechanism by which we can excuse those deemed to be not responsible may be why even abolitionists like Norval Morris allow for the introduction of psychiatric evidence on a defendant's mental state,[256] and why, in jurisdictions where the

---

252. Willens, *Structure, Content and the Exigencies of War: American Prison Law After Twenty Five Years, 1962-87*, 37 AMER. U. L. REV. 41, 154 (1987) (footnote omitted). *See also,* Pillsbury, *supra* note 175, at 773-74 ("The legitimation and even celebration of punishment as *punishment* may encourage the native cruelties of the prison as an institution"); *see generally,* M. FOUCAULT, DISCIPLINE AND PUNISH: THE BIRTH OF THE PRISON (A. Sheridan trans. 1977); Rafter, *The Social Construction of Crime and Crime Control*, 27 J. RES. CRIME & DELINQ. 376 (1990); Blecker, *supra* note 209, at 1166-68. On the historical roots of the idea of imprisonment as punishment, *see* Wolfgang, *Crime and Punishment in Renaissance Florence*, 81 J. CRIM. L. & CRIMINOL. 567, 576-78 (1990).

      The idea of imprisonment as a *positive* experience is explored in Duncan, *"Cradled on the Sea:" Positive Images of Prison and Theories of Punishment*, 76 CAL. L. REV. 1201 (1988).
253. This assumes even greater importance in the interrelationship among punitiveness, personality style, and authoritarianism. *See e.g.,* Vidmar & Miller, *Sociopsychological Processes Underlying Attitudes Toward Legal Punishment*, 14 LAW & SOC'Y REV. 565, 590-91 (1980), and *see generally infra* chapter 7 D.
254. The paradigm statement of this position is found in Judge Thurman Arnold's oft-cited opinion in United States v. Holloway, 148 F. 2d 665, 666-67 (D.C. Cir. 1945) (emphasis added):

Legal tests of criminal insanity are not and cannot be the result of scientific analysis and objective judgment...They must be based on the instinctive sense of justice of ordinary men. *This* sense of justice assumes that there is a faculty called reason, which is separate and apart from instinct, emotion, and impulse, that enables an individual to distinguish between right and wrong and endows with moral responsibility for his acts. *This* ordinary sense of justice still operates in terms of punishment...*Our collective conscience does not allow punishment where it cannot impose blame.*

255. Note, *Due Process Concerns With Delayed Psychiatric Evaluations and the Insanity Defense: Time Is of the Essence*, 64 B.U.L. REV. 861, 860 (1985).
256. N. MORRIS, MADNESS AND THE CRIMINAL LAW (1982), discussed in Homant & Kennedy, *Judgment of Legal Insanity as a Function of Attitudes Toward the Insanity Defense*, 8 INT'L J. L. & PSYCHIATRY 67, 78-79 (1986). Morris's views on this point are characterized as "neo-reactionary" in Kadish, *supra* note 84, at 277. *See also,* R. SIMON, THE JURY AND THE DEFENSE OF INSANITY 220 (1967)

insanity defense has been "abolished," defendants retain the right to present testimony as to their lack of *mens rea*.[257] Herbert Packer has even speculated that the "urge to 'punish' may have a common source in some dark recess of the human psyche with the urge to 'cure.'"[258]

These principles seem to reflect some cognitive dissonance or psychological reactance:[259] if some mentally ill individuals are deemed to not be criminally culpable (and if we accept the notion that some individuals will receive "special treatment" from the law by reason of their mental disability), such exemptions can exist only where those so selected accurately reflect society's moral judgments that such special treatment is warranted.[260] This may help to explain why there is increasing support for relaxing the legal protections available to the mentally ill, by making them equally subject to the same "draconian penalties" now generally in good currency.[261] It may

---

(public outrage following the M'Naghten acquittal was, in part, precipitated by a general fear of crime that had been stimulated by a series of recent assassination attempts, and, in part, by a belief that lifetime confinement in Broadmoor was inadequate punishment for the underlying deed).

257. *See e.g.*, State v. Korell, 213 Mont. 316, 690 P. 2d 992 (Mont. 1984) (abolition not unconstitutional); MONT. CODE ANN. §46-14-102 (1985) (retaining *mens rea* defense); State v. Searcy, 118 Id. 632, 798 P. 2d 914 (1990) (due process does not include right to present insanity defense); State v. Beam, 109 Idaho 616, 710 P. 2d 526, 531 (1985) (abolition statute, *see* IDAHO CODE §18-207 (1986 Supp.), does not presume that no defendant can lack such mental capacity to form criminal intent); *see also*, State v. Young, 1993 WL 79648, at **47-49 (Utah 1993) (explaining motivating factors leading to abolition in Utah). *Searcy* is criticized in Note, 104 HARV. L. REV. 1132 (1991). On the abolition of the insanity defense in general, *see* 3 M.L. PERLIN, *supra* note 4, §15.10 at 314-17; *see generally infra* chapter 3 C.

258. Packer, *Enemies of Progress*, N.Y. REV. 17, 21 (Oct. 23, 1969).

259. *See* S. BREHM & J. BREHM, PSYCHOLOGICAL REACTANCE: A THEORY OF FREE-DOM AND CONTROL 30-31 (1981) ("Given that a person believes he or she has a specific freedom, any force on the individual that makes it more difficult for him or her to exercise the freedom constitutes a threat to it. Thus, any kind of attempted social influence...that work[s] against exercising the freedom can be defined as threats"); *see generally*, Perlin, *Morality and Pretextuality, Psychiatry and the Law: Of "Ordinary Common Sense," Heuristic Reasoning, and Cognitive Dissonance*, 19 BULL. AM. ACAD. PSYCHIATRY & L. 131, 138-39 (1991); *see also*, Perlin, *Pretexts and Mental Disability Law: The Case of Competency*, 47 U. MIAMI L. REV. (1993) (in press).

260. Note, *The Insanity Defense: Effects of an Abolition Unsupported by a Moral Consensus*, 9 AM. J. L. & MED. 471, 477-78 (1984).

261. Forer, *supra* note 166, at 191. On the question of whether we are, in fact, "criminalizing" mental patients, *see* Lurigio & Lewis, *The Criminal Mental Patient: A Descriptive Analysis and Suggestions for Future Research*, 14 CRIM.

also explain why so much of our insanity defense debate is obsessively dominated by our fear of defendants "faking" so as to "beat the rap."[262] In reality, research shows that offenders often *deny* mental illness and its symptomatology,[263] even where recognition of the existence of such symptoms might, literally, save their lives.[264]

Thus, in analyzing the decision of the legislature in Idaho (an isolated, highly religious state)[265] to reduce the insanity defense to solely a consideration of *mens rea*,[266] Geis and Meier have found that that state's residents strongly held the view that *all* human beings ought to take personal responsibility for their behavior.[267] As a result,

---

JUST. & BEHAV. 283, 283 (1987) (little empirical evidence found to support thesis); *see also*, Belcher, *Are Jails Replacing the Mental Health System for the Homeless Mentally Ill?* 24 COMMUN. MENT. HEALTH J. 185 (1988) (recommending increased use of outpatient commitment to avoid criminalizing homeless mentally ill individuals); Arvanites, *The Impact of State Mental Hospital Deinstitutionalization on Commitments for Incompetency to Stand Trial*, 26 CRIMINOL. 307, 318 (1988) (no evidence that deinstitutionalization has resulted in "wholesale criminalization" of the mentally ill); *see generally*, Perlin, *Competency, Deinstitutionalization and Homelessness: A Story of Marginalization*, 28 HOUS. L. REV. 63, 115 n. 303 (1991).

262. According to Foucault, the public's obsession with madness dates to at least 1500. *See generally*, Midelfort, *supra* note 126, at 249-50, discussing M. FOUCAULT, *supra* note 132, at 13.

263. *See e.g.*, Grossman & Cavanaugh, *Do Sex Offenders Minimize Psychiatric Symptoms?* 34 J. FORENS. SCI. 881 (1989).

264. *See e.g.*, findings reported in Lewis, Pincus, Bard, Richardson et al, *Neuropsychiatric, Psychoeducational, and Family Characteristics of 14 Juveniles Condemned to Death in the United States*, 145 AM. J. PSYCHIATRY 584, 588 (1988) (death row juveniles "almost uniformly" tried to hide evidence of cognitive deficits and psychotic symptoms), and in Lewis, Pincus, Feldman, Jackson & Bard, *Psychiatric and Psychoeducational Characteristics of 15 Death Row Inmates in the United States*, 143 AM. J. PSYCHIATRY 838, 841 (1986) (Lewis) (all but one of sample of death row inmates studied attempted to *minimize* rather than exaggerate their degree of psychiatric disorders); *see also*, State v. Stevens, 158 Ariz. 595, 764 P. 2d 724, 729 (1988) (evidence showed that fifty percent of all individuals with certain neurological lesions would be led "in the direction of anti-social behavior").

265. Geographical and regional variation is generally significant. *See* Way, Dvoskin & Steadman, *supra* note 49, at 412 (lowest rates of inpatient beds used for insanity acquittees found in Southern states; authors speculate that states in question, "many of which are known for relatively harsh prison systems, are places where religious values stress personal responsibility and punishment for crimes"). *But see* Hawley & Messner, *The Southern Violence Construct: A Review of Arguments, Evidence, and the Normative Context*, 6 JUST. Q. 481 (1989) (questioning popular picture of a "distinctively Southern culture of violence").

266. *See* 3 M.L. PERLIN, *supra* note 4, §15.41 at 404-6.

267. Geis & Meier, *Abolition of the Insanity Plea in Idaho: A Case Study*, 477

Idaho residents concluded that mentally disabled criminal defendants should not be able to avoid punitive consequences of criminal acts by reliance on either a "real *or* faked plea of insanity,"[268] an attitude recently endorsed by a member of the Louisiana Supreme Court.[269] This may help explain why, despite recidivism of thirty-five to sixty-five percent reported by all prison systems, the public is more incensed at the crimes of insanity acquittees than it is by those of ex-convicts.[270] Crimes by individuals identified as mentally ill con-

---

ANNALS 72, 73 (1985); *see also*, Balkin, *supra* note 248, at 238 (discussing view that Hinckley's emotional problems were "his own *fault*") (emphasis added); People v. Dobben, 187 Mich. App. 462, 468 N.W. 2d 527, 532 (1991), *rev'd on other gds.*, 440 Mich. 679, 488 N.W. 2d 726 (1992) (not reversible error where prosecutor argued in summation that defendant's drug use was "triggering factor instigating his mental illness" leading to involuntary civil commitment two years prior to criminal act in question) (defendant had placed his children in a foundry ladle). *Compare* Hamm, *Legislator Ideology and Capital Punishment: The Special Case for Indiana Juveniles*, 6 JUST. Q. 219, 220 (1989), reporting on findings of Cullen, Clark, Cullen & Mathers, *Attribution, Salience, and Attitudes Toward Criminal Sanctioning*, 12 CRIM. JUST. & BEHAV. 305 (1985) (male legislators who attributed crime to "free will" gave statistically significantly greater support to capital punishment than did those who attributed such behavior to social factors).

268. Geis & Meier, *supra* note 267, at 73 (emphasis added). The authors suggest that the Idaho legislation might reflect "the response of the uneasy good against the acting out wicked:"

> [T]here exist in all of us impulses toward wickedness that we suppress at some cost. As a reward for our suppression, we would like to make certain that those who have not forced themselves to repress their evil impulses suffer suitably for that lapse so we ourselves can be reassured that our sacrifice was not for nothing.

Id. at 77. *Cf.* Weihofen, *Institutional Treatment of Persons Acquitted By Reason of Insanity*, 38 TEX. L. REV. 849, 861 (1960) (frequent requests for psychiatric assistance seen as evidence of malingering).

269. *See* State v. Perry, 610 So. 2d 746, 781 (La. 1992) (Cole, J., dissenting) ("Society has the right to protect itself from those who would commit murder and seek to avoid their legitimate punishment by a subsequently contracted, or feigned, insanity").

270. Rappeport, *The Insanity Plea Scapegoating the Mentally Ill—Much Ado About Nothing*, 24 SO. TEX. L.J. 687, 695 (1983). On the conflict in the research about recidivism by insanity acquittees, *see* Bogenberger, Pasewark, Gudeman & Beiber, *Follow-Up of Insanity Acquittees in Hawaii*, 10 INT'L J. L. & PSYCHIATRY 283 (1987); *see also*, Scott, Zonana & Getz, *supra* note 6, at 982 (discussing clinicians' resistance to treating insanity acquittees, "the most despised and feared group in society"); Leong, Silva & Weinstock, *Dangerous Mentally Disordered Criminals: Unresolvable Societal Fear?* 36 J. FORENS. SCI. 210, 215 (1991) ("assuaging public fear of dangerous individuals may be an impossible task").

tinue to vividly set the terms for the debate over the future of the insanity defense.[271]

These attitudes also create a residual problem: empirical studies have shown, clearly and consistently, that a significant percentage of offenders suffer from mental illness,[272] and that the act of incarceration may either exacerbate underlying psychiatric conditions or precipitate mental illness in vulnerable individuals.[273] To some extent, this percentage, which absorbs mental health and criminal justice resources "at an alarming pace,"[274] includes defendants unable to avail themselves of a nonresponsibility defense who are subsequently

---

271. The vividness effect is a phenomenon through which vivid information about a specific case overwhelms the abstract data on which rational choices should be based. See Rosenhan, supra note 6, at 13 (1984); see generally infra chapter 6 C. On the way such a case affects legislative policy, see People v. Seefeld, 95 Mich. App. 197, 290 N.W. 2d 123, 124 (1980) (adoption of guilty but mentally ill status); see also, Commonwealth v. Trill, 374 Pa. Super. 549, 543 A. 2d 1106, 1119 (Super. Ct. 1988), appeal den. 522 Pa. 603, 562 A. 2d 826 (1989) (discussing reaction to case in which defendant "falls through the cracks").

On the implications of such vivid crimes for formulation of administrative police policies, see Finn & Sullivan, Police Handling of the Mentally Ill: Sharing Responsibility With the Mental Health System, 17 J. Crim. Just. 1, 4 (1989) (Los Angeles' law enforcement policy toward the mentally ill restructured after two vivid incidents involving crimes by mentally ill persons).

272. See e.g., Perlin, supra note 109, at 85, (percentage of death row inmates with serious psychiatric problems "staggeringly high") discussing Lewis, supra note 264; Daniel & Harris, Female Offenders Referred for Pre-Trial Psychiatric Evaluation, 9 Bull. Am. Acad. Psychiatry & L. 40, 46 (1979) (ninety percent of referred female offenders found to have at least one "recognizable psychiatric condition"); Gudjonsson & Petrusson, Some Criminological and Psychiatric Aspects of Homicide in Iceland, 26 Med., Sci., & L. 299 (1986) (two-thirds of offenders considered mentally abnormal).

These, of course, are not new discoveries. See W. White, supra note 198, at 3 ("Upwards of fifty percent of the criminals who are convicted and sent to prison are, upon arrival, suffering from some form of mental deficiency or psychosis") citing two studies reported in Glueck, A Study of 608 Admissions to Sing Sing Prison, 2 Ment. Hyg. No. 1 (1918), and Glueck, Concerning Prisoners, 2 Ment. Hyg. No. 2 (1918).

273. Prins, Mental Abnormality and Criminality—An Uncertain Relationship, 30 Med., Sci. & L. 247, 248-49 (1990). On the need for correctional programmers to understand the psychology of criminal conduct, see Andrews, Bonta & Hoge, supra note 188, at 22.

274. Lurigio & Lewis, supra note 261, at 282. A symposium at a American Psychological Association's yearly conference was thus provocatively titled, "The Nation's Largest Psychiatric Hospital—Los Angeles County Jail" (August, 1990, San Francisco, CA).

imprisoned.[275] This "overlapping clientele"[276] of individuals—often "twice-cursed"[277] as "mad and bad"[278]—will inevitably increase as judicial hostility toward the insanity defense and insanity defense pleaders increases, fueled by the punitive spirit that sparks the "negative pattern of fear and repression" that again dominates penology.[279] It is this spirit that best exemplifies our "culture of punishment."[280]

---

275. On the implications of recent adoptions of the guilty but mentally ill verdict for this population, see 3 M.L. PERLIN, supra note 4, §15.09 at 307-13; see generally infra chapter 3 A 1 c (4).

276. Toch & Adams, In the Eye of the Beholder? Assessments of Psychopathology Among Prisoners By Federal Prison Staff, 24 J. RES. CRIME & DELINQ. 119 (1987), discussing L. TEPLIN, MENTAL HEALTH AND CRIMINAL JUSTICE (1984). See also, Teplin, Criminalizing Mental Disorder: The Comparative Arrest Rate of the Mentally Ill, 39 AM. PSYCHOLOGIST 794 (1984); Teplin, The Criminality of the Mentally Ill: A Dangerous Misconception, 142 AM. J. PSYCHIATRY 593 (1985); Teplin, The Prevalence of Severe Mental Disorder Among Male Urban Jail Detainees: Comparison with the Epidemiologic Catchment Area Program, 80 AM. J. PUB. HEALTH 663 (1990) (most recent studies reveal that the prevalence rate of severe mental disorder is significantly higher in typical urban jails than in the general population).

277. Hochstedler, Twice-Cursed? The Mentally Disordered Criminal Defendant, 14 CRIM. JUST & BEHAV. 251, 252 (1987).

278. See generally, German & Singer, Punishing the Not Guilty: Hospitalization of Persons Found Not Guilty By Reason of Insanity, 29 RUTGERS L. REV. 1011, 1074 (1976); Prins, Mad or Bad—Thoughts on the Equivocal Relationship Between Mental Disorder and Criminality, 3 INT'L J. L. & PSYCHIATRY 421 (1980). The fear of criminal defendants who are seen as both "mad" and "bad" is, of course, intensified. See Leong, Silva & Weinstock, supra note 270, at 210. On the relationship between different mental disorders and crime, see Prins, supra note 272, at 250-54. On the special factors involved in sex offender cases, see e.g., Walsh, Twice Labeled: The Effect of Psychiatric Labeling on the Sentencing of Sex Offenders, 37 SOC'L PROBS. 375 (1990).

279. See Menzies, Cycles of Control: The Transcarceral Careers of Forensic Patients, 10 INT'L J. L. & PSYCHIATRY 233, 246 (1987), describing the "mutual encroachment of legal and medical systems of penalty," and see id. at 233 (citations omitted):

Forensic patients are highly accessible targets for both medical and legal intervention. Like criminal defendants generally, individuals facing psychiatric assessment are typically dependent, dispossessed, powerless people...who are 'put into order'...by a system over which they exercise little knowledge or control. They are the semi- or pre-institutionalized populations...who are immersed within the expanding web of welfare, justice, and mental health, and whose deviant careers repeatedly penetrate into this triadic system of supervision and constraint. At the frontier between law and medicine, forensic patients become the subjects of a control display in which parallel agencies mutually reinforce each other's capacity to promote order.

280. The closest prior use I have found of this phrase is in Clear, The Punishment Addiction: Twenty Years of Compulsive Punishment Lifestyle, in 150 PLI/Crim

D. Conclusion

Our efforts to simultaneously understand and reconstruct an insanity defense jurisprudence must begin then with this foundation. The *Hinckley* trial breathed vivid life into a series of social, empirical and behavioral myths. Congress responded to the public fury that followed the *Hinckley* acquittal by passing legislation that, basically, repudiated 150 years of scientific and behavioral knowledge. It did this knowing fully that the public's fears were based upon a numbing level of misinformation.

For many reasons, the insanity defense serves as the perfect scapegoat for all that is perceived as inexplicable about our criminal justice system. It symbolizes "the most profound issues in social and criminal justice"[281] and serves as the "screen upon which the community has projected its visions" of that system.[282] It underscores the gap—a chasm, actually—between the public's perceptions of how the criminal justice system should operate and the way that, in a handful of cases, a "factually guilty" person can be diverted from criminal punishment because of moral or legal nonresponsibility.

Beyond this, the insanity defense flies in the face of the way that we have traditionally conflated sin, evil and madness. Although modern psychiatry and psychology illuminates many of the reasons why certain criminal defendants commit apparently-incomprehensible "crazy" acts, we reject such psychodynamic explanations, both on personal and justice-system levels.

We do this because such explanation—indeed, the existence of the insanity defense itself—robs us of our need (our desire, our compulsion) to mete out punishment to the transgressor. Most strikingly, we do this even when we are faced with incontrovertible evidence that the "successful" use of an insanity defense can lead to significantly longer terms of punishment in significantly more punitive facilities than the individual would have been subjected to had he pled guilty or been found guilty after a trial.[283]

55, Criminal Law and Urban Problems: National Conference on Sentencing Advocacy (P.L.I. ed. 1989) ("Our culture suffers from a punishment addiction").

281. Keilitz, *supra* note 69, at 322.

282. Virgin Islands v. Fredericks, 578 F. 2d 927, 936-37 (3d Cir. 1978) (Adams, C.J., dissenting).

283. *See generally infra* chapter 3 B 1 b (1).

What is there about the insanity defense that inspires such massive societal irrationality? Why do we adhere to these myths, ignore the reams of rational data that patiently rebut them, and wilfully blind ourselves to the behavioral and empirical realities that are well known to all serious researchers in this area? It is to these questions that I now turn.

A History of Myths

A. The Development of Insanity Defense Doctrine[1]

1. Substantive Tests

a. Pre-M'Naghten history.[2] The development of the insanity defense prior to the mid-nineteenth century tracked both the prevailing scientific and popular concepts of mental illness, "craziness," responsibility[3] and blameworthiness. In existence since at least the twelfth century,[4] the defense has always "aroused more discussion" than any

---

1. *See generally,* 3 M.L. PERLIN, MENTAL DISABILITY LAW: CIVIL AND CRIMINAL §§15.02-15.03, 279-86 (1989).
2. This has been a particularly fertile topic for legal and behavioral scholars. *See e.g.,* R. SMITH, TRIAL BY MEDICINE: INSANITY AND RESPONSIBILITY IN VICTORIAN TRIALS 1-46 (1981); D. HERMANN, THE INSANITY DEFENSE (1983); 1 N. WALKER, CRIME AND INSANITY IN ENGLAND (1973); Walker, *The Insanity Defense Before 1800,* 477 ANNALS 25 (1985); Platt & Diamond, *The Origins of the "Right and Wrong" Test of Criminal Responsibility and Its Subsequent Development in the United States: An Historical Survey,* 54 CALIF. L. REV. 1227 (1966); Eule, *The Presumption of Sanity: Bursting the Bubble,* 25 U.C.L.A. L. REV. 637 (1978).
3. *See e.g.,* Glueck, *Ethics, Psychology and the Criminal Responsibility of the Insane,* 14 J. CRIM. L. & CRIMINOL. 208, 248 (1924) ("The basis of responsibility is not a condition, but a process; a process of scientific study of the factors of criminality in the individual case and of the balancing by trained, experienced scientists, of the individual and social interests involved in each individual case, and with reference to the ideals of our day and age").
4. *See* Sendor, *Crime and Communication: An Interpretive Theory of the Insanity*

other topic of substantive criminal law.[5] While there were few insanity pleas entered prior to the mid-eighteenth century,[6] the questions of the *scope* of the defense, the appropriate substantive test, and the social implications of the test were already matters of great concern.[7]

Prior to *M'Naghten*, the substantive insanity defense went through three significant stages: the "good and evil" test, the "wild beast" test, and the "right and wrong" test. The employment of *each* of these tests reflected (1) prevailing cultural and social myths, (2) the triumph of superstition and demonology over enlightenment and reason, and (3) the spurious use of science to justify the imposition of specific behavioral norms.

(1) "Good and evil." The "good and evil" test—which apparently first appeared in a 1313 case involving the capacity of an infant

---

Defense and the Mental Elements of Crime, 74 GEO. L. J. 1371, 1380 (1986) ("for six centuries before M'Naghten's Case, commentators, judges and attorneys identified a number of specific capacities as relevant to the exculpatory character of the insanity defense"); *see generally,* Rodriguez, LeWinn & Perlin, *The Insanity Defense Under Siege: Legislative Assaults and Legal Rejoinders,* 14 RUTGERS L.J. 397, 406-407 n. 56 (1983) (*quoting* 2 H. BRACTON, DE LEGIBUS ET CONSUETUDINIBUS ANGLIAE 424 (S. Thorne trans. 1968); D. HERMANN, *supra* note 2, at 22 (insanity as excuse in the time of Henry II (1216-1272)). Noting that the doctrine's origins are "hidden in the mists of the Bosporous," Nigel Walker has traced the first use of insanity as a *pardonable* excuse to Justinian's Digest in the third century. Walker, *supra* note 2, at 26.

On pre-common law roots, *see* T. PLUNCKETT, A CONCISE HISTORY OF THE COMMON LAW 261-262 (5th ed. 1956). Dr. Jordan Scher has traced the historical concern with the impact of mental illness on responsibility to 400 B.C. Scher, *Expertise and the Post Hoc Judgment of Insanity or the Antegnostician and the Law,* 57 Nw. U. L. REV. 4-6 (1962). On the Talmudic roots of the defense, *see* Quen, *Anglo-American Criminal Insanity,* 2 BULL. AM. ACAD. PSYCHIATRY & L. 115, 115 (1973).

5. Crotty, *The History of Insanity as a Defence to Crime in English Common Law,* 12 CALIF. L. REV. 105, 105 (1924). Added Crotty, "The discussion breaks out with renewed violence every time that this defence is raised in a criminal case." *Id.*

6. From 1760 to 1815, an average of three insanity pleas a year were entered in London's criminal courts. Eigen, *Historical Developments in Psychiatric Forensic Evidence: The British Experience,* 6 INT'L J. L. & PSYCHIATRY 423, 425 (1984).

7. This phenomenon has not changed significantly in the past three centuries; we continue to be preoccupied with the insanity defense in spite of its rarity. The incidence of successful insanity defense pleas has been described as rarer than poisonous snake bites in Manhattan. Eule, *supra* note 2, at 655, *quoting* Cohen, *Book Review,* 13 CONTEMP. PSYCHIATRY 386 (1968). On the increased frequency of insanity pleas in nineteenth century England, *see e.g.,* 1 N. WALKER, *supra* note 2, at 88 (approximately eight insanity defense cases per year at Old Bailey in London).

under the age of seven—reflected the "moral dogmata reflected in [the medieval] theological literature."[8] The insane, like children, were incapable of "sin[ning] against [their] will" since man's freedom "is restrained in children, in fools, and in the witless who do not have reason whereby they can choose the good from the evil."[9] Thus, as Professor Stephen Golding has recently suggested, the operative assumption was that "the mental anguish and suffering of the insane is sufficient to account for any retributive feelings we might have towards them concerning their misdeeds."[10] In short, to further punish the insane would create a sort of moral double jeopardy.

During the fourteenth through sixteenth centuries, this test—the source of which was most likely biblical—remained constant in English law,[11] and, by the end of that time (coinciding with the reign of Elizabeth I), insane persons who met this test were treated as "nonpersons" not fit subjects for punishment, "since they did not comprehend the moral implications of their harmful acts." Most likely, only the "most gross and dramatic kinds of mental illness"[12] qualified for mitigation of responsibility.[13] It was thus no surprise when this test was transfigured in 1724 to the "wild beast test."

(2) "Wild beast." Under this formulation, in *Rex. v. Arnold,* a case in which the defendant had shot and wounded a British Lord in a homicide attempt, and one characterized by Dr. Jacques Quen the "first of the historically significant" insanity defense trials,[14] Judge Tracy instructed the jury that it should acquit by reason of insanity in the case of:

> a mad man...must be a man that is totally deprived of his understanding and memory, and doth not know what he is doing, no more than *a brute, or a wild beast,* such a one is never the object of punishment.[15]

---

8. Platt & Diamond, *supra* note 2, at 1231-33, *discussing* Y.B., 6 & 7 Edw. 2, in 24 Selden Society 109 (1909).
9. Platt & Diamond, *supra* note 2, at 1233, *quoting* Michel, Ayenbit of Inwyt, Or Remorse of Conscience 86 (Morris ed. 1866) (treatise written in 1340).
10. Golding, Mental Health Professionals and the Courts: The Ethics of Expertise, 13 Int'l J. L. & Psychiatry 281, 287 (1990).
11. Platt & Diamond, supra note 2, at 1233-34.
12. Id. On the development of the "compartmentalized mind" theory (with different functions allocated to different parts of the brain), *see e.g.* V. Hans & N. Vidmar, Judging the Jury 187-88 (1986).
13. *See* Sendor, *supra* note 4, at 1373-76 (analyzing role of theories crafted by thirteenth through sixteenth century commentators).
14. Quen, *supra* note 4, at 116, *quoted* in Eule, *supra* note 2, at 978.
15. Rex v. Arnold, 16 How. St. Tr. 695 (1724), in 16 A Complete Collection of

According to Platt and Diamond, this test represented a "medley of legal theories of responsibility mixed with popular superstitions about mental illness."[16] The word "brute" was a mistranslation of Bracton's use of the Latin word *brutis*.[17] Further, the phrase "wild beast" never appeared in any prior definition of insanity;[18] according to Quen, "'brute' referred to farm animals and [in 1724] wild beasts in England were pretty much restricted to badgers, foxes, deer and rabbits."[19]

In short, the emphasis was on lack of *intellectual ability*, rather than the violently wild, ravenous beast image that the phrase calls to mind. Yet, the "wild beast" image of mental illness remained a powerful and long-lasting one, and the test stood as "a significant archetype in the history of law and medicine."[20]

(3) "Right and wrong." While the "good and evil" test continued to be used until at least 1840,[21] the following step—the "right and wrong" test which is the true forerunner of *M'Naghten*—emerged in two 1812 cases;[22] in the second of the two, the jury was charged that

---

STATE TRIALS 695 (T.B. Howell, ed. 1812) (emphasis added).

16. Platt & Diamond, *The Origins and Development of the "Wild Beast" Concept of Mental Illness and Its Relation to Theories of Criminal Responsibility*, 1 J. HIST. BEHAV. SCI. 355, 360 (1965); *see also*, Gray, *The Insanity Defense: Historical Development and Contemporary Relevance*, 10 AM. CRIM. L. REV. 559, 563 n. 20 (1972) (wild beast concept developed "from the medieval superstition of demonic possession, the accepted church psychology which distinguished man from beast on the basis of reason and a mistranslation of the word *Brutus*").

17. Platt & Diamond, *supra* note 16, at 360. See also, *id.* at 365 n. 61 (explaining source of error).

18. *Id.*

19. Quen, *Isaac Ray and Charles Doe: Responsibility and Justice*, in LAW AND THE MENTAL HEALTH PROFESSIONS: FRICTION AT THE INTERFACE 235, 237 (Barton & Sanborn eds. 1978).

20. Platt & Diamond, *supra* note 16, at 365.

21. *See* Platt & Diamond, *supra* note 2, at 1236 (listing cases). The test was temporarily abandoned in the aberrational Hadfield's Case, 27 How. St. Tr. 1281 (1800), *see generally*, 3 M.L. PERLIN, *supra* note 1, §15.04 at 286-89; D. HERMANN, *supra* note 2, at 31-33. However, the basis for this idiosyncratic decision is universally be ascribed to defense counsel Thomas Erskine's "brilliance and oratory," and the "bewildering effect of [his] adroitness, rhetoric and eloquence," H. WEIHOFEN, MENTAL DISORDER AS A CRIMINAL DEFENSE 58 (1954); as a result, the case was seen as idiosyncratic, and not contemporaneously perceived as persuasive authority, D. HERMANN, *supra* note 2, at 33.

22. Platt & Diamond, *supra* note 2, at 1237, discussing *Parker's Case* and *Bellingham's Case, cited* in G.D. COLLINSON, IDIOTS, LUNATICS, AND OTHER PERSONS NON COMPOS MENTIS 477, 636 (1812); Quen, *supra* note 4, at 119.

it must decide whether the defendant "had sufficient understanding to distinguish good from evil, right from wrong..."[23] It was finally expanded upon in 1840 in *Regina v. Oxford*,[24] where Lord Denman charged the jury that it must determine whether the defendant, "from the effect of a diseased mind," knew that the act was wrong, and that the question that must thus be answered was whether "he was quite unaware of the nature, character, and consequences of the act he was committing."[25]

Even with these rigid tests in place, the public's perceptions of abuse of the insanity defense differed little from its reactions in the aftermath of the Hinckley acquittal. Thus, addressing the House of Commons in 1800 (at the time of the employment of the "wild beast" test), the English Attorney General warned:

> It has been found that persons who have done the most shocking acts, and who have been acquitted on the grounds of being deranged in their intellects, having been allowed again to go at large afterwards committed similar acts again.[26]

In short, the public's representatives demanded an "all or nothing" sort of insanity, a conceptualization which has been "peculiarly foreign" to psychiatry since the middle of the nineteenth century.[27]

---

23. Lewinstein, *The Historical Development of Insanity as a Defense in Criminal Actions, Part I*, 14 J. FORENS. SCI. 275, 279 (1969), *quoting* G.D. COLLINSON, *supra* note 22, at 671 (*Bellingham's Case*). In the other case (*Parker's*), the Attorney General had argued that the defendant could be acquitted by reason of insanity only if the jury were "perfectly satisfied" that the defendant "did not really know right from wrong." Platt & Diamond, *supra* note 2, at 1237, *quoting* G.D. COLLINSON, *supra* note 22, at 477.
24. 9 Carr. & P. 525 (1840).
25. *Id.*, *quoted* in D. HERMANN, *supra* note 2, at 33.
26. Eule, *supra* note 2, at 646 (*quoting* 1 N. WALKER, *supra* note 2, at 84). *See generally*, Roberts, Golding & Fincham, *Implicit Theories of Criminal Responsibility: Decision Making and the Insanity Defense*, 11 LAW & HUM. BEHAV. 207, 226 (1987): "Judge Tracy's 'wild beast' conception of insanity is representative of most people's implicit theories of responsibility."
27. Diamond, *Criminal Responsibility of the Mentally Ill*, 14 STAN. L. REV. 59, 62 (1961); *see e.g.*, J. BUCKNILL, UNSOUNDNESS OF MIND IN RELATION TO CRIMINAL ACTS 2 (1856):

> Insanity is a condition of the human mind ranging from the slightest aberration from positive health to the wildest incoherence of mania, or the lowest degradations of cretinism. Insanity is a term applied to conditions measurable by all the degrees included between these widely separated poles, and to all the variations which are capable of being produced by partial or total affection of the many faculties into which the mind can be analyzed.

Similarly, the "demonological" concept of mental illness[28] retained its power centuries after it became clear that such a view was never supported by scientific data; Seymour Halleck has thus noted, "Even today, [mental] illness is characterized as a separate and pernicious external agent."[29]

Psychiatry can thus be seen as having always "inextricably tied" to the values of the prevailing culture.[30] As Professors Romanucci-Ross and Tancredi have pointed out, "Forensic psychiatry is always accompanied by a set of cultural attitudes [representing] an anthropology concerning the nature of man and the nature of culture."[31]

b. M'Naghten.[32] Even before M'Naghten's trial, Isaac Ray severely criticized the "right and wrong" test as inconsistent and "hopelessly out of step" with psychological and scientific knowledge,[33] and as an example of the criminal law's clinging to "crude and imperfect notions" of insanity. Wrote Ray in 1838:

> In their zeal to uphold the wisdom of the past, from the fancied desecrations of reformers and theorists, the ministers of the law seem to have forgotten that, in respect to this subject, the real dignity and respectability of their profession is better upheld by yielding to the improvements of the times and thankfully receiving the truth from whatever quarter it

---

This demand did not die in the nineteenth century. *See e.g.,* Holloway v. United States, 148 F. 2d 665, 667 (D.C. Cir. 1945) ("For the purposes of conviction there is no twilight zone between abnormality and insanity. An offender is wholly sane or wholly insane"); Johnson v. State, 292 Md. 405, 439 A. 2d 542, 552 (1982) ("For the purposes of guilt determination, an offender is either wholly sane or wholly insane").

28. *See generally supra* chapter 2 B.

29. S. Halleck, Psychiatry and the Dilemmas of Crime: A Study of Causes, Punishment and Treatment 210 (1971); *see also,* Golding, *supra* note 10, at 287 ("the key to understanding the level of emotionality" surrounding the insanity defense is the "deeply rooted moral and religious tension which surrounds the attribution of individual responsibility for 'good' and 'evil'").

30. Romanucci-Ross & Tancredi, *Psychiatry, The Law and Cultural Determinants of Behavior,* 9 Int'l J. L. & Psychiatry 265, 291 (1986).

31. *Id.* at 265. *See also,* L. Romanucci-ross, D. Moerman & L. Tancredi, The Anthropology of Medicine: From Culture to Method 262 (1983): "Because it is concerned with disorders of mood, thought and behavior, psychiatry must eke out of the panorama of everyday life…disturbances which involve an infusion of the symbols, imageries and metaphors of the culture into the content of specific patterns of behavior."

32. This section is partially adapted from 3 M.L. Perlin, *supra* note 1, §15.04.

33. Hovenkamp, *Insanity and Responsibility in Progressive America,* 57 N.D. L. Rev. 541, 552 (1981).

may come than by turning away with blind obstinacy from everything that conflicts with long-established maxims and decisions.[34]

Five years later, the "most significant case in the history of the insanity defense in England" arose out of the shooting by Daniel M'Naghten of Edward Drummond, the secretary of the man he mistook for his intended victim: Prime Minister Robert Peel.[35] After *nine* medical witnesses testified that M'Naghten was insane, and after the jury was informed that an insanity acquittal would lead to the defendant's commitment to a psychiatric hospital, M'Naghten was found not guilty by reason of insanity.[36]

Enraged by the verdict, Queen Victoria questioned why the law was of "no avail," since everybody is morally convinced that "[the]

---

34. I. RAY, MEDICAL JURISPRUDENCE OF INSANITY 13 (3d ed. 1853), as quoted in Platt & Diamond, *supra* note 2, at 1250. Three years before the publication of his famous treatise, Ray characterized the law of insanity as "greatly behind the present state of our knowledge of that disease." Ray, *Criminal Law of Insanity*, 28 AM. JURIST 253, 253 (1835).

35. Hermann & Sor, *Convicting or Confining? Alternative Directions in Insanity Law Reform: Guilty But Mentally Ill Versus New Rules for Release of Insanity Acquittees*, 1983 B.Y.U. L. REV. 449, 508; *see generally*, DANIEL MCNAUGHTON: HIS TRIAL AND THE AFTERMATH (D.J. West & A. Walk eds. 1977); Quen, *An Historical View of the M'Naghten Trial*, in 1 THE PSYCHOLOGICAL FOUNDATIONS OF CRIMINAL JUSTICE 93 (H. Vetter & R. Rieber eds. 1978).

36. R. MORAN, KNOWING RIGHT FROM WRONG: THE INSANITY DEFENSE OF DANIEL MCNAUGHTAN 18 (1981); *see* P. LOW, J. JEFFRIES & R. BONNIE, THE TRIAL OF JOHN W. HINCKLEY, JR.: A CASE STUDY IN THE INSANITY DEFENSE 10 (1986) (summarizing testimony). Judge Tindal charged the jury with the following language:

> The question to be determined is, whether at the time the act in question was committed, the prisoner had or had not the use of his understanding, so as to know that he was doing a wrong or wicked act. If the jurors should be of the opinion that the prisoner was not sensible, at the time he committed it, that he was violating the laws both of God and man, then he would be entitled to a verdict in his favour: but if, on the contrary, they were of the opinion that when he committed the act he was in a sound state of mind, then their verdict must be against him.

M'Naghten's Case, 8 Eng. Rep. 718, 719-720 (H.L. 1843), as quoted in Hermann & Sor, *supra* note 35, at 509.

M'Naghten spent the rest of his life in Broadmoor, a mental institution, Weiner, *Not Guilty By Reason of Insanity—A Sane Approach*, 56 CHICAGO-KENT L. REV. 1057, 1059 (1980); nonetheless, the public outrage that followed the M'Naghten acquittal was "partly fueled" by the belief that M'Naghten was not being "adequately punished" by this disposition of the case. Ellsworth, Bukaty, Cowan & Thompson, *The Death Qualified Jury and the Defense of Insanity*, 8 LAW & HUM. BEHAV. 81, 83 (1984) (Ellsworth).

malefactor...[was] perfectly conscious and aware of what he did,"[37] and demanded that the legislature "lay down the rule" so as to protect the public "from the wrath of madmen who they feared could now kill with impunity."[38] In response, the House of Lords asked the Supreme Court of Judicature to answer five questions regarding the insanity law,[39] and the judges' answers to two of these five became the *M'Naghten* test:

> [T]he jurors ought to be told in all cases that every man is presumed to be sane, and to possess a sufficient degree of reason to be responsible for his crimes, until the contrary be proved to their satisfaction; and that to establish a defence on the ground of insanity, it must be clearly proved that, at the time of the committing of the act, the party accused was labouring under such a defect of reason, from disease of the mind, as not to know the nature and quality of the act he was doing; or, if he did know it, that he did not know he was doing what was wrong.[40]

37.　*See* Eule, *supra* note 2, at 644; R. MORAN, *supra* note 36, at 20, *quoting Queen Victoria's Letters*, Royal Archives File No. A 14/8.

38.　Hermann & Sor, *supra* note 35, at 510, *quoting* 1 BENSON, THE LETTERS OF QUEEN VICTORIA, 1837-1861 587 (1907); R. MORAN, *supra* note 36, at 19.

　　The parallels to the Hinckley trial and to post-trial reactions are astonishing. *See* Hermann & Sor, *supra* note 35, at 510; Perlin, *"The Things We Do For Love:" John Hinckley's Trial and the Future of the Insanity Defense in the Federal Courts* (book review of L. CAPLAN, THE INSANITY DEFENSE AND THE TRIAL OF JOHN W. HINCKLEY, JR. (1984)), 30 N.Y.L. SCH. L. REV. 857, 862 n.21 (1985) ("The NGRI verdict in the *M'Naghten* case inspired virtually the same sentiments as did the *Hinckley* verdict nearly a century and a half later"). *See supra* chapter 2 A 1 a, at n. 12.

39.　*See* United States v. Freeman, 357 F. 2d 606, 617 (2d Cir. 1966) (Lord Tindal wrote "with the Queen's breath upon him"); *id.* at 625 ("The outrage of a frightened Queen has for too long caused us to forego the expert guidance that modern psychiatry is able to provide"). The press agreed with the Queen. *See* Moran, *The Modern Foundation for the Insanity Defense: The Cases of James Hadfield (1800) and Daniel McNaughten (1843)*, 477 ANNALS 31, 39-40 (1985) (citations omitted; emphasis added):

The *Times* of London expressed its concern that the physicians had invaded the traditional province of the jury. 'The judge in his treatment of the madman yields to the decision of the physician, and the physician in his treatment becomes the judge.' The *Illustrated London News* added that those who indulge themselves in the doctrines of socialism and infidelity, and thereby *willingly undergo* a 'process of mental intoxication,' cannot claim to be entirely without legal or moral responsibility.

　　The text of the questions is reproduced in Hermann & Sor, *supra* note 35, at 510-11 n.56.

40.　*M'Naghten*, 8 Eng. Rep. at 722.

This rigid, cognitive-only responsibility test, established under royal pressure, reflected "the prevailing intellectual and scientific ideas of the times," and stemmed from an "immutable philosophical and moral concept which assumes an inherent capacity in man to distinguish right from wrong and to make necessary moral decisions."[41]

The test has been severely and regularly criticized as rigid and inflexible, "untrustworthy," a "facade," "absolutist," an illustration of "a fiction being a fetish," "an absurd dictum which has long been discredited by medical science," and "outmoded and unrealistic."[42] It has been characterized as having been based on "an entirely obsolete and misleading conception," on outmoded views of the human psyche, and of bearing "little relation to the truths of mental life."[43] Critics have argued that it reflects "antiquated and outworn medical and ethical concepts," and have called it "the impenetrable wall behind which sits entrenched the almost unconquerable prosecutor

---

41. Hovenkamp, *supra* note 33, at 551; Brancale, *More on M'Naghten: A Psychiatrist's View*, 65 DICK. L. REV. 277, 277 (1961). Dr. Robert Waelder has likened the use of M'Naghten to requiring a physicist to testify about radioactivity "in the language of Aristotle," or a surgeon as to the consequences of an accident "in the language of Galen." Waelder, *Psychiatry and the Problem of Criminal Responsibility*, 101 U. PA. L. REV. 378, 381 (1952).

42. On the full scope of criticisms, *see generally*, Sendor, *supra* note 4, at 1380-83; *see e.g.*, S. GLUECK, LAW AND PSYCHIATRY: COLD WAR OR ENTENTE CORDIALE 43-48 (1966) ("rigid and inflexible"); R. REYNOLDS, SCIENTIFIC VALUE OF THE LEGAL TESTS OF INSANITY 34 (1872), as quoted in Parsons v. State, 81 Ala. 577, 2 So. 854, 861 (1887) ("untrustworthy"); Dubin, Mens Rea *Reconsidered: A Plea For a Due Process Concept of Criminal Responsibility*, 18 STAN. L. REV. 322, 388 (1966) ("a facade"); J. ROBITSCHER, PURSUIT OF AGREEMENT: PSYCHIATRY AND THE LAW 58 (1966) ("outmoded and unrealistic"); J. MARSHALL, INTENTION IN LAW AND SOCIETY 117 (1968) ("absolutist"); Guttmacher, *The Psychiatrist as an Expert Witness*, 22 U. CHI. L. REV. 325, 325 (1955) (*quoting* Dr. Henry Maudsley) ("an absurd dictum"); Trowbridge, *Competency and Criminal Responsibility in Washington*, 21 GONZAGA L. REV. 691, 712 (1985-86) ("outmoded and unrealistic").

    Professor Hovenkamp has stressed that the "discovery" of the unconscious (*see generally supra* chapter 2 B 2) made the psychological paradigm underlying M'Naghten "obsolete." Hovenkamp, *supra* note 33, at 551; *see also*, Hoedemaker, *"Irresistible Impulse" as a Defense in Criminal Law*, 23 WASH. L. REV. 1, 3 (1948) (discussing influence of Freud's discoveries on application of M'Naghten test).

43. United States v. Smith, 404 F.2d 720, 725 (6 Cir. 1968), *quoting* Sobeloff, *Insanity and the Criminal Law: From M'Naghten to Durham, and Beyond*, 41 A.B.A. J. 793, 794 (1955); Cardozo, *What Medicine Can Do For Law*, in LAW AND LITERATURE AND OTHER ESSAYS AND ADDRESSES 70, 106 (K. Menninger ed. 1931); Hermann & Sor, *supra* note 35, at 512 n. 60.

[and which prevents the introduction] into the courtroom true understanding of human psychology and the psychology of the criminal act."[44]

Further, the use of language such as "know" and "wrong" was "ambiguous, obscure, unintelligible, and too narrow."[45] Professor Hermann and a colleague have summarized the arguments:

> [T]he human being's psyche is an integrated entity of cognition and affect; therefore, one single aspect of personality—namely cognition—cannot solely be determinative of behavior. Critics also maintain that the narrow scope of the expert testimony required by the *M'Naghten* test deprives the jury of a complete picture of the psychological profile of the defendant.[46]

The M'Naghten Rules, in short, reflected a theory of responsibility that was outmoded far prior to its adoption, and which bore little resemblance to what was known about the human mind, even at the time of their promulgation. The Rules were developed at a time when it was generally believed that the mind was each person's "link with God or the supernatural." Predicated on the notion that the human mind was "dark and mysterious," they rejected the principle at the core of modern psychology, that man functions as a "unitary being."[47]

Nonetheless, with almost no exceptions, they were held as "sacrosanct"[48] by American courts that eagerly embraced this formulation, and codified it as the standard test "with little modification" in virtually all jurisdictions[49] until the middle of the twentieth century. Thus, the Kentucky Supreme Court sternly noted four decades after the *M'Naghten* decision:

> There is no law which will excuse or palliate a deliberate murder on the ground that the perpetrator of it is unlearned, passionate, ignorant, or even of weak mind, unless the weakness of mind amounts to such a defect

---

44. W. White, Twentieth Century Psychiatry 493 (1936); G. Zilboorg, The Psychology Of The Criminal Act And Punishment 10 (1954).

45. Hermann & Sor, *supra* note 35, at 512.

46. *Id.* at 512-13 (footnotes omitted).

47. Hovenkamp, *supra* note 33, at 544; Hall, *Psychiatry and Criminal Responsibility*, 65 Yale L.J. 761, 775 (1956).

48. Guttmacher, *The Quest for a Test of Criminal Responsibility*, 111 Am. J. Psychiatry 428 (1954).

49. Weiner, *supra* note 36, at 1060; for a more recent statutory review, *see* Callahan, Meyer & Steadman, *Insanity Defense Reform in the United States—Post-Hinckley*, 11 Ment. & Phys. Dis. L. Rep. 54 (1987).

of reason as to render him incapable of knowing the nature and quality of his act, or, if he does know it, that he does not know it is wrong to commit it.

It is no excuse for murder that the perpetrator has not power to control his actions when aroused or in a passion. It is the duty of men who are not insane or idiotic to control their evil passions and violent tempers or brutal instincts, and if they do not do so, it is their own fault, and their moral and legal responsibility will not be destroyed or avoided by the existence of such passions, or by their conduct resulting from them.[50]

The significance of the law's adamant adherence to *M'Naghten* for more than a century has not gone unnoticed. As early as 1924, Goodwin pointed out in his treatise on *Insanity and the Criminal*, "there are signs that lawyers are beginning to realize that for them to persist indefinitely in an attitude of indifference to the march of psychological science will result only in bringing the law into contempt in the eyes of the man on the street."[51] More recently, Professor Jay Katz has pinpointed one source of the law's hesitation to alter *M'Naghten*'s foundations as "the tension between the traditions of law and psychiatry in relation to free will."[52]

Yet, *M'Naghten* has not been without its academic supporters. In the most important defense of the doctrine, Professors Livermore and Meehl concluded that the test—in its reliance on the cognitive mental function— was sounder than any of its successors, in large part, because it takes into account "societal views on the blameworthiness of conduct engaged in by mentally abnormal people," by isolating specifically that group of offenders "that is popularly viewed as insane."[53] On this point, the Ninth Circuit has observed

---

50. Fitzpatrick v. Commonwealth, 81 Ky. Rep. 357, 361 (1883). This position has been consistently reiterated in American M'Naghten jurisdictions until the present day. *See* Commonwealth v. Banks, 513 Pa. 318, 521 A. 2d 1, 15 (1987), quoting Commonwealth v. Neill, 362 Pa. 514, 67 A. 2d 276, 280 (1949):

     Certainly, neither social maladjustment, nor lack of self-control, nor impulsiveness, nor psycho-neurosis, nor emotional instability, nor chronic malaria, nor all of such conditions combined, constitute insanity within the criminal conception of that term.

51. F. GOODWIN, INSANITY AND THE CRIMINAL 236 (1924).
52. Katz, *Law, Psychiatry, and Free Will*, 22 U. CHI. L. REV. 397 (1954).
53. Livermore & Meehl, *The Virtues of M'Naghten*, 51 MINN. L. REV. 789, 855-56 (1967) (emphasis added). For a recent example of a court's careful reading of *M'Naghten* on the question of whether "moral wrong" is to be measured by a societal standard or by a defendant's subjective understanding of an act's

that M'Naghten persisted as the major insanity defense test for over a century, "not because it is scientifically perfect, but because the courts regard it as the best criteria yet articulated for ascertaining criminal responsibility *which comports with the moral feelings of the community*."[54] More recently, Third Circuit Judge Arlin Adams, in dissenting from a panel decision affirming a manslaughter verdict, characterized the law of criminal responsibility as the "screen upon which the community has projected its visions of criminal justice."[55] As I will discuss subsequently, it is precisely this reflection of majoritarian community feelings—a value prized highly by the Burger and Rehnquist Supreme Courts[56]—which remains the "joker" in *any* attempt to analyze the development of an insanity defense jurisprudence.

c. Post-M'Naghten developments.

(1) Irresistible impulse. Although there was some interest in the post-*M'Naghten* years in the so-called "irresistible impulse" exception—allowing for the acquittal of a defendant if his mental disorder caused him to experience an "irresistible and uncontrollable impulse to commit the offense, even if he remained able to understand the nature of the offense and its wrongfulness"[57]—this formulation was

---

legality, *see* People v. Serravo, 823 P. 2d 128 (Colo. 1992) (using societal standard); *see generally*, Goldstein, *The Psychiatrist's Guide to Right and Wrong: Part II: A Systematic Analysis of Exculpatory Delusions*, 17 BULL. AM. ACAD. PSYCHIATRY & L. 61 (1989).

54. Sauer v. United States, 241 F. 2d 640, 649 (9th Cir. 1957) (emphasis added), *overruled on other gds.* in Wade v. United States, 426 F. 2d 64 (9th Cir. 1970).
55. Virgin Islands v. Fredericks, 578 F. 2d 927, 936, 937 (3d Cir. 1978).
56. Perlin, *State Constitutions and Statutes as Sources of Rights for the Mentally Disabled: The Last Frontier?* 20 LOYOLA L.A. L. REV. 1249, 1258 (1987) (discussing majoritarianism of Burger and Rehnquist Supreme Courts). *See infra* chapter 4, text accompanying notes 204-7. *But compare*, Marshall, *The Supreme Court and the Grass Roots: Whom Does the Court Represent Best?* 76 JUDICATURE 22, 28 (1992) (concluding that modern Supreme Court has been "relatively evenhanded in representation of different social and demographic group attitudes").
57. Dix, *Criminal Responsibility and Mental Impairment in American Criminal Law: Responses to the Hinckley Acquittal in Historical Perspective*, in 1 LAW AND MENTAL HEALTH: INTERNATIONAL PERSPECTIVES 1, 7 (D. Weisstub ed. 1986). The test flows from Stephen's arguments:

If it is not, it ought to be the law of England that no act is a crime if the person who does it is at the time...prevented either by defective mental power or by any disease affecting his mind from controlling his own conduct, unless the absence of the power of control has been produced by his own default.

not more than a transitory detour in the development of an insanity jurisprudence,[58] notwithstanding U.S. Attorney Giuliani's remarks to Congress following the Hinckley verdict.[59]

(2) Durham. The first important theoretical alternative to M'Naghten emerged in the District of Columbia in the case of Durham v. United States.[60] Writing for the court, Judge David Bazelon rejected both M'Naghten and the irresistible impulse tests[61] on the theory that the mind of man was a functional unit, and that a far broader test would be appropriate.[62] Durham thus held that an accused would not

---

2 J. STEPHEN, A HISTORY OF THE CRIMINAL LAW OF ENGLAND 168 (1883).
On the relationship between this test and "moral insanity," see supra chapter 2 B 2; see Lewinstein, The Historical Development of Insanity as a Defense in Criminal Actions (Part II), 14 J. FORENS. SCI. 469, 469 (1969).

58. While it was subsequently adopted—at its high-water mark—in approximately eighteen jurisdictions, it was rejected firmly by others, for a variety of reasons "ranging from the principled to the pragmatic." 3 M.L. PERLIN, supra note 1, §15.05 at 295-96; Hermann & Sor, supra note 35, at 516 n. 79; see also, Low, Jeffries & Bonnie, supra note 36, at 15.

59. See supra chapter 2 A 2 b (3).

60. 214 F. 2d 862 (D.C. Cir. 1954), overruled in United States v. Brawner, 471 F. 2d 969, 981 (D.C. Cir. 1972). In contradistinction to Hinckley and M'Naghten, Durham involved a nonjury conviction for housebreaking in a case with an "unknown" defendant.
The Durham test is a reformulation of the standard articulated in State v. Pike, 49 N.H. 399, 442 (11870) (Doe, J., dissenting), overruled on other gds. in Hardy v. Merrill, 56 N.H. 227 (1875), that, in turn, partially emanated from Dr. Isaac Ray's criticisms of M'Naghten, see Low, Jeffries & Bonnie, supra note 36, at 16-17; Reik, The Doe-Ray Correspondence: A Pioneer Collaboration in the Jurisprudence if Mental Disease, 63 YALE L.J. 183-84 (1953).

61. Durham, 214 F. 2d at 874:

We find that as an exclusive criterion the right-wrong test is inadequate in that (a) it does not take sufficient account of psychic realities and scientific knowledge, and (b) is based upon one symptom and so cannot validly be applied in all circumstances. We find that the 'irresistible impulse' test is also inadequate in that it gives no recognition to mental illness characterized by brooding and reflection and so relegates acts caused by such illness to the application of the inadequate right-wrong test. We conclude that a broader test should be adopted.

62. Id. at 870-71 (discussing criticisms of M'Naghten test); compare People v. Horton, 308 N.Y. 1, 123 N.E. 2d 609, 616, 618 (1954) (Van Voorhis, J., dissenting):

The development of psychiatry appears to have transferred the main professional attention from disorganization of the intellect to emotional disturbances. The legal definition remains focused upon intellectual disorientation,...regardless of how distorted his own standards of behavior may have been due to emotional disintegration.

be criminally responsible if his "unlawful act was the product of mental disease or mental defect."[63] This test would provide for the broadest range of psychiatric expert testimony, "unbound by narrow or psychologically inapposite legal questions."[64] Further, it reiterated the jury's function in such a case:

> Juries will continue to make moral judgments, still operating under the fundamental precept that "Our collective conscience does not allow punishment where it cannot impose blame." But in making such judgments, they will be guided by wider horizons of knowledge concerning mental life. The question will be simply whether the accused acted because of a mental disorder, and not whether he displayed particular symptoms which medical science has long recognized do not necessarily or even typically, accompany even the most serious disorder.[65]

Durham was the first modern, major break from the *M'Naghten* approach, and created a "feeling of ferment" as the District of Columbia "became a veritable laboratory for consideration of the details of insanity, in its fullest substantive and procedural ramifications."[66] Although it was hailed as "the zenith of legal and psychiatric optimism,"[67] it soon came under rigorous criticism.[68] Critics sug-

---

63. *Durham*, 214 F. 2d at 874-75. Added the court:

   We use 'disease' in the sense of a condition which is considered capable of either improving or deteriorating. We use 'defect' in the sense of a condition which is not considered capable of either improving or deteriorating and which may be either congenital, or the result of injury, or the residual effect of a physical or mental disease.

64. Weiner, *Mental Disability and Criminal Law*, in S. BRAKEL, J. PARRY & B. WEINER, THE MENTALLY DISABLED AND THE LAW 693, 710 (ed 3d. 1985).
65. *Durham*, 214 F. 2d at 876 (footnotes omitted), *quoting* Holloway v. United States, 148 F. 2d 665, 666 (D.C. Cir. 1945), *cert. den.*, 334 U.S. 852 (1948).
66. A. GOLDSTEIN, THE INSANITY DEFENSE 83 (1967); *see also*, H. FINGARETTE, THE MEANING OF CRIMINAL INSANITY 12 (1972). On the way that insanity defense reforms such as *Durham* were part of a larger "liberal agenda of the time," *see* Trubek, *Back to the Future: The Short, Happy Life of the Law and Society Movement*, 18 FLA. ST. U. L. REV. 4, 39 (1990).
67. Bennett & Sullwold, *Qualifying the Psychiatrist as a Lay Witness: A Reaction to the American Psychiatric Association Petition in* Barefoot v. Estelle, 30 J. FORENS. SCI. 462, 462 (1985).
68. *See e.g.*, Sauer v. United States, 241 F. 2d 640, 646-50 (9th Cir. 1957), *overruled on other gds.* in Wade v. United States, 426 F. 2d 64 (9th Cir. 1970) (summarizing criticisms). At least some of the criticism carries with it a particularly rueful or regretful tone. *See e.g.*, Burt, *Of Mad Dogs and Scientists: The Perils of the "Criminal-Insane,"* 123 U. PA. L. REV. 258-59 (1974):

gested that its vague definitions failed to provided helpful guidelines, that it was—at its core—a "non-rule," providing the jury with "no standard by which to judge the evidence," that it misidentified the "moral issue of responsibility with the scientific issues of diagnosis and causation," that it was too heavily dependent upon expertise, leading to the usurpation of jury decision making by psychiatrists, and allowing the insanity defense to "draw upon anything medicine could bring to it."[69] In addition, it appeared that, in practice, it was frequently honored only in the breach.[70]

Within a few years, *Durham* was judicially criticized,[71] modified[72] and ultimately dismantled by the D.C. Circuit, its burial being

---

The *Durham* experiment has succeeded by graphically demonstrating a proposition of considerable social importance: the conjoining of psychiatry and the criminal law frequently (perhaps inevitably) produces mutual misunderstandings and defeats optimistic expectations on all sides.

69. Hermann & Sor, *supra* note 35, at 520; H. FINGARETTE, *supra* note 66, at 30; R. GERBER, THE INSANITY DEFENSE 47 (1984); A. GOLDSTEIN, *supra* note 66, at 84 (discussing criticism); *see e.g.*, Wechsler, *The Criteria of Criminal Responsibility*, 22 U. CHI. L. REV. 367, 373 (1955) (*Durham* puts forth "a legal principle beclouded by a central ambiguity, both unexplained and unsupported by its basic rationale"). While one contemporaneous study found that, after *Durham*, there was a statistically significant increase in the number of insanity pleas offered in District of Columbia felony trials, *see* Arens, *The* Durham *Rule in Action: Judicial Psychiatry and Psychiatric Justice*, 1 LAW & SOC'Y REV. 41, 46 (1967), a more recent careful evaluation of the same data concludes that it is "problematic" to attribute the increase "simply" to the application of the *Durham* rule. *See* Keilitz, *Researching and Reforming the Insanity Defense*, 39 RUTGERS L. REV. 289, 300-1 (1987).
70. In a post-*Durham* survey of experienced criminal defense lawyers in Washington, D.C., 26 of 27 respondents reported that District Court judges viewed the insanity defense "with suspicion and at times hostility." Arens & Susman, *Judges, Jury Charges and Insanity*, 12 HOWARD L.J. 1, 6 (1966). Concluded the authors (*id.* at 23):

[T]he symbols of M'Naghten, clearly inconsistent with the *Durham* jurisprudence, have maintained a curious 'co-existence' with the *Durham* symbols in the jury instructions of the District Court.

71. Frigillana v. United States, 307 F. 2d 665, 667 (D.C. Cir. 1962) ("This case vividly illustrates the tangled web we have spun for ourselves under the ambiguous labels of *Durham v. United States*").
72. *See e.g.*, McDonald v. United States, 312 F. 2d 847, 851 (D.C. Cir. 1962), clarifying that the terms "mental disease and defect" include "any abnormal condition of the mind which substantially affects mental or emotional processes or substantially impairs behavior control."

completed by the decision in *United States v. Brawner* to adopt the Model Penal Code/American Law Institute test.[73]

Durham retains significance for several interrelated reasons. First, as a historical document, it stands as a reflection of the judiciary's—or, at least, Judge Bazelon's—ultimate faith in psychiatry (and especially in *forensic* psychiatry) to illuminate underlying issues of causation, responsibility and blameworthiness. The fact that the *Durham* alternative was explicitly rejected in twenty-two states within seven years of the court's decision suggests that this faith was not replicated elsewhere.[74] Next, the response to *Durham* reflects the myths that control jurisprudential developments in this area. It was a perfect foil for those who rejected psychodynamic explanations of interpersonal behavior, and was contemporaneously misread as an open floodgate that could ultimately "excuse all mentally or emotionally disturbed persons from criminal responsibility."[75]

This sort of distorted overreading is common in lay interpretations of court cases involving mentally disabled litigants.[76] What is significant here is that this distortion came from a panel of the same Court of Appeals that had decided *Durham* only eight years previously. Indeed, it has been suggested that the evisceration of *Durham* stemmed from the Court's response to two cases in which hospital administrative psychiatric staff reversed, as a policy decision, its position on a patient's diagnosis;[77] as I will discuss sub-

---

73. 471 F. 2d 969, 973 (D.C. Cir. 1972); *see infra* text accompanying notes 86-91.
74. *See* Krash, *The* Durham *Rule and Judicial Administration of the Insanity Defense in the District of Columbia*, 70 YALE L.J. 905, 906 n. 8 (1961). Maine legislatively adopted *Durham*, and subsequently repealed the statute in question thirteen years later. *See* ME. REV. STAT., tit. 15 § 102 (1963) (repealed 1976).
75. *Frigillana*, 307 F. 2d at 668.
76. *See e.g.*, E.B. WILLIAMS, ONE MAN'S FREEDOM 256 (1962) (national news magazine characterized *Durham* as "easing up on murderers"). On the way that *Durham* was mischaracterized in the Congressional post-Hinckley insanity defense hearings, *see supra* chapter 2 A 2 b. On the way that distortions of mental disability law decisions affect subsequent clinical practice, *see* Perlin, Tarasoff *and the Dilemma of the Dangerous Patient: New Directions for the 1990's*, 16 LAW & PSYCHOL. REV. 29 (1992).
77. *See* Perlin, *The Supreme Court, the Mentally Disabled Criminal Defendant, and Symbolic Values: Random Decisions, Hidden Rationales, or "Doctrinal Abyss?"* 29 ARIZ. L. REV. 1, 24 n. 215 (1987); B. BURSTEN, BEYOND PSYCHIATRIC EXPERTISE 23-26 (1984); Uelman, *The Psychiatrist, the Sociopath and the Courts: New Lines for an Old Battle*, 14 LOY. L.A. L. REV. 1, 12-13 (1980) (discussing decisions in *In re* Rosenfeld, 157 F. Supp. 18 (D.D.C. 1957) (known as the "weekend flip-flop case), discussed in *Brawner*, 471 F. 2d at 978), and in Blocker v. United States, 288 F. 2d 853, 858 (D.C. Cir. 1961) (hospital doctors

sequently, it is precisely the use of this sort of heuristic cognitive device that has insured the continuing incoherence of insanity defense policy.[78]

Finally, *Durham* inspired pretextuality on the part of suspicious and hostile trial judges.[79] Jury charges under *Durham* reinforced pre-existing juror concepts that mental illness must be reflected in "bizarre behavior manifestations,"[80] avoided the "product" language of *Durham* and "reflected an overwhelming number of symbols suggestive of the cognitive [*M'Naghten*] formulation."[81] Such behavior by trial judges overtly subverted the attempt of the *Durham* court to "extend...[the] courtroom back into the world."[82]

The decision in *Durham* must be read in light of Judge Adams' metaphor of the "screen upon which the community has projected its vision of criminal justice."[83] The decision was so cognitively dissonant[84] from "the moral feelings of the community"[85] that its collapse was inevitable. That collapse reflected the depths of our societal discomfort with the approach urged heroically, if unsuccessfully, by Judge Bazelon.

(3) United States v. Brawner. Brawner discarded *Durham's* "product" test, but added a *volitional* question to *M'Naghten's* cognitive inquiry. Under this test:

---

reversed policy on administrative decision as to whether "psychopathy" or "sociopathy" would be included as mental illnesses).

78. *See generally infra* chapter 6 C.
79. Arens & Susman, *supra* note 70, at 6. By "pretextuality," I refer to the way courts engage in dishonest (frequently meretricious) decision making. *See* Perlin, *Pretexts and Mental Disability Law: The Case of Competency,* 47 U. Miami L. Rev. (1993) (in press), manuscript at 3 n. 3. *See generally infra* chapter 8 C.
80. Arens, Granfield & Susman, *Jurors, Jury Charges, and Insanity,* 14 Cath. U. L. Rev. 1, 26 (1965). On how this sort of "sanist" behavior frequently dominates judicial discourse, *see* Perlin, *On "Sanism,"* 46 SMU L. Rev. 373 (1992); *see generally infra* chapter 8 B.
81. Arens & Susman, *supra* note 70, at 33.
82. Wales, *The Rise, the Fall, and the Resurrection of the Medical Model,* 63 Geo. L.J. 63, 87 (1974).
83. Virgin Islands v. Fredericks, 578 F. 2d 927, 936 (3d Cir. 1978) (Adams, C.J., dissenting).
84. *See* Perlin, *Morality and Pretextuality, Psychiatry and Law: Of "Ordinary Common Sense," Heuristic Reasoning, and Cognitive Dissonance,* 19 Bull. Am. Acad. Psychiatry & L. 131, 139 (1991).
85. Sauer v. United States, 281 F. 2d 640, 649 (9th Cir. 1957), *overruled on other gds.* in Wade v. United States, 426 F. 2d 64 (9th Cir. 1970).

A defendant would not be responsible for his criminal conduct if, as a result of mental disease or defect, he "lack[ed] substantial capacity either to appreciate the criminality of his conduct or to conform his conduct to the requirements of law.[86]

Although the test was rooted in *M'Naghten,* there were several significant differences. *First,* its use of the word "substantial" was meant to respond to caselaw developments which had required "a showing of total impairment for exculpation from criminal responsibility." *Second,* the substitution of the word "appreciate" for the word "know" showed that "a sane offender must be emotionally as well as intellectually aware of the significance of his conduct," and "mere intellectual awareness that conduct is wrongful when divorced from an appreciation or understanding of the moral or legal import of behavior, can have little significance." *Third,* by using broader language of mental impairment than had *M'Naghten,* the test "capture[d] both the cognitive and affective aspects of impaired mental understanding." *Fourth,* its substitution in the final proposed official draft of the word "wrongfulness" for "criminality" reflected the position that the insanity defense dealt with "an impaired moral sense rather than an impaired sense of legal wrong."[87]

It was assumed that the spreading adoption of *Brawner* would augur the death of *M'Naghten.*[88] That assumption, of course, has

---

86. MODEL PENAL CODE §4.01(1) (Tent. Draft No. 4 1955).
87. A. GOLDSTEIN, *supra* note 66, at 87; United States v. Freeman, 357 F. 2d 606, 623 (2d Cir. 1966); Hermann & Sor, *supra* note 35, at 522; MODEL PENAL CODE §4.01 (Prop. Off'l Draft 1962). For a recent explanation of why one state discarded *M'Naghten* for the ALI test, *see* State v. Gardner, 616 A. 2d 1124, 1125-26 (R.I. 1992).
88. *See e.g.,* Diamond, *From* M'Naghten *to* Currens *and Beyond,* 50 CALIF. L. REV. 189, 189 (1962) ("I shall start with the assumption that *M'Naghten* is dead"). *Compare* Roth, *Preserve But Limit The Insanity Defense,* 58 PSYCHIATRIC Q. 91, 96 (1986-87):

The operation of the insanity defense under the *M'Naghten* rules resulted in what Bernard Diamond has recently called 'the dead days' of the 1930s and 1940s. Many psychiatrists would like to return to the dead days.

Brawner was eventually adopted by over half of the states, Weiner, *supra* note 64, at 712, and, in some form, by all but one of the federal circuits. *See* United States v. Lyons, 731 F. 2d 243, 253 n. 3 (5th Cir. 1984) (Rubin, J., concurring in part & dissenting in part); Note, *The Proposed Federal Insanity Defense: Should the Quality of Mercy Suffer for the Sake of Safety?* 22 AM. CRIM. L. REV. 49, 55-56 nn. 42, 46 (1984) (circuit-by-circuit listing).

proven to be mortally inaccurate.[89] *Brawner*, did, however, serve as the final burial for the *Durham* experiment.[90] As Professor Wales has concluded:

> After all the buildup—...the 18 years of a national debate [after *Durham*], and the half-dozen cases heralding the coming of *Brawner*—the court simply rolled over and died. Chief Judge Bazelon's concurrence revealed the agony of his disappointment over the court's failure to match wits with the issues.[91]

(4) Guilty But Mentally Ill.[92] Perhaps the most important development in substantive insanity defense formulations in the twenty years post-*Brawner* has been the adoption in over a dozen jurisdictions[93] of the hybrid "guilty but mentally ill" (GBMI) verdict. Heuristically, it received its initial recent impetus in 1975 in Michigan as a reflection of legislative dissatisfaction with and public outcry over a state Supreme Court decision that prohibited automatic commitment of insanity acquittees.[94] The GBMI statute was adopted to "protect

---

89. *Brawner* and other federal cases adopting the ALI test were legislatively overruled by Congress in the Insanity Defense Reform Act, passed as part of the Comprehensive Crime Control Act of 1984. *See* 18 U.S.C. §17 (1988); *see supra* chapter 2 A 2 c.
90. *See* Diamond, *From* Durham *to* Brawner, *A Futile Journey,* 1973 WASH. U. L.Q. 109.
91. Wales, *supra* note 82, at 103. See *Brawner*, 471 F. 2d at 1013 (Bazelon, C.J., concurring and dissenting): "[T]he Court's current attitude...is...sharply at odds with the spirit of experimentation, inquiry and confrontation that have characterized so much of our work in this field." In his separate opinion, Judge Bazelon urged adoption of this alternative formulation (*Id.* at 1032 (emphasis in original)):

   Our instruction to the jury should provide that a defendant is not responsible *if at the time of his unlawful conduct his mental or emotional processes or behavior controls were impaired to such an extent that he cannot justly be held responsible for his act.*

92. Much of the material in text *infra* accompanying notes 93-107 is adapted from 3 M.L. PERLIN, *supra* note 1, §15.09 at 307-13.
93. *See* McGraw, Farthing-Capowich & Keilitz, *The "Guilty But Mentally Ill" Plea and Verdict: Current State of the Knowledge,* 30 VILL. L. REV. 117, 128-142 (1985) (McGraw) (Tables 1-3), for a full compilation of all statutes, discussing substance, procedure and disposition.
94. *See* People v. McQuillan, 392 Mich. 511, 221 N.W. 2d 569, 576 (1974); *see generally,* Mickenberg, *A Pleasant Surprise: The Guilty But Mentally Ill Verdict Has Succeeded in Its Own Right and Successfully Preserved the Insanity Defense,* 55 U. CIN. L. REV. 943, 973-74 (1987). The public's response followed the rearrest of two former patients on new charges of violent crimes. *See* McGraw, *supra* note 93, at 124.

the public from violence inflicted by persons with mental ailments who slipped through the cracks of the criminal justice system."[95] This experience has been replicated in virtually *every* jurisdiction that has enacted a GBMI statute.[96]

The rationale for the passage of GBMI legislation was that the implementation of such a verdict would decrease the number of persons acquitted by reason of insanity, and would assure treatment of those who were GBMI within a correctional setting.[97] A GBMI defendant would purportedly be evaluated upon entry to the correc-

---

95. People v. Seefeld, 95 Mich. App. 197, 290 N.W. 2d 123, 124 (Ct. App. 1980). While three other states adopted GBMI after Michigan and before the Hinckley verdict, the rest did so in the immediate aftermath of Hinckley. *See* Weiner, *supra* note 64, at 714 n. 264 (noting that, although the GBMI tide has ebbed, "it is likely to be revived in those states where a crime occurs which enrages the public when the defendant raises and/or succeeds with the insanity defense").

   GBMI also seems to mirror the majoritarian position as to how an appropriate mental status defense should operate. *See* Roberts, Golding & Fincham, *supra* note 26, at 222-23 (jurors predisposed to use GBMI alternative); Poulson, *Mock Juror Attribution of Criminal Responsibility: Effects of Race and the Guilty But Mentally Ill (GBMI) Verdict Option*, 20 J. APPL. SOC'L PSYCHOLOGY 1596, 1608 (1990) (GBMI a "very attractive compromise" to jurors).

96. *See* Mickenberg, *supra* note 94, at 972, *citing* Hagen, *The Insanity Defense: A Review of Recent Statutory Changes*, 3 J. LEG. MED. 617, 618 (1982) (GBMI laws enacted "as a direct response to a highly publicized crime committed by a former NGRI mental patient"); *see also*, Keilitz, *supra* note 69, at 308.

97. *See* Robey, *Guilty But Mentally Ill*, 6 BULL. AM. ACAD. PSYCHIATRY & L. 374, 379-80 (1978); People v. Smith, 124 Ill. App. 3d 805, 465 N.E. 2d 101, 106 (1984) (legislature intended GBMI to reduce number of insanity acquittals; statute is "clearly rationally designed to accomplish that goal"). Under a prototypical GBMI law, a defendant could be found GBMI—as an *alternative* to the NGRI verdict—if the following were found by the trier of fact beyond a reasonable doubt:
   (a) That the defendant is guilty of an offense.
   (b) That the defendant was mentally ill at the time of the commission of the offense.
   (c) That the defendant was not legally insane at the time of the commission of the offense.
   See e.g., MICH. STAT. ANN. §28.1044(1) (1985). *Cf.* MICH. STAT ANN. §28.1059 (1986) (NGRI statute).
   In at least one state, the GBMI verdict had no empirical impact on the NGRI rate as, prior to the passage of the GBMI law, there were only one or two insanity verdicts in a universe of 24,000 felony indictments. *See* Morgan, McCullough, Jenkins & White, *Guilty But Mentally Ill: The South Carolina Experience*, 16 BULL. AM. ACAD. PSYCHIATRY & L. 41, 42 (1988). *But see* H. STEADMAN ET AL., REFORMING THE INSANITY DEFENSE: AN EVALUATION OF PRE- AND POST-HINCK-LEY REFORMS (1993) (in press), manuscript at 202 (H. STEADMAN, REFORMING) ("GBMI may diminish use of the insanity defense, especially for those committing violent offenses").

tional system and be provided appropriate mental health services either on an in-patient basis as part of a definite prison term or, in specific cases, as a parolee or as an element of probation.[98]

Practice under GBMI statutes reveals that the verdict does little or nothing to ensure effective treatment for mentally disabled offenders. As most statutes vest discretion in the director of the state correctional or mental health facility to provide a GBMI prisoner with such treatment as she "determines necessary," the GBMI prisoner is not ensured treatment "beyond that available to other offenders."[99] A comprehensive study of the operation of the GBMI verdict in Georgia revealed that only three of the 150 defendants who were found GBMI during the period in question were being treated in hospitals. [100]

In Illinois, an appellate court explicitly held that such a statute provides no right to treatment for offenders beyond their constitutionally minimal right to adequate medical care;[101] in at least two other states, treatment is available to GBMI offenders only to the extent that available state money permits.[102] This may be especially pernicious as the building of "false treatment expectations" may mislead defendants, their lawyers, courts and the general public into believing that GBMI defendants are accorded special post-conviction treatment.[103] Sentencing decisions also show the vacuity of the GBMI

---

98. Weiner, *supra* note 64, at 715. *See generally*, People v. Booth, 414 Mich. 343, 324 N.W. 2d 741, 745 (1982); People v. McLeod, 407 Mich. 632, 288 N.W. 2d 909, 918-19 (1980); *see also*, People v. Boatright, 137 Ill. App. 3d 888, 486 N.E. 2d 926 (1986).

99. *See* Slobogin, *The Guilty But Mentally Ill Verdict: An Idea Whose Time Should Not Have Come*, 53 GEO. WASH. L. REV. 494, 513 (1985); McGraw, *supra* note 93, at 187.

100. H. STEADMAN, REFORMING, *supra* note 97, at 195. *Accord*, People v. Smith, 124 Ill. App. 3d 805, 465 N.E. 2d 101, 103 (1984) (not a single one of first 44 defendants found GBMI in Illinois received hospital treatment).

101. People v. Marshall, 124 Ill. App. 3d 217, 448 N.E. 2d 969, 980 (1983); *see also*, *Smith*, 465 N.E. 2d at 106 (failure to ensure treatment to GBMI prisoners does not render statute unconstitutional).

102. 42 PA. CODE STAT. ANN. §9727(b) (1986); GA. CODE ANN. §17-7-131(g) (1985). On the paucity of resources available to such prisoners, *see* People v. Ramsey, 422 Mich. 500, 375 N.W. 2d 297, 316-17 n. 56 (1985), *rehearing den.* (1985) (Levin, J., dissenting) (state correctional health care official concedes that adequate care not provided for mentally ill prisoners).

103. McGraw, *supra* note 93, at 188; Slobogin, *supra* note 99, at 514. Subsequent research confirms that jurors in simulated cases often select this verdict with precisely this expectation in mind. *See e.g.*, Finkel, *The Insanity Defense: A Comparison of Verdict Schemes*, 15 LAW & HUM. BEHAV. 533 (1991).

verdict. Courts have thus found that it was constitutional to sentence a GBMI defendant to death,[104] or to a term that exceeds his life expectancy.[105]

A recent Kentucky case reflects the emptiness of the GBMI option. A defendant was sentenced to twenty years in prison for murdering her infant daughter after a jury rejected her insanity defense and found her GBMI. On appeal, the state Supreme Court rejected her argument that it had been error for the trial court to refuse to allow her counsel to comment on the meaning of a GBMI verdict:

> She argues that the jurors are totally confused as to what the consequences of their actions in returning a particular verdict will actually be...She claims that well meaning jurors do not want to bear the public stigma of having turned loose a child killer even though they may believe this can be accomplished by the middle ground of guilty but mentally ill verdict. [Defendant] asserts that such is not the case.[106]

The majority merely concluded cursorily that "future consequences...have no place in the jury's finding of fact and may serve to distort it," and affirmed the conviction.[107]

---

104. Harris v. State, 499 N.E. 2d 723 (Ind. 1986); People v. Crews, 122 Ill. 2d 266, 522 N.E. 2d 1167 (1988). *But see* Sanders v. State, 585 A. 2d 117 (Del. 1990) (GBMI verdict established mitigating factor as matter of law; case remanded for new penalty hearing); *see generally,* Emanuel, *Guilty But Mentally Ill Verdicts and the Death Penalty: An Eighth Amendment Analysis,* 68 N.C. L. Rev. 37 (1989).

105. Whitt v. State, 497 N.E. 2d 1059 (Ind. 1986); *but see* People v. Newell, 196 Ill. App. 3d 373, 553 N.E. 2d 722 (1990), *rehearing den.* (1990) (60 year sentence excessive in GBMI case).

106. Mitchell v. Commonwealth, 781 S.W. 2d 510, 511 (Ky. 1989), *reh. den.* (1990). Paradoxically, matricide prosecutions comprise one of the few subsets of insanity defense cases in which jurors appear to *over*-acquit. *See generally infra* chapter 4 D 2-3.

107. *Id.* at 511. In dissent, Justice Liebson took sharp issue with the majority's stance (*Id.* at 513-14 (Liebson, J., dissenting)):

Few, if any [jurors] will realize that the 'but mentally ill' finding is, for all practical purposes, empty of legal consequences
* * *   * * *   * * *
The bizarre result in the Hinckley case has always been only a remote possibility in Kentucky [because of the placement in Kentucky of the burden of proof in insanity cases on the defendant], and the [GBMI] statute was at best an unnecessary overreaction. But, since we have this statute, albeit essentially meaningless and inherently confusing, the least we can do is to provide the triers of fact an explanation so they can understand what it means.

The GBMI verdict is a perfect exemplar of insanity defense ambivalence and popular attitudes. We rationalize that we are "doing something" for the mentally disabled criminal defendant, but the results of this legislative "reform" are, at best, cosmetic, and, at worst, meretricious. With no meaningful promise of treatment or rehabilitative services, and with the countenancing of punitive sentencing, the GBMI verdict becomes deceptive and hollow.[108]

(5) Conclusion. As I have already discussed, Congress' direct response to the *Hinckley* acquittal was to adopt an even more restrictive version of the *M'Naghten* test. Given the political strength of the insanity defense abolitionists at that time, this formulation was seen as a victory by the defense's supporters.[109] How can this be?

A line can be drawn from *M'Naghten* to *Hinckley* on which the public's negative reaction to "vivid" cases and its fear of abuse of the insanity defense can be charted. The boldest experiment—*Durham* (a case that, not coincidentally, involved a non-famous defendant and a nondescript crime)—faded quickly and ingloriously in *Brawner*. *Brawner*, which itself had been seen as the death of *M'Naghten*, was then overruled by the Insanity Defense Reform Act (IDRA). Although only a handful of states abolished the insanity defense outright, twelve adopted the GBMI verdict,[110] notwithstanding a nearly-unanimous empirical record suggesting that that alternative was truly a meretricious one. The expansive approach urged passionately by Judge Bazelon in *Durham* was, to be blunt, dead, buried and unmourned.[111]

The adoption of the IDRA—like *M'Naghten* before it—was animated by the public's negative reaction to the vividness of the Hinckley case and by its fear of "abuse" of the insanity test. In

---

108. *See* H. STEADMAN, REFORMING, *supra* note 97, at 195, 203-4; Roberts, Golding & Fincham, *supra* note 26, at 223 (GBMI "obfuscates meaningful distinctions in the insanity defense;" effect of GBMI option is to "truncate the traditional meaning of both insanity and guilt").

109. Perlin, *supra* note 38, at 862; *see generally*, 3 M.L. PERLIN, *supra* note 1, §§15.38-15.39.

110. Fentiman, *"Guilty But Mentally Ill:" The Real Verdict Is Guilty*, 26 B.C. L. REV. 601, 603-4 (1985); H. STEADMAN, REFORMING, *supra* note 97, at 64.

111. *See* Schulhofer, *Just Punishment in an Imperfect World*, 87 MICH. L. REV. 1263, 1272 (1989) (book review of D. BAZELON, QUESTIONING AUTHORITY: JUSTICE AND CRIMINAL LAW (1985)) (tide of public opinion now "strongly against" Bazelon's position).

Hinckley's wake, though, came additional changes: changes in the procedures by which insanity cases are tried.

2. The importance of procedure.   Although most of the attention to changes in the insanity defense has focused on shifts in the language of substantive standards, it is necessary to also consider the many procedural issues that affect the trial and disposition of insanity defense cases.[112] The most significant of these procedural issues is the allocation of the burden of proof at an insanity defense trial. Recent changes in the allocation of this burden illuminate many of the important underlying jurisprudential concerns.

When John Hinckley was tried, the burden of proof in all federal courts (and in about half the states) was on the prosecution to prove a defendant's sanity beyond a reasonable doubt.[113] Many observers placed the "blame" for the jury's subsequent acquittal on this allocation, and the question of burden shifting became a major subject of controversy at the subsequent Congressional insanity defense hearings.[114]

The IDRA responded to these concerns and placed the burden of proof in insanity defense cases on the defendant, and specified a

---

112. Some of these will be discussed subsequently in an investigation of how jurors process insanity defense testimony and construe insanity defense cases, *see generally infra* chapter 6 D 6 (discussing jury interpretation of lay and expert evidence in such cases, and the question of informing jurors of the consequences of an insanity verdict), and others will be considered in an inquiry into the factors affecting the disposition of cases involving hospitalized insanity acquittees, *see generally infra* chapter 4 E 2 d. As to other procedural issues, on notice, *see generally,* 3 M.L. PERLIN, *supra note 1, §15.11; on the privilege against self-incrimination, see generally, id. §15.15; on bifurcated trial procedures, see generally, id., §15.17; on other trial practice issues, see generally, id. §15.19.*

113. *See e.g.,* 3 *id.,* §15.12 at 320; Weiner, *supra* note 64, at 778-84 (Table 12.6); Comment, *Recent Changes in the Criminal Law: The Federal Insanity Defense,* 46 LA. L. REV. 337, 356 n. 127 (1985).

114. *See e.g.,* Low, *supra* note 60, at 122 n. f; Ellis, *The Consequences of the Insanity Defense: Proposals to Reform Post-Acquittal Commitment Laws,* 35 CATH. U. L. REV. 961, 963 (1986). Jurors in the *Hinckley* trial told Congressional investigators that the placement of the burden on the government "played a role" in their ultimate verdict. R. SIMON & D. AARONSON, THE INSANITY VERDICT: A CRITICAL ASSESSMENT OF LAW AND POLICY IN THE POST-HINCKLEY ERA 59 (1988), *discussing The Insanity Defense,* Hearings Before the Committee on the Judiciary, U.S. Senate, 97th Cong., 2d Sess. 81 (1982) (statement of Sen. Cochran); J. Q. LA FOND & M. DURHAM, BACK TO THE ASYLUM: THE FUTURE OF MENTAL HEALTH LAW AND POLICY IN THE UNITED STATES 68-69 (1992); *see also,* authorities cited in Northrup, *Guilty But Mentally Ill: Broadening the Scope of Criminal Responsibility,* 44 OHIO ST. L.J. 797, 800 n. 43 (1983).

burden of proof of "clear and convincing evidence."[115] Fifteen states quickly followed suit in shifting the burden to the defendant.[116]

This change was significant for two main reasons. First, symbolically, it underscored Congress's dissatisfaction with a system that appeared to make it "easier" for jurors to acquit in insanity cases.[117] Second, empirically, by making the quantum greater than a preponderance (previously, the standard allocation in jurisdictions where the burden was on the defendant to prove insanity),[118] it gave researchers the opportunity to investigate the "real life" impact of both the burden shift (as to party) and the especially heavy quantum of proof that the defendant will be responsible to prove. There is no question that Congress recognized the heaviness of this burden. Indeed, in reporting out its version of the bill, the House Judiciary Committee had *rejected* this burden as "a radical departure...not justified by the evidence of problems with the current operation of the defense."[119]

Every aspect of insanity defense jurisprudence is laden with symbolic value.[120] By making this change in the law, Congress sought to make it even more difficult for defendants to successfully plead insanity, and thus even more unlikely that "mistaken" verdicts (i.e., jury findings of insanity where the defendant did not meet the nonresponsibility standard) would ever be entered.[121] Even though it is

---

115. 18 U.S.C. §17 (1988); HANDBOOK ON THE COMPREHENSIVE CRIME CONTROL ACT OF 1984 AND OTHER CRIMINAL STATUTES ENACTED BY THE 98TH CONGRESS 60-61 (1984); *see generally*, 3 M.L. PERLIN, *supra* note 1, §15.39.

116. Callahan, Meyer & Steadman, *supra* note 49, at 55 (Table 2).

117. *See e.g.*, United States v. Pohlot, 827 F. 2d 889, 899-900 (3d Cir. 1987), *cert. den.*, 484 U.S. 1011 (1988) (discussing Congressional hearings); Note, 61 TEMP. L. Q. 955, 955 n. 5 (1988) (same). On how legislatures and courts are especially sensitive to prosecutors' needs for more "convicting power" in this area, *see* Gershman, *The New Prosecutors*, 53 U. PITT. L. REV. 393, 411-18 (1992).

118. *See e.g.*, Eule, *supra* note 2, at 670 n. 162.

119. *Insanity Defense and Related Criminal Procedure Matters*, H. Rep. No. 98-577, 98th Cong., 1st Sess. 15 (1983).

120. *See supra* chapter 2 A 3. *See also*, Homant & Kennedy, *Subjective Factors in Clinicians' Judgments of Insanity: Comparison of a Hypothetical Case and an Actual Case*, 18 PROF'L PSYCHOL.: RES. & PRAC. 439, 455 (1987):

> [I]nsanity defense trials will continue to play an important symbolic role. They will underline the fact that reasons for criminal behavior are indeed important, and that a principled and effective response to offenders must follow from an understanding of the individuals involved.

121. One of the arguments made in favor of changing the burden was that its

often taken for granted that burden shifts "may have little practical impact in some contexts," commentators and judges seem to agree that such changes have "more than symbolic importance" in insanity cases.[122] In short, "common sense" would lead us to believe that this shift will have some actual impact on the number of successful insanity acquittals in federal courts.[123]

The research that has been done on the significance of substantive jury standards in insanity defense cases suggests that the choice of test may not always be dispositive in a jury's deliberations. The comprehensive California study done by Dr. Henry Steadman and his associates, for instance, revealed that that state's change from the Model Penal Code test to M'Naghten "altered nothing in the volume of the insanity pleas, their success rate, the characteristics of who pled insanity or who was acquitted, or how long those acquitted by

---

placement on the government by the beyond a reasonable doubt quantum made it virtually impossible for the government to disprove such a defense. Former Attorney General Meese was thus quoted as having said, "You couldn't even prove the White House staff sane beyond a reasonable doubt. It's a tremendous burden." *See* J.Q. La Fond & M. Durham, *supra* note 114, at 68 (statement by Congressman Lagomarsino in Congressional hearings, quoting Meese). The statistical evidence, however, suggests that the impossibility argument was a gross exaggeration. *See e.g.*, Jonakait, *Two Proposals for Abolishing the Insanity Defense* (book reviews of W. Winslade & J. Ross, The Insanity Plea (1983) and N. Morris, Madness and the Criminal Law (1982)), 35 Hastings L.J. 403, 409 (1983); Smith, *Limiting the Insanity Defense: A Rational Approach to Irrational Crimes*, 47 Mo. L. Rev. 605, 606 (1982).

122. American Bar Association, Criminal Justice Mental Health Standards, Commentary to Standard 7-6.9, at 385 (1989); *see also*, State v. Krol, 68 N.J. 236, 344 N.J. 289, 311 (1975) (Clifford, J., dissenting) (debunking view that distinction between burdens of proof is nothing more than "so much academic claptrap"); Miller, *Recent Changes in Criminal Law: The Federal Insanity Defense*, 46 La. L. Rev. 337, 355 (1985) ("Who bears the burden of persuasion...is a matter of considerable legal importance"). *But compare*, Weiner, *supra* note 64, at 721 (shift in federal standard will most likely not reduce number of successful pleas).

For an outline of a potential constitutional challenge to the placement of the clear and convincing burden on defendants, *see* Lefcourt & Becker, *The New Insanity Defense and Mental Condition Defense*, 140 PLI/Crim 347, PLI Order No. C4-4174 (1985), WESTLAW pagination at 6-7.

123. *See* Comment, *supra* note 113, at 359-60. On the perils of "ordinary common sense" in insanity defense decision making, *see generally infra* chapter 6 D; *see also* Perlin, *supra* note 84. On the relationship between the question of the burden in insanity cases and burden of proof in tort cases seeking to hold an "insane" person responsible for his tortious behavior, *see* Delahanty v. Hinckley, 799 F. Supp. 184 (D.D.C. 1992).

insanity stayed in confinement."[124] It is not at all clear, though, that the combination of the change in allocation of burden from the state to the defendant and the increase in the burden on the defendant will yield the same results.

First, most judges seem to translate a burden of "clear and convincing evidence" to be the equivalent of about seventy to eighty percent of the evidence.[125] In the insanity defense context, this would appear to be an especially "heavy burden that cannot be carried successfully."[126] Second, we know that, in mental capacity cases in general, jury behavior depends not simply upon the quality of the expert testimony, the presentation of other evidence, and the coherence of jury instructions,[127] but, perhaps, most importantly, on the jurors' pre-existing views of the relationship between mental illness and criminal behavior.[128] Will these variables add even more weight

---

124. H. STEADMAN, REFORMING, *supra* note 97, at 12-13.
    See generally, J. WARREN & W.L. FITCH, VIRGINIA'S FORENSIC INFORMATION MANAGEMENT SYSTEM ANNUAL REPORT, 1990-1991 16 (1992); N. FINKEL, INSANITY ON TRIAL 155-81 (1988); V. HANS & N. VIDMAR, JUDGING THE JURY 192-98 (1986); *see generally infra* chapter 6 D 6. On the difference in results when a GBMI option is added, *see e.g,* Poulos, *supra* note 95. On the different ways forensic psychiatrists apply different substantive insanity standards, *see* Wettstein, Mulvey & Rogers, *A Prospective Comparison of Four Insanity Defense Standards*, 148 AM. J. PSYCHIATRY 21 (1991) (logical division seen between application of cognitive and volitional standards, but little difference seen in the application of differing cognitive standards; most defendants who met cognitive criteria also met volitional criteria).

125. *See e.g.*, McCauliff, *Burdens of Proof: Degrees of Belief, Quanta of Evidence, or Constitutional Guarantees?* 35 VAND. L. REV. 1293 (1982).

126. Duncan, *Confronting the Burden of Proof Under the Federal Insanity Defense*, in CRIMINAL COURT CONSULTATION 79, 90 (R. Rosner & R. Harmon eds. 1989).
    On the impact of this burden in a contested insanity case, *see* State v. Zmich, 160 Ariz. 108, 770 P. 2d 776 (1989). In *Zmich*, the defendant had pled NGRI to murdering his mother. Three expert witnesses found him severely mentally ill and insane under the M'Naghten test; the fourth witness stated, "I believe he was suffering from a mental disorder at the time, involving paranoid thought processes. However, I believe that he knew what he was doing (assaulting his mother) and also that it was wrong to do so." *Id.* at 776-77. Although the appellate court conceded that, based upon the expert reports, "it would appear that" the defendant had carried his burden of proving insanity under M'Naghten, it nonetheless affirmed the trial judge's finding of sanity, based, in large part, on the testimony of the defendant's stepfather that the defendant was malingering and appeared to be feigning mental illness. *Id.* at 778-79.

127. *See* Keilitz, *supra* note 69, at 316.

128. N. FINKEL, *supra note 124*, at 174-77. *See generally, Roberts & Golding, The Social Construction of Criminal Responsibility and Insanity*, 15 LAW & HUM.

to the defendant's burden? A study of the experience in Georgia and New York reveals that the shift in burden of proof reduced the rate of insanity pleas in both of those jurisdictions.[129]

The ultimate empirical impact of this weightier burden on case disposition is not yet clear. On the other hand, its "fit" into insanity defense symbolism is obvious: because placement of the burden on the government is seen as a contributing cause to the "wrong" verdict entered in the Hinckley case, the burden is shifted in all future insanity defense cases. The message here is clear: if all things are equal (i.e., the balance of evidence is in homeostasis), the societal preference is for conviction, not for an insanity acquittal.[130] Combined with what we know about the New York and Georgia experiences, we can expect that the shift in burden *will have* a significant impact on future insanity defense practice.

B. The Role of Externalities

One underlying constant throughout the centuries of insanity defense test formulation has been the intermittent calibration and recalibration of the degree to which *externalities*[131]—empirical research, scientific advances, political confrontations, and teachings of moral philosophers—have had a significant impact on the actual structuring of the substantive legal formula for responsibility. As a result of the tension created by this relationship (between "law" and "externalities"), insanity defense scholarship has been caught up in an elaborate "paper covers rock" game: Moral Philosopher #1 "trumps" Moral Philosopher #2 as a result of his or her new interpretation of what Kant *would have said* about the Hinckley case had he known of it, or in which Law Professor #1 plays *his* evaluation of psychological studies against Law Professor #2's evaluation of *other*

BEHAV. 349 (1991) (attitudes and beliefs about insanity defense more important in decision making than data change).

129. H. STEADMAN, REFORMING, *supra* note 97, at 13, 107-41.
130. *Cf.* Medina v. California, 112 S. Ct. 2572, 2587 (1992) (Blackmun, J., dissenting from opinion upholding constitutionality of state statutory scheme placing burden of proof in incompetency to stand trial proceeding on defendant) (subjecting defendant to trial where evidence is inconclusive introduces a "systematic and unacceptably high risk" of convictions of individuals unable to participate in court proceedings).
131. I am unaware of any prior use of the word "externality" in this context. *Cf.* Smith, *The Technology of Transnational Environmental Externalities*, in PUBLIC GOODS AND PUBLIC POLICY 177 (1978).

studies,[132] or in which Behavioral Scientist #1 fronts *his* responsibility assessment construct against the alternative model developed by Behavioral Scientist #2.[133]

I believe that it is futile to be terribly concerned with the question of *which* school of moral philosophy "wins" or *which* set of scientific data is soundest or *which* database of empirical evidence is most persuasive. For the empiricist, the scientist, and the moral philosopher all bottom their arguments on one important but unarticulated premise: that fact-finders are ready, willing, and able to be rational, fair and bias-free in their assessment of insanity defense cases, and it is only the absence of a missing link—the additional, irrefutable data as to NGRI demographics, the newest discovery in brain biology, the exact calibration of moral agency in the allocation of responsibility—that stands in the way of a coherent and well-functioning system. Yet, there is virtually no evidence that the addition of any (or all) of these extra factors really would make any such difference.

What is necessary is for us to shift the focus of the debate. We must ask a *different* question: *how* has this reality (the omnipresence of the "externalities" and our hyper-attentiveness to them)[134] helped, psychodynamically, to shape an insanity defense jurisprudence? *Do* the positions of moral philosophers (or of contemporaneous scholars advocating the positions of such philosophers) really matter? *Does* the fact that virtually every belief held dear by the public (and by its elected representatives) as to *who* pleads the insanity defense, *how* it is abused, *what happens* to such defendants following an NGRI verdict, *where* such individuals are institutionalized (and for how long) is a *myth*—that ordinary common sense is, to be blunt, dead wrong—actually matter? *Does* the fact that scientists *appear* to understand more about brain chemistry, physiology, neurology, and the effect of physical and psychological trauma on criminally irresponsi-

---

132. *Compare e.g.*, Bonnie & Slobogin, *The Role of Mental Health Professionals in the Criminal Process: The Case for Informed Speculation*, 66 VA. L. REV. 427 (1980), to Morse, *Failed Explanations and Criminal Responsibility: Experts and the Unconscious*, 68 VA. L. REV. 971 (1982).

133. *See e.g.*, Rogers, Seman & Clark, *Assessment of Criminal Responsibility: Initial Validation of the R-CRAS with the M'Naghten and GBMI Standards*, 9 INT'L J. L. & PSYCHIATRY 67 (1986).

134. I plead, in part, *mea culpa*. *See e.g.*, Rodriguez, LeWinn & Perlin, *supra* note 4, at 400-4 (empirically-based rebuttal of popular myths surrounding insanity defense plea).

ble behavior matter?[135]

If the resolutions of these questions have not, up until this time, seemed to matter, several other issues are raised: First, is it worthwhile expending time and effort to explore these issues further?[136] My sense is it is worthwhile on several different levels: (1) there remains the possibility that additional research will significantly "influence reform and public policy;"[137] (2) there is a value in learning for learning's sake;[138] (3) the more extensive our database, the more likely that we will not repeat past mistakes (or, if we *do*, we will have a better idea of *why* we are repeating them);[139] (4) additional knowledge will aid in the process of demystifying the myths[140] which have largely controlled jurisprudential developments in this area; and (5) *if* we can begin to understand and "work through" the underlying psychodynamic issues,[141] then, perhaps we will be ready, as a society,

---

135. Professor David Wexler has been one lonely voice, calling for "careful empirical research relating to the roots of dissatisfaction with the [insanity] defense," while noting that such research has "yet to be performed." Wexler, *Redefining the Insanity Problem*, 53 GEO. WASH. L. REV. 528, 540 (1985).

136. *See* Monahan, *Abolish the Insanity Defense? Not Yet*, 26 RUTGERS L. REV. 719, 739-40 (1973) (before there can be major reform of the substantive criminal law, it is necessary to establish "a solid body of empirical evidence to guide the development of that reform"); *accord*, Sales & Hafemeister, *Empiricism and Legal Policy on the Insanity Defense*, in MENTAL HEALTH AND CRIMINAL JUSTICE 253 (L. Teplin ed. 1984). *Cf.* Keilitz, *supra* note 69, at 289-90 (the empirical approach to insanity defense operations and outcomes "is a healthy development which should be encouraged") (writing in 1988). *See generally,* Steadman, *Mental Health Law and the Criminal Offender: Research Directions for the 1990's*, 39 RUTGERS L. REV. 323, 337 (1988) (suggesting areas "that could profit from research in the remaining 1980s and the 1990s").

137. Keilitz, *supra* note 69, at 290. Dr. Keilitz acknowledges that this possibility "remains to be gauged." *Id. See also*, Phillips, Wolf & Coons, *Psychiatry and the Criminal Justice System: Testing the Myths*, 145 AM. J. PSYCHIATRY 605, 609 (1988) ("Legislators, jurists, and mental health administrators need a realistic [empirical] overview before they can rationally devise and implement policies for the management of mentally ill offenders").

138. *See generally,* M. Perlin, "The Government's Effect on Patients' Lives: A Challenge to Scholars" (paper delivered at the annual meeting of the American Psychological Association, Atlanta, GA, August 1988), manuscript at 7 ("Challenge to Scholars").

139. *Cf.* G. SANTAYANA, THE LIFE OF REASON 284 (1905) ("Those who cannot remember the past are condemned to repeat it"). For the most recent empirical studies, *see* 3 M.L. PERLIN, *supra* note 1, §15.37, at 164-65 n. 694 (1992 pocket part).

140. *See* "Challenge to Scholars," *supra* note 138, at 7-8.

141. *See id.* at 8.

to engage in a rational discourse about the future of the insanity defense. Only then will there be even a possibility that our insanity defense jurisprudence can ever become a coherent one.[142]

Second, if we now understand so much more about science, human behavior, and empiricism than we did at the time of, say, the M'Naghten verdict, *why* have we shrunken our insanity defense to the point where it now approximates but is even *more* restrictive than what was scientifically, empirically, and morally out of date 145 years ago?[143] The answer to this question may be the answer to the "gridlock" that has plagued insanity defense jurisprudence for seven centuries: until we understand *why* society feels the way it does about the insanity defense and the criminally insane, the empirical evidence, the scientific discoveries, the competing philosophical interests, the new behavioral constructs simply do not "matter." In short, we must "unpack" the symbols that control insanity defense decision making so that we can attempt to understand the meta-mythology that underlies the empirical myths that continue to animate insanity defense developments.

This is because the powerful symbolic values that surround, and, in some important ways, strangle, the development of an insanity defense jurisprudence have little (if anything) to do with empiricism, with science, or with philosophy. Contrarily, they reflect and illuminate the importance of *psychodynamic* factors—unconscious decision making, political personality styles, authoritarianism—in the creation of an insanity defense doctrine which, paradoxically, overtly rejects psychodynamic factors when offered as an explanation for what would otherwise be criminal behavior. In order to understand *why* insanity defense jurisprudence has developed as it has, it is necessary to examine these psychodynamic factors as well.

For it is these psychodynamic factors that are at the root of our discomfort with the insanity defense. That discomfort is, in large measure, psychodynamically-based, and has political and psychological components. It is a function of our psychodynamic "outrage," of our authoritarian personality styles, and of our rejection of "psychological man." The insanity defense is, to a significant majority of

---

142. It is certainly possible that the construction of such a jurisprudence may lead to a greater number of insanity pleas entered and verdicts returned. Of course, that may be precisely the reason why such a jurisprudence has never been developed.
143. *See* English, *The Light Between Twilight and Dusk: Federal Criminal Law and the Volitional Insanity Defense*, 40 HASTINGS L.J. 1, 8 (1988).

the American public, counterintuitive. We are generally uncomfortable with the entire notion of "excuse" defenses (putting aside self-
defense); the use of the others (duress, choice of evils, etc.), however,
does not appear to imperil the operation of the criminal justice
system (as the insanity defense appears to do).[144] This imperilment, of
course, has nothing to do with the "reality" of empirical issues (i.e.,
the frequency with which the defense is used, the type of cases in
which it is used, the actual disposition of insanity defense cases, the
rate of subsequent institutionalization of insanity acquittees),[145] of
philosophical issues (i.e., the way in which we choose to balance free
will and determinism, assuming that these "emotionally freighted"[146]
constructs can be given meaningful content in this context),[147] or of
scientific issues (i.e., the way that scientific "advances" are translated
into insanity defense doctrinal development).[148]

Thus, I will look at the relevant "externalities" (for they are
external to the processes that actually animate our decision making
in this area), I will explore what I call the "mythology of insanity
defense myths." I will examine the empirical myths that have "frozen" insanity defense decision makers and insanity defense decision
making,[149] and will then attempt to "unpack" these myths in an effort

---

144. *See* W. LAFAVE & A. SCOTT, CRIMINAL LAW §5.3 (2d ed. 1986); *see*, for helpful
    overviews, Dressler, *Justification and Excuses: A Brief Review of the Concepts
    and the Literature*, 33 WAYNE L. REV. 1155 (1987); Dressler, *Reflections on
    Excusing Wrongdoers: Moral Theory, New Excuses, and the Model Penal Code*,
    19 RUTGERS L. J. 671 (1988). *Compare* English, *supra* note 143, at 41-42
    (continued existence of the duress defense is a "strong paradigm" for perpetuat-
    ing the insanity defense's volitional prong).
145. I *agree* emphatically with Drs. Steadman (*supra* note 136, and *see also*, Stead-
    man, *Empirical Research on the Insanity Defense*, 477 ANNALS 58 (1985); H.
    STEADMAN, REFORMING, *supra* note 97, at 252-54), and Keilitz, (*supra* note 69)
    that more empirical research *is* necessary to "fill in the puzzle." And, once that
    is done, we will know better what *other* myths are lurking, and where we should
    be better channeling our fiscal and scholarly resources. Yet, there is no firm
    evidence that this will extract us from the seemingly-intractable dilemma: *why*
    do we feel the way we do about insanity defense pleaders? *See infra* chapter 8
    B-D. *But see* H. STEADMAN, REFORMING, *supra* note 97, at 258-59 (authors'
    data solicited by mass media, and thus helped "influence how the insanity defense
    was depicted for millions of Americans").
146. *See* Monahan, *supra* note 136, at 721.
147. *See generally infra* chapter 3 B 4.
148. *See generally infra* chapter 3 B 3.
149. Prof. Stephen Morse rightfully characterizes many of these myths as "insubstan-
    tial." Morse, *Excusing the Crazy: The Insanity Defense Revisited*, 58 S. CAL. L.
    REV. 777, 795-801 (1985). Yet, this characterization misses an important reality:
    in spite of (or, perhaps, *because of*) the *banality* of these myths, they have served

to determine the source of their power and longevity. I will do this by suggesting a series of *meta*-myths that lie at the roots of the "insubstantial" empirical myths, and by demonstrating how these meta-myths—the true animator of insanity defense decision making—have driven us back, beyond *M'Naghten*, into the time warp of Justice Tracy and the "wild beast" test, articulated in the 1724 case of *Rex v. Arnold*.[150]

This test—the wild beast standard—speaks to a significant portion of the American public. It speaks to the person on the street, to legislators, to the President, and to members of the judiciary (including, pointedly, the Chief Justice).[151] It is only when this is understood that we may begin to deal rationally—and on a conscious level—with the insanity defense issue.

1. Empirical Data and Myths[152]

a. Introduction. In the past several years, commentators have urged that "scholars and practitioners in law and mental health…look more often to social science research to determine the effect of the insanity defense."[153]

---

to set the focus (and the limits) of the insanity defense debate for centuries. Until we attempt to understand *why* that is, we will remain their prisoner. *Compare* Kaplan & Rinella, *Jurisprudence and the Appropriation of the Psychoanalytic: A Study in Ideology and Power*, 11 INT'L J. L. & PSYCHIATRY 215, 246 (1988) ("Human psychology has an intra-psychic structure that retains cultural attitudes long after such attitudes are dysfunctional for self or society").

150. *See* Roberts, Golding & Fincham, *supra* note 26, at 226.
151. *See generally*, Perlin, *supra* note 77.
152. It is universally acknowledged that, at least until very recently, there has been "an extreme dearth of empirical data" relating to the insanity defense plea. Pasewark, *Insanity Plea: A Review of the Literature*, 9 J. PSYCHIATRY & L. 357 (1981). Even now, the research has focuses almost entirely on NGRI defendants, their sociodemographic characteristics, and their subsequent postacquittal dispositions (including institutionalization and rearrest rates); virtually *no* attention has been paid to the clinical assessment of such defendants and the relevant trial processes (including attitudes of defense counsel, judges and prosecutors). Rogers, *APA's Position on the Insanity Defense: Empiricism Versus Emotionalism*, 42 AM. PSYCHOLOGIST 840, 845 (1987).
153. Keilitz, *supra* note 69, at 291-92. Interestingly, Keilitz then states and rebuts a potential counterargument. He notes that opponents might say "that by its emphasis on outcome data, the empirical approach ignores the logic, intuition, and rational analysis of legal doctrine that is the center of the debate on the insanity defense," *id.* at 292, but demurs, suggesting that his approach will "help rather than hinder understanding" because it helps to "sidestep much of the dogma," *id.*

When such research is examined, it is clear how much a series of myths—utterly discredited by scholars and practitioners alike—dominates the insanity defense landscape. What must now be done is to examine *why* these myths have sprung up, *why* we continue to honor them, and *why* the revelations that they *are* myths continue to have absolutely no impact on insanity defense jurisprudence. These myths remain "firmly rooted in our cultural subconscious."[154] The question we must try to answer is, "Why?"

The failure of courts and states to collect adequate statistical data "is testimony to the indifference of bureaucracy, societal avoidance and neglect of the criminally insane."[155] Until we begin to understand *why* we are indifferent to something as seemingly-non-emotionally charged as statistical data collection and retrieval, we will not make any meaningful progress toward understanding the true roots of insanity defense mythology.

What makes this problem even more confounding is the *concession* that the empirical data belie the common wisdom that has dominated the insanity defense legislative landscape. Thus, the House Report accompanying the House version of the IDRA explicitly acknowledged:

> Although abuses of the insanity defense are few and have an insignificant direct impact upon the criminal justice system, the Committee *nonetheless* concluded that the present defense and the procedures surrounding its use are in need of reform...

          * * *   * * *   * * *   * * *

---

154. de Vito, *Some New Alternatives to the Insanity Defense*, 1 AM. J. FORENS. PSYCHIATRY 38, 40 (1980). As I will subsequently explore, these myths are the roots of our sanist legal discourse and pretextual decision making, and are the reason why courts respond teleologically to the use of social science in deciding mental disability law cases. *See generally*, Perlin & Dorfman, *Sanism, Social Science, and Mental Disability Law Jurisprudence*, 11 BEHAV. SCI. & L. 47 (1993).

    While I agree completely with Keilitz that such an approach is an important one, my sense is that its most powerful opponents are *not* moral philosophers committed to the construction of a defense based upon "logic, intuition, and rational analysis," but are, rather, majoritarian, authoritarian, ordinary common sensical and pretextual sanists, who will continue to ignore the *illogical* and the *irrational* components of the developing jurisprudence. It is necessary to articulate the roots of *this* opposition to come to a meaningful understanding of the true issues in the debate. *See generally infra* chapter 8 B-D.

155. Roth, *supra* note 88, at 92.

The insanity defense has an impact on the criminal justice system that goes beyond the actual cases involved. The uses of the defense in highly publicized cases, *and the myths surrounding its use*, have undermined public faith in the criminal justice system.[156]

It is this concession—that, even though the myths are nothing more than myths, the Congress must act to assuage *erroneous* public sentiments (based on what all acknowledge to be false beliefs)[157]— that is astounding, and to which serious attention must be paid.

b. Deconstructing the myths[158]   In the wake of the Hinckley verdict, commentators began to examine carefully the "myths" which had developed about the insanity defense, in an effort to determine the extent "to which this issue has been distorted in the public eye."[159] The empirical research revealed that at least half a dozen myths had arisen and been perpetuated, but that all were "unequivocally disproven by the facts."[160] The research shows that (1) the insanity defense opens only a "small window of nonculpability,"[161] (2) defendants who successfully use the NGRI plea "do not beat the rap,"[162]

---

156. H. Rep. 98-577 (98th Cong., 1st Sess) 9-10 (1983) (emphasis added).
157. *Compare* City of Cleburne v. Cleburne Living Center, 473 U.S. 432, 448 (1985), quoting Palmore v. Sidotti, 466 U.S. 429, 432-34 (1984) ("Private biases may be outside the reach of the law, but the law cannot, directly or indirectly, give them effect") (implications of equal protection clause for local zoning ordinance seeking to bar congregate housing for the mentally retarded).
158. The text *infra* accompanying notes 159-76 is partially adapted from 3 M.L. PERLIN, *supra* note 1, §15.37.
159. Rodriguez, LeWinn & Perlin, *supra* note 4, at 400; *see e.g.*, Steadman, *supra* note 136, at 330: "Legal scholars and federal legislative committees with meaningful data on the insanity defense immediately following the 1982 insanity acquittal of John W. Hinckley, Jr., who had attempted to assassinate President Reagan." *But see*, Rodriguez, LeWinn & Perlin, *supra* note 4, at 397 n. ‡ (following receipt of testimony based on cited article empirically refuting insanity defense myths, New Jersey State Senate Judiciary Committee rejected all efforts to abolish or modify insanity defense). For the most recent research, *see* sources cited at 3 M.L. PERLIN, *supra* note 1, §15.37, at 164-65 n. 694 (1992 pocket part).
160. Perlin, *Whose Plea Is It Anyway? Insanity Defense Myths and Realities*, 79 PHILA. MED. 5, 6 (1983). *See also*, Morse, *supra* note 149, at 795-801, characterizing the arguments based on some of these myths as "insubstantial objections to the insanity defense." For the most recent comprehensive overviews, *see* Steadman, *supra* note 136; Keilitz, *supra* note 69.
161. Jeffrey, Pasewark & Bieber, *Insanity Plea: Predicting Not Guilty By Reason of Insanity Adjudications*, 16 BULL. AM. ACAD. PSYCHIATRY & L. 35, 39 (1988).
162. Pogrebin, Regoli & Perry, *Not Guilty By Reason of Insanity: A Research Note*, 8 INT'L J. L. & PSYCHIATRY 237, 240 (1986) (Pogrebin).

and, perhaps more importantly, (3) the "tenacity of these [false] beliefs in the face of contrary data" is profound.[163]

(1) Eight empirical myths.

•*Myth #1*: The insanity defense is overused.

All empirical analyses have been consistent: the public at large and the legal profession (especially legislators) "dramatically" and "grossly" overestimate both the frequency and the success rate of the insanity plea, an error which is "undoubtedly...abetted" by the media's "bizarre depictions," "distortion[s]," and inaccur[acies]" in portraying mentally ill individuals charged with crimes.[164] The most recent research reveals, for instance, that the insanity defense is used in only about one percent of all felony cases, and is successful just about one-quarter of the time.[165]

What is as startling as any other fact unearthed by empiricists is the realization that, as recently as 1985, directors of forensic services in only ten of the fifty states could even provide researchers with baseline information regarding the frequency of the insanity plea and its success, and that officials in twenty states could provide no information whatsoever about the use of the plea.[166] In short, not only are

---

163. Rogers, *supra* note 152, at 840; Jeffrey & Pasewark, *Altering Opinions About the Insanity Plea*, 11 J. PSYCHIATRY 29 (1983). *See generally*, Phillips, Wolf & Coons, *supra* note 137.

164. *See* Rodriguez, LeWinn & Perlin, *supra* note 4, at 401 (footnotes omitted), relying on sources at *id.* nn. 21-28; *see also*, Jeffrey & Pasewark, *supra* note 163; J. OGLOFF, THE USE OF THE INSANITY DEFENCE IN BRITISH COLUMBIA: A QUANTITATIVE AND QUALITATIVE ANALYSIS (1991). On the specific role of attorney attitudes, *see* Hans, *An Analysis of Public Attitudes Toward the Insanity Defense*, 26 CRIMINOL. 393 (1986). On juror attitudes, *see* People v. Seuffer, 144 Ill. 2d 482, 582 N.E. 2d 71, 79 (1991) (trial judge restatement of juror's voir dire response that insanity defense was "overused" not reversible error).

165. *See* Callahan, Steadman, McGreevy & Robbins, *The Volume and Characteristics of Insanity Defense Pleas: An Eight-State Study*, 19 BULL. AM. ACAD. PSYCHIATRY & L. 331 (1991) (Callahan et al); H. STEADMAN, REFORMING, *supra* note 97, at 44-46 (reporting on data in Georgia, New York, California and Montana). *Compare* Rodriguez, LeWinn & Perlin, *supra* note 4, at 401 (in New Jersey in 1982, successful NGRI pleas were entered in one-twentieth of one percent of all cases handled by state public defender); J. OGLOFF, *supra* note 164, at 7 (in British Columbia in 1989, successful NGRI pleas were entered in one-fiftieth of one percent of all cases); Janofsky, Vandewalle & Rappeport, *Defendants Pleading Insanity: An Analysis of Outcome*, 17 BULL. AM. ACAD. PSYCHIATRY & L. 203 (1989) (1.2 percent of defendants pled NGRI; plea successful in one-tenth of those cases); Phillips, Wolf & Coons, *supra* note 137 (insanity defense successful in less than .1 percent of all criminal cases).

166. Pasewark & McGinley, *Insanity Plea: National Survey of Frequency and Suc-*

the estimates as to the use of the plea mythic, but the small discrete universe of individuals who might logically be expected to represent the *one* group that could dispel the myth is as self-admittedly ignorant as the rest of us as to the myth's scope.[167]

•*Myth #2*: Use of the insanity defense is limited to murder cases.

In one jurisdiction where the data has been closely studied, contrary to expectations, slightly less than one third of the successful insanity pleas entered over an eight year period were reached in cases involving a victim's death.[168] Further, individuals who plead insanity in murder cases are no more successful in being found NGRI than persons charged with other crimes.[169]

•*Myth #3*: There is no risk to the defendant who pleads insanity.

Defendants who asserted an insanity defense at trial, and who were ultimately found guilty of their charges, served significantly longer sentences than defendants tried on similar charges who did not assert the insanity defense. The same ratio is found when only homicide cases are considered.[170]

•*Myth #4*: NGRI acquittees are quickly released from custody.

Of the entire universe of individuals found NGRI over an eight year period in one jurisdiction, only fifteen percent had been released from all restraints; thirty-five percent remained in full custody, and

---

cess, 13 J. PSYCHIATRY & L. 101, 106 (1985).

167. The first successful attempt to collect nationwide data about forensic inpatient populations is reported in Way, Dvoskin & Steadman, *Forensic Psychiatric Inpatients Served in the United States: Regional and System Differences*, 19 BULL. AM. ACAD. PSYCHIATRY & L. 405 (1991).

168. Rodriguez, LeWinn & Perlin, *supra* note 4, at 402. Among the other underlying charges were writing of false checks, carrying an unloaded starter's pistol, and drug use. *Id.*; *see also*, Jones v. United States, 463 U.S. 354, 359 (1983) (attempted petit larceny). The most recent multi-state study reveals that 13.6 percent of those pleading NGRI were charged with murder, while another 36 percent were charged with crimes of violence. Callahan et al., *supra* note 165, at 336.

169. Steadman, Keitner, Braff & Arvanites, *Factors Associated With a Successful Insanity Plea*, 140 AM. J. PSYCHIATRY 401, 402-3 (1983).

170. Rodriguez, LeWinn & Perlin, *supra* note 4, at 401-2, and *id.* at 402 n. 32. A possible explanation for this is discussed in Perlin, *supra* note 77, at 98 ("They have made a 'play' for our unconscious, and have come up short"). *Cf.* Braff, Arvanites & Steadman, *Detention Patterns of Successful and Unsuccessful Insanity Defendants*, 21 CRIMINOL. 439, 445 (1983) (unsuccessful NGRI pleaders are incarcerated for a twenty-two percent longer time than individuals who never raise the plea).

forty-seven percent were under partial court restraint following conditional release.[171]

A comprehensive study of California practice showed that only
one percent of insanity acquittees were released following their
NGRI verdict and that another four percent were placed on conditional release, the remaining ninety-five percent being hospitalized.[172]
In other recent research, Dr. Stephen Golding and a colleague discovered, in their study of all persons found NGRI in the Canadian
province of British Columbia over a nine year period, that the average time spent in secure hospitalization or supervision was slightly
over nine and a half years.[173]

> •*Myth #5*: NGRI acquittees spend much less time in custody than
> do defendants convicted of the same offenses.

Contrarily, NGRI acquittees spend almost *double* the amount of
time that defendants convicted of similar charges spend in prison
settings, and often face a lifetime of post-release judicial oversight.[174]
In California, while the length of confinement for individuals acquitted by reason of insanity on murder charges was less than for those
convicted, defendants found NGRI for other violent crimes were
confined twice as long as those found guilty of such charges, and

---

171. Rodriguez, LeWinn & Perlin, *supra* note 4, at 403. *Compare Primetime Live*
(ABC News broadcast, May 30, 1991) (full text available on NEXIS) (remarks
of commentator Sylvia Chase, discussing case of Mark Austin, who had found
NGRI in a celebrated Arizona case) (emphasis added):

>   And what about Mark Austin? He's now in a mental hospital, *but it's almost certain that
>   he'll soon be free*, perhaps as early as July...

172. H. STEADMAN, REFORMING, *supra* note 97, at 93.
173. Golding, Eaves & Kowaz, *The Assessment, Treatment and Community Outcome of Insanity Acquittees*, 12 INT'L J. L. & PSYCHIATRY 149 (1989).
174. Rodriguez, LeWinn & Perlin, *supra* note 4, at 403-4; *see also*, Pogrebin, *supra*
note 162, at 240 (insanity acquittees do not spend fewer days in confinement
via an NGRI plea than had they been convicted and sentenced). On the
operational implications of a post-release conditional release system, *see*
McGreevy, Steadman, Dvoskin & Dollard, *New York State's System of Managing Insanity Acquittees in the Community*, 42 HOSP. & COMMUN. PSYCHIATRY
512 (1991). On the question of rearrest rates of released insanity acquittees, *see
e.g.*, Silver et al., *Follow-Up After Release of Insanity Acquittees, Mentally
Disordered Offenders, and Convicted Felons*, 17 BULL. AM. ACAD. PSYCHIATRY
& L. 401 (1989) (insanity acquittees' rearrest rate statistically significantly lower
than rates of convicted felons or of mentally disordered prisoners transferred for
hospital treatment).

those found NGRI of non-violent crimes were confined for periods over *nine* times as long.[175]

• *Myth #6*: Criminal defendants who plead insanity are usually faking.

This is perhaps the oldest of the insanity defense myths, and is one that has bedeviled American jurisprudence since the mid-nineteenth century.[176] Of the 141 individuals found NGRI in one jurisdiction over an eight year period, there was no dispute that 115 were schizophrenic (including 38 of the 46 cases involving a victim's death), and in only three cases was the diagnostician unwilling or unable to specify the nature of the patient's mental illness.[177] Also, most studies show that a large number of NGRI defendants have significant histories of prior hospitalizations.[178]

Looking at the same issue from a different perspective, Dr. Henry Steadman and his colleagues studied all defendants who pled NGRI in Erie County, New York, from 1970 to 1980: the *only* statistically significant factor which consistently correlated positively with a clinical finding of insanity was a diagnosis of psychosis, and

---

175. H. STEADMAN, REFORMING, *supra* note 97, at 94.
176. *See* I. RAY, MEDICAL JURISPRUDENCE OF INSANITY §247, at 243 (3d ed. 1853); *see generally infra* chapter 5 C 1. For the most recent research, *see* 3 M.L. PERLIN, *supra* note 1, §15.37, at 166 n. 719.1 (1992 pocket part) (citing cases and studies).
177. Rodriguez, LeWinn & Perlin, *supra* note 4, at 404. Paradoxically, at least one recent empirical survey has concluded that a return from the ALI to the M'Naghten test "may systematically exclude from a successful plea of insanity that class of psychotic patients whose illness is clearest in symptomatology, most likely biologic in origin, most eminently treatable, and potentially most disruptive in penal detention." Silver & Spodak, *Dissection of the Prongs of ALI: Retrospective Assessment of Criminal Responsibility by the Psychiatric Staff of the Clifton T. Perkins Hospital Center*, 11 BULL. AM. ACAD. PSYCHIATRY & L. 383, 390 (1983).
178. *See* Hawkins & Pasework, *Characteristics of Persons Utilizing the Insanity Plea*, 53 PSYCHOLOGICAL REP. 191, 194 (1983) (citing studies). A recent British Columbia study revealed that eighty percent of all NGRI acquittees had "significant mental health histories including frequent hospitalizations." Golding, Eaves & Kowaz, *supra* note 173, at 15. *Accord*, Callahan et al, *supra* note 165, at 336 (eighty-four percent had diagnosis either of schizophrenia or other major mental disorder); H. STEADMAN, REFORMING, *supra* note 97, at 49 (eighty-two percent of those found NGRI had major mental disorder); Kranhold, *Insanity Plea Leads to Longer Term; Escapee Can't Shake Treatment After Insanity Plea*, Hartford Courant (Dec. 13, 1992), at B1 (full text available on NEXIS) (according to Martha Lewis, executive director of Connecticut's Psychiatric Security Review Board, only five of 176 insanity acquittees in that state did not have a major psychosis).

the "key" to a successful insanity defense was the forensic evaluation done by the county's mental health service.[179] This reflects another empirical truth: there is an unusually high degree of concordance between clinical evaluations of sanity and subsequent legal dispositions.[180]

•*Myth #7*: Most insanity defense trials feature "battles of the experts."

The public's false perception of the circus-like "battle of the experts" is one of the most telling reasons for the rejection of psychodynamic principles by the legal system. A dramatic case such as the *Hinckley* trial thus "reinforced the public's perception that the insanity defense is characterized by battles of experts" who "overwhelm[]" the jury,[181] engendering judicial and public skepticism as to the ability of psychiatrists to actually come to reasoned and reasonable judgments in cases involving mentally disabled individuals charged with crime.[182]

---

179. Steadman, Keitner, Braff & Arvanites, *supra* note 169, at 401-4. In only 3 of the 131 cases in which a forensic clinic found a defendant sane did the court acquit by reason of insanity. *Id* at 402. *See also*, Rice & Harris, *The Predictors of Insanity Acquittal*, 13 INT'L J. L. & PSYCHIATRY 217, 222 (1990) (successful insanity pleaders demonstrate "clear evidence of psychosis"). On the relationship between major mental illness and criminal acts, *see* Cirincione, Steadman, Robbins & Steadman, *Schizophrenia as a Contingent Risk Factor for Criminal Violence*, 15 INT'L J. L. & PSYCHIATRY 347 (1992).

180. *See e.g.*, Philips, Wolf & Coons, *supra* note 137 (79%); Rogers, Cavanaugh, Seman & Harris, *Legal Outcome and Clinical Findings: A Study of Insanity Evaluations*, 12 BULL. AM. ACAD. PSYCHIATRY & L. 75, 80 (1984) (88% concordance); Jeffrey, Pasewark & Bieber, *supra* note 161 (88%); Janofsky, Vanewalle & Rappeport, *supra* note 165 (85%); Rogers, Bloom & Manson, *Insanity Defense: Contested or Conceded?* 141 AM. J. PSYCHIATRY 885 (1984); Fukunaga et al., *Insanity Plea: Interexaminer Agreement in Concordance of Psychiatric Opinion and Court Verdict*, 5 LAW & HUM. BEHAV. 325 (1981) (93% concordance). Dr. Rogers and his colleagues have thus concluded that "the legal outcome is closely related to the clinical evaluation and not unduly influenced by sociodemographic factors." Rogers, Cavanaugh, Seman & Harris, *supra*, at 82.

181. Anchor, *Expert Witness Testimony in the John Hinckley Trial*, 6 AM. J. TRIAL AD. 153 (1982); Rogers, Bloom & Manson, *supra* note 180, at 885. More recent research suggests that prospective jurors—contrary to popular judicial myth, *see e.g.*, Barefoot v. Estelle, 463 U.S. 880, 919 (1983) (Blackmun, J., dissenting) (discussing expert testimony's "aura of scientific infallibility")—are *not* unduly influenced by experts' ultimate opinions. *See generally*, Rogers, Bagby & Chow, *Psychiatrists and the Parameters of Expert Testimony*, 15 INT'L J. L. & PSYCHIATRY 387 (1992).

182. *See* Note, *The Right to a Partisan Psychiatric Expert: Might Indigency Preclude Insanity?* 61 N.Y.U. L. REV. 703, 721 (1986), and sources cited at *id*. n. 116.

The empirical reality is quite different. In a Hawaii survey, there was examiner congruence on insanity in ninety-two percent of all cases; in Oregon, prosecutors agreed to insanity verdicts in eighty percent of all cases;[183] Most importantly, these are not recent developments: over twenty-five years ago, a study of the impact of the *Durham* decision in Washington, D.C., found that between two-thirds and three-quarters of all insanity defense acquittals were uncontested.[184] In short, the empirical evidence refuting this myth has been available to judges, legislators, and scholars since almost a decade *prior* to the adoption of the ALI-Model Penal Code test in *Brawner*.

• *Myth #8*: Criminal defense attorneys—perhaps inappropriately—employ the insanity defense plea solely to "beat the rap."

Attorneys representing mentally disabled defendants have been routinely criticized for "seeking refuge" in the insanity defense as a means of technically avoiding a deserved conviction.[185] In reality, the facts are quite different. First, the level of representation afforded to mentally disabled defendants is frequently substandard, a fact noted pointedly a decade ago by the President's Commission on Mental Health's Task Force on Legal and Ethical Issues.[186] Second, the few

---

Conflicts in the Hinckley testimony are discussed at *id.* n. 115, and in L. CAPLAN, *supra* note 38, at 66-84; *see* Perlin, *supra* note 38, at 863-65.

183. Rogers, Bloom & Manson, *supra* note 180, at 885; Fukunaga et al., *supra* note 180, at 326.

184. Acheson, McDonald v. United States: *The* Durham *Rule Redefined*, 51 GEO. L.J. 580, 589 (1963).

185. *See e.g.*, M. KAVANAGH, THE CRIMINAL AND HIS ALLIES 90 (1928) (charging that, because "skillful criminal lawyers" can turn insanity defense trials into emotional disputes,"…in cases where insanity is presented as a defense, so many verdicts which outrage justice are returned"). This position is articulated forcefully in Justice Morris's well-traveled dissent in State v. Strasburg, 110 P. 2d 1020, 1029 (Wash. 1910):

No defense has been so much abused and no feature of the administration of our criminal law has so shocked the law-loving and law-abiding citizen as that of insanity, put forward not only as a shield to the poor unfortunate bereft of mind or reason, but more frequently as a cloak to hide the guilty for whose act astute and clever counsel can find neither excuse, justification, nor mitigating circumstances either in law or fact.

186. *See e.g.*, *Mental Health and Human Rights: Report of the Task Panel on Legal and Ethical Issues*, 20 ARIZ. L. REV. 49, 61 (1978) (in provision of counsel to indigent criminal defendants, few states provide for "special problems endemic to representation…when there are questions…as to [the defendant's] responsibility for the criminal act in question"); *see generally*, Perlin, *Fatal Assumption: A Critical Evaluation of the Role of Counsel in Mental Disability Cases*, 16 LAW

studies that have been done paint an entirely different picture; lawyers also enter an insanity plea to obtain immediate mental health treatment of their client, as a plea-bargaining device to insure that their client ultimately receives mandatory mental health care, and to avoid malpractice litigation.[187] Third, the best available research suggests that jury biases exist relatively independent of lawyer functioning, and are generally "not induced by attorneys."[188]

(2) An alternative view on empiricism. Not all commentators are as eager as I am to incorporate empiricism into this debate. For example, in arguing that empiricism improperly elevates the values of objectivity and verifiability over the value of justice, Professor Serena Stier draws on the Supreme Court's contrasting opinions in *Barefoot v. Estelle,*[189] in the context of the on-going debate about the propriety of testimony about dangerousness at capital punishment penalty hearings, and on the controversy over dangerousness as an involuntary civil criterion, and concludes that excessive reliance on "naive empiricism...corrupts the dialogue." Because such empirical testimony is value-laden, she argues, its apparent "objectivity" is meretricious; jurors will eagerly "buy into" scientific claims of expertise when the claims appear supportable by "objective" or "verifiable" facts.[190]

& HUM. BEHAV. 39 (1992).

187. Pasewark & Craig, *Insanity Plea: Defense Attorneys' Views,* 8 J. PSYCHIATRY & L. 413 (1980). Attorneys also entered the insanity plea as a plea-bargaining chip, as a device through which to gain time to allow community outrage to subside, and to introduce relevant background and motivational information either to mitigate verdict or sentence. *Id.*

188. Tanford & Tanford, *Better Trials Through Science: A Defense of Psychologist-Lawyer Collaboration,* 66 N. C. L. REV. 741, 748-49 (1988). *See also,* Perlin, *After* Hinckley: *Old Myths, New Realities, and the Future of the Insanity Defense,* 5 DIRECTIONS IN PSYCHIATRY, Lesson 22 (1985), at 4, *quoting* Rodriguez, LeWinn & Perlin, *supra* note 4, at 425:

> Clearly, this data reflects the extent to which myths have permeated the debate [on] the insanity defense, and the extent to which much of the new legislation represents 'an unnecessary and extreme reaction to a group of serious misconceptions.'...What is clear is that 'each and every one of the false premises' raised in support of abolition or evisceration of the defense is disproved by the evidence.

189. 463 U.S. 880 (1983); *see* Perlin, *supra* note 77, at 7-12; 3 M.L. PERLIN, *supra* note 1, §§17.12-17.14 at 527-40.

190. Stier, *Privileging Empiricism in Legal Dialogue: Death and Dangerousness,* 21 U.C. DAVIS L. REV. 271, 273, 287-309 (1987). On the relationship between dangerousness and civil commitment, *see e.g.,* State v. Krol, 68 N.J. 236, 344 A. 2d 289 (1975); *see generally infra* chapter 6 C 3.

Stier's argument is an appealing one, but may be slightly off the mark with regard to the specific questions addressed here: in the dangerousness and civil commitment models, she fears that jurors and judges will accept—unhesitatingly—the delphic pronouncements of expert testimony in *support of* institutionalization (or a death sentence).[191] Here, she appropriately relies on the teachings of cognitive psychology in such areas as heuristic decision making, attribution theory and the vividness effect to explain this behavior by fact-finders.[192]

The discourse in insanity defense decision making is, however, quite different. Here, the evidence is fairly clear that jurors (and courts) employ the same distortive decision making devices to *ignore* empirical evidence, where, if it were to be accepted, it (most frequently) would lead to a finding *against* penal incarceration.[193] Jurors in these instances do *not* buy into expertise where it conflicts with their heuristic experiences. Just as judges deny the existence of empirical evidence when it conflicts with their fantasy of how the legal system should theoretically work,[194] so do jurors employ similar devices in insanity defense cases.

In their recent analysis of mental disability law policy, Professors John La Fond and Mary Durham focus on exactly this discontinuity:

> Neoconservative insanity defense and civil commitment reforms value psychiatric expertise when it contributes to the social control functions of the law and disparage it when it does not. In the criminal justice system, psychiatrists are now viewed skeptically as accomplices of defense lawyers who get criminals "off the hook" of responsibility. In the commitment system, however, they are more confidently seen as therapeutic helpers who get patients "on the hook" of treatment and control. The result will be

---

191. *But compare* Rogers, Bagby & Chow, *supra* note 181, at 394 (juries are, at best, highly ambivalent about the worth of psychological, theories and the value of such testimony in insanity trials); Perlin, *supra* note 84, at 138 (juries are "'mildly interested' in, but not 'thunderstruck' by such testimony") (citations omitted).

192. Stier, *supra* note 190, at 295-300; *see generally infra* chapter 6 C.

193. *See e.g.*, Slobogin, *Dangerousness and Expertise*, 133 U. PA. L. REV. 97, 145 (1984) ("scientific evidence is particularly potent when it confirms the state's decision to prosecute"). On the teleological way such evidence is used in mental disability law cases, *see* Perlin & Dorfman, *supra* note 154; *see generally infra* chapter 8 D.

194. *See* Geimer & Amsterdam, *Why Jurors Vote Life or Death: Operative Factors in Ten Florida Death Penalty Cases*, 15 AM. J. CRIM. L. 1, 4 (1987-88). On judicial use of heuristic devices, *see* Perlin & Dorfman, *supra* note 154, at 63 n. 114.

increased institutionalization of the mentally ill and greater use of psychiatrists and other mental health professionals as powerful agents of social control.[195]

Insanity defense decision makers are teleological in their use of social science data and in their valuing and devaluing of expert testimony.[196] It is not empiricism that is the villain (as Professor Stier seems to suggest), but our sanist and pretextual use of empirical data that is villainous.

(3) Conclusion. We have known for 150 years of the depths of insanity defense mythology. Over the past fifteen years, researchers and other scholars have been patiently rebutting these myths. The recent publication by Dr. Henry Steadman and his colleagues of their extended multi-jurisdiction study of virtually every empirical facet of insanity defense pleading proves—beyond *any* doubt—that the basic tenets are mythic. It is essential that we realize this, and that we realize the inevitable corollary: that our continued adherence to these myths is irrational and based on sanist thought processes that continue to contaminate our jurisprudence.

Steadman is optimistic that the dissemination of his data may alter the terms of the debate, and I believe that there are some grounds for this optimism.[197] I believe also, though, that those of us interested in making this area of the law coherent cannot simply rest on this record (as impressive as it is). We must inquire further—into our societal approach to the development of behavioral assessment instruments, to scientific advances, and to the insights of moral philosophy—to try to assess the impact of all of these factors on our jurisprudence, and then, finally, to consider the other variables that must be weighed in this jurisprudential reconstruction.

---

195. J. LA FOND & M. DURHAM, *supra* note 114, at 156.
196. Perlin & Dorfman, *supra* note 154, at 52-54, 62-63; *see generally infra* chapter 8 D.
197. *See* H. STEADMAN, REFORMING, *supra* note 97, at 258-59 (authors' data solicited by mass media, and thus helped "influence how the insanity defense was depicted for millions of Americans").

    My own anecdotal experience reveals some change as well. For years, when I had been called by radio or television stations to comment on an insanity defense case, the questioner began by saying something to the effect of, "Well, Professor Perlin, we all know that the insanity defense is the subject of great abuse, and lets thousands of defendants get away with murder." More recently, though, the phraseology has changed: "Well, Professor Perlin, it's always been assumed that the insanity defense is the subject of great abuse....Now, is this really so?"

2. The Use of Assessment Tools

Since the first outpouring of literature focusing on the pervasive myths which infect the insanity defense system, behaviorists have continued to examine the data which have been developed about insanity defense pleaders in an effort to further illuminate the relevant issues.[198] For the first time, there has been a significant and meaningful focus upon the provision of standardized and empirically-based approaches to criminal responsibility,[199] through the use of such instruments as the Mental State at the Time of the Offense Screening Evaluation (MSO),[200] the Schedule of Affective Disorders and Schizophrenia (SADS),[201] the Research Diagnostic Criteria

---

198. See generally, Keilitz, A Model Process For Forensic Mental Health Screening and Evaluation, 8 LAW & HUM. BEHAV. 355 (1984). On the important question of whether such research can be truly "objective," see Berk, The Role of Subjectivity in Criminal Justice Classification and Prediction Methods, 9 CRIM. JUST. ETHICS 35, 36-37, 44 (Winter/Spring 1988), arguing that (1) all statistical procedures "necessarily rest on subjective elements that can drastically affect the numbers produced," and (2) "objectivity in all classification and forecasting schemes is multidimensional and a matter of degree," but (3) quantitative methods still lead to the best results "we can currently produce," results that are "certainly better than conventional wisdom, bureaucratic convenience, seat-of-the-pants calculations or clinical judgments." On the scientific limits of expertise, see Wasyliw, Cavanaugh & Rogers, Beyond the Scientific Limits of Expert Testimony, 13 BULL. AM. ACAD. PSYCHIATRY & L. 147 (1985) (expert testimony a product of legal and societal forces).

199. Rogers, Seman & Clark, supra note 133; see generally, Rogers & Cavanaugh, Differences in Psychological Variables Between Criminally Responsible and Insane Patients: A Preliminary Study, 1 AM. J. FORENS. PSYCHIATRY 29 (1980). On the related question of assessment instruments to evaluate incompetency to stand trial (IST), see e.g., Bagby, Nicholson, Rogers & Nussbaum, Domains of Competency to Stand Trial: A Factor Analytic Study, 16 LAW & HUM. BEHAV. 491 (1992); Everington, The Competence Assessment for Standing Trial for Defendants With Mental Retardation, 17 CRIM. JUST. & BEHAV. 147 (1990); Nicholson, Briggs & Robertson, Instruments for Assessing Competency to Stand Trial: How Do They Work? 19 PROF'L PSYCHOLOGY: RES. & PRAC. 383 (1988). On the relationship between IST and NGRI findings, see Johnson, Nicholson & Service, The Relationship of Competency to Stand Trial and Criminal Responsibility, 17 CRIM. JUST. & BEHAV. 169 (1990).

200. Slobogin, Melton & Showalter, The Feasibility of A Brief Evaluation of Mental State at the Time of the Offense, 8 LAW & HUM. BEHAV. 305 (1984); see generally, G. MELTON, J. PETRILA, N. POYTHRESS & C. SLOBOGIN, PSYCHOLOGICAL EVALUATION FOR THE COURTS: A HANDBOOK FOR MENTAL HEALTH PROFESSIONALS AND LAWYERS 147-56 (1987) (G. MELTON).

201. The SADS was developed to facilitate diagnosticians' ability to obtain accurate and reliable diagnoses. See Endicott and Spitzer, A Diagnostic Interview: The Schedule of Affective Disorders and Schizophrenia, 35 ARCG. GEN'L PSYCHIATRY

(RDC),[202] and the Rogers Criminal Responsibility Assessment Scales (R-CRAS).[203] These instruments were designed to translate legal insanity concepts into quantifiable variables that will meet the standard of reasonable scientific certainty.[204]

In a series of studies, R-CRAS has been validated for the ALI/ Model Penal Code standard, and for M'Naghten and GBMI as well.[205] The instrument tellingly revealed that malingering was not

---

837 (1978). Its development followed the publication of studies that revealed that an astounding ninety-five percent of diagnostic disagreements among psychiatrists could be accounted for by the usage of differing and unreliable interviewing techniques and diagnostic standards. Rogers & Cavanaugh, *Application of the SADS Diagnostic Interview to Forensic Psychiatry*, 9 J. PSYCHIATRY & L. 329, 330 (1981).

The SADS has been adapted successfully to forensic evaluations, *see* Rogers & Cavanaugh, *supra*, and, preliminarily, to criminal responsibility assessments, *see* Rogers, Thatcher & Cavanaugh, *Use of the SADS Diagnostic Interview in Evaluating Legal Insanity*, 40 J. CLIN. PSYCHOLOGY 1538 (1984).

202. Spitzer, Endicott & Robins, *Research Diagnostic Criteria For Use in Psychiatric Research*, 35 ARCH. GEN'L PSYCHIATRY 773 (1978).

203. Rogers, Seman & Clark, *supra* note 133; Rogers, Cavanaugh, Seman & Harris, *supra* note 179. The R-CRAS instrument measures patients on five scales: patient reliability, organicity, psychopathology, cognitive control, and behavioral control. Rogers, Seman & Clark, *supra* note 133, at 68.

204. Golding & Roesch, *The Assessment of Criminal Responsibility: A Historical Approach to a Current Controversy*, in HANDBOOK OF FORENSIC PSYCHOLOGY 395, 418 (1987). *See* G. MELTON, *supra* note 200, at 144-47. They also were created, in important part, in response to research suggesting that some evaluating clinicians were both "biased and unknowledgeable" about the evaluations they performed, and that experts' own subjective judgments about the justifications for the insanity defense substantially affected their judgments in evaluations of marginal cases. Rogers, *supra* note 152, at 844-45; *see generally*, Rogers & Turner, *Understanding Insanity: A National Survey of Forensic Psychiatrists and Psychologists*, 7 HEALTH LAW IN CANADA 71 (1987); Rogers, Turner, Helfield & Dickens, *Forensic Psychiatrists and Psychologists Understanding of Insanity: Misguided Expertise?* 35 CANAD. J. PSYCHIATRY 691 (1988); Beckham, Annis & Gustafson, *Decision Making and Examiner Bias in Forensic Expert Recommendations for Not Guilty By Reason of Insanity*, 13 LAW & HUM. BEHAV. 79 (1989).

205. *See e.g.*, Rogers & Cavanaugh, *supra* note 201; Rogers, Dolmetsch & Cavanaugh, *An Empirical Approach to Insanity Evaluations*, 37 J. CLIN. PSYCHOLOGY 683 (1981); Rogers, Seman & Wasyliw, *The R-CRAS and Legal Insanity: A Cross Validation Study*, 39 J. CLIN PSYCHOLOGY 554 (1983), and Rogers, Wasyliw & Cavanaugh, *Evaluating Insanity: A Study of Construct Validity*, 8 LAW & HUM BEHAV. 293 (1984) (all ALI); Rogers, Seman & Clark, *supra* note 133, at 74 (four of five scales consistent with *a priori* hypotheses). *See also*, Rogers, *Assessment of Criminal Responsibility: Empirical Advances and Unanswered Questions*, 15 J. PSYCHIATRY & L. 73 (1987) (M'Naghten and GBMI); Rogers & Ewing, *The Measurement of Insanity: Debating the Merits of the*

associated in criminal defendants either with severe psychopathology or expert opinion regarding sanity.[206]Whether or not these or other instruments prove ultimately to be of significant global value in assessing responsibility,[207] they reflect an important development and concomitant reality: psychologists and other behavioralists *are* developing new empirical tools to help us understand "crazy behavior." These tools remain, however, virtually irrelevant both to the policy debate over the future of the insanity defense, and to the substantive and procedural contours of the defense itself. It is *this* reality that needs sober reflection.[208]

R-CRAS and Its Alternatives, 15 INT'L J. L. & PSYCHIATRY 113 (1992). In a more recent paper, Rogers suggests that accurate assessment tools may be of greater reliability in volitional than in cognitive determinations, Rogers, *supra,* at 78, and that arguments that volitional prong non-responsibility cannot be measured are "an intellectual charade played for the benefit of an uninformed public." *Id.*

On the impact of the standard on forensic examiners' conclusions, *see* Wettstein, Mulvey & Rogers, *supra* note 124. On the frequently negligible empirical impact of a substantive change in an insanity defense standard, *see* H. STEADMAN, REFORMING, *supra* note 97, at 12 (change in substantive standard in California made very little difference). /

206. Rogers, Dolmetsch & Cavanaugh, *supra* note 205, at 687; Rogers, Gillis & Bagby, *The SIRS as a Measure of Malingering: A Validation Study With a Correctional Sample,* 8 BEHAV. SCI. & L. 85 (1990). *See generally infra* chapter 5 C 1.

207. The R-CRAS has been gently criticized by Professors Roesch and Golding (substantively and operationally, because it may not appropriately clarify the association between organic disturbance and control/moral judgment capacities, and empirically, because its published validity data uses "criterion contaminated groups," that is, groups characterized as sane or insane on the basis of the R-CRAS itself), *see* Golding & Roesch, *supra* note 204, at 419. They thus fear that the use of such instruments may "deflect attention away from the critical need to develop a better understanding of the behavioral, perceptual, cognitive, affective, and judgmental correlates" of mental disorders. *Id.* at 417-18. *See also,* G. MELTON, *supra* note 200, at 147:

The weakness of the R-CRAS include its misplaced emphasis on addressing ultimate-issue questions; its claims to quantify in areas of judgment that are actually logical and/or intuitive in naturel and the manual's claim to scientific rigor, which assures that R-CRAS-based opinions have 'reasonable medical and scientific certainty.' The major risk involved in its use at this time is that clinicians or courts may, in light of the unsubstantiated claims in the manual, attribute undeserved scientific status to judgments that remain, ordinal ratings notwithstanding, logical and commensensical in nature.

208. *Cf.* R. ROGERS, CONDUCTING INSANITY EVALUATIONS 16 (1986): "[T]he relevant question is whether the standardized measures represent a substantial improvement in the quality of forensic evaluations. The issue is not whether these measures represent a perfect synchronicity of any law professor's armchair interpretation of the legal standard."

3. *The Significance of Scientific Evidence*

a. Introduction.   The elements of the empirical picture are thus fairly clear, although its contours remain opaque. Myths regarding the operation of the insanity defense system developed, and became locked into place; commentators empirically rebutted these myths; other empiricists developed new data leading to a significant measure of clarity regarding certain elements of responsibility decision making; scholars continue to call for additional empirical evidence to illuminate the underlying issues more coherently; regardless of the wealth of new empirical data, public attitudes have not changed.

Virtually all of the data and instruments discussed, however, focus on the *court process*: what happens to insanity pleaders once they are arrested, tried and institutionalized, and how forensic assessors come to their determinations of responsibility. None of this touches on another critical aspect of insanity defense jurisprudence: the interplay—if any—between scientific "discoveries" and changes in the law. If the insanity defense is inevitably and inextricably intertwined with notions of mental disease, then it might be assumed that, as our data base of the etiology, epidemiology, pathology and physiology of mental disability increases, our construct of mental responsibility becomes increasingly more sophisticated, especially in light of the recent attention being paid by legal commentators to the scientific method and its implications for the law.[209] Of course, no such thing has happened.

In the lengthy Congressional hearings held in the wake of the Hinckley acquittal, there was apparently only one witness whose testimony focused on the development and utility of any of these tools. *See* U.S. House of Rep., Comm. on Judiciary, Subcomm. on Crim. Justice, *Reform of the Federal Insanity Defense* (Apr. 21, 1983), at 416 (statement of Stephen L. Golding, Ph. D.). Nothing in either the final committee report or the IDRA as enacted suggests that Congress paid any particular heed to Dr. Golding's recommendations. *See also,* English, *supra* note 143, at 47-48 (decrying fact that Dr. Rogers' empirical research "never informed the Congressional debate").

209. *Compare* Fuller, *Playing Without A Full Deck: Scientific Realism and the Cognitive Limits of Legal Theory,* 97 YALE L.J. 549 (1988); Note, *The Scientific Model in the Law,* 75 GEO. L.J. 1968, 1970-71 (1987) (Note, *Scientific Model*) (three elements generally found in the "scientific model of judicial lawmaking" are (1) an objective inquirer, (2) a process of hypothesis and empirical testing, and (3) a belief in some underlying coherent system that assures that the first two principles will produce accurate and reproducible answers).

b. Models of illness.[210] Development of insanity defense jurisprudence has proceeded with extreme indifference to new scientific discoveries. If anything, the retrenchment of the cognitive-only test (as reflected in the M'Naghten rules and the even more restrictive IDRA) may have reflected a conscious decision on the part of legal decision makers to ignore the Freudian revolution and its aftermath.[211]

It may be helpful to consider these seemingly-paradoxical developments in light of the various dominant models of mental illness which have been constructed in an effort to explain aberrant behavior:[212] the medical model,[213] the psychoanalytic model,[214] the behaviorist model,[215] and the social model.[216] It might also be helpful to examine the basis of recent scientific "discoveries" in an effort to determine whether (a) the choice of model, in fact, makes any difference,[217] and (b) whether such discoveries have had any significant impact on insanity defense jurisprudence.[218]

---

210. *See generally,* M. SIEGLER, & H. OSMOND, MODELS OF MADNESS, MODELS OF MEDICINE (1976) (MODELS); *see also,* Wolfgang, *The Medical Model Versus the Just Deserts Model,* 16 BULL. AM ACAD. PSYCHIATRY & L. 111 (1988).
211. *See e.g.,* State v. Pike, 49 N.H. 399, 438 (1869) (Doe, J., concurring) ("The law does not change with every advance of science; nor does it maintain a fantastic consistency by adhering to medical mistakes which science has corrected"); *compare,* Livermore & Meehl, *The Virtues of* M'Naghten, 51 MINN. L. REV. 789, 855 (1967) (M'Naghten test broad enough to allow for application of psychodynamic theory).
212. In addition to the models listed below, *see also,* MODELS, *supra* note 210, at 16-18 (discussing moral model, impaired model, psychedelic model, conspiratorial model, and family interaction model).
213. *Id.* at 23-27.
214. *Id.* at 43-52. The use of this model in criminal justice problem-solving is demonstrated in Schoenfeld, *Law and Unconscious Motivation,* 8 HOWARD L.J. 15 (1962). On the question of the scientific basis of psychodynamic theory, *see* Morse, *supra* note 132, at 994-1018.
215. MODELS, *supra* note 210, at 27-35. For a helpful discussion of this model in a non-insanity defense context, *see* Wexler, *Token and Taboo: Behavior Modification, Token Economies, and the Law,* 61 CALIF L. REV. 81 (1973).
216. MODELS, *supra* note 210, at 52-58. *See e.g.,* Weiss & Bergen, *Social Supports and the Reduction of Psychiatric Disability,* 31 PSYCHIATRY 107 (1968).
217. *See e.g.,* Lazare, *Hidden Conceptual Models in Clinical Psychiatry,* 288 N. ENG. J. MED. 345 (1973) (choice of model is implicitly determined by several variables, including diagnosis, effectiveness of available treatments, immediacy of social situation, patient's social class, and therapist's ideology).
218. On the relationship between biology and crime, *see e.g.,* Mednick & Volavka, *Biology in Crime,* in CRIME & JUSTICE: AN ANNUAL REVIEW OF RESEARCH 85 (N. Morris & M. Tonry eds. 1980).

The "medical model" hypothesizes that the various kinds of behavior that result in individuals being labelled mentally ill are caused by underlying physical malfunctions and which insist upon "scientific investigation" (classification, observation and testing).[219] In a recent paper, Professor Jules Gerard extols this as the appropriate model to be embraced by the legal system in insanity defense and civil commitment decision making, and asserts that psychiatry's failures in describing illnesses in such a way that patients could be appropriately clinically diagnosed were "an inevitable by-product of the *dominance* in America of the psychoanalytic model."[220]

Nothing is more significant to Professor Gerard in his position than the adoption by the American Psychiatric Association of DSM-III.[221] It is ironic, he stresses, that, while critics of the mental health legal system were, historically, "essentially correct" in arguing that psychiatry's descriptions of illnesses were vague, overlapping and confusing, their criticism "reached its apogee" at the precise time that psychiatry was remediating the problem through the elaborate diagnostic criteria and both clinical and operational descriptions of men-

---

219. Gerard, *The Usefulness of the Medical Model to the Legal System*, 39 RUTGERS L. REV. 377, 382-83 (1987).

220. *Id.* at 378, 414. Such a model, Professor Gerard charges, "viewed diagnosis as unnecessary," *id.*, at 414; only with the publication of the third edition of the Diagnostic and Statistical Manual did medical model supporters "win the war." *Id.* at 415. *But compare* Commonwealth *ex rel.* Grimes v. Yack, 289 Pa. Super. 495, 433 A. 2d 1363, 1381 (1981), *quoting,* in part, J. ROBITSCHER, THE POWERS OF PSYCHIATRY 38 (1980):

> For the law to base itself on [the medical model...], however, would transform the nature of the law as we have conceived of it and would entail great risk....The medical model proposes that conditions have discernable causes and scientific cures, and that the nonexperts, the rest of the population, should submit to the authority of these experts. Such legal considerations as procedurally protected rights need not be given major consideration since the experts would presumably only be operating in the interests of those they serve.

221. *See e.g.*, Spitzer, Williams & Skodol, *DSM-III: The Major Achievements and an Overview*, 137 AM. J. PSYCHIATRY 151 (1980); *see generally*, 1 M.L. PERLIN, *supra* note 1, *§2.03 n.123, and sources cited. DSM-III has since been supplemented by a new manual, DSM-IIIR. See* AMERICAN PSYCHIATRIC ASSOCIATION, DIAGNOSTIC AND STATISTICAL MANUAL IIIR (1988). *See e.g.,* Cooper & Michels, *DSM-III-R: The View From Here and Abroad*, 145 AM. J. PSYCHIATRY 1300, 1301 (1988) (book review) (majority of changes in DSM-III-R "improve the manual and provide both a better basis for current diagnosis and better opportunities for future research").

tal illness in DSM-III.[222]

The reascendancy of the medical model becomes even more significant in light of contemporaneous "discoveries" regarding the alleged physiological bases of mental illnesses and the use of "hard science" diagnostic tools such as CT scanning, Magnetic Resonance Imaging (MRI), Positron Emission Tomography (PET), and others to determine the presence of such illnesses.[223] Even Professor Stephen Morse concedes that recent "real biological differences between normals and various types of disordered people" may reflect some "valid differences."[224] While the impact of neuroscience on forensic medicine is "still somewhat in its infancy,"[225] scientific papers about such developments are frequently written in an ebullient tone brimming with the promise of yet *further* developments "just around the corner."[226]

---

222. Gerard, *supra* note 219, at 414-15.
223. *See e.g.*, Bear & Fedio, *Quantitative Analyses of Interictal Behavior in Temporal Lobe Epilepsy*, 34 ARCH. NEUROL. 454 (1977); Skeen, *The Genetically Defective Offender*, 9 WM. MITCHELL L. REV. 217 (1983); Luchins, *Computed Tomography in Schizophrenia: Disparities in the Presence of Abnormalities*, 39 ARCH. GEN'L PSYCHIATRY 859 (1982); Garber et al., *Use of Magnetic Resonance Imaging in Psychiatry*, 145 AM. J. PSYCHIATRY 164 (1988); Ellis, *Religiosity and Criminality From the Perspective of Arousal Theory*, 24 J. RES. CRIME & DELINQ. 215-222 (1987) (unusually large proportion of slow brain wave cortical activity found in criminal population); Miyabo, Asato & Mizushima, *Psychological Correlates of Stress-Induced Cortisol and Growth Hormone Releases in Neurotic Patients*, 41 PSYCHOSOMAT. MED. 515 (1979) (high growth hormone levels positively associated with personality features such as hostility and distorted thinking processes).
224. Morse, *Treating Crazy People Less Specially*, 90 W. VA. L. REV. 353, 365 (1987), and *id.* n. 25, *citing* Egeland et al., *Bipolar Affective Disorders Linked to DNA Markers on Chromosome 11*, 325 NATURE 783 (1987); Hodgkinson et al., *Molecular Genetic Evidence for Heterogeneity in Manic Depression*, 325 NATURE 805 (1987); Wong et al., *Positron Emission Tomography Reveals Elevated D_2 Dopamine Receptors in Drug-Naive Schizophrenics*, 234 SCIENCE 1558 (1986). On the other hand, Morse argues that the presence of a distinguishing biological variable would have no necessary relevance for *legally* and *socially* "distinguishing crazy people from normals." Morse, *supra*, at 365.
   On the relationship between biology and crime, *see e.g.*, Walters & White, *Heredity and Crime: Bad Genes or Bad Research?* 27 CRIMINOL. 455 (1989).
225. Cavanaugh & Rogers, *Forensic Psychiatry and the Neurosciences*, 5 BEHAV. SCI. & L. 221 (1987).
226. *See e.g.*, Swayze, Yates & Andreason, *Brain Imaging: Applications in Psychiatry*, 5 BEHAV. SCI. & L. 223, 224 (1987) ("Exciting new developments in a multiplicity of brain imaging techniques capable of studying not only structure but physiology have rekindled psychiatric interest in brain science"); *id.* at 235 ("The

But there can be no debating the limitations of science.[227] The history of psychiatry as a means of altering the social order has been, to some extent, a history of failed promises.[228] In each of the past several generations, psychiatrists have developed new treatments, new tests, and new methods of diagnosis; inevitably, a counterliterature develops, criticizing the new developments.[229] On an individualized basis, while the problems may be more apparent regarding therapeutic *interventions* which are later found to be wanting (because of irreversible side effects, civil rights violations and/or their invasion of personal autonomy),[230] they are still of significance in

---

foregoing has been just a taste of what these new technologies are like and what they may allow psychiatric researchers and clinicians to explore regarding the brain and its secrets"). *But compare* Denno, *Human Biology and Criminal Responsibility: Free Will or Free Ride?* 137 U. PA. L. REV. 615, 617 (1988) (scientific research has not successfully demonstrated a sufficiently strong link between biological factors and criminal behavior to warrant major consideration in determining criminal responsibility).

227. *See* Note, *Scientific Model, supra* note 209, at 1987-88 (discussing the Heisenberg Uncertainty Principle); *see generally*, Korn, *Law, Fact and Science in the Courts*, 66 COLUM L. REV. 1080 (1966).

228. J. LA FOND & M. DURHAM, *supra* note 114, at 169 ("Pronouncements of scientific breakthroughs that will cure the minds of the mentally ill are still, at present, promises that cannot be kept"). What is significant for this inquiry is that, historically, since at least the 1930s, psychiatrists have consciously attempted to "increase the legitimacy and expand the influence" of their science by establishing a linkage between psychiatry and law at a time when the public was becoming "increasingly aware of the promise of psychiatry." *See* Weisberg, *The "Discovery" of Sexual Abuse: Experts' Role in Legal Policy Formulation*, 18 U.C. DAVIS. L. REV. 1, 18; (1984); *see also*, S. GLUECK, LAW AND PSYCHIATRY: COLD WAR OR ENTENTE CORDIALE? 171 (1962):

Psychiatric research is following psychological, physiological and chemical paths. This is wise; for mental illness appears to be the outcome of chemistry at one end and culture at the other, and limitation of inquiry to psychological symptoms may mean that investigators are dealing more with the smoke than with the fire.

229. For helpful historical overviews, *see e.g.*, G. GROB, MENTAL ILLNESS AND AMERICA SOCIETY, 1875-1940 (1983); A. SCULL, MUSEUMS OF MADNESS (1979); G. ROSEN, MADNESS IN SOCIETY (1968); M. FOUCAULT, MADNESS AND CIVILIZATION: A HISTORY OF INSANITY IN THE AGE OF REASON (1963); Scull & Favreau, *"A Chance To Cut Is a Chance To Cure:" Sexual Surgery for Psychosis in Three Nineteenth Century Societies*, 8 RESEARCH IN LAW, DEVIANCE & SOC'L CONTROL ANN. 3 (1986).

230. *See e.g.*, Kaimowitz v. Michigan Dep't of Mental Health, Civil No. 73-19434-AW (Mich. Cir. Ct., Wayne Cty., July 10, 1973), reprinted in A. BROOKS, LAW. PSYCHIATRY AND THE MENTAL HEALTH SYSTEM 902 (1974); *see e.g.*, Note, Kaimowitz v. Department of Mental Health: *A Right to Be Free From Experimental Psychosurgery*, 54 B.U. L. REV. 301 (1974).

matters involving testing and diagnosis.[231]

Just because many of the new scientific "discoveries" appear closer to "hard science" than do traditional psychoanalytic constructs does not suggest that there is no conflict in the "hard sciences" in diagnostic matters.[232] Also, while the psychoanalytic model may not be an appropriate *diagnostic* model,[233] the criticisms raised by adherents to the medical model should not obscure the correlate reality that *other* contemporaneous studies show that—as a *treatment* intervention—psychotherapy's benefits have been found to be "on a par with other expensive and ambitious interventions, such as...medicine."[234]

Thus, whether Professor Gerard is correct or not may be largely irrelevant, whether from the vantage point of empiric "reality," of moral philosophy, of the rules of evidence, of legal theory, or of science.[235] As a student commentator has recently observed, "The absolute truth Cardozo found lacking in the law is not present in scientific theories either."[236] Like law, science is interpretive and

---

231. *See e.g.*, Comment, *The Psychologist as Expert Witness: Science in the Courtroom?* 38 MD. L. REV. 539, 577-88 (1979) (on reliability of psychiatric diagnosis), and *id.* at 565-77 (on reliability of psychological testing).

232. Indeed, Gerard explicitly concedes as much. *See* Gerard, *supra* note 219, at 417 n. 144 (discussing cardiologic diagnosis and toxicologic analyses); *see generally*, Note, *Scientific Model, supra* note 209, at 1986-88.

233. *Cf.* Kaplan & Rinella, *supra* note 149, at 216 (reasons why psychoanalysis remains a "marginal tool for legal analysis").

234. M. SMITH, G. GLASS & T. MILLER, THE BENEFITS OF PSYCHOTHERAPY 183 (1980) (discussing the "near monotonous regularity" with which psychotherapy's efficacy continues to be demonstrated).

235. *See e.g.*, Boorse, *On the Distinction Between Disease and Illness*, 5 J. PHIL & PUB. AFFS. 49, 67 (1975) ("one cannot expect to substitute psychiatry for moral debate, any more than moral evaluations can be substituted for psychiatric theory"); Note, *Scientific Method, supra* note 209, at 1971: "Scientists themselves have questioned whether their own disciplines are capable of the kind of objectivity, strict empiricism, and theoretical coherence the traditional model describes." On the question of whether law is "scientific" (e.g., "objectively observable, analytically determinate, or conceptually coherent") or indeterminate and subjective, *see id.* at 1968-69, 1983-90.

236. *Id.* at 1980; *see generally* T. KUHN, THE STRUCTURE OF SCIENTIFIC REVOLUTIONS (1962). Over twenty years ago, Professor Harold Korn argued that attacks on the *M'Naghten* test were "misconceived," as *M'Naghten*, a legal standard, reflected "not a purely scientific" formulation, and was thus one that could not be resolved solely by reference to the learning of psychiatry. Korn, *supra* note 219, at 1094. *M'Naghten*, he explained, "explicitly authorize[d]" the jury to make "an inferential jump from psychiatric concepts to the value-laden legal

contextual.[237]

It is especially ironic that the key common denominator between law and science is a central emphasis on "the critical method of hypothesis formulation and empirical testing."[238] For it is here that one of the great ironies of insanity defense jurisprudence—the ultimate *irrelevance* to decision makers of the results of empirical testing[239]—glares at us; as I will demonstrate, even where we are made aware of the inaccuracy of the myths that form the underpinning of that jurisprudence, we continue, via a process known as attribution theory,[240] to ignore overwhelming and virtually uncontradicted evidence, and to, instead, adhere to the persistent myths. Just as we have demurred to uncontested empirical evidence, so do we demur, in large part, to "interpretive and contextual" scientific explanations of mentally disordered criminal behavior.[241]

The other side of this coin may be even more stark. While science continues to offer "new insights and techniques applicable to the law and to all aspects of human understanding," it is not at all clear that society is prepared to accept these insights and expand its base of understanding. Perhaps we reject scientific explanations be-

---

ones." *Id.* at 1095. This, of course, implies that psychiatric concepts are *not* "value-laden," an assumption that, today, nearly all would agree is erroneous. *See also, id.* at 1101 ("The normative and prescriptive attitudes of the legal system inject value and policy ingredients with which scientific learning is not concerned"). *Compare* Posner, *The Jurisprudence of Skepticism*, 86 MICH. L. REV. 827, 842-43 (1988):

Scientific authority, on which nonscientists rely in forming their beliefs on scientific matters, is derivative from the genuine power and well-deserved prestige of scientific methodology; science works. Judicial activity is essentially political.

237. Note, *Scientific Method, supra* note 209, at 1988. *See e.g.*, Wessel, *Adversary Science and the Adversary Scientist: Threats to Responsible Dispute Resolution*, 28 JURIMETRICS J. 379 (1988).
238. Note, *Scientific Method, supra* note 209, at 1981; *see generally*, C. HEMPEL, PHILOSOPHY OF NATURAL SCIENCE 2 (1966).
239. *See e.g.*, Tancredi & Volkow, *Neural Substrates of Violent Behavior: Implications for Law and Public Policy*, 11 INT'L J. L. & PSYCHIATRY 13, 28 (1988) ("[H]ow do we arrive at understanding the significance of biophysiological research that has the potentiality of objectively identifying those who can be considered as not capable of evidencing free will?").
240. *See generally infra* chapter 6 C 1.
241. *See e.g,* Kaplan & Rinella, *supra* note 149, at 226 ("the efficacy of conceptualizing criminal responsibility on a universal level is extremely questionable and tenuous"); *see also*, Berk, *supra* note 198, at 36-37, 44.

cause we are terrified that they will tell us what we do not want to confront—that far more criminal defendants are "not responsible" than we had thought.

If this number goes beyond some abstract "pressure point," new dilemmas for society are then created. The empirical reality is that few defendants plead insanity and fewer are successful. Yet, if we accept new scientific evidence (and integrate those findings into our jurisprudence), we would then have to deal with an insanity defense system which has a potentially significant impact on the judicial system and the criminal process. That might plausibly lead to new pressure to abolish the defense because its legitimate use would—for the first time in history—actually have an operational impact on the crime control model of criminal law.[242]

An analogy may help. The development of new types of social science research data has created new factual issues, by challenging long-held assumptions which underlie criminal trial factfinding. Thus, statistical studies have shown, e.g., that white jurors have a disproportionate tendency to convict black defendants, and that indigent criminal defendants often do not have an adequate opportunity to prepare a defense or rebut the state's evidence in cases in which scientific evidence is crucial.[243] Society's instinctive response is to reject the studies that inform us of these disparities so that we can maintain our adherence to the status quo.[244]

In short, where science does appear to inform us of ways in which the criminal justice system is operating "unfairly," we choose to reject it rather than to confront the underlying issues that are

---

242. *See* S. Brehm & J. Brehm, Psychological Reactance: A Theory of Freedom and Control 79 (1981), discussing the "hydraulic principle" articulated in R.A. Wicklund, Freedom and Reactance 86 (1974): "When a freedom cannot be regained directly, the motivation resulting from that freedom will push over into a second freedom." *See generally infra* chapter 8 A. On the impact that similar cognitive dissonance has on the mental disability law system, *see* Perlin, *supra* note 84.

243. Note, *Scientific Model, supra* note 209, at 1991.

244. *E.g.*, McCleskey v. Kemp, 481 U.S. 279 (1987), rejecting statistics and results of social science survey offered to show systemic racial discrimination in Georgia prosecutors' decisions to seek death penalty, and in jurors' decisions to impose death sentences. After *McCleskey*, in order to prevail, a defendant must show that, in *his* case, the decision makers acted with discriminatory purpose. *Id.* at 292. Presumably, intelligent prosecutors will be able to avoid this outcome. *See* Perlin, *supra* note 84, at 134.

raised.[245] To some extent, this may reflect another self-referential heuristic: in order to retain our concepts of intentionality of the mind "as understood in scholastic medieval philosophy," we need to reject the apparent scientific reality that, because of "defects in the limbic area" or differences in "receptor systems of the brain," all of us simply do not react—indeed, cannot—react the same way to external stimuli.[246]

Scientific "advance" is clearly not without its internal dissonance. Yet, acknowledging both its inherent and inevitable subjectivism and contextuality, as well as its history of failed promises as a means of controlling deviance, one even more implacable problem must still be confronted: society's dogged heuristic adherence to its "common sense" conceptions of free will and behavior control, in the face of remarkable contrary evidence.[247] Until this paradox is confronted, the impact of scientific "advance" on our ability to craft new solutions to perennial dilemmas will be little more than illusory.[248]

4. The Meaning of Moral Philosophy

No perspective is more ubiquitous in insanity defense literature than that of the moral philosopher. The insanity defense is, to be sure, a "natural" for philosophic debates, as it involves so many of the philosopher's "high cards:" notions of free will, of determinism, of responsibility, of rationality, of community standards, of ethical perspectives.[249] Without *too* much distortion, one can read the his-

---

245. *See* R. Rogers & C. Ewing, "Frye or Scrambled? A Response to Goldstein's Critique of the R-CRAS," paper presented at annual conference of American Psychology-Law Society, March 1990, manuscript at 13 (characterizing "deliberate avoidance of further knowledge" as a "virulent form of prejudice"); *see also*, Rogers & Ewing, *Ultimate Opinion Proscriptions: A Cosmetic Fix and A Plea for Empiricism*, 13 LAW & HUM. BEHAV. 357 (1989).

246. Tancredi & Volkow, *supra* note 239, at 34.

247. *See generally*, T. KUHN, *supra* note 236 (science can be seen as "normal" only when community accepts new conceptual structures).

248. *Compare* McHenry, *The Judicial Evolution of Ohio's Insanity Defense*, 13 U. DAYTON L. REV. 49, 78 (1987) (speculating that Ohio's insanity test will probably remain static until the time that "all human behavior, emotions, and thoughts will be discernible from examining a string of DNA on the end of a pin").

249. *See generally*, FREEDOM AND RESPONSIBILITY (H. Morris ed. 1962); for a more recent formulation, *see* Morris, *The Decline of Guilt*, 99 ETHICS 62 (Oct. 1988). *Compare* D. BAZELON, *supra* note 111, at 25-26 (insanity defense "illuminates the complex moral judgments made in finding guilty a person who commits a

tory of the insanity defense debate as a history of philosophical positions.

This history has been paralleled by an important development in the field of criminal law scholarship: the ascendancy of moral philosophy as a tool by which to analyze substantive criminal law doctrine.[250] As a result, scholars and academics began the "immense undertaking"[251] of crafting and retooling insanity defense doctrines in reliance on schools of philosophical thought. From this body of work, the writings of Stephen Morse[252] and Michael Moore[253] have

---

moral act").
250. See e.g., Arenella, *Rethinking the Functions of Criminal Procedure: The Warren and Burger Courts' Competing Ideologies,* 72 GEO. L.J. 185, 214 (1983) (criticizing Herbert Packer—see H. PACKER, THE LIMITS OF THE CRIMINAL SANCTION (1968)—for "ignor[ing] the moral quality of substantive guilt"). For other recent important inquiries, see e.g., Arenella, *Convicting the Morally Blameless: Reassessing the Relationship Between Legal and Moral Accountability,* 39 UCLA L. REV. 1511 (1992); Simons, *Rethinking Mental States,* 72 B.U. L. REV. 463 (1992); Boldt, *The Construction of Responsibility in Criminal Law,* 140 U. PA. L. REV. 2245 (1992); Dan-Cohen, *Responsibility and the Boundaries of the Self,* 105 HARV. L. REV. 959 (1992); Siegel, *On Narcissism and Veiled Innocence: Prolegomena to a Critique of Criminal Law,* 15 INT'L J. L. & PSYCHIATRY 339 (1992); Beahrs, *Volition, Deception, and the Evolution of Justice,* 19 BULL. AM. ACAD. PSYCHIATRY & L. 81 (1991). On the role of responsibility in civil law, see Kuklin, *The Asymmetrical Conditions of Legal Responsibility in the Marketplace,* 44 U. MIAMI L. REV. 893 (1990).
251. Ross, *Some Philosophical Considerations of the Legal-Psychiatric Debate of Criminal Responsibility,* 1 ISSUES IN CRIMINOL. 34, 35 (1965); see also, Boorse, supra note 235. For a recent thoughtful inquiry into the relationship between criminal responsibility and free will, see Rychlak & Rychlak, *The Insanity Defense and the Question of Human Agency,* 8 NEW IDEAS IN PSYCHOLOGY 3 (1990).
252. See e.g., Morse, supra notes & 224; Morse, *Diminished Capacity: A Moral and Legal Conundrum,* 2 INT'L J. L. & PSYCHIATRY 271 (1979).
253. In Moore's monumental work, *Law and Psychiatry: Rethinking the Relationship,* he explicitly articulates the importance of moral philosophy to the inquiries in question:

I shall return to the ultimate theses of the book: first, that both lawyers and psychiatrists need to know more about the philosophy of science, the philosophy of the mind, and the philosophy of law if either group is to get straight the relationship between the two disciplines; and second, that a rethinking of the relationship in terms of such knowledge should show that neither the legal nor the psychiatric theory of the person departs significantly from the ancient and commonsense idea that persons are beings who are sufficiently rational, 'in charge' of their actions, and unified in their purposes, that they may justly be the subjects of praise and blame, justly the holders of rights and responsibilities.

M. MOORE, LAW AND PSYCHIATRY: RETHINKING THE RELATIONSHIP 5 (1984).

emerged as the most important.[254]

Both Morse and Moore appear to be comfortable with retetionist positions,[255] at least in cases involving the "extremely crazy."[256] That is, while Moore acknowledges the role of the insanity defense as a "morality play," he also suggests that the only "appropriate" ques-

---

See also, Moore, *Responsibility and the Unconscious*, 53 So. CAL. L. REV. 1563 (1980); Moore, *Responsibility for Unconsciously Motivated Action*, 2 INT'L J. L. & PSYCHIATRY 323 (1979); Moore, *Mental Illness and Responsibility*, 39 BULL. MENNINGER CLIN. 308 (1975) (Moore, *Responsibility*); Moore, *Causation and the Excuses*, 73 CALIF. L. REV. 1091 (1985); Moore, *Moral Reality Revisited*, 90 MICH. L. REV. 2424 (1992). For a helpful (and generally laudatory) review of Moore's work, *see* Slobogin, *A Rational Approach to Responsibility*, 83 MICH. L. REV. 820 (1985) (review essay of M. MOORE, *supra*).

254. Moore and Morse have also greatly influenced the work of others working in the area of moral philosophy and criminal responsibility. *See e.g.*, Mitchell, *Culpable Mental Disorder and Criminal Liability*, 8 INT'L J. L. & PSYCHIATRY 273 (1986). *Compare* Saunders, *Voluntary Acts and the Criminal Law: Justifying Culpability Based on the Existence of Volition*, 49 U. PITT. L. REV. 443, 475-76 n. 130 (1988) (distinguishing his approach from Moore's).

This is not to denigrate the work of many other commentators in this area, specifically that of Richard Bonnie and Christopher Slobogin, *see e.g.*, Slobogin, *supra* note 99; Slobogin, *supra* note 194; Bonnie & Slobogin, *supra* note 132; Bonnie, *The Moral Basis for the Insanity Defense*, 69 A.B.A. J. 194 (1983); Bonnie, *Morality, Equality, and Expertise: Renegotiating the Relationship Between Psychiatry and the Criminal Law*, 12 BULL. AM. ACAD. PSYCHIATRY & L. 5 (1984) (Bonnie, *Morality*). A careful reading of their work, however, reveals that they are both as concerned with empirical data and with the underlying evidential and doctrinal issues as with the "pure" issues of moral philosophy. *See also*, Sendor, *supra* note 4 (articulating an interpretative theory of the insanity defense).

255. *See* Slobogin, *supra* note 253, at 828 (Moore's thesis "strongly affirms the role of the insanity defense as a necessary and integral aspect of the criminal law"); Morse, *supra* note 149, at 836 ("We should not abolish the insanity defense unless we truly believe that every perpetrator of a criminal act deserves to be punished, no matter how crazy"); *see also*, Kadish, *Excusing Crime*, 75 CALIF. L. REV. 257, 280 (1987) (abolition "would open a dramatic gap between moral and legal requirements of blaming").

256. Morse, *supra* note 149, at 820. On the use of the vernacular word "crazy," *compare* Fletcher, *The Universal and the Particular in Legal Discourse*, 1987 B.Y.U. L. REV. 335, 341 ("language shapes cultural identity and part of that identity seems to be an indigenous style of legal argument and legal theory"), to Toulmin, *Introductory Note: The Multiple Aspects of Mental Health and Mental Disorder*, 2 J. MED. & PHIL. 191 (1977) (discussing the "confused and confusing" colloquial language used for talking about the mentally disabled). On the relationship between such language and "sanist" behavior, *see* Perlin, *supra* note 80.

tion to ask jurors is whether the accused is "so irrational as to be nonresponsible."[257] Morse, on the other hand, suggests a new alternative formulation:

> A defendant is not guilty by reason of insanity if, at the time of the offense, the defendant was so extremely crazy, and the craziness so substantially affected the criminal behavior that the defendant does not deserve to be punished.[258]

While these tests are, to be sure, narrow ones, they are certainly based on defensible moral constructs. More problematic are the "real world" predicates for Moore's and Morse's positions which disregard (1) the inherent irrationality in legal insanity defense decision making, and, (2) the inherent dissonance between the insanity defense and the "peacekeeping function" of the criminal law. Thus, Moore expects that jurors, the primary representatives of the "shared moral sentiments of the community,"[259] will ultimately come to a "moral" decision as to a defendant's responsibility. Morse similarly relies on factfinder compassion to insure that the "extremely crazy" are found not responsible.[260]

These seemingly unobjectionable views rest on a premise which may be far shakier than Moore and Morse appear to acknowledge: the expectation that factfinders will be "fair" in determining criminal liability in cases involving mentally disabled criminal defendants.[261] It is simply not clear what normative standards Morse expects jurors will employ in coming to moral decisions as to who "deserves" to be punished. This lack of clarity is troubling, because the hope (or expectation) articulated by both Morse and Moore flies squarely in the face of the empirically-demonstrated *irrationality* of jurors acting as fact-finders in insanity defense decision making.[262]

---

257. M. MOORE, *supra* note 253, at 244, 245. *Compare* Kadish, *supra* note 256, at 279 ("the concept of mental disease serves to identify *so complete* a breakdown of the human capacities of judgment and practical reason that the afflicted person cannot fairly be held liable") (emphasis added).

258. Morse, *supra* note 149, at 820. *See also, id.* at 781 ("The basic precondition for desert in all contexts...is the actor's responsibility as a moral agent").

259. Moore, *Responsibility, supra* note 253, at 322.

260. *See e.g.*, Morse, *supra* note 132, at 1081 ("an evaluation of the rich available data, using common sense and compassion, is all that one can reasonably expect").

261. *See e.g.*, Kadish, *supra* note 254, at 279 (presuming such fairness).

262. *See e.g.*, Roberts, Fincham & Golding, *supra* note 26; Slater & Hans, *Public Opinion of Forensic Psychiatry Following the Hinckley Verdict*, 141 AM. J.

Similarly, Morse suggests a defendant should be "entirely excused" if his or her irrationality is the product of extreme mental disorder over which, "to the best of our knowledge, the person has little control."[263] This argument presupposes rational and cognitively-driven decision making, a scenario that bears little resemblance to reality in the trial of insanity defense cases, and which may be largely irrelevant to insanity defense decision makers.

To some extent, Moore's formulation also begs the political question. Thus, he quotes, with seeming endorsement, an observation from the Royal Commission on Capital Punishment's report:

> However much you charge a jury as to the M'Naghten Rules or any other test, the question they would put to themselves when they retire is—"Is this man mad or not?"[264]

But, if this were so, then *why* the furor over Hinckley or other "wrong" verdicts where something about the *victim* or the surrounding social or political circumstances or the highly publicized nature of the case animates the public's post-verdict furor?[265]

Moral philosophy illuminates the underlying issues and forces us to make careful discriminations between types of behavior, to look closely at concepts of reason and rationality, and to question causational relationships. Scholars such as Professors Morse and Moore who have written extensively in this area help define the baseline issues and provide us with a rich vocabulary for assessing insanity questions. Yet, our predictable social hysteria that follows a verdict such as Hinckley's hammers home the inevitable conclusion that we must turn elsewhere if we are to have any measure of success in clarifying the jurisprudential incoherences.[266]

PSYCHIATRY 675 (1984).

263. Morse, *Justice, Mercy, and Craziness*, 36 STAN. L. REV. 1485, 1490 (1984) (review of N. MORRIS, MADNESS AND THE CRIMINAL LAW (1982)).

264. M. MOORE, *supra* note 253, at 245, *quoting* REPORT OF ROYAL COMMISSION ON CAPITAL PUNISHMENT §322 (1953).

265. *See* Wexler, *supra* note 135, at 541; *see also, id.*, discussing the use by the American Bar Association's Criminal Justice Mental Health Standards Project of the phrase "moral mistake," referring, in Wexler's view, to a "substantial disharmony between the good faith judgment of a criminal jury and the public reaction to that judgment."

266. Most contemporaneous schools of scholarship generally ignore or marginalize mental disability law. *See* M. Perlin & D. Dorfman, "The Invisible Renaissance of Mental Disability Law: A Case Study of Subordination" (manuscript in progress).

C. The Abolitionist Movement

While the movement to abolish the insanity defense dates to the turn of the century,[267] its contemporaneous revival can be traced to the Nixon Administration's unsuccessful attempts to "gut the [insanity] defense"[268] by limiting it to cases where the defendant, by mental disease or defect, "lacked the state of mind required as an element of the offense charged."[269]

This is not, though, to say that other schools of jurisprudential thought have nothing to offer the intellectualist insanity defense debate; for instance, it is clear that the insanity defense is an important one to feminist scholars, especially as it relates to cases in which traditional stereotypes of women's behavior have traditionally been reflected in judicial decision making, where the defense's uses are purportedly connected "to notions of women's frailty, mental confusion, emotional instability, defective reasoning capacities, and receptivity to manias." MacKinnon, *Toward Feminist Jurisprudence*, 34 STAN L. REV. 703, 720 (1982) (*discussing* A. JONES, WOMEN WHO KILL 158-66 (1980)). While discussion generally focuses on the defense's potential use in battered spouse syndrome cases, the description is also applicable to cases involving pre-menstrual stress syndrome, post-partum depression syndrome and rape trauma syndrome. *See e.g.,* Schwartz & Clear, *Feminism and Rape Law Reform*, 6 BULL. AM. ACAD. PSYCHIATRY & L. 313 (1978); Lustberg & Jacobi, *The Battered Woman as Reasonable Person: A Critique of the Appellate Division Decision in* State v. McClain, 22 SETON HALL L. REV. 365 (1992); Lewis, *Premenstrual Syndrome as a Criminal Defense*, 19 ARCH. SEXUAL BEHAV. 425 (1990); Provine, *Gender, Crime and Criminal Justice: Edwards's* WOMEN ON TRIAL, 1987 AM. BAR FOUND. RES. J. 571 (review essay).

267. *See generally,* 3 M.L. PERLIN, *supra* note 1, §15.10. A New York State Bar Association report recommended that the law "relegate to the realm of the obsolete the assumption that an insane man cannot commit crime." Hermann & Sor, *supra* note 38, at 534-535, *quoting* Rood, *Statutory Abolition of the Defense of Insanity in Criminal Cases*, 9 MICH. L. REV. 126 (1911) (*quoting* report).

Interestingly, Professor Rood—writing over seventy-five years ago —began his paper anecdotally by focusing on the then-recent Thaw case "as a striking illustration of the disgraceful farce made of criminal trials by the allowance of the defense of insanity under the present practice"). On the way that "anecdotal justice"—formulating a jurisprudence from the heuristic of an isolated case—is largely responsible for the state of insanity defense jurisprudence, *see generally infra* chapter 6 C.

268. Perlin, *supra* note 38, at 860.

269. *See* Wales, *An Analysis of the Proposal to "Abolish" the Insanity Defense in S. 1: Squeezing a Lemon*, 124 U. PA. L. REV. 687, 687 (1976), *quoting* S. 1, 94th Cong., 1st Sess. §522 (1975). A forerunner to this section had been proposed by a consultant to the National Commission on Reform of Federal Criminal Laws in 1970, but was rejected by the Commission. Wales, *supra*, at 688; *see also,* Hermann & Sor, *supra* note 35, at 539-40.

This proposed limitation has been characterized as the "lemon squeezer" exception: the defense would apply only where the defendant thought the strangulation-victim's head was a lemon.[270]

President Nixon had charged that this limitation was necessary so as to end the "unconscionable abuse" to which the defense had been subjected by unscrupulous defendants.[271] Although the source of this charge has never been made clear, there has been informed speculation that it flowed from press accounts of the case of one Garrett Trapnell, who allegedly boasted that he had successfully feigned the defense.[272] If so, it is but one additional instance of the way that the "fear of faking" myth and the solitary vivid case have combined, heuristically, to stunt the growth of a rational insanity discourse.[273]

By Nixon's time, a "strange bedfellow"[274] coalition of abolitionists had begun to form: scholars and libertarians (who feared the excesses of a "therapeutic state"),[275] retributionists (such as President

270. *See* American Law Institute, MODEL PENAL CODE, Tent, Draft No. 4, Comments to §4.01 (1956), at 156: "A madman who believes that he is squeezing lemons when he chokes his wife...is plainly beyond reach of the restraining influence of law;" *but see* Bonnie, *Morality*, *supra* note 254, at 15 ("Such cases... simply do not exist"). *But compare* Regina v. Machekequonabe, 28 Ont. Rep. 309 (1896) (defendant "pagan Indian" shot and killed second Indian, based on erroneous belief victim was a Wendogo, "an evil spirit clothed in human flesh...[who] would eat [another] human being;" manslaughter conviction affirmed).

271. *See* Mackenzie, *New Code Would Alter Rules on Insanity*, Wash. Post (Oct. 12, 1975), at C6, as quoted in Perlin, *Overview of Rights in the Criminal Process*, in 3 LEGAL RIGHTS OF MENTALLY DISABLED PERSONS 1879, 1889 (P. Friedman ed. 1979).

272. On the possible roots of this charge, *see* Gerber, *The Insanity Defense Revisited*, 1984 ARIZ. ST. L. J. 183, 117-18 (discussing case of Garrett Trapnell); *see also*, Gerard, *supra* note 219, at 410; *see infra* chapter 5 C 1, note 40. On the lack of empirical data supporting President Nixon's allegations, *see e.g.*, Pasewark & Pasewark, *Insanity Revised: Once More Over the Cuckoo's Nest*, 6 J. PSYCHIATRY & L. 481 (1978).

273. *See generally infra* chapter 6 C.

274. Perlin, note 271, at 1889. On the relationship between the political left and right wings in this venture, *see* Packer, *Enemies of Progress*, N.Y. REV. (Oct. 23, 1969), at 17 (essay reviewing A. GOLDSTEIN, *supra* note 66, and K. MENNINGER, THE CRIME OF PUNISHMENT (1969)).

On the concomitant "political realignment" of insanity defense supporters (leading to passage of the compromise Insanity Defense Reform Act legislation), *see supra* chapter 2 A; *see* Johnson, book review of N. MORRIS, *supra* note 262, 50 U. CHI. L. REV. 1534, 1549 (1983).

275. *See e.g.*, Goldstein & Katz, *Abolish the Insanity Defense—Why Not?* 72 YALE L.J. 853, 865 (1963); N. KITTRIE, THE RIGHT TO BE DIFFERENT 398-99 (1973). For a recent restatement of this position, *see* Szasz, *The Insanity Defense Is, Well,*

Nixon), and the mostly-invisible "bureaucratic center."[276] This latter group consisted of officials at state departments of mental health and forensic hospital staffs who wanted to rid their institutions of insanity acquittee defendants who served as "political albatrosses," as well as those in the criminal justice system who opposed the insanity defense because of the "grave problems of administration" it caused.[277]

Perhaps the most important—and persistent—criminal law scholar supporting abolition has been Norval Morris.[278] According to Professor Morris, the "moribund" insanity defense is "anachronistic[,] manifestly inefficient," and "a sop to our conscience, a comfort for our failure to address the difficult arena of psychopathology and crime,"[279] In marshaling his abolitionist arguments, Morris continues to repeat the same myths based upon what Professor Morse has characterized as "insubstantial objections"[280] to the insanity defense: that its use is limited to "sensational cases" or "particularly ornate homicide cases where the lawyers, the psychiatrists, and the community seem to enjoy their plunge into the moral debate," and that it is "not raised for minor crimes."[281]

Insane, Newsday, Mar. 10, 1993, at 85 (full text available on NEXIS) (on the "immorality" of insanity defense). On the "embarrassing inconsistency" of civil libertarians' position on abolition, *see* Stone, *The Insanity Defense and the Civil Libertarian*, 20 HARV. CIV. RTS.-CIV. LIBS. L. REV. 525, 528 (1985) (book review of L. CAPLAN, *supra* note 38); on the split among civil rights lawyers on libertarian based abolitionism, *see* Ledwith, Jones v. Gerhardstein: *The Involuntarily Committed Mental Patient's Right to Refuse Treatment with Psychotropic Drugs*, 1990 WIS. L. REV. 1367, 1372 n. 38.

276. *See generally*, Bloom & Rogers, *The Legal Basis of Forensic Psychiatry: Statutorily Mandated Psychiatric Diagnoses*, 144 AM. J. PSYCHIATRY 847, 849 (1987), studying the use of the insanity defense in Oregon ("Support for excluding defendants with personality disorders from the insanity defense came from those responsible for the hospitalized [Psychiatric Security Review Board] clients"). On the ways that institutional psychiatrists are "indirectly influenced" by such external demands, *see* D. BAZELON, *supra* note 111, at 36-37.

277. Perlin, *supra* note 271, at 1891; Kadish, *The Decline of Innocence*, 26 CAMB. L.J. 273, 279 (1968), and *see id.* (administrative difficulty argument no more makes out case for abolition of insanity defense than it does for jury abolition in cases involving defenses such as unintentionality or ignorance).

278. *See e.g.*, Morris, *Psychiatry and the Dangerous Criminal*, 41 S. CAL. L. REV. 514 (1968); N. MORRIS, *supra note 263*.

279. Morris, *supra* note 278, at 516-19.

280. *See* Morse, *supra* note 149, at 795-801.

281. Bonnie & Morris, *Debate: Should the Insanity Defense Be Abolished?* 1 J. L. & HEALTH 113, 118 (1986) (remarks of Prof. Morris).

Morris' adherence to these myths is striking and raises an important sub-text issue. If a careful, well-respected scholar such as Norval Morris can continue to perpetuate such myths, we should not be surprised when we discover similar distortions on the part of mass media or political figures.[282] This reliance is especially ironic given the careful way that Morris has debunked criminal justice system myths that do not relate to the insanity defense—myths about purported racial and genetic propensities for crime.[283]

Interestingly, Morris also asserts that it is error to "assume benevolence" on the part of a mental health system to which such insanity acquittees would be predictably committed,[284] and that it is also error to premise retention upon reliance on the community's "moral intuitions:" "the history of the insanity defense is that the community thinks it is a mechanism for letting people off; that it is characterized historically by leniency, fraud, and all sorts of complexities."[285] In short, Morris—the abolitionist—recognizes the irrationality of the community's anti-insanity defense animus, but, remarkably, *endorses* the community's lack of information on the "moral subtleties" involved, since the subtleties "are very difficult indeed."[286]

This may all resemble a philosophical shell game. Professor Morse *limits* the defense, but retains it because we can rely on juror compassion;[287] Morris *abolishes* it because we cannot rely on systemic benevolence on the part of mental health professionals charged with administering state systems. In both instances, the proponent relies upon an acontextual argument to support his major philosophical premise—in Morse's case, the "given" that jurors show compassion in the "right" cases; in Morris's, the "given" that mental health system workers may be more venal than prison workers. Both positions beg the question: *why* do decision makers really feel the way that they do about these cases?

---

282. *See also*, Wexler, *supra* note 135, at 543, discussing Morris's near-exclusive concern with murder cases.
283. *See* Morris, *Race and Crime: What Evidence Is There That Race Influences Results in the Criminal Justice System?* 72 JUDICATURE 111 (1985) (characterizing myths as "balderdash").
284. Morris, *supra* note 278, at 522.
285. Bonnie & Morris, *supra* note 281, at 127 (remarks of Prof. Morris).
286. *Id.*
287. *See supra* note 260.

In the recent Jeffrey Dahmer trial, for instance, the prosecutor—
apparently without defense objection—relied on a metaphor like the
"lemon squeezer"[288] in an effort to discredit a defense psychiatrist.
According to a press account:

> Holding his hands out as if to strangle the defense psychiatrist, [the
> district attorney] roared, "This was not a fish he choked the life out of, was
> it, doctor? It was a human being."[289]

Had Wisconsin "abolished" the insanity defense leaving only a
mens rea exception, then this question would have been appropriate.
In an ALI jurisdiction such as Wisconsin,[290] however, the question
was, at least theoretically, objectionable. More importantly, it probably captured precisely the flavor sought by the prosecutor: notwithstanding the correct substantive standard, only *if* Dahmer *had*
thought that the victim was a fish (or some other non-human entity),
should the jury then consider the propriety of an insanity acquittal. If
he had not, then conviction should follow (as it did).

The elegance and academic underpinnings of much of the opposition to the insanity defense[291] should not mask a simple reality: the
only significant influence in this country—either rejecting a "liberal"
test or adopting a "conservative" test—over the past forty years has
been that of prosecutors, district attorneys, and their legislative allies.[292] While the language and supporting arguments of scholars and
theoreticians as diverse as Thomas Szasz, Norval Morris and Jay

---

288. *See supra* note 270.
289. Howlett, *The Dahmer Debate // Sanity Trial Raises Legal Questions*, USA Today
     (Feb. 10, 1992), at 3A (full text available on NEXIS).
290. *See e.g.*, State v. Bergenthal, 47 Wis. 2d 668, 178 N.W. 2d 16 (1970), *cert. den.*,
     402 U.S. 972 (1971); Steele v. State, 97 Wis. 2d 72, 294 N.W. 2d 2 (1980).
291. Subsequently, I will discuss separately the opposition of Dr. Abraham Halpern,
     the most articulate abolitionist among forensic psychiatrists. Dr. Halpern has
     for many years been an implacable foe of the defense, and his contributions to
     the ongoing debate have been extraordinary. I believe, though, that his position
     depends implicitly on a strong system of jury nullification (*see e.g.*, Halpern,
     Uncloseting the Jury—A Justly Acquitted Doctrine, 52 PSYCHIATRIC ANN. 144
     (1980)), and I thus discuss his views in connection with jury issues. *See generally*
     infra chapter 6 D 6 a (1).
292. *See generally*, Gray, *The Insanity Defense: Historical Development and Con-
     temporary Relevance*, 10 AM. CRIM. L. REV. 559, 576 (1972), discussing
     prosecutorial distortion of "the real issues involved in the determination of
     criminal responsibility;" *see generally*, Sherry, *The Politics of Law Reform*, 21
     AM. J. COMPAR. L. 201, 212-17 (1973); Allen, *Criminal Law and the Modern
     Consciousness: Some Observations on Blameworthiness*, 44 TENN. L. REV. 735,
     752 (1977).

Goldstein have been cited to bolster their arguments, there can be no doubt that insanity defense "law reform agendas" have been animated by one and only one significant motivation:[293] to lessen the number of criminal defendants—the non-"truly crazy"—who can avail themselves of a non-responsibility defense, and, simultaneously, to increase the number of convictions and insure longer and more punitive terms of imprisonment.[294]

D. The Hinckley Verdict "Fit"

By its very nature, the Hinckley case was guaranteed to stoke the fires of the abolitionist movement. It left no question that, in a controversial case, political pragmatism would "trump" clinical needs.[295] In his analysis of the operation of the insanity defense system in Missouri, John Petrila, former director of that state's Forensic Services Office, thus charged forensic administrators with por-

---

293. Professors Wexler and Winick have raised the important question of the therapeutic jurisprudence implications of insanity defense abolition. *See* Wexler & Winick, *Therapeutic Jurisprudence and Criminal Justice Mental Health Issues*, 16 MENT. & PHYS. DIS. L. REP. 225, 228 (1992); *see also,* Wexler, *Criminal Commitment Contingency Structures*, in THERAPEUTIC JURISPRUDENCE: THE LAW AS A THERAPEUTIC AGENT 23 (D. Wexler ed. 1990), and Fein, *How the Insanity Acquittal Retards Treatment*, in *id.* at 49. I subsequently will discuss the role of therapeutic jurisprudence in this inquiry; *see generally infra* chapter 9 B.

294. *See* Keilitz, *supra* note n. 97 (*citing* Strasser, *Reagan to Resubmit Meese Nomination*, NAT'L L.J., Dec. 24, 1984, at 3, col. 8):

   In a chapter on the workings of the U.S. Department of Justice the influential conservative Heritage Foundation called for the elimination of the insanity defense as a priority in the criminal justice field in 1985.

295. Thus, one critic has noted, "The disrepute into which the insanity defense appears to be falling has profound impact upon both the criminal justice system and the mental health system." Where an insanity defense acquittal appears to reflect "official permissiveness," the public's faith in the judicial system may be further disturbed. Prevost, *Foreward*, in A REPORT TO GOV. HUGH L. CAREY ON THE INSANITY DEFENSE IN NEW YORK 1, 4 (1978) (NY REPORT), as quoted in Sherman, *Guilty But Mentally Ill: A Retreat From the Insanity Defense*, 7 AM. J. L. & MED. 237, 251 n. 111 (1981). Such a loss of faith has profound implications for the system's "gatekeepers" who must enforce the system's values, and becomes explicitly more problematic in controversial cases, such as John W. Hinckley's. *Id.* at 252 & *id.* n. 113.
   On the need for integration between the justice and mental health systems, *see e.g.*, Casey, Keilitz & Hafemeister, *Toward an Agenda for Reform of Justice and Mental Health Systems Interactions*, 16 LAW & HUM. BEHAV. 107 (1992).

traying the defense as "the last refuge of sociopathic individuals who manipulate mental health-criminal justice systems in order to escape confinement in a penitentiary:"[296]

> Administrators found that this view is often held by staff charged with caring for forensic patients. The author has been assured on several occasions by staff "there isn't one of them (in the state's maximum security unit) that's really crazy."[297]

Political abolitionists also focus on a defendant's moral weakness in "becoming insane." One of the virulent myths of "sanism" is that "Mentally disabled persons simply don't try hard enough. They give in too easily to their basest instincts and do not exercise appropriate self-restraint."[298] Thus, the Hinckley prosecutor suggested to the jury that "if Hinckley had emotional problems they were largely his own fault."[299] Similarly, it was not error for a trial judge to refuse to excuse a juror who felt a defendant would be responsible for his acts as long as he "wanted to do them."[300] Commentators argue that failure to take prescribed neuroleptic medication should be barred from raising the defense.[301] "Fault" is a significant element in our assessing the value of insanity defenses, and Hinckley—to many—fell clearly on the far side of the fault line.

Hinckley's case, of course, was also saddled down by an excess of political baggage. As I have already pointed out, federal prosecutors frequently look to potential political controversy, and not to clinical conditions, in assessing whether to oppose conditional release.[302] An NIMH special report thus stressed, discussing procedures at the hospital where Hinckley is housed, "From the perspective of the Hospital, *in controversial cases such as Hinckley*, the U.S. Attorney's Office *can be counted upon* to oppose *any* conditional release

---

296. Petrila, *The Insanity Defense and Other Mental Health Dispositions in Missouri*, 5 INT'L J. L. & PSYCHIATRY 81, 91 (1982).
297. *Id.* at 91 n. 36.
298. Perlin, *supra* note 80, at 396.
299. Balkin, *The Rhetoric of Responsibility*, 76 VA. L. REV. 197, 238 (1990).
300. State v. Duckworth, 496 So. 2d 624, 635 (La. App. 1986). *See also*, People v. Dobben, 187 Mich. App. 462, 468 N.W. 2d 527, 532 (1991) (prosecutor's charge in summation that defendant's drug use was a "triggering factor instigating his mental illness" two years prior to criminal act did not violate defendant's right to a fair trial; conviction reversed on other grounds).
301. *See e.g.*, Slodov, *Criminal Responsibility and the Noncompliant Psychiatric Offender: Risking Madness*, 40 CASE W. RES. L. REV. 271 (1989-90).
302. *See supra* chapter 2 A 2 b (2), at note 36.

recommendation."[303] The bureaucratic issue is not one of moral philosophy, of treatment philosophy, of clinical conditions: it is the *political* reality that the government will be *sure* to oppose release of a "controversial" patient.[304]

The movement to abolish the insanity defense has largely been a symbolic one, albeit a symbolic one with "potentially pervasive consequences."[305] After the Hinckley acquittal, the Reagan Administration called loudly for abolition, but dropped that position when it became clear that the relevant professional groups presented a "nearly unified front" in urging Congress to retain the defense in some form.[306] This willingness to accept modified retention, of course, was dissonant with the earlier calls by the Reagan Justice Department for abolition; its quiet change in position[307] ensured that the symbolic call for abolition would be the lasting public image.

The intellectual vacuity among politically-motivated abolitionists is illuminated by the striking lack of interest that has been shown in the empirical data in those jurisdictions where abolition has been attempted. The *mens rea* reduction in Montana, Idaho and Utah[308] should provide an "ideal opportunity" for emulating the "laboratory" conditions envisioned by Justice Brandeis in *New State Ice Co. v. Liebmann*.[309] It is ironic that so little attention has been paid to the

---

303. *Final Report of the National Institute of Mental Health (NIMH) Ad Hoc Forensic Advisory Panel*, 12 MENT. & PHYS. DIS. L. REP. 77, 96 (1988) (emphasis added).

304. *But see* 18 U.S.C. §4243(f) (1988) (mandating that when the director of a facility housing a person hospitalized following an insanity acquittal determines that the person has sufficiently recovered so that his outright or conditional release "would no longer create a substantial risk of bodily injury to another," he "*shall* promptly file a certificate to that effect with the [committing] court," at which time the court shall either order discharge or, upon motion by the government, schedule a release hearing) (emphasis added). This statutory section was enacted as part of the Insanity Defense Reform Act.

305. Schulhofer, *supra* note 111, at 1292.

306. Perlin, *supra* note 38, at 860.

307. *See* 3 M.L. PERLIN, *supra* note 1, §15.39, at 398-99.

308. *See supra* chapter 2 A 2 d, text accompanying n. 72.

309. 285 U.S. 262, 311 (1932) (Brandeis, J., dissenting) ("A single courageous state may, if its citizens choose, serve as a laboratory; and try novel social and economic experiments to the rest of the country"). *See e.g.*, Keilitz, *supra* note 69, at 304-6 decrying the "conspicuous...absence of such data"); *see also*, Brooks, *The Merits of Abolishing the Insanity Defense*, 477 ANNALS 125, 135 (1985) (recommending experimentation with and study of the *mens rea* alternative).

experiences in the *mens rea* states,[310] especially since, empirically, there has been some evidence that, as a result of the new legislation, there may be "more claims of mental disturbance" rather than fewer.[311]

Henry Steadman and his colleagues are now beginning to publish data giving us some inklings as to what actually *happens* when abolition is attempted.[312] Their research reveals that, basically, "abolition" in Montana was a pretext. First, "abolition" had no meaningful statistical impact on the number of defendants pleading NGRI.[313] Defendants continued to allege that they lacked the requisite mens rea for criminal responsibility.[314] Although the success rate dropped precipitously, Steadman speculates that it was perhaps "still advantageous" for defendants to raise the plea.[315]

Perhaps the explanation comes in another major research finding. Defendants who previously would have been found NGRI are now found incompetent to stand trial.[316] Two-thirds of these were subsequently committed indefinitely to state hospitals where they were frequently treated on the same units as patients who had been found NGRI prior to abolition "reform." In short, "the insanity statutes were reformed, but the detention system was not."[317] It is certainly possible that some of the post-"abolition" pleas were the result of defense counsel wanting to "flag" for the court that the

---

310. *But see*, Geis & Meier, *Abolition of the Insanity Plea in Idaho: A Case Study*, 477 ANNALS 72, 74 (1985) (evaluating the Idaho legislation in light of that state's "highly conservative" population "notably hostile to mental health concepts," and "wont to proclaim that the mental health movement was dominated by left-wingers"). *Compare* Steadman, Callahan, Robbins & Morrisey, *Maintenance of an Insanity Defense Under Montana's "Abolition" of the Insanity Defense*, 146 AM. J. PSYCHIATRY 357 (1989) (Steadman et al.) (discussing forces motivating similar legislation in Montana).

311. Keilitz, *supra* note 69, at 305. *See also*, T. MAEDER, CRIME AND MADNESS 157 (1985) (discussing U.S. Senator Howell Heflin's fears that the *mens rea* test could greatly *increase* psychiatric testimony).

312. H. STEADMAN, REFORMING, *supra* note 97, at 214-51.

313. *Id.* at 213-14.

314. *Id.* at 214.

315. Only five of 466 insanity pleaders in post-abolition Montana were found NGRI. *Id.* at 218.

316. On the incompetency process, *see* 3 M.L. PERLIN, *supra* note 4, chapter 14. On the pretextual use of this process, *see* Perlin, *Pretexts and Mental Disability Law: The Case of Competency*, 47 U. MIAMI L. REV. (1993) (in press).

317. Steadman et al., *supra* note 310, at 359; H. STEADMAN, REFORMING, *supra* note 97, at 220-22.

defendants were seriously mentally ill and in need of psychiatric hospitalization. This is precisely the same strategy often employed by counsel in jurisdictions where the defense has not been abolished.[318]

It is not yet clear what impact Steadman's empirical break-through will have on politically-motivated abolitionist measures. If the Montana experience is a representative one, then the full measure of the abolition charade is clear. The defense is "abolished" in name, but the plea is entered for pretextual reasons. Severely mentally ill criminal defendants are treated in the same wards of the same forensic hospitals to which they would have been sent had they been found NGRI. This suggests the meretriciousness of much of the politically-based abolition movement: voters are being told that their representatives are "doing something" about the crime problem, but only the labels describing the patients' forensic status change.

In short, the "abolitionist movement" is a textbook example of the way that insanity defense mythology and opportunistic politicians have helped corrupt our jurisprudence. Empiricism, science and philosophy are subverted; old shibboleths are repeated, and little changes. In order to understand how this can be, I will shift my attention now to the way that the legal system generally treats psychodynamic principles, and how the ambivalence of this treatment comes to a head in our treatment of the insanity defense, of insanity defense pleaders, and of other mentally disabled individuals in the criminal justice system.

---

318. See *supra* text accompanying note 186, and Pasework & Craig, *supra* note 186.

CHAPTER

. . .

4

The Law and
Psychodynamic Principles

A. Introduction

The legal system's continuing and unremitting failure to take
seriously either empirical or scientific data about virtually all aspects
of the insanity defense reflects its ongoing and generalized rejection
of psychodynamic principles as a means of explaining human behavior.[1] Three aspects of this rejection are especially important: the roots
of the legal system's profound ambivalence about psychiatry and
toward psychiatrists, the importance of punishment to the Anglo-
American systems of criminal justice, and the specific, obsessive fears
that are regularly uncabined in response to any suggestion that psychodynamic principles can be of assistance to the law in its disposition of cases of mentally disabled offenders.[2]

---

1. *See* Comment, *Legal and Psychiatric Concepts and the Use of Psychiatric
   Evidence in Criminal Trials*, 73 CALIF. L. REV. 411, 428 (1985): "[L]egal
   decisionmakers behave rather like scientists faced with disruption of an imperfect
   but functioning paradigm: they find ways to limit the defense, and to preserve
   the ability of law to achieve its policy goals."
2. This rejection reveals itself in at least five different ways: in the way the legal
   system expresses its feelings about insanity defense pleaders, in the persistence
   of insanity defense myths (specifically, the overarching fear that the presence of
   the insanity defense allows responsible defendants to "beat the rap" through
   "bought" testimony adduced by "shifty" lawyers), in the lack of consciousness
   on the part of legal decisionmakers as to the psychodynamic principles which

B. The Law's Ambivalence About Psychiatry

1. Introduction

The law remains "paradoxically fascinated and repelled" and "overwhelmingly ambivalent" about psychiatry's role in the adjudicative process.[3] This frequently noted tragic ambivalence is most simply reflected in the courts' frantic desires to have mental health experts testify as to future dangerousness (an expertise which psychiatrists themselves freely acknowledge they do not have) and to "take the weight" on difficult decisions as to commitment or release (especially in the cases of individuals hospitalized following insanity acquittals),[4] while, at the same time, characterizing psychiatry as "the ultimate wizardry" and psychiatrists as "medicine m[e]n" or "shamanistic wizards."[5] This leads to another ambivalence: the conflict between the aid that the legal system desires from psychiatrists and

---

help animate their behavior, in the way the political system has shaped the insanity defense critique (exemplified most starkly and most recently by the Congressional hearings called in the wake of the Hinckley acquittal), and in the way that social science data of all sorts are flatly rejected in insanity defense jurisprudence.

3.   See e.g., Perlin, *The Supreme Court, the Mentally Disabled Criminal Defendant, and Symbolic Values: Random Decisions, Hidden Rationales, or "Doctrinal Abyss?"* 29 ARIZ. L. REV. 1, 86-87 (1987); Zilboorg, *Misconceptions of Legal Insanity*, 9 AM. J. ORTHOPSYCHIATRY 540, 543 (1939) (ideological attitudes of law and psychiatry, while both motivated by "deepest and greatest altruistic feelings, appear in practice extremely antagonistic;" relationship between law and psychiatry marked by "mutual suspicion and even open hostility"); for a psychological analysis of why lawyers resist psychology, *see* P. REIWALD, SOCIETY AND ITS CRIMINALS 21-41 (T. James trans. 1950). But see, Sadoff, Insanity: Evolution of a Medicolegal Concept, 9 TRANSACTIONS & STUD. COLL. PHYSICIANS PHILADELPHIA 237, 240 (1987) ("Historically, medical writers and legal scholars dovetailed their writings and influenced each others' thinking"); Smith, Scientific Proof and Relations of Law and Medicine, 10 U. CHI. L. REV. 243 (1943) ("The anvil of law has always responded to the striking iron of science").

4.   See e.g., Barefoot v. Estelle, 463 U.S. 880 (1983); Perlin, *supra* note 3, at 7-12; Wasyliw, Cavanagh & Rogers, *Beyond the Scientific Limits of Expert Testimony*, 13 BULL. AM. ACAD. PSYCHIATRY & L. 147, 152 (1985) ("Public decisions are often so close to impossible that those charged with making them are more than anxious to pass their burdens to unwilling experts"); Suarez, *A Critique of the Psychiatrist's Role as Expert Witness*, 12 J. FORENS. SCI. 172 (1967) ("The judicial system lumps the conflicts, needs and fears of its terrible responsibility on psychiatry").

5.   Perlin, *supra* note 3, at 87.

its fear that, as a result of the acceptance of that aid, an unacceptable amount of power over legal decision making will accrete to psychiatrists.[6]

This ambivalence is even more ironic when we juxtapose it with what we now know about juror behavior. Jurors "do not appreciate the tentativeness of much scientific work" and thus privilege the ability to reach "firm conclusions" as more important in determining believability than either a witness's impressive educational credentials or professional reputation.[7] This rejection of expert ambivalence further confounds the other ambivalences under discussion.

This ambivalence permeates mental disability law. Psychiatric expertise is valued when it serves a social control function of the law (such as in testifying in involuntary civil commitment proceedings in support of commitment applications) but is devalued when it appears to subvert that purpose (such as in testifying in insanity defense cases in support of a defendant's non-responsibility claim).[8] It is manifested in the teleological way that judges deal with social science evidence in mental disability law cases.[9]

Justice Thomas's recent opinion in *Foucha v. Louisiana*[10]—dissenting from an opinion declaring unconstitutional a state law allowing for the continued commitment of NGRI acquittees who are no longer mentally ill—is a textbook example of this sort of judicial behavior. There, he based much of his conclusion that such retention is constitutionally permissible on a variety of sources, including the 1962 commentary to the Model Penal Code, a 1933 text by Henry Weihofen, and a 1956 Supreme Court opinion that had stressed psychiatry's "uncertainty of diagnosis."[11]

---

6. *See e.g.*, Freckleton, *Court Experts, Assessors, and the Public Interest*, 8 INT'L J. L. & PSYCHIATRY 161, 161-62 (1986). *Compare* Sallett, *After Hinckley: The Insanity Defense Reexamined*, 94 YALE L.J. 1545, 1553 (1985) ("It is possible that opposition to verdicts such as that in the Hinckley trial springs, at least in part, from widespread societal distrust of psychiatry...").

7. Champagne, Shuman & Whitaker, *Expert Witnesses in the Courts: An Empirical Examination*, 76 JUDICATURE 5, 8 (1992).

8. *See* J. LA FOND & M. DURHAM, BACK TO THE ASYLUM: THE FUTURE OF MENTAL HEALTH LAW AND POLICY 156 (1992).

9. *See generally*, Perlin & Dorfman, *Sanism, Social Science, and the Development of Mental Disability Law Jurisprudence*, 11 BEHAV. SCI. & L. 47 (1993); *see generally infra* chapter 8 D.

10. 112 S. Ct. 1780 (1992).

11. *See id.* at 1797, 1801 (Thomas, J., dissenting) (relying on, *inter alia*, H. WEIHOFEN, INSANITY AS A DEFENSE IN CRIMINAL LAW 294-332 (1933) (for the

His opinion is astounding. It relies on legal scholarship that predates (by ten to forty years) the Supreme Court's application of the due process clause to cases involving the institutionalization of mentally disabled defendants.[12] It endorses a mid-1950s characterization of psychiatric imprecision in diagnosis to suggest that psychiatry is so inexact that the court should discount expert testimony saying that an individual once acquitted on grounds of insanity is not mentally ill; yet—no doubt because it fits well with his *a priori* position on the case—he finds that psychiatric predictions of dangerousness are sufficiently reliable to require the acquittee's future institutionalization.[13] He privileges psychiatry where it supports him, and denigrates it when it does not.

Similarly, the Supreme Court's majority opinion in *Colorado v. Connelly*—upholding the voluntariness of a confession made by a severely mentally disabled criminal defendant (who followed the "voice of God" that directed him to either confess to a killing or to commit suicide)[14]—makes it clear that "'free will' is simply not a topic for constitutional consideration."[15]

In rejecting a constitutional link between the defendant's state of mind and the voluntariness of his confession in a case where the only expert witness had testified unequivocally that the defendant was "incapable" of making a "free decision" about waiving his *Miranda* rights,[16] the Court chose to ignore the reality of police and prosecutorial practice that had recognized the limiting impact of mental condition on such a waiver as well as the well-developed body of scientific studies documenting the disabling effects of such mental conditions on *Miranda* waiver.[17] The refusal of the court to consider

---

proposition that there is a long history of states providing for the continued institutionalization of dangerous insanity acquittees), and Greenwood v. United States, 350 U.S. 366, 375 (1956) (on the "uncertainty of diagnosis")).

12. *See* Jackson v. Indiana, 406 U.S 715 (1972).

13. Perlin & Dorfman, *supra* note 9, at 60-62.

14. 479 U.S. 157, 161 (1986).

15. Perlin, *Criminal Confessions and the Mentally Disabled:* Colorado v. Connelly *and the Future of Free Will,* in CRIMINAL COURT CONSULTATION 157, 167 (R. Rosner & R. Harmon eds. 1989).

16. *See Connelly,* 479 U.S. at 187 (Brennan, J., dissenting).

17. *See* 3 M.L. PERLIN, MENTAL DISABILITY LAW: CIVIL AND CRIMINAL §16.14, at 472 (1989), *citing, inter alia,* F. INBAU, CRIMINAL INTERROGATION AND CONFESSIONS 57 (3d ed. 1986), and Wulach, *The Assessment of Competency to Waive* Miranda *Rights,* 9 J. PSYCHIATRY & L. 209 (1981). On the reasons why some defendants confess falsely, *see* Gudjonsson, *The Psychology of False*

the defendant's free will is a clear reflection of its inability to grasp psychodynamic explanations for human behavior.

This type of decision making reflects "ambiguous...feelings in need of self-rationalization: unconscious feelings of awe, of fear, of revulsion, of wonder."[18] It may also reflect a profound discomfort on the part of judges hearing cases involving aberrant behavior.[19] There are at least three separate (but interconnected) elements in this sort of decision making: the view of psychiatry as "soft," exculpatory, and confusing; the view of psychiatry as an "invisible" and "imprecise" science; and the view of psychiatrists as "wizards" or charlatans. It also reads history to reveal a record of empirical psychiatric error (invariably focusing on the numerically-insignificant "false negatives") in the areas of diagnosis, release decisions and dangerousness evaluations, and a tableau of demeaning and circus-like "battles of the experts" in trials where psychiatric evidence is a critical issue.

2. Psychiatry as "Soft," "Exculpatory," and "Confusing"

The legal critique of psychiatry is bottomed on the innate feeling that psychiatry is inappropriately "soft" or unduly exculpatory, as reflected in what is seen as psychiatrists' "peculiarly tolerant attitude toward criminal behavior, which is born out of his recognition of the welter of antisocial impulses occurring in noncriminal individuals."[20]

Confessions, 57 MEDICO-LEG. J. 93 (1989); Gudjonsson, *Suggestibility and Compliance Among Alleged False Confessors and Resisters in Criminal Trials*, 31 MED., SCI., & L. 147 (1991).

18. Perlin, *The Supreme Court, the Mentally Disabled Criminal Defendant, Psychiatric Testimony in Death Penalty Cases, and the Power of Symbolism: Dulling the Ake in Barefoot's Achilles Heel*, 3 N.Y.L. SCH. HUM. RTS. ANN. 91, 168 (1985); *see generally*, Goldstein & Katz, *Abolish the Insanity Defense—Why Not?* 72 YALE L.J. 853 868-69 (1963) (discussing public's ambivalence toward mentally disabled criminal defendant); *see also*, Roth, *Preserve but Limit the Insanity Defense*, 58 PSYCHIATRIC Q. 91, 93 (1986-87) ("It is difficult to educate the public about psychiatry and the Insanity Defense within a climate of fear and violence, where conscious and unconscious associations inevitably intrude").

19. *See e.g.*, Matter of Clements, 440 N.W. 2d 133, 137 (Minn. App. 1989) (Irvine, J., dissenting), *review den.* (1989) ("It is undisputed that for at least 10 years, [the defendant] has engaged in conduct that makes a *normal person's skin crawl* (exposing himself in public while masturbating). It is easy to lose one's objectivity while dealing with such a highly emotional situation") (emphasis added); *compare* People v. P.T., 233 Ill. App. 3d 386, 599 N.E. 2d 79 (1992) (evidence that defendant had had sexual contact with a cow 30 years ago admissible in trial charging defendant with incestuous child molestation).

20. Guttmacher, *The Psychiatric Approach to Crime and Correction*, 23 LAW &.

According to popular columnist Charles Krauthammer in his critique of post-traumatic stress disorder (PTSD)-based defenses, "some of these newfangled psychiatric syndromes are so elastic that one can always find an expert witness willing (for a fee) to pin an extenuating diagnosis on just about anybody."[21]

Psychiatry, it is believed, expands the concept of illness "continually at the expense of the concept of moral failure," and interjects improper "rehabilitative impulses" which doom the legal system to "contradiction, confusion and frequent public criticism." For this reason, "many people simply do not trust psychiatrists with anything so obvious as the determination of criminal responsibility," while others insist on "near total lack of comprehension" on a defendant's part if the insanity standard is to be met.[22] The psychiatric suggestion that disability less than an illness "obviously reflective of psychotic psychopathology" or "a severe psychotic disorientation" might be exculpatory has simply traditionally been rejected by the law and by the general public as well.[23] It is not coincidental that, when President

---

CONTEMP. PROBS. 633, 633 (1958). *See also*, M. GUTTMACHER, THE ROLE OF PSYCHIATRY IN CRIMINAL LAW 95 (1968) (urging retention of the insanity defense because it "gives the criminal law a heart"); Halleck, *A Critique of Current Psychiatric Roles in the Legal process*, 1966 WIS. L. REV. 379, 395 ("The most important reason for psychiatric participation in the criminal trial is humanitarian zeal to temper the harshness of punishment").

   It is a serious mistake to infer from these statements that all psychiatrists (especially all forensic psychiatrists) endorse these sentiments. *See e.g.*, J. ROBITSCHER, THE POWERS OF PSYCHIATRY 24, 262 (1980) (discussing prosecution-minded psychiatrists); *see supra* chapter 2 C 1, notes 186-89.

21. Krauthammer, *Jeffrey Dahmer's Ghastly, Pitiless Cruelty Is Proof of Evil, Not of Madness*, Houston Chronicle (Feb. 11, 1992), at A12 (full text available on NEXIS); *see also*. Perkins v. General Motors Corp., 709 F. Supp. 1487, 1495 (W.D. Mo. 1989), *aff'd sub. nom.* Perkins v. Spivey, 911 F. 2d 22 (8th Cir. 1990), *cert. den.*, 111 S. Ct. 1309 (1991) (labeling PTSD the "diagnosis of choice"); *but see*, Appelbaum et al., *Use of Post Traumatic Stress Disorder to Support an Insanity Defense*, 150 AM. J. PSYCHIATRY 229 (1993) (PTSD diagnosis present in only .3 percent of insanity defense pleas).

22. Wootton, *Sickness or Sin?* 159 TWENTIETH CENTURY 433, 434 (1956); Watson, *On the Preparation and Use of Psychiatric Expert Testimony: Some Suggestions in an Ongoing Controversy*, 6 BULL. AM. ACAD. PSYCHIATRY & L. 226, 226 (1978); Comment, *The Psychiatrist's Role in Determining Accountability for Crimes: The Public Anxiety and an Increasing Expertise*, 52 MARQ. L. REV. 380, 385 (1969); Hans & Slater, *"Plain Crazy:" Lay Definitions of Legal Insanity*, 7 INT'L J. L. & PSYCHIATRY 105, 111 (1984).

23. Arens, Granfield & Susman, *Jurors, Jury Charges and Insanity*, 14 CATH. U. L. REV. 1, 9 (1965); *see e.g.*, A. GOLDSTEIN, THE INSANITY DEFENSE 42 (1967) (behavior not regarded by public as reflecting severe mental disorder without

Reagan warned in 1986 of the dire consequences that would flow from the impending Democratic control of the Senate, he spoke indirectly to this fear: "We don't need a bunch of sociology majors on the bench."[24]

To some extent, the public's attitude partially mimics Justice Stewart's famous *dictum* in *Jacobellis v. Ohio*:[25] they "know [insanity] when they see it."[26] Beyond this, the law is also convinced that psychiatrists are *not* better in finding it than are members of the lay public.[27] Chief Justice Rehnquist's allegedly common-sensical vision of severe mental disability is a near-perfect exemplar of the public's views.[28]

---

breakdown of intellect, serious loss of self-control, and markedly inappropriate behavior, conditions "reminiscent of the major characteristics of psychosis").

Professor Goldstein further suggests, *see id.* at 26, that, if the expert does his "educative job" well, jurors will learn that "the psychotic is much less 'crazy' than the general public imagines him to be." On the other hand, I think it can be fairly argued that members of the public has a major emotional investment in insuring that the psychotic be seen as "truly crazy" so as to distance themselves from such individuals. Also, *see generally*, Perlin, *On "Sanism,"* 46 SMU L. Rev. 373 (1992) (our attitudes toward mentally disabled persons reflect irrational and prejudiced views); Perlin & Dorfman, *supra* note 9 (same).

24. Rowland, Songer & Carp, *Presidential Effects on Criminal Justice Policy in the Lower Federal Courts: The Reagan Judges*, 22 Law & Soc'y Rev. 191, 194 (1988). *Compare* House v. State, 1993 WL 48244 (Fla. Dist. App. 1993), at *1 (prosecutor justified peremptory challenge to juror on grounds that "someone who works in mental health would be more liberal than conservative, therefore I struck her") (conviction reversed; alleged rationale was pretext for impermissible race-based challenge).

25. 378 U.S. 184, 197 (1964) (Stewart, J., concurring).

26. Writing in an entirely different science-and-law context, Prof. Nancy Rhoden characterized Justice Stewart's test as a combination of "common sense plus social values." *See* Rhoden, *Trimesters and Technology: Revamping* Roe v. Wade, 95 Yale L.J. 639, 691-92 (1986).

27. Thus, Dr. Andrew Watson quotes an 1843 broadside: "Doctors were not subpoena'd, to shield of knave from common justice, righteous retribution—by flimsy barefaced artifice to save a brutal murderer from execution—to prove him mad, who'd ne'er been heard to rave, or labour under mental prostitution; to prove him mad, by theories too wild, too weak, too silly, to deceive a child." Watson, *supra* note 21, at 245 n.1 (quoting *Monomania*, an 1843 broadside, written by "Dry Nurse").

28. *See* Perlin, *supra* note 3, at 82-83; Perlin, *supra* note 23, at 401; *see generally infra* chapter 4 D. *See* D. Bazelon, Questioning Authority: Justice and Criminal Law 6 (1988): "As H.L. Mencken once said, for every complex problem in our society, there is a solution that is simple, plausible—and wrong." *Compare* M. Moore, Law and Psychiatry: Rethinking the Relationship 244 (1984) (discussing the "popular moral notion of mental illness").

Finally, the legal system, reflecting community custom and consciousness, is dissatisfied with psychiatry because it is perceived as simply too confusing, both internally (reflected by concern that psychiatrists have never been able to come to accord on the meaning of such terms as responsibility, mental illness, or dangerousness)[29] and externally (reflected by concern that psychiatry has never satisfactorily explained to the law why mentally disabled individuals act as they do).[30] Thus, Dr. Stephen Golding has recently noted perceptively:

> When the expert is asked covertly to relieve us of the moral burden of deciding who is on which side of a fuzzy boundary marked by considerable tension and conflict, we displace our anxiety, our punitiveness, and perhaps our resentment about being held to the moral standard and the psychological tension it causes.[31]

Similarly, Dr. Richard Rogers has noted, "Both attorneys and psychiatrists attempted to disavow the Hinckley case, seeking their *own* exculpation through proposals for a more restrictive standard."[32]

Perhaps this reflects the reality that mental disease *is* "too complex to 'make it simple and understandable to everyone just by inventing simple words or phrases to describe it.'"[33] Thus, in his role

---

29. See e.g., Quen, *Isaac Ray and Charles Doe, Responsibility and Justice,* in Law and the Mental Health Professions 237, 247 (1978): "As for the 'battle of the experts,' I confess that I've never been able to understand why, when psychiatrists disagree, it is proof positive that they don't know what they're talking about and it demeans our profession; while, when our Supreme Court decides the law of the land by a disagreement of 5-4, they are scholars dealing with profound, difficult, and complicated issues, and one must respect their differences in judgment."

30. For a helpful overview, *see* Bonnie & Slobogin, *The Role of Mental Health Professionals in the Criminal Process: The Case for Informed Speculation,* 66 Va. L. Rev. 427 (1980).

31. Golding, *Mental Health Professionals and the Courts: The Ethics of Expertise,* 13 Int'l J. L. & Psychiatry 281, 287 (1990); *see also,* Bazelon, *Veils, Values, and Social Responsibility,* 37 Am. Psychologist 115, 116 (1982) ("Too often a decision that should integrate expert diagnosis with public morality becomes, instead, little more than an official ratification of an overreaching and inadequately justified expert opinion on the ultimate issue").

32. Rogers, *Assessment of Criminal Responsibility: Empirical Advances and Unanswered Questions,* 15 J. Psychiatry & L. 73, 76 (1987).

33. Comment, *supra* note 22, at 395 (*quoting* 112 Cong. Rev. 2975 (1966) (remarks of Sen. Dodd). *Compare,* Scharf, *Send In the Clowns: The Image of Psychiatry During the Hinckley Trial,* 36 J. Commun. 80, 86 (1986) (testimony on enlarged ventricles in Hinckley trial held psychiatry up to public ridicule, lending itself easily to "visual satire"), and *see id.,* Figure 3 (reproducing editorial

as a court of appeals judge, former Chief Justice Burger observed,
"[N]o rule of law can possibly be sound or workable which is dependent upon the terms of another discipline whose members are in
profound disagreement about what those terms mean."[34]

3. Psychiatry as "Unseeable" and "Imprecise"

The legal system rejects psychodynamic principles because, unlike the case of the biological sciences, the subject matter of psychological sciences is not visible.[35] The imprecision of psychiatry and
psychology is seen as a given: judges should not "harbor the illusion"
that they will ever become "exact...: that is, precise, quantitative,
experimentally verified, and with substantially unanimous agreement
of all behavioral scientists as to observation and theory."[36]

Or, as stated by Dr. Jonas Rappeport, a leading forensic psychiatrist, "there is no scientifically valid method for measuring 'scientific
capacity' to appreciate criminality or to conform behavior."[37] Why,
Rappeport asks elsewhere, "are we embarrassed to let the public
know that the state of our art is such that we do not know everything
and that there are different schools and theories in psychiatry?"[38]
This observation has been used regularly as a major weapon in the

cartoon from the Chicago Sun-Times, featuring a witness, pointing to an
enlargement of the brain, and testifying, "...And this obsession with peanut
butter clearly affects the desire for disco music which obviously impairs the sense
of...," while the judge, *sotto vocce*, murmurs, "I'm beginning to hate these
insanity defenses").

34. Blocker v. United States, 288 F. 2d 853, 860 (D.C. Cir. 1961) (Burger, J.,
concurring). *Compare*, Wertham, *Psychoauthoritarianism and the Law*, 22 U.
CHI. L. REV. 336, 338 (1955) ("Judge Bazelon's legal openmindedness shows
that lawyers are eager to receive concrete psychiatric information. If we have
nothing to offer but psychological speculations and highhanded pronouncements, no progress is possible. Only if we overcome this psychoauthoritarianism
will psychiatry find its proper place in the courtroom, and play, as it should, a
strong but subordinate role").

35. Diamond & Louisell, *The Psychiatrist as an Expert Witness: Some Ruminations
and Speculations*, 63 MICH. L. REV. 1335, 1340 (1965); *see also*, Kuh, *The
Insanity Defense—An Effort to Combine Law and Reason*, 110 U. PA. L. REV.
771, 791 (1962) ("Mental disease or defect is most often unaccompanied by
tissue pathology").

36. Diamond & Louisell, *supra* note 35, at 1342.

37. Rappeport, *The Insanity Plea Scapegoating the Mentally Ill—Much Ado About
Nothing*, 24 SO. TEX. L.J. 687, 698 (1983).

38. Rappeport, *Ethics and Forensic Psychiatry*, in PSYCHIATRIC ETHICS 255, 259 (S.
Bloch & P. Chodoff eds. 1981); *see also*, Rappeport, *The Insanity Plea: Getting
Away With Murder?* 1983 MD. ST. MED. J. 1, 3.

judicial attack on psychiatric testimony.[39]

The perceived "invisibility" of mental illness is important for several reasons. It appears implicitly to lead to inexactitude in measurement and observation, an inexactitude which is contrasted with the "exact" "hard" sciences.[40] It gives courts the power to say, without citation to any authority, that it is less likely that medical patients will "fabricate descriptions of their complaints" than will "psychological patients."[41] This is especially troubling in the context of the "all or nothing" role of mental illness in determining responsibility questions;[42] thus, one of the important reasons that the diminished responsibility defense has traditionally been so unpopular is simply because it appears to establish a "middle ground" between responsibility and irresponsibility.[43] It is also dissonant with juror demand that expert witnesses reach "firm conclusions."[44]

It also appears to lead to a set of circumstances where the pivotal terminology and constructs are beyond the ken of jurors who rely on "ordinary common sense." The D.C. Circuit's decision to overrule *Durham*[45] and substitute the ALI-Model Penal Code insanity test in *United States v. Brawner*[46] underscores how insanity tests "cannot be the result of scientific analysis or objective judgment," but must be based "on the instinctive sense of justice of ordinary men."[47] This is

---

39. *See e.g.*, Suggs v. LaVallee, 570 F. 2d 1092, 1119 (2d Cir. 1978) (Kaufman, C.J., concurring) ("[P]sychiatry is at best an inexact science, if, indeed, it is a science, lacking the coherent set of proven underlying values necessary for ultimate decisions on knowledge and competence").

40. *See e.g.*, Nesbitt v. Community Health of South Dade, Inc., 467 So. 2d 711, 717 (Fla. Dist. App. 1985) (Jorgensen, J., concurring in part and dissenting in part) (physicians' diagnoses can be verified whereas psychiatrists' cannot (*quoting* Almy, *Psychiatric Testimony: Controlling the "Ultimate Wizardry" in Personal Injury Actions*, 19 *Forum* 223, 243 (1984)).

41. People v. LaLone, 432 Mich. 103, 437 N.W. 2d 611, 613 (1989), *reh. den.* (1989).

42. *See e.g.*, Robitscher & Haynes, *In Defense of the Insanity Defense*, 31 EMORY L.J. 9, 26-27 (1982).

43. *See* Arenella, *The Diminished Capacity and Diminished Responsibility Defenses: Two Children of a Doomed Marriage*, 77 COLUM. L. REV. 827, 849 (1977).

44. Champagne, Shuman & Whitaker, *supra* note 7, at 8.

45. Durham v. United States, 214 F. 2d 862, 874-75 (D.C. Cir. 1954); *see generally supra* chapter 3 A 1 c 2.

46. 471 F. 2d 969 (D.C. Cir. 1972). *See generally supra* chapter 3 A 1 c 3.

47. *Brawner*, 471 F. 2d at 977 n. 6.

all the more important in a universe where we know a lay juror "puts his own 'value' on [the defendant's] asocial behavior."[48]

Further, it clarifies why neurological and biological testimony as to brain disease (as reflected in tests such as CAT scans) may be embraced more readily by jurors and courts in sensational[49] and unknown[50] trials alike. Such "hard" data may simply be more persuasive to lay jurors than "soft" psychological explanations.[51] There is an interesting extra measure of ambivalence here: if Professor Rhoden was right when she asserts that the judicial process "cannot become value-free and remain judicial,"[52] it is ironic that the more purportedly "pure" scientific testimony (e.g., CAT scans) is embraced by jurors precisely because it appears to be "value-free," while the "softer" and less visible psychodynamic testimony—implicitly embodying "values" just as the legal system embodies values—is to be rejected.[53]

This also gives credence to what is basically a fundamentalist view: if we cannot see it, how can we be sure it exists, and if it does, how can we assess or measure it?[54] Here, psychiatric language serves an additional symbolic function: it reemphasizes to the judge and to

---

48. Comment, *supra* note 22, at 390.
49. *See generally,* L. CAPLAN, THE INSANITY DEFENSE AND THE TRIAL OF JOHN W. HINCKLEY, JR. 69-84 (1984); *see also,* Elliott, *An Introduction to Brain Syndromes,* 5 BEHAV. SCI. & L. 287, 305 (1987) ("Thus, a scan of the brain dome on would-be presidential assassin John Hinckley, showing enlarged ventricles, may have helped to persuade the jury that he indeed did have 'something wrong' with his brain"). *Compare* Scharf, *supra* note 33 (on jury's response to this testimony).
50. *See e.g.,* Commonwealth v. Monico, 396 Mass. 793, 488 N.E. 2d 1168, 1172-1173 (1986) (neurological testimony as to frontal lobe dysfunction sufficient basis for giving of insanity instructions); Boykin v. State, 149 Ga. App. 457, 254 S.E. 2d 457, 458 (App. 1979) (no failure to charge insanity based on delusional compulsion where witness "did not see the defendant suffering from any compulsion").
51. Elliott, *supra* note 49, at 305.
52. Rhoden, *supra* note 26, at 696.
53. *Id.* ("For while science seeks to be value free, law is the ultimate articulation of social values"). On the role of "scientific policymaking," *see e.g.,* Wells, *Scientific Policymaking and the Torts Revolution: The Revenge of the Ordinary Observer,* 26 GA. L. REV. 725 (1992); Alexander, *Takings, Narrative and Power,* 88 COLUM. L. REV. 1752, 1761 n. 54 (1988).
54. *Compare* People v. Guzman, 47 Cal. App. 3d 385, 121 Cal. Rptr. 69, 72 (1975): "How far should the courts go in allowing so-called scientific testimony, such as that of polygraph operators, hypnotists, 'truth drug' administrants, as well as purveyors of general psychological theories, to substitute for the commonsense of the jury?"

the lay juror how idiosyncratic the expert's views truly are. This stands in stark contrast with what Craig Haney has called the law's epistemological authoritarianism.[55] It is no surprise that an authoritarian system instinctively rejects the values of an "invisible" science.

Its concomitant imprecision and inexactitude stand in stark juxtaposition to the legal system's emphasis on certainty, an emphasis seen by some as "the primacy of the legal form in modern society."[56] Finally, even among mental health professionals, surveys seem to indicate that public attitudes are more favorable to the "strictly medical professions" than to those involving "psychologically designated roles."[57] This reflects the public's "commonsense" feeling that scientists specializing in an imprecise, invisible branch of study are simply not as trustworthy as those dealing with "objective" data.

On the other hand, it is not at all clear that "the precision and finality often associated with the x-ray and microscope" really is either precise or final.[58] As Dr. Rappeport reminds us, "[H]eart sounds may be interpreted differently by various physicians, and even the revered EKG may be interpreted differently,"[59] an observation amply borne out by the scientific literature.[60]

---

55. Haney, *Psychology and Legal Change: On the Limits of a Factual Jurisprudence*, 4 LAW & HUM. BEHAV. 159 n. 23 (1980), *quoting* J. SKLAR, LEGALISM: AN ESSAY ON LAW, MORALS AND POLITICS 10 (1964) ("law is itself a conservativizing ideal and institution").

56. Haney, *supra* note 55, at 165.

57. McGuire & Borowy, *Attitudes Toward Mental Health Professionals*, 10 PROF. PSYCHOLOGY 74, 78 (1979); *see also*, Nunnally & Kittross, *Public Attitudes Toward Mental Health Professions*, 13 AM. PSYCHOLOGIST 589 (1958).

58. Soboleff, *From M'Naghten to Durham and Beyond*, in CRIME AND INSANITY 136, 142 (R. Nice ed. 1958).

59. Rappeport, *supra* note 37, at 702.

60. *See e.g.*, Resnekov et al., *Task Force IV: Use of Electrocardiograms in Practice*, 41 AM. J. CARDIOLOGY 170 (1978); Patterson et al., *The Pre-Operative Electrocardiogram: An Assessment* 28 SCOT. MED. J. 116 (1983); Moorman et al., *The Yield of the Routine Admission Electrocardiogram: A Study in the General Medical Service*, 103 ANN. INTERN. MED. 590 (1985); Goldberger & O'Konski, *Utility of the Positive Electrocardiogram Before Surgery and On General Hospital Admission*, 105 ANNALS INTERNAL MED. 552 (1986).
  Similarly, there is significant parallel controversy in many other, seemingly more-tangible areas of medicine. *See e.g.*, Blery, Chastang & Gaudy, *Critical Assessment of Routine Pre-Operative Investigations*, 1 EFF. HEALTH CARE 111 (1983); Myers & Kuhn, *Informed Consent Issue in the Cardiac Transplantation Evaluation*, 16 BULL. AM. ACAD. PSYCHIATRY & L. 59 (1988); *see generally*, Lasagna, *Consensus Among Experts: The Unholy Grail*, 19 PERSPECTIVES IN BIOL. & MED. 537 (1976).
  The popular analysis rebutted by Rappeport is also to be found wanting by

Thus, the statement in a District of Columbia appellate opinion—that psychiatric predictivity of dangerousness is not unlike predictions made by oncologists as to the consequences of an untreated malignancy[61]—miscomprehends both the accuracy of psychiatric predictions and the false objectivity of much physiological medical data. Like many other sanist opinions in mental disability law, it is unsupported by either behavioral or scientific authority.[62]

4. Psychiatrists as Wizards or Charlatans

Perhaps no attitude contributes as much to the legal system's ambivalence about psychiatry and psychiatrists as the attribution of shamanistic or wizard-like qualities to psychiatric practitioners.[63] We have historically invested psychiatrists with "the special powers of reading and healing minds, powers that are magical," calling upon them as the "medicine men" who have the ability to heal our anxiety and take away our fears.[64]

There is significant support for the argument that the origins of law "[lay] buried deep in primitive religion and superstition."[65] When

---

recent research explorations of the wide range of physical diseases that masquerade as psychiatric disorders, leading to the discovery that physiological disorders such as endocrine disturbances, neurologic diseases, a variety of other tumors, tissue disorders, and electrolyte and fluid imbalances, epilepsy, cerebral tumor, head trauma, encephalitis, and cerebral arteriosclerosis may play an important part in creating disabling mental conditions. *See e.g.*, Peterson and Martin, *Organic Disease Presenting as a Psychiatric Syndrome*, 54 POSTGRAD. MED. 78 (1973); Hall et al., *Physical Illness Presenting as Psychiatric Disease*, 35 ARCH. GEN'L PSYCHIATRY 1315 (1978); Hall et al., *Physical Illness Manifesting as Psychiatric Disease II: Analysis of a State Hospital Inpatient Population*, 37 ARCH. GEN'L PSYCHIATRY 989 (1980), and *see id.* at 995 nn. 1-9; Martin, *A Brief Review of Organic Disease Masquerading as Functional Illness*, 34 HOSP. & COMMUN. PSYCHIATRY 328, 329-32 (1983).

61. *In re* Melton, 597 A. 2d 892, 898 (D.C. 1991) (involuntary civil commitment case).

62. *See* Perlin & Dorfman, *supra* note 9, at 55.

63. On shaminism and cultural relativism in the labelling of mental illness, *see* Kaplan, *The Mad and the Bad: An Inquiry Into the Disposition of the Criminally Insane*, 2 J. MED. & PHIL. 244, 257 (1977).

64. Walter Bromberg traces this investiture to the use by Bronze Aid shamans of magical aids. W. BROMBERG, FROM SHAMAN TO PSYCHOTHERAPIST: A HISTORY OF THE TREATMENT OF MENTAL ILLNESS 2-3 (1975 rev. ed.); Gunn, *An English Psychiatrist Looks at Dangerousness*, 10 BULL. AM. ACAD. PSYCHIATRY & L. 143, 147 (1982).

65. Loevinger, *Law and Science as Rival Systems*, 8 JURIMETRICS J. 63, 63 (1966); *see also*, Weyrauch, *Law as Mask—Legal Ritual and Relevance*, 66 CALIF. L.

a king decided a dispute by a sentence, "the judgment was assumed to be the result of direct [divine] inspiration."[66] Thus, legal constructs are metaphorically characterized as "magical tools for objectification which make persons and human emotions disappear," with masks serving to "objectify human conflict," as "tools for the enforcement of social policies," benefitting the legal system's peace-keeping functions.[67] Simply put, modern thought systems of our professions are not without ritual, magic, belief in incantations, and a certain a-mount of liturgy.[68]

It should be no surprise that there is such dissonance between this peace-keeping function and the apparent role of the insanity defense, especially given the traditional link seen between insanity and demonology.[69] While one of the main functions of the insanity defense is to act as a corrective where society abandons its need for

---

REV. 699, 716 (1978) (*citing* O.W. HOLMES, THE COMMON LAW 5 (1881)):

> The idea that our legal system has magical and religious roots and that there is an identity of functions between tribal masks and legal concepts and rules, is hard to accept because of our belief in the intrinsic rationality of modern law. But this idea is not very different from Holmes' observation that rules survive the forces that give rise to them

66. Loevinger, *supra* note 65, at 63-64, *quoting* H. MAINE, ANCIENT LAW 4 (3d Amer. ed. 1888).
67. Weyrauch, *supra* note 65, at 713-14 (discussing, in part, J. NOONAN, PERSONS AND MASKS OF THE LAW—CARDOZO, HOLMES, JEFFERSON, AND WYTHE AS MAKERS OF THE MASKS (1976); *see also*, Weyrauch, *Taboo and Magic in Law*, 23 STAN. L. REV. 782, 798 (1973) (reviewing A. EHRENZWEIG, PSYCHOANALYTIC JURISPRUDENCE (1971)):

> Magic attempts to control the environment primarily by manipulative and mechanistic incantations of words. Spells are cast by the uttering of words in an exacting ritual, any deviation from which destroys the spell and may turn it against the actor. In addition, magic establishes standards of *rationality,* channels behavior, and permits prediction of the future

68. Romanucci-Ross & Tancredi, *Psychiatry: The Law and Cultural Determinants of Behavior*, 9 INT'L J. L. & PSYCHIATRY 265, 265 (1986), *citing* L. ROMANUCCI-ROSS, D. MOERMAN & L. TANCREDI, THE ANTHROPOLOGY OF MEDICINE: FROM CULTURE TO METHOD 347-48 (1983).
69. *See e.g.*, Crotty, *The History of Insanity as a Defence to Crime in English Common Law*, 12 CALIF. L. REV. 105 (1924) ("The medieval notions that insanity was a visitation from the Almighty, or that the insane were possessed with demoniacal influences, were not confined to laymen alone, but were generally current among all classes"); S. HALLECK, PSYCHIATRY AND THE DILEMMAS OF CRIME: A STUDY OF CAUSES, PUNISHMENT AND TREATMENT, 210 (1967) (reviewing "demonological concept" of mental illness).

vengeful punishment,[70] it is paradoxical that the defense is perceived as most frequently being pled in cases of so-called "Oedipal crimes:"[71] crimes where the fear of punishment is ineffective to restrain an offender once there is an overpowering urge to commit the act.[72]

As John Gunn has noted:

> Man seems to need to invest his physician with superior, almost supernatural, powers....The psychiatrist is after all the medicine man who heals anxiety, the man we call upon to take away our fears. This is partly why we give him legal powers to protect us from insane violent people...
>
> It may be that man's inherent fear of irrationality is intimately mixed with an understandable fear of violence. If this be the case then it is a very short, although unwarranted step, to believe that all violence is a form of madness and alien.[73]

This mystification is two-sided. While it serves a preservative function in alleviating our fears of irrationality and of violence,[74] it also increases public skepticism of psychiatry. It does this for several reasons: it is frequently contrary to "ordinary common sense,"[75] it appears that it can be manipulated for ideological purposes,[76] it

---

70. Weyrauch, *supra* note 67, at 791, discussing A. EHRENZWEIG, *supra* note 67, at 230-41.

71. The image of President Reagan (a paradigmatic father figure) as a victim of an "Oedipal crime" cannot pass unnoticed. *See generally infra* chapter 6 C 2, chapter 7 B 2 c-d.

72. A. EHRENZWEIG, *supra* note 67, at 211-12, 220-21. "Oedipal crime" is meant to signify the severity of the crime and the emotional repulsion it causes. Weyrauch, *supra* note 67, at 790 n. 26.

73. Gunn, *supra* note 64, at 147. On the continued role of magic in the civil commitment process, *see* Méstrovic, *Magic and Psychiatric Commitment in India,* 9 INT'L J. L. & PSYCHIATRY 431 (1986).

74. Gunn, *supra* note 64, at 147.

75. *See generally infra* chapter 6 D; Sherwin, *Dialects and Dominance: A Study of Rhetorical Fields in the Law of Confessions,* 136 U. PA. L. REV. 729 (1988); Perlin, *Morality and Pretextuality, Psychiatry and Law: Of "Ordinary Common Sense," Heuristic Reasoning, and Cognitive Dissonance,* 19 BULL. AM. ACAD. PSYCHIATRY & L. 131 (1991); *see also,* Kaplan, *supra* note 63, at 254:

The fact that contemporary medicine (psychiatry) and psychology have generated models of man which vary from the original simple dichotomy of responsibility/ nonresponsbility articulated by the law creates an ideological tension with traditional legal notions concerning responsibility.

76. *See e g.,* Wasyliw, Cavanagh & Rogers, *supra* note 4, at 149 (discussing concern that expert testimony may reflect statements of personal or political beliefs

appears that the testifying psychiatrist too often abandons the role of "healer" (inappropriately becoming an advocate),[77] it appears to establish the "parameters of 'normal' for the mental sphere of life,"[78] and it appears to represent itself as being all-inclusive.[79] Psychiatrists thus appear to be engaged in a policy of "turf" annexation via their claims of expertise "in almost all areas of human behavior."[80]

The insanity defense has thus been traditionally seen as a part of the "complex of cultural forces that keep alive the moral lessons, and the myths, which are essential to the continued order of society,"[81] and as "a crucial prop in a 'public morality play,'" serving a "ritual function."[82] However, we must consider the reverse side of this facade as well. As I have already argued, public outrage at a Hinckley-type acquittal fills a special symbolic need: the need to expiate our-

---

"inappropriately disguised as expert testimony"); Rogers, *Ethical Dilemmas in Forensic Evaluations*, 5 BULL. AM. ACAD. PSYCHIATRY & L. 149, 151 (1987) (distortion caused by "forensic identification," an unintentional process by which clinicians adopt theory or fact statement of attorneys with whom they have initial contact); *see generally*, Perlin, *Power Imbalances in Therapeutic and Forensic Relationships*, 9 BEHAV. SCI. & L. 111 (1991).

On the significance of an expert's legal attitudes in the formulation of his testimonial judgments, *see* Homant & Kennedy, *Subjective Factors in Clinicians' Judgments of Insanity: Comparison of a Hypothetical Case and an Actual Case*, 8 PROF. PSYCHOLOGY: RES. & PRAC. 439 (1987). On the related question of the ways in which a psychiatrist's personal feelings and emotions may color his testimony, *see e.g.*, Schetky & Colbach, *Countertransference on the Witness Stand: A Flight From Self?* 10 BULL. AM. ACAD. PSYCHIATRY & L. 115 (1982); Colbach, *American Forensic Psychiatry in the Eighties*, 29 INT'L J. OFFENDER THER. & COMPAR. CRIMINOL. 99 (1985).

77. Note, *Hearsay Bases of Psychiatric Opinion Testimony: A Critique of Federal Rule of Evidence 703*, 51 SO. CAL. L. REV. 129, 137 (1977); *see also*, Needell, *Psychiatric Expert Witnesses: Proposals for Change*, 6 AM. J. L. & MED. 425 (1980).

78. Boswell, *Jews, Bicycle Riders, and Gay People: The Determination of Social Consensus and Its Impact on Minorities*, 1 YALE J. L. & HUMAN. 205, 218 (1989).

79. Weitzel, *Public Skepticism: Forensic Psychiatry's Albatross*, 5 BULL. AM. ACAD. PSYCHIATRY & L. 456, 462 (1977).

80. Wasyliw, Cavanagh & Rogers, *supra* note 4, at 151. On the question of whether forensic psychiatric decision making is truly different from that engaged in by other mental health professionals, lawyers, and lay persons, *see* Jackson, *Lay and Professional Perceptions of Dangerousness and Other Forensic Issues*, 30 CANAD. J. CRIMINOL. 215 (1988).

81. A. GOLDSTEIN, *supra* note 23, at 233.

82. Monahan, *Abolish the Insanity Defense? Not Yet*, 26 RUTGERS L. REV. 719, 721 (1973); Heinbecker, *Two Years' Experience Under Utah's Mens Rea Insanity Law*, 14 BULL. AM. ACAD. PSYCHIATRY & L. 185, 190 (1986).

selves because of the system's failure to mete out "appropriate" pun-ishment.[83] Even some of the outraged state legislators who intro-duced post-Hinckley bills modeled after the federal Insanity Defense Reform Act acknowledged that this attempt served, at most, to fulfill a symbolic function: to help create public confidence in the criminal justice system.[84]

Similarly, because trust—the willingness of citizens to cooperate with governmental decisions and leaders—plays a key role in the authoritativeness and the legitimacy of government, and because empirical research seems to indicate that lack of such public support may lead to a willingness to disobey the law and engage in antisocial behaviors, it is a high priority for governmental officials to minimize the hostility that "unsatisfactory government decisions might engen-der."[85] As the perception of unequal treatment is "the single most important source of popular dissatisfaction with the American legal system,"[86] it becomes almost essential for public authorities to take at least symbolic action to reflect to the public their symbolic outrage at a perceived "unfair" judicial decision.

Thus, speaking at the District of Columbia's Judicial Conference on the Insanity Defense, Assistant United States Attorney General Stephen Trott has stated:

> [W]e have a right as people to expect that the state will vindicate our individual rights as human beings and citizens and the state has an

---

83. *See supra* chapter 2 C 3; *see* J. FEINBERG, DOING AND DESERVING 100 (1970): "[P]unishment generally expresses more than judgments of disapproval; it is also a symbolic way of getting back at the criminal, of expressing a kind of vindictive resentment...[The criminal's] punishment bears the aspect of legitimatized vengefulness."

84. Kaufman, *Should Florida Follow the Federal Insanity Defense?* 15 FLA. ST. U. L. REV. 793, 823, n. 144 (1987), quoting a sponsor of a series of Florida bills that would have codified M'Naghten in a M'Naghten caselaw state ("Bureau-cratically, there is not a felt need to make that change. I believe, though, that it would be a substantial value to the public in helping create confidence in the criminal justice system").

85. Tyler, *The Role of Perceived Injustice in Defendants' Evaluations of Their Courtroom Experience*, 18 LAW & SOC'Y REV. 51-52 (1984); *see also*, Wahlke, *Policy Demands and System Support: The Role of the Represented*, 1 BRIT. J. POLI. SCI. 271 (1971).

86. Tyler, *supra* note 85, at 55. Professor Tyler has recently concluded that fair judicial hearings "will have positive psychological consequences" on those who are the subject of involuntary civil commitment hearings. *See* Tyler, *The Psycho-logical Consequences of Judicial Procedure: Implications for Civil Commitment Hearings*, 46 SMU L. REV. 433, 444 (1992).

obligation to deliver a level of redress and protection that makes up for the renouncement of rights. And I think that's a good way to go, it's a government that's organized along the right lines. And whenever we see the government doing strange and bizarre things that fail to take into consideration in that balance of our individual rights, I think we ought to be disturbed and that is partially what is at the bottom of all this insanity defense business.[87]

The legal system serves as a type of social mask that is essential as a means of minimizing conflict and avoiding social confrontation.[88] The concept of law as a mask is "an ancient device to invoke a higher authority in a dramatic ceremony, and to channel emotions and events into [aesthetically appealing and persuasive] fixed styles of reasoning."[89] The social outrage that followed in the wake of the Hinckley acquittal thus threatened public faith in the judicial system and its masking function.

The vividness of an on-camera assassination attempt of an enormously popular president followed by the seeming exculpation of his putative assassin via a retreat into obfuscatory, self-contradictory psychiatric jargon, served to threaten the uneasy homeostasis that has traditionally surrounded the use of the insanity defense at criminal trials. Only through a decisive and symbolic response of "reform" legislation such as the Insanity Defense Reform Act (and its state-level cognates) could the masking function of the use of psychiatry in law be maintained. Our evisceration of the insanity defense must be seen in this light as well: as a perpetuation of a mask that both reflects and hides our underlying rejection of psychodynamic principles.

---

87. *Proceedings of the Forty-Sixth Judicial Conference of the District of Columbia Circuit*, 111 F.R.D. 91, 226 (1985).
88. Weyrauch, *supra* note 65, at 718-19; *see* Ingber, *Procedure, Ceremony and Rhetoric: The Minimization of Ideological Conflict in Deviance Control*, 56 B.U.L. Rev. 266, 269 (1976).
89. Weyrauch, *supra* note 65, at 725-26.

C. The Law's Ambivalence About the Psychiatric Method

1. Psychiatry and Crime

As I have already demonstrated, there has always been a great measure of dissonance between the visionary theories of psychiatrists such as Benjamin Karpman (who viewed criminality solely as a "symptom of abnormal mental states")[90] and a public convinced that such statements served as "soft" excuses that could be use to rationalize all criminality.[91] Perceptions of rising crime rates, public dissatisfaction with the "rehabilitative ideal,"[92] and heuristic reasoning (that inaccurately attributed views such as Karpman's to *all* mental health professionals)[93] led to an environment that rejected all psychodynamic explanations for behavior.[94] It also called into question psychiatric claims of expertise on issues of diagnosis and dangerousness.[95]

---

90. Karpman, *Criminality, Insanity, and the Law*, 39 J. CRIM. L., CRIMINOL. & POL. SCI. 584, 584 (1949). *see also, id.* at 605:

> We have to treat [criminals] as psychically sick people, which in every respect they are. It is no more reasonable to punish these individuals for a behavior over which they have no control than it is to punish an individual for breathing through his mouth because of enlarged adenoids, when a simple operation will remove the cause. There can be no question of responsibility when there is no evidence of conscious guilt; and there can be no question of guilt, if there is in the individual a strong psychic barrier that does not allow him to see it.

91. *See generally supra* chapter 2 B 2.
92. *See e.g.*, Harris, *Constitutional Limits on Criminal Presumptions as an Expression of Changing Concepts of Fundamental Fairness*, 77 J. CRIM. L. & CRIMINOL. 308, 353-54 (1986); Bonnie, *Morality, Equality, and Expertise: Renegotiating the Relationship Between Psychiatry and Law*, 12 BULL. AM. ACAD. PSYCHIATRY & L. 5, 6 (1984).
93. *See e.g.*, *supra* note 20; Zimring & Hawkins, *Dangerousness and Criminal Justice*, 85 MICH. L. REV. 481 (1986).
94. *See e.g.*, State v. Sikora, 44 N.J. 453, 210 A. 2d 193, 202 (1965) ("Criminal responsibility must be judged at the level of the conscious"); Colorado v. Connelly, 479 U.S. 157, 169 (1987) (rejecting state court opinion for "importing into this area of constitutional law [*Miranda* waivers] notions of 'free will' that have no place there").
95. Any apparent ambiguity between these arguments and those presented in the discussion of the public's adherence to behavioral and empirical myths dealing with insanity defense pleas and the operational impact of the defense is only illusory. We have consciously chosen to ignore data that focuses on the insanity

2. The Ambivalence of Diagnosis

The criminal justice system's dependence on psychiatry was traditionally found diagnostically wanting for at least two reasons: the ambiguity of the confusing diagnostic categories themselves,[96] and the "highly subjective application" of the relevant diagnostic instruments (e.g., intelligence and personality tests, psychiatric observational interviews), often subject to "inconsistency and change" and suffering from "bias."[97] Although recent editions of the American Psychiatric Association's *Diagnostic and Statistical Manual* have eliminated much of the ambiguity of the diagnostic categories and have provided specific diagnostic criteria to enhance diagnostic reliability,[98] the problem of subjective application and bias remains.[99]

As "diagnosis is a social act" which takes place in a social context, and because the "facts" that an interviewer perceives "can easily be distorted by his or her presuppositions, expectations, and sheer random errors,"[100] significant divergences of psychiatric opin-

---

pleader and the disposition of his case, but, paradoxically, we choose to read carefully data that considers the question of how much "expertise" a forensic mental health "expert" actually has. As I will explain subsequently, *see generally infra* chapters 6 and 8, this seeming inconsistency can be explained by an examination of heuristic reasoning and the power of teleology, pretextuality and sanism in insanity defense decision making.

96. Note, *The Right to a Partisan Psychiatric Expert: Might Indigency Preclude Insanity?* 61 N.Y.U. L. Rev. 703, 719 (1986). *But see generally*, Gerard, *The Usefulness of the Medical Model to the Legal System*, 39 Rutgers L. Rev. 377 (1987) (discussing utility of DSM-III in this regard); *see supra* chapter 3 B 3 b.

97. Reich, *Psychiatric Diagnosis as an Ethical Problem*, in Psychiatric Ethics, *supra* note 38, at 63, and see sources cited in *id.* at 85 nn. 8-12; Note, *supra* note 96, at 719; Faust & Miner, *The Empiricist and His New Clothes: DSM-III in Perspective*, 143 Am. J. Psychiatry 962, 963 (1986) (diagnostic categories' appearance of objectivity "largely illusory").

98. Campbell, *The Psychopath and the Definition of "Mental Disease or Defect" Under the Model Penal Code Test of Insanity: A Question of Psychology or a Question of Law?* 69 Neb. L. Rev. 190, 204 (1991).

99. *See e.g.*, Bernstein, *Termination of Parental Rights on the Basis of Mental Disorder: A Problem of Policy and Interpretation*, 22 Pac. L.J. 1155, 1178 n. 116 (1991) (arguing that DSM-IIIR diagnoses remain "notoriously subjective"); Winick, *The Right to Refuse Mental Health Treatment: A First Amendment Perspective*, 44 U. Miami L. Rev. 1, 46 (1989) (criteria remain "imprecise and value-laden"). For a recent debate, *see* Himmelhoch, Mezzich & Ganguli, *Controversies in Psychiatry: The Usefulness of DSM-III*, 21 Psychiatric Ann. 621 (1991).

100. Reich, *supra* note 97, at 64; United States v. Byers, 740 F. 2d 1104, 1138, 1169 n. 187 (D.C. Cir. 1984) (Bazelon, J., dissenting).

ion are thus inevitable.[101] Thus, there have been increasing recent suggestions that experts limit their testimony to "explaining the psychodynamics of a defendant's behavior, and avoid testifying on the ultimate issue of legal responsibility, which should be left to a value judgment of the jury."[102]

Conflict is intensified in forensic cases. Beyond the potentially conflicting interests of the forensic mental health professional's employer,[103] and the additional set of variables to be considered in weighing the specific ethical proscriptions for lawyers dealing with forensic experts,[104] the forensic evaluator may also weigh—consciously *or* unconsciously—community, social and political values (for example, in determining whether a notorious insanity acquittee should be conditionally released),[105] or the availability of public hospital space or potential fear of liability in weighing the need for involuntary civil commitment.[106] Ben Bursten sees the problem even more broadly. In his view, any decision as to whether any behavior is a product of mental illness is *not* a matter of scientific expertise, "but a matter of social policy."[107]

Even in therapeutic relationships, neutrality is never to be presumed. In his towering work, *The Powers of Psychiatry*, Dr. Jonas

---

101. *See e.g.*, Liston, Yager & Strauss, *Assessment of Psychotherapy Skills: The Problem of Interrater Agreement*, 138 AM. J. PSYCHIATRY 1069 (1981) (extent of agreement among thirteen experienced supervising psychotherapists evaluating interviews of residents was "uniformly low"); for an earlier view, *see* Spitzer & Fleiss, *Re-Analysis of the Reliability of Psychiatric Diagnosis*, 125 BRIT. J. PSYCHIATRY 341 (1974).

102. Homant & Kennedy, *Subjective Factors in the Judgment of Insanity*, 14 CRIM. JUST. & BEHAV. 38, 58 (1987); *see also*, Homant & Kennedy, *supra* note 76. For a comprehensive analysis, *see* Eastman, *Metaphor and Madness, Law and Liberty*, 40 DE PAUL L. REV. 281, 339-45 (1991).

103. *But see* Stitt v. State Dep't of Mental Health & Mental Retardation, 562 So. 2d 259, 262 (Ala. Civ App. 1990), *quoting* Williams v. Wallis, 734 F. 2d 1434, 1438 (11th Cir. 1984) (court can "safely assume that hospitals and medical professionals [are] disinterested decisionmakers [who] certainly have no bias against the patient or against release").

104. *See* Fitch, Petrella & Wallace, *Legal Ethics and the Use of Mental Health Experts in Criminal Cases*, 5 BEHAV. SCI. & L. 105, 109-16 (1987).

105. *See* Shestack, *Psychiatry and the Dilemmas of Dual Loyalties*, 60 A.B.A. J. 1521, 1522 (1974).

106. Thompson & Ager, *An Experimental Analysis of the Civil Commitment Recommendations of Psychologists and Psychiatrists*, 6 BEHAV. SCI. & L. 119, 120 (1988).

107. B. BURSTEN, BEYOND PSYCHIATRIC EXPERTISE 167 (1984). *See generally*, Perlin, *supra* note 76, at 117.

Robitscher was clear in his critique of the alleged neutrality or value-freedom of the therapeutic relationship. A whole "constellation of values—personal, economic, political, philosophical, therapeutic—determines the treatment relationship,"[108] Robitscher wrote, and it is "foolish" for mental health professionals to claim that their disciplines are "objective and value free:"

> The purpose of the therapeutic encounter is to permit one person to have enough effect on another person to change behavior and personality, and such a situation is rife with values...The values that psychiatrists provide for their patients and for society are the most influential expressions of the great authority that psychiatry exerts.[109]

Seymour Halleck saw the power issue even more specifically, arguing that, by participating in individual psychotherapy, a patient "regularly experiences either a gain or a loss of power" and that the "vectors" in the therapy encounter that favor conformity "tend to be the most powerful."[110] These concerns suggest that the power issues that are embedded in the diagnostic process must always be seen as hovering near the surface.[111]

On the other hand, the diagnostic process remains an attractive means of solving or avoiding complex problems, through its "fetching[ly] beaut[iful]" capacity to instantly explain odd, troublesome or objectionable behavior. This "quick fix" solution may be a meretricious one, since it encourages "temptation even in cases in which such illness does not exist, or is at best, only marginally present." Also, diagnosis may serve a reassuring function in that it encourages a shift of "the frame of the behaviour from the threatening personal or social arena to a safer medical one."[112]

By the same token, diagnosis can be seen as excluding and dehumanizing:

> When we want to do unto others as we would not have them to unto ourselves, we find some way of turning them into others. We usually do that by labelling them, by excluding them from our own group, and by

---

108. J. ROBITSCHER, THE POWERS OF PSYCHIATRY 399 (1980).
109. *Id.* at 400.
110. S. HALLECK, THE POLITICS OF THERAPY 33-34 (1971).
111. *See* Perlin, *supra* note 76, at 121-22.
112. Reich, *supra* note 97, at 71-74.

dehumanizing them—by defining their status as less than ours, and, therefore less human.[113]

Through this characteristic, diagnosis allows the psychiatrist to "harden his heart" by seeing the person as a patient, "one whose pleas are not simple, soulful, human importunings but rather the routine and expected reactions of ill patients to the illnesses that have possessed them and to the treatments to which they have been subjected."[114]

Similarly, diagnosis has the capacity for "inevitable self-confirmation:" once an individual is labelled as "crazy" or "weird," all his subsequent actions "can be attributed to, and dismissed as a result of, [such] epithets." Finally, diagnosis can be a weapon of discreditation and punishment, "the attribution of a person's views, politics, actions, or conclusions to a mind gone sick."[115]

3. Predictivity of Dangerousness[116]

The voluminous literature examining the ability of psychiatrists (or other mental health professionals) to testify reliably as to an individual's "dangerousness" in the indeterminate future has been virtually unanimous:[117] "psychiatrists have absolutely no expertise in predicting dangerous behavior—indeed, they may be *less* accurate predictors than laymen—and that they usually err by overpredicting violence."[118] These errors are known as "false positives," *i.e.*, a per-

---

113. *Id.* at 77. The roots of this impulse, Reich adds, are "primitive, powerful, and universal." *Id.*

114. *Id.* at 79.

115. *Id.* at 81-82.

116. The material *infra* accompanying notes 117-35 is partially adapted from 1 M.L. PERLIN, *supra* note 17, §2.15.

117. For an excellent overview, *see* Slobogin, *Dangerousness and Expertise*, 123 U. PA. L. REV. 97 (1984); for the most recent comprehensive studies, *see* Monahan, *Risk Assessment of Violence Among the Mentally Disordered: Generating Useful Knowledge*, 11 INT'L J. L. & PSYCHIATRY 249 (1989); Monahan, *Mental Disorder and Violent Behavior: Perceptions and Evidence*, 47 AM. PSYCHOLOGIST 511 (1992) (Monahan, *Mental Disorder*); Grisso & Appelbaum, *Is It Unethical to Offer Predictions of Future Violence?* 16 LAW & HUM. BEHAV. 621 (1992); Hoge & Grisso, *Accuracy and Expert Testimony*, 20 BULL. AM. ACAD. PSYCHIATRY & L. 67 (1992).

118. *See* Ennis & Litwack, *Psychiatry and the Presumption of Expertise: Flipping Coins in the Courtroom*, 62 CALIF. L. REV. 693, 734-35 (1974) (*Flipping Coins*) (emphasis in original); Barefoot v. Estelle, 463 U.S. 880, 916, 933-36 (Blackmun, J., dissenting), and see sources cited at *id.* nn. 2-4.

son falsely predicted to be dangerous, as opposed to "false negatives," *i.e.*, a person falsely predicted to be *not* dangerous; generally,
"false positives" have been seen as "preferable" errors for medical
predictors to make.[119]

The American Psychiatric Association has thus informed the
Supreme Court that two out of three predictions of long-term future
violence made by psychiatrists are wrong.[120] According to Professor

---

119. H. STEADMAN & J. COCOZZA, CAREERS OF THE CRIMINALLY INSANE 110 (1974);
    Wilkins, *The Case for Prediction*, in 3 CRIME & JUSTICE 375 (Radzinowicz &
    Wilkins eds. 1971).

    Ironically, researchers have suggested that the false negative rate is much
    lower than the false positive rate. *See* Wenk, Robison & Sineth, *Can Violence
    Be Predicted?* 18 CRIME & DELINQ. 393, 394 (1972), as quoted in *Flipping
    Coins, supra* at 715: "The best prediction available today...is that any member
    of a [studied control group] *will not* become violent" (emphasis in *Flipping
    Coins*). *See generally,* Petrunik, *The Politics of Dangerousness*, 5 INT'L J. L. &
    PSYCHIATRY 225, 244 (1982) (discussing heavy media focus on the problem of
    "false negatives[—]individuals diagnosed as insufficiently dangerous enough to
    confine (or as safe enough to release) who are later found to have committed
    serious acts of personal violence or nonconsensual sexual offences") (footnote
    omitted).

120. In *Barefoot*, the United States Supreme Court *rejected* the arguments made by
    the American Psychiatric Association based on this data, and ruled that, in the
    context of a penalty phase of a capital case, "it makes little sense, if any, to submit
    that psychiatrists, out of the entire universe of persons who might have an
    opinion on the issue, would know so little about the subject that they should not
    be permitted to testify." *Barefoot*, 463 U.S. at 896.

    Compare id. at 916 (Blackmun, J., dissenting): "The Court holds that
    psychiatric testimony about a defendant's future dangerousness is admissible,
    despite the fact that such testimony is wrong two times out of three....[W]hen a
    person's life is at stake—no matter how heinous his offense—a requirement of
    greater reliability should prevail. In a capital case, the specious testimony of a
    psychiatrist, colored in the eyes of an impressionable jury by the inevitable
    untouchability of a medical specialist's words, equates with death itself."

    See generally, Perlin, *supra* note 18, at 108-111; Perlin, *supra* note 3, at 7-12;
    Schroeder, *Ethical and Moral Dilemmas Confronting Forensic Scientists*, 29 J.
    FORENS. SCI. 966, 979 (1984) ("Where public law generates such error by its use
    of unscientific facts and opinions in the administration of criminal justice is there
    not an obligation for the forensic science professions, especially forensic psychia-
    try, to establish ethical standards with appropriate sanctions to assure at least a
    modicum of scientific authenticity to psychiatric testimony?") Psychiatric aspects
    of *Barefoot* are placed in a cultural perspective in Romanucci-Ross & Tancredi,
    supra note 68, at 286. Professor Michael Saks and his colleagues have concluded
    flatly, "We have yet to find a single word of praise for, or in defense of, *Barefoot*
    anywhere in the literature of science or law." Risinger, Denbeaux & Saks,
    *Exorcism of Ignorance as a Proxy for Rational Knowledge: The Lessons of
    Handwriting Identification "Expertise,"* 137 U. PA. L. REV. 731, 780 n. 215
    (1989).

John Monahan, "the leading thinker on this issue:"[121]

> Outcome studies of clinical prediction with adult populations under-
> score the importance of past violence as a predictor of future violence, yet
> lead to the conclusion that psychiatrists and psychologists *are accurate in*
> *no more than one out of three predictions of violent behavior over a several*
> *year period among institutionalized populations that had both committed*
> *violence in the past and were mentally ill.*[122]

In their earlier exhaustive study, Ennis and Litwack reviewed the
then-available empirical evidence of the validity of psychiatric diagnosis, of the predictivity of dangerousness, of the predictivity of the
need for hospitalization and treatment, and of the predictivity of the
effect of hospitalization and treatment, and concluded:

> [P]sychiatrists often disagree in their judgments and...even when they
> do agree those judgments—especially predictive judgments—are often
> wrong. In particular, psychiatric predictions that an individual is dangerous
> are usually wrong. Furthermore, perceptions of symptoms and behavior
> vary dramatically among examining psychiatrists and for some diagnostic
> categories there is little relationship between the symptoms and behavior
> perceived by the psychiatrist and the eventual diagnosis. For specific
> diagnostic categories, there is little evidence that the symptoms and behav-
> ior perceived by the psychiatrist were actually exhibited by the patient....In
> short, diagnoses often convey more inaccurate than accurate information
> about patients.[123]

There is some recent evidence of a counterassault,[124] and Professor Monahan has found a "modest, positive relationship between

---

121. *Barefoot*, 463 U.S. at 901 (*quoting* state's expert witness).
122. J. MONAHAN, THE CLINICAL PREDICTION OF VIOLENT BEHAVIOR, 92 (1981)
    (emphasis added).
123. *Flipping Coins, supra* note 118, at 719. According to the authors, courts should
    limit psychiatric testimony to "descriptive statements and should exclude psy-
    chiatric diagnoses, judgments and predictions." *Id.* at 696. *See also*, Morse,
    Crazy Behavior, Morals, and Science: An Analysis of Mental Health Law, 51 S.
    CAL. L. REV. 527, 619 (1978) ("Experts should simply present descriptive data
    that would otherwise be unknown and hard, relevant probability data"); *see*
    generally, Eastman, *supra* note 102, at 341-43.
124. *See generally*, Haddad, *Predicting the Supreme Court's Response to the Criti-*
    cisms of Psychiatric Predictions of Dangerousness in Civil Commitment Pro-
    ceedings, 64 NEB. L. REV. 190, 238-44 (1985), and *id.* at 246 ("[R]ecent research
    does indicate that psychiatrists can provide useful and sufficiently reliable
    information to aid the trier-of-fact in determining the need for emergency and
    extended involuntary detention") (footnote omitted).

some mental disorders and some violent behavior.[125] Not all commentators continue to couch the issue in as vivid terms as Professor Dix's aphorism that, under certain circumstances, a psychiatrist who predicts future dangerousness brings himself to "the brink of quackery,"[126] Yet, current research still reveals, at best, a "false positive" rate of over forty percent.[127] Professor Gary Melton and his colleagues have thus recommended that forensic witnesses focus in their testimony on "risk variables:"

> If a clinician is going to make statements about an individual's violence potential, he or she may do so either by describing the risk factors with a particular class of individuals whose violence potential is known and to which the subject belongs, or by concluding a careful inquiry into the personal and situational factors that have contributed to the individual's violent behavior in the past, in an effort to identify those conditions under which the likelihood of a future aggressive act is increased.[128]

---

125. Monahan, *Mental Disorder, supra* note 117, at 514.

    In earlier research, Monahan had determined that predictions might be more accurate as to the presence of certain social variables associated with dangerousness: sex, age, employment, prior history, J. MONAHAN, *supra* note 122, at 127, and had begun to differentiate between predictive abilities as to long-term, indeterminate future dangerousness and as to short-term emergency confinement and treatment, *see e.g.,* Monahan, *Prediction Research and the Emergency Commitment of Dangerous Mentally Ill Persons: A Reconsideration,* 135 AM. J. PSYCHIATRY 198 (1978); *see also,* McNiel & Binder, *Clinical Assessment of the Risk of Violence Among Psychiatric Inpatients,* 148 AM. J. PSYCHIATRY 1317 (1991) (reliability and validity of short-term estimates of risk of violence among acutely disturbed inpatients may be higher than suggested by past research). Monahan now takes the position that "there maybe a relationship between mental disorder and violence, one that cannot be fobbed off as chance," and that while the relationship "probably is not large," it "may be important both for legal theory and for social policy." Monahan, *Mental Disorder, supra* note 117, at 511.

    For the most recent research, *see* 1 M.L. PERLIN, *supra* note 17, §2.15, at 26-27 n. 525 (1992 pocket part) (listing studies).

126. Dix, *The Death Penalty, "Dangerousness," Psychiatric Testimony and Professional Ethics,* 5 AM. J. CRIM. L. 151, 172 (1977), discussing testimony of Dr. James P. Grigson, *see supra* chapter 2, note 189.

127. *See* Bersoff, *Judicial Deference to Nonlegal Decisionmakers: Imposing Simplistic Solutions on Problems of Cognitive Complexity in Mental Disability Law,* 46 SMU L. REV.329, 356 (1992), discussing research reported in Sepejak et al., *Clinical Predictions of Dangerousness: Two-Year Follow-up of 408 Pre-Trial Cases,* 11 BULL. AM. ACAD. PSYCHIATRY & L. 171 (1983), and in Klassen & O'Connor, *A Prospective Study of Predictors of Violence in Adult Male Mental Health Admissions,* 12 LAW & HUM. BEHAV. 143 (1988).

128. G. MELTON. J. PETRILA, N. POYTHRESS & C. SLOBOGIN, PSYCHOLOGICAL EVALUATIONS FOR THE COURTS: A HANDBOOK FOR MENTAL HEALTH PROFES-

As Professor Bersoff has recently noted, "These results may exhibit more accuracy relative to older studies, but they do not inspire much confidence that mental health professionals can predict violent behavior very precisely." This predictive rate of error reflects the inappropriate use of the representative and vividness heuristics.[129] Thus, in a study of over 250 individuals, the only variable that distinguished those determined to be dangerous from those determined not to be dangerous was the alleged crime: the more serious the crime, the more likely that the examiner would find dangerous.[130]

Ennis and Litwack's conclusion that "training and experience do not enable psychiatrists adequately to predict dangerous behavior," based on research studies done by psychiatrists, psychologists and sociologists,[131] has been supported warmly by the psychiatric establishment.[132] On the other hand, the "vast majority" of clinicians

---

SIONALS AND LAWYERS 205 (1987) (G. MELTON).

129. Bersoff, *supra* note 127, at 356, *citing*, in part, Menzies et al., *The Nature and Consequences of Forensic Psychiatric Decision-Making*, 27 CAN. J. PSYCHIATRY 463 (1982); Palermo et al., *On the Predictability of Violent Behavior: Considerations and Guidelines*, 36 J. FORENS. SCI. 1435, 1439 (1991) (possibility of future dangerousness can not be deduced from isolated individual trait).

130. Cocozza & Steadman, *The Failure of Psychiatric Predictions of Dangerousness: Clear and Convincing Evidence*, 29 RUTGERS L. REV. 1084, 1096 (1976). I discuss the implications of these findings in Perlin, *Pretexts and Mental Disability Law: The Case of Competency*, 47 U. MIAMI L. REV. (1993) (in press), manuscript at 67-68.

131. *Flipping Coins*, *supra* note 118, at 733.

132. Eminent forensic psychiatrist Robert L. Sadoff has stated: "We do not have treatment for dangerousness...[; furthermore, a] psychiatrist ha[s] no expertise in the prediction of dangerousness." Sadoff, *Dangerousness as a Criterion for Involuntary Commitment*, DIRECTIONS IN PSYCHIATRY Lesson 22 (1981), at 4. In his influential monograph *Mental Health and Law: A System in Transition*, Alan Stone, the past president of the American Psychiatric Association, went even further: "It can be stated flatly...that neither objective actuarial tables nor psychiatric intuition, diagnosis, and psychological testing can claim predictive success when dealing with the traditional population of mental hospitals." A. STONE, MENTAL HEALTH AND LAW: A SYSTEM IN TRANSITION 33 (1976). The American Psychiatric Association has formally agreed with this position. AMERICAN PSYCHIATRIC ASS'N, CLINICAL ASPECTS OF THE VIOLENT INDIVIDUAL 28 (1974):

Neither psychiatrists nor anyone else have reliably demonstrated an ability to predict future violence or 'dangerousness.' Neither has any special psychiatric expertise in this area been established.

Dr. Sadoff has subsequently endorsed the views of Melton and his colleagues on the importance of risk variables. *See* R.I. SIMON & R.L. SADOFF, PSYCHIATRIC

continue "either in ignorance or with misplaced confidence, [to] ignore relevant factors that contribute to more accurate decisionmaking."[133]

Nonetheless, the public and the courts continue to invest psychiatrists with "superior, almost superhuman powers...and continue to demand that psychiatrists predict violence.[134] Definitions of "dangerousness" are thus "based on the pressures—'real' or alleged—the general public and particular interest groups exert on policy makers and prevalent ideologies of social control."[135] Similarly, jurors, judges *and* the lay public are all influenced to believe in "the subterfuge of 'dangerousness' (1) by their respect for science, (2) by the participation of doctors, and (3) by the slippery nature of clinical testimony."[136]

In short, even though the track record of dangerousness predictivity ranges from terrible to spotty, we continue to reify psychiatric expertise here because it fits well with our own need to manipulate this expertise for external social ends. It again reflects our ambiva-

---

MALPRACTICE: CASES AND COMMENTS FOR CLINICIANS 201 (1992).

133. Bersoff, *supra* note 127, at 361. On the relationship between the use of antipsychotic medications and dangerousness predictions, *see* Zenoff, *Controlling the Dangers of Dangerousness: The ABA Standards and Beyond*, 53 GEO. WASH. L. REV. 562, 582 (1985).

134. Gunn, *supra* note 64, at 147; Beck, *Psychiatric Assessment of Potential Violence: A Reanalysis of the Problem*, in THE POTENTIALLY VIOLENT PATIENT AND THE TARASOFF DECISION IN PSYCHIATRIC PRACTICE 84 (J. Beck ed. 1985). Dr. Beck adds, however, that "none of us knows whether we can predict violence or not, although most of us [in clinical practice] believe we can." *Id.* at 90. Alan Stone's metaphor is helpful:

I once did some empirical research on humor. It turns out that of 280 students 280 thought they had a very good sense of humor. Similarly, it seems to me that every psychiatrist thinks he/she has very good clinical judgment.

Stone, *The Ethical Boundaries: The View from the Ivory Tower*, 12 BULL. AM. ACAD. PSYCHIATRY & L. 209, 213 (1984) (footnote omitted).

On the ways jurors respond to different levels of confidence on the part of forensic examiners, *see* Rogers, Bagby & Chow, *Psychiatrists and the Parameters of Expert Testimony*, 15 INT'L J. L. & PSYCHIATRY 387, 394-95 (1992) (testimony with an expressed confidence of 80% appears to exert a greater influence on perceptions of criminal sanity or insanity than expressions at 60% or 100%); *accord*, Cutler, Penrod & Dexter, *The Eyewitness, the Expert Psychologist, and the Jury*, 13 LAW & HUM. BEHAV. 311 (1989).

135. Petrunik, *supra* note 119, at 226.

136. Worrell, *Psychiatric Prediction of Dangerousness in Capital Sentencing: The Quest for Innocent Authority*, 5 BEHAV. SCI. & L. 433, 438 (1987).

lence about the psychiatric method. While we criticize mental health professionals for being "soft on crime" (and gullible about allegedly feigned insanity defenses), we glorify their predictive abilities to identify dangerous individuals (even when their record at such identifications is, at best, slightly better than random chance, and where professional leadership has repudiated claims to accuracy).

This tension becomes especially important when we consider the post-acquittal retention and recommitment process. Much of the public's post-Hinckley outrage was centered on its inaccurate perceptions that, once acquitted, an insanity defendant would generally be released from all custodial restraints quickly, and much of the insanity defense reform movement targeted this (mis)perception as a focal point for legislative change.[137] To insure that insanity acquittees do not "slip through the cracks" and re-enter society, the public demands lengthy post-acquittal terms of confinement. To justify these terms, it requires expert testimony on the acquittees' continuing dangerousness.[138] Evidence that forensic witnesses are *not* accurate in these predictions ("not much better than arbitrary judgment")[139] leads to further cognitive dissonance, and exacerbates the public's ambivalence about the role of psychiatry here.[140]

D. The Specific Rejection of Psychodynamic Principles: The Insanity Defense as Case Study

1. Introduction

As we saw in the prior section, the *notion* of psychodynamics has been rejected by the legal system for a variety of reasons. This rejection is seen in starkest form in the legal response to both the substance of the insanity defense and the *personality characteristics* of the insanity defense pleader. A century ago, Sir James Stephen

---

137. *See e.g.*, Ellis, *The Consequences of the Insanity Defense: Proposals to Reform Post-Acquittal Commitment Laws*, 35 CATH. U. L. REV. 961, 962 (1986) ("the public's concern is less with ascertaining whether blame properly can be assigned to a particular defendant than with determining when he will get out").

138. *Compare* Foucha v. Louisiana, 112 S. Ct. 1780 (1992) (state statute permitting continued retention of non-mentally ill insanity acquittee unconstitutional).

139. Bersoff, *supra* note 127, at 362.

140. *See generally*, Perlin, *supra* note 75 (on the power and role of cognitive dissonance in mental disability law decision making).

wrote: "I think it highly desirable that criminals should be hated;"[141] this attitude—"dramatiz[ing] the differences between the 'we' and the 'they'"[142]—requires accused criminals to go through rituals "which allow status degradation."[143]

The insanity defense has served, to some extent, to control retribution;[144] thus, it is seen as "cheating" this degradation and as dissipating the opportunity for expressing hatred; by "thwarting" punishment, it runs counter to the "mythology of justice, creating the illusion that the world is fair;" by downplaying emotions of vengeance, it threatens social solidarity and raises "the terrifying anxiety that the forces of good might not triumph against the forces of evil after all."[145] As a "moral judgment that mental illness is relevant to our determination of criminal culpability,"[146] it is a judgment that society frequently wishes to decline making.[147] Thus, researchers reporting on Idaho's insanity defense abolition concluded that the legislature's actions might have reflected "the response of the uneasy good against the acting out wicked:"

> There exist in all of us impulses toward wickedness that we suppress at some cost. As a reward for our suppression, we would like to make certain that those who have not forced themselves to repress their evil impulses suffer suitably for that lapse so we ourselves can be reassured that our sacrifice was not for nothing.[148]

Media depictions rely on stereotypes and distort images of mental illness; television portrayals of mentally ill persons are touched

---

141. 2 J. STEPHEN, A HISTORY OF THE CRIMINAL LAW OF ENGLAND 81 (1883).
142. Ingber, *A Dialectic: The Fulfillment and Decrease of Passion in Criminal Law*, 28 RUTGERS L. REV. 861, 911 (1975).
143. *Id.* at 907, *citing* Goldstein, *Police Discretion Not To Invoke the Criminal Process: Low Visibility Decisions in the Administration of Justice*, 69 YALE L. J. 543, 590 (1960).
144. Rappeport, *supra* note 37, at 690.
145. Diamond, *From* Durham *to* Brawner: *A Futile Journey*, 1973 WASH. U. L. Q. 109, 110.
146. Note, *The Insanity Defense: Effects of an Abolition Unsupported by a Moral Consensus*, 9 AMER. J. L. & MED. 471, 495 (1984).
147. *See* People v. Wallace, 160 Mich. App. 1, 408 N.W. 2d 87, 92 (1987): "We recognize that in a particularly brutal case where the defendant admits perpetrating the acts and raises the defense of insanity, the temptation will be great to place the insanity defense on trial along with the defendant."
148. Geis & Meier, *Abolition of the Insanity Plea in Idaho: A Case Study*, 477 ANNALS 72, 77 (1985).

with a "sense of evil that justifies their continued mistreatment."[149] Prosecutors in insanity defense cases often tap into this vein in their portrayals of defendants, their counsel, and of expert witnesses who testify on defendants' behalf.[150] Courts have historically seen mental illness as an all-or-nothing category (and a condition that must be demonstrated by certain overt, graphic, physiological characteristics),[151] and judges often attribute blame to criminal defendants for their mental illness, ascribing their problems to "weak character or poor resolve."[152]

Decisions such as these—and others that generally reject psychodynamic principles that have the potential to illuminate issues for jurors to give them some insight into mentally disabled defendants[153]—help explain further the incoherence of our insanity de-

---

149. Wahl & Roth, *Television Images of Mental Illness: Results of a Metropolitan Washington Media Watch*, 26 J. BROADCASTING 599, 601 (1982), discussing research reported on in Gerbner, *Dreams That Hurt: Mental Illness in the Mass Media*, in THE COMMUNITY IMPERATIVE 19 (R. Baron et al. eds. 1980); *see* Perlin, *supra* note 23, at 389; Kaufman, *"Crazy" Until Proven Innocent: Civil Commitment of the Mentally Ill Homeless*, 19 COLUM. HUM. RTS. L. REV. 333, 363 (1988); Snow et al., *The Myth of Pervasive Mental Illness Among the Homeless*, 33 SOC. PROBS. 407, 407-08 (1986); Hyler et al., *Homicidal Maniacs and Narcissistic Parasites: Stigmatization of Mentally Ill Persons in the Movies*, 42 HOSP. & COMMUN. PSYCHIATRY 1044 (1991).

150. *See e.g.*, Fleming, Annotation, *Negative Characterization or Description of Defendant by Prosecutor During Summation of Criminal Trial, As Ground for Reversal, New Trial, or Mistrial—Modern Cases*, 88 A.L.R. 4th 8 (1991); Sinclair v. Wainwright, 814 F. 2d 1516, 1522 (11th Cir. 1987) (defendant described as a "lunatic"); Brown v. People, 8 Ill. 2d 540, 134 N.E. 2d 760, 762 (1956) (judge asked defendant "You are not crazy at this time, are you?"); Commonwealth v. Musolino, 320 Pa. Super. 425, 467 A. 2d 605 (1983) (reversible error for trial judge to refer to expert witnesses as "headshrinkers"); State v. Blasus, 445 N.W. 2d 535, 539 (Minn. 1989) (reversible error where prosecutor accused expert witnesses of "mak[ing] their living testifying for the defense"); *see generally*, Perlin, *supra* note 129, manuscript at 79-80.

151. *See e.g.*, Johnson v. State, 292 Md. 405, 439 A. 2d 542, 552 (1982) ("For the purposes of guilt determination, an offender is either wholly sane or wholly insane"); Battalino v. People, 118 Colo. 587, 199 P. 2d 897, 901 (1948) (finding no evidence of defendant exhibiting "paleness, wild eyes and trembling" in affirming jury's rejection of insanity defense).

152. Perlin, *supra* note 129, manuscript at 80-81. *See also, id.*, manuscript at 81, discussing K. Gould, I. Keilitz & J.R. Martin, "Criminal Defendants With Trial Disabilities: The Theory and Practice of Competency Assistance" (unpublished manuscript), at 68 (reporting on trial judge's response to National Center for State Courts survey, expressing belief that defendants who were incompetent to stand trial could have understood and communicated with counsel and the court "if they [had] only wanted").

153. *See e.g.*, Braley v. State, 741 P. 2d 1061 (Wyo. 1987) (psychiatric expert

fense jurisprudence. They also shed some light on the way we, simultaneously, have difficulty in judicially expressing empathy for insanity pleaders, while being able to sympathize (perhaps to an exaggerated degree) with a minute subclass of individuals who enter that plea. They also help explain how our "community tolerance threshold" helps define the way the insanity defense operates.

2. The Ambivalence of Empathy

The use of stereotypes precludes empathic behavior. We think of the stereotyped as "them" and not as "us" and we are therefore less likely to share in their pain and humiliation.[154] Empathy encompasses three interrelated phenomena:

> (1) feeling the emotion of another; (2) understanding the experience or situation of another, both affectively and cognitively, often achieved by imagining oneself to be in the position of the other; and (3) action brought about by experiencing the distress of another (hence the confusion of empathy with sympathy and compassion).[155]

The public, simply put, cannot empathize with an insane defendant,[156] especially where the definition of "insane" appears to be "a highly restrictive and legalistic definition of responsibility."[157] This lack of empathy leads to irrational fears (as to the defense's overuse, the perceived "soft" treatment of insanity acquittees, the deviousness

---

testimony not required to explain defendant's reactions to fear and stress); Stano v. Dugger, 883 F. 2d 900 (11th Cir. 1990), *on rehearing*, 901 F. 2d 898 (11th Cir. 1990) (testimony of psychiatrist that mentally ill persons often confess to crimes that they did not commit inadmissible).

154. Perlin, *supra* note 23, at 380, *quoting* Ross, *The Rhetoric of Poverty: Their Immorality, Our Helplessness*, 72 GEO. L.J. 1499, 1542 (1991).

155. Henderson, *Legality and Empathy*, 85 MICH. L. REV. 1574, 1579 (1987); *see generally*, N. EISENBERG & J. STRAYER, EDS., EMPATHY AND ITS DEVELOPMENT (1987); Ellmann, *Empathy and Approval*, 43 HASTINGS L.J. 991 (1992). On the relationship between empathy and sympathy, *see* Rosenberg, *In Defense of Mediation*, 33 ARIZ. L. REV. 467, 477 (1991); Pillsbury, *Emotional Justice: Moralizing the Passions of Criminal Punishment*, 74 CORNELL L. REV. 655, 695-98 (1989). On the role of compassion in the law, *see* Zipursky, DeShaney and the Jurisprudence of Compassion, 65 N.Y.U. L. REV. 1101 (1990).

156. *See* V. HANS & N. VIDMAR, JUDGING THE JURY 131 (1986) *quoting* Clarence Darrow: "Jurymen seldom convict a person they like, or acquit one that they dislike. The main work of a trial lawyer is to make a jury like his client, or, at least, to feel sympathy for him; facts regarding the crime are relatively unimportant."

157. S. HALLECK, *supra* note 69, at 208.

of counsel and expert witnesses in proffering the defense), symbolizing "society's frustrated vengeance."[158] With the insanity defense seen as the "lynch-pin that holds together the broader system of responsibility-desert-punishment"[159] through its "courtroom ritualization," we must reject the notion that insanity defense pleaders are "much like us, even just like us 'but for the grace of God.'"[160] This expresses our societal frustration that the defense does not seem to serve its alleged metaphysical purpose of "distinguishing between bad guys and good guys, between normal guys and sick guys, between free-willing guys and determined guys; between guys we feel satisfied about torturing and guys we are satisfied with treating."[161]

This frustration may result in increased punitiveness by juries towards certain defendants—e.g., women charged with murdering their husbands—"for not conforming to the stereotype [of sounding truly insane]."[162] Rejection of the insanity defense may similarly be

---

158. *See e.g* Arafat & McCahery, *The Insanity Defense and the Juror*, 22 DRAKE L. REV. 538, 548 (1973) ("the presence of an unfavorable attitude toward psychiatry was strongly associated with the decision against the use of the insanity plea"); Arenella, *Reflections on Current Proposals to Abolish or Reform the Insanity Defense*, 8 AMER. J. L. & MED. 271 (1982); S. HALLECK, *supra* note 69, at 250-51.

159. Homant & Kennedy, *supra* note 102, at 78.

160. Burt, *Of Mad Dogs and Scientists: The Perils of the "Criminal-Insane,"* 123 U. PA. L. REV. 258, 273, 282 (1974). It is, of course, this sort of thought process that might have led to the Bernhard Goetz self-defense acquittal. *See generally,* G. FLETCHER, A CRIME OF SELF-DEFENSE: BERNHARD GOETZ AND THE LAW ON TRIAL (1988).

161. Seney, *"When Empty Terrors Overawe"—Our Criminal Law Defenses,* 19 WAYNE L. REV. 947, 984 (1973). On the difficulties arising from jury assessments of whether or not defendants behaved "reasonably" when raising a provocation defense to a murder charge, *see* State v. Hoyt, 21 Wis. 2d 284, 128 N.W. 2d 645, 652, 654 (1964) (Hoyt, J., concurring) (emphasis added):

[W]e must place ourselves empathetically in the actual situation in which the defendant was placed, a situation which may be relatively unique [To find provocation, t]he trier-of-fact must be able to say, 'Although I would have acted differently, and I believe most persons would have acted differently, *I can understand why* this person gave way to an impulse to kill.'

162. Schneider & Jordan, *Representation of Women Who Defend Themselves in Response to Physical or Sexual Assault,* 4 WOMEN'S RIGHTS L. RPTR. 149, 160 (1978), and *see* Wilczynski, *Images of Women Who Kill Their Infants: The Mad and the Bad,* 2 WOMEN & CRIM. JUST. 71 (1991); *see also,* Napier, *Civil Incest Suits: Getting Beyond the Statute of Limitations,* 68 WASH. U. L. Q. 995, 1008 (1990) (on the way that such insanity defenses perpetuate inaccurate stereotypes of women). On the relationship between "ordinary common sense" and jury

seen as an expression of "ancient convictions" that society can punish an offender "because the punishment is a sort of justified collective purge or vengeance; a purge to rid society of the offender and thereby to protect it, and vengeance to show retribution on the transgressor and thus to protect society."[163]

Both the frustration and the punitiveness are seen in sharpest focus in public attitudes towards defendants following insanity acquittals. For it is here that the rare "false negative"—the individual predicted to be not dangerous who subsequently commits a violent act—enthralls the system. Repressive legislation regularly follows disclosure of the public's worst fantasy: such a violent crime committed by an insanity acquittee.[164] Yet, there is virtually no empirical basis for this pattern of legislation-in-response-to-horror-story: in 1983, researchers could point to only one person acquitted by reason of insanity in New York state—ever—who subsequently killed someone after his release.[165]

---

behavior in such cases, *see* Kromsky & Cutler, *The Battered Wife Syndrome: A Matter of Common Sense?* 2 FORENS. REP. 173 (1989); Dodge & Greene, *Jurors and Expert Conceptions of Battered Women*, 6 VIOLENCE & VICTIMS 271 (191); Schuller, *The Impact of Battered Wife Syndrome on Jury Decision Processes*, 16 LAW & HUM. BEHAV. 597 (1992); Follingstad, *Factors Predicting Verdicts in Cases Where Battered Women Kill Their Husbands*, 13 LAW & HUM. BEHAV. 253 (1989). The most recent comprehensive multi-state study confirms that women are statistically disproportionately likely to be successfully acquitted on an insanity defense than are men. *See* H. STEADMAN ET AL., REFORMING THE INSANITY DEFENSE: AN EVALUATION OF PRE- AND POST-HINCKLEY REFORMS (1993) (in press), manuscript at 49 (H. STEADMAN, REFORMING).

163. People v. Nash, 52 Cal. 2d 36, 338 P. 2d 416, 424 (1959).

164. See e.g., Mickenberg, A Pleasant Surprise: The Guilty But Mentally Ill Verdict Has Succeeded in Its Own Right and Successfully Preserved the Traditional Role of the Insanity Defense, 55 U. CIN. L. REV. 943 (1987); Fentiman, "Guilty But Mentally Ill": The Real Verdict Is Guilty, 26 B.C. L. REV. 601 (1985) *See also*, Fisher, Pierce & Appelbaum, *How Flexible Are Our Civil Commitment Statutes?* 39 HOSP. & COMMUN. PSYCHIATRY 711 (1988) (more restrictive *civil* commitment legislation also frequently follows on the heels of such an act by an insanity acquittee); J. LA FOND & M. DURHAM, *supra* note 9, at 118.

Such responses are sometimes precipitated by "outside events" having virtually no likelihood of recurring in the jurisdiction in question. *See e.g.*, Morgan et al., *Guilty But Mentally Ill: The South Carolina Experience*, 16 BULL. AM. ACAD. PSYCHIATRY & L. 41, 42 (1988) (GBMI legislation in South Carolina partially inspired by Hinckley insanity acquittal notwithstanding fact that, in that state, insanity defense used successfully in no more than two out of 24,000 felony indictments per year).

165. Steadman et al., *Factors Associated With a Successful Insanity Plea*, 140 AM. J. PSYCHIATRY 403 (1983).

Such public pressure reflected in "vindictive community attitudes…subverts the humane intention of the law."[166] This subversion is made easier because of the law's "active avoidance of any true, psychological understanding of the defendants who come before the courts."[167] Where a defendant, then, does not show "flagrant psychotic symptomatology," or does not behave like a "wild beast," or where his behavior does not have apparent organic roots,[168] "pervasive judicial hostility" toward the use of the defense constantly surfaces.[169] Thus, a recent simulated study of nearly 200 college psychology students (a group that, presumably, would be more sensitive to the underlying issues than a random sample from the general public) revealed the following:

> The present study suggests strongly that the only defendant who will be found universally insane is the *totally mad individual* who acts impulsively to a *glaringly psychotic process* that is itself tied thematically to a criminal action. *Judge Tracy's "wild beast" conception of insanity is representative of most people's implicit theories of responsibility.* Even with respect to such a prototypically insane person, the concept of guilt still has appeal to the lay public, despite several hundred years of religiously toned jurisprudential logic that flatly opposes the morality of such attributions… [I]t is clear…that the public as a whole does not trust the underlying logic nor the administration of the insanity defense.[170]

---

166. S. HALLECK, *supra* note 69, at 251.
167. Curran, *Expert Psychiatric Evidence of Personality Traits*, 103 U. PA. L. REV. 999 (1955), *citing* G. ZILBOORG, THE PSYCHOLOGY OF THE CRIMINAL ACT AND PUNISHMENT 14 (1954).
168. V. HANS & N. VIDMAR, *supra* note 156, at 194-95, discussing, *inter alia* Ellsworth et al., *The Death-Qualified Jury and the Defense of Insanity*, 8 LAW & HUM. BEHAV. 81 (1984) (Ellsworth).
169. Arens & Susman, *Judges, Jury Charges, and Insanity*, 12 HOWARD L.J. 1, 2 (1966).
170. Roberts, Golding & Fincham, *Implicit Theories of Criminal Responsibility: Decision Making and the Insanity Defense*, 11 LAW & HUM. BEHAV. 207, 226 (1987) (emphasis added). *See also*, Finkel, *Maligning and Misconstruing Jurors' Insanity Verdicts: A Rebuttal*, 1 FORENS. REP. 97 (1988) (verdicts of mock jurors using "wild beast" test not significantly different from verdicts of jurors using M'Naghten test). For another empirical assessment of jury decision making in insanity defense cases, *see* Miller, Stava & Miller, *The Insanity Defense for Sex Offenders: Jury Decisions After Repeal of Wisconsin's Sex Crimes Law*, 39 HOSP. & COMMUN. PSYCHIATRY 186, 188 (1988) (insanity defense decision making based upon considerations of defendants' "apparent need for treatment and the right of the public to protection but not particularly influenced by legal definitions of insanity").

3. The Paradox of Sympathy

This atavistic picture of societal conceptions of responsibility may, however, be incomplete. Paradoxically, *other* research has revealed that there are certain groups to whom jurors have appeared to be inordinately (and, perhaps, even inappropriately) sympathetic in cases where insanity pleas are proferred.[171] When *these* cases are looked at, however, it appears that the results are consistent: that insanity defense decisionmaking regularly and systemically is based on a host of social and psychological factors which share a common thread: the *rejection* of psychodynamic principles.[172]

Thus, a series of New York studies identified at least three groups of insanity acquittees who not only did not appear to be "insane" under the prevailing substantive test, but seemed to be the recipients of jury *sympathy*: (1) certain women committing infanticide; (2) law enforcement officials; and (3) a category labeled by Dr. Richard Pasewark as the "we can feel sorry for you group" (in short, individuals with whom the jurors *could* empathize).[173] Over a ten

---

171. The categories to be discussed below are independent of the groupings where we have traditionally accepted (albeit in a grudging manner) the use of the defense: cases involving defendants who are probably entitled to outright acquittal on *mens rea* grounds (the archetypal lemon squeezer, *see supra* chapter 3, note 267), and those where the defendant meets the "wild beast" test of 1724, *see* Roberts, Golding & Fincham, *supra* note 170, at 226. For a parallel inquiry as to the way sympathy affects our attitudes toward the sentencing of white-collar criminals, *see* Benson, *The Influence of Class Position on the Formal and Informal Sanctioning of White-Collar Offenders*, 30 SOCIOLOG. Q. 465, 475 (1989).

172. For a recent call for further research in this area, *see* R. ROGERS, CONDUCTING INSANITY EVALUATIONS 9-10 (1986).

173. Steadman, Pasewark & Pantle, *The Use of the Insanity Defense*, in THE INSANITY DEFENSE IN NEW YORK 37, 57, 68-69 (1978) (NY DEFENSE) (of 28 female NGRIs in sample, 16 had been tried for infanticide; police officers disproportionately represented—four of 239 acquittees—in sample); *see e.g.*, Tornsney v. Gold, 47 N.Y. 2d 667, 394 N.E. 2d 262, 420 N.Y.S. 2d 192 91979) (police officer); *see also*, Pasewark, *Insanity Plea: A Review of the Research Literature*, 9 J. PSYCHIATRY & L. 357 (1981); Pasewark, Pantle & Steadman, *The Insanity Plea in New York State, 1965-19076*, 51 N.Y. ST. B.J. 186, 224 (1979). *See also*, Howard & Clark, *When Courts and Experts Disagree: Discordance Between Insanity Recommendations and Adjudications*, 9 LAW & HUM. BEHAV. 385, 394 (1985):

> [W]hen courts find defendants insane in spite of contrary expert opinion from state examiners, the discordance is not haphazard. The offenses are likely to be unusual ones, occupying neither the clearly rational nor clearly irrational ends of the spectrum. It is in the middle grounds, where subjective judgment is most needed to determine whether the test if insanity has been met, that discordance occurs.

year period, in fact, over two-thirds of all insanity acquittees in that jurisdiction fell into categories "of classes not necessarily predisposed to commit additional crimes."[174]

Different rationales for making "special allowances" appear to be employed in the case of each subgroup.[175] Henry Steadman and his colleagues inferred that we categorize women who murder their children as "insane" as a means of "preserv[ing] our illusions about 'mother love,'" and that institutionalized sexism, masquerading as "judicial chivalry," allows us to accept "certain cultural transgressions" more readily from women than from men.[176] Thus, in a recent high-profile matricide case, one of the expert witnesses told the court, "Mothers in our society simply do not kill their children unless they are seriously disturbed individuals, usually psychotic."[177]

---

174. Sherman, *Guilty But Mentally Ill: A Retreat From the Insanity Defense*, 7 AM. J. L. & MED. 237, 261 (1981) (e.g., individuals with no prior arrest record). Here, Dr. Loren Roth suggests, "We forgive, if not condone, a patient's past behavior on the basis of psychological determinism, or at times on heuristic reasons." Roth, *supra* note 18, at 100. *Compare e.g.*, Tayler, *Insanity: Hard Sell for Reza; Juries Disinclined to "Buy" the Defense*, Newsday (Sept. 21, 1992), at 4 (speculating whether physician charged with murdering his wife would fit into this category), to Riley, *Sol Wachtler Preparing a Defense; Could Be a Crazy Idea; Experts Doubt Effectiveness of Wachtler Insanity Plea*, Newsday (Feb. 7, 1993), at 44 (speculating whether state Court of Appeals chief judge charged in sexual extortion scheme would fit into this category) (full text of both articles available on NEXIS).

175. Pasewark, Pantle & Steadman, *supra* note 173, at 224; *see also*, Stokman & Heiber, *The Insanity Defense Reform Act in New York State, 1980-1983*, 7 INT'L J. L. & PSYCHIATRY 367, 373 (1984) (compared to New York state prison inmates, recent NGRIs of Islamic religion significantly underrepresented while Jewish NGRIs similarly overrepresented).

176. Pasewark, Pantle & Steadman, *supra* note 173, at 224; *see also*, Stokman & Heiber, *supra* note 175, at 382, *quoting* Steadman & Braff, *Defendants Not Guilty By Reason of Insanity*, in MENTALLY DISABLED OFFENDERS: PERSPECTIVES IN LAW AND PSYCHOLOGY 109 (J. Monahan & H. Steadman eds. 1983). *See also*, Ford, *The Role of Extralegal Factors in Verdicts*, 11 JUST. SYS. J. 16, 24 (1986) (perceptions of attractiveness associated with leniency in jury verdicts and unattractiveness associated with jury severity); Faulstich & Moore, *The Insanity Plea: A Study of Societal Reactions*, 8 LAW & PSYCHOLOGY REV. 129, 132 (1984) (in simulated study, insanity plea was viewed as more acceptable when accused was female). The most recent research shows that a high percentage of *all* victims of female killers are small children. *See* Goettling, *When Females Kill One Another: The Exceptional Case*, 15 CRIM. JUST. & BEHAV. 179, 186 (1988). Only four cases of *paternal* filicide have ever been reported. *See* Kaye, Borenstein & Donnelly, *Families, Murder and Insanity: A Psychiatric Review of Paternal Neonaticide*, 35 J. FORENS. SCI. 133 (1990).

177. Nelson, *Postpartum Psychosis: A New Defense?* 95 DICK. L. REV. 625, 625

As to police officers, the same authors speculate that "society, investing the officer with the sacred trust of protecting society and providing him with weapons for that purpose, is highly reluctant to accept the fact that this trust might be violated." We thus are willing to show this group "special leniency."[178]

Also, the "feel-sorry-for-you" group included those individuals who least met the *criminal* stereotype: "previously respectable, middle class individuals with whom the courts and/or juries can empathize,"[179] persons with no prior psychiatric or criminal record and no reported psychotic symptomatology[180] whose crimes appear "reactive to an immediate stressful situation."[181]

(1991), *quoting* report prepared in connection with the sentencing hearing in Commonwealth v. Comitz, 365 Pa. Super. 59, 530 A. 2d 473 (1987); *see also*, Waldron, *Postpartum Psychosis as an Insanity Defense: Underneath a Controversial Defense Lies a Garden Variety Insanity Defense Complicated by Unique Circumstances for Recognizing Culpability in Causing*, 21 RUTGERS L. REV. 669 (1990).

    Such defenses are not always successful. *See e.g.*, People v. Carlson, 179 Ill. App. 3d 1050, 535 N.E. 2d 79 (1989) (defendant's motion to vacate GBMI plea denied); State v. Jenner, 451 N.W. 2d 710 (S.D. 1990) (defendant's second-degree murder conviction affirmed; insufficient evidence presented to support insanity instruction to jury).

178. Sherman, *supra* note 174, at 261; Pasewark, Pantle & Steadman, *supra* note 173, at 224. Elsewhere, the authors also questioned whether there was an additional reluctance to place police officers in prison "with their former felon enemies." Steadman, Pantle & Pasewark, *supra* note 173, at 69.

179. Pasewark, Pantle & Steadman, *supra* note 173, at 224.

180. Pasewark, *supra* note 173, at 375. *But see* Resnick, *Perceptions of Psychiatric Testimony: A Historical Perspective on the Hysterical Invective*, 14 BULL. AM. ACAD. PSYCHIATRY & L. 203, 208 (1986) ("The closer a defendant is to normality, the more public opinion is outraged by insanity acquittals").

    This analysis may not be discordant with the data. Thus, if we can empathize with the defendant (and say, "*we'd* break down"), then we are more comfortable acquitting; if we feel, on the other hand, that "we'd be strong[er]", then we will reject the insanity defense. As our collective consciousness shifts, so does our perception of a defendant's breaking point shift. This analysis is consonant with the discovery by Stokman and Heiber that, compared with the period of 1971-76, the percentage of insanity acquittees diagnosed as suffering from personality disorders decreased from eleven to one percent in 1980-83. Stokman & Heiber, *supra* note 175, at 374. The researchers speculated that the "current opinion" regarding the insanity defense and the concepts of personality disorder as a mental disorder thus "discourages the use of personality disorder as a primary diagnosis in insanity defenses." *Id.* at 375.

181. Steadman, Pasewark & Pantle, *supra* note 173, at 70. *But see* Faulstich & Moore, *supra* note 176, at 132 (contradictory findings, showing that simulated study sample was *more likely* to accept insanity defense where defendant had psychiatric history; authors offer potential explanation based on the increased

Dr. Steadman and his colleagues use this example: "A professional male who was a compulsive gambler and had accumulated extensive gambling debts. Harassed by his debtors, threatened with harm and under severe stress, he committed robbery." [182] More recent studies have indicated that a greater degree of education (at least the completion of high school) is also frequently associated with a legal decision of nonresponsibility, leading to speculation that (1) triers of fact may more readily identify and empathize with more educated individuals presumably more similar to themselves, (2) there may be different criteria in referring better educated individuals for sanity evaluations, or (3) more educated individuals are more articulate and thus better able to participate meaningfully in legal proceedings.[183]

Finally, it has been suggested, without apparent contradiction, that in some cases in these categories, "the puny efforts of some of the prosecutors...greatly increased the chances of the defendants to gain [an insanity] acquittal."[184] To some extent, such cases appear to reflect a sort of *prosecutorial* nullification: prosecutors, like other citizens, "feel sorry" for this tiny sub-group of insanity pleaders, and choose to allow such defendants to "evade" responsibility. Illustratively, Professor Morse discusses a tax evasion prosecution hypothetical as an example of what he characterizes as an illegitimate use of mental disorder as a defense.[185] He posits a "nice middle-class" businesswoman who, in defense of her intentional failure to file income tax returns, claims that "strains on her produced mental disorder," thus giving the IRS a more "class-neutral ground for pursuing civil rather than criminal remedies." [186]

---

amount of information given to jurors in real cases). On the paradoxical question as to whether *bizarreness* of the criminal act itself is seen as indicative of insanity, see Stokman & Heiber, *supra* note 175, at 382; *compare* L. CAPLAN, *supra* note 49, at 56 (discussing case in which jury convicted defendant of five counts in a murder-rape indictment, but found defendant not guilty by reason of insanity on sixth charge that he sodomized victim after her death since "[it's] not a normal thing, for a man to sodomize a dead body").

182. Pasewark, Pantle & Steadman, *supra* note 173, at 224.
183. Rogers, Seman & Stampley, *A Study of Socio-Demographic Characteristics of Individuals Evaluated for Insanity*, 28 INT'L J. OFFENDER THER. & COMPAR. CRIMINOL. 3, 8 (1984).
184. Ireland, *Insanity and the Unwritten Law*, 32 AM. J. LEG. HIST. 157, 170 (1988).
185. Morse, *supra* note 123, at 376.
186. *Id. But see e.g.*, United States v. Barta, 888 F. 2d 1220 (8th Cir. 1989) (jury rejected defendant's "detail phobia"-based insanity defense in tax evasion case).

While Morse is undoubtedly right—that this solution allows society to avoid "facing the hard question of prosecutorial policy that is really involved"—the focus on the way "mental disorder may be used illegitimately to evade responsibility" misses the more important point. Our choice to (perhaps "improperly") exculpate a very few is simply the flip side of our decision to (improperly) inculpate many, a societal decision based on our conceptions of good and evil, right and wrong, and reflected in a "community sense of justice" that remains frozen in medieval views of responsibility.

Popular press coverage of legal troubles of famous athletes helps illuminate the underlying issues. Thus, *New York Post* columnist Phil Mushnick criticized Pete Rose's lawyers for "leaving him in the lurch" by *not* raising a mental status defense based on pathological gambling.[187] On the other hand, *New York Times* columnist Murray Chass quoted former baseball commissioner Fay Vincent's criticism of an arbitrator reinstating Yankee pitcher Steve Howe (following a guilty plea to a drug offense):

> "We're fortunate [the arbitrator] doesn't review the criminal convictions of most felons," Vincent said. "Otherwise we'd have them all out on the streets. No one would be in jail. If you pushed these medical, psychological reasons, you'd have no justice system. No one would be guilty. It's psychology run wild."[188]

Rose, the archetypal hero who gambled, is the recipient of public sympathy (and thus, an excellent choice for an insanity acquittal); Howe, a seven-time "loser" (that is, he had been suspended from baseball on six other occasions for drug-related activity), is the recipient of public scorn and anger (and thus, a prototype of the mental-defense-system abuser).[189]

4. The "Community Tolerance Threshold"

Dr. Caryl Boehnert has thus suggested that individuals who commit crimes that fall below the "community tolerance threshold"

---

187. Mushnick, *Lawyers Left Pete in the Lurch*, N.Y. Post (July 20, 1990), at 86.
188. Chass, *Howe's Endless Game of Chance*, N.Y. Times (Nov. 13, 1992), at B11.
189. *Compare* Kriegel, *Howie Gets 2 1/2 Years: "Criminal" Spira Is Really a Small, Tragic Figure*, N.Y. Post (Dec. 11, 1991), at 58 (criticizing prison sentence imposed on Howard Spira, "a genuinely sick man," who had been paid by former New York Yankees owner George Steinbrenner to attempt to discover material that would incrimnate or embarrass former Yankee player Dave Winfield).

(and thus would not trigger a concomitantly high level of community outrage) are more readily found not guilty by reason of insanity.[190] Professor David Wexler, in suggesting an "offense-victim approach" to the insanity defense debate, has similarly focused on the community tolerance threshold.[191] Accepting as his basic premise the need for the administration of the insanity defense to be harmonious with the "community sense of justice," Wexler has urged retention of the "morally-appropriate" defense "except in areas where its retention would likely enrage the community sense of justice and protection."[192]

As he views public concern over the insanity defense's use to be largely aimed at mentally disabled defendants who kill strangers (or, even, non-relatives), he would disallow the defense in such instances "that may well exceed bounds of public tolerance."[193] Adds Professor Wexler: "The public is far less fearful of the intrafamilial killer and possesses greater empathy for insanity acquittees in domestic homicide cases than it does in cases involving strangers."[194] Thus, even

---

190. Boehnert, *Psychological and Demographic Factors Associated With Individuals Using the Insanity Defense*, 13 J. PSYCHIATRY & L. 9, 27-28 (1983). On the use of the "community tolerance threshold" in other areas, *see* Rubinowitz & Trosman, *Affirmative Action and the American Dream: Implementing Fair Housing Policies in Federal Homeownership Programs*, 74 Nw. U. L. REV. 491, 538 n. 180 (1979) (discussing the "tipping" point involved following an influx of minority residents into a previously predominantly-white neighborhood). On its application to battered spouse cases, *see* Finkel, Meister & Lightfoot, *The Self-Defense Defense and Community Sentiment*, 15 LAW & HUM. BEHAV. 585 (1991).

191. *See* Wexler, *An Offense-Victim Approach to Insanity Defense Reform*, 26 ARIZ. L. REV. 17 (1984).

192. *Id.* at 20. *Compare* Packer, *Homicide and the Insanity Defense: A Comparison of Sane and Insane Murderers*, 5 BEHAV. SCI. & L. 25, 34 (1987) (juries are more sympathetic to defendants where victim is a family member).

193. Wexler, *supra* note 191, at 21-22. *See also,* Willis & Wells, *The Police and Child Abuse: An Analysis of Police Decisions to Report Illegal Behavior*, 26 CRIMINOL. 695, 710 (1988) (police reaction stronger if race or class of victim and offender different; in such cases "the degree of social intimacy is low"). *But see* H. STEADMAN, REFORMING, *supra* note 162, at 90 (California data revealed that type of victim had little to do with success of insanity plea).

194. Wexler, *Redefining the Insanity Problem*, 53 GEO. WASH. L. REV. 528, 552 (1985). A British study has revealed that the victims of 70-75% of homicides committed by mentally disabled defendants were related to the assailants. Parker, *The Victims of Mentally Disordered Female Offenders*, 125 BRIT. J. PSYCHIATRY 51 (1974). *See also,* Reidel, *Stranger Violence: Perspectives, Issues, and Problems*, 78 J. CRIM. L. & CRIMINOL. 223 (1987) ("Stranger violence represents one of the most frightening form of criminal victimization"); *see also,*

though Jeffrey Dahmer's murders appeared to *bespeak* insanity (leading a *Chicago Tribune* editorial writer to ask, "How could anyone kill so many people as Jeffrey Dahmer has admitted doing unless he was crazy?"),[195] the jury's rejection of the insanity defense in his case was seen as a necessary act in order that the defense itself survive.[196] The Dahmer prosecutor displayed photographs of each of Dahmer's victims to the jury so that the jurors could "remember their suffering," a tactic that, Professor David Dolinko rightly points out, might have been "quite relevant to determining the punishment for Dahmer's wicked deeds, yet surely out of place in assessing whether he was responsible, and hence 'wicked' in the first place."[197]

A victim-focused reduction would also eliminate much of the concern about repeat offenses by insanity acquittees: research has revealed a recidivism rate ranging from zero to "very low" in the cases of defendants who are found NGRI in cases involving family

---

DeStefano, *A Question of Sanity*, Newsday (July 7, 1991), at 5 ("The insanity defense has a better chance of working if a defendant was provoked, particularly if the victim was a relative," *quoting* forensic psychiatrist Dr. Daniel Schwartz) (full text available on NEXIS).

195. *"I Know I Was Sick or Evil,"* Chi. Tribune (Feb. 18, 1992), at 16 (editorial) (full text available on NEXIS). *See also, So Guilty They're Innocent; Criminal Innocence and the Sanity Plea: The Case of Serial Killer Jeffrey Dahmer*, 44 NAT'L REV., No. 4 (Mar. 2, 1992), at 17 (editorial). *Compare e.g.*, People v. Wilbur, 226 Ill. App. 3d 733, 589 N.E. 2d 1143, 1147 (1992) (Stouder, J., dissenting) ("In closing arguments, the prosecutor advised the jury numerous times to reject the 'popular myth' that someone who would commit this type of brutal murder must be 'sick'").

196. De Benedictis, *Sane Serial Killer; Experts Say Insanity Plea Alive and Well, Thanks Partly to Dahmer Jury*, 78 A.B.A. J. 22 (Apr. 1992); Worthington, *When Fantasy Becomes Reality: Dahmer's Illusions Turned Into the Most Deadly of Acts*, Chi. Trib. (Feb. 26, 1992), at C12 ("Once again, we learned that insanity defenses do not work for serial killers") (full text available on NEXIS); *but compare* Royko, *Verdict Aside, Dahmer's Nuts*, Trentonian (Feb.24, 1992), at 20, to Lillek, *He's A Monster—and He's One of Us*, Trenton Times (Aug. 1, 1991), at A16 ("Jeffrey Dahmer is no monster; he's human. That's his problem and our challenge.").

197. Dolinko, *Three Mistakes of Retributivism*, 39 U.C.L.A. L. REV. 1623, 1649 (1992). *Compare Psychobabblers Failed To Sell Evil as Illness*, L.A. Daily J. (Mar. 2, 1992), at 6 (editorial, reprinted from Tacoma (Wash.) Morning News Tribune):

If Dahmer's crimes are proof of his insanity, and hence his innocence, then what justifies sending any violent criminal to prison? The psychobabble that would exonerate Jeffrey Dahmer could exonerate Ted Bundy or Jack the Ripper. The greater the evil, the less the guilt....Evil is conscious and responsible; insanity is neither...

murders.[198] Wexler has stressed that this limitation is not a "moral model" but that it arises from a "pragmatic concern that, once a certain level of intolerance is exceeded, abstract moral discourse will simply not carry the day, and legislative revision will follow suit."[199] Thus, while the public is "inured" to a thirty percent-plus recidivism rate among released felons, "*any* criminal recidivism by insanity acquittees offends the public's sense of justice."[200]

Certainly, the research literature bears out at least the last part of Wexler's premise: that we do have, as Boehnert suggested, a community tolerance level which is triggered in NGRI cases. It is not so clear that the family member/stranger dichotomy is the only variable with which we must be concerned. Thus, the most recent research shows that, "[a]lmost without exception," women and whites are still over-represented significantly in virtually all categories of mentally disordered offenders being treated in inpatient psychiatric services.[201] While there are many possible explanations for this statistically significant disparity,[202] the "community tolerance threshold" suggestion

---

198. Wexler, *supra* note 191, at 23; *see also*, J. MONAHAN, *supra* note 122, at 96, 113-14. Acquittals in such cases can also sometimes be seen as a reflection of jury empathy. *See e.g.*, Layton, *Insanity Ruling in Garfield Death: Dad Shot Child's Alleged Rapist*, Bergen-Hudson (N.J.) Record (Oct. 15, 1992), at B1.

199. Wexler, *The "Offense-Victim" Insanity Limitation: A Rejoinder*, 27 ARIZ. L. REV. 335, 336 (1985). Prof. Finkel's jury research echoes Wexler's concerns. *See* Finkel, *supra* note 170, at 112 (in certain insanity cases, "jurors weigh the *victim's* actions and character along with the defendant's in their delicate calculus") (emphasis added). *See generally infra* chapter 7 A (discussing law's "tensile strength" in insanity defense cases).

200. Roth, *supra* note 18, at 94 (emphasis added). *See also*, Rappeport, *supra* note 37, at 695 (despite recidivism rate of 35 to 65 percent reported by all prison systems, public is more incensed by crimes of insanity acquittees than by those of ex-convicts).

201. Steadman et al., *A Profile of Mentally Disordered Offenders Admitted to Inpatient Psychiatric Services in the United States*, 12 LAW & HUM. BEHAV. 91, 98 (1988); for the most recent research *see*, H. STEADMAN, REFORMING, *supra* note 162, at 49 (women overrepresented); Packer, *supra* note 192, at 27 (9.4% of evaluated males found NGRI, compared to 23.3% of evaluated females; 4.7% of evaluated whites so found, compared to 2.6% of evaluated non-whites) (1987 study of 1980-83 sample); Morgan et al., *supra* note 164 (whites and women overrepresented in GBMI sample as well). *But see* Schneider & Jordan, *supra* note 162, at 159-60 (arguing that many women on whose behalf insanity pleas were entered in spousal homicide cases should have been viewed as acting in self-defense).

202. Steadman et al., *supra* note 201, at 98: "Do attorneys differentially advise clients to raise these questions? Do county prosecutors differentially accept such pleas or requests? Do judges and/or juries respond differently to these determinations?

of Dr. Boehnert's appears to provide the most likely answers.[203]

This employment of a "community tolerance threshold" is entirely consistent with the general methodology of the Rehnquist Supreme Court.[204] Over the past decade, the Supreme Court has become far more sympathetic to *majoritarian* claims, a change in course that has revealed itself in a series of hostile decisions to many disenfranchised groups, including, notably, the mentally disabled.[205] This hostility has led the courts to read the Constitution increasingly "through the eyes of mainline America" through means that are "insensitive or at least unempathetic to those most in need of its protection."[206] Contained in its opinions is at least the implicit endorsement of such a threshold, one that is frequently consonant with the imposition of the justices' own psychological, social, economic or moral preconceptions.[207] Our insanity defense jurisprudence reflects this threshold and this implicit judicial endorsement.

Do clinicians differentially recommend clients for evaluation or formal determinations? Do these patterns reflect differences in the detection of pathology?"
Dr. Daniel Schwartz, a prominent forensic witness, has suggested that the success of an insanity plea frequently hinges on the defendant's "likeability." Schwartz, *The Proper Use of a Psychiatric Expert*, in SCIENTIFIC AND EXPERT EVIDENCE IN CRIMINAL ADVOCACY 97, 111 (1975).

203. On the question of whether acceptance of the insanity defense in these cases may be little more than an example of jury nullification, an issue which has rarely been examined in the context of insanity cases, *see generally infra* chapter 6 D 6 a (1). For two exceptions, *see* Note, *supra* note 147, at 492-93 (nullification may "incorporate evidence of mental illness"), and Packer, *supra* note 192, at 34 (discussing case—involving young defendant without mental disorder who killed extremely abusive and threatening father—where judge rendered insanity verdict "as a means of exculpating a defendant who did not appear to warrant imprisonment but who did not qualify for any other exculpating verdict").

204. *See* Perlin, *Competency, Deinstitutionalization, and Homelessness: A Story of Marginalization*, 28 HOUS. L. REV. 63, 137-38 (1991).

205. *See* Perlin, *State Constitutions and Statutes as Sources of Rights for the Mentally Disabled: The Last Frontier?* 20 LOYOLA L.A. L. REV. 1249, 1258-59 (1987); *see*, for a recent empirical investigation, Mishler & Sheehan, *The Supreme Court as a Countermajoritarian Institution? The Impact of Public Opinion on Supreme Court Decisions*, 87 AM. POLI. SCI. REV. 87 (1993).

206. Stone, O.T., *1983 and the Era of Aggressive Majoritarianism: A Court in Transition*, 19 GA. L. REV. 15, 19, 22 (1984).

207. *See e.g.*, Pennhurst State School & Hospital v. Halderman, 465 U.S. 89, 106-12 (1984) (greatly expanding states' eleventh amendment immunity from suit in cases involving the right of institutionalized mentally disabled persons to community treatment); *see generally*, Rudenstine, Pennhurst *and the Scope of Federal Judicial Power to Reform Social Institutions*, 6 CARDOZO L. REV. 71, 76 (1984) (cases such as *Pennhurst* reflect court's wish to limit judiciary's power to

E. The Law's Ambivalence About Punishing the Mentally Disabled

1. Introduction

The legal system's overwhelming ambivalence toward psychiatry, psychiatrists and the psychiatric method's role in the adjudication process takes many forms, and is reflected consistently in a series of tensions: between our desire and need to punish individuals who threaten our social order, our fear and loathing of the mentally disabled individual who is "factually guilty,"[208] our fear that behavioral explanations are inherently too exculpatory, our attempt to throw off the shackles of the medievalist and punitive spirit that still dominates us,[209] and our desperate thirst for a mechanism that can accurately identify those few individuals whose mental disabilities are "so extreme" that their exculpation "bespeaks no weakness in the law."[210]

These tensions create ambivalence in six critical areas: (a) our views on whether it is "right" to punish a mentally disabled person charged with crime, (b) the way the insanity defense has been calibrated to accommodate psychodynamic explanations of behavior and our punitive urges, (c) the way we are pretextual in our assessment of the role of the psychiatric method in the legal process, and the role of behavioral expert testimony in criminal cases, (d) the way we treat individuals who have been found not guilty by reason of insanity, (e) the way we consider mental disability in other sentencing decisions, and (f) the way we assess mental disability as a potentially mitigating factor in death penalty cases.

---

vindicate federal civil rights in institutionally-based cases); Finer, Gates, Leon, and the Compromise of Adjudicative Fairness (Part II): Of Aggressive Majoritarianism, Willful Deafness, and the New Exception to the Exclusionary Rule, 34 CLEVE. ST. L. REV. 199, 205-06 (1986).

208. See generally, Seidman, Factual Guilt and the Burger Court: An Examination of Continuity and Change in Criminal procedure, 80 COLUM. L. REV. 436 (1980).

209. See Society for Good Will to Retarded Children, Inc. v. Cuomo, 572 F. Supp. 1300, 1304 (E.D.N.Y. 1983).

210. Kadish, The Decline of Innocence, 26 CAMB. L. J. 273, 284 (1968), quoting Wechsler, The Criteria of Criminal Responsibility, 22 U. CHI. L. REV. 367, 374 (1955).

2. Six Areas of Ambivalence

a. The "right" to punish the mentally disabled. Our actions have always reflected a special ambivalence toward the need to punish mentally ill individuals charged with crime. On one hand, there has been some sort of insanity defense operative since at least the twelfth century.[211] On the other, the tradition of the Middle Ages treated the mentally ill harshly whether or not they were "factually guilty" of the underlying criminal charge. Such individuals were regularly flogged "to drive the devils out of them;" their insanity was seen as criminal *in se*.[212] Mercier argued in one of the first treatises in this area, "The doctrine, upheld by so many medical men, that no insane person should under any circumstances be punished, appears to me both unjust and impracticable."[213] Treatment was simply not the purpose of confinement.[214]

One of the most persistent, vivid and profound pictures that has survived of the mentally ill (especially of the mentally ill criminal) is that of the madman as a beast. Foucault's imagery is especially vivid:

> Madness discloses a secret of animality which is its own truth…In the reduction to animality, madness finds both its truth and its cure; when the madman has become a beast, this presence of the animal in man, a presence which constituted the scandal of madness, is eliminated: not that the animal is silenced, but man himself is abolished. In the human being who has become a beast of burden, the absence of reason follows wisdom and its order: madness is then cured, since it is alienated in something which is no less than its truth.[215]

---

211. *See supra* chapter 3 A 1 a.
212. C. Hibbert, The Roots of Evil: A Social History of Crime and Punishment 201 (1968); Guth v. Walker, 92 Ga. App. 490, 88 S.E. 2d 821, 823 (1955). *See also* C. Hibbert, supra, at 201: "In case a man be a lunatic, take skin of a mereswine or porpoise, work it into a whip, swinge the man well therewith, soon he will be well." (quoting 2 O. Cockayne, Leechdoms, Wortcunning and Starcraft 335 (1864)).

On the use of whips and chains in institutions for the mentally ill generally, see Scull, *Moral Treatment Reconsidered: Some Sociological Comments on an Episode in the History of British Psychiatry*, in Madhouses, Mad-Doctors, and Madmen: The Social History of Psychiatry in the Victorian Era 105, 106-07 (A. Scull ed. 1988) (A. Scull); *see also*, C. Harding & R. Ireland, Punishment: Rhetoric, Rule and Practice 143 (1989) (Punishment).
213. C. Mercier, Criminal Responsibility 214 (1926).
214. Ellis, *supra* note 137, at 965. On the way that, historically, English insanity acquittees were historically imprisoned and chained, *see id.*
215. M. Foucault, Madness and Civilization 76 (1965), and *see generally id.* at

Andrew Scull explains that this stems from the seventeenth and eighteenth century conception that one who has lost his capacity to reason "has lost his claim to be treated as a human being." According to Scull:

> The division between apes and men was a permeable, not an absolute, one in eighteenth century conceptions of nature—an assumption which was exemplified in a number of different ways: the portrayal of criminals in animalistic terms, and the assimilation of the mad to the ranks of brute creation....And in the case of lunatics, the apparent insensitivity of the maniac to heat or cold, hunger or pain, his refusal to abide clothing, and so forth were simply taken as confirmatory of the correctness of the basic explanatory scheme.[216]

Foucault is again even more explicit: "Madness borrowed its face from the mask of the beast." Those chained to walls in early asylums "were no longer men whose minds have wondered but beasts preyed upon by a natural frenzy." Madness was thus ultimately seen "in immediate relation to [man's] animality, without any reference, without any recourse." A man without reason, concluded Pascal, would be "a stone or a brute."[217] Thus, according to Scull, resort to "fear, force and coercion" is seen as a "tactic entirely appropriate to the management of 'brutes.'"[218]

Many of the institutions in which such individuals were eventually confined had previously housed lepers and individuals with vene-

---

72-85. On the way that Foucault "connected the history of madness to the history of civilization and society," *see* Midelfort, *Madness and Civilization in Early Modern Europe: A Reappraisal of Michel Foucault,* in AFTER THE REFORMATION: ESSAYS IN HONOR OF J.H. HEXTER 247, 248 (B. Malamut ed. 1980).

It is not merely coincidental that the insanity defense test that comes closest to the public's notion of an appropriate measure of exculpation is the "wild beast" test. *See* Roberts, Golding & Fincham, *supra* note 170, at 226.

216. Scull, *supra* note 212, at 108-09.
217. Scull, *supra* note 212, at 109, *quoting* B. PASCAL, OEUVRES COMPLETES 1156 (1954); M. FOUCAULT, supra note 214, at 72, 77. On the medieval roots of the penal-like sequestration of the mentally ill, see Jones v. State, 52 Mich. App. 628, 218 N.W. 2d 89, 93 (1974).
218. Scull, supra note 212, at 109-10. *See also,* PUNISHMENT, *supra* note 212, at 143:

> [We do not know] to what extent responses to the diagnosis of illness, such as the whipping of the insane, may have reflected similar feelings of hatred and distrust, and a similar desire to distance the normal from the abnormal to those which we may find in the punishment of the wrongdoer.

real disease.[219] Often, they were used to confine "a motley assortment of criminals, aged, orphans, prostitutes, the poor, the mentally defective, and the mad." Always, an important purpose of such institutions was to deal with "immorality and antisocial behavior."[220]

"Treatment" of the mentally disabled in such institutions was generally punitive,[221] and the attitudes of the keepers towards their "patients"[222] were dominated by "superstition, moral condemnation, ignorance, and apathy."[223] As Harding and Ireland point out:

> [T]he leper colony may look very like the penal colony, and the stripes on the back of the madman who in earlier periods in Britain was whipped as part of his treatment would be practically indistinguishable from those on the back of a petty thief of the same time.[224]

Yet, even within the framework of this brutalization, the insanity defense developed steadily over an 800 year period.[225] The early formulations—satisfying the public's demands for an all-or-nothing test[226]—mirrored the "moral dogmata reflected in the [medieval]

---

219. M. FOUCAULT, *supra* note 215, at 3-23; PUNISHMENT, *supra* note 212, at 141; *see also*, Midelfort, *supra* note 215, at 261 n. 14 (Foucault's discussion of venereal disease cut from abridged English version of his text commonly in use).
220. Midelfort, *supra* note 215, at 251; G. ROSEN, MADNESS IN SOCIETY: CHAPTERS IN THE HISTORICAL SOCIOLOGY OF MENTAL ILLNESS 163 (1969 ed.).
221. In Great Britain, only by 1744 did the government recognize a need to provide treatment for the institutionalized mentally ill. *See* 1 M.L. PERLIN, *supra* note 17, §2.02, at 36-37, and sources cited at *id*. nn. 33-39.
222. The use of quotation marks around the word "patients" is purposeful. The horrors of St. Mary's of Bethlehem (Bedlam), the most famous English refuge for the insane, have been well-documented. *See e.g.*, F. ALEXANDER & S. SELESNICK, THE HISTORY OF PSYCHIATRY 114 (1966):

Should they survive the filthy conditions, the abominable food, the isolation and the darkness, and the brutality of their keepers, the patients of Bedlam were entitled to treatment—emetics, purgatives, bloodletting, and various so-called harmless tortures.

Compare In re Mazzara, 133 Ill. App. 3d 146, 478 N.E. 2d 567 (1985) (Webber, J., dissenting) ("[T]he term ['Bedlam'] has come to mean tumultuous uproar and confusion characteristic of early asylums").
223. K. JONES, A HISTORY OF THE MENTAL HEALTH SERVICES 10 (1972).
224. PUNISHMENT, *supra* note 212, at 141.
225. *See* Note, *A Continuing Source of Aggravation: The Improper Consideration of Mitigating Factors in Death Penalty Sentencing*, 41 HASTINGS L.J. 409, 418 (1990) ("The American penal system, without exception, has accorded special consideration and leniency to criminals suffering from mental abnormality").
226. *See supra* chapter 3 A 1 a. *Compare* Commonwealth v. Rightnour, 435 Pa. 104, 253 A. 2d 644, 653 (Roberts, J., dissenting), *overruled*, Commonwealth v. Walczak, 468 Pa. 40, 360 A. 2d 914 (1976), *quoting* Taylor, *Partial Insanity as*

theological literature"[227] and established the rationales that are still followed today: the insane, being childlike, could not distinguish between good and evil; the extent to which they suffered by reason of their state of insanity was "sufficient to account for any retributive feelings we might have towards them concerning their misdeeds."[228] To further punish the insane would create a sort of "moral double jeopardy."

That society was willing to suppress its punitive urges toward the mentally disabled criminal defendant and allow for a limited insanity defense, as long as the defendant was "utterly and obviously" beyond the reach of the law.[229] The more that such a defendant was "different," the less need there was to fear mob passions (in case of an insanity acquittal) since his "'getting away with it' would not call into question the validity of the repressive guilt which forbids violation of the social order."[230] We thus have grudgingly sanctioned the use of the insanity defense in cases involving defendants who appear to be "mad to the man on the street."[231]

Affecting the Degree of Crime—A Commentary on Fisher v. United States, 34 CALIF. L. REV. 625, 629 (1946), *quoting* W. WHITE, INSANITY AND THE CRIMINAL LAW 89 (1923) (Da Capo ed. 1981):

To conceive that an individual is either absolutely responsible or absolutely irresponsible is to fly in the face of perfectly patent facts that are in everybody's individual experience and is only comparable to such beliefs of the Middle Ages that a person is possessed of a Devil or is not possessed of a Devil, and therefore is or is not a free moral agent.

227. Platt & Diamond, The Origins of the "Right and Wrong" Test of Criminal Responsibility and Its Subsequent Development in the United States: An Historical Survey, 54 CALIF. L. REV. 1227, 1231 (1966); *see also,* Fentiman, *supra* note 164, at 651.
228. Platt & Diamond, *supra* note 227, at 1233; Golding, *supra* note 31, at 287.
229. Kadish, *supra* note 210, at 284. *See also,* M. MOORE, LAW AND PSYCHIATRY: RETHINKING THE RELATIONSHIP 198 (1984) (national research opinion survey found "there is an old, socially-sanctioned, well-established set of views which supports the identification of mental illness only with the violent, extreme psychoses and, within this context of ideas, mental illness emerges as the ultimate catastrophe that can happen to a human being"), and *id.* at 244 ("What is ...needed is an analysis of [the] popular moral notion of mental illness").
230. Ingber, *supra* note 142, at 956. We also are sometimes willing to apply it to cases involving family members or nonstrangers as victims, since we feel we have less to fear from a defendant whose target is one personally known to him. *See supra* chapter 4 D 4.
231. A. STONE, *supra note 132, at 219. See also, Bromberg & Cleckley, The Medico-Legal Dilemma: A Suggested Solution, 42* J. CRIM. L. & CRIMINOL. 729, 738 (1952) (to the lay person, the temporarily delirious patient "leaping over

The dominant image of brutality may also serve to helpfully explain why there are the few tiny categories in which juries seem to *overapply* the insanity defense—that is, where the insanity defense exculpates certain defendants who do not meet the defense's typically-rigid statutory criteria.[232] Jurors can be paradoxically sympathetic to these "empathy outlier" defendants—mothers committing infanticide, law enforcement officials, and a category labeled as the "we-can-feel-sorry-for-you people"—because these individuals do not conform to our pre-reflective and allegedly "common-sensical" views of the mentally disabled defendant as a "madman" or "beast." We thus do not have the same needs to punish them to "even out" the transgressor's evil in the usual way.

b. The role of the insanity defense. The development of the insanity defense reflects the uneasy détente between law and psychiatry (especially *forensic* psychiatry) over the past two centuries in a way that "threads the needle" by applying deterministic principles in what is, allegedly, a free will-based judicial system.[233] This balance is made even more tenuous by society's difficulty in separating the actions it sees as "wrong" from those it sees as symptomatic of illness.[234] It is no wonder that our attributions of responsibility are so "shaky."[235]

---

chairs and taking the broomstick to hallucinatory monsters [still] looks more genuinely psychotic than a deeply disordered but calm and brittle-worded schizophrenic"); Kadish, *supra* note 210, at 275 ("the law absolves a person precisely because his deficiencies of temperament, personality or maturity distinguish him *so utterly* from the rest of us") (emphasis added); United States v. Torniero, 520 F. Supp. 721, 724 (D. Conn. 1983), *aff'd*, 735 F. 2d 725 (2d Cir. 1984), *cert. den.*, 469 U.S. 1110 (1985) (insanity defense should be limited to cases involving defendants "alienated from human experience").

232. *See supra* chapter 4 D 2-3.
233. *See supra* chapter 4 B & C.
234. PUNISHMENT, *supra* note 212, at 141. In some traditional cultures, illness is still explicitly seen as a symptom of a wrong. *Id.* at 143.
    These tensions are reflected in the lengthly legislative and judicial battles over the appropriate procedures to be invoked following an insanity acquittal. *See* Jones v. United States, 463 U.S. 354 (1983); Foucha v. Louisiana, 112 S. Ct. 1780 (1992); *see generally infra* chapter 4 E 2 d.
235. Kaplan, *Unhappy Pierre: Foucault's Parracide and Human Responsibility*, 83 Nw. U. L. REV. 321, 323 (1989). *See also id.*:

We know the blame is contaminated with the social need to displace fault or flaw on the individual from the community, from the family, from the social order itself.

Except for cases involving "empathy outliers," we demand that defendants utilizing the insanity defense "seem clearly and totally crazy."[236] As a result, pre-existing attitudes toward the insanity defense become more important in verdict decision making than do factual variances or changes in the wording of the substantive responsibility test.[237] The resulting rigid, fixed, inaccurate picture is the dominant metaphor to jurors and to witnesses,[238] the dominant

---

236. Morse, *supra* note 123, at 654. This conclusion may need to be further unpacked to determine if there is a difference between (1) jurors' attitudes, (2) jurors' perceptions of general social attitudes, and (3) politicians' perceptions of either (a) jurors' attitudes or (b) jurors' perceptions of social attitudes. (Personal communication, Prof. Norman Finkel, Sept. 29, 1991).

   While research by Professor Finkel and his colleagues seems to contradict other findings that any evidence of "planfulness," *see supra* chapter 2 A 2 e, note 85, will result in rejections of insanity defenses, other characteristics about the simulated cases used in Finkel's studies—both involving female defendants, one a severely mentally ill paranoid schizophrenic (who had earlier sought psychiatric treatment) and the other an abused spouse—might have "overridden" the evidence of planfulness and led to NGRI findings. *See e.g.,* Finkel, *DeFacto Departures From Insanity Instructions: Toward the Remaking of Common Law,* 14 LAW & HUM. BEHAV. 105 (1990); Finkel & Handel, *Jurors and Insanity: Do Test Instructions Instruct?* 1 FORENS. REP. 65 (1988); Finkel, *The Insanity Defense: A Comparison of Verdict Schemes,* 15 LAW & HUM. BEHAV. 533 (1991); Finkel, Shaw, Bercaw & Koch, *Insanity Defenses: From the Jurors' Perspectives,* 9 LAW & PSYCHOL. REV. 77 (1985). On the impact of a defendant having sought therapy prior to the commission of the criminal act in question, *see* White, *The Mental Illness Defense in the Capital Penalty Hearing,* 5 BEHAV. SCI. & L. 411, 416-18 (1987).

237. Roberts & Golding, *The Social Construction of Criminal Responsibility and Insanity,* 15 LAW & HUM. BEHAV. 349, 372-73 (1991) (factors associated with jurors' subjective processing and construing of cases may be "powerful determinants" of predeliberational verdict outcomes); *see also,* C. Roberts, E. Sargent & A. Chan, "Juror Construal and Verdict Selection in Insanity Cases: A Research Note" (unpublished manuscript, 1991); *see generally,* Hans, *An Analysis of Public Attitudes Towards the Insanity Defense,* 24 CRIMINOLOGY 393 (1986); Finkel & Handel, *How Jurors Construe "Insanity,"* 13 LAW & HUM. BEHAV. 41 (1989). *Compare In re* New York Times Co., Misc. #82-0124 (D.D.C. June 19, 1982), *discussed in* Raskopf, *A First Amendment Right of Access to a Juror's Identity: Toward a Fuller Understanding of the Jury's Deliberative Process,* 17 PEPPERDINE L. REV. 357, 373 n. 111 (1990) (Hinckley trial court judge granted request for post-trial juror interviews because "publicity about the case is likely to play a large role in shaping public and legislative attitudes toward the insanity defense in the future").

238. For an example of how the insanity defense is construed by jurors in a "real life" case, *see generally infra* chapter 5 B (the case of Josee McNally). On witness perceptions, *see* State v. Clayton, 656 S.W. 2d 344, 350 (Tenn. 1983) (insanity defense rejected by fact-finder in light of police testimony that defendant "looked okay," in spite of "overwhelming, even staggering evidence" of severe mental

metaphor to counsel[239] and to trial courts,[240] and, ultimately, to Chief Justice Rehnquist.[241] Congress's response to the Hinckley acquittal reveals the power of this image.

c. The role of psychiatry in the legal process. Again, as I have already argued, our legal system is tragically ambivalent about psychiatry, forensic psychiatrists, the psychiatric method, and the role of psychiatry in the judicial process. We see psychiatry as "soft, exculpatory and confusing" and as "unseeable and imprecise," view psychiatrists as "wizards" or "charlatans." Through our reliance on heuristic cognitive errors, we reject much of contemporary behavioral scholarship on issues of interpretation of empirical data, classification, diagnosis, and predictivity of dangerousness.[242]

On the other hand, we turn—relentlessly and regularly—to psychiatry both to explain "inexplicable" deviant behavior[243] and to "take the weight" in decisions about an individual defendant's re-

---

disability; defendant's conviction subsequently reversed).

239. *See e.g.,* Franklin v. United States, 589 F. 2d 192, 194 (5th Cir. 1979), *cert. den.,* 441 U.S. 950 (1979) (no Sixth Amendment ineffectiveness violation where counsel failed to inquire into defendant's mental status when defendant seemed "alert and coherent").

240. *See e.g.,* Rogers v. State, 514 N.E. 2d 1259, 1261 (Ind. 1987) (affirming trial court's rejection of insanity plea where defendant's girl friend testified he did not act "crazy").

241. The Chief Justice's crystallized positions reveal a vision of mental disability that virtually mirror public perceptions in cases of Wainwright v. Greenfield, 474 U.S. 284, 297 (1986) (Rehnquist, J., concurring), Ake v. Oklahoma, 470 U.S. 68, 90-91 (1985) (Rehnquist, J., dissenting), Ford v. Wainwright, 477 U.S. 399, 435 (1986) (Rehnquist, J., dissenting), and Colorado v. Connelly, 479 U.S. 157, 169 (1987)). *See generally* Perlin, *supra* note 3, at 82-83.

242. *See supra* chapter 4 C 2-3; *see also,* Platt, *The Proposal to Abolish the Federal Insanity Defense: A Critique,* 10 CAL. WEST. L. REV. 449, 471 (1974); *see also,* Zilboorg, *Misconceptions of Legal Insanity,* 9 AM. J. ORTHOPSYCHIATRY 540, 543 (1939) (ideological attitudes of law and psychiatry, while both motivated by "deepest and greatest altruistic feelings, appear in practice extremely antagonistic;" relationship between law and psychiatry marked by "mutual suspicion and even open hostility").

243. *See supra* chapter 4 C 1; *see e.g.,* People v. Lopez, 233 Cal. Rptr. 199, 201 (1986), *review den.* (1987) (ordered not published; full text available on WESTLAW) (psychiatric testimony as to defendant's "inexplicable violent behavior"); Louisiana State Bar Ass'n v. Cryer, 441 So. 2d 734, 736 (1983) (psychiatric testimony "sheds some light" on respondent's "otherwise inexplicable behavior"); United States v. Stine, 521 F. Supp. 808, 811 (E.D. Pa. 1981), *aff'd* 675 F. 2d 69 (3d Cir. 1982) (psychological counseling ordered as part of probationary term where defendant committed "unusual, and often inexplicable behavior").

sponsibility, competency, or dangerousness.[244] This ambivalence leads to both pretextual and teleological decision making: that is, we privilege psychiatric expertise where it supports other instrumental social goals, yet we subordinate it where it is dissonant with such goals.[245]

The presence of experts in criminal justice proceedings may have additional impacts as well: it may validate elements of the criminal justice system itself, and it may reinforce (in the minds of judges, jurors, legislators and the general public) the idea that a legal definition of insanity, for instance, has scientific validity.[246]

As I will explore in more depth subsequently, I believe that much of the explanation of the incoherence of our insanity defense jurisprudence can be found in the way that courts are pretextual in their treatment of psychiatric evidence in mental health cases (both civil and criminal).[247] Trial judges ignore the impressive data base that suggests that the insanity defense is rarely pled, is more rarely successful, is a high-risk maneuver with a significant "backfire penalty,"[248] and, even when successful, is followed by lengthy incarcera-

---

244. *See e.g.*, Appelbaum, *Psychiatrists' Role in the Death Penalty*, 32 HOSP. & COMMUN. PSYCHIATRY 761, 762 (1981) (we use psychiatrists when we do not want to deal directly with what troubles us; "society's demand for psychiatric input [may] substitute for some hard thinking about the purposes of punishment and particularly about the role of the death sentence in the modern world"); Wasyliw, Cavanagh & Rogers, *supra* note 4, at 152, *discussing* Bazelon, *supra* note 31 ("Public decisions are often so close to impossible that those charged with making them are more than anxious to pass their burdens to unwilling experts"), and Suarez, *A Critique of the Psychiatrist's Role as Expert Witness*, 12 J. FORENS. SCI. 172 (1967) ("The judicial system lumps the conflicts, needs and fears of its terrible responsibility on psychiatry"). As forensic psychiatrist (and law professor) Alan Stone suggests, "The more they hate us, the more they need us." Stone, *supra* note 134, at 209; *see generally*, Perlin, *supra* note 75, at 133-34.
245. *See generally*, Perlin & Dorfman, *supra* note 9; Perlin, *supra* note 75; Perlin, *supra* note 130.
246. Wasyliw, Cavanaugh & Rogers, *supra* note 4, at 153.
247. *See generally infra* chapter 8 C; Perlin, *supra* note 129; Perlin, *supra* note 75, at 133-35. As I will demonstrate, there is a dramatic tension between those areas in which courts accept (either implicitly or explicitly) dishonesty in certain subject matter areas and those where they erect "unsurmountable barriers" to guard against what is perceived as feigning or malingering.
248. That is, when it is unsuccessfully pled, defendants receive significantly larger sentences than do defendants tried on similar charges who did not assert the defense. *See supra* chapter 3 B 1 d (1); Braff, Arvanites & Steadman, *Detention Patterns of Successful and Unsuccessful Insanity Defendants*, 21 CRIMINOL. 439, 445 (1983).

tions in maximum security facilities. They blind themselves to the unrebutted empirical reality and "continue to see the insanity defense as a wily lawyer's ploy, in which 'soft, bleeding heart' expert witnesses dupe gullible jurors into returning inappropriately-exculpatory verdicts," and assume that intelligent insanity pleaders were simply knowledgeable about psychiatric testing procedures and could thus "lie" and "fak[e] test results."[249] As a result,

> the legal system winks broadly at testimony that talismanically finds "dangerousness" (based on behavior that, in reality, shows either a need for treatment or an ability to provide optimal care for oneself) or that denies nonresponsibility in criminal *and* civil cases where a defendant's acts reflect textbook levels of mental disorder and pathology.[250]

Lawyers' passive-aggressive behavior here compounds the problems.[251] Because many lawyers have traditionally regarded mental disorders as "arcane and disturbing phenomena that are beyond their comprehension,"[252] they have made little effort to comprehend psychodynamic theory or diagnostic terminology.[253] This is especially

---

249. State v. Mercer, 191 Mont. 418, 625 P. 2d 44, 50 (1981); *see also*, People v. Kurbegovic, 138 Cal. App. 3d 731, 188 Cal. Rptr. 268, 273 (1982), speculating that defendant had had the opportunity to review courts' accounts of the relationship between mental illness and competency to stand trial. *See generally supra* chapter 3 B 1 b (1).

250. Perlin, *supra* note 75, at 134. *See e.g.*, Francois v. Henderson, 850 F. 2d 231 (5th Cir. 1988). On the significance and impact of courts' "fear of faking" in the development of insanity defense jurisprudence, *see generally infra* chapter 5 C 1.

251. I discuss such behavior in related contexts in Perlin, Tarasoff *and the Dilemma of the Dangerous Patient: New Directions for the 1990's*, 16 LAW & PSYCHOL. REV. 29, 57-58 (1992) (Perlin, *Tarasoff*); Perlin, *Reading the Supreme Court's Tea Leaves: Predicting Judicial Behavior in Civil and Criminal Right to Refuse Treatment Cases*, 12 AM. J. FORENS. PSYCHIATRY 37, 54 (1991) (Perlin, *Tea Leaves*), and Perlin, *Are Courts Competent to Decide Questions of Competency? Stripping the Facade from* United States v. Charters, 38 U. KAN. L. REV. 957, 984-85, 989 (1990) (Perlin, *Charters*).

252. Morse, *Law and Mental Health Professionals: The Limits of Expertise*, 9 PROF'L PSYCHOLOGY 389, 391 (1978).

253. *See e.g.*, Perlin & Sadoff, *Ethical Issues in the Representation of Individuals in the Commitment Process*, 45 LAW & CONTEMP. PROBS. 161, 166 (Summer 1982) ("many lawyers possess scant knowledge about psychiatric decisionmaking, diagnoses and evaluation tools"), and *id.* at 166-167 n. 49, *discussing* Poythress, *Psychiatric Expertise in Civil Commitment: Training Attorneys to Cope With Expert Testimony*, 2 L. & HUM. BEHAV. 1, 15 (1978); Perlin, *Fatal Assumption: A Critical Evaluation of the Role of Counsel in Mental Disability Cases*, 16 LAW & HUM. BEHAV. 39 (1992); Commonwealth v. Trill, 374 Pa. Super. 549, 543 A. 2d 1106, 1128 (1988), *appeal denied* 522 Pa. 603, 562 A. 2d 826 (1989) ("The

problematic in light of the fact that the presentation of the insanity defense "probably is the most demanding task of the defense lawyer."[254] This almost-helpless attitude on the part of the bar may be contrasted with the legal system's belated recognition of the need to reconstruct its views regarding rape and the traditional misogynist attitudes that shaped criminal law-rape policies over the past three centuries.[255]

In the specific context of the insanity defense, the bar's omissions are exacerbated by the failure of psychiatrists to systematically study the procedures used in clinical evaluations or the way clinical judgments are made in such evaluations; thus, the actual clinical practice of assessing insanity remains "largely idiosyncratic and invalidated."[256] In short, while the psychiatrist's role in the insanity defense is to attempt to reconstruct the defendant's state of mind at the time of the crime,[257] the legal system remains resolutely skeptical of psychiatry's ability to do just that.[258]

This skepticism is reinforced by evidence that expert witnesses' testimonial judgments may be colored by their *legal* attitudes,[259] by political ideology,[260] by the existence of an "identification bias"

----

concepts of the mind held by psychiatry and law are so disparate that it is difficult for the two professions to agree as to responsibility for behavior, especially criminal behavior").

254. Kwall, *The Use of Expert Services by Privately Retained Criminal Defense Attorneys*, 13 LOYOLA U. L.J. 1, 17 (1981). *See e.g.*, Miller v. State, 338 N.W. 2d 673, 678 (S. Dak. 1983) (Henderson, J., dissenting) (on defense counsel's failure to adequately explore a potential Post-Traumatic Stress Disorder-based insanity defense); on lawyers' failures to comprehend scientific testimony in general, *see e.g.*, United States v. Baynes, 687 F. 2d 659, 668-69 (3d Cir. 1982).

255. *See e.g.*, Geis & Geis, *Rape Reform: An Appreciative-Critical Review*, 6 BULL. AM. ACAD. PSYCHIATRY & L. 301, 310 (1978) ("Few self-respecting lawyers and psychiatrists today would endorse most of the mythology that passed for the lode of scientific information regarding rape a decade or so ago").

256. Rogers, *APA's Position on the Insanity Defense: Empiricism Versus Emotionalism*, 42 AM. PSYCHOLOGIST 840, 844 (1987).

257. Note, *Due Process Concerns With Delayed Psychiatric Evaluations and the Insanity Defense: Time Is of the Essence*, 64 B.U. L. REV. 861, 871 (1985).

258. *See e.g.*, Morse, *Failed Explanations in Criminal Responsibility: Experts and the Unconscious*, 68 VA. L. REV. 971, 972-76, 1083-84 (1982).

259. *See e.g.*, Homant & Kennedy, *supra* note 76; Homant & Kennedy, *supra* note 102.

260. *See e.g.*, Homant & Kennedy, *Judgment of Legal Insanity as a Function of Attitudes Toward the Insanity Defense*, 8 INT'L J. L. & PSYCHIATRY 67 (1986); Wasyliw, Cavanaugh & Rogers, *supra* note 4, at 149. *Compare* Estelle v. Smith, 451 U.S. 454, 477 (1981) (decision regarding psychiatric evaluation in death penalty case is especially difficult because it requires, on counsel's part, knowl-

through which the witness's "secret hope for victory" can lead to "innumerable subtle testimonial distortions and bias,"[261] and by their prior personal experiences.[262] This sort of evidence all helps to define the *power imbalances* inherent in systems in which forensic evaluators may come to their decisions for reasons of social policy rather than scientific expertise.[263]

d. Treatment of persons found NGRI. Insanity acquittees are perceived as perhaps the "most despised" and "morally repugnant" group of individuals in society.[264] They are the criminal defendants who have "gotten away with it," who have "beaten the rap," and been exculpated because of lack of criminal responsibility. The realities that this universe is a tiny one, that insanity acquittees are subject to long term institutionalization in maximum security facilities and a lifetime of follow-up supervision are obscured by our enmity.[265] We grudgingly accept the existence of the insanity defense as long as it is followed by lengthy periods of preventive detention.[266]

In the early 1970s, some courts began to read the due process clause expansively, and found that insanity acquittees were basically entitled to the same sort of commitment and release system as individuals subject to the involuntary civil commitment process. In *State v. Krol*, for instance, the New Jersey Supreme Court was explicit:

---

edge of "the particular psychiatrist's biases and predilections," *quoting* Smith v. Estelle, 602 F. 2d 694, 708 (5th Cir. 1979), *aff'd*, 451 U.S. 454 (1981)).

261. Diamond, *The Fallacy of the Impartial Expert*, 3 ARCHIVES CRIM. PSYCHODYNAMICS 221, 222 (1959).

262. *See e.g.*, Colbach, *American Forensic Psychiatry in the Eighties*, 29 INT'L J. OFFENDER THER. & COMPAR. CRIMINOLOGY 99 (1985).

263. B. Bursten, *supra* note 107, at 167; *see generally*, Perlin, *supra* note 76, at 117-19. *Compare* United States v. Segna, 555 F. 2d 226, 231 (9th Cir. 1977) (reversing conviction where prosecutor argued to jury that it must reject defendant's insanity defense unless defendant could convince jurors "by scientific evidence" that he was not sane).

264. Scott, Zonana & Getz, *Monitoring Insanity Acquittees: Connecticut's Psychiatric Security Review Board*, 41 HOSP. & COMMUN. PSYCHIATRY 980, 982 (1990); Perlin, *supra* note 23, at 396.

265. *See supra* chapter 3 B 1 b (1). Personality and behavioral characteristics of insanity acquittees are described in Nicholson, Norwood & Enyart, *Characteristics and Outcomes of Insanity Acquittees in Oklahoma*, 9 BEHAV. SCI. & L. 487 (1991).

266. *See* H. STEADMAN, REFORMING, *supra* note 162, at 156 (discussing New York experience). *See also*, Ellis, *supra* note 137, at 962 (public's major concern is length of time insanity acquittees remain institutionalized following NGRI finding).

"The labels 'criminal commitment' and 'civil commitment' are of no constitutional significance."[267] Decisions such as *Krol* were decidedly neither sanist nor pretextual; they rejected the underlying insanity acquittal as a principled basis upon which to premise a retention and release system that was significantly more restrictive than the one in place for individuals civilly committed.[268]

In *Jones v. United States*,[269] however, the U.S. Supreme Court made it clear that different rules for persons found not guilty by reason of insanity were constitutional, limiting its decision in *Addington v. Texas* (that had required proof by at least clear and convincing evidence) to civil cases.[270] *Jones* revealed the depths of the Supreme Court's discomfort with the status of insanity acquittees, even in the context of a case that involved a trivial offense—attempted petit larceny (shoplifting).[271]

The court approved a post-insanity acquittal recommitment scheme that placed the burden of proof on the patient to prove his lack of mental illness or dangerousness and that countenanced longer post-acquittal commitments than the maximum sentence the defendant could have received had he been convicted of the underlying charge.[272] Rejecting the patient's argument that the commission of prior "dangerous" acts had no predictive value as an indicia of future dangerousness, the court refused to distinguish between acts of violence and crimes such as the one under which Jones had been charged. Here it noted that it was appropriate to "pay *particular* deference to reasonable legislative judgments" made by Congress in this context.[273]

---

267. 68 N.J. 236, 344 A. 2d 289, 297 (1975); *see generally*, 1 M.L. PERLIN, *supra* note 17, §§2.10-2.11, at 88-89, on *Krol's* subsequent impact on involuntary civil commitment law.
268. *But see e.g.,* Whitfield v. State, 158 Ga. App. 660, 281 S.E. 2d 643 (1981) (finding of NGRI reflects factual determination that defendant met involuntary civil commitment standard).
269. 463 U.S. 354 (1983).
270. 441 U.S. 418 (1979); *see generally*, 1 M.L. PERLIN, *supra* note 17, §3.38, at 308-15. Prior to *Jones*, nineteen states committed insanity acquittees under the same procedures used to commit persons subject to involuntary civil commitment. Note, *Throwing Away the Key: Due Process Rights of Insanity Acquittees in Jones v. United States*, 34 AM. U.L. REV. 479, 480-81 n.7 (1985).
271. *Jones*, 463 U.S. at 359.
272. *Id.* at 370.
273. *Id.* at 364 n. 13 (emphasis added).

Over the vigorous objection of Justice Brennan (joined by Justices Marshall and Blackmun),[274] the majority quoted from an opinion that Chief Justice Burger had written while on the District of Columbia Court of Appeals:

> [T]o describe the theft of watches and jewelry as "nondangerous" is to confuse danger with violence. Larceny is usually less violent than murder or assault, but in terms of public policy the purpose of the statute is the same.[275]

The court also concluded that it was reasonable to presume that the defendant's mental illness continued; "someone whose mental illness was sufficient to lead him to commit a criminal act is likely to remain ill and in need of treatment."[276]

There is, self-evidently, no social science basis upon which to rest these assumptions. The court noted, for example, that it was not unreasonable for Congress to determine that insanity should be presumed to continue, in light of a Congressional committee report that had expressed the fear that "dangerous criminals, particularly psychopaths, [may] win acquittals of serious criminal charges on grounds of insanity yet still "escape hospital commitment."[277] There was no evidence whatsoever before the court in *Jones* that the defendant was a psychopath, that the insanity defense was in any way spurious or that the underlying criminal charges were "serious."

Jones was an utterly indeterminate decision that reflected perfectly the court's "unwillingness to contradict public sentiment [soon after the Hinckley acquittal] in such a controversial area."[278] It complemented the post-Hinckley statutory cutbacks in the insanity defense, and, perhaps, paradoxically served as a means of *preserving* the substantive defense: legislatures could now countenance a retained (albeit limited) defense if they knew that a successful insanity acquittee could be retained for lengthy periods of time in maximum confinement.[279] *Jones* provided the court with a vehicle through

---

274. *Id.* at 371. Justice Stevens dissented separately. *Id.* at 387.
275. *Id.* at 365 n. 14, *quoting* Overholser v. O'Beirne, 302 F. Supp. 852, 861 (D.C. Cir. 1961).
276. *Id.* at 366.
277. *Id.* at 364.
278. Note, Jones v. United States: *Automatic Commitment of Individuals Found Not Guilty By Reason of Insanity*, 68 MINN. L. REV. 822, 840 (1984).
279. *Compare* Note, *Automatic and Indefinite Commitment of Insanity Acquittees: A Procedural Straightjacket*, 37 VAND. L. REV. 1233, 1261 (1984) (on whether

which the court could impose its dissatisfaction with the insanity defense on defendants who succeeded in the use of the plea by a means that would make it likely that the plea be used even less frequently in the future.[280]

Jones may also be simply the reflection of the Supreme Court's inability to confront the complicated issues at the heart of the insanity defense.[281] While it has not proven to be "the death knell for the constitutional rights of insanity acquittees,"[282] it reflects the court's underlying larger agenda:

> [*Jones*'s] truncated review failed to take into account the powerful punitive urge which the public and its elected representatives, as well as some of our most noted judges, have displayed toward insanity acquittees. The Court's upholding of a lower standard of proof for acquittees than for civil commitment candidates in effect encourages this punitive urge, along with the overprediction of dangerousness to which acquittees are also subjected.[283]

Jones, at its base, was a *political* decision, "reflecting the Court's reluctance to contradict what it perceives as public sentiment."[284] It teleologically ignored social science, heuristically focused on a "worst case" fact pattern not before the court (that of the psychopath who avoids post-acquittal institutionalization), and encouraged the public's punitive urges. Its gratuitous use of the phrase *"particular* deference" in describing its response to Congressional judgments is strik-

---

Jones condoned surreptitious punishment of such individuals). On the "punitive motives" that generally underlie standard justifications for lenient commitment and stringent release standards for insanity acquittees, *see* Polstein, *Throwing Away the Key: Due Process Rights of Insanity Acquittees in* Jones v. United States, 34 AM. U. L. REV. 479, 479-80 (1985).

280. Note, *supra* note 270, at 521; Singer, *The Aftermath of an Insanity Acquittal: The Supreme Court's Recent Decision in* Jones v. United States, 477 ANNALS 114 (1985); *see also* Schmidt, *Supreme Court Decision Making on Insanity Acquittees Does Not Depend on Research Conducted by the Behavioral Science Community:* Jones v. United States, 12 J. PSYCHIATRY & L. 507, 515 (1984).

281. *See* Note, *Mistreating a Symptom: The Legitimatizing of Mandatory, Indefinite Commitment of Insanity Acquittees*—Jones v. United States, 11 PEPPERDINE L. REV. 569, 588 (1984) ("The Court appears to have succumbed to the ideological complexities of the insanity defense").

282. *See* Note, *supra* note 270, at 521; *compare* Foucha v. Louisiana, 112 S. Ct. 1780 (1992), *discussed infra* text accompanying notes 285-319.

283. Margulies, *The "Pandemonium Between the Man and the Bad:" Procedures for the Commitment and Release of Insanity Acquittals After* Jones v. United States, 36 RUTGERS L. REV. 793, 836 (1984).

284. 1 M.L. PERLIN, *supra* note 17, §3.44, COMMENT at 388.

ing in this context: what *is* it about mental disability law decision making (or, more precisely, post-insanity acquittal retention/release decision making) that makes this extra level of deference especially appropriate? *Jones* represents sanist judicial behavior at its worst.

Interestingly, the Supreme Court's other case involving an insanity acquittee was decided quite differently. In *Foucha v. Louisiana*,[285] the court held that the retention of a non-mentally ill insanity acquittee (who had originally been charged with weapons and drug offenses) in a forensic mental hospital violated the due process clause.[286]

It rejected on three different bases the state's argument that Foucha's anti-personality diagnosis provided a permissible rationale for further institutionalization. First, Foucha could not be civilly committed as currently mentally ill and dangerous, since antisocial personality disorder was not, under Louisiana state law, viewed as a "mental illness."[287] Second, relying on *Jackson v. Indiana*, the court found that if he could no longer be held as an insanity acquittee, he was entitled to constitutionally adequate procedures to establish permissible grounds for his confinement.[288] Finally, stressing the "fundamental nature" of the individual's "right to liberty,"[289] the court concluded that Foucha—who had never been convicted of a crime— could not be punished.[290]

At the hearing below, no expert had testified "positively" that Foucha would be a danger if he were to be released; one witness stated, "I don't think I would feel comfortable in certifying that he was not a danger to himself or to other people"; this testimony, the court found, was not enough to sustain further institutionalization.[291] The court concluded that the state had *not* shown, by clear and convincing evidence, that the defendant was mentally ill and

---

285. 112 S. Ct. 1780 (1992); *see generally*, 3 M.L. PERLIN, *supra* note 17, §15.25A, at 149-56 (1992 pocket part); Perlin & Dorfman, *supra* note 9, at 60-61.
286. *Foucha*, 112 S. Ct. at 1784.
287. *Id.* at 1784-85.
288. *Foucha*, 112 S. Ct at 1785, *discussing* 406 U.S. 715 (1972); *see* 1 M.L. PERLIN, *supra* note 17, at §2.08; 3 *id.* at §14.15.
289. *See* Youngberg v. Romeo, 457 U.S. 307, 316 (1982); United States v. Salerno, 481 U.S. 739, 746 (1987).
290. *Foucha*, 112 S. Ct. at 1785, *citing* Jones v. United States, 463 U.S. 354, 369 (1983).
291. *Id.*

dangerous, and Foucha could thus no longer be kept institutional-ized.[292]

Justice O'Connor concurred, stressing the uncertainty of scientific knowledge[293] as a basis for courts to pay "particular deference" to legislative judgments about the relationship between dangerous behavior and mental illness.[294] She also emphasized that nothing in the majority's opinion could be construed as suggesting either that the insanity defense was constitutionally mandated, that guilty-but-mentally-ill statutes might be constitutionally suspect,[295] or that the court's decision in *Jones* was in any way modified or overturned.[296]

Justice Kennedy dissented in an opinion joined by the Chief Justice, arguing that, notwithstanding the jury's verdict of not guilty by reason of insanity in Foucha's underlying criminal trial, the case does not differ substantially from one in which a defendant had been convicted of the precedent crime, and that earlier civil cases relied upon by the majority (such as *O'Connor v. Donaldson*[297] and *Addington v. Texas*)[298] should thus be inapplicable, characterizing the distinction between an NGRI and a GBMI verdict as a trivial "choice of nomenclature."[299]

Justice Thomas also dissented in an opinion joined by the Chief Justice and Justice Scalia. He based his conclusion that Foucha's continued retention in a forensic psychiatric hospital (notwithstanding a finding that he was not mentally ill) was permissible on a variety of sources, including the 1962 commentary to the Model Penal Code, a 1933 text by Henry Weihofen, and a 1956 Supreme Court case that had stressed psychiatry's "uncertainty of diagnosis."[300] He focused at some length on the possibility of "calculated

---

292. *Foucha*, 112 S. Ct. at 1786.
293. *Id.* at 1789 (O'Connor, J., concurring in part & concurring in judgment), *citing Jones*, 463 U.S. at 354, *quoting* Greenwood v. United States, 350 U.S. 366, 375 (1966).
294. *Foucha*, 112 S. Ct at 1789, *quoting Jones*, 463 U.S. at 365 n. 13.
295. *Foucha*, 112 S. Ct. at 1790. *See supra* chapter 3 A 1 c (4).
296. *Foucha*, 112 S. Ct. at 1789-90.
297. 422 U.S. 563 (1975) (constitutional right to liberty).
298. 441 U.S. 418 (1979) (clear and convincing evidence required as burden of proof in civil commitment hearing).
299. *Foucha*, 112 S. Ct at 1793-94 (Kennedy, J., dissenting).
300. *See id.* at 1797 (Thomas, J., dissenting) (referring to "current provisions of the American Law Institute's Model Penal Code), *cf. id.* at 1787 n. 6 (majority opinion) (charging that sections in question "fail to incorporate or reflect substantial developments in the relevant decisional law during the intervening

abuse of the insanity defense" by defendants who might feign the plea, and speculated as to how the public might react to the specter of a "serial killer...returned to the streets immediately after trial."[301]

The opinions in *Foucha* raise a series of difficult questions.[302] Had the dissenters prevailed and Foucha's recommitment order upheld, what impact would this have had for the staff at the forensic facility at which Foucha was institutionalized? How would he have been treated if he were no longer mentally ill? What impact would this have had on the other patients institutionalized there?[303]

Will *Foucha* lead to the creation of an intermediate type of facility for "dangerous-but-no-longer-mentally-ill" individuals? Would the creation of such a facility be constitutionally permissible? Is Foucha—who had been involved in several altercations with other patients while institutionalized[304]—exculpated, by reason of the NGRI verdict, from taking responsibility for what would otherwise be considered criminal acts committed at a forensic facility? Does it make sense to prosecute such cases?[305]

Justice Thomas's opinion is especially remarkable for several reasons.[306] First, he relies on legal scholarship that precedes (by ten to 40 years) the Court's application of the due process clause to cases involving the institutionalization of mentally disabled criminal defendants.[307] Second, he relies on a mid-1950s characterization of psychiatric precision in diagnosis to suggest that psychiatry is so inexact that the court should discount expert testimony saying that an individual once acquitted on grounds of insanity is not mentally ill; yet he

---

three decades"); *id.* at 1801 (Thomas, J., dissenting) (*citing* Greenwood v. United States, 350 U.S. 366, 375 (1956), for proposition that there is "uncertainty of diagnosis" in psychiatry), *and id.* at 1806 (*citing, inter alia*, HENRY WEIHOFEN, INSANITY AS A DEFENSE IN CRIMINAL LAW 294-332 (1933), for proposition that there is a long history of states providing for the continued institutionalization of dangerous insanity acquittees).

301. *Id.* at 1801-02; *see also, id.* at 1797 (Kennedy, J., dissenting).
302. *See generally*, M. Perlin, "Law as a Therapeutic and Anti-Therapeutic Agent," paper presented at the Massachusetts Department of Mental Health's Division of Forensic Mental Health's annual conference, Auburn, MA (May 1992), at 14-16.
303. *See* Perlin, *Tarasoff, supra* note 251, at 48-49, discussing *Foucha*'s potential influence in this context.
304. *See Foucha*, 112 S. Ct. at 1782-83.
305. *See e.g.*, Norko, Zonana & Phillips, *Prosecuting Assaultive Psychiatric Inpatients*, 42 HOSP. & COMMUN. PSYCHIATRY 193 (1991).
306. *See generally*, Perlin & Dorfman, *supra* note 9, at 60-61.
307. *See* Jackson v. Indiana, 406 U.S. 715 (1972).

finds that psychiatric predictions of dangerousness are sufficiently reliable to require the acquittee's future institutionalization (although, here, the experts hedged on even this prediction).[308]

Third, his twin foci on the sanist judges' worst fears about insanity acquittees—that they "faked" the insanity defense in the first place and that the improper use of the defense will allow for the speedy release of serial killers profoundly demonstrates how judges can distort social science evidence. His reference to "serial killers" is even more perplexing here, given the fact that Foucha's underlying charges were burglary and firearms offenses.[309]

In short, while *Foucha* clarifies the narrow question before the court, it raises a host of other difficult mental disability law issues. Justice Kennedy's opinion, characterizing the distinction between an NGRI and a GBMI verdict as a trivial "choice of nomenclature,"[310] is especially troubling. Centuries of insanity defense jurisprudence have rested on the proposition that "our collective consciousness does not allow punishment where it cannot impose blame."[311] A finding of NGRI is an expression by the community's representatives of that lack of blame. A GBMI verdict, on the other hand, is a finding of guilty with an additional aspirational (but optional) hope that the convicted defendant—subjected to harsh penal punishment—receive some sort of treatment while institutionalized.[312]

Beyond this, if Kennedy were right, would that have meant that a "forensic mental health facility" was inevitably nothing more than a prison who were found not responsible for their crimes? Courts have held that insanity acquittees—like other institutionalized men-

---

308. *See Foucha*, 112 S. Ct. at 1808-09 (Thomas, J., dissenting) ("I see no basis for holding that the Due Process Clause per se prohibits a state from continuing to confine in a 'mental institution'...an insanity acquittee who has recovered his sanity"). *Compare id.* at 1783 n. 3 (Justice White's response to this argument). On the inability of psychiatrists to consistently predict long-term dangerous behavior accurately, *see supra* chapter 4 C 3.

309. *Foucha*, 112 S. Ct at 1782.

310. *Id.* at 1793.

311. Holloway v. United States, 148 F. 2d 665, 666 (D.C. Cir. 1945), *cert. denied*, 334 U.S. 852 (1948).

312. *See e.g.*, Slobogin, *The Guilty But Mentally Ill Verdict: An Idea Whose Time Should Not Have Come*, 53 GEO. WASH. L. REV. 494, 513 (1985); McGraw, Farthing-Capwich & Keilitz, *The "Guilty But Mentally Ill" Plea and Verdict: Current State of the Knowledge*, 30 VILL. L. REV. 117, 187 (1985); People v. Marshall, 124 Ill. App. 3d 217, 448 N.E. 2d 969, 980 (1983); People v. Smith, 124 Ill. App. 3d 805, 465 N.E. 2d 101 (1984); *see supra* chapter 3 A 1 c (5).

tally disabled persons—have a constitutional right to treatment[313] and a constitutional right to refuse treatment.[314] These rights are generally far broader than those afforded to prison inmates.[315] If the difference between NGRI and GBMI is only one of "nomenclature," how will these rights-based discrepancies be resolved?

The majority opinion in *Foucha*, then, certainly erodes some of the sanist and teleological bases of *Jones*. Yet, suggestions raised by the dissenters suggest that the Court is still uneasy about affording insanity acquittees substantial substantive or procedural due process rights. Also, because the evidence showed that Foucha was not mentally ill, it might have been easier for the majority to resolve (or at least bypass) its ambivalence about this question. Prior Supreme Court decisions in other areas of mental disability law have taken as a given that the litigants are, in fact, genuinely mentally ill.[316] Faced with uncontradicted testimony that Foucha did not fall into this category (under Louisiana's own definition of the term), five members of the court were able to throw off the usual sanist shackles, and decide the case in a principled manner.

It may be impossible for this court—or any court—to "assuag[e] public fear of dangerous individuals,"[317] especially individuals such

---

313. *See e.g.*, Rouse v. Cameron, 373 F. 2d 451 (D. C. Cir. 1966); Davis v. Watkins, 384 F. Supp. 1196 (N.D. Ohio 1974); Marshall v. Kort, 690 P. 2d 219 (Colo. 1984); State v. Kupchun, 373 A. 2d 1325 (N.H. 1977); Parry, *The Civil-Criminal Dichotomy in Insanity Commitment and Release Proceedings: Hinckley and Other Matters*, 11 MENT. & PHYS. DIS. L. REP. 218 (1987).

314. *See e.g.*, Davis v. Hubbard, 506 F. Supp. 915 (N.D. Ohio 1980); Williams v. Wilzack, 319 Md. 485, 573 A. 2d 809 (1990), *reconsid den.* (1990); State v. Nording, 485 N.W. 2d 781 (N. Dak. 1992); Perlin, *Tea Leaves, supra* note 251, at 47-48; 2 M.L. PERLIN, *supra* note 17, §5.65, at 76-78 (1992 pocket part). *But compare*, Perlin, *Pretexts, supra* note 130, manuscript at 90 (disposition of post-insanity acquittal release hearing often hinges on court's assessment of whether defendant will take antipsychotic medication in community setting); *see e.g*, State v. Jacob, 669 P. 2d 865, 869 (Utah 1983); Clark v. State , 151 Ga. App. 853, 261 S.E. 2d 764 (1979).

315. *See e.g.*, Hoptowit v. Ray, 682 F. 2d 1237 (9th Cir. 1982) (limited right to treatment); Washington v. Harper, 494 U.S. 210 (1990) (limited right to refuse treatment); 3 M.L. PERLIN, *supra* note 17, §16.22, at 485-86, and 2 *id.*, §5.64A, at 62-74 (1992 pocket part).

316. *See* Perlin, *An Invitation to the Dance: An Empirical Response to Chief Justice Warren Burger's "Time-Consuming Procedural Minuets Theory in* Parham v. J.R., 9 BULL. AM. ACAD. PSYCHIATRY & L. 149, 151 (1981), and 1 M.L. PERLIN, *supra* note 17, §3.72, at 423-24, critiquing the court's decision in Parham v. J.R., 442 U.S. 584 (1979) (more relaxed procedural due process constitutionally permissible in cases involving involuntary civil commitment of juveniles).

317. Leong, Silva & Weinstock, *Dangerous Mentally Disordered Criminals: Unre-*

as insanity acquittees, so "despised and feared" that many clinicians resist providing them with mental health treatment.[318] However, it should not be impossible for members of the Court to set aside sanist prejudices and resist pretextual decision making. It is *not* an axiom of criminal procedure that rights be denied "to all because of the fear that a few might abuse them."[319] If the court was serious in the exclusionary zoning case of *City of Cleburne v. Cleburne Living Center* when it declared, "Private biases may be outside the reach of the law, but the law cannot directly or indirectly give them effect,"[320] then its members should not give such biases lasting effect in the context of judicial opinions.

e. Mental disability and the federal sentencing guidelines.[321] In response to criticisms of indeterminate sentencing,[322] Congress passed the 1984 Sentencing Reform Act in an attempt to bring about a measure of regularity and uniformity in federal sentencing procedures.[323] Under statutorily-mandated *Sentencing Guidelines*, a sen-

---

solvable Societal Fear? 36 J. FORENS. SCI. 210, 215 (1991).
318. Scott, Zonana & Getz, *supra* note 264, at 982. *See also*, Parry, *The Civil-Criminal Dichotomy in Insanity Commitment and Release Proceedings: Hinckley and Other Matters*, 11 MENT. & PHYS. DIS. L. REP. 218, 223 (1987) ("hospitals have been pressured by public outrage to bend over backwards to make sure no insanity acquittee is released too soon, even if such public pressure is contrary to the intent and spirit of being found not guilty by reason of insanity").
319. Bolton v. Harris, 395 F. 2d 642, 649 n. 35 (D.C. Cir. 1968).
320. 473 U.S. 432 (1985), *quoting* Palmore v. Sidoti, 466 U.S. 429, 433 (1984) (local ordinance excluding group homes for the retarded violated "rational basis" equal protection test).
321. The material *infra* text accompanying notes 321-33 is largely adapted from 3 M.L. PERLIN, *supra* note 17, §16.18A at 186-89 (1992 pocket part).
322. *See* Mistretta v. United States, 488 U.S. 361, 365 (1989) (discussing sentencing disparities).
323. *See* 18 U.S.C. §§3551-3742, and 28 U.S.C. §§991-998 (1988). Under this law, a Sentencing Commission was created, *see* 28 U.S.C. §991, and was directed to issue Sentencing Guidelines in accordance with the Act, *see* 28 U.S.C. §994(a)(1). Under the Act, a series of permissible sentencing ranges is created for each federal criminal offense. *See* 28 U.S.C. §994(b)(2). The constitutionality of the Guidelines—a binding set of rules that courts must use in imposing sentences—has been upheld by the Supreme Court in Mistretta, *supra; see generally*, Nagel, *Structuring Sentencing Discretion: The New Federal Sentencing Guidelines*, 80 J. CRIM. L. & CRIMINOL. 883 (1990).
  These Guidelines, of course, do not bind state sentencing tribunals. *See e.g.*, State v. Anderson, 789 P. 2d 27 (Utah 1990) (despite defendant's mental retardation, no error in sentence of two consecutive five year terms to state prison instead of to state hospital); State v. Notch, 1988 WL 83673 (Minn. Ct. App. 1988), at 3 (affirming 78% upward departure from state sentencing guidelines

tencing court may depart from the prescribed ranges where "the defendant committed a nonviolent offense while suffering from significantly reduced mental capacity[324] not resulting from voluntary use of drugs or other intoxicants."[325] In such cases, a lower sentence "may be warranted" to reflect the extent to which the reduced mental capacity contributed to the commission of the offense, so long as the defendant's criminal history "does not indicate a need for incarceration to protect the public."[326] On the other hand, a different guideline suggests that a defendant's mental condition may be relevant as either a "mitigating or aggravating" factor in determining conditions of probation and/or supervised release.[327]

In several recent cases, courts have invoked the Guidelines to reduce a defendant's sentence based on reduced mental capacity.[328] In

---

in case of mentally ill defendant); Commonwealth v. Faulkner, 528 Pa. 57, 595 A. 2d 28, 38 (1991) (finding of substantial mental impairment does not bar death penalty); State v. Watson, 211 Mont. 401, 686 P. 2d 879 (1984) (sentence of 300 years without parole not cruel and unusual punishment despite substantial evidence of mental disease); State v. Allert, 117 Wash. 2d 156, 815 P. 2d 752 (1991), rev'g, 58 Wash. App. 200, 791 P. 2d 932 (1990) (improper for court below to have imposed exceptional sentence below statutory range on mentally disabled defendant); compare id., 815 P. 2d at 759 (Johnson, J., dissenting) (urging affirmance of intermediate appellate court's decision upholding trial court's downward departure).

324. On the question of whether a compulsive gambling disorder satisfies the Guidelines, see United States v. Katzenstein, 1991 WL 24386 (S.D.N.Y. 1991) (unless defendant could demonstrate that total rehabilitation had been achieved, she would have to introduce evidence showing lack of correlation between compulsive gambling disorder and increased propensity for criminal activity); United States v. Rosen, 896 F. 2d 789 (3d Cir. 1990), rehearing & en banc den. (1990) (defendant's compulsive gambling did not warrant downward departure).

325. United States Sentencing Commission Guideline Manual §5k2.13 (Manual). Compare Denno, Human Biology and Criminal Responsibility: Free Will or Free Ride? 137 U. Pa. L. Rev. 615, 617 (1988) (mitigating factors should not reduce sentence but should only determine the type of facility used for detaining or treating convicted prisoner).

326. Id. Great discretion is vested in the trial courts in determining when a sentence reduction is appropriate under the Guidelines. See e.g., United States v. Yellow Earrings, 891 F. 2d 650, 654-55 (8th Cir. 1989).

327. Manual, supra note 414, at §5h1.3; see T. Hutchison & D. Yellen, Federal Sentencing Law and Practice, Annotations to §5h1.3 (1989) (quality of mental condition needed to trigger section's operation undefined). Compare Berkman, Mental Illness as an Aggravating Circumstance in Capital Sentencing, 89 Colum. L. Rev. 291 (1989) (considering aggravating circumstances that flow from defendant's mental illness in death penalty cases is constitutionally impermissible).

328. See also, United States v. Morales, 905 F. 2d 599 (2d Cir. 1990) (upholding departure from Guidelines based on defendant's likely "extreme vulnerability"

United States v. Speight,[329] the court found that a defendant (con-victed of drug and firearm offenses) who suffered from schizophrenia and other emotional disturbances met all the criteria of the Guide-lines, and that a sentence reduction was thus warranted.[330] In *United States v. Ruklick,*[331] the court emphasized that, under the Guidelines, it was not necessary to find that the defendant's reduced mental capacity amounted to "but-for causation" in order to reduce a sen-tence, as long as his diminished mental capacity "comprised a con-tributing factor in the commission of the offense."[332]

On the other hand, determinations to *not* depart from the Guidelines have been upheld where the underlying crime was violent, and where the defendant's violent criminal record raised the possibil-ity that he would threaten public safety,[333] and in another case where the jury had rejected the defendant's insanity defense.[334] Again, this series of decisions reflects the courts' profound ambivalence about the effect of mental disability on the severity of criminal punishment.

f. Mental disability and the death penalty. Our ambivalence about the insanity defense is reflected in a series of four related conundrums raised in cases involving mentally disabled criminal defendants in areas relating to death penalty determinations. I will thus address (1) the extent to which expert testimony is admissible on the question of

---

in a correctional facility).

There are limits to the use of mental disability as a reductive element. *See* Sentencing Commission's Policy Statement Regarding Mental and Emotional Conditions, Guideline 5H1.3 ("Mental and emotional conditions are not ordi-narily relevant in determining whether a sentence should be outside the guide-lines, except as provided in the general provisions of Chapter 5"); *see generally,* Houser, *Downward Departures: The Lower Envelope of the Federal Sentencing Guidelines,* 31 Duq. L. Rev. 361 (1993).

329. 726 F. Supp. 861 (D.D. C. 1989).
330. *Id.* at 867-68. *See also,* United States v. Adonis, 744 F. Supp. 336 (D.D.C. 1990). *Compare* United States v. Doering, 909 F. 2d 392 (9th Cir. 1990) (prohibiting *upward* departure where evidence reflected need for psychiatric care).
331. 919 F. 2d 95 (8th Cir. 1990).
332. *Id.* at 97-98. *Compare* United States v. Gentry, 925 F. 2d 186, 188-89 (7th Cir. 1991), *rehearing den.* (1991) (sentencing court must assess whether defendant possesses "*significantly* reduced mental incapacity" in justifying downward departure from Guidelines) (emphasis in original).
333. United States v. Wilson, 891 F. 2d 293 (6th Cir. 1989) (Table) (full text available on WESTLAW); *see also,* United States v. Lauzon, 938 F. 2d 326 (1st Cir. 1991) (defendant's mental impairment insufficient to justify downward departure); United States v. Poff, 926 F. 2d 588 (7th Cir. 1991) (same): United States v. Wilson, 920 F. 2d 1290 (6th Cir. 1990) (same).
334. United States v. Spedalieri, 910 F. 2d 707 (10th Cir. 1990).

future dangerousness in death penalty cases; (2) the extent to which jurors accept mental disability as a mitigating factor in such cases; (3) the way courts factor in mental disability in determining whether a defendant on death row is competent to be executed, and (4) the extent to which a death row inmate can be medicated to make him competent to be executed. In each instance, our failure to resolve the tension between our punitive urges and our need to exculpate the profoundly mentally disabled reflects our culture's core values.

(1) Expert testimony and future dangerousness.[335] In *Jurek v. Texas,* the Supreme Court specifically upheld the constitutionality of a state statute that required a jury to determine, beyond a reasonable doubt, whether there was a "probability that the defendant would commit criminal acts of violence that would constitute a continuing threat to society."[336] The role of expert testimony in *Jurek* cases was subsequently clarified and expanded upon in *Barefoot v. Estelle.*[337] In *Barefoot,* in the face of unanimous scholarly and academic opposition,[338] the United States Supreme Court affirmed the denial of a habeas corpus petition in a death penalty case where expert witnesses (who had not examined the defendant) testified in response to hypotheticals that the defendant "would probably commit further acts of violence and represent a continuing threat to society."[339]

The court rejected the position of the American Psychiatric Association (as *amicus*) that such testimony was invalid due to "fundamentally low reliability" and that any such predictions as to long-term dangerousness should be based on "predictive statistical or actuarial information that is fundamentally nonmedical in nature."[340] It found, given its prior decision in *Jurek,* that death penalty statutes requiring findings as to future dangerousness were constitutional, and that it made "little sense" to exclude only psychiatrists

---

335. *See generally,* Perlin, *supra* note 3, at 7-12, 64-66; Perlin, *supra* note 18, at 101-21; 3 M.L. PERLIN, *supra* note 17, §17.13, at 529-36.

336. 428 U.S. 262, 264 (1976); *see generally,* 3 M.L. PERLIN, *supra* note 17, §17.12, at 527-28.

337. 463 U.S. 880 (1983).

338. *See id.* at 916, 920-23 (Blackmun, J., dissenting), and sources cited at nn. 1-5; *see supra* chapter 4 C 3.

339. *Id.* at 884. Justice Blackmun dissented vigorously, concluding "When the court knows full well that psychiatrists' predictions of dangerousness are specious, there can be no excuse for imposing on the defendant, on the pain of his life, the heavy burden of convincing a jury of laymen of the fraud." *Id.* at 924.

340. *Amicus* Brief of American Psychiatric Association, Barefoot v. Estelle, 463 U.S. 880, at 14.

from the "entire universe of persons who might have an opinion on this issue."[341] Also, if it were to accept defendant's argument as to inadmissibility, that would "call into question those other contexts in which predictions of future behavior are constantly made."[342]

Barefoot should be contrasted with the obscure case of *Thomas v. State.* There, the state Supreme Court affirmed a trial court decision disallowing—on the grounds of "irrelevancy and questionable scientific reliability"—expert testimony that mental health professionals could *not* "predict future behavior."[343] The dissonance between *Barefoot* (accepting testimony that flies in the face of all professional expertise in this area) and *Thomas* (disallowing testimony that is in accord with such expertise) should be apparent. On the other hand, both decisions had the same impact: the affirmance of criminal convictions.[344]

Two points can be made here. First, organized psychiatry is being, to some extent at least, hoist by its own petard. Our legal system regularly accepts, condones (and demands) psychiatric expertise as to dangerousness questions in involuntary civil commitment cases.[345] To a significant extent, this determination has been "encouraged, indeed fostered" by individual clinicians' assertions that they have this ability.[346] When psychiatrists say they cannot make such predictions in death penalty cases, the Supreme Court is simply not willing to call into question what it perceives as the testimonial

---

341. *Barefoot,* 463 U.S. at 896. *Compare id.* at 916-19 (Blackmun, J., dissenting) (laymen do as well as psychiatrists in making such predictions; the majority cites no "single reputable source" for the proposition that such predictions are more likely than not to be accurate; "crystal-clear" that witnesses in case "had no expertise whatever"; such testimony "baseless").

342. *Id.* at 898. Here the court relied on O'Connor v. Donaldson, 422 U.S. 563, 576 (1975) (nondangerous mentally ill person could not be institutionalized against his will), and Addington v. Texas, 441 U.S. 418, 429 (1979) (commitment determination turns on "*meaning* of facts which must be interpreted by expert") (emphasis in original). On the way that the acceptance of predictive testimony is used like a whipsaw to shape jurisprudence in other areas of mental disability law, *see* Perlin, *Tarasoff, supra* note 251, at 40-41.

343. 259 Ga. 202, 378 S.E. 2d 686, 687 (1989).

344. On the teleological ways in which courts read social science data, *see* Perlin, *supra* note 75, at 136-37; Perlin & Dorfman, *supra* note 9; Perlin, *supra* note 130; Appelbaum, *The Empirical Jurisprudence of the United States Supreme Court,* 134 AM. J. L. & MED. 335, 349 (1987); *see generally infra* chapter 8 D.

345. Indeed, this is precisely the point made by the *Barefoot* majority. *See supra* note 321. *See generally,* Perlin, *supra* note 75, at 133-35.

346. Rubenstein, *The Paradox of Professional Liability,* 39 HOSP. & COMMUN. PSYCHIATRY 815 (1988).

predicate for the entire civil commitment system.[347] According to Doctor Robert Miller and his colleagues:

> The psychiatric profession, which has demonstrated its willingness to predict future dangerousness when such predictions were required in order to effect the involuntary commitment of patients who appeared to need it clinically, or to facilitate the release of forensic patients who were perceived not to require future hospitalization, is now surprised to find that other courts are holding them accountable for that claim of expertise in areas where they had not chosen to assert it.[348]

Second, there is again significant cognitive dissonance here between the "ordinary common sense" view of psychiatry as being inherently soft and inappropriately exculpatory, and the role for psychiatry that is urged by criminal prosecutors in cases such as *Barefoot*. For instance, one of the expert witnesses in *Barefoot* (Dr. Grigson) testified in 1985 that he had already testified in 120 capital cases, and that, in every one, he found future dangerousness within the Texas statute.[349]

---

347. I consider a parallel dilemma in Perlin, *Tarasoff, supra* note 251, at 41 (judges who see psychiatrists regularly predicting dangerousness in involuntary civil commitment cases "simply do not buy the argument" that predictions made in "duty to protect" tort cases are any "murkier").

348. Miller, Doren, Van Rybroek & Maier, *Emerging Problems for Staff Associated With the Release of Potentially Dangerous Forensic Patients*, 16 BULL. AM. ACAD. PSYCHIATRY & L. 309, 314 (1988); *compare* Poythress, *Concerning Reform in Expert Testimony: An Open Letter From a Practicing Psychologist*, 6 LAW & HUM. BEHAV. 39 (1982) (describing court's heated and hostile reaction when expert witness refused to give conclusory opinion).

349. Nethery v. State, 692 S.W. 2d 686, 708 (Tex. Crim. App. 1985). A 1988 television broadcast reported that jurors agreed with Grigson's death penalty recommendations 104 of 114 times. Fuller v. State, 829 S.W. 2d 191, 213 n. 5 (Tex. Cr. App. 1992), *rehearing den.* (1992) (Baird, J., concurring in part and dissenting in part).

Grigson continues as a regular witness in Texas courtrooms and a subject of consideration by Texas appellate courts. *See e.g.,* Fuller, *supra*; Murphy v. State, 1991 WL 107536 (Tex. App.-Dallas 1991); Hupp v. State, 801 S.W. 2d 920 (Tex. Cr. App. 1991); Amis v. Ashworth, 802 S.W. 2d 374 (Tex. App.-Tyler 1990); Duckett v. State, 797 S.W. 2d 906 (Tex. Cr. App. 1990); Hartley v. State, 790 S.W. 2d 332 (Tex. Cr. App. 1990); Bennett v. State, 766 S.W. 2d 227 (Tex. Cr. App. 1989); Cook v. State, 821 S.W. 2d 600 (Tex. Cr. App. 1991), *rehearing den.* (1991).

It is estimated that Grigson—who claims to have examined more than 12,000 prisoners, *see* Redmen v. State, 828 P. 2d 394, 402 (Nev. 1992) (Rose, J., concurring)—has testified for the state in as many as 1/3 of all modern Texas death penalty cases. Sorensen & Marquart, *Prosecutorial and Jury Decision-Making in Post-Furman Texas*, 18 N.Y.U. REV. L. & SOC. CHANGE 743, 749

The role of psychiatry in our insanity defense system must be weighed in light of these dissonances. While we reject psychodynamic explanations for why certain criminal defendants exhibit "crazy behavior," we still require behavioral testimony as to "future dangerousness" to palliate our feelings about punishing such defendants.

(2) Is mental disability a mitigating factor to jurors?
Contemporary death penalty jurisprudence requires the sentencing authority to consider any relevant mitigating evidence that a defendant offers as a basis for a sentence less than death.[350] In its most recent decision on this question involving a mentally disabled defendant, the Supreme Court held that evidence as to the defendant's mental retardation was relevant to his culpability and that, without such information, jurors could not express their "reasoned moral response" in determining the appropriateness of the death penalty.[351]

While this requirement has recently been the target of bitter attack by Justice Scalia,[352] the Supreme Court continues to pay at least lip service to this doctrine.[353] Empirical inquiries, however, illuminate society's degree of ambivalence about this proposition.

Scholars have expressed their skepticism about the use of a mental illness defense in a capital punishment penalty phase, suggesting that such testimony raises issues of unpredictability and dangerousness to potentially suggest to the jury that the defendant "poses a continuing risk to society."[354] While expert witnesses have predicted

---

(1990-91). For a recent consideration of Dr. Grigson's testimony, *see* Note, *A Reasoned Moral Response: Rethinking Texas' Capital Sentencing Statute After Penry v. Lynaugh*, 69 TEX. L. REV. 407, 447 n. 188 (1990).

350. *See* Lockett v. Ohio, 438 U.S. 586, 604 (1978); Eddings v. Oklahoma, 455 U.S. 104, 114 (1982). *See generally*, 3 M.L. PERLIN, *supra* note 17, §17.09, at 521-23.

351. Penry v. Lynaugh, 492 U.S. 302, 304 (1989). *See generally*, 3 M.L. PERLIN, *supra* note 17, §17.09, at 209-11 (1992 pocket part). On the traditional role of clemency in such cases, *see* Kobil, *The Quality of Mercy Strained: Wresting the Pardoning Power From the King*, 69 TEX. L. REV. 569, 624-27 (1991).

352. *See* Penry, 492 U.S. at 359 (Scalia, J., concurring in part & dissenting in part): "It is an unguided, emotional, 'moral response' that the Court demands to be allowed—an outpouring of personal reaction to all the circumstances of a defendant's life and personality, an unfocused sympathy." On the role of "empathy" evidence in death penalty litigation, *see* Geimer, *Law and Reality in the Capital Penalty Trial*, 18 N.Y.U. REV. L. & SOC'L CHANGE 273, 285-86 (1990-91).

353. *See e.g.*, McKoy v. North Carolina, 494 U.S. 433, 443 (1990) (citing and discussing *Penry*); Payne v. Tennessee, 111 S. Ct. 2597, 2614 (1991) (Souter, J., concurring) (same).

354. Dix, *Psychological Abnormality and Capital Sentencing: The New "Diminished Responsibility*," 7 INT'L J. L. & PSYCHIATRY 249, 264 (1984); *see generally*,

(with near unanimity) that such a defense would be successful,[355] research with mock jurors (and archival research in cases involving actual jurors) has revealed that (1) a defendant's unsuccessful attempt to raise an insanity defense positively correlates with a death penalty verdict,[356] (2) a mental illness defense is rated as a less effective strategy than other alternatives at the penalty phase (even including the alternative of raising no defense at all),[357] and (3) jurors who are "death qualified"[358] are more likely to convict capital defendants who suffer from nonorganic mental disorders.[359]

As discussed previously, fact-finders demand that defendants conform to popular, common-sensical visual images of "looking crazy."[360] This further "ups the ante" for defendants raising such a defense. On the other hand, some empirical evidence suggests that a mental illness defense may be successful where the defendant presents expert testimony, where he has a history of psychiatric impairment (especially where he has sought treatment), and where he is able to present "objective" evidence of psychopathology.[361] Also, empirical

---

White, *supra* note 236, at 414-19.

    A significant number of defendants facing execution are mentally disabled. *See* Mello, *On Metaphors, Mirrors, and Murders: Theodore Bundy and the Rule of Law*, 18 N.Y.U. REV. L. & SOC. CHANGE 887, 919 n. 162 (1990-91) (collecting studies); on the ways that imprisonment negatively affects mental health, *see* Hodgins & Côté, *The Mental Health of Penitentiary Inmates in Isolation*, 33 CANAD. J. CRIMINOL. 175 (1991)

355. *See* White, *supra* note 236, at 414-15, discussing findings reported in White, *Trial Consultants, Psychologists, and Prediction Errors*, COURT CALL 1 (Spring 1986).

356. Note, *A Study of the California Penalty Jury on First-Degree Murder Cases*, 21 STAN. L. REV. 1296 (1969). This article, of course, predates the "modern" death penalty jurisprudence that follows the U.S. Supreme Court's decision in Gregg v. Georgia, 428 U.S. 153 (1976). *Compare* Berkman, *supra* note 327 (arguing that considering aggravating circumstances that flow from defendant's mental illness is constitutionally impermissible).

357. White, *Juror Decision Making in the Capital Penalty Trial: An Analysis of Crimes and Defense Strategies*, 11 LAW & HUM. BEHAV. 113 (1987).

358. *See e.g.*, Lockhart v. McCree, 476 U.S. 162, 171-83 (1986) (upholding process of "death qualifying" jurors by which potential jurors with "conscientious scruples" against the death penalty are excluded from jury service).

359. Ellsworth, *supra* note 168.

360. *See e.g.*, State Farm Fire & Casualty Ltd. v. Wicka, 474 N.W. 2d 324, 327 (Minn. 1991) (both law and society always more skeptical about putatively mentally ill person who has a "normal appearance" or "doesn't look sick").

361. White, *supra* note 236, at 416-18; Ellsworth, *supra* note 168; *see also* White, *supra* note 357 (besides simply feeling that "mental illness is no excuse," jurors hostile to a mental illness defense focused on the possibility that the defendant

evidence reveals that fact-finders will be more receptive to a mental status defense that does not involve "planful" behavior,[362] and that, in coming to their conclusions, jurors are likely to rely upon "implicit theories about the causes of violence."[363]

The riskiness of a mental illness defense must be considered in the context of yet other evidence that a significant percentage of actual jurors saw certain aspects of a defendant's demeanor—whether he looked passive, unremorseful, or emotionless—as a critical operative factor in determining whether or not to return a death sentence.[364] This finding is particularly problematic in light of the fact that a significant percentage of mentally disabled criminal defendants receive powerful psychotropic medication while awaiting trial.[365] Among the side effects of such medications are akinesia and akathesia, conditions that may mislead jurors by making the defendant appear either apathetic and unemotional or agitated and restless.[366]

---

was malingering, and on his prior failure to seek help for his problems). *But compare*, Geis & Meier, *supra* note 145, at 73 (irrelevant to Idaho residents whether defendant's reliance on insanity defense was real or feigned); Weihofen, *Institutional Treatment of Persons Acquitted by Reason of Insanity*, 38 Tex. L. Rev. 849, 861 (1960) (request for psychiatric assistance seen as evidence of malingering); State v. Perry, 610 So. 2d 746, 781 (La. 1992) (Cole, J., dissenting) ("Society has the right to protect itself from those who would commit murder and seek to avoid their legitimate punishment by a subsequently contracted, or *feigned*, insanity") (emphasis added).

362. See Roberts, Golding & Fincham, *supra* note 170, at 209-10; Golding & Roesch, *The Assessment of Criminal Responsibility: A Historical Approach to a Current Controversy*, in Handbook of Forensic Psychology 395, 400 (I. Weiner & A. Hess eds. 1987)

363. Costanzo & Costanzo, *Jury Decision Making in the Capital Penalty Phase: Legal Assumptions, Empirical Findings, and a Research Agenda*, 16 Law & Hum. Behav. 185, 199 (1992).

364. See Geimer & Amsterdam, *Why Jurors Vote Life or Death: Operative Factors in Ten Florida Death Penalty Cases*, 15 Am. L. Crim. L. 1, 40-41, 51-52 (1987).

365. See e.g., Perlin, *Tea Leaves, supra* note 251; Perlin, *Charters, supra* note 251.

366. See United States v. Charters, 829 F. 2d 479, 494 (4th Cir. 1987), *on reh'g* 863 F. 2d 302 (4th Cir. 1988) (en banc), *cert. denied*, 494 U.S. 1016 (1990), and *see id.* at 493 (heavily medicated defendant might give jury "false impression of defendant's mental state at the time of the crime"); *see also*, Note, *The Identification of Incompetent Defendants: Separating Those Unfit for Adversary Combat From Those Who Are Fit*, 66 Ky. L.J. 666, 668-71 (1987) (defendant can alienate jury "if he displays such inappropriate demeanor as grinning when gruesome details are discussed, losing his temper when witnesses maintain he is a violent man, or acting indifferent to the proceedings").

The Supreme Court was confronted with this issue last term in *Riggins v. Nevada*, a case that may have signaled a shift in the court's jurisprudence in this area. *Riggins* presented the court with the dilemma of whether involuntary administration of antipsychotic drugs to a criminal defendant during the pendency of his trial violated his right to a fair trial by impeding his ability to consult with counsel, by interfering with the content of his own testimony, or by negatively affecting his capacity to follow the proceedings.[367]

Riggins had been charged with the murder of an acquaintance by multiple stab wounds. After he was arrested and jailed pending trial, he told a jail psychiatrist that he was "hearing voices in his head and having trouble sleeping," and informed him that, in the past, he had been prescribed the antipsychotic drug, Mellaril.[368] The psychiatrist then prescribed Mellaril, and subsequently increased the dosage to 800 milligrams per day, an unusually large amount (considered to be within the "toxic range" by one expert and a sufficient dosage to "tranquilize an elephant" by another).[369] About ten weeks later, a competency to stand trial hearing was held (by which time Riggins' dosage had been reduced to 450 milligrams), at which Riggins was found competent to stand trial.[370]

The defendant then sought a court order that would have terminated the administration of antipsychotic drugs during the pendency of the trial, on the theory that, as the defendant was proferring an insanity defense, he had a right to have the jury see him in "his true mental state."[371] After hearing conflicting expert testimony,[372] the

---

367. 112 S. Ct. 1810, 1814 (1992); *see generally*, Perlin, Riggins v. Nevada: *Forced Medication Collides With the Right to a Fair Trial*, 16 NEWSLETTER AM. ACAD. PSYCHIATRY & L. 81 (1992); 2 M.L. PERLIN, *supra* note 17, §5.65A at 78-85 (1992 pocket part); Perlin & Dorfman, *supra* note 98, at 57-58.

368. *Id.* at 1812.

369. *See id.* at 1816 (800 mgs within the "toxic range"); *see also, id.* at 1819 (Kennedy, J., concurring) (expert testified that 800 mgs. was a sufficient dosage with which to "tranquilize an elephant"). Other experts testified that the drug could make the defendant "uptight," or could cause "drowsiness or confusion;" as *amicus*, the American Psychiatric Association stated that, in extreme cases, the sedative properties of the drug, might even "affect thought processes." *Id.* at 1816.

370. *Id.* at 1812.

371. *Id.* On the ways that jurors make stereotypic assumptions about mentally disabled individuals based on visual imagery, *see* Perlin, *supra* note 23; Perlin, *supra* note 130.

372. *See Riggins*, 112 S. Ct. at 1813.

trial judge denied defendant's motion; by this time, the defendant was receiving 800 milligrams again.[373]

Defendant presented an insanity defense at trial, and testified that "voices in his head" had told him that killing the victim would be justifiable homicide.[374] He was found guilty and sentenced to death.[375] The Supreme Court reversed, holding that the use of antipsychotic drugs violated defendant's right to a fair trial, citing language from the Court's previous opinion in *Washington v. Harper*[376] as to the impact of drug side-effects on constitutional decision making, and construing *Harper* to require "an overriding justification and a determination of medical appropriateness" prior to forcibly administering antipsychotic medications to a prisoner.[377]

The *Riggins* court focused on what might be called the "litigational side-effects" of antipsychotic drugs, and discussed the possibility that the drug use might have "compromised" the substance of the defendant's trial testimony, his interaction with counsel, and his comprehension of the trial.[378] In a concurring opinion, Justice Kennedy (the author of *Harper*, and, even more remarkably, the author of a *Foucha* dissent) took an even bolder position. He would not allow the use of antipsychotic medication to make a defendant competent to stand trial "absent an *extraordinary* showing" on the state's part, and noted further that he doubted this showing could be made "given our present understanding of the properties of these drugs."[379]

Justice Thomas dissented, suggesting (1) the administration of the drug might have *increased* the defendant's cognitive ability,[380] (2) since Riggins had originally asked for medical assistance (while a jail inmate, he had "had trouble sleeping" and was "hearing voices"), it could not be said that the state ever "ordered" him to take medication,[381] (3) if Riggins had been aggrieved, his proper remedy was a

---

373. *Id.*
374. *Id.*
375. *Id.*
376. 494 U.S. 210 (1990) (limited right to refuse treatment for prison inmates).
377. *Riggins*, 112 S. Ct. at 1815.
378. *Id.* at 1816; *see generally*, Bonnie, *The Competence of Criminal Defendants: A Theoretical Reformulation*, 10 BEHAV. SCI. & L. 291 (1992).
379. *Riggins*, 112 S. Ct. at 1817 (Kennedy, J., concurring).
380. *Id.* at 1822-23 (Thomas, J., dissenting).
     Trial testimony had indicated that Riggins' daily drug regimen (800 mgs. of Mellaril) was enough to "tranquilize an elephant." *Id* at 1819 (Kennedy, J., concurring), *quoting* trial record.
381. *Id.* at 1823-24 (Thomas, J., dissenting).

§1983 civil rights action,[382] and (4) under the majority's language, a criminal conviction might be reversed in cases involving "penicillin or aspirin."[383]

Riggins is the Court's most expansive reading of the effect of psychotropic drugs' side-effects on an individual's functioning.[384] Justice Kennedy's concurrence highlights the ways that such side-effects could imperil a fair trial:

> At all stages of the proceedings, the defendant's behavior, manner, facial expressions, and emotional responses, or their absence, combine to make an overall impression on the trier of fact, an impression that can have a powerful influence on the outcome of the trial. If the defendant takes the stand, as Riggins did, his demeanor can have a great bearing on his credibility, his persuasiveness, and on the degree to which he evokes sympathy.[385]

This is the clearest articulation of this position in any opinion by any Supreme Court justice.

Kennedy's observations as to jurors' responses to defendants who fail to display the proper "remorse and compassion" is also telling. Here he continues:

> The prejudice can be acute during the sentencing phase of the proceedings, when the sentencer must attempt to know the heart and mind of the offender and judge his character, his contrition or its absence, and his future dangerousness. In a capital sentencing proceeding, assessments of character and remorse may carry great weight and, perhaps, be determinative of whether the offender lives or dies.[386]

His reliance here on a law review article that reports on the experiences of *real* jurors in *real* cases[387] reflects an important sensitivity to the ways that jurors process clues and cues about the *persona* of capital defendants, and his integration of that data into an analysis of the ways that jurors may potentially respond to medicated defendants demonstrates a similar sensitivity to the way that visual images of

---

382. *Id.* at 1825-26. At his trial, Riggins had been sentenced to death.
383. *Id.* at 1826.
384. *Compare* Harper, *supra*; *see generally*, 2 M.L. PERLIN, *supra* note 17, §5.65A, at 83-84.
385. *Riggins*, 112 S. Ct. at 1819.
386. *Id.* at 1819-20.
387. *See* Geimer & Amsterdam, *supra* note 359.

mentally disabled defendants may be dispositive of juror decision making on this question.

On the other hand, Justice Thomas's opinion raises grave issues for defense counsel; had his position prevailed, would concerned and competent defense lawyers feel as if they were assuming a risk in *ever* seeking psychiatric help for an awaiting-trial defendant?[388] His analogizing antipsychotic drug side effects to penicillin or aspirin may be disingenuous or it may be cynical. What *is* clear is that nowhere in the lengthy *corpus* of "right to refuse treatment" litigation is this position ever seriously raised.[389] Its use here appears, again, to reflect the sanist use of "social science."

Riggins, like *Foucha*,[390] may augur a shift in the Supreme Court's insanity defense jurisprudence. On the other hand, Riggins' victory could be seen as the triumph of a different kind of sanism: even though the court agreed that the involuntary imposition of medication violated his fair trial rights, it may be that the justices' internal, visual images of a person who "looked crazy" inspired the decision. Also, the case did not give the court an opportunity to express an opinion on either the operative substantive insanity test, or the procedures employed either at trial or following an insanity acquittal. Perhaps the court's reading of the case as a "fair trial" case allowed it to avoid the cognitive dissonance[391] that would have been caused had the case been seen as an "insanity defense" case. In short,

---

388. *Compare* Buchanan v. Kentucky, 483 U.S. 402 (1987) (no error to admit, in rebuttal of defendant's "extreme emotional disturbance" defense, report prepared following pretrial detainee's request to be treated at state hospital pending trial), discussed in 3 M.L. PERLIN, *supra* note 17, §16.04A at 425-29. This decision also raises profound questions under a therapeutic jurisprudential analysis. *See* M. Perlin, "Law as a Therapeutic and Anti-Therapeutic Agent," paper presented at the Massachusetts Department of Mental Health's Division of Forensic Mental Health's annual conference, Auburn, MA (May 1992). *See generally infra* chapter 9 B.

389. The only case in which a similar issue is raised is Matter of Salisbury, 138 Misc. 2d 361, 524 N.Y.S. 2d 352, 354 (Sup. Ct. 1988), holding that prior court authorization was not necessary before a state mental hospital could administer antibiotics to a patient, citing "overwhelming public policy considerations" that made it "imperative" that hospitals could perform such "routine, accepted, non-major medical treatment which poses no significant risk, discomfort, or trauma to the patient." *Salisbury* has never been cited in any subsequent case nor has it been mentioned in the law review literature.

390. *See supra* chapter 4 E 2 d.

391. *See generally*, Perlin, *supra* note 75.

it is *not* clear what wider impact *Riggins* will have on insanity defense jurisprudence.[392]

It is also not clear how subsequent judicial responses to cases such as *Riggins* will affect jurors in later cases. Will it have an impact on the use of mental disability as a mitigating factor in death penalty cases in general? Specifically, will it make it any less risky for capital defendants to raise mental illness in mitigation? The answers to these questions may well determine *Riggins'* ultimate impact.

(3) Execution of the "insane."[393]   The issue of executing the insane has plagued the legal system for centuries.[394] In his classic treatise, *Insanity and the Criminal Law*, Dr. William White focused on the "general feeling of abhorrence against executing a person who is insane."[395] Although the roots of the policy against execution of insane offenders are ancient, "no consensus exists about the reasons for it, about the meaning of 'insane' in this context, or the procedures which should be used to determine it."[396] One commentator suggests that

---

392. As of yet, there have been few important constructions of *Riggins* by the lower courts. In one case, a District of Columbia appellate court judge dissented from a rehearing denial arguing—unsuccessfully—that *Riggins* compelled reconsideration of a decision allowing for the administration of forcible medication of a presently-incompetent to stand trial defendant. Van Kheim v. United States, 612 A. 2d 160, 174 (D.C. 1992) (Ferren, J., dissenting from denial of petition for en banc rehearing). In another, the Seventh Circuit relied in part on *Riggins* to find that parolees had a qualified liberty interest in remaining free from the administration of unwanted antipsychotic drugs. Felce v. Fiedler, 974 F. 2d 1484, 1494 (7th Cir. 1992). In perhaps its most important application, the Louisiana Supreme Court read *Riggins* to confirm its broad reading of *Harper* that such drugs "may not be used as a tool for punishment." State v. Perry, 608 So. 2d 594, 603 (La. 1992) (violation of state constitution to involuntarily medicate death row prisoner so as to make him competent to be executed).

393. Much of the material *infra* text accompanying notes 394-439 is adapted from 3 M.L. PERLIN, *supra* note 12, §§17.02-17.06.

394. In their seminal study, Professors Hazard and Louisell examined arguments made by Blackstone, Hale and Coke specifically opposing such execution, and looked also at the writings of St. Thomas Aquinas and Shakespeare for the religious and cultural roots of the doctrine. *See* Hazard & Louisell, *Death, the State, and the Insane: Stay of Execution,* 9 U.C.L.A. L. REV. 381 (1962). *See also,* A. KOESTLER, REFLECTIONS ON HANGING 162 (1957) (suggestion that insane murderers be subject to capital punishment akin to doctrine "preached and practiced" in Nazi Germany, and "repugnant to the moral traditions of Western civilization").

395. W. WHITE, *supra* note 226, at 245.

396. Zenoff, *Can an Insane Person Be Executed?* [1985-1986] ABA PREVIEW, Issue No. 16 (June 27, 1986), at 465, 466.

attempts at prescribing appropriate standards "have proved incoherent because they failed to confront the reality that law and psychiatry rarely, if ever, exist separately from culture and politics."[397]

As capital punishment is today "probably a stronger force in American society than it has been in thirty years,"[398] it should be no surprise that this issue again assumes great significance both to forensic psychiatry and to the law. This has become especially important in the post-*Hinckley* universe of a shrunken (or abolished) insanity defense that cannot be relied upon as "an impenetrable bulwark to prevent execution of the insane."[399] More mentally ill offenders will be imprisoned,[400] and many death row inmates will suffer serious mental disorder.[401]

The issues involved in psychiatric participation in capital punishment decision making raise a series of "intractable"[402] *operational* problems for mental health professionals: the responsibility of psychiatrists to appropriately construe the key terms in operative statutes (such as a Florida law that prohibited execution if the defendant did not have "the mental capacity to understand the nature of the death penalty"); assessment of the appropriate standard of proof; reliability of diagnoses; and the possibility of regression between evaluation and execution.[403] Thoughtful forensic clinicians and legal

---

397. Ward, *Competency for Execution: Problems in Law and Psychiatry*, 14 FLA. ST. U. L. REV. 35, 100 (1986).

398. Perlin, *supra* note 18, at 97; *see generally,* H. BEDEAU, THE DEATH PENALTY IN AMERICA 3-95 (3d ed. 1982).

399. Perlin, *supra* note 18, at 96. *See e.g.,* sources cited at *id.* nn. 27-30.

400. *See* Steadman, Monahan, Hartstone, Davis & Robbins, *Mentally Disordered Offenders: A National Survey of Patients and Facilities,* 6 LAW & HUM. BEHAV. 31 (1982). On the specific problems of mentally ill prisoners, *see* George, *The American Bar Association's Mental Health Standards: An Overview,* 53 GEO. WASH. L. REV. 338, 371-74 (1985). At least one *physically* disabled prisoner has recently been executed. *See* Miller, *The Execution of a Disabled Killer Rekindles the Debate on Capital Punishment,* Wash. Post (Feb. 2, 1993), at Z10 (case of Charles Sylvester Stamper, *see* Stamper v. Wright, 983 F. 2d 1057 (4th Cir. 1993), *cert. den.,* 113 S. Ct. 1069 (1993)).

401. It has been estimated that "as many as fifty percent of Florida's death row inmates become intermittently insane." Ward, *supra* note 397, at 42, relying on Sherrill, *Electrocution Binge: In Florida, Insanity Is No Defense,* 239 NATION 537 (1984).

402. Ward, *supra* note 397, at 100. *See also,* Note, *Medical Ethics and Competency to be Executed,* 96 YALE L.J. 167, 173-179 (1986). *See id.* at 184 (characterizing dilemma as "insoluble").

403. Radelet & Barnard, *Ethics and the Psychiatric Determination of Competency to be Executed,* 14 BULL. AM. ACAD. PSYCHIATRY & L. 37, 43 (1986); Hazard

commentators have carefully staked out competing positions on the ways that these problems can be resolved;[404] yet, it is clear that there is no current professional consensus on the underlying issues.

The Supreme Court's 1986 decision in *Ford v. Wainwright*[405] brought limited doctrinal coherence to this question. In *Ford*, a fractured court[406] concluded that the Eighth Amendment did prohibit the imposition of the death penalty on an insane prisoner.[407] On this point, Justice Rehnquist dissented on behalf of himself and the Chief Justice.[408] In his view, the Florida procedures were "fully consistent with the 'common-law heritage' and current practice on which the Court purport[ed] to rely," and, in their reliance on executive-

---

& Louisell, *supra* note 394, at 400; FLA. STAT. ANN. §922.07(3) (1986 Supp.). This statute was the subject of the litigation in Ford v. Wainwright, 447 U.S. 399 (1986); *see infra* text accompanying notes 404-11.

404. *See e.g.*, Mossman, *Assessing and Restoring Competency to be Executed: Should Psychiatrists Participate?* 5 BEHAV. SCI. & L. 397 (1987); Mossman, *The Psychiatrist and Execution Competency:* Ford-*ing Murky Ethical Waters*, 43 CASE W. RES. L. REV. 1 (1992); Bonnie, *Dilemmas in Administering the Death Penalty: Conscientious Abstention, Professional Ethics, and the Needs of the Legal System*, 14 LAW & HUM. BEHAV. 67 (1990); Brodsky, *Professional Ethics and Professional Morality in the Assessment of Competence for Execution: A Reply to Bonnie*, 14 LAW & HUM. BEHAV. 91 (1990); Heilbrun, *The Assessment of Competency for Execution: An Overview*, 5 BEHAV. SCI. & L. 383 (1987): Heilbrun & Dvoskin, *The Debate on Treating Individuals Incompetent for Execution*, 149 AM. J. PSYCHIATRY 596 (1992); Schopp, *Wake Up and Die Right: The Rationale, Standard, and Jurisprudential Significance of the Competency to Face Execution Requirement*, 51 LA. L. REV. 995 (1991); Deitschman, Kennedy & Beckham, *Self-Selection Factors in the Participation of Mental Health Professionals in Competency for Execution Evaluations*, 15 LAW & HUM. BEHAV. 287 (1991); Small & Otto, *Examinations of Competency to Be Executed: Legal Contours and Implications for Assessment*, 18 CRIM. JUST. & BEHAV. 146 (1991); Showalter, *Psychiatric Participation in Capital Sentencing Procedures: Ethical Considerations*, 13 INT'L J. L. & PSYCHIATRY 261 (1990).

405. 477 U.S. 399 (1986).

406. On the question of what procedures were appropriate to satisfy the constitution, three other justices joined Justice Marshall. *Id.* at 410. Justice Powell concurred on that issue, and wrote separately on the issue of the appropriate procedures to be followed in such a case. *Id.* at 418. Justice O'Connor (for herself and Justice White) concurred in part and dissented in part. *Id.* at 427. Justice Rehnquist (for himself and the Chief Justice) dissented. *Id.* at 431.

407. *Id.* at 402-10. On the question of what procedures were appropriate in such a case, the court was sufficiently fragmented that no opinion commanded a majority of justices. In a four-justice opinion, Justice Marshall concluded that a *de novo* evidentiary hearing on Ford's sanity was required unless "the state-court trier of fact has after a full hearing reliably found the relevant facts." *See* Townsend v. Sain, 372 U.S. 293, 312-13 (1963).

408. *Id.* at 431 (Rehnquist, J., dissenting).

branch procedures, "faithful to both traditional and modern practice."[409] He thus rejected the majority's conclusion that the Eighth Amendment created a substantive right not to be executed while insane.[410]

Ford is a curious and difficult opinion, that reflects the ambiguity and ambivalence that permeate this subject-matter.[411] It is especially perplexing in light of the Court's subsequent decision in *Penry v. Lynaugh*,[412] in which it rejected the argument that defendant's mental *retardation* barred capital punishment.[413] Although she conceded that the execution of the "profoundly or severely retarded" might violate the Eighth Amendment, Justice O'Connor suggested that such persons were unlikely to be convicted or face that penalty in light of "the protections afforded by the insanity defense today."[414]

To some extent, *Ford* and *Penry* serve as paradigms both for the court's confusion about, and for its use of rationalization to deal with many of the cases it has decided in recent years about mentally disabled criminal defendants.[415] Justice Rehnquist's and Justice O'Connor's opinions in *Ford* and Justice O'Connor's opinion in *Penry* are especially troubling. Their *Ford* opinions remain infused with the obsessive fear that defendants will raise "false" or "spurious claims"[416] in desperate attempts to stave off execution. This fear—a *doppelganger* of the public's "swift and vociferous...outrage"[417] over what it perceives as "abusive" insanity acquittals, thus allowing

---

409. *Id.* at 431-33.
410. Writing for herself and Justice White, Justice O'Connor agreed fully with this aspect of Justice Rehnquist's two-justice dissent. *Id.* at 427 (O'Connor, J., concurring in part and dissenting in part).
411. *See* Perlin, *supra* note 18, at 167-69. An early analysis of *Ford* saw it as "sanctioning a double paradox: condemned prisoners are killed if they are sane, but spared if they are insane; insane prisoners are cured in order that they may be killed." *The Supreme Court, 1985 Term,* 100 HARV. L. REV. 100, 106 (1986) (footnote omitted).
412. 492 U.S. 302 (1989).
413. *Id.* at 332-34. *See supra* text accompanying notes 351-52. On the relationship between *Ford* and *Penry, see* 3 M.L. PERLIN, *supra note 12, §17.06A, at 198-205 (1992 pocket part).*
414. *Penry,* 492 U.S. at 333.
415. *See generally,* Perlin, *supra* note 3; Perlin, *supra* note 18.
416. *Ford,* 477 U.S. at 429 (O'Connor, J., concurring in part and dissenting in part); *id.* at 435 (Rehnquist, J., dissenting).
417. *See* I. KEILITZ & H. FULTON, THE INSANITY DEFENSE AND ITS ALTERNATIVES: A GUIDE FOR POLICYMAKERS 3 (1984).

"guilty" defendants to "beat the rap"—remains the source of one of the ultimate insoluble dilemmas here.

Justice O'Connor's Penry assertion that the insanity defense protects against conviction and punishment of the severely mentally disabled stands in disingenuous and stark contrast to counsel's dismal track record in this area.[418] Certainly, post-*Ford* litigation on this issue[419] gives no support whatsoever to this groundless assertion.[420]

(4) Medicating defendants prior to execution.[421] Neither *Ford* nor *Penry* directly addressed whether a state can forcibly involuntarily medicate an individual under a death sentence so as to make him competent to be executed.[422] Thus, when the Supreme Court granted *certiorari* in *Perry v. Louisiana*[423]—presenting this precise question —it appeared that this gap would be closed.

After Perry was found competent to stand trial on multiple murder charges (involving five family members), he withdrew his previously-entered not guilty by reason of insanity plea (against counsel's advice), and entered a not guilty plea.[424] He was convicted and sentenced to death.[425] On appeal, the Louisiana Supreme Court affirmed both his conviction and death sentence, but ordered an adversarial hearing on his then-present competence to be executed.[426]

---

418. *See* 3 M.L. PERLIN, *supra* note 17, §15.23; *see*, for a stark case example, Alvord v. Wainwright, 469 U.S. 956, 957 (1984) (Marshall, J., dissenting from denial of certiorari).

419. *See e.g.*, Rector v. Bryant, 111 S. Ct. 2872 (1991) (Marshall, J., dissenting from denial of *certiorari*); Hamilton v. Texas, 497 U.S. 1016 (1990) (Brennan, J., dissenting from denial of stay of execution); Demosthenes v. Baal, 495 U.S. 731 (1990): Johnson v. Cabana, 481 U.S. 1061 (1987) (Brennan, J., dissenting from denial of stay of execution & denial of *certiorari*).

420. *See* Perlin, *supra* note 253 (on general inadequacy of counsel in capital cases involving mentally disabled criminal defendants).

421. Much of the material *infra* text accompanying notes 422-38 is adapted from 3 M.L. PERLIN, *supra* note 12, §17.06B, at 205-08 (1992 pocket part).

422. On refusal of medication generally, *see* 2 M.L. PERLIN, *supra* note 17, chapter 5. On prisoners' right to refuse medication, *see id.*, §5.64A; *see generally*, Washington v. Harper, 494 U.S. 210 (1990); Perlin & Dorfman, *supra* note 9, at 56-57.

423. 494 U.S. 1015 (1990).

424. State v. Perry, 502 So. 2d 543, 546-47 (La. 1986), *cert. denied*, 484 U.S. 872 (1987), *rehearing denied*, 484 U.S. 992 (1987).

425. *Id.* at 545. Following his conviction, Perry was treated on several occasions in the prison's psychiatric unit, where he received an antipsychotic drug (Haldol). Richardson, *Involuntary Medication on Death Row: Is It Cruel and Unusual?* 1990-91 ABA PREVIEW 18 (Sept. 28, 1990).

426. Perry, 502 So. 2d at 563-64.

At that competency hearing, the four expert witnesses agreed that Perry was psychotic and that his condition improved when he was properly medicated.[427] The trial court subsequently ordered two of the experts to reexamine the defendant, after it had received new reports from the prison hospital. At this hearing (held five months after the initial hearing), witnesses testified that Perry now knew why he was to be executed.[428]

The trial court then found that (1) Perry was competent to be executed, and (2) that any due process right to refuse medication that he might have had was outweighed by two compelling state interests: the provision of proper psychiatric care, and carrying out a valid death penalty. It thus ordered Perry medicated—by force if necessary—so that he would remain competent to be executed.[429] The Louisiana Supreme Court declined to review this order.[430]

The United States Supreme Court subsequently granted *certiorari* to resolve the question of whether the Eighth Amendment prohibits states from forcibly medicating death row inmates to make them competent to be executed.[431] Rather than deciding the case on the merits, however, the Court ultimately vacated and remanded[432] to the Louisiana Supreme Court for further reconsideration in light of its earlier decision in *Washington v. Harper*[433] on the scope of a convicted prisoner's right to refuse treatment.[434]

Why did the Supreme Court chose to deal with *Perry* this way?[435] Perhaps the justices, on reflection, felt that the only issue

---

427. Perry v. Louisiana, No. 89-5120 (May 24, 1990), Petitioner's Brief on Merits, J.A. 126-49 (Petitioner's Brief). Two of the witnesses found that he would be competent to be executed if he were to receive medication; a third, who did not believe Perry understood the purpose of his sentence, was not sure if the medication would make him competent; the fourth remained unconvinced that the defendant understood that he had really committed the murders in question. Id.

428. *Id.*

429. *Id.*

430. State v. Perry, 543 So. 2d 487 (La. 1989), *rehearing denied,* 545 So. 2d 1049 (1989).

431. Perry v. Louisiana, 494 U.S. 1015, 58 U.S.L.W. 3584 (1990).

432. 498 U.S. 38 (1990), *rehearing denied,* 111 S. Ct. 804 (1991).

433. 494 U.S. 210 (1990).

434. *See generally,* 2 M.L. PERLIN, *supra* note 17, §5.64A at 62-74 (1992 pocket part). Interestingly, the Supreme Court had decided *Harper* about one week before it granted *certiorari* in *Perry.*

435. *See e.g.*, Greenhouse, *New Hearing on Forced Medication of Inmate,* N.Y. Times (Nov. 14, 1990), at A30.

presented was that of forcible medication, finding the execution
consequences irrelevant, and that it was thus essential that the state
court consider, after *Harper*, whether the difference in long-term
harm in a case like *Perry* (his execution) outweighed the state's
interests in involuntarily medicating him.[436] Maybe, since Justice
Souter did not participate in *Perry*,[437] the court felt the issue was too
important to decide without the benefit of nine sitting justices.
Maybe the Supreme Court simply could not—or would not—resolve
the tensions and ambivalences raised by this case.[438]

It is likely that this specific case will not reach the Court again.
On remand, the Louisiana Supreme Court found, under state constitutional law, that the state was prohibited from medicating Perry to
make him competent to be executed.[439] Concluded the court:

> For centuries no jurisdiction has approved the execution of the insane.
> The state's attempt to circumvent this well-settled prohibition by forcibly
> medicating an insane prisoner with antipsychotic drugs violates his rights
> under our state constitution...First, it violates his right to privacy or
> personhood. Such involuntary medication requires the unjustified invasion
> of his brain and body with discomforting, potentially dangerous and
> painful drugs, the seizure of control of his mind and thoughts, and the
> usurpation of his right to make decisions regarding his health or medical
> treatment. Furthermore, implementation of the state's plan to medicate
> forcibly and execute the insane prisoner would constitute cruel, excessive
> and unusual punishment. This particular application of the death penalty
> fails to measurably contribute to the social goals of capital punishment.
> Carrying out this punitive scheme would add severity and indignity to the
> prisoner's punishment beyond that required for the mere extinguishment
> of life. This type of punitive treatment system is not accepted anywhere in
> contemporary society and is apt to be administered erroneously, arbitrarily
> or capriciously.[440]

---

436. *Supreme Court Sidesteps Issue of Restoring Inmates' Competency to Allow
Execution*, Psychiatric News (Dec. 21, 1990), at 6 (*quoting* Dr. Paul Appelbaum).
437. *See* 498 U.S. at 38.
438. *Cf.* Haney, *The Fourteenth Amendment and Symbolic Legality: Let Them Eat
Due Process*, 15 LAW & HUM. BEHAV. 183, 202 (1991) (discussing McCleskey
v. Kemp, 481 U.S. 279, 339 (1989) (Brennan, J., dissenting) (majority's refusal
to grant defendant's statistically-based claim of racial discrimination in capital
punishment decision making reflects a "fear of too much justice").
439. State v. Perry, 610 So. 2d 746 (La. 1992).
440. *Id.* at 757-48.

This decision has not been re-appealed to the Supreme Court (no doubt because of its state constitutional law basis). It is certainly possible, however, that a similar case will unfold in another jurisdiction. If it does, the Court may then choose to address the relationship between *Harper*, *Ford*, and even *Riggins*. We may then understand better how the members of the current Court will resolve their ambivalences about the underlying questions.

F. Conclusion

Our ambivalent feelings—about the mentally ill criminal defendant, the use of the insanity defense, the roots of punishment, and the significance of expert mental disability testimony—reflect the social conflicts that dominate insanity defense jurisprudence. These ambivalent feelings, in turn, have spawned a series of tensions that have contributed substantially to our doctrinal incoherence. The legislative debate that followed the Hinckley acquittal reflected the way that these tensions animated legislative change that returned the federal insanity standard to a more restrictive version of a test that was seen as hopelessly outdated 150 years ago. To understand the impact that this doctrinal incoherence will have on the trials of mentally disabled criminal defendants who still seek to maintain a defense of nonresponsibility, I turn next to consider why the myths that drive insanity defense jurisprudence have persisted as they have. I will consider the roots of the myths, how the myths play out in a "real life" case (one that was not attended by any of the publicity or national attention that was focused on the Hinckley trial), and will then identify the meta-myths that appear to be the most responsible for our doctrinal incoherence.

5

The Roots of Insanity Defense Myths

A. Why Do Myths Persist?

As I have already demonstrated, one of the driving forces behind the movement to abolish or sharply limit the insanity defense has been the persistence of insanity defense mythology. It is taken as "common wisdom" that the insanity defense is an abused, over-pleaded and over-accepted "loophole" used as a "last-gasp" plea solely in grisly murder cases to thwart the death penalty;[1] that most

---

1. W. WHITE, INSANITY AND THE CRIMINAL LAW 3 (1923) (Da Capo ed. 1981); Hans, *An Analysis of Public Attitudes Toward the Insanity Defense*, 24 CRIMINOL. 393, 408 (1986); Roberts, Golding & Fincham, *Implicit Theories of Criminal Responsibility Decision Making and the Insanity Defense*, 11 LAW & HUM. BEHAV. 207, 211 (1987); Slater & Hans, *Public Opinion of Forensic Psychiatry Following the Hinckley Verdict*, 141 AM. J. PSYCHIATRY 175, 202 (1984); Hans & Slater, *"Plain Crazy:" Lay Definitions of Legal Insanity*, 7 INT'L J. L. & PSYCHIATRY 105, 110 (1984) (two- thirds of study sample "strongly agreed" that defense was a "loophole"); *see e.g.*, Moore v. State, 525 So. 2d 870, 871-73 (Fla. 1988) (reversible error where court failed to excuse challenged juror who felt insanity defense was overused, and thought his beliefs would probably "prevent him from following court's instructions").

   Prior to the eighteenth century, at least sixty percent of all insanity pleas were entered in petty larceny cases. Eigen, *Historical Developments in Psychiatric Forensic Evidence: The British Experience*, 6 INT'L J. L. & PSYCHIATRY 423, 426 (1984). To some extent, this pattern continues today. *See e.g.*, Fentiman, *"Guilty But Mentally Ill:" The Real Verdict Is Guilty*, 26 B.C. L. REV. 601, 648

successful pleaders are not truly mentally ill;[2] that most acquittals follow sharply-contested "battles of the experts;"[3] that most successful pleaders are sent for short stays to civil hospitals. By now, each of these myths—the substantial and insubstantial ones alike—has been clearly, definitively, and empirically disproved; yet, they remain powerful, and show no sign of abating.[4] What is more, even when the inaccuracy of public perceptions is demonstrated, the public remains resistent to change, even in the face of contrary data.[5] Thus, a *USA*

---

n. 281 (1985) (*citing* authorities); *see generally*, H. STEADMAN ET AL., REFORMING THE INSANITY DEFENSE: AN EVALUATION OF PRE-AND POST-HINCKLEY REFORMS (1993) (manuscript at 51) (H. STEADMAN) (forty percent of insanity pleas are entered in cases involving property or drug offenses or other nonviolent crimes; less than one quarter of pleas entered in homicide cases). Yet, the underlying assumptions (that the predicate acts are necessarily heinous crimes) are accepted by even the most thoughtful and perceptive of scholars working in this area. *See e.g.*, Morse, *Excusing the Crazy: The Insanity Defense Revisited*, 58 S. CAL. L. REV. 777, 809 (1985) (perception that insanity acquittees have "almost always" committed serious acts is legitimate one); *but compare id.* at 795-801 (discussing and dismissing other insubstantial insanity defense myths).

2. Hans, *supra* note 1, at 408.

3. *See e.g.*, Acheson, McDonald v. U.S.: *The* Durham *Rule Redefined*, 51 GEO. L.J. 580, 589 (1963) (even after the "highwater" insanity acquittal level in the years immediately following the *Durham* decision, between two- thirds and three-fourths of acquittals were uncontested bench trials following stipulations by both parties, reflecting unanimous medical opinion). *See also*, THE INSANITY DEFENSE: HEARINGS BEFORE THE COMM. ON THE JUDICIARY OF THE U.S. SENATE TO AMEND TITLE 18 TO LIMIT THE INSANITY DEFENSE, 97th Cong., 2d Sess. 267, 278 (1982) (THE INSANITY DEFENSE) (remarks of Prof. Bonnie); S. HALLECK, THE MENTALLY DISORDERED OFFENDER 51 (1986) (battle of experts "rare").

4. *See* Morse, *supra* note 1, at 795-801 (discussing insubstantiality of certain myths); *see generally supra* chapter 3 B 1 b (1), and *see* United States v. Lyons, 739 F. 2d 994, 995-999 (5 Cir. 1984) (Rubin, J., dissenting) (answering each "mythic" argument); H. STEADMAN, *supra* note 1 (same). A study by two psychologists concluded that, *despite* recent efforts to educate the public about insanity defense issues, "professionals and laymen continue to exhibit a lack of accurate understanding regarding the mechanics and use of the mechanics and use of the NGRI plea and its success rate." Faulstich & Moore, *The Insanity Plea: A Study of Societal Reactions*, 8 LAW & PSYCHOL. REV. 129, 129 (1984), *citing* D. Van Speybroeck, "A Comparison of the Opinions of Professionals and Laypersons Toward the Insanity Plea and the Criminal Behavior of Mental Patients," (Dissertation Abstracts International, 8111615, 1980).

5. Rogers & Ewing, *Ultimate Opinion Proscriptions: A Cosmetic Fix and Plea for Empiricism*, 13 LAW & HUM. BEHAV. 357, 361 (1989); Jeffrey & Pasework, *Altering Opinions About the Insanity Plea*, 11 J. PSYCHIATRY & L. 29, 33-35 (1983); *see e.g.*, United States v. Wright, 511 F. 2d 1311, 1313 n. 11 (D.C. Cir. 1975) (from 1968 to 1975, not a *single* defendant found NGRI in Washington, D.C. was released from custody where doctors from St. Elizabeth's Hospital opposed such release); Kirschner, *Constitutional Standards for Release of the*

Thus, a *USA Today* editorial by Paul Kamenar (executive legal director of the Washington Legal Foundation) charged:

> The insanity defense on the books in most states allows criminals to
> escape moral culpability and punishment for crimes ranging from mass
> murder to tax evasion, even when they know their conduct is wrong. They
> get off by arguing fuzzy and vague concepts such as the inability to
> emotionally appreciate their wrongdoing.[6]

It should have been fairly easy for a staff citechecker to do some
rudimentary research and discover that Kamenar was factually
wrong.[7] This research was apparently not done, and Kamenar's
myths were reified for the newspaper's readers.

It is thus necessary to examine *why* these myths originally
emerged, *why* these myths have shown such remarkable longevity,
why cases such as Hinckley's have had such a profound effect on the
perpetuation of the myths, *why* they appear essential to the continued order of society,[8] *why* they continue to capture a significant
portion of the general public and the legal community,[9] *how* they
reflect a "community consciousness,"[10] and *why* their persistence

---

    Civilly Committed and Not Guilty By Reason of Insanity, 20 ARIZ. L. REV. 223,
    276 n. 380 (1978) (discussing legislative fear of public outcry was infamous
    insanity acquittee is released).

6.   Kamenar, *Insanity Defense Is Crazy*, USA Today (Feb. 6, 1992), at 8A (full text
    available on NEXIS).

7.   *See* H. STEADMAN, *supra* note 1, at 60 (ALI substantive standard employed in
    20 states, but burden of proof allocated to state in only five jurisdictions). On
    the infrequency of insanity defense pleas and its low success rate, *see supra*
    chapter 3 B 1 b (1).

8.   A. GOLDSTEIN, THE INSANITY DEFENSE 233 (1967).

9.   The fact that the insanity defense "is in many ways the acid test of our attitudes
    toward the insane and toward the criminal law itself," Herman, *The Insanity
    Defense in Fact and Fiction: On Norval Morris's Madness and the Criminal Law*,
    1985 AM. B. FOUND. RES. J. 385, 385, certainly helps to explain the phenome-
    non.

10.   *See supra* chapter 4 D 4. In his paper counseling rejection of expert testimony
    based upon psychodynamic psychology, Morse, *Failed Explanations and Crimi-
    nal Responsibility: Experts and the Unconscious*, 68 VA. L. REV. 971, 1042
    (1982), Professor Morse explains the appeal of dynamic theory to "lawyers,
    historians and literary critics" (*id.* at 991 n. 74):

    They are constantly interpreting language and behavior in order to make sense of them.
    If a psychodynamic theorist is asked to explain a human action, he or she will tell a story
    about a human life, explaining the behavior by reference to motives—sex, aggression—that
    we can all understand. It will be a human story about human beings, rather than an account

may doom any attempt to establish a rational insanity defense jurisprudence,[11] no matter how much conflicting empirical data is revealed.[12] To answer these questions it is thus necessary to look at the myths' roots.[13]

An examination of the literature and the caselaw reveals at least four reasons for the myths' persistence:[14]

•The (irrational) fear that defendants will "beat the rap" through fakery, a millennium-old fear which has its roots in a general

---

that treats behavior as nothing more than mechanistic effects of biological, psychological, or sociological variables.

It may be precisely this *lack* of "mechanistic"-ness that engenders jury suspicion, and insures that testimony based upon *psychological* motives will never truly "fit" within a jury's reflection of a community consciousness.

11. *See e.g.*, Roberts, Golding & Fincham, *supra* note 1, at 208 ("Unfortunately, calls for [insanity] reform did not stem from an increased understanding of the purpose and appropriate limits of the insanity defense, but, rather, arose from a sense of emotional outrage, a series of factual and attitudinal misconceptions, and a belief that insanity acquittals undermined the public's faith in the criminal justice system").

12. We have known for at least a half century that the empirical data refutes these myths. Guttmacher, *The Quest For a Test of Criminal Responsibility*, 111 AM. J. PSYCHIATRY 428 (1954) (discussing William White's studies showing insanity acquittees spent more time confined than those convicted in cases dealing with similar offenses).

13. *See e.g.*, Bidney, *Myth, Symbolism and Truth*, in MYTH: A SYMPOSIUM 3, 16 (T. Sebeok ed. 1955) (myths symbolize "fundamental metaphysical and religious truth"), and *id.* at 20-21:

[Myth] is beyond truth and falsity. The 'truth' of a myth is a function of its pragmatic and dramatic effectiveness in moving men to act in accordance with typical, emotionally charged ideals. The effectiveness of myth depends in large part upon ignorance or unconsciousness of its actual motivation. That is why myth tends to recede before the advance of reason and self-conscious reflection.

See generally, de Vito, *Some New Alternatives to the Insanity Defense*, 1 AM. J. FORENS. PSYCHIATRY 30 (1980) (myths rooted in "cultural subconscious"); E. BERGLER & A. MEERLOO, JUSTICE AND INJUSTICE 144 (1963) (stumbling blocks in developing a legal system that appeal's to "man's sense of justice," include "(1) widespread and timebound popular misconceptions; (2) blind prejudice based on inner fear; (3) fallacies of judgment based on 'probabilities;' (4) panic reactions").

14. This analysis accepts as given the continued vitality of the presumption regularly indulged in by the courts: that a defendant's sanity can be presumed. *See e.g.*, Mullaney v. Wilbur, 421 U.S. 684, 702-03 n. 31 (1975), *quoting* Davis v. United States, 160 U.S. 469 (1895); Ake v. Oklahoma, 470 U.S. 68, 72-73 (1985). This presumption has been challenged—convincingly, in my view—in Eule, *The Presumption of Sanity: Bursting the Bubble*, 25 U.C.L.A. L. REV. 637 (1978).

disbelief in mental illness, and a deep-seeded distrust of manipulative criminal defense lawyers invested with the ability to "con" jurors into accepting spurious expert testimony.[15]

- The sense (among the legal community and the general public) that there is "something different" about mental illness and organic illness, so that, while certain *physiological* disabilities may be seen as legitimately exculpatory, "mere" emotional handicaps will not.
- The demand that a defendant conform to popular images of extreme "craziness" in order to be "legitimately" "insane," a demand with which Chief Justice Rehnquist and other members of the current Supreme Court appear entirely comfortable.[16]
- A fear that the "soft," exculpatory sciences of psychiatry and psychology, claiming expertise in almost all areas of behavior, will somehow overwhelm the criminal justice system by thwarting the system's crime control component.[17]

---

15. *See* Resnick, *Perceptions of Psychiatric Testimony: A Historical Perspective on the Hysterical Invective*, 14 BULL. AM. ACAD. PSYCHIATRY & L. 203, 206 (1986) (concerning dates to the tenth century); *Lyons*, 739 F. 2d at 998 (Rubin, J., dissenting) ("[A] defendant pleading insanity typically faces both a judge and a jury who are skeptical about psychiatry in general and the insanity plea in particular"), and *id.* at 997-98 (discussing public's perceived difference between objectively-determined exculpatory defenses and subjectively-weighed ones, such as insanity); for a more realistic appraisal of counsel's *inabilities* in this area, *see* Miller v. State, 338 N.W. 2d 673, 678 (S. Dak. 1983) (Henderson, J., dissenting) (criticizing defense counsel for failure to research and raise Vietnam Stress Syndrome defense); *see generally*, Perlin, *Fatal Assumption: A Critical Evaluation of the Role of Counsel in Mental Disability Cases*, 16 LAW & HUM. BEHAV. 39 (1992).

16. There is an important exception to this. We are willing to exculpate certain defendants who may not look crazy at all in those very limited and fact-specific cases where our sense of sympathy, understanding, and/or empathy outweighs our punitive, disbelieving and/or vengeful feelings. *See supra* chapter 4 D 2-3. As I will demonstrate subsequently, these feelings are reflective of precisely the same personality characteristics that make us reject the insanity defense in many "legitimate" cases (that is, where the defendant *is* mentally ill and not responsible as a result of that mental illness).

17. Wasyliw, Cavanagh & Rogers, *Beyond the Scientific Limits of Expert Testimony*, 13 BULL. AM. ACAD. PSYCHIATRY & L. 147, 151 (1985); H. PACKER, THE LIMITS OF THE CRIMINAL SANCTION (1968). Studies have demonstrated clearly that reactions towards the insanity defense "are part of a cluster of crime and justice attitudes." Hans, *supra* note 1, at 410; *see generally*, Fitzgerald & Ellsworth, *Due Process vs. Crime Control: The Impact of Death Qualification on Jury Attitudes*, 8 LAW & HUM. BEHAV. 31 (1984).

To some extent, each of these reasons reflects Judge Adams' dissent in *Government of Virgin Islands v. Fredericks*, that the law of criminal responsibility acts "as a screen upon which the community has projected its visions of criminal justice."[18] The eminent psychiatrist William A. White similarly saw the jury as representing "the mind of the community," and as "project[ing] its own feelings upon the accused."[19] In this way, jury verdicts in insanity defense cases represented "the affective orientation of the herd towards the offender."[20] Within the community, it is thus "aberrant behavior by those sufficiently similar to ourselves [which] is truly threatening to our core beliefs."[21]

The projections on this screen are seriously distorted,[22] and it is necessary to explore the depths of these distortions if any sense is to be made of the intractability of the myths under discussion.[23] Unless this exploration is successful, any attempt to develop a coherent jurisprudence is doomed to failure, "since insanity must always be at bottom a matter of custom and opinion of the community."[24] Where the doctrine is based on the community's "personal biases or fears,"[25] attempts at structuring a rational body of law appear to be even more deeply doomed.

---

18. 578 F. 2d 927, 937 (3d Cir. 1978).
19. W. WHITE, *supra* note 1, at 91.
20. *Id.* at 205. Similarly, the Ninth Circuit found *M'Naghten*'s longevity to flow from its most closely comporting with "the moral feelings of the community." Sauer v. United States, 241 F. 2d 640, 649 (9th Cir. 1957), *cert. denied*, 354 U.S. 940 (1957), *overruled on other grounds*, Wade v. United States, 426 F. 2d 64, 73 (9th Cir. 1970).
21. Ingber, *Ideological Boundaries of Criminal Responsibility* (review of H. FINGARETTE & A. HASSE, MENTAL DISABILITIES AND CRIMINAL RESPONSIBILITY (1979)), 27 U.C.L.A. L. REV. 816, 826-27 (1980).
22. *Cf.* Spring, *The Insanity Issue in a Public Needs Perspective*, 4 DET. COLL. L. REV. 603, 609 (1979): "What we are witnessing [in insanity defense cases] is jury vigilantism, and the effects run deep because it occurs in the most celebrated of cases. It mocks the entire process of criminal justice and fuels a lack of confidence in the whole system."
23. *See e.g.*, Lyons, 739 F. 2d at 999-1000 (Rubin, J., dissenting), discussing the need for judges to insulate themselves from "uninformed public opinion."
24. Guttmacher, *Criminal Responsibility in Certain Homicide Cases Involving Family Members*, in PSYCHIATRY AND THE LAW 73, 77 (Hoch & Zubin eds. 1955) (*quoting* DeGrazia, *The Dog Must Wag the Tail*, N.Y. Times (May 3, 1952), at 18 (Book Review section).
25. *See* Note, *The Syndrome Syndrome: Problems Concerning the Admissibility of Expert Testimony on Psychological Profiles*, 37 U. FLA. L. REV. 1035, 1045 (1985) (discussing how "syndrome" jurisprudence may reflect such biases and fears in Vietnam Veterans' or rape trauma syndrome cases).

B. The Myths in "Real Life"

Because so much of our insanity defense jurisprudence is informed by sensational cases (such as M'Naghten's or Hinckley's), it is all too easy to lose sight of the way jurors respond in less celebrated trials. A recent journalistic account of one such case focuses our attention on some of the critical issues.

Josee Trani McNally, a fifty-two year old white, middle-class professional, has suffered from "complex partial seizures," a form of epilepsy that renders its victims semiconscious and may lead to irrational behavior, since she underwent brain surgery in 1980 to eradicate the *grand mal* epileptic convulsive seizures that she had suffered since she sustained head injuries in an auto accident at age seventeen.[26] Since 1982, she has been arrested on at least four occasions for shoplifting or petit larceny. She pled guilty to the first charges; after her fourth arrest, she entered an insanity plea, relying on testimony by her treating psychologist,[27] arguing that, while in the throes of a seizure, she could not understand the nature and consequences of her act.

The jury rejected her defense[28] and, following her conviction, she was placed on probation. As a condition of probation, she was ordered to wear an electronic sensor to monitor her controlled trips from her home (to church, her doctor and a weekly hour-long walk). Post- verdict interviews with the judge, the forensic expert, and jurors appeared to reveal these important points:

---

26. Abrams, *Confined for Crimes She Can't Remember*, Newsday (Mar. 4, 1989), at 2, 10.
27. According to the press accounts, the prosecutor stressed that the psychologist did not have "medical credentials." *Id.* On the extent to which jurors demand testimony by *physicians* in insanity cases, *compare* Perlin, *The Legal Status of The Psychologist in the Courtroom*, 5 J. Psychiatry & L. 41 (1977) (nonmedical witnesses often viewed as "second rate" experts), *to* Yarmey & Popiel, *Judged Value of Medical Versus Psychological Expert Witnesses*, 11 Int'l J. L. & Psychiatry 195 (1988) (distinction between professional backgrounds not as salient as individual witness's training and experience). *But see e.g.*, Satterwhite v. Texas, 486 U.S. 249, 259 (1988) (prosecutor highlighted expert witness's credentials in summation: "Dr. Grigson was the only physician to take the stand").
28. There is no indication from the press account as to whether the state produced its own forensic expert witness.

•Since the jurors had never heard of this type of epilepsy,[29] "they could not understand how somebody could be in this state while looking and acting normal."

•"If she had fallen to the floor in convulsions—then they would have believed."

•"There was nothing wrong with the woman we saw," said a juror. "She dressed well, was obviously intelligent, and answered questions very precisely. She seemed all there."

•According to the judge, "That stuff about being unconscious while seeming conscious sounded like a lawyer's ploy. The jury obviously didn't believe her defense—and, frankly, neither did I."

Each of these arguments reflects an important and fixed vision of "crazy behavior," a vision with which the defendant clearly did not comport. The defendant neither looked nor acted "insane," her intelligence was not impaired, there were no outward physical manifestations of her disorder demonstrated at the time of trial, and the entire defense seemed to be a "lawyer's ploy."[30] It is the sort of paradigmatic case that precisely reflects the little value placed by jurors on the externalities of scientific research and empirical evidence, and the persistence of the meta-myths that still dominate the insanity defense landscape.

C. Unpacking the Myths

1. Fear of Faking

Historically, it has been believed that insanity was too easily feigned, that psychiatrists were easily deceived by such simulation, and that the use of the defense has thus been "an easy way to escape punishment."[31] Because it could not be demonstrated conclusively

---

29. According to a spokesperson from the Epilepsy Foundation, 25% of the nation's two million epileptics suffer from complex partial seizures. Abrams, *supra* note 26, at 10.

30. *But see supra* chapter 4 D 3 (jurors usually exhibit *sympathy* toward defendants who fell into a "we can feel sorry for you" category). Perhaps, while the defendant here obviously did not strike the jurors as a violent or dangerous *personal* threat, the fact that she was perceived as a recidivist offender (albeit for a minor charge) robbed her of this expected sympathy.

31. Note, State v. Field: *Wisconsin Focuses on Public Protection by Reviving Automatic Commitment Following a Successful Insanity Defense*, 1986 Wis. L.

that insanity had some "observable 'material' existence," charges of "counterfeit[ing]" insanity quickly arose.[32] When Judge Darling characterized insanity in 1911 as "the last refuge of a hopeless defence,"[33] the factual basis of his assertion went unchallenged.

This fear of successful deception, which has "permeated the American legal system for over a century,"[34] was seen as significantly weakening the deterrent effect of the criminal law.[35] The fear is one which has held some of this century's most respected jurists in its thrall.[36] The public's fear of feigned insanity defenses meshes with its fears of released insanity acquittees. If a defendant can successfully feign insanity, it is feared, he will likely be quickly released from

REV. 781, 784. For what is probably the first recorded example of feigned insanity, see Cohn, *Some Psychiatric Phenomena in Ancient Law*, in PSYCHIATRY, LAW AND ETHICS 59, 61 (A. Carmi, S. Schneider & A. Hefez eds. 1986) (David's decision to feign mental disorder so as to escape from King Saul; see 1 *Samuel* 21:13-16); see also, Brittain, *The History of Legal Medicine: The Assizes of Jerusalem*, 34 MEDICO-LEGAL J. 72 (1966) (feigned illness to avoid trial in 1100).

32. Eigen, *supra* note 1, at 427. Thus, in 1681, Sir Robert Holbrun wrote, "[A] man may counterfeit himself to be mad, he may do it so cunningly as it cannot be discerned whether he be mad or no." *Id.* at 427-28, *quoting* G. COLLINSON, A TREATISE ON THE LAW CONCERNING IDIOTS, LUNATICS, AND OTHER PERSONS "NON COMPOTES MENTIS" (1812).

33. Rex v. Thomas, 7 Cr. App. R. 36 (1911), discussed in Crotty, *The History of Insanity as a Defence to Crime in English Criminal Law*, 12 CALIF. L. REV. 105, 119 n.87 (1924).

34. Perlin, *The Supreme Court, the Mentally Disabled Criminal Defendant, and Symbolic Values: Random Decisions, Hidden Rationales, or "Doctrinal Abyss?"* 29 ARIZ. L. REV. 1, 98 (1987). *Cf.* Winiarz v. State, 752 P. 2d 761, 763 (Nev. 1988) (reversible error for psychiatric expert to testify defendant was "feigning" in homicide cased where defendant pled mistake and misadventure as defenses). The alleged ease with which insanity can be feigned is also cited as a rationale for the tort law doctrine imposing tort liability on the "insane." *See e.g.*, Williams by Williams v. Kearbey by and through Kearbey, 13 Kan. App. 2d 564, 775 P. 2d 670, 672 (1989), citing RESTATEMENT (SECOND) OF TORTS §895J, comment a (1977).
    For a recent historical analysis, *see* Geller et al., *Feigned Insanity in Nineteenth Century America: Experts, Explanations and Exculpations*, 20 ANGLO-AMER. L. REV. 443 (1991).

35. Eule, *supra* note 14, at 649. For an analysis of how a release hearing opinion in what was apparently a "nullification" NGRI verdict case—*see* Matter of Tornsney, 47 N.Y. 2d 667, 420 N.Y.S. 2d 192, 394 N.E. 2d 292 (1979)—reflected the public's response to the original verdict, *see* Block, *The Semantics of Insanity*, 36 OKLA. L. REV. 561, 587-90 (1983).

36. *See e.g.*, Lynch v. Overholser, 369 U.S. 705, 715 (1962) (Harlan, J.); United States v. Brown, 478 F. 2d 606, 611 (D.C. Cir. 1973) (Leventhal, J.) (*quoting Lynch*).

confinement, thus both escaping his "justly deserved punishment" and endangering other potential victims in the community.[37] Thus, even lawyers for insanity acquittees repeat these myths. In a press interview following a bench trial acquitting his client, defense counsel Jerome Ballarotto stated, "Everybody who knew [the defendant] knew something wasn't right about this...Prosecutors generally scoff at this type of defense, but *in this case, it was true.*"[38]

Yet there is virtually no evidence that feigned insanity has ever been a remotely significant problem of criminal procedure, even after more "liberal" substantive insanity tests were adopted. A survey of the case law reveals no more than a handful of cases in which a defendant free of mental disorder "bamboozled"[39] a court or jury into a spurious insanity acquittal.[40]

---

37. Neumann, *Territorial Discrimination, Equal Protection, and Self- Determination*, 135 U. Pa. L. Rev. 261, 361 (1987); Zenoff, *Controlling the Dangers of Dangerousness: The ABA Standards and Beyond*, 53 Geo. Wash. L. Rev. 562, 569 (1985); ABA Criminal Justice Mental Health Standards, Commentary to Standard 7-7.3, at 409-10 (1989).

38. Booth, *Trenton Firefighter Acquitted; Temporary Insanity Cited in 1991 Attack*, The (Trenton, NJ) Times, March 17, 1993, at A19. The defendant, a fireman, had suffered organic brain damage after having been struck on the head by a rock eight months prior to the incident that gave rise to the criminal charges. *Id.*

39. United States v. Carter, 415 F. Supp. 15, 16 (D.D.C. 1975). *See* Mickenberg, *A Pleasant Surprise: The Guilty But Mentally Ill Verdict Has Both Succeeded On Its Own Right and Successfully Preserved the Traditional Role of the Insanity Defense*, 55 U. Cin. L. Rev. 943, 981 (1987) (footnote omitted):

Even the most vociferous opponents of the insanity defense are usually unable to cite actual cases of defendants who escaped justice by pretending to be mentally ill. United States Attorney Guiliani, when pressed on this point, cited the novel Anatomy of a Murder as a 'perfect example of how you can manipulate and use the insanity defense.' Needless to say, while Anatomy of a Murder is an excellent novel, it is still only fiction.

40. *See Carter, supra*; People v. Lockett, 121 Misc. 2d 549, 468 N.Y.S. 2d 802 (Sup. Ct. 1983) (granting state's motion to vacate defendant's NGRI plea on ground defendant defrauded court); Sollars v. State, 316 P. 2d 917 (Nev. 1957); People v. Schmidt, 216 N.Y. 324, 110 N.E. 2d 945 (1915). The defendant was *unsuccessful* in his effort in State v. Simonson, 100 N.M. 297, 669 P. 2d 1092 (1983). *Lockett* and *Simonson* are discussed in Note, *Vietnam Stress Syndrome and the Criminal Defendant*, 19 Loy. L.A. L. Rev. 473, 505-06 (1985).

Other anecdotal instances of feigned insanity are discussed in Sauer v. United States, 241 F. 2d 640, 648 n. 21 (9th Cir. 1957) (case of Martin Leven, discussed in F. Wertham, The Show of Violence (1949)), and in Gerber, *The Insanity Defense Revisited*, 1984 Ariz. St. L.J. 83, 117-118 (speculating that President Nixon's charges that the insanity defense had been subject to "unconscionable abuse by defendants" stemmed from his reading press accounts of the case of United States v. Trapnell, 495 F. 2d 22 (2d Cir. 1974), *cert. den.*, 419 U.S. 851

Recent carefully-crafted empirical studies have clearly demonstrated that malingering among insanity defendants is, and traditionally has been, statistically low.[41] Even where it is attempted, it is fairly easy to discover (if sophisticated diagnostic tools are used).[42] Clinicians correctly classify ninety-two to ninety-five percent of all sub-

---

(1974), where the court admitted evidence that Trapnell, while a patient at a hospital, had counseled a fellow patient, Padilla, about how to feign insanity. Padilla subsequently had charges against him dropped and attributed his success to Trapnell's teachings on the art of acting insane. *Id.* at 24. For the complete story of Trapnell, *see* E. Asinof, The Fox Is Crazy Too: The True Story of Garrett Trapnell, Adventurer, Skyjacker, Bank Robber, Con Man, Lover (1976); *see generally,* Robitscher & Haynes, *In Defense of the Insanity Defense,* 31 Emory L.J. 9, 36-37 n. 99 (1982).

41. Cornell & Hawk, *Clinical Presentation of Malingerers Diagnosed by Experienced Forensic Psychologists,* 13 Law & Hum. Behav. 375, 381-83 (1989); Grossman & Wasyliw, *A Psychiatric Study of Stereotypes: Assessment of Malingering in a Criminal Forensic Group,* 52 J. Personal. Assessment 549 (1988). For earlier inquiries, *see e.g.,* Eissler, *Malingering,* in Psychoanalysis and Culture: Essays in Honor of Géza Rohéim 218 (G. Wilbur & W. Muensterburger eds. 1951); H. Davidson, Forensic Psychiatry 159-73 (1952); Resnick, *The Detection of Malingered Mental Illness,* 2 Behav. Sci. & L. 21 (1984).

42. *See e.g.,* Wettstein & Mulvey, *Disposition of Insanity Acquittees in Illinois,* 16 Bull. Am. Acad. Psychiatry & L. 11, 15 (1988) (one of 137 insanity acquittees seen as malingering).

For the most recent efforts to validate assessment tools designed to screen malingering, *see* Rogers, Bagby & Gillis, *Improvements in the M Test as a Screening Measure for Malingering,* 20 Bull. Am. Acad. Psychiatry & L. 101 (1992); Rogers et al., *Standardized Assessment of Malingering: Validation of the Structured Interview of Reported Symptoms,* 3 Psycholog. Assessment: J. Consulting & Clin. Psychology 89 (1991); Rogers, *Development of a New Classificatory Model of Malingering,* 18 Bull. Am. Acad. Psychiatry & L. 323 (1990); *see also,* Gummow & Gregory, *To Catch a Cheat: The Use of Intentional Deception in Forensic Psychological Examinations,* 8 Am. J. Forens. Psychol. 41 (1990); Roman et al., *Evaluating MMPI Validity in a Forensic Psychiatric Population: Distinguishing Between Malingering and Genuine Psychopathology,* 17 Crim. Just. & Behav. 186 (1990). Wasyliw et al., *The Detection of Malingering in a Criminal Forensic Group: MMPI Validation Scales,* 52 J. Personal. Assessment 321 (1988).

But see Faust, *Declarations Versus Investigations: The Case for the Special Reasoning Abilities and Capabilities of the Expert Witness in Psychology/Psychiatry,* 13 J. Psychiatry & L. 33 (1985) (little evidence found to support clinical claims of expert capacity to accurately detect malingering). Although Professor Donald Bersoff is generally critical of clinician accuracy in malingering detection, he exempts Rogers' structured interview format from his criticism. *See* Bersoff, *Judicial Deference to Nonlegal Decisionmakers: Imposing Simplistic Solutions on Problems of Cognitive Complexity in Mental Disability Law,* 46 SMU L. Rev. 323, 360 n. 162 (1992).

jects as either faking or not faking.[43] Some of these cases involve defendants who, although feigning, are nonetheless severely mentally ill.[44]

Reported cases also reveal that attempted feigning is a risky gambit: feigned attempts result in abandoned insanity defenses and/ or convictions.[45] This, of course, should not surprise. Almost two centuries ago, it was observed that feigning attempts would be "doomed to failure" because to "'sustain the character of a paroxysm of active insanity would require a continuity of exertion beyond the power of the sane person.'"[46]

In reality, the empirical evidence is quite to the contrary: it is much more likely that seriously mentally disabled criminal defendants will feign *sanity* in an effort to not be seen as mentally ill, even

---

43. Schretlen & Arkowitz, *A Psychological Test Battery to Detect Prison Inmates Who Fake Insanity or Mental Retardation*, 8 BEHAV. SCI. & L. 75 (1990).

44. *See e.g.*, Gellman, *Acting Skills Gain Defendant an Extended Run in Prison: Mental Illness "Charade" Doesn't Fool Court*, Wash. Post (July 6, 1989), at C1 (case of Tyrone Robinson) (data was consistent "both with psychosis and with desperate malingering"); People v. Kurbegovic, 138 Cal. App. 3d 731, 188 Cal. Rptr. 268 (1983) ("alphabet bomber case").

   Other individuals suffer from Munchausen's Syndrome, a mental disorder in which individuals voluntarily produce or simulate illness for no apparent purpose other than to assume a sick role. *See* Cohen v. Albert Einstein Med. Center, 405 Pa. Super. 392, 592 A. 2d 720, 724 (1991).

45. *See e.g.*, People v. Bey, 167 A.D. 2d 868, 562 N.Y.S. 2d 896 (1990) (defendant convicted; conviction affirmed); People v. Swan, 158 A.D. 2d 158, 557 N.Y.S. 2d 791 (1990) (same); Ross v. Kemp, 260 Ga. 312, 393 S.E. 2d 244 (1990) (defendant convicted; conviction reversed on other grounds); Daniel v. Thigpen, 742 F. Supp. 1535, 1544-46 (M.D. Ala. 1990) (insanity defense abandoned; writ of habeas corpus granted on other grounds); *compare* State v. Ondek, 584 So. 2d 282, 291 (La. App. 1991), *rev. den.* (1991) (determination that defendant was malingering consistent with testimony that defendant was reading psychiatric diagnostic manual during forensic observation).

46. *See* Eigen, *supra* note 1, at 428, discussing J. HASLAM, JURISPRUDENCE AS IT RELATES TO INSANITY ACCORDING TO THE LAWS OF ENGLAND 60 (1817). *See also*, People v. Schmidt, 216 N.Y. 324, 110 N.E. 945, 950 (1915) (emphasis added):

   Cases will doubtless arise where criminals will take shelter behind a professed belief that their crime was ordained by God just as this defendant attempted to shelter himself behind that belief. *We can safely leave such fabrications to the common sense of juries.*

   But see, Dietz, *Why the Experts Disagree: Variations in the Psychiatric Evaluation of Criminal Insanity*, 477 ANNALS 80, 82 (1985) ("To ask a murder defendant claiming hallucinations whether the voices encouraged the killing is to invite self-serving fabrication").

where such evidence might serve as powerful mitigating evidence in death penalty cases.[47] Thus, juveniles imprisoned on death row were quick to tell Dr. Dorothy Lewis and her associates, "I'm not crazy," or "I'm not a retard." [48]

In spite of this track record, the public remains highly skeptical of the abilities of forensic psychiatrists to determine legal insanity.[49] Prosecutors have offered, as evidence of sanity, expert testimony that a defendant was "intelligent enough to feign sanity."[50] Anti-insanity defense prosecutors suggest that only "a defendant who is faking insanity" can reasonably fear disclosure of his response to post-arrest *Miranda* warnings.[51] Prosecutors characterize the defense as a "fake"

---

47. *See e.g.*, People v. McCleary, 208 Ill. App. 3d 466, 567 N.E. 2d 434, 437 (1990) (defendant "malingered sanity"); Grossman & Cavanaugh, *Do Sex Offenders Minimize Psychiatric Symptoms?* 34 J. FORENS. SCI. 881 (1989) (answering question affirmatively); Grossman & Wasyliw, *supra* note 41 (22-39 percent of all insanity defendants studied showed evidence of minimizing their psychopathology).

    In the "pecking order" of prisoners, the mentally ill have always been plagued by an exceptionally low status. *See* Halleck, *The Criminal's Problem With Psychiatry*, in READINGS IN LAW AND PSYCHIATRY 51 (R. Allen et al. eds., 1975), and *see generally*, Resnick, *supra* note 15, at 23-24.

48. *See e.g.*, Lewis et al., *Neuropsychiatric, Psychoeducational, and Family Characteristics of 14 Juveniles Condemned to Death in the United States*, 145 AM. J. PSYCHIATRY 584, 588 (1988) (Lewis I) (juveniles on death row "almost uniformly tried to hide evidence of cognitive deficits and psychotic symptoms"); Lewis et al., *Psychiatric and Psychoeducational Characteristics of 15 Death Row Inmates in the United States*, 143 AM. J. PSYCHIATRY 838, 841 (1986) (all but one of sample of death row inmates studies attempted to *minimize* rather than exaggerate their degree of psychiatric disorders); Taylor, *Motives for Offending Among Violent and Psychotic Men*, 147 BRIT. J. PSYCHIATRY 491, 496-97 (1985) (in sample of 211 prisoners studied, nonpsychotic men never claimed psychotic justification for their offenses but half the psychotic men claimed ordinary, nonpsychotic motives).

49. *See e.g.*, Slater & Hans, *supra* note 1, at 677 (40% of those polled had "no confidence" in expert testimony in Hinckley trial; another 20% had only "slight" confidence); *see generally*, Homant & Kennedy, *Judgment of Legal Insanity as a Function of Attitude Toward the Insanity Defense*, 8 INT'L J. L. & PSYCHIATRY 67, 79-80 (1986)

50. Fulgham v. Ford, 850 F. 2d 1529, 1534 (11th Cir. 1988). *Compare* Francois v. Henderson, 850 F. 2d 231, 235 (5th Cir. 1988), a case involving an insanity acquittee's habeas corpus application for release, in which the state alleged that the defendant was "faking sanity." Expert testimony was unanimous that sanity could be feigned for only a few hours; "No schizophrenic can feign sanity for years on end." *Id.*

51. Daley & Fryklund, *The Insanity Defense and the "Testimony By Proxy" Problem*, 21 VALPARAISO U. L. REV. 497, 521 (1987) (authors are Illinois state attorneys).

and the ensuing convictions are affirmed.[52]

In its application for *certiorari* to the United States Supreme Court in *Colorado v. Connelly*, on the question of whether mental illness vitiates a *Miranda* waiver, the state prosecutor's office appended this editorial from a local paper following the decision by that state's Supreme Court to suppress the confession:

> You may well wonder how the [Colorado] Supreme Court can be sure Connelly lacked free will. Silly you! The court knows because a psychiatrist says so, and the psychiatrist knows because Connelly says so...Perhaps next time the Supreme Court should find an expert who is willing to go the distance—someone who will contend that no confession is ever the product of free will   Surely the court should find that notion appealing: It's simple but abstract, and it's a bold departure in legal theory. Best of all, though, it helps the guilty go free.[53]

Indeed, it may not even matter to some segment of the public whether an insanity defense is feigned or authentic; in *either* case, it is equally rejected.[54] Even insanity defense supporters such as Professor Richard Bonnie recommend that "an exculpatory doctrine of insanity should be framed in a way that minimizes the risk of fabrication, abuse, and moral mistake."[55] Dr. Isaac Ray, the father of American forensic psychiatry, discussed the impact of these misperceptions more than a century ago:

---

52. *See* United States *ex rel* Ford v. O'Leary, 1990 WL 106498 (N.D. Ill. 1990), at *2 (denying writ of habeas corpus).

53. Benner, *Requiem for* Miranda: *The Rehnquist Court's Voluntariness Doctrine in Historical Perspective*, 67 WASH. U. L. Q. 59, 143 n. 379 (1989), *quoting* Exhibit "E," Colorado v. Connelly, Petition for Certiorari (from Rocky Mountain News, July 11, 1985). In *Connelly*, 479 U.S. 157 (1986), the Supreme Court held that a defendant's free will irrelevant to voluntariness inquiry under *Miranda*; *see infra* text accompanying notes 148-52.

54. *See* Geis & Meier, *Abolition of the Insanity Plea in Idaho: A Case Study*, 477 ANNALS 72, 73 (1985) (Idaho residents hold view that persons should not be avoid to avoid punitive consequences of criminal acts by reliance on "either a real or a faked plea of insanity"); State v. Perry, 610 So. 2d 746, 780 (La. 1992) (Cole, J., dissenting) ("Society has the right to protect itself from those who would commit murder and seek to avoid their legitimate punishment by a subsequently contracted, or feigned, insanity").

55. Bonnie, *Morality, Equality, and Expertise: Renegotiating the Relationship Between Psychiatry and the Criminal Law*, 12 BULL. AM. ACAD. PSYCHIATRY & L. 5, 15 (1984).

The supposed insurmountable difficulty of distinguishing between feigned and real insanity has conduced, probably more than all other causes together, to bind the legal profession to the most rigid construction and application of the common law relative to this disease, and is always put forward in objection to the more humane doctrines.[56]

Courts are extraordinarily casual in their admission of both lay and expert testimony as to feigning.[57] Thus, an expert's testimony that a defendant might have been feigning "because he could be released from an institution in only a few months" if he were found NGRI[58] was considered improper (albeit harmless error) only because there was no evidence in the case that the defendant had knowledge about the possibility of his potential release following such an insanity acquittal.[59] Nowhere in the court's brief opinion is there any indication as to how such testimony fits within psychiatric expertise as to mental states.

In another case, testimony by a psychiatrist that an institutional chaplain had told him that he (the chaplain) felt the defendant "had tendencies to be a manipulative type of person," was admissible since that issue was "clearly relevant to...whether...[the defendant] was a malingerer."[60] Again, there is no discussion of *why* this is "clearly relevant" nor of the relationship that this testimony bears to the witness's expertise. This is especially telling in light of Professor Ogloff's conclusion that "unstructured interviews and projective tests are the least effective ways to identify malingerers."[61]

---

56. I. RAY, MEDICAL JURISPRUDENCE OF INSANITY § 247, at 243 (1962 ed.); *see generally*, Rogers, *Feigned Mental Illness*, 26 PROF'L PSYCHOLOGY 312, 313 (1989)(labeling current model of malingering as "puritanical," and concluding it is "scientifically indefensible").

   The issue of how jurors respond to fabricated defenses in general is discussed in State v. Eaton, 30 Wash. App. 288, 633 P. 2d 921, 925 (1981) (defendant claimed alcohol-induced blackout). *See also*, Singer, *On Classism and Dissonance in the Criminal Law: A Reply to Professor Meir Dan-Cohen*, 77 J. CRIM. L. & CRIMINOL. 69, 76 (1986) (discussing courts' fears of fabrication in cases involving prison inmates claiming duress in escape cases).

57. In addition to the cases discussed *infra* accompanying notes 58-62, *see also*, Capps v. State, 573 N.E. 2d 459 (Ind. App. 1991); State v. Perkins, 248 Kan. 760, 811 P. 2d 1142 (1991).

58. *But see supra* chapter 3 B 1 b (1).

59. People v. Christopher, 170 A.D. 2d 1020, 566 N.Y.S. 2d 167, 168 (1991).

60. Sanders v. Commonwealth, 801 S.W. 2d 665, 678 (Ky. 1990), *rev. den.* (1991).

61. Ogloff, *The Admissibility of Expert Testimony Regarding Malingering and Deception*, 8 BEHAV. SCI. & L. 27, 35 (1990).

On the other hand, a conviction was reversed on state Confrontation Clause grounds when an expert's deposition was taken out of the defendant's presence; at the deposition, the expert had testified that he felt a defendant's IQ score of fifty-nine may have evidenced malingering to avoid criminal prosecution (since, three years earlier, the defendant had scored eighty-one on a similar test, and the witness believed that that score was "the most accurate" one).[62] While the conviction was reversed, there was no consideration of the witness's basis for this testimony. On what basis did the witness decide that the eighty-one IQ score was "right" and the fifty-nine score "wrong?" This question is never asked.

Courts are pretextual and teleological in the way they construe malingering testimony.[63] Where a defendant who committed a brutal murder gave himself up to police authorities, confessed and showed no remorse for the killing, the court found that this evidence "wholly refute[d]" expert testimony as to defendant's insanity, leading to the initial conclusion that the defendant "concocted" evidence of delusions,[64] and to the broader holding that expert opinions are "especially entitled to little or no weight" when based upon a "feigned state of mind."[65] Elsewhere, a court supported a finding that the defendant had "feigned incoherence" on evidence that his previous institutionalizations had made him "aware" of how to act during a psychological evaluation.[66] In neither of these instances is there any social science basis offered by the court to support its conclusions.

No one is guiltier of "buying into" the feigning meta-myth than Chief Justice Rehnquist. In *Ake v. Oklahoma*, which held that when an indigent defendant makes a preliminary showing that his sanity at trial time "is likely to be a significant factor at trial," he is constitutionally entitled to psychiatric assistance,[67] he was the lone dissenter, expressing fears of feigned insanity defenses[68] "in the face of staggeringly-unanimous professional diagnosis and lay observation as to the

---

62. Dean v. Commonwealth, 777 S.W. 2d 900, 901-2 (Ky. 1989).
63. *See* Perlin, *Morality and Pretextuality, Psychiatry and Law: Of "Ordinary Common Sense," Heuristic Reasoning, and Cognitive Dissonance*, 19 BULL. AM. ACAD. PSYCHIATRY & L. 131, 134 (1991).
64. Commonwealth v. Patskin, 375 Pa. 368, 100 A. 2d 472, 473 (1953).
65. *Id.* at 475.
66. State v. Carr, 231 Neb. 127, 435 N.W. 2d 194, 196-97 (1989).
67. 470 U.S. at 68, 83 (1985). *See generally,* Perlin, *supra* note 34, at 18-22.
68. *Id.* at 87, 91 (Rehnquist, J., dissenting).

profundity of Ake's mental illness."[69] In *Ford v. Wainwright*,[70] holding that the Eighth Amendment prohibits the execution of an insane prisoner, he dissented, raising the specter that sane, capitally-sentenced defendants will seek to "'cheat' death by raising spurious, multiple claims of insanity."[71] In *Foucha v. Louisiana*,[72] holding that a non-mentally ill insanity acquittee could not be retained in a forensic mental health facility, he and Justice Scalia joined in Justice Thomas's dissent, focusing on the possibility of the "calculated abuse of the insanity defense" by those who might feign the plea.[73] Rehnquist's views here suffer from an abject lack of empirical support and perfectly mirror the public's sanist views on this question.

Lurking beneath the surface of this meta-myth is another truism: that the "'insanity dodge' has come into existence by popular concept as a symbol of sharp practice by unscrupulous attorneys and none

---

69. Perlin, *supra* note 34, at 83. Ake's lawyer characterized his client to the court as "goofier than hell," Brief of Petitioner, Ake v. Oklahoma, 470 U.S. 68 (1985), at 10, *quoting* Joint Appendix at 27; a consulting psychiatrist characterized Ake as "a psychotic [diagnosed as suffering from] paranoid schizophrenia—chronic with exacerbation..." *Id.* at 2-3. See Perlin, *supra* note 34, at 18-19 nn. 156, 158.

70. 477 U.S. 399 (1986); *see generally*, Perlin, *supra* note 34, at 53-62.

71. Perlin, *supra* note 34, at 83. *See e.g.*, *Ford*, 477 U.S. at 435 (Rehnquist, J., dissenting):

A claim of insanity may be made at any time before sentence, and, once rejected, may be used again; a prisoner found sane two days before execution might claim to have lost his sanity the next day thus necessitating another judicial determination of his sanity and presumably another stay of execution.

Picking up on this argument, a student note has suggested that, when such a prisoner raises "frivolous claims of insanity," he could thus be deemed to waive the right to a judicial inquiry into present sanity. *See* Note, *Ford v. Wainwright: The Eighth Amendment, Due Process and Insanity on Death Row*, 1986 No. ILL. U. L. REV. 89, 110. *But see*, Note, *The Eighth Amendment and the Execution of the Presently Incompetent*, 32 STAN. L. REV. 765, 790 (1980) (empirical evidence "undermines forecast of a stampede of unmeritorious claims").

72. 112 S. Ct. 1780 (1992); *see supra* chapter 4 E 2 d; *see generally*, 3 M. L. PERLIN, MENTAL DISABILITY LAW: CIVIL AND CRIMINAL (1989), §15.25A, at 149-56 (1992 pocket part).

73. *Foucha*, 112 S. Ct. at 1801-2; *see also id.* at 1797 (Kennedy, J., dissenting). Similar concerns emerge in Justice O'Connor's concurrence in Medina v. California, 112 S. Ct. 2572, 2582-83 (1992) (placement of burden of proof on defendants in incompetency to stand trial proceedings not unconstitutional) (expressing fear that defendants will feign incompetency).

too honest medical men."[74] Thus, a comprehensive survey in the District of Columbia—the true laboratory for most major insanity defense developments in the past four decades—showed that court distrust of psychiatrists was "fully matched by distrust of defense counsel who appeared unorthodox in their approach to the insanity defense."[75] The parallels to the perception of the role of lawyers in death penalty cases[76] and in challenges to involuntary civil commitment standards[77] are remarkable.

Forensic psychiatrists testifying in criminal cases were similarly viewed "as attempting to cloud our moral standards and to ignore the limits of community tolerance."[78] From their first involvement in

---

74. W. WHITE, *supra* note 1, at 3; H. WEIHOFEN, MENTAL DISORDER AS A CRIMINAL DEFENSE 8 (1954); *see generally*, Comment, *The Use of Illegally Obtained Evidence to Rebut the Insanity Defense: A New Exception to the Exclusionary Rule?* 74 J. CRIM. L. & CRIMINOL. 391, 402 (1983).

75. Arens & Susman, *Judges, Jury Charges, and Insanity*, 12 How. L.J. 1, 5 (1966). Of twenty-seven defense lawyers interviewed, all but one expressed the view that D.C. District Court judges "viewed the insanity defense with suspicion and at times hostility." *Id.* at 6; *see also*, Keilitz, *Researching and Reforming the Insanity Defense*, 39 RUTGERS L. REV. 289, 315 (1987) ("the promise of treatment" may draw defense counsel to the GBMI plea in cases where the insanity defense is unlikely to succeed).

76. *See* Burt, *Disorder in the Court: The Death Penalty and the Constitution*, 85 MICH. L. REV. 1741, 1793 (1987), characterizing Justice Rehnquist's dissent from *certiorari* in Coleman v. Balkcom, 451 U.S. 949, 958 (1981) (criticizing extensive judicial inquiry into capital punishment as a "mockery of our criminal justice system"), as reflective of the fear that "shyster lawyers [have been] so successful in tricking gullible federal and state judges." On the relationship between death penalty views and insanity defense views, *see* Ellsworth et al., *The Death-Qualified Jury and the Defense of Insanity*, 8 LAW & HUM. BEHAV. 81, 90 (1984).

77. *See* Perlin, *Book Review of* ANN B. JOHNSON, OUT OF BEDLAM: THE TRUTH ABOUT DEINSTITUTIONALIZATION (1990), 8 N.Y.L. SCH. J. HUM. RTS. 557, 558-60 (1991) (refuting arguments blaming post-deinstitutionalization social problems on patients' rights' lawyers); *see generally*, Perlin, *Fatal Assumption: A Critical Evaluation of the Role of Counsel in Mental Disability Cases*, 16 LAW & HUM. BEHAV. 39 (1992).

78. Weitzel, *Public Skepticism: Forensic Psychiatry's Albatross*, 5 BULL. AM. ACAD. PSYCHIATRY & L. 456, 459 (1977).

On the public's "scapegoating" of forensic psychiatry following its "outrage" at the Hinckley verdict, *see* Sharf, *Send In the Clowns: The Image of Psychiatry During the Hinckley Trial*, 36 J. COMMUN. 80 (1986) (arguing that forensic psychiatrists portrayed an "alien rhetorical vision" during the trial). Religious racism and xenophobia have also played a part as well. *See* 1 N. WALKER, CRIME AND INSANITY IN ENGLAND 82 (1973), *quoting* this question by crown's counsel of a forensic witness from an 1801 trial: "Prosecutor: Have you not been here as a witness and a *Jew physician* to give an account of a prisoner as a madman,

court proceedings, "'alienists'...have been perceived as a threat to public security and a fancy means for 'getting criminals off.'"[79] Yet, as long as sixty-five years ago, William A. White responded to these charges: "[I]n my personal experience I have *never* known a criminal to escape conviction on the plea of 'insanity' where the evidence did not warrant such a verdict [except in jury nullification cases]."[80]

In short, the fear of feigned insanity and the distrust of expert witnesses' ability to identify malingering behavior continue to dominate insanity defense jurisprudence. The empirical data suggesting that this problem is minimal continues to be trivialized, and judges, legislators and jurors continue to adhere to this most powerful of all myths.

2. *"Mental Illness Is 'Different'"*

The public's suspicion of mental illness is significantly fueled by its perception of mental illness's "invisibility." Professors Diamond

---

to get him off upon the ground of insanity?" (emphasis in original)

Compare C. ROSENBERG, THE TRIAL OF THE ASSASSIN GUITEAU: PSYCHIATRY AND LAW IN THE GILDED AGE 166, 186 (1968) (assassination of President Garfield) (prosecutorial bias toward defendant's forensic expert as "foreigner" and as a "weak echo of a class of modern crazy German pagans, who are trying...to break down all the safeguards of our Christian civilization"); *see also*, Spiegel & Spiegel, *Prosecution Tactics Against an 1865 Paroxysmal Insanity Plea*, THE PROSECUTOR 12, 14 (Summer 1992), discussing prosecutor's "ruthless" tactics in attacking court's expert as a "propagator of the new and dangerous doctrine—this modern philosopher of the humbug of paroxysmal insanity").

79. Watson, *On the Preparation and Use of Psychiatric Expert Testimony: Some Suggestions in an Ongoing Controversy*, 6 BULL. AM. ACAD. PSYCHIATRY & L. 226, 226 (1978). *Cf.* Stone, *The Ethical Boundaries of Forensic Psychiatry: A View From the Ivory Tower*, 12 BULL. AM. ACAD. PSYCHIATRY & L. 209, 214 (1984):

Indeed it seems there is a very comfortable ideological fit between being a forensic psychiatrist and being against capital punishment; being therapeutic rather than punitive; being against the prosecution and what was seen as the harsh status quo in criminal law. This ideological fit has begun to come apart in recent history, but during the days when David Bazelon and American psychiatry had their love affair, the fit was real. Those were the halcyon days when the concept of treatment and the concept of social justice were virtually indistinguishable.

On the pro-prosecution bias of many forensic psychiatrists, *compare supra* chapter 4, note 349, and *supra* chapter 2, note 189.

80. W. WHITE, *supra* note 1, at 3. On nullification in insanity defense cases, *see generally infra* chapter 6 D 6 a (1).

and Louisell's observation still rings true: "The psychological sciences differ from the biological sciences in that the subject matter of the former is not visible."[81]

This invisibility leads jurors to reject insanity if the defendant does not demonstrate "highly persuasive evidence of severe psychotic disorientation,"[82] and to rely most strongly on physiological evidence of insanity. It is not coincidental or insignificant that the testimony in the *Hinckley* trial that appeared to be the most persuasive (e.g., CAT scans, brain x-rays)[83] (1) was *organic* at base, and (2) astonishingly mimicked the type of testimony frequently presented in nineteenth century cases as evidencing insanity.[84]

For the American psychiatric orientation toward the etiology of "insanity" and the nature and cause of mental disorder was, traditionally, nearly exclusively "an anatomico-pathological one," the product of "brain mythology" and what Zilboorg termed a "psychiatry without psychology."[85] Thus, in testifying at the trial of Guiteau (President Garfield's assassin), Dr. Walter Kempster, a prominent state psychiatric superintendent, stated, "In every case of insanity there is disease of the brain which may be discovered if the proper methods are made to discover it. I have never yet examined a case in which I did not discover marked disease of the brain."[86]

---

81. Diamond & Louisell, *The Psychiatrist as Expert Witness: Some Ruminations and Speculations*, 63 MICH. L. REV. 1335, 1340 (1965).

82. Arens, Granfield & Susman, *Jurors, Jury Charges, and Insanity*, 14 CATH. U. L. REV. 1, 9 (1965).

83. White, *The Mental Illness Defense in the Capital Penalty Hearing*, 5 BEHAV. SCI. & L. 411, 417 (1987) ("observers of the John Hinckley trial seem to agree that the abnormal CAT scans of Hinckley's brains were highly instrumental in his acquittal"); *see generally*, L. CAPLAN, THE INSANITY DEFENSE AND THE TRIAL OF JOHN W. HINCKLEY, JR. 79-85 (1984).

84. *See* Pantkratz, *Murder and Insanity: Nineteenth Century Perspectives from the "American Journal of Insanity,"* 28 INT'L J. OFFENDER THER. & COMPAR. CRIMINOL. 37, 38-39 (1984) (discussing cases in which pulse rates, "peculiar odors," head measurements, and ophthalmoscopic measurements of brain congestion were used as evidence of insanity); *Thoughts on the Causation of Insanity*, 28 AM. J. INSAN. 264 (1872) (same); *but see*, Eigen, *supra* note 1, at 426 (pre-nineteenth century cases noteworthy for lack of physicalist imagery).

85. Bunker, *American Psychiatric Literature During the Past One Hundred Years*, in ONE HUNDRED YEARS OF AMERICAN PSYCHIATRY 195, 207 (Amer. Psych. Ass'n eds. 1944).

86. Zilboorg, *Misconceptions of Legal Insanity*, 9 AM. J. ORTHOPSYCHIATRY 540, 557 (1939) (*quoting* from 38 AM. J. INSAN. 384 (1881-82)). Earlier, in an 1839 treatise, John Shapland Stock recommended inquiry into "any of those circumstances which are generally acknowledged to be the cause of [insanity] had

Critics of psychiatric testimony have traditionally attacked such forensic evidence for being less accurate than the allegedly-"objective" methods employed by medical specialists such as surgeons, who base their diagnoses upon "probable objective facts."[87] This rests on the faulty assumption that other medical specialties are more "objective" and are more likely to reflect unanimity in areas of diagnosis, prognosis and choice of treatment modality;[88] yet, the power of this myth remains constant.[89]

It should thus come as no surprise when a contemporaneous court deems critical—in determining that diminished capacity was not established—that the expert witnesses failed to testify "that appellant's dyssocial personality was caused by trauma *or other damage to the brain*,"[90] or where the lack of "organic manifestations" is seen as a significant factor in a decision affirming a jury's insanity defense rejection in a case of a schizophrenic defendant.[91]

The "differentness" between mental and physical illness also led to the wide suspicion that insanity could be more easily feigned,[92]

---

occurred—as injuries of the head, mercurial preparations largely or injudiciously administered, attacks of paralysis, suppression of customary evacuations, etc." J. STOCK, A PRACTICAL TREATISE ON THE LAW OF NON COMPOTES MENTIS, OR PERSONS OF UNSOUND MIND 70-71 (1839). On the Guiteau trial generally, *see* C. ROSENBERG, *supra* note 78. This continues today. *See* Booth, *supra* note 38 (insanity defense accepted where defendant suffered organic brain injury after having been struck by rock).

87. Note, *The Right to a Partisan Psychiatric Expert: Might Indigency Preclude Insanity?* 61 NYU L. REV. 703, 718 (11986).

88. White, *supra* note 83, at 417 (jurors probably unaware of interpretational problems involved in neurological and psychological testing and thus place inappropriately greater weight on brain scans and test scores).

89. *Cf.* Stone, *supra* note 79, at 211 ("the mind-brain problem...plagues all our endeavors to account for human actions").

90. Commonwealth v. Terry, 513 Pa. 381, 521 A. 2d 398, 406 n.17 (1987) (emphasis added). The court, in a "*cf*" reference, cited to the leading diminished capacity case of Commonwealth v. Walzack, 468 Pa. 210, 360 A. 2d 914 (1976), noting that, in that case, the defendant had undergone a lobotomy (i.e., a surgical procedure organically altering brain tissue). *See also e.g.*, Commonwealth v. Tempest, 496 Pa. 396, 437 A. 2d 952, 954 (1981) ("mental illness alone cannot absolve [a defendant] from criminal responsibility") (infanticide case).

91. United States v. Dube, 520 F. 2d 250, 252 (1st Cir. 1975). *See e.g.*, D. NELKIN & L. TANCREDI, DANGEROUS DIAGNOSTICS: THE SOCIAL POWER OF BIOLOGICAL INFORMATION 143 (1989) (courts increasingly look to biological explanations in insanity defense cases as part of a trend toward "medicalizing deviance").

92. *Cf.* Bonnie & Slobogin, *The Role of Mental Health Professionals in the Criminal Process: The Case for Informed Speculation*, 66 VA. L. REV. 427, 434 n. 14 (1980) (citation omitted):

and to the conclusion that defendants *could* control their own actions if they truly "wanted to."[93] These assumptions fly in the face of
the uncontroverted scientific evidence.[94] They are, however, regularly
reified both in case law and in other writings of members of the
judiciary.[95]

On the other hand, insanity acquittals are *more* likely when the
defendant's pathology is organically based,[96] and, thus, presumably
less easily feigned.[97] While some physical diseases are also difficult to

---

> Although the issue is not much discussed, the skeptics appear to be intuitively more
> confident about the precision of the inquiry when it concerns neuropsychological expla-
> nations for aberrant behavior rather than psychogenic ones. Thus, they might permit the
> defendant to offer evidence of epilepsy and trauma to negate the 'voluntariness' (conscious
> direction) of his criminal act. These investigations, however, usually are every bit as
> speculative as those concerning functional mental disorder.

93. *See e.g.*, State v. Ducksworth, 496 So. 2d 624, 635 (La. App. 1986) (refusal to
    dismiss prospective juror who felt defendant would be legally responsible for his
    actions if he "wanted to do them" was proper). *Cf.* State v. Kelly, 118 N.J. Super.
    38, 285 A. 2d 571 (App. Div. 1972) (not abuse of discretion to fail to grant
    defendant's request to conduct *voir dire* inquiry on potential juror's predisposi-
    tions as to potential insanity defense).
94. *See e.g.*, Lewis I, *supra* note 48, at 504 (40 percent of juvenile death row
    population multiply handicapped; nine of fourteen had major neurological
    impairment, seven evidenced "significant organic dysfunction" on neurological
    testing).
95. *In re* Melton, 597 A. 2d 892, 898 (D.C. 1991) (equating oncologist's ability to
    predict cancer patient's future progress to psychiatrist's ability to predict future
    dangerousness); K. Gould, I. Keilitz & J. Martin, "Criminal Defendants With
    Trial Disabilities: The Theory and Practice of Competency Assessment" (unpub-
    lished manuscript at 68) (trial judge responding to National Center for State
    Courts survey indicated that, in his mind, defendants who were found incompe-
    tent to stand trial could have understood and communicated with counsel and
    the court "if they [had] only wanted"); *see generally*, Perlin & Dorfman, *Sanism,
    Social Science, and the Development of Mental Disability Law Jurisprudence*,
    11 BEHAV. SCI. & L. 47 (1993); Perlin, *Pretexts and Mental Disability Law: The
    Case of Competency*, 47 U. MIAMI L. REV. (1993) (in press).
96. Ellsworth et al., *supra* note 76; *see also*, White, *supra* note 83, at 417. *Cf.* Biddy
    v. State, 138 Ga. App. 4, 225 S.E. 2d 448 (1976) (not failure to charge
    "delusional insanity" in case involving defendant whose "behavioral aberrations
    [were] connected with traumatic brain damage").
97. The development of the law of criminal responsibility in cases involving *physi-
    ological* disabilities underscores the gap between (verifiable) organic illness and
    (purportedly feignable) mental illness. *See generally*, S. HALLECK, PSYCHIATRY
    AND THE DILEMMAS OF CRIME: A STUDY OF CAUSES, PUNISHMENT, AND
    TREATMENT 159-66 (1967); Fox, *Physical Disorder, Consciousness, and Crimi-
    nal Liability*, 63 COLUM. L. REV. 645 (1963). For case-by-case consideration of
    the issues involved, *see e.g.*, R. v. Charlson, 1 A.E. Rep. 859 (1955) (automatism

prove, courts rarely display the sort of hostility to testimony in such cases that is frequently exhibited in the "usual" insanity defense trial; "when it comes to the insanity defense, however, the public appears to demand near perfection."[98] As Professor Moran has observed:

> [W]hen two ballistics experts disagree as to whether the defendant's pistol fired the fatal bullets. the science of ballistics is not discredited. Again, the public understands the limits of scientific knowledge, that much of what is known in science is a matter of interpretation....Yet, when two psychiatrists disagree as to whether a defendant's behavior was the product of a mental disease, or whether the defendant knew the difference between right and wrong, the profession of psychiatry is often discredited.[99]

The Josee McNally case serves to illustrate the operative bias.[100] Even though her disorder was neurological (epilepsy), the testimony she offered was by a psychologist who, in the words of the prosecutor, "lacked medical credentials." Since the defendant "look[ed] and act[ed] normal," the jury rejected her insanity plea.[101]

---

arising from case involving cerebral tumor); R. v. Sibbles, 1959 CRIM. L. REV. 660 (automatism arising from case involving high blood pressure); R. v. Kemp, 1 Q.B. 399 (1957) (arteriosclerosis) (distinguishing Charlson); State v. Parker, 416 So. 2d 545 (La. 1982); People v, Morton, 100 A.D. 2d 637, 473 N.Y.S. 2d 66 (1984) (hypoglycemia); State v. Werlein, 136 Wis. 2d 445, 401 N.W. 2d 848 (Ct. App. 1987) (organic brain dysfunction); Gov't of Virgin Islands v. Smith, 278 F. 2d 169 (3d Cir. 1960); Clark v. State, 436 N.E. 2d 779 (Ind. 1982) (epilepsy).

98. Moran, *Preface*, 477 ANNALS 9 (1985).

99. *Id.* at 10. *Compare* R. Rogers & C. Ewing, "'Proscribing Ultimate Opinions:' The Quick and Cosmetic Fix," (paper presented at the American Psychological Association annual meeting, August 1988), manuscript at 9 (jurors appear "mildly interested" in mental health expert testimony, but are not "thunderstruck" by it), and Rogers, Bagby & Chow, *Psychiatrists and the Parameters of Expert Testimony*, 15 INT'L J. L. & PSYCHIATRY 387, 394 (1992) (jurors "highly ambivalent" about value of psychiatric testimony in insanity trials), to Gramble, *The Admissibility of Laboratory Reports in Criminal Trials: The Reliability of Scientific Proof*, 49 OHIO ST. L.J. 671, 672 (1988) (25 percent of jurors surveyed indicated that, but for "hard" scientific evidence presented by prosecutor, "they would have changed their verdict—from guilty to not guilty"), *quoting* Peterson et al., *The Uses and Effects of Forensic Science in the Adjudication of Felony Cases*, 32 J. FORENS. SCI. 1730, 1748 (1987).

100. *See supra* chapter 5 B.

101. Abrams, *supra* note 26, at 10.

3. "The Defendant Doesn't 'Look Crazy' "

The public has also demanded that mentally ill defendants comport with its *visual* images of "craziness."[102] The persistence of this phenomenon was noted nearly fifty years ago by Thurman Arnold:

> For the basic premises upon which the jury operates are false in the light of the modern science of psychology. But erroneous as these legally supported assumptions may be, they are defensible as an institutional matter if they comport with the "instinctive sense of justice of the ordinary man." The ordinary juror, when he considers the mechanism of human behavior, sees a "little picture" of a "separate little man in the top of one's head called reason whose function it is to guide another unruly little man called instinct, emotion, or impulse in the way he should go."[103]

The lay public *cannot*, by using its intuitive "common sense" (based on a combination of media images, religious iconography and unconscious rationalizations),[104] effectively determine who is or is not criminally responsible by whether or not the individual "looks crazy."[105] Thus, cases hinge on witnesses' failure to describe defendants as "raving maniacs,"[106] on lay testimony that "there was nothing unusual about defendant's appearance" in the days before the murder, or on police testimony that the same defendant "was neatly dressed and...seemed aware and mentally alert",[107] or on jail or sheriff personnel's testimony that the defendant exhibited no "un-

---

102. *See generally*, S. GILMAN, SEEING THE INSANE (1982) for a full historical overview. On the role of this demand in the development of mental disability law in general, *see* Perlin, *On "Sanism,"* 46 SMU L. REV. 373 (1992).

103. Hill, *The Psychological Realism of Thurman Arnold*, 22 U. CHI. L. REV. 377, 382-83 (1955), discussing Arnold's opinion in Holloway v. United States, 148 F. 2d 665 (D.C. Cir. 1945).

104. *See e.g.*, Baur, *Legal Responsibility and Mental Illness*, 57 Nw. U. L. REV. 12 (1962) (discussing religious, moral and cultural roots of responsibility concepts). Again, this is hardly a problem of recent vintage. *See* Eigen, *supra* note 1, at 429, discussing J. HASLAM, supra note 46, at 16 (discounting "popular" images of bizarre behavior derived from literary images). On the role of "ordinary common sense," *see generally infra* chapter 6 D. On its role in mental disability law in general, *see* Perlin, *supra* note 63.

105. State Farm Fire & Cas. Co., v. Wicka, 474 N.W. 2d 324, 327 (Minn. 1991); *see e.g.*, S. GLUECK, MENTAL DISORDER AND THE CRIMINAL LAW 31 (1925), *quoting* Lind, *Cross-Examination of the Alienist*, 13 J. CRIM. L., CRIMINOL. & POL. SCI. 228, 229, (1922) (setting out "typical" juror response in cases of conflicting expert testimony: "the man doesn't look very crazy to us, anyhow.")

106. State v. Brantley, 514 So. 2d 747, 751 (La. App. 1987) (defendant found to be "outgoing," "very friendly," and a "nicely dressed 'person of means'").

107. People v. Tylkowski, 171 Ill. App. 3d 93, 524 N.E. 2d 1112, 1117 (1988).

usual" behavior.[108] Revealingly, in describing the procedures that must be followed in pretrial psychiatric evaluations, a New York trial court judge set up this juxtaposition:

> If the physician examines the defendant within hours or days of the event, he or she may observe that the defendant was disoriented and agitated or, at the other extreme, composed or feigning symptoms.[109]

Jury studies have shown "pervasive judicial hostility" toward the insanity defense where it was not founded on "flagrant psychotic symptomatology."[110] To the lay person (the juror *or* the judge), the temporarily delirious patient "leaping over chairs and taking the broom-stick to hallucinatory monsters" still *looks* more genuinely psychotic than "a deeply disordered but calm and brittle schizophrenic."[111]

Jurors "look for bizarre acts, sudden episodes, a defendant's genuine obliviousness to his own best concerns, and a pervasive inability to lead an ordinary life."[112] A paper prepared by a former Texas Attorney General for the National District Attorneys Association notes anecdotally, "Our verdicts in Dallas indicate that if a man can earn a living, support himself and perhaps family, up to time of crime *without drawing attention to self by crazy acts*, they'll find him

---

108. Fulgham v. Ford, 850 F. 2d 1529, 1532 (11th Cir. 1988).
109. People v. McNamee, 145 Misc. 2d 187, 547 N.Y.S. 2d 519, 524 (Sup. Ct. 1989).
110. Arens & Susman, *supra* note 75, at 2, discussing results reported in Arens, Granfield & Susman, *supra* note 82; see *id.* at 9 (most jurors perceive insanity defense as calling for nothing short of "highly persuasive evidence of severe psychotic disorientation"); Gabriel, *The Psychiatrist Who Pleaded Insanity*, N.Y. Times (May 12, 1991), Mag. §, at 36 (*quoting* forensic psychologist Leonard Haber, "Jurors tend to dismiss the insanity defense. It has to be so apparent that the average person almost doesn't need an expert.") (full text available on NEXIS).
111. Bromberg & Cleckley, *The Medico-Legal Dilemma: A Suggested Solution*, 42 J. CRIM. L., CRIMINOL., & POL. SCI. 729, 738 (1952). *Cf.* State v. Van Horn, 528 So. 2d 529, 530 (Fla. Dist. Ct. App. 1988) (state rebuttal lay witnesses provided sufficient "probative perceptions of normalcy"). *See* Abrams, *supra* note 26, at 10 (jurors would have accepted defendant's insanity defense if she had "fallen to the ground in convulsions") (Josee McNally case).
    The same imagery continues today. In accepting New York State Chief Judge Sol Wachtler's guilty plea in a bizarre sexual extortion case, the prosecuting attorney focused on the defendant's apparent "normalcy." Said U.S. Attorney Michael Chertoff in describing Wachtler: "This was not a man who was staying home in a bathrobe or going around like a screaming banshee." Kleinfield, *Admitting Guilt, Wachtler Offers Account of Plot*, N.Y. Times. April 1, 1993, at A1 (full text available on NEXIS).
112. T. MAEDER, CRIME AND MADNESS 109 (1985).

sane."[113] In short, for the insanity defense to be successful, the defendant must still appear "mad to the man on the street."[114]

There may be one exception to this rule. If a defendant's acts are *so* heinous and bestial, the jury may still reject the insanity defense.[115] This exception may simply be another example of the "tensile strength" doctrine: certain cases are so emotionally loaded that the defense might not "survive" a verdict of non-responsibility.[116]

---

113. W. Alexander, "How To Meet the Insanity Defense," (undated manuscript), at 4. *See also*, A. GOLDSTEIN, *supra* note 6, at 114:

> The jury will have heard counsel for each side promise to prove conflicting states of fact. Witnesses will have been presented in support of each version: on one side, policemen will have told how 'normal' the defendant 'looked' to them, employers will have described satisfactory work records, acquaintances will have spoken of adequate performance in day-to-day living; on the other, members of the defendant's family will have told of odd behavior previously kept secret, of emotional problems in school and psychiatric clinics. Psychiatrists will probably have testified to entirely different inferences from the examination of the defendant and from his prior history. And before their own eyes, the jurors will have seen in the defendant an apparently rational man who asserts he was insane at some prior time.

114. A. STONE, MENTAL HEALTH AND LAW: A SYSTEM IN TRANSITION 219 (1976). To some extent, it may be necessary for a defendant to look like this to convince a forensic psychiatrist as well. *See* White, *supra* note 83, at 416-17, discussing Daniel et al., *Factors Correlated With Psychiatric Recommendations of Incompetency and Insanity*, 12 J. PSYCHIATRY & L. 527 (1984) (psychiatrists more likely to recommend diminished capacity when defendant exhibits "bizarre behavior"). *Cf.* People v. Jackson, 152 Cal. App. 3d 961, 199 Cal. Rptr. 848, 850 (1984) (expert testified that defendant "can look and function in a controlled manner to the point where most other people wouldn't take notice").

115. The Jeffrey Dahmer case is the most recent vivid example. *See e.g.*, Worthington, *When Fantasy Becomes Reality: Dahmer's Illusions Turned Into the Most Deadly of Acts*, Chi. Trib. (Feb. 26, 1992), at C 12 ("[I]nsanity defenses do not work for serial killers") (full text available on NEXIS). *So Guilty They're Innocent: The Case of Serial Killer Jeffrey Dahmer*, 44 NAT'L REV. (Mar. 2, 1992), at 17 (editorial) (*So Guilty*), *quoting* Charles Krauthammer:

> It is absurd to permit the heinousness of a crime to become self-acquitting. That sets up a perverse standard: the more terrible the crime, the crazier, therefore the less culpable the criminal. The man who commits incomprehensible torture is acquitted. the father who steals bred to feed his children is convicted.

> *Compare e.g.*, People v. Wilbur, 226 Ill. App, 3d 733, 589 N.E. 2d 1143, 1147 (1992) (Stouder, J., dissenting), discussed *supra* chapter 4, note 95.

116. *See* Glynn, *If Dahmer's Not Crazy, Who Is?* Nat'l L.J. (Mar. 9, 1992), at 13. On "tensile strength," *see generally infra* chapter 8 A.

Insanity claims are also generally rejected where jurors find any significant measure of "planfulness" in the defendants' pre-crime actions:[117]

> The closer a defendant is to normality, the more public opinion is outraged by insanity acquittals. People are unwilling to excuse conduct that appears to have a rational criminal motive. Evidence of the ability to plan and premeditate a crime flies in the face of the public's perception of mental disease.[118]

Chief Justice Rehnquist's vision duplicates popular sentiment, a sentiment also exhibited in the Josee McNally case.[119] He concurred in *Estelle v. Smith*,[120] urging a limited reading of the Court's holding.[121] Using reasoning "reveal[ing] a vision of mental disability that virtually mirrors public perceptions,"[122] Justice Rehnquist stressed the *Estelle* defendant's failure to "invoke...[his] rights when confronted with [the state's expert's questions];"[123] in short, "since [the defendant] wasn't 'really crazy,' his failure to complain would be seen

---

117. Roberts, Golding & Fincham, *supra* note 1, at 209-10. *See also, So Guilty, supra* note 115, at 17 ("Dahmer had enough sense to hide his deeds; that should be evidence enough of sanity for the law").

118. Resnick, *supra* note 15, at 208. *See also*, Golding & Roesch, *The Assessment of Criminal Responsibility: A Historical Approach to a Current Controversy*, in HANDBOOK OF FORENSIC PSYCHOLOGY 395, 400 (Weiner & Hess eds. 1987) (planfulness will rule out exculpation in "strict interpretation" jurisdictions).

M'Naghten reflects these misperceptions: "[The M'Naghten] rules, to put it as simply as possible, labor under the illusion that a 'criminotic'...is 'crazy' in the *popular* sense of that word. The popular conception of mental disease envisages a raving maniac devoid of all reason. The *scientific* conception of psychosis is quite different; a person may appear to the layman quite rational and still harbor psychotic delusions which prompt his actions. Criminosis is not characterized by the ability or inability to distinguish between 'right and wrong,' but by a tendency to commit acts, punishable by the specific society, under the influence of an *unconscious defense mechanism*." E. BERGLER & A. MEERLOO, *supra* note 13, at 118 (emphasis added).

119. *See e.g.*, Abrams, *supra* note 26, at 10 (since jurors were unfamiliar with type of epilepsy, "they could not understand how somebody could be in this state while looking and acting normal;" defendant "dressed well, was obviously intelligent, and answered questions very precisely[; s]he seemed all there").

120. 451 U.S. 454 (1982), holding that *Miranda* applies to statements given to psychiatric expert witnesses called by the state to testify either as to a defendant's sanity or the appropriate penalty to be imposed following conviction. *See generally*, Perlin, *supra* note 34, at 23-28.

121. *See Estelle*, 451 U.S. at 474-76 (Rehnquist, J., concurring).

122. Perlin, *supra* note 34, at 82.

123. *Estelle*, 451 U.S. at 475 (Rehnquist, J., concurring).

as probative."[124] In *Wainwright v. Greenfield*,[125] holding that defendant's request for counsel following the administration of *Miranda* warnings was not probative of sanity, he again concurred:

> [The request for counsel] is a perfectly straightforward statement tending to show that an individual is able to understand his rights and is not *incoherent or obviously confused or unbalanced.*[126]

Again, Rehnquist focuses strictly on the defendant's external appearance.[127] Like the defendant described by Drs. Bromberg and Cleckley who did not "leap over chairs,"[128] the defendant in *Greenfield* did not, by lay concepts, "look" "clearly and totally" crazy.[129]

Rehnquist's opinions reveal a fixed, unidimensional vision of the sort of externalities that must be present if mental disability is to be an exculpatory defense.[130] His views incorporate a kind of "ordinary

---

124. Perlin, *supra* note 34, at 82.

125. 474 U.S. 284 (1986); *see generally*, Perlin, *supra* note 34, at 29-33.

126. *Greenfield*, 474 U.S. at 297 (Rehnquist, J., concurring) (emphasis added). A better understanding of mental illness was demonstrated nearly two centuries ago by Thomas Erskine, counsel for defendant in James Hadfield's treason trial:

> Delusions, Erskine continued, unaccompanied by 'frenzy or raving madness [were] the true character of insanity.' A person may reason with great skill and subtlety, but if the 'premises from which they reason' are uniformly false, and cannot be shaken even with the clearest evidence, then it can be said that he is suffering from the disease of insanity....

Moran, *The Origin of Insanity as a Special Verdict: The Trial For Treason of James Hadfield*, 19 LAW & SOC'Y REV. 487, 503 (1985) (citations omitted).

127. The judicial roots of the Chief Justice's vision may partially be found in the writings of former Chief Justice Burger when he was a District of Columbia Court of Appeals judge. These writings reflect Burger's sense of "normalcy:"

> [The presumption of sanity] is grounded on the premise that the generality of mankind is made up of persons within the range of 'normal,' rational human beings and can be said to be accountable or responsible for their conduct; this premise is rooted in centuries of experience, [and] has not been undermined by contemporary medical knowledge.

Keyts v. United States, 346 F. 2d 824, 826 (D.C. Cir. 1965), *cert. den.*, 382 U.S. 869 (1968).

128. Bromberg & Cleckley, *supra* note 110, at 738.

129. *See* Morse, *Crazy Behavior, Morals, and Science: An Analysis of Mental Health Law*, 51 S. CAL. L. REV. 527, 564 (1978). *See also*, Mestrovic, *Need for Treatment and New York's Revised Commitment Law: An Empirical Assessment*, 6 INT'L J. L. & PSYCHIATRY 75, 78 (1983) (in assessing admission to facility, public hospital staff "essentially concerned with [the] idea of 'normal craziness' that enables one to function versus 'more than normal craziness'").

130. For the historical antecedents of this position, *see* Quen, *Anglo-American Criminal Insanity: A Historical Perspective*, 2 BULL. AM. ACAD. PSYCHIATRY &

common sense-icality" that rejects the notion that a defendant who does not conform to the visual images of a "madman" or who is not a "raving maniac or complete imbecile"[131] can avail himself of the insanity defense.[132]

Other judges reflect the same vision. Thus, in a "textbook classic" case, a Tennessee intermediate appellate court affirmed a conviction where a jury rejected defendant's insanity defense in light of *police* testimony that, upon apprehension, the defendant "was sitting with his head down and looked okay," despite the presentation of "overwhelming, even staggering evidence" of an overtly-psychotic, paranoid schizophrenic, actively-hallucinating defendant.[133] Similarly, the Indiana Supreme Court affirmed a conviction in another rejected-insanity defense case where victim's girlfriend testified that, while defendant was first acting "nervous" with a " 'weird' facial expression," she subsequently found his speech and actions "calmer" and testified he did not act "crazy."[134]

In a recent study, Professors Hans and Slater concluded that so many individuals see the insanity defense as a "loophole" because of their insistence "on a near total lack of comprehension" as an insanity defense standard, a test not unlike the "wild beast" inquiry of the early eighteenth century.[135] The Colorado Supreme Court thus focused on the lack of such evidence in an opinion rejecting defendant's argument that his mental state should have served to reduce the degree of homicide:

L. 115, 120 (1974).

131. Jones v. State, 289 So. 2d 725, 729 (Fla. 1974).

132. *See* Quen, *supra* note 130, *quoting* I. RAY, A TREATISE ON THE MEDICAL JURISPRUDENCE OF INSANITY 46-47 (3d ed. 1953) ("[I]f in the disturbance of your moral and intellectual perceptions you take *a* step for which a sane man would have been punished, insanity will be no bar to your punishment") (emphasis added).

133. State v. Clayton, 656 S.W. 2d 344, 348-50 (Tenn. 1983) (reversing conviction).

134. Gardner v. State, 514 N.E. 2d 1259, 1260 (Ind. 1987); *see also*, State v. Alley, 776 S.W. 2d 506, 513 (Tenn. 1989) (not error to allow testimony by "psychiatric technician" [presumably a security officer] that "defendant was malingering and...did not act like persons who were really insane").

135. Hans & Slater, *supra* note 1, at 111. Of 434 Delaware residents surveyed, only *one* "gave a reasonably good approximation" of the definition of legal insanity then operative in that jurisdiction. *Id.* at 105-6; *see also*, Roberts, Golding & Fincham, *supra* note 1, at 226; Daniel et al., *supra* note 113, at 527 (bizarre behavior at time of offense among the most influential factors in forensic finding of nonresponsibility).

[W]e find that here there was no evidence of the defendant suddenly going berserk...no evidence of mental weakness...no[r] evidence of *burst of passion with paleness, wild eyes and trembling....*[136]

The court refused to reverse as erroneous a jury charge cautioning jurors "not to confuse...mental disease [amounting to insanity] with moral obliquity, mental depravity, or...kindred evil conditions."[137]

Society is also confident that it is *accurate* in its assessment of serious mental illness.[138] This failure to acknowledge "shades of gray" reinforces more subtly our fixed image of "crazy behavior," especially in assessments of criminal responsibility.

4. Mental Illness as an (Improperly) Exculpatory Excuse.

Finally, the insanity defense myths are premised on a persistent meta-myth that has lost little of its power over the centuries: that mental illness, simply, is not an "appropriate" excuse, and that, but for the inappropriate "social engineering" engaged in by the mental health professionals, society would be able to appropriately punish those who have engaged in criminal acts.[139]

---

136. Battalino v. People, 118 Colo. 587, 199 P. 2d 897, 901 (1948) (emphasis added).
137. *Id.* at 902.
138. Swartz, *Mental Disease: The Groundwork for Legal Analysis and Legislative Action,* 111 U. PA. L. REV. 389, 413 (1963), *quoting* Redlich in Milbank Memorial Fund, *Interrelations Between the Social Environment and Psychiatric Disorders* 120-21 (1953):

> We know what the seriously ill person in a given culture is. That we do know. In this respect we agree, incidentally, with the policeman, with the clerk in the drug store. Our crude diagnostic criteria are reasonably similar...

139. On the question of defendants who "cause" their own insanity either through substance abuse or failure to comply with prescribed medications, *see e.g.,* People v. Smith, 124 Ill. App. 3d 805, 465 N.E. 2d 101, 103 (1984); Slodov, *Criminal Responsibility and the Noncompliant Psychiatric Offender: Risking Madness,* 40 CASE W. RES. L. REV. 271 (1989); Sherlock, *Compliance and Responsibility: New Issues for the Insanity Defense,* 12 J. PSYCHIATRY & L. 483 (1984); Bunt, *New Perspectives in the Legal Psychiatry of Cocaine-Related Crimes,* 37 J. FORENS. SCI. 894 (1992); L. TIFFANY & M. TIFFANY, THE LEGAL DEFENSE OF PATHOLOGICAL INTOXICATION, WITH RELATED ISSUES OF TEMPORARY AND SELF-INFLICTED INSANITY (1991); Tiffany, *The Drunk, The Insane, and the Criminal Courts: Deciding What To Make of Self-Induced Insanity,* 69 WASH. U. L.Q. 221 (1991); Bidwell & Katz, *Injecting New Life Into an Old Defense: Anabolic Steroid- Induced Psychosis as a Paradigm of Involuntary Intoxication,* 7 U. MIAMI ENT. & SPORTS L. REV. 1 (1989); *see generally,* Robinson, *Causing the Conditions of One's Own Defense: A Study in the Limits of Theory in*

The "indiscriminate and often irresponsible glorification of psychiatry" of the past half century has frequently encouraged the public to see psychiatry as the "magic" solution to all of society's ills.[140] The sentiment of psychiatrists such as Dr. Manfred Guttmacher that the insanity defense should be retained because "it gives the criminal law a heart"[141] was *precisely* the type of expression which led a public that dislikes the insanity defense for *both* utilitarian and retributive reasons to express its revulsion at exculpatory psychological defenses.[142] In short, the public could *not* be satisfied with the insanity defense if it were to be left "with the inner sense that justice [had not] been done."[143]

The public's disproportionate and institutional hostility to mental illness and the mentally disabled criminal offender arises from a complex combination of sources: its historic negative view of psychiatry (and, specifically, forensic psychiatry),[144] its negative stereo-

---

Criminal Law Doctrine, 71 VA. L. REV. 1 (1985). On the therapeutic jurisprudential implications (*see generally infra* chapter 9 B) of mandating insanity acquittees to comply with certain treatment regimens, *see* Wexler, *Health Care Compliance Principles and the Insanity Acquittee Conditional Release Process*, 27 CRIM. L. BULL. 18 (1991).

140. Schmideberg, *The Promise of Psychiatry: Hopes and Disillusionment*, 57 NW. U. L. REV. 19, 20 (1962); *see e.g.*, Weitzel, *Public Skepticism: Forensic Psychiatry's Albatross*, 5 BULL. AM. ACAD. PSYCHIATRY & L. 456, 462 (1977) ("The skepticism we meet in the public forum seems to come from the *mystification* of the knowledge we possess about mental illness and the *all-inclusiveness* some of us claim as our own medical turf") (emphasis added).

141. M. GUTTMACHER, THE ROLE OF PSYCHIATRY IN LAW 95 (1968); *see also* S. HALLECK, *supra* note 3, at 222 ("The most important reason for psychiatric participation in the criminal trial is a humanitarian zeal to temper the harshness of punishment."). The reality is, of course, quite different. *See supra* chapter 2, note 189.

142. Hans, *supra* note 1, at 407.

143. Davidson, *Criminal Responsibility: The Quest for a Formula*, in PSYCHIATRY AND THE LAW, *supra* note 24, at 61, 67.

144. These comments reflect over a century of informed wisdom. In an 1885 article in the *Journal of Insanity*, a psychiatrist asserted:

Experts are almost as much a necessity in a court of justice as the judge himself, yet our customs are stripping their testimony of almost all its value. To laugh at them, to worry out and get ahead of them in the battle of wits—which is dignified by courts as a cross-examination—is much of the business of the modern attorney.

Wood, *The Law of Insanity*, 41 AM. J. INSANITY 476 (1885).

For more contemporaneous readings, *see e.g.*, McGuire & Borowy, *Attitudes Toward Mental Health Professionals*, 10 PROF. PSYCHOLOGY 74 (1979); *see generally*, Slater & Hans, *supra* note 1; Hans & Slater, *supra* note 1; Rogers,

types of the mentally ill,[145] its tendency to link mental illness and criminality,[146] the vagueness of mental health concepts and their apparent imprecise relationship to criminal behavior,[147] and the awareness that psychiatrists frequently are erroneous in their prediction of future dangerous behavior.[148]

Case law developments track these myths. Decisions such as *State v. Sikora*, holding that criminal responsibility must be judged at the "level of the conscious,"[149] were premised on the notion that the psychodynamic theory of determinism was "too speculative"[150] a basis upon which to bottom a criminal law system.[151] This position—

Bagby & Chow, *supra* note 99.

145. *See generally,* Perlin, *supra* note 102; Perlin & Dorfman, *supra* note 95; *see also,* Sarbin & Mancusco, *Failure of a Moral Enterprise: Attitudes of the Public Toward Mental Illness,* 35 J. CONSULT. & CLIN. PSYCHOLOGY 159 (1970); Roberts, Golding & Fincham, *supra* note 1, at 211; Slater & Hans, *supra* note 1.

146. *See e.g.,* Steadman & Cocozza, *Selective Reporting and the Public's Misconception of the Criminally Insane,* 41 PUB. OPIN. Q. 523, 525-29 (1977-78); Slater & Hans, *supra* note 1, at 675. These feelings are often abetted by frequent media linkages between crime and mental illness. *See* Hans & Slater, *supra* note 1, at 112 (speculating that television's distortion of the link between crime and mental illness "may affect views of the insanity defense and help shape people's definitions"); *see generally,* Haney & Manzolati, *Television Criminology: Network Illusions of Criminal Justice Realities,* in READINGS ABOUT THE SOCIAL ANIMAL 125 (E. Aronson ed., 3d ed. 1981); Slater & Elliott, *Television's Influence on Social Reality,* 68 Q.J. SPEECH. 69 (1982).

147. MacBain, *The Insanity Defense: Conceptual Confusion and the Erosion of Fairness,* 67 MARQ. L. REV. 1, 6 (1983).

148. *See generally,* Poythress & Stock, *Competency to Stand Trial: A Historical Review and Some New Data,* 8 J. PSYCHIATRY & L. 131 (1980); *see also,* Menzies, Webster & Sepejak, *The Dimensions of Dangerousness: Evaluating the Accuracy of Psychometric Predictions of Violence Among Forensic Patients,* 9 LAW & HUM. BEHAV. 49, 67 (1985) ("Violence *does* play a substantial role in shaping public attitudes and legal policy, the fear of violence has expanded in North American society, and the predictive components of the decisionmaking are not easily exorcised from the medicolegal system...") (emphasis in original; citations omitted).

149. 44 N.J. 453, 210 A. 2d 193, 202 (1965).

150. *See* Lewin, *Psychiatric Evidence in Criminal Cases for Purposes Other Than the Defense of Insanity,* 26 SYR. L. REV. 1051, 1065 n. 60 (1975).

151. *See also,* State v. Lucas, 30 N.J. 37, 152 A. 2d 50, 74 (1959) (Weintraub, C.J., concurring).

Chief Justice Weintraub concurred in *Sikora* as well:

Finally, we could amend our concept of criminal responsibility by eliminating the requirement of an evil-meaning mind, That is the true thrust of this psychiatric view of human behavior,...To grant a role in our existing structure to the theme that the conscious is just the innocent puppet of a nonculpable unconscious is to make a mishmash of the

reflecting a "fear of engag[ing] in a philosophical discussion of determinism and free will when the product could be the acquittal of one
who in his conscious state was aware of the consequences and illegal-
ity of his conduct"[152] — has remained the dominant one in American
jurisprudence.[153]

More recently, in *Colorado v. Connelly*, the Supreme Court held
that serious mental disability was not a factor to consider in determining the validity of a *Miranda* waiver absent police misconduct.[154]
Chief Justice Rehnquist stated unequivocally:

> *Miranda* protects defendants against government coercion leading
> them to surrender rights protected by the Fifth Amendment; it goes no
> further than that. Respondent's perception of coercion flowing from the
> "voice of God," however important or significant such a perception may
> be in other disciplines, is a matter to which the United States Constitution
> does not speak.[155]

Connelly is a clear descendant of *Sikora* and the *Lucas* concurrence, reflecting a dogged adherence to a vision of criminal law and
procedure that does its decision making on a conscious level.[156]
While this may be because, as Professor Lewin suggested, "the state
of science has not advanced to the stage where general agreement has
been reached on the nature of the unconscious, the role it plays on

---

criminal law,...It would be absurd to decide criminal blameworthiness upon a psychiatric
thesis which can find no basis for personal blame. So long as we adhere to criminal
blameworthiness, *mens rea* must be sought and decided at the level of conscious behavior.

Sikora, 210 A. 2d at 204, 206-7 (Weintraub, C.J., concurring).

152. Lewin, *supra* note 150, at 1096.

153. *See also*, M. MOORE, LAW AND PSYCHIATRY: RETHINKING THE RELATIONSHIP
141-43 (1984)(discussing how the "discovery of the unconscious" appears to
have inherently "apparently contradictory implications" for the law); Sendor,
*Crime as Communication: An Interpretative Theory of the Insanity Defense and
the Mental Elements of Crime*, 74 GEO. L.J. 1371, 1406 n. 142 (1986).

154. 479 U.S. 157, 163-69 (1987).

155. *Id.* at 170-71. *See also, id.* at 169 (rejecting state court analysis for "importing
into this area of constitutional law notions of 'free will' that have no place
there"). On the psychiatric implications of *false* confessions, *see* Gudjonsson &
MacKeith, *Retracted Confessions: Legal, Psychological and Psychiatric Aspects*,
28 MED. SCI. & L. 187 (1988).

156. *See generally*, Perlin, *Criminal Confessions and the Mentally Disabled*: Colorado
v. Connelly *and the Future of Free Will*, in CRIMINAL COURT CONSULTATION
157 (R. Rosner & R. Harmon eds. 1989); Benner, *supra* note 53; Dix, *Federal
Constitutional Confession Law: The 1986 and 1987 Supreme Court Terms*, 67
TEX. L. REV. 234, 244 (1988) (*Connelly* "undoubtedly" the court's most
significant confessions case in previous two terms).

the conscious and the means by which to test and identify it,"[157] this may simply be a sophisticated explanation for another reality: psychiatry's reliance on schemes of unconscious (unseeable, unverifiable) motivations are "soft" and that undue reliance on them will subvert the crime control component of the criminal justice system.[158]

D. Conclusion

Our insanity defense jurisprudence remains the prisoner of medievalist concepts of sin and punishment, and of rigid constructs of "good and evil" and "right and wrong." Because these concepts hold us so firmly in their grasp, we reject evidence that counsels reconsideration. We thoughtlessly repeat disproved empirical myths, and adhere to them, in spite of ample empirical and scientific refutation.

We adhere to these myths because they enable us to retain our allegiance to an underlying social vision that rejects psychodynamic thinking and the importance of psychodynamic motivation on human behavior. Cases such as John Hinckley's create "heightened arousal," causing us to retreat more deeply into our eighteenth century visions of crime and mental illness. Because of the "hydraulic pressure" of these visions, our jurisprudence does not have the "tensile strength" necessary to withstand the type of vivid imagery raised by such cases.[159]

When the underlying myths are "unpacked," they reveal yet another set of fundamentalist meta-myths that serve as the true structural basis for the jurisprudence that has developed. These myths remain powerful whether the decision maker is a state legislature, Chief Justice Rehnquist, or a Long Island juror.[160] By adhering to these meta-myths, jurors can invoke a type of "conventional community morality," punishing the defendant whose "crazy" behavior is truly threatening to our "core beliefs."[161]

We must now ask the next logical question: *why* do we continue to adhere to these myths? To answer this, I will turn to the field of cognitive psychology in a search for answers.

---

157. Lewin, *supra* note 150, at 1096.
158. *See generally*, H. PACKER, THE LIMITS OF THE CRIMINAL SANCTION 131-35 (1968).
159. *See generally infra* chapter 8 A.
160. *See* Abrams, *supra* note 26.
161. Ingber, *supra* note 21, at 827.

6

Piercing the Veil of Consciousness

A. Introduction

It is not enough to merely assert that insanity defense mythology is persistent and impervious to scientific developments, philosophical reasoning and empirical discoveries. We must inquire into the unique roots of the implacability of public opinion in this area of the law. Many of these myths have their roots in theology, in medieval superstition, in concepts of "masks" and "magic."[1] It is necessary to explore beyond these fairly rudimentary drives and motivations if we are to ferret out the true meaning of why our insanity defense jurisprudence has developed the way it has.

Our further attention must be focused on at least four sets of additional phenomena: the singular way in which "wrong verdicts" bring immediate calls for the abolition of the insanity defense (in a way that "wrong" verdicts based on self-defense, alibi, or mistake do not inspire public outcries for the abolition of those defenses); the use of heuristic thinking and behavior theory as an explanation for such decision making, the role of alleged "ordinary common sense" (OCS) in decision making, and the reasons *why* heuristics and OCS dominate insanity defense decision making. In this chapter, I will examine each of these phenomena in turn.

---

1.   *See supra* chapter 4 B 4.

B. The Significance of "Wrong" Verdicts

Writing over eighty years ago in a railroad case, Justice Holmes wrote that "great cases like hard cases make bad law" because of "some accident of immediate, overwhelming interest which appeals to feelings and distorts the judgment."[2] According to Holmes, these "immediate interests" exercise a kind of "hydraulic pressure which makes what previously was clear seem doubtful and before which even well settled principles of law will bend."[3]

So it is with insanity defense cases. The call for abolition of the insanity defense followed quickly the "strafing of the cuckoo's nest" in the Hinckley case.[4] In responding to the "hydraulic pressure" of public opinion and by "overreacting to a single astonishing incident,"[5] it replicated similar calls which have followed almost every

---

2.   No. Sec. Co. v. United States, 193 U.S. 197, 400 (1904). *See also*, P. DEVLIN, TRIAL BY JURY 124 (1966):

Hard cases make bad law; the jury is sometimes too frightened of the hard case and the judge of the bad law. This is the eternal conflict between law in the abstract and the justice of the case—how to do what is best in the individual case and yet preserve the rule. It is out of this dialect that the just verdict comes....

3.   *No. Sec. Co.*, 193 U.S. at 400-1.
     See Morse, *Excusing the Crazy: The Insanity Defense Reconsidered*, 58 S. CAL. L. REV. 777, 779 (1985): "Unpopular or even 'wrong' verdicts occur in all areas of law, however, and should not spur intemperate attempts to change fundamentally just laws." *But see*, Shah, *Criminal Responsibility*, in W. CURRAN, A.L. McGARRY & S. SHAH, FORENSIC PSYCHIATRY AND PSYCHOLOGY: PERSPECTIVES AND STANDARDS FOR INTERDISCIPLINARY PRACTICE 167, 200 (1986):

There is also reason for concern that the shocking cases tends to have a very disproportionate influence in shaping public policies and related practices. Notorious cases seem in many instances to function like the proverbial tails that tend to wag and influence policies the much larger (albeit less visible) class of people.

4.   English, *The Light Between Twilight and Dusk: Federal Criminal Law and the Volitional Insanity Defense*, 40 HASTINGS L. REV. 1, 10 (1988).
5.   Kaufman, *Should Florida Follow the Federal Insanity Defense?* 15 FLA. ST. U. L. REV. 793, 836 (1987); R. Christiansen, "From Hadfield to Hinckley: The Insanity Plea in Politically-Related Trials," (paper delivered at the 1983 Academy of Criminal Justice Sciences' Annual Meeting, March 22, 1983), manuscript at 46; *see also*, Herman, *The Insanity Defense in Fact and Fiction: On Norval Morris's Madness and the Criminal Law*, 1985 AM. B. FOUND. RES. J. 385, 393: "In the wake of such traumatic events [as political assassination and assassination attempts], public opinion cannot be measured reliably. Comment on the insanity defense now is not likely to be reaction to the insanity defense in general but rather to its operation in the exceptional case of John Hinckley."

unpopular insanity verdict since the M'Naghten trial.[6] These calls reflected a "tenuous logic: if the verdict was wrong, then the standard [must have been] wrong."[7]

It is thus not surprising that *some* homicide insanity acquittees are regarded as "moral mistakes" while others are not. Whereas "stranger killings" evoke feelings of "fear, anger, and rage," intrafamilial killings sometimes evoke contrary feelings of "pity and shock."[8] When there is the rare discordance between responsibility recommendations by state forensic examiners and subsequent adjudications, it emerges where defendants' offenses were "unusual,...impulsive, emotionally charged, or without apparent motivation."[9]

---

6.   *Cf.* Tighe, *Francis Wharton and the Nineteenth Century Insanity Defense: The Origins of a Reform Tradition,* 27 AM. J. LEG. HIST. 223 (1983) (Hinckley acquittal *rejuvenated* insanity defense reform movement); *see* R. MORAN, KNOWING RIGHT FROM WRONG: THE INSANITY DEFENSE OF DANIEL MCNAUGHTAN 191-95 (1981).

   Rogers and Ewing have speculated that, if the Hinckley jury *rejected* his insanity defense, that decision would have probably resulted in "a public affirmation of our court system and its experts in the pursuit of justice." R. Rogers & C. Ewing, *Proscribing Ultimate Opinions: The Quick and Cosmetic Fix,* (unpublished manuscript), at 2 (delivered at American Psychological Association convention, Atlanta, Georgia, August 1988). This was precisely the relieved public response to the jury's rejection of the insanity defense in the Jeffrey Dahmer trial. *See supra* chapter 4, text accompanying notes 194-96; De Benedictis, *Sane Serial Killer: Experts Say Insanity Plea Alive and Well, Thanks Partly to Dahmer Jury,* 78 A.B.A. J. 22 (April 1992). For links between the Hinckley and M'Naghten verdicts, *see supra* chapter 2, note 12.

7.   Rogers, *The American Psychological Association's Position on the Insanity Defense: Empiricism Versus Emotionalism,* 42 AM. PSYCHOLOGIST 840 (1987); *compare* Tanford & Tanford, *Better Trials Through Science: A Defense of Psychologist-Lawyer Collaboration,* 66 N.C. L. REV. 741, 765 (1988) (social acceptance of a verdict does not automatically follow from verdict accuracy). Verdicts and post-acquittal release decisions in individual insanity defense cases (where either the verdict or the post-acquittal release were perceived as outrageous) have thus led speedily to the consideration and adoption of the guilty but mentally ill (GBMI) verdict in many jurisdictions. *See generally,* McGraw, Farthing-Capowich & Keilitz, *The "Guilty But Mentally Ill" Plea and Verdict: Current State of the Knowledge,* 38 VILL. L. REV. 117 (1985); *see supra* chapter 3 A 1 c (4).

8.   Wexler, *Redefining the Insanity Problem,* 53 GEO. WASH. L. REV. 528, 551-52 (1985). *See supra* chapter 4 D 2-3.

9.   Howard & Clark, *When Courts and Experts Disagree: Discordance Between Insanity Recommendations and Adjudications,* 9 LAW & HUM. BEHAV. 385, 394 (1985). Concordance rates of 79-93 percent have been uniformly found in the empirical literature. *See supra* chapter 3 B 1 b (1).

While the "bad case" phenomenon has been noted,[10] there appears to be little discussion in the literature of the *uniqueness* of this ultimate drown-the-baby-to-get-rid-of- the-bath-water response. It is accepted, almost as a *given*, that an unpopular verdict will lead to abolition cries.[11] Yet, unpopular verdicts based on other "excusing" criminal law defenses do not lead to similar "reform" suggestions,[12] notwithstanding the common law's "deeply rooted hostility" toward all such excuse defenses.[13]

There have been few recent criminal cases that have polarized major metropolitan areas in the same way as did the Bernhard Goetz trial.[14] While the specific legal question was a fairly narrow one that has provoked criminal law scholars for centuries—the standard to be used in assessing whether a defendant's use of deadly force was

---

10. *See e.g.*, Gerard, *The Usefulness of the Medical Model to the Legal System*, 39 RUTGERS L. REV. 377, 410 (1987) (discussing case of Garrett Trapnell who allegedly feigned insanity successfully on six occasions) ("Such cases stimulate the current uproar over the insanity defense because society perceives that it is improperly being denied protection"). On the heuristic significance of the Trapnell case in animating President Nixon's attempt to abolish the insanity defense, *see* Gerber, *The Insanity Defense Revisited*, 1984 ARIZ. ST. L.J. 83, 117-18.

11. *See e.g.*, Adler, *Not Guilty By Reason of Insanity: A System Plagued by Madness*, 29 ARIZ. ATTORNEY 18 (Nov. 1992) (NGRI abolition bill in Arizona dubbed "Laura's Law" after name of victim of successful insanity pleader). In this case, the victim was the defendant's estranged wife, and her family was apparently the impetus for the proposed legislation. The legislation —which would create a "guilty but insane" verdict and would place oversight of such defendants in the hands of a five-member psychiatric review board—has passed the state Senate Judiciary Committee, and, as of this writing, is before the full state Senate. *See* Cook, *"Guilty but Insane" Bill Clears Senate Panel*, Ariz. Daily Star (Feb. 24, 1993), at 1B. *Compare* Wexler, *An Offense-Victim Approach to Insanity Defense Reform*, 26 ARIZ. L. REV. 16 (1984) (urging limiting insanity defense to cases not involving "stranger victims"); *see supra* chapter 4 D 4.

12. *See e.g.*, Kadish, *The Decline of Innocence*, 26 CAMB. L.J. 273, 279 (1968). This does not suggest that the public does not become regularly enraged about individual jury acquittals or its perceptions of the overall rate of jury acquittals. While these may lead to outcries against the perceived incompetence of jurors or the deficiencies inherent in the jury system, *see e.g.*, V. HANS & N. VIDMAR, JUDGING THE JURY 133 (1986), discussing J. BALDWIN & M. McCONVILLE, JURY TRIALS (1979), the attacks are rarely, if ever, focused on a specific substantive defense.

13. Fletcher, *The Individualization of Excusing Conditions*, 47 S. CAL. L. REV. 1269, 1295 (1974).

14. People v. Goetz, 68 N.Y. 2d 96, 497 N.E. 2d 41, 506 N.Y.S. 2d 18 (1986); *see e.g.*, L. RUBIN, QUIET RAGE: BERNIE GOETZ IN A TIME OF MADNESS (1986); G. FLETCHER, A CRIME OF SELF-DEFENSE: BERNHARD GOETZ AND THE LAW ON TRIAL (1988).

justified under the circumstances[15]— the combination of the location of the shooting (a New York City subway) and the contrasting socio-economic statuses of the (white, middle-class) defendant and the (black, inner-city) victims led to an emotionally-charged, publicity-driven trial.[16] That trial, "part of the folklore of American law, like the Leopold and Loeb case,"[17] resulted in a verdict which was seen by a significant number of observers as "outrageous." [18] Also, self-defense is a defense that, by all anecdotal and observational accounts, is used frequently in criminal courts.[19] Yet, there were no cries for the abolition of the self-defense defense.[20]

Similarly, when auto manufacturer John DeLorean was acquitted of narcotics and conspiracy charges based on his successful use of the entrapment defense, no bills were introduced into Congress to eliminate entrapment as a criminal law defense.[21] It does not appear that society is ready to do what Professor Mickenberg suggests would

15. *See e.g.*, W. LaFave & A. Scott, Criminal Law §§3.7(g), 5.7(c) (2d ed. 1986).
16. *See generally*, Comment, *Bernard Goetz, A "Reasonable Man:" A Look At New York's Justification Defense*, 53 Brooklyn L. Rev. 1149 (1988); Note, *The Proper Standard for Self-Defense in New York: Should People v. Goetz Be Viewed as Judicial Legislation or Judicial Restraint?* 39 Syr. L. Rev. 845 (1988). *Compare* Tesner, *Racial Paranoia as a Defense to Crimes of Violence: An Emerging Theory of Self-Defense or Insanity*, 11 B.C. Third World L.J. 307 (1991) (discussing Goetz case as example).
17. Heller, *A Professor Watches the Law Come to Life*, Chron. Higher Ed. (June 24, 1987), at 3 (*quoting* Prof. George Fletcher). *See also*, Rosenfeld, *Afterthoughts on the Goetz Case*, N.Y.L.J. (Aug. 11, 1987), at 2 (Editorial).
18. *See e.g.*, *Goetz Verdict Will Endanger Young Black Males, Leaders Say*, 72 Jet (July 6, 1987), at 18; Rosenfeld, *supra* note 18, at 2.
19. This, of course, contrasts with the *low* number of insanity defense pleas. *See supra* chapter 3 B 1 b (1); *see generally*, H. Steadman et al., Reforming the Insanity Defense: An Analysis of Pre-and Post-Hinckley Reforms (1993) (in press) (H. Steadman, Reforming).
20. Of course, many observers strongly *supported* Goetz. *See* Carter, *When Victims Happen To Be Black*, 97 Yale L.J. 420, 422-24 (1988) (stories like Goetz's become true "because the popular culture demands their truth;" Goetz becomes a folk- hero, and the central message of the hero-worshippers is clear: "We *know* that what he did was right"). On how the Goetz debate served as "an indirect way of talking about race," *see* Chase, *In the Jungle of Cities*, 84 Mich. L. Rev. 737, 739 (1986), and *see id.* at 739-40 n. 11 (discussing "socioeconomic and sexual-psychological fear of blacks" as "undercurrent" of law-and-order politics).
21. The DeLorean case is discussed in Comment, *Entrapment, DeLorean and the Undercover Operation: A Constitutional Connection*, 18 J. Marshall L. Rev. 365 (1985).

appear to be the next logical step following the Hinckley-inspired call for insanity defense abolition:

> If criminal responsibility must attach to all who commit a bad act regardless of issues of free will, then not just insanity but all other defenses should be abolished. Thus, the individual who injures another in self-defense should be as guilty of assault as the crazy person who injures another because of his mental illness.[22]

What is it about the insanity defense which animates the public's response? Why does the sensational case appear to have such a disproportionate impact on the development of a jurisprudence? To some extent, the insanity defense *is* different.[23] It involves unconscious motivations; it inevitably involves profound issues such as free will, responsibility and blame. It incorporates religious ideology, medieval superstition, and anthropological roots, and draws on rich lodes of myths in such a way that "symbolic values" remain necessarily paramount.[24]

Because of *these* factors (many of which are *not* frequently present in cases involving the use of other criminal defenses), the distortion of the "sensational" case appears to be even grosser. To try to make sense of this, I propose it is necessary to examine cognitive behavior decision theory and recent social cognition research in an effort to learn *why* we respond to these phenomena the way we do.[25]

---

22. Mickenberg, *A Pleasant Surprise: The Guilty But Mentally Ill Verdict Has Both Succeeded On Its Own Right and Successfully Preserved the Traditional Role of the Insanity Defense*, 55 U. CINN. L. REV. 943, 962 (1987).

23. Researchers have suggested that *criminal justice attitudes* may be formed in ways that separate them from other attitudes because of the public's lack of a clear idea as to how the criminal justice system actually operates. *See* Doob & Roberts, *Social Psychology, Social Attitudes, and Attitudes Toward Sentencing*, 16 CANAD. J. BEHAV. SCI. 269, 270 (1984); *see also*, Stalans & Diamond, *Formation and Change in Lay Evaluations of Criminal Sentencing: Misperception and Discontent*, 14 LAW & HUM. BEHAV. 199 (1990). The public's specific misperceptions about the operation of the insanity defense within the criminal justice system are even more distorted. *See supra* chapter 3 B 1 b.

24. *See supra* chapter 2 A 3 (discussing Jungian views of myths as "projections from the unconscious"). *See generally*, Perlin, *The Supreme Court, the Mentally Disabled Criminal Defendant, and Symbolic Values: Random Decisions, Hidden Rationales, or "Doctrinal Abyss?"* 29 ARIZ. L. REV. 1 (1987).

25. *See* Bersoff, *Judicial Deference to Nonlegal Decisionmakers: Imposing Simplistic Solutions on Problems of Cognitive Complexity in Mental Disability Law*, 46 SMU L. REV. 329 (1992); Saks & Kidd, *Human Information Processing and Adjudication: Trial By Heuristics*, 15 LAW & SOC'Y REV. 123, 125 (1980-81); COGNITION AND SOCIAL BEHAVIOR (J. Carroll & J. Payne eds. 1976) (J. Carroll

C. The Behavioral Roots of Insanity Defense Decision Making: The Power of Heuristic Reasoning[26]

1. On Heuristics

Behaviorists are aware of the power of what Dr. David Rosenhan has characterized as the "distortions of vivid information." As part of this phenomenon, "concrete and vivid information" about a specific case "overwhelms" the abstract data...upon which rational choices are often made."[27] Thus, "the more vivid and concrete is better remembered, over recitals of fact and logic."[28] Studies have

---

& J. Payne); R. NISBETT & L. ROSS, HUMAN INFERENCE: STRATEGIES AND SHORTCOMINGS OF SOCIAL JUDGMENT (1980).

26. For a comprehensive one volume survey of the issues discussed in this section, *see* JUDGMENT UNDER UNCERTAINTY: HEURISTICS AND BIASES (D. Kahneman, P. Slovic & A. Tversky eds. 1982) (D. Kahneman). For helpful overviews of related areas, *see* Bersoff, *supra* note 25; C. SHERIF, M. SHERIF & R. NEBERGALL, ATTITUDE AND ATTITUDE CHANGE: THE SOCIAL JUDGMENT- INVOLVEMENT APPROACH (1965); J. Carroll & J. Payne, *supra* note 25; S. BREHM & J. BREHM, PSYCHOLOGICAL REACTANCE: A THEORY OF FREEDOM AND CONTROL (1981); Edwards & von Winterfeldt, *Cognitive Illusions and Their Implications for the Law*, 59 S. CAL. L. REV. 225 (1986) (Edwards); Moore, *Trial By Schema: Cognitive Filters in the Courtroom*, 37 UCLA L. REV. 273 (1989); Scott & Stuntz, *Plea Bargaining As Contract*, 101 YALE L.J. 1909 (1992). *But compare*, Gigerenzer, *How to Make Cognitive Illusions Disappear: Beyond "Heuristics and Biases,"* 2 EUR. REV. SOC'L PSYCHOLOGY 83 (1991) (criticizing standard interpretations of heuristic biases), and *see* Bersoff,*supra* note 25, at 339-40 n. 47, explaining the roots of the disagreements between Gigerenzer and researchers such as Tversky and Kahneman.

27. Rosenhan, *Psychological Realities and Judicial Policies*, 10 STAN. LAW. 10, 13, 14 (1984).

    Professor Joel Finer has explicitly recognized the impact of the "vividness effect" on the post-Hinckley debate. Finer, *Should the Insanity Defense Be Abolished? An Introduction to the Debate*, 1 J. HEALTH & L. 113 (1986-87). *See also*, D. BAZELON, QUESTIONING AUTHORITY: JUSTICE AND CRIMINAL LAW 28 (1988) ("Run-of-the-mill muggings by street toughs are too common for the front pages, but even the most banal burglary is newsworthy if committed by someone with a psychiatric history").

28. Ford, *The Role of Extralegal Factors in Jury Verdicts*, 11 JUST. SYS. J. 16, 23 (1986); *see also*, Bank & Poythress, *The Elements of Persuasion In Expert Testimony*, 10 J. PSYCHIATRY & L. 173. On the psychological tendency to employ the defense mechanism of avoidance following a vivid, stressful incident, *see* Horowitz, Wilner & Alvarez, *Impact of Event Scale: A Measure of Subjective Stress*, 41 PSYCHOSOMATIC MED. 209 (1979). On the way that surprise, consequentiality and emotional arousal contribute to the "flashbulb memory" effect (e.g., where one was when they heard the news about the assassination of President Kennedy), *see* Brown & Kulik, *Flashbulb Memories*, 5 COGNITION 73

shown further that the "vividness" effect is actively present in judicial proceedings,[29] and in our *perceptions* of judicial proceedings.[30]

This distortion results in "trial by heuristics,"[31] the use of problem-solving methods to keep "the information-processing demands of a task within the bounds of [individuals'] limited cognitive capacity."[32] Through the use of social cognitive research and behavior decision theory,[33] I will examine how the use of such principles which

---

(1977).

29. *See e.g.*, Bell & Loftus, *Vivid Persuasion in the Courtroom*, 49 J. PERSONALITY ASSESSMENT 659, 663 (1985) (vivid information at trial may "garner more attention, recruit more attention from memory, cause people to spend more time in thought, be more available in memory, be perceived as having a more credible source, and have a greater affective impact"); Doob & Roberts, *supra* note 23, at 279, *citing* Hamill, Wilson & Nisbett, *Insensitivity to Sample Bias: Generalizing From Atypical Cases*, 39 J. PERSONAL. & SOC'L PSYCHOLOGY 578 (1980) (subjects presented with information about one welfare recipient generalized data to all recipients even when told the particular exemplar was "highly atypical of the population at large"). On the impact that vivid events have on police policies dealing with mentally disabled persons, *see* Finn & Sullivan, *Police Handling of the Mentally Ill: Sharing Responsibility With the Mental Health System*, 17 J. CRIM. JUST. 1, 4 (1989).

30. *See e.g.*, Diamond & Stalans, *The Myth of Judicial Leniency on Sentencing*, 7 BEHAV. SCI. & L. 73, 87-88 (1989) (vividness of media stories about particularly violent criminal offenses has a "disproportionate impact" on public perceptions about crime); Alschuler, *"Close Enough For Government Work:" The Exclusionary Rule After Leon*, 1984 SUP. CT. REV. 309, 347-48 (fear that application of exclusionary rule might potentially free "next year's Son of Sam" will overwhelm empirically-based arguments in support of rule); Nisbett et al., *Popular Induction: Information Is Not Necessarily Informative*, in D. Kahneman, *supra* note 26, at 101, 113 (comparing "influenceability" by abstract and concrete information); Slovic, Fischhoff & Lichtenstein, *Facts Versus Fears: Understanding Perceived Risk*, in *id.* at 463, 468 (impact of biased newspaper coverage on perceived risks in cases of various disaster scenarios); Stalans & Lurigio, *Law and Professionals' Beliefs About Crime and Criminal Sentences: A Need for Theory, Perhaps Schema Theory*, 17 CRIM. JUST. & BEHAV. 333 (1990) (lay persons rely disproportionately on unrepresentative impressions in forming beliefs about punishment and crime).

31. Saks & Kidd, *supra* note 25. *See generally*, Tanford & Tanford, *supra* note 7, at 748-49; Tversky & Kahneman, *Judgment Under Uncertainty: Heuristics and Biases*, in D. Kahneman, *supra* note 26, at 3 (Tversky & Kahneman I); Walker & Monahan, *Social Frameworks: A New Use of Social Science in Law*, 73 VA. L. REV. 559, 576-78 (1987); Tversky, *Features of Similarity*, 84 PSYCHOLOG. REV. 327 (1977).

32. Carroll & Payne, *The Psychology of the Parole Decision Process: A Joint Application of Attribution Theory and Information Processing Psychology*, in J. Carroll & J. Payne, *supra* note 25, at 13, 21.

33. Saks & Kidd, *supra* note 25, at 125. For a full elaboration, *see e.g.*, Kahneman & Tversky, *On the Psychology of Prediction*, 80 PSYCHOLOG. REV. 237 (1973);

appear to guide the simplification of complex, information-processing tasks—"simplifying heuristics"—actually lead to distorted and systematically erroneous decisions,[34] and lead decision makers "to ignore or misuse items of rationally useful information."[35]

These principles include the following:

- *Representativeness.* We erroneously view a random sample drawn from a population as highly representative of that population, i.e., similar in all essential characteristics.[36]

Thus, the high rate of false positives (the consistent overprediction of dangerousness by psychiatrists and clinical psychologists) is due, in part, to inappropriate reliance on the representative heuristic where a person facing involuntary civil commitment is compared to the stereotype of a dangerous person.[37] Because the rare false negative receives such extensive negative publicity, we overattribute representativeness to that category.[38]

- *Insensitivity to sample size.* We "intuitively" reject the statistical reality that larger samples are more likely to approximate the characteristics of the population from which they are drawn.[39] As Tversky and Kahneman have noted, "This fundamental notion of statistics is evidently not part of people's repertoire of intuitions."[40]

Tversky & Kahneman I, *supra* note 31; Tversky & Kahneman, *Availability: A Heuristic for Judging Frequency and Probability,* 5 COGNITIVE PSYCHOL. 207 (1973) (Tversky & Kahneman II); Tversky & Kahneman, *Belief in the Law of Small Numbers,* in D. Kahneman, *supra* note 26, at 23 (Tversky & Kahneman III); *see generally,* Tanford & Tanford, *supra* note 7, at 749-52. Saks and Kidd's research is ably summarized in McCord, *A Primer for the Nonmathematically Inclined on Mathematical Evidence in Criminal Cases:* People v. Collins *and Beyond,* 47 WASH. & LEE L. REV. 741, 783-84 n. 173 (1990).

34. Saks & Kidd, *supra* note 25, at 132. *See also,* Edwards, *supra* note 26, at 227 (discussing elements of cognitive illusions).

35. Carroll & Payne, *supra* note 32, at 21.

36. *See generally,* Bersoff, *supra* note 25, at 342-44.

37. *See supra* chapter 4 C 3; Saks & Kidd, *supra* note 25, at 133, discussing Kahneman & Tversky, *Subjective Probability: A Judgment of Representativeness,* 3 COGNITIVE PSYCHOLOGY 430 (1972), reprinted in D. Kahneman, *supra* note 26, at 32; *see also,* Tversky & Kahneman, *Belief in the Law of Small Numbers,* in D. Kahneman, *supra* note 26, at 23.

38. *See* Edwards, *supra* note 26, at 237, discussing Kahneman & Tversky, *supra* note 33.

39. *See* Edwards, *supra* note 26, at 235, discussing Tversky & Kahneman III, *supra* note 33.

40. Saks & Kidd, *supra* note 25, at 134, *quoting* Tversky & Kahneman I, *supra* note 31. Like the *illusion of validity* (see *infra* text accompanying notes 41-43, this

• *The illusion of validity.* Individuals tend to make intuitive predictions by selecting an outcome most similar to a pre-existing stereotype, and express extreme confidence in such predictions, even where they are given scanty, outdated or unreliable information about an unknown. Moreover, we frequently fill in the gaps in our evidence base with information consistent with our "preconceived notions of what evidence should support our belief," a phenomenon also known as "filling." [41]

• *Availability.* People are likely to judge the probability or frequency of an event based on the ease with which they can recall instances or occurrences of the event. [42] Thus, extensive publicity about "some atrocious crime...greatly enhances lay assessment of how probable the event is." [43] However, as the most salient experiences are the ones which are the most bizarre and extreme, they are precisely the "poorest instances on which to construct decision making policies." [44]

An example of the availability heuristic in a collateral area should be illustrative: when asked about whether a sentencing judge was too lenient in an individual case, eighty percent of all respondents who had read a newspaper account of the case agreed while only 14.8 percent of those who had read court transcript came to the same conclusion. [45] As a correlative of this phenomenon, Professors

---

heuristic may be viewed as a subcategory of representativeness.

41. Saks & Kidd, *supra* note 25, at 135; Bersoff, *supra* note 25, at 345-48; *see* D. BINDER & S. PRICE, LEGAL INTERVIEWING AND COUNSELING: A CLIENT-CENTERED APPROACH 45 (1977); *see also,* D. BINDER, P. BERGMAN & S. PRICE, LAWYERS AS COUNSELORS: A CLIENT-CENTERED APPROACH (1991); *see generally,* Snyder, Tanke & Berscheid, *Social Perception and Interpersonal behavior: On the Self-Fulfilling Nature of Social Stereotypes,* 35 J. PERS. & SOC'L PSYCHOLOGY 656, 657 (1977) (Snyder).

42. Saks & Kidd, *supra* note 25, at 137, *citing* Tversky & Kahneman I, *supra* note 31, at 1127; *see also,* Tversky & Kahneman II, *supra* note 33, at 163; Slovic, Fischhoff & Lichtenstein, *Cognitive Processes and Societal Risk Taking,* in J. Carroll & J. Payne, *supra* note 25, at 165; *see generally,* Bersoff, *supra* note 25, at 339-42.

43. Edwards, *supra* note 26, at 248.

44. Saks & Kidd, *supra* note 25, at 139. *See also,* Merz & Fischhoff, *Informed Consent Does Not Mean Rational Consent: Cognitive Limitations on Decision-Making,* 11 J. LEG. MED. 321, 344-45 (1990).

45. Diamond & Stalans, *supra* note 30, at 88, *citing* Doob & Roberts, *supra* note 23. *See also,* Harris & Harvey, *Attribution Theory: From Phenomenal Causality to the Intuitive Social Scientist and Beyond,* in THE PSYCHOLOGY OF ORDINARY SOCIAL BEHAVIOUR 57, 83 (C. Antaki ed. 1981):

Saks and Kidd also report studies confirming that experts reporting scientific and/or statistical data are likely to have less of an impact on fact-finders than a person who reports a case study, relates a compelling personal experience, or offers anecdotal evidence. Such anecdotal evidence is viewed as "more concrete, vivid and emotion-arousing" and thus more accessible to factfinders.[46] According to Professor Van Zandt:

> Anecdotal evidence plays a major role in people's understanding of their society. The most obvious examples are the use of oral stories, tales, and myths. Individuals routinely accept as highly probative evidence that would constitute hearsay.[47]

On a CNN call-in broadcast of *Sonya Live*, for example, in response to a discussion of the Dahmer case, a caller from North Carolina told the national audience that his father had been murdered by a defendant who pled the insanity defense and was hospitalized for less than a year.[48] Assuming that this in fact was so, the case disposition was clearly anomalous;[49] yet, employment of the availability heuristic will make this accessible personal story the dominant image retained by listeners.

[T]he use of the availability heuristic can account for frequently seen types of attributional bias....[I]f one had to judge the chances of a discharged mental patient being dangerous, one might only access dramatic memories of particular discharged patients (e.g., memories of their violent behaviour) presumably because such memories are more available. If so, then one would judge a particular patient as having a greatly inflated chance of being dangerous, ignoring data which suggest, in general, that discharged mental patients are most likely to be docile and non-violent.

46. Saks & Kidd, *supra* note 25, at 137, *citing* Nisbett & Temoshok, *Is There an "External" Cognitive Style?* 33 J. PERSONAL. & SOCIAL PSYCHOLOGY 36 (1976); *see also*, G. MELTON, J. PETRILA, N. POYTHRESS & C. SLOBOGIN, PSYCHOLOGICAL EVALUATIONS FOR THE COURTS: A HANDBOOK FOR MENTAL HEALTH PROFESSIONALS AND LAWYERS 10-12 (1989), for *idiographic* (case-centered) testimony. It is not coincidental that political commentators have credited much of the personal popularity of President Reagan—Hinckley's victim—to his facility with precisely this sort of heuristic, "anecdotal evidence." *See generally infra* chapter 6 C 2.

47. Van Zandt, *Common Sense Reasoning, Social Change and the Law*, 81 Nw. U. L. REV. 894, 917 n. 120 (1987) (citation omitted); *see generally infra* chapter 6 D.

48. *Sonya Live*, CNN News (March 9, 1992), transcript #6-2, at 3 (full text available on NEXIS).

49. *See supra* chapter 3 B 1 b (1); H. STEADMAN, REFORMING, *supra* note 19.

- *Illusory correlation*. We erroneously report correlations between two classes of events which, in reality, are not correlated, are correlated to a lesser extent than is reported, or are correlated in an opposite direction.[50]
- *Adjustment and anchoring*. Our adjustments or revisions of initial estimates frequently depend heavily on initial values. Even where new information is introduced, initial decisions are often not subsequently corrected or altered in light of the additional data.[51]
- *Overconfidence in judgments*. Fact-finders tend to overestimate how much they already know and underestimate how much they have recently learned.[52] Lawyers, by way of example, are found to be significantly overconfident in predicting their chances of winning a hypothetical case, and very *difficult* judgments produce the most overconfidence.[53]
- *Under-incorporation of statistical information*. Contrary to the common belief that statistical reliance results in the production of "unduly persuasive" data, individuals do not process prob-

---

50. Saks & Kidd, *supra* note 25, at 139, *citing, inter alia,* Chapman & Chapman, *The Genesis of Popular But Erroneous Psychodiagnostic Signs,* 74 J. ABNORMAL PSYCHOLOGY 193 (1967). This is a subcategory of *availability,* see *supra* text accompanying notes 42-49.

51. Bersoff, *supra* note 25, at 348, discussing Turk et al., *Psychotherapy: An Information- Processing Perspective,* in REASONING, INFERENCE AND JUDGMENT IN CLINICAL PSYCHOLOGY 1, 9 (C. Turk & P. Salovey eds. 1988) (TURK & SALOVEY). The phenomenon that differing initial values lead to differing final estimates is known as "anchoring." Saks & Kidd, *supra* note 25, at 140-41; *see e.g.,* Roberts & Edwards, *Contextual Effects in Judgments of Crimes, Criminals and the Purposes of Sentencing,* 19 J. APP. SOC. PSYCHOLOGY 902 (1989) (anchoring effect controlled respondents' assessments of seriousness of criminal behavior).

52. Saks & Kidd, *supra* note 25, at 143. Accordingly, jurors rank expert witnesses' firmness of conclusion as more important in assessing believability than either the expert's educational credentials or reputation. Champagne, Shuman & Whitaker, *Expert Witnesses in the Courts: An Empirical Examination,* 76 JUDICATURE 5, 8 (1992); *see also,* McGaffey, *The Expert Witness and Source Credibility—The Communication Perspective,* 1 AM. J. TRIAL AD. 57, 68-69 (1978) ("strength of witness" was significant determination of extent to which jurors found testimony believable).

53. *See* Loftus & Wagenaar, *Lawyers' Predictions of Success,* 28 JURIMETRICS J. 437 (1988); Edwards, *supra* note 26, at 239, *citing* Pitz, *Subjective Probability Distribution for Imperfectly Known Quantities,* in KNOWLEDGE AND COGNITION (L. Gregg ed. 1984); *see generally,* Oskamp, *Overconfidence in Case-Study Judgments,* in D. Kahneman, *supra* note 26, at 287.

abilistic information well, and, as a result, unduly ignore statistical information.[54]

• *The myth of particularistic proofs.* We misassume that case-specific, *anecdotal* information is *qualitatively* different from base-rate, *statistical* information.[55]

When acknowledged, considered and understood, these heuristic reasoning devices can shed new light on the hidden issues underlying insanity defense decision making. For example, the simplifying heuristic of *attribution theory*[56] teaches that, once a stereotype is adopted, a wide variety of evidence can be read to support that stereotype, including events that could equally support the opposite interpretation.[57] This process is sometimes characterized as "dispositional consistency."[58] There is also a "well-documented tendency for people to seek information which confirms rather than disconfirms their beliefs."[59]

A stereotype, in short, functions as a self-fulfilling prophecy; once formed, beliefs about the self, others, or relationships can even survive and persevere in light of "the total discrediting of the evidence

---

54. Saks & Kidd, *supra* note 25, at 149; *see also,* Goodman, *Jurors' Comprehension and Assessment of Probabilistic Evidence,* 16 Am. J. Trial Ad. 361 (1992).

55. Saks & Kidd, *supra* note 25, at 151; *see also,* Walker & Monahan, *supra* note 31, at 576 ("It appears that aggregate 'statistical' information is likely to be highly *undervalued* by lay decision makers") (emphasis in original); J. Monahan & L. Walker, Social Science in Law: Cases and Materials 248-49 (on impacts of probabilistic versus particularistic evidence).

56. *See e.g.,* Kelley, *The Process of Causal Attribution,* 28 Am. Psychologist 107 (1973); Nisbet & Temoshok, *supra* note 46.

57. Snyder, *supra* note 41, at 657; *see generally,* Zadny & Gerard, *Attributed Intentions and Informational Selectivity,* 10 J. Exper. Soc'l Psychology 34 (1974); Russell, *The Causal Dimension Scale: A Measure of How Individuals Perceive Causes,* 42 J. Pers. & Soc'l Psychology 1137; Carroll & Burke, *Evaluation and Prediction in Expert Parole Decisions,* 17 Crim., Just. & Behav. 315 (1990); Weiner, *Metaphors in Motivation and Attribution,* 46 Am. Psychologist 921 (1991); Cullen et al., *Attribution, Salience, and Attitudes Toward Criminal Sanctioning,* 12 Crim. Just. & Behav. 305 (1985).

58. Fiske, *Attention and Weight in Person Perception: The Impact of Negative and Extreme Behaviors,* 38 J. Personal. & Soc'l Psychology 889 (1980). *See also,* Ross & Anderson, *Shortcomings in the Attribution Process: On the Origins and Maintenance of Erroneous Social Assessments,* in D. Kahneman, *supra* note 26, at 129 (attribution theory deals with "naive psychology").

59. Doob & Roberts, *supra* note 23, at 279, *citing* Snyder & Swann, *Hypothesis-Testing Processes in Social Interaction,* 36 J. Personal. & Soc'l Psychology 1202 (1978).

that first gave rise to such beliefs."[60] Thus, the biased assimilation processes "may include a propensity to remember the strengths of confirming evidence, but not the weaknesses of disconfirming evidence, to judge confirming evidence as relevant and reliable but disconfirming evidence as irrelevant and unreliable, and to accept confirming evidence at face value while scrutinizing disconfirming evidence hypercrticially."[61] As I will demonstrate subsequently, stereotypes drive the sanist thought processes and judicial opinions that are at the root of our insanity defense jurisprudence.[62]

Evidence shows that belief polarization will *increase*, rather than decrease or remain unchanged, when mixed or inconclusive findings are assimilated by proponents of opposite viewpoints. This polarization hypothesis stems from the assumption that data relevant to a belief are not processed impartially.[63] People who hold strong opin-

---

60. Lord, Ross & Lepper, *Biased Assimilation and Attitude Polarization: The Effects of Prior Theories on Subsequently Considered Evidence*, 37 J. PERS. & SOC'L PSYCHOLOGY 2098, 2108 (1979); *see e.g.*, Ross, Lepper & Hubbard, *Perseverance in Self-Perception and Social Perception: Biased Attributional Processes in the Debriefing Paradigm*, 32 J. PERS. & SOC'L PSYCHOLOGY 880 (1975); Ross & Anderson, *supra* note 58, at 144-45. There is substantial evidence that simplifying devices may lead to systematic errors in perception and action. *See* Van Zandt, *supra* note 48, at 918 n. 125 (citing sources).

These principles control, whether the topic is law, psychology, or sports. Thus, in an essay reviewing a book about Joe DiMaggio's 1941 fifty-six game hitting streak, Stephen Jay Gould relies on heuristic theories (*quoting, inter alia,* D. Kahneman, *supra* note 26), to demonstrate that, statistically, DiMaggio's one-season streak is "the greatest factual achievement in the history of baseball." Gould, *The Streak of Streaks*, N.Y. REV. OF BOOKS (Aug. 18, 1988), at 8. Yet, well-known sports odds-maker Danny Sheridan continues to quote significantly longer odds (100 to 1 as opposed to 75 to 1) on the longevity (and unbeatability) of Hank Aaron's *career* record of 755 home runs. *Pursuing Baseball's Elusive Records*, USA Today (Sept. 30, 1988), at 7C. *But compare* Case, *Say It Ain't So, Joe: DiMaggio's Streak Stricken?* 253 NATION 225 (Aug. 26/Sept. 2, 1991) (arguing that other baseball players have had far better fifty-six game stretches than did DiMaggio during his hitting streak). On heuristics and the "hot hand" phenomenon in basketball, *see* Camerer, *Does the Basketball Market Believe in the "Hot Hand?"* 79 AM. ECON. REV. 1257 (1989).

61. Lord, Ross & Lepper, *supra* note 60, at 2099. See *id.*: "Indeed [we] may even come to regard the ambiguities and conceptual flaws in the data *opposing* their hypotheses as somehow suggestive of the fundamental *correctness* of those hypotheses. Thus, completely inconsistent or even random data—when 'processed' in a suitably biased fashion—can maintain or even reinforce one's preconceptions" (emphasis added).

62. *See generally infra* chapter 8 B; *see* Perlin, *On "Sanism,"* 46 SMU L. REV. 373 (1992).

63. Lord, Ross & Lepper, *supra* note 60, at 2099; *see also,* Edwards, *supra* note 26,

ions on complex social issues are likely to examine relevant empirical evidence in a biased manner.[64] As a corollary, individuals will irrationally exaggerate a person's causal responsibility for an event while underestimating *other* causal factors that are logically involved in the event's occurrence.[65] Our reasoning is also distorted by the "hindsight illusion" through which we "consistently exaggerate what could have been anticipated in foresight," a phenomenon characterized as "a probabilistic version of 'I told you so.'"[66]

Public perceptions of a legal order and judicial system "burdened by citizen demands and assailed by unprecedented efforts to use courts as a vehicle for social engineering" have been found to be based upon "a handful of 'worst' case studies" or "an anecdotal parade of horribles."[67] We thus respond to social policies "in terms of the symbols or metaphors they evoke, or in conformity with views expressed by opinion leaders we like or respect." The "evidence" brought to bear in the formulation of such policies is apt to be "incomplete, biased, and of marginal probative value—typically, no

---

at 23, *quoting* Bar-Hillel, *The Base Rate Fallacy in Probability Judgments*, 44 ACTA PSYCHOLOGICA 211, 230 (1980):

> People integrate two items of information only if both seem to them equally relevant. Otherwise, high relevance information renders low information irrelevant. One item of information is more relevant than another if it somehow pertains to it more specifically.

64. White, *Juror Decision Making in the Capital Penalty Trial: An Analysis of Crimes and Defense Strategies*, 11 LAW & HUM. BEHAV. 113, 127 (1987), *citing* Lord, Ross & Lepper, *supra* note 60; *see also*, Ross & Anderson, *supra* note 58, at 149-50 (discussing "confirmation bias").

65. Landy & Aronson, *The Influence of the Character of the Criminal and His Victim on the Decisions of Simulated Jurors*, 5 J. EXPERIMENTAL SOC'L PSYCHOLOGY 141 (1969).

66. Edwards, *supra* note 26, at 243, *quoting*, in part, Fischhoff, *For Those Condemned to Study the Past: Reflections on Historical Judgments*, in NEW DIRECTIONS FOR METHODOLOGY OF SOCIAL AND BEHAVIORAL SCIENCE: FALLIBLE JUDGMENT IN BEHAVIORAL RESEARCH (R. Schweder & D. Fiske eds. 1980), reprinted in modified form in D. Kahneman, *supra* note 26, at 325.

67. Cavanagh & Sarat, *Thinking About Courts: Toward and Beyond a Jurisprudence of Judicial Competence*, 14 LAW & SOC'Y REV. 371, 373, *citing* D. HOROWITZ, THE COURTS AND SOCIAL POLICY (1977), and *id.* at 396; *see* Edwards, *supra* note 26, at 241 (even intelligence analysts "overestimate the probabilities of occurrence of dire events"); V. HANS & N. VIDMAR, *supra* note 12, at 133. On the way that attributional thought processes shape individuals' explanations of crimes and criminal sanctioning by the courts, *see* Cullen et al., *supra* note 57.

more than a couple of vivid, concrete, but dubiously representative instances or cases."[68]

In the same vein, individuals tend to generalize from specific cases to the population from which such cases were drawn, and tend to remember and recall negative and extreme behaviors more easily than positive, more moderate behaviors.[69] Thus, (1) individuals who are statistically rare, rare in context, or "visually highlighted...all have been shown to attract [disproportionate] attention," (2) impressions are most influenced "by their extreme terms," and (3) individuals "read" negative cues as more important than positive ones, in part because they "stand out by virtue of being rare."[70] Also, when multiple forces contribute to an unfortunate outcome, people select the most blameworthy as the predominant causal factor.[71] In short, heuristics and biases shed significant light on our perceptions of the insanity defense.

2. The Insanity Defense and Human Inference: Reagan-as-victim

Public perceptions of the insanity defense comprise a prime exhibit in the case against the soundness of human cognition and inference. Heuristics and biases such as vividness and representativeness distort public perceptions. These effects combine to produce invidious scenarios which doggedly resist rational correction.

For example, insanity defense defenders attempt to use statistics (to rebut empirical myths), scientific studies (to demonstrate that "responsibility" is a valid, externally verifiable term, and that certain

---

68. Lord, Ross & Lepper, *supra* note 60, at 2098. Congress's "fixating" on the Hinckley case clearly reflects this "vividness" effect. *See* English, *supra* note 4, at 37 n. 211. On the role of this sort of "horror story" in the legislative reduction of Idaho's insanity defense, *see* Geis & Meier, *Abolition of the Insanity Plea in Idaho: A Case Study*, 477 ANNALS 72, 74-5 (1985).

69. Diamond & Stalans, *supra* note 30, at 87, *citing* S.FISKE & S. TAYLOR, SOCIAL COGNITION (1984), and Fiske, *supra* note 58; *see also*, Roberts & White, *Public Estimates of Recidivism Rates*, 28 CANAD. J. CRIMINOL. 229 (1986).

70. Fiske, *supra* note 58, at 890-91, 904, *citing, inter alia*, Taylor & Fiske, *Salience, Attention and Attribution: Top of the Head Phenomena*, in 11 ADVANCES IN EXPERIMENTAL SOCIAL PSYCHOLOGY (L. Berkowitz ed. 1978); Warr & Jackson, *The Importance of Extremity*, 32 J. PERSONAL. & SOC'L PSYCHOLOGY 278 (1975); Kanouse & Hanson, *Negativity in Evaluations*, in ATTRIBUTION: PERCEIVING THE CAUSES OF BEHAVIOR (E.E. Jones et al eds. 1972).

71. Alicke, *Culpable Causation*, 63 J. PERSONAL. & SOC'L PSYCHOLOGY 368 (1992).

insanity-pleading defendants are, simply, "different") and principles of moral philosophy (to "prove" that responsibility and causation questions are legitimate ones for moral and legal inquiry).[72]

On the other hand, President Reagan—the *victim* of an insanity-pleader—owed his remarkable popularity with the anti-insanity defense American public, in large part, to an anecdotal, case-specific style that relied on the concrete, the vivid and the emotion-arousing, instinctively more accessible to the fact-finder.[73] It is no surprise that counterdemands by empiricists that change be based on scientific evidence rather than emotionalism receive "scant attention."[74]

Insanity defense decision making is a uniquely fertile field in which the distortive "vividness" effect can operate, and in which the legal system's poor mechanisms of coping with "systematic errors in intuitive judgment" made by heuristic "information processors" become especially troubling.[75] The chasm between perception and reality on the question of the frequency of use of the insanity defense, its success rate, and the "appropriateness" of its success rate all reflect this effect.[76] This is especially problematic in light of what are known as "oddities of measurement" (the law's attempt to impose an all-or-nothing construct on what is, behaviorally, a "fundamentally continuous dimension") and "adversarial investments" (the nature of the adversary system itself will inevitably breed *some* disagreement on

---

72. *See supra* chapter 3 B 4. These efforts have had negligible effects on insanity defense jurisprudential developments. *See generally infra* chapters 8-9.
73. *See* Saks & Kidd, *supra* note 25, discussing Nisbett & Temoshok, *supra* note 46. In a radio broadcast commentary recapping the Reagan Presidency, National Public Radio Commentator Jim Angle characterized Reagan by his "ability to ignore any fact contrary to his views." *All Things Considered* (Jan. 20, 1989) (Angle Broadcast). On the question of political party identification as a heuristic device, *see* Fitts, *Can Ignorance Be Bliss? Imperfect Information as a Positive Influence in Political Institutions?* 88 MICH. L. REV. 917, 945 n.93 (1990).
74. Rogers, *supra* note 7, at 840; *see also,* Alschuler, *supra* note 30.
75. Saks & Kidd, *supra* note 25, at 145. The members of the National Institute of Mental Health Forensic Advisory Panel implicitly recognized the importance of anecdotal notoriety in the shaping of an insanity defense jurisprudence: "From the perspective of [St. Elizabeth's] Hospital, in *controversial* cases such as Hinckley, the United States Attorney's office can be counted upon to oppose *any* conditional release recommendations." *Final Report of the NIMH Ad Hoc Forensic Advisory Panel*, 12 MENT. & PHYS. DIS. L. RPTR. 77, 96 (1988) (emphasis added).
76. *See also,* Finkel, *De Facto Departures From Insanity Instructions*, 14 LAW & HUM. BEHAV. 105 (1990) (mock jurors "keep shifting their relevant and determinative constructs from case to case").

questions of a defendant's sanity).[77]

Distortions are similarly likely in the context of the type of legislative hearing which typically followed the Hinckley acquittal.[78] Academic research psychologists have concluded that such hearings are highly suspect as accurate fact-finding procedures. As such hearings rely "respectively on the phenomenologies of the people called to testify and of the Congressmen and the Senators who ask the questions," at best, "they may be useless public rituals," while, at worst, the self-serving motives of the participants, and the pitfalls of relying on phenomenological accounts to reach crucial decisions, potentially makes them seriously misleading. Similarly, "journalistic uses of the interview are equally suspect, misleading, and possibly socially detrimental, especially when they are—as in the case, for example of 60 Minutes, the TV program—weekly paraded as serious, informed, and socially responsible fact-finding efforts to audiences of millions." [79]

Key court personnel also succumb to heuristics. Dr. Henry Steadman and his colleagues report that, when they described their data collection process to court clerks, those clerks tended to remember only successful insanity pleas even though those examples are only a minor percentage (twenty-five percent) of total pleas.[80]

Finally, not even scholars are immune from the temptation of heuristics:

> The similarity of the political reactions to the M'Naghten and Hinckley cases is understandable...Less understandable, however, is the similarity of scholarly reactions to the two trials. In each instance, opponents of the insanity defense have cited the controversial case, and often grossly distorted its facts, as evidence that exculpation by insanity fosters lawlessness,

---

77. Rosenhan, *supra* note 27, at 14-15. *But see supra* chapter 3 B 1 b (1) (high percentage of uncontested "walkthrough" insanity defense cases) In the study reported by Rosenhan, there was a 15% split among doctors on defendants' sanity. Rosenhan, *supra* note 27, at 15.
78. *See e.g.*, THE INSANITY DEFENSE: HEARINGS BEFORE THE SENATE COMMITTEE ON THE JUDICIARY, 97th Cong., 2d Sess. (1982); *Reform of the Federal Insanity Defense: Hearings Before the Subcommittee on Criminal Justice of the House Committee on the Judiciary*, 98th Cong., 2d Sess. (1983); *see supra* chapter 2 A 2 b.
79. Konecini & Ebbesen, *The Mythology of Legal Decision Making*, 7 INT'L J. L. & PSYCHIATRY 5, 17 (1984).
80. H. STEADMAN, REFORMING, *supra* note 19, at Appendix A, 19; *see generally supra* chapter 3 B 1 B (1) (on empirical data).

frees the guilty, and undermines public confidence in the criminal justice system....[81]

There appears to be some connection between these heuristic fallacies and reliance on "ordinary common sense" (OCS)[82] In his dissent from the Fifth Circuit's decision abandoning the control component of the Model Penal Code's substantive test,[83] Judge Alvin Rubin focused astutely and presciently on one aspect of the majority's (unconscious) decision making process:

> Judges are not, and should not be, immune to popular outrage over this nation's crime rate. Like everyone else, judges watch television, read newspapers and magazines, listen to gossip. and are sometimes themselves victims. They receive the message trenchantly described in a recent book criticizing the insanity defense: "Perhaps the bottom line of all these complaints is that *guilty people go free*—guilty people who do not have to accept judgment or responsibility for what they have done and are not held accountable for their actions....These are not cases in which the defendant is *alleged* to have committed a crime. *Everyone knows he did it.*" Although understandable as an expression of uninformed public opinion, such a viewpoint ought not to serve as the basis for judicial decisionmaking; for it misapprehends the very meaning of guilt....[84]

The Justice Department's position on post-Hinckley insanity defense reform illuminated the issue: "What [the IDRA Act] is really saying [is], how do we get a hook into this person, so that he isn't going to go out and do this again to me, to any of my family, or to my brothers and sisters...If, you are so disturbed mentally that it mani-

---

81. Mickenberg, *supra* note 22, at 948; see also *id.* (discussing heuristic response of defense's supporters). On the impact of psychological data on legislators, *see* Lasswell, *Legislative Policy, Conformity and Psychiatry*, in BY REASON OF INSANITY: ESSAYS ON PSYCHIATRY AND THE LAW 47, 58-59 (L.Z. Freedman ed. 1983).

82. This is made explicit in Kelley, *supra* note 56, at 108 ("it is precisely common sense with which attribution theory is concerned"). *See generally,* Sherwin, *Dialects and Dominance: A Study of Rhetorical Fields in the Law of Confessions,* 136 U. PA. L. REV. 729 (1988).

83. United States v. Lyons, 731 F. 2d 243 (5th Cir. 1984). *Lyons* preceded the adoption of the Insanity Defense Reform Act of 1984 (IDRA). *See* 18 U.S.C. §20 (1988); *see supra* chapter 2 A 2 c.

84. *Lyons,* 739 F. 2d 994, 999-1000 (5th Cir. 1984) (Rubin, J., dissenting) (footnote omitted), *quoting,* in part, W. WINSLADE & J. ROSS, THE INSANITY PLEA 2-3 (1983) (emphasis added in opinion). *See* English, *supra* note 4, at 4 (post-*Hinckley* abolitionist movement the result of "reflexive, rather than reasoned, legislative action").

fests itself in…assassinations…, society has a right to put a hook into you …until I think it's demonstrated beyond a shadow of a doubt that you are no longer that type of danger to the community…The people really don't care if he couldn't help himself. They want to know what do you do to protect me."[85]

This type of decision making mimics what is characterized as "implicit personality theory:" "an untested, unconfirmed collection of ideas that people rely on to explain or predict others."[86] Thus, if OCS is a "prereflective attitude"—exemplified by the attitude of "What I know is 'self-evident;' it is 'what everybody knows'"[87]—then

---

85. *Proceedings of the Forty-Sixth Judicial Conference of the District of Columbia Circuit*, 111 F.R.D. 91, 227 (1985) (remarks of Assistant U.S. Attorney General Stephen Trott). *See generally*, Nisbett et al., *Popular Induction: Information Is Not Necessarily Informative*, in J. Carroll & J. Payne, *supra* note 25, at 113, 128 (in assessing impact of "sheer number of instances" as against "instances of some emotional interest," researchers have found that "emotional instance *in every case* carried the day") (emphasis added).

On the role of heuristic decision making in involuntary *civil commitment* law (following the commission of a criminal act by an individual whose application for civil hospitalization had been denied), *see* Perlin, *Morality and Pretextuality, Psychiatry and Law: Of "Ordinary Common Sense," Heuristic Reasoning, and Cognitive Dissonance*, 19 BULL. AM. ACAD. PSYCHIATRY & L. 131 (1991) (Perlin, *Morality*); Bagby & Atkinson, *The Effects of Legislative Reform on Civil Commitment Admission Rates: A Critical Analysis*, 6 BEHAV. SCI. & L. (1988) ("publicly salient events such as a heinous murder of an innocent victim at the hands of a discharged mental patient, or community intolerance of deviance, may have the effect of increasing the rate of commitment"). On its role in incompetency to stand trial proceedings, *see* Perlin, *Are Court Competent to Decide Questions of Competency? Stripping the Facade from* United States v. Charters, 38 U. KAN. L. REV. 957 (1990) (Perlin *Charters*). On how heuristics influence pretextual legal decisions, *see* Perlin, *Pretexts and Mental Disability Law: The Case of Competency*, 47 U. MIAMI L. REV. (1993) (in press) (Perlin, *Pretexts*).

86. Saks & Kidd, *supra* note 25, at 135 n. 15, *citing* Bruner & Tagiuri, *The Perception of People*, in 2 HANDBOOK OF SOCIAL PSYCHOLOGY (G. Lindzey ed. 1954).

87. Sherwin, *supra* note 82, at 737. *See also*, Sherwin, *A Matter of Voice and Plot: Belief and Suspicion in Legal Story Telling*, 87 MICH. L. REV. 543, 595 (1988) ("Common sense probably would not surrender concrete evidentiary truth to abstract constitutional principle…"). Professor Cunningham has offered this "translation:"

More commonly, the phrase suggests a kind of practical wisdom shared by people generally that enables them to manage and solve life's problems. This kind of common sense is often opposed to intellectual learning, usually with the observation that common sense is sufficient, or even superior, for navigating through the world in a sound and stable way.

Cunningham, *A Linguistic Analysis of the Meanings of "Search" in the Fourth*

the use of the heuristic bias becomes even more pernicious in insanity defense decision making.[88]

3. The Heuristic Life of Expert Witnesses and Clinicians

The problem before us is exacerbated by the reality of an impressive universe of evidence that demonstrates persuasively that mental health professionals are just as susceptible to heuristic biases as are lay persons.[89] These biases affect clinical judgment and psychiatric decision making in much the same way that they affect decisions made by individuals without mental health backgrounds.[90]

Amendment: A Search for Common Sense, 73 Iowa L. Rev. 541, 545 (1988).

For a paradigmatic judicial characterization in a collateral area, *see* State v. Vaughan, 268 S.C. 119, 232 S.E. 2d 328, 331 (1977) ("The effect of drunkenness on the mind and on men's actions...is a fact known to everyone"), *quoting* 22 C.J.S., Criminal Law §66 (1961).

88. The public's view that the use of the insanity defense exculpates the factually guilty makes this even more problematic. *See e.g.* Sherwin, *supra* note 87, at 595: "Can common sense make sense of interpretive principles, deriving, say, from a constitutional text, which trump our 'natural' inclination to blame the factually guilty?" On the important difference between *factual* guilt and *moral* guilt, *see* Seidman, *Factual Guilt and the Burger Court: An Examination of Continuity and Change in Criminal Procedure*, 80 Colum. L. Rev. 436 (1980); Arenella, *Rethinking the Functions of Criminal Procedure: The Warren and Burger Courts' Competing Ideologies*, 72 Geo. L.J. 185 (1983).

89. *See generally*, Bersoff, *supra* note 25, at 351-62; *see also*, Jackson, *Psychiatric Decision-Making for the Courts: Judges, Psychiatrists, Lay People?* 9 Int'l J. L. & Psychiatry 507 (1986) (psychiatric decisionmakers may be as susceptible to heuristic bias as lay persons); Bagby, *The Indigenous Paraprofessional and Involuntary Civil Commitment: A Return to Community Values*, 25 Canad. Psychol. 167, 172 (1984) (psychiatric judgment is often "inextricably woven with social class bias"); *see generally*. Perlin, *supra* note 62, at 397-98 n. 170 (*citing* sources).

There is some evidence that these biases affect different mental health professionals in different ways. *See e.g.*, Rogers & Webster, *Assessing Treatability in Mentally Disordered Offenders*, 13 Law & Hum. Behav. 19, 24 (1989), discussing findings reported in M. Jackson, "Understanding the Concepts of Need for Treatment/Treatability" (paper presented at the annual conference of the American Academy of Psychiatry and Law, Albuquerque, NM, Oct. 1985) (social workers most optimistic about patients' treatability, psychiatric nurses the least so); *compare* Homant & Kennedy, *Subjective Factors in Clinicians' Judgments of Insanity: Comparison of a Hypothetical Case and an Actual Case*, 18 Prof. Psychology: Res. & Prac. 439 (1987) (psychiatrists surveyed significantly more sympathetic to insanity defense than were psychologists).

90. *See* Jackson, *supra* note 89, at 519 ("in clinical practice, a knowledge of how heuristics and biases work to affect judgment may be every bit as important as clinical acumen *per se*"); Jackson, *The Clinical Assessment and Prediction of Violent Behavior: Toward a Scientific Analysis*, 16 Crim. Just. & Behav. 114,

Mental health professionals—even *experienced* mental health professionals[91]—have been found to be susceptible to the availability heuristic, the representative heuristic and the illusion of validity heuristic.[92] So, if a clinician has been repeatedly exposed to a certain type of disorder, that diagnostic category may show a relatively permanent increase in availability.[93] And, the representativeness bias can cause "scripted thinking" which leads clinicians to make erroneous predictions of violence in involuntary civil commitment settings.[94] Finally, the illusion of validity causes clinicians to place an inappropriately high level of confidence in judgments that are based upon data that actually decreases diagnostic accuracy, and to be resistant

---

115-18 (1989) (same); C. WEBSTER, R. MENZIES & M. JACKSON, CLINICAL ASSESSMENTS BEFORE TRIAL 121 ("The rules of psychiatric decision-making are not substantially divergent from the canons and heuristics of everyday life"). On lawyers' susceptibility to heuristic thinking, *see* Bundy, *The Policy in Favor of Settlement in an Adversary System*, 44 HASTINGS L.J. 1, 19 (1992).

91.   *See* Bersoff, *supra* note 25, at 360; Oskamp, *supra* note 53; Garb, *Clinical Judgment, Clinical Training, and Professional Experience*, 105 PSYCHOLOG. BULL. 387 (1989). *Compare* Mack & Weinland, *Not Guilty By Reason of Insanity Evaluations: A Study of Defendants and Examiners*, 17 J. CRIM. JUST. 39 (1989) (insanity assessments varied with examiner's length of professional experience).

92.   On availability, *see* Bersoff, *supra* note 25, at 340-41, discussing research reported in Snyder & Thomsen, *Interactions Between Therapists and Clients: Hypothesis Testing and Behavioral Confirmation*, in TURK & SALOVEY, *supra* note 51, at 133, and in Higgins et al., *Individual Construct Accessibility and Subjective Impressions and Recall*, 43 J. PERSONALITY & SOC. PSYCHOLOGY 35. On representativeness, *see* Bersoff, *supra* note 25, at 342-43, discussing research reported in Kahneman & Tversky, *supra* note 37, and in Jordan et al., *Attributional Biases in Clinical Decision Making*, in TURK & SALOVEY, *supra* note 51, at 90, 99. On the illusion of validity, *see* Bersoff, *supra* note 25, at 346-47, discussing research reported in, *inter alia*, Snyder & Thomsen, *supra*, at 131, and in Houts & Galante, *The Impact of Evaluative Disposition and Subsequent Information on Clinical Impressions*, 3 J. SOC'L & CLIN. PSYCHOLOGY 201 (1985).

93.   Snyder & Thomsen, *supra* note 92; Higgins, *supra* note 92. On the ethical implications of clinicians' "slotting" their patients, *see* Perlin, *Power Imbalances in Therapeutic and Forensic Relationships*, 9 BEHAV. SCI. & L. 111 (1991).
      The same heuristic affects non-clinical staff. *See Sonya Live, supra* note 48, at 4: "I work at Koskoney Jail in Chicago in the psych unit. And I find my experience with a lot of people is that the malingerers…if they are going to trial and pleading the insanity plea, they go off to a mental hospital, they come back. A lot of times they fool the psychiatrist…" (comments of "Pamela in Illinois," a telephone caller).

94.   Kahneman & Tversky, *supra* note 37; Saks & Kidd, *supra* note 25; Jordan et al., *supra* note 92.

to change from their initial clinical impressions.[95]

The use of such heuristic devices may also explain why clinicians frequently rely on a wide array of nonclinical factors—including sociodemographic and legal variables—in making treatment recommendations. One retrospective study, for example, revealed that marital status, personality characteristics and prior criminal history were the strongest discriminants, while clinical variables such as prior treatment response, psychometric data and diagnosis were relied on minimally.[96] Another investigation showed that the only variable that distinguished those determined to be dangerous from those determined not to be was the alleged crime: the more serious the crime, the more likely that the examiner would find dangerousness.[97] Further, there was a discrepancy between the criteria actually used by the examiners (the crime's seriousness) and the criteria that the examiners reported actually animated their decisions (presence of impaired or delusional thinking).[98]

In reviewing the literature, Professor Bersoff has thus concluded:

> These incorrect intuitive judgments result from the use of simplifying heuristic strategies in all situations where decisionmakers' cognitive capacities cannot otherwise efficiently process information. As the research illustrates, judgmental errors are not limited to lay decisionmakers but have been observed in the work of mental health professionals arriving at diagnoses, formulating treatment regimens, and predicting behavior.[99]

---

95. Snyder & Thomson, *supra* note 92; Houts & Galante, *supra* note 92; Dawes et al., *Clinical Versus Actuarial Judgment*, 243 SCIENCE 1668, 1672 (1989); R. NISBETT & L. ROSS, *supra* note 25, at 160.

96. Ashford, *Factors Used in Treatment Discriminations Used in Ohio Drug Legislation*, 6 BEHAV. SCI. & L. 139 (1988); *see also*, Rogers, *Ethical Dilemmas in Forensic Evaluations*, 5 BEHAV. SCI. & L. 149, 152 (1987) (mental health professionals unduly influenced by "extraneous sociodemographic variables" such as status, race and sex); Menzies, Webster & Sepejak, *Dimensions of Dangerousness: Evaluating the Accuracy of Psychometric Predictions of Violence Among Forensic Patients*, 9 LAW & HUM. BEHAV. 49 (1985) (same).

97. Cocozza & Steadman, *The Failure of Psychiatric Predictions of Dangerousness: Clear and Convincing Evidence*, 29 RUTGERS L. REV. 1084, 1096 (1976); *see also*, Quinsey & Ambtman, *Variables Affecting Psychiatrists' and Teachers' Assessments of the Dangerousness of Mentally Ill Offenders*, 47 J. CLIN. & CONSULTING PSYCHOLOGY 353 (1978).

98. Cocozza & Steadman, *supra* note 97, at 1096.

99. Bersoff, *supra* note 25, at 350; *see generally*, TURK & SALOVEY, *supra* note 51.

These heuristic errors infect clinician decision making in incompetency to stand trial decisions, in predictions of violence, and in malingering assessments,[100] as well as in insanity defense evaluations.[101] One study thus found that experts' pre-existing attitudes about the insanity defense substantially and significantly affected their evaluations of marginal test cases.[102] In another study, clinical psychology graduate students who believed they had been appointed to evaluate a defendant by defense counsel were significantly more likely to find the defendant insane than were those who believed that they had been appointed by the prosecution.[103]

While a third study did not find this appointment bias,[104] its results showed that, in the face of ambiguity, clinicians were likely to form ultimate opinions (rather than state that they required more information upon which to base such a conclusion), that much of the clinical decision making was idiosyncratic, and that experienced cli-

---

100. *See* Bersoff, *supra* note 25, at 354-60, discussing research reported in, *inter alia*, Menzies et al., *The Nature and Consequences of Forensic Psychiatric Decision-Making*, 27 CAN. J. PSYCHIATRY 463 (incompetency to stand trial); Klassen & O'Connor, *A Prospective Study of Predictors of Violence in Adult Male Mental Health Admissions*, 12 LAW & HUM. BEHAV. 143 (1988) (violence predictions); Ogloff, *The Admissibility of Expert Testimony Regarding Malingering and Deception*, 8 BEHAV. SCI. & L. 27 (1990) (malingering). *See supra* chapter 5 C 1.

101. Another collateral question asks the extent to which clinicians actually know what the insanity standard is. Research by Dr. Richard Rogers and his colleagues reveals that an astounding eighty-eight percent of experienced forensic mental health professionals surveyed did not know the operative insanity standard in their jurisdiction. Rogers et al., *Forensic Psychiatrists' and Psychologists' Understanding of Insanity: Misguided Expertise?* 33 CAN. J. PSYCHIATRY 691 (1988); *see also*, Rogers & Turner, *Understanding Insanity: A National Survey of Forensic Psychiatrists and Psychologists*, 7 HEALTH L. IN CAN. 71 (1987); *see generally*, Perlin, *Pretexts*, *supra* note 85, manuscript at 31 n. 77 (collecting sources on the frequency with which mental health evaluators confuse the concepts of insanity and incompetency).

102. Homant & Kennedy, *Judgment of Legal Insanity as a Function of Attitude Toward the Insanity Defense*, 8 INT'L J. L. & PSYCHIATRY 67 (1986); *see also*, Homant & Kennedy, *supra* note 89. The correlation between attitude and a determination of whether a hypothetical defendant was insane was so high that, according to the authors, it would occur less than one time in 1000 by chance. *Id.* at 442.

103. Otto, *Bias and Expert Testimony of Mental Health Professionals*, 7 BEHAV. SCI. & L. 267 (1989).

104. Beckham et al., *Decision Making and Examiner Bias in Forensic Expert Recommendations for Not Guilty By Reason of Insanity*, 13 LAW & HUM. BEHAV. 79 (1989).

nicians came to "highly divergent conclusions" about the defendant's mental state.[105]

Again, Professor Bersoff has summed this research up in this manner:

> Despite attempts to educate clinicians about heuristics, behavior decision theory, information processing, and the availability of actuarial or mechanical methods that have been shown for decades to produce markedly more accurate and less biased clinical decisions,[106] the vast majority of clinicians persist, either in ignorance or with misplaced confidence, in using instruments of questionable validity and ignore relevant factors that contribute to more accurate decision making.[107]

In reviewing some of these studies, Michael Bagby concluded that they revealed that intuitive or implicit beliefs rather than expert knowledge often guided examiners' decisions.[108] We ignore these findings, though, and continue to assume that true expertise drives the forensic assessment process. The social significance of this error is dramatically magnified when it is next weighed in the context of the power of "ordinary common sense" (OCS).

D. "Ordinary Common Sense" (OCS): The Unconsciousness of Legal Decision Making

1. Introduction

The positions frequently taken by Chief Justice Rehnquist in criminal procedure cases best highlight the power of "ordinary common sense" (OCS) as an unconscious animator of legal decision making.[109] Such positions frequently demonstrate a total lack of awareness of the underlying psychological issues and focus on such

---

105. Bersoff, *supra* note 25, at 353-54 n. 120.
106. *See* Dawes et al., *supra* note 95, at 1668.
107. Bersoff, *supra* note 25, at 360.
108. *See* Bagby, *supra* note 89, at 170-71; Bagby, *The Deprofessionalization of Civil Commitment*, 29 CANAD. PSYCHOLOGY 234 (1988).
109. *See e.g.*, Grigsby v. Mabry, 569 F. Supp. 1273, 1332 (E.D. Ark. 1983), *aff'd*, 758 F. 2d 226 (8th Cir. 1985), *rev'd sub. nom.* Lockhart v. McCree, 476 U.S. 162 (1986), relying on, *inter alia*, Berry, *Death- Qualification and the "Fireside Induction*," 5 U. ARK.-L.R. L. REV. 1 , to define "fireside induction" as "those common sense, empirical generalizations about human behavior which derive from introspection, anecdotal evidence, and culturally transmitted beliefs").

superficial issues as whether a putatively mentally disabled criminal defendant bears a "normal appearance."[110]

The Chief Justice is not the first jurist to exhibit this sort of closed-mindedness.[111] Trial judges will typically say, "he [the defendant] doesn't look sick to me," or, even more revealingly, "he is as healthy as you or me."[112] In short, where defendants do not conform to "popular images of 'craziness,'"[113] the notion of a handicapping

---

110. Perlin, *supra* note 24 at 83 n. 811; *see supra* V C 3. Rehnquist's opinions reflect the "meta-myths" of "fear of feigning," *see* Ake v. Oklahoma, 470 U.S. 68, 87, 91 (1985) (Rehnquist, J., dissenting); Ford v. Wainwright, 477 U.S. 399, 435 (1986) (Rehnquist, J., dissenting), of stereotypical visions of mental disability informed primarily by surface views of defendants' external appearance, *see* Wainwright v. Greenfield, 474 U.S. 284, 297-98 (1986) (Rehnquist, J., concurring), and of mental illness as an improperly exculpatory excuse, *see* Colorado v. Connelly, 479 U.S. 157, 163-69 (1987).

   In a revealing speech, the Chief Justice discussed the impact of public opinion on judicial decision making: "Somewhere 'out there'—beyond the walls of the courthouse—run currents and tides of public opinion which lap at the courthouse door...[I]f these tides of public opinion are sufficiently great and sufficiently sustained, they will very likely have an effect upon the decision of some of the cases decided within the courthouse. This is not a case of judges "knuckling under" to public opinion, and cravenly abandoning their oaths of office. Judges, *so long as they are relatively normal human beings*, can no more escape being influenced by public opinion in the long run than can people working at other jobs." Rehnquist, *Constitutional Law and Public Opinion*, 20 SUFFOLK L. REV. 751, 768 (1986) (emphasis added).

   The degree to which Rehnquist's views mirror public consensus on "craziness," the appearance of normality, and criminal nonresponsibility as an exculpating condition is probably not coincidental.

111. *See also*, Haney, *Psychology and Legal Change: On the Limits of a Factual Jurisprudence*, 4 LAW & HUM. BEHAV. 147, 154 (1980) ("Courts regularly and routinely make assumptions about how and why people behave in certain ways"). For a rare example of a judicial opinion "unpacking" the mythology that serves as the building blocks of "ordinary common sense," *see* United States v. Lyons, 739 F. 2d 994, 999-1000 (5th Cir. 1984) (Rubin, J., dissenting), discussed *supra* text accompanying note 84.

112. Perlin, *Psychiatric Testimony in a Criminal Setting*, 3 BULL. AM. ACAD. PSYCHIATRY & L. 143, 147 (1975).

113. Lasswell, *Foreword*, in R. ARENS, THE INSANITY DEFENSE xi (1974). For an empirical evaluation of how defendants who do so conform are differentially treated by prosecutors and by courts, *see* Hochstedler, *Twice-Cursed? The Mentally Disordered Criminal Defendant*, 14 CRIM. JUST. & BEHAV. 251, 260 (1987) (mentally disabled defendants were prosecuted in "significant[ly]" different ways from the general population; courts commonly subjected mentally disabled defendants to court-ordered treatment and were reluctant to release on their own recognizance previously hospitalized defendants; prosecutors showed "selective leniency," issuing charges *less* frequently to the formerly-hospitalized, but *more* frequently to defendants with histories of chronic health problems).

mental disability condition is flatly, and unthinkingly, rejected.[114] Similarly, the "slippery slope" conflation of mental illness and dangerousness is blindly accepted.[115] Views such as these[116] reflect a false kind of "ordinary common sense."[117] In criminal procedure, OCS presupposes two "self-evident" truths: "First, everyone knows how to assess an individual's behavior. Second, everyone knows when to

---

On the ways that correctional officials perceive mentally ill inmates less favorably than other inmates, *see* Kropp et al., *The Perceptions of Correctional Officers Toward Mentally Disordered Offenders*, 12 INT'L J. L. & PSYCHIATRY 181 (1989).

114. Arens graphically reproduces transcripts of two competency hearings conducted by the same judge on the same day in which the judge merely asks the defendant the date, the names of the President and the Vice-President, and the Washington Senators' standing in the American League. R. ARENS, *supra* note 113, at 77-79. The motion of the defendant who answered the questions correctly was denied, while the defendant who knew only the President's name was ordered held for psychiatric evaluation. *Id. See generally*, Perlin, *supra* note 24, at 83-84 n.811.

115. Jones v. United States, 463 U.S. 354, 365 n. 14 (1983), *quoting* Overholser v. O'Beirne, 302 F. 2d 852, 861 (D. C. Cir. 1961) (Burger, J.) ("To describe the theft of watches and jewelry as 'nondangerous' is to confuse danger with violence. Larceny is usually less violent than murder or assault, but in terms of public policy the purpose of the [post- insanity acquittal commitment] statute is the same as to both"). *Compare* Schmidt, *Supreme Court Decision Making on Insanity Acquittees Does Not Depend on Research Conducted By The Behavioral Science Community:* Jones v. United States, 12 J. PSYCHIATRY & L. 507, 512 (1984) ("The empirical evidence does not support the 'common sense' of the majority in *Jones* as much as it supports the responding speculation of the dissent").

116. *See also*, Amsterdam, *The Supreme Court and the Rights of Suspects in Criminal Cases*, 45 N.Y.U. L. REV. 785, 805-09 (1980) (discussing Supreme Court's implicit use of OCS in deciding the lead confession-coercion case of Brown v. Mississippi, 297 U.S. 278 (1936)).

Such judgments are not limited to cases involving mentally disabled defendants. Complaining that "[f]ar too little systematic attention has been focused upon the influence of political, racial, and moral idiosyncratic factors in judicial decisionmaking," Professor Randall Kennedy has noted Chief Justice Burger's "sympathy" and "admiration" for the "'law-abiding' and 'self-sufficient'" Amish people, as reflected in his opinion in Wisconsin v. Yoder, 406 U.S. 205, 212-13 (1972). Kennedy, McCleskey v. Kemp: *Race, Capital Punishment, and the Supreme Court*, 101 HARV. L. REV. 1388, 1417 n. 141 (1988).

117. Sherwin, *supra* note 82, at 737. One important example of such thinking is reflected in courts' persistent adherence to patterns of jury instructions in spite of overwhelming social science evidence as to the instructions' confusion. *See infra*...Professors Steele and Thornburg thus articulate the OCS position: "Since [judges and lawyers] understand the instructions, they believe that jurors understand them as well." Steele & Thornburg, *Jury Instructions: A Persistent Failure to Communicate*, 67 N. C. L. REV. 77, 99 (1988).

blame someone for doing wrong."[118]

Empirical investigations similarly corroborate the inappropriate application of OCS to insanity defense decision making.[119] Judges "unconsciously express public feelings...reflect[ing] community attitudes and biases because they are 'close' to the community."[120] Virtually no members of the public can actually articulate what the substantive insanity defense test is.[121] The public is seriously misinformed about both the "extensiveness and consequences" of an insanity defense plea.[122] And, the public explicitly and consistently rejects any such defense substantively broader than the "wild beast" test.[123]

---

118. Sherwin, *supra* note 82, at 738; *see also*, Doob & Roberts, *supra* note 23, at 275 (public "appears simply to accept the information they have as adequate" in assessing perceived leniency of criminal sentences); Stalans & Diamond, *Formation and Change in Lay Evaluations of Criminal Sentencing: Misperception and Discontent*, 14 LAW & HUM. BEHAV. 199 (1990); *see generally*, PUBLIC ATTITUDES TO SENTENCING: SURVEYS FROM FIVE COUNTRIES (N. Walker & M. Hough eds. 1988). *Cf.* Kelman, *Interpretive Construction in the Substantive Criminal Law*, 33 STAN. L. REV. 591, 671-72 (1981) ("dominant legal thought is nothing but some more or less plausible common-wisdom banalities, superficialities, and generalities").

119. *See e.g.*, Finkel et al., *Insanity Defenses: From the Jurors' Perspectives*, 9 LAW & PSYCHOL. REV. 77, 92 (1985) (characterizing the layman's perspective toward the insanity defense as reflecting "intuitive, common sense"). *Cf.* State v. Van Horn, 528 So. 2d 529, 530 (Fla. Dist. App. 1988) (rebuttal lay witness provided jury with "probative perceptions of *normalcy*") (emphasis added).

120. Arens & Susman, *Judges, Jury Charges, and Insanity*, 13 HOWARD L.J. 1, 34 n. 43 (1966). The caselaw reflects each of these traps. *See e.g.*, Regina v. Turner, 1 Q.B. 834, 841 (1975) ("Jurors do not need psychiatrists to tell them how ordinary folk who are not suffering from any mental illness are likely to react to the stresses and strains of life"). Professor Finkel's research suggests that *expert witnesses* reinforce this sense of conventional morality as well. N. FINKEL, INSANITY ON TRIAL 349 (1985).

121. Of 434 Delaware residents surveyed, only one gave a "reasonably good approximation" of the insanity test then operative in that jurisdiction. Hans & Slater, *"Plain Crazy:" Lay Definitions of Legal Insanity*, 7 INT'L J. L. & PSYCHIATRY 105-06 (1984). *See also*, Rogers et al., *supra* note 101 (eighty-eight percent of experienced forensic witnesses did not know the correct substantive insanity standard in their jurisdiction).

122. Hans, *An Analysis of Public Attitudes Toward the Insanity Defense*, 24 CRIMINOL. 393, 411 (1986).

123. Roberts, Golding & Fincham, *Implicit Theories of Criminal Responsibility Decision Making and the Insanity Defense*, 11 LAW & HUM. BEHAV. 207, 226 (1987). *Cf.* Washington v. United States, 390 F. 2d 444, 445 (D.C. Cir. 1967) ("Presumably, [the 18th century] jury and the witnesses knew a wild beast when they saw one"). The nineteenth century prosecutors also knew the powers of

These realities may lead into yet one more trap. While judges and attorneys are accustomed to weighing and interpreting several factors at once, conflict arises here "from the attorney's fear that a jury will reject, or will be less impressed by, explanations that require complex analysis and a lengthy rationale."[124] Yet other research shows that mock jurors often use their own "schemas" when deciding the outcome of an insanity defense trial, and that variables such as the burden or standard of proof may not have a significant effect on their deliberations.[125]

OCS is an incomplete and imperfect tool by which to assess criminality. Anthropologists have shown that the content and style of expression of common sense varies markedly from one place from one place to another.[126] Also, OCS cannot answer such questions as "how can a reasoned argument hope to dissuade a court that is committed to a contrary view of human nature?"[127] Thus, the truth claims to which OCS gives rise are "complex and conflicting and revelatory perhaps of diverse situational factors, such as geography, class, education, familial background, religion, and current events..."[128]

OCS. *See e.g.*, Spiegel & Spiegel, *Not Guilty of Murder By Reason of Paroxysmal Insanity: The "Mad" Doctors Vs. "Common Sense" Doctors in an 1865 Trial*, 62 PSYCHIATRIC Q. 51 (1991).

124. Anderten, Staulcup & Grisso, *On Being Ethical in Legal Places*, 11 PROF'L PSYCHOLOGY 764, 769 (1980). *See also id.*: "Thus, the psychologist might be led into this more simplistic manner of reasoning that scientifically and ethically misrepresents the complexity of most psychological conclusions and potentially distorts the results."

125. Ogloff, *A Comparison on Insanity Defense Standards on Juror Decision Making*, 15 LAW & HUM. BEHAV. 509, 524 (1991); *see also*, Severance & Loftus, *Improving the Ability of Jurors to Comprehend and Apply Criminal Jury Instructions*, 17 LAW & SOC'Y REV. 153 (1992).

126. Sherwin, *supra* note 82, at 738, and see sources cited at *id.* n. 19. *See generally*, C. LÉVI-STRAUSS, STRUCTURAL ANTHROPOLOGY (1965). For a historical reading suggesting that insanity defense decision making flowed from "the prevailing Protestant religious morality," *see* Dain & Carlson, *Moral Insanity in the United States, 1835-1866*, 117 AM. J. PSYCHIATRY 785, 787 (1960). *Cf.* N. WALKER, CRIME AND INSANITY IN ENGLAND 82 (1973) (prosecutor's characterization of defense forensic expert witness as a "Jew physician" in 1801 trial), *see supra* chapter 5, note 78.

127. Sherwin, *supra* note 82, at 755.

128. *Id.* at 829. On the way different ethnic and socioeconomic groups perceive and define deviance, *see* Dohrenwend & Chin-Song, *Social Status and Attitudes Toward Psychological Disorder: The Problem of Tolerance of Deviance*, 32 AM. SOC. REV. 417 (1967); *see also*, Gusfield, *On Legislating Morals: The Symbolic Process of Designating Deviance*, 56 CALIF. L. REV. 54, 55-56 (1968) ("To

The dominance of OCS is reflected in the Supreme Court's opinions in *Coy v. Iowa*,[129] a constitutional criminal procedure decision holding that the placement of a screen between a child sexual assault victim and the defendant violated the latter's confrontation clause rights. In *Coy*, Justice Scalia first precedentially invoked the literary and cultural underpinnings of OCS by citing to the Bible and to Shakespeare, and then explained his use of references to and quotations from antiquity as part of his effort to convey "that there is something deep in human nature that regards face-to-face confrontation...as 'essential to a fair trial.'" [130]

To ultimately buttress his conclusion that this condition persists, Scalia quotes at length from remarks made by former President Eisenhower on the role played by face-to-face confrontation in the code of social justice in his home town of Abilene, Kansas:

> In Abilene, he said, it was necessary to "[m]eet anyone face to face with whom you disagree. You could not sneak up on him from behind, or do any damage to him, without suffering the penalty of an outraged citizenry...In this country, if someone dislikes you, he must come up in front. He cannot hide behind the shadow."[131]

---

assume a common culture or a normative consensus in American society, as in most modern societies, is to ignore the deep and divisive role of class, ethnic, religious, status, and regional culture conflicts which often produce widely opposing definitions of goodness, truth, and moral virtue"). *Compare* Myers, *Social Background and the Sentencing Behavior of Judges*, 26 CRIMINOL. 649, 669 (1988) (older judges found to be more lenient to the "selected, advantaged offenders, in particular, those who were white and older"), to Willis & Willis, *The Police and Child Abuse: An Analysis of Police Decisions to Report Illegal Behavior*, 26 CRIMINOL. 695, 711 (1988) (police more likely to report white families for child physical and sexual abuse, perhaps reflecting "negative stereotyping of black life-style and behavior").

129. 487 U.S. 1012 (1988). Justice Scalia's majority opinion was for an "odd bedfellows" majority of himself, Justices Brennan, White, Marshall, Stevens and O'Connor.

130. *See id.* at 1015-16, *quoting* Acts 25:16, and Richard II, act 1, sc. 1; *id.* at 1017, *quoting*, in part, Pointer v. Texas, 380 U.S. 400, 404 (1965). Directly after citing to the biblical and Shakespearian sources, Scalia added: "We have never doubted, *therefore*, that the Confrontation Clause guarantees the defendant a face-to-face meeting with witnesses appearing before the trier of fact." *Id.* at 1016 (emphasis added)

131. *Id.* at 1017, *quoting* Pollitt, *The Right of Confrontation: Its History and Modern Dress*, 8 J. PUB. L. 381 (1959). Scalia followed with this observation: "The phrase exists, 'Look me in the eye and say that.'" *Id.*

As a result of "these human feelings of what is necessary for fairness,"[132] the right to confrontation "contributes to the establishment of a system in which the perception as well as the reality of fairness prevails."[133]

Dissenting Justice Blackmun (joined by Chief Justice Rehnquist) specifically criticized the "weakness" of the majority's opinion as reflected in its reliance on "literature, anecdote, and dicta."[134] Demurring to the assertion that "there is something deep in human nature" that considers confrontation critical, Blackmun relied instead on Wigmore's treatise (that expressed a contrary opinion as to the essentiality of confrontation at common law), and concluded, somewhat archly: "I find Dean Wigmore's statement infinitely more persuasive than President Eisenhower's recollection of Kansas justice...or the words Shakespeare placed in the mouth of his Richard II concerning the best means of ascertaining the truth."[135]

Here, in a case that, like the insanity defense, can be expected to raise powerful unconscious feelings in jurors, judges, academics and others,[136] the dilemma of OCS as a vehicle for the establishment of constitutional policy should be clear: Justice Scalia invests human nature (based on the archetypal historical stories of the Bible and Shakespeare, and on President Eisenhower's *fin de siècle* notions of "justice") with a constitutional dimension only tepidly replied to in Justice Blackmun's dissent.[137] Neither considers the meretricious power of OCS in the formulation of this policy; neither acknow-

---

132. *Coy*, 487 U.S. at 1017.
133. *Id.* at 1019, *quoting* Lee v. Illinois, 476 U.S. 530, 540 (1986).
134. *Coy*, 487 U.S. at 1028 (Blackmun, J., dissenting). The Chief Justice apparently failed to see the irony in this critique of Scalia's opinion. *Cf.* Wainwright v. Greenfield, 474 U.S. 284, 297-98 (1986) (Rehnquist, J., concurring) (relying on an OCS-ical "reading" of external manifestations of mental illness in determining whether a request for counsel following administration of *Miranda* warnings was probative of sanity, noting that the defendant was not "incoherent or obviously confused or unbalanced").
135. *Coy*, 487 U.S. at 1028-29, *quoting*, in part, *id.* at 1017.
136. The defendant had been charged with sexually assaulting two thirteen year old girls while they were camped out in the back yard of an adjoining home. *See id.* at 1014.
137. On the other hand, Blackmun noted that Wigmore had discussed the passage from *Richard II* used by Scalia in his majority opinion, and that, according to Wigmore, the view of confrontation there expressed reflected an "earlier conception" that had merged with the principle of cross-examination by the time the Bill of Rights was ratified. *Id.* at 1029 n. 3 (Blackmun, J., dissenting).

ledges the "diverse situational factors" that inform our individualized concepts of OCS.[138]

Contemporaneous psychologists and researchers are no strangers to this issue. In a study of the beliefs of one hundred psychologists about depression and antidepressive behavior, consensus as to the truth of certain assertions ranged from near-complete to total disagreement. This prompted the study's director to conclude that far greater study was needed in exploring "the paradoxically unknown territory of 'what everybody knows' about depression."[139]

Similarly, the terrain of "what everybody knows" about insanity is perilously unchartered.[140] Yet, courts and legislatures regularly base decisions upon perceptions (or, more likely, misperceptions) about OCS and mental illness.[141] In a related context, for instance, recent research demonstrates that all segments of the public lacked substantial knowledge about battered woman syndrome, but subsamples of police officers and individuals eligible to be jurors knew the least.[142]

Just as OCS cannot be employed as the tool by which confessions or confrontation clause law developments can be charted, neither is it applicable to insanity defense law jurisprudence, where human behavior is very often opposite to what OCS would suggest. The reliance on such propositions by legal decisionmakers is risky, at best, and probably reflective, at its base, of a refusal to acknowledge the bases and applicability of psychodynamic principles to the questions at hand.[143]

---

138. Sherwin, *supra* note 82, at 755. The question remains open as to whether judges truly comprehend the reasons that animate their decision making. *See* Konecini & Ebbesen, *External Validity of Research in Legal Psychology*, 3 LAW & HUM. BEHAV. 39 (1979), as discussed in J. MONAHAN & L. WALKER, *supra* note 55, at 158 (great discrepancy found between "reasons" judges gave for sentencing decisions and factors that actually seemed to determine sentences).

139. Rippere, *Commonsense Beliefs About Depression and Antidepressive Behaviour: A Study of Social Consensus*, 15 BEHAV. RES. & THERAPY 465, 467 (1977); *see also*, Rippere, *"What's the Thing To Do When You're Feeling Depressed?"— A Pilot Study*, 15 BEHAV. RES. & THERAPY 185 (1977).

140. *See* Rogers et al., *supra* note 101 (on high level of misinformation on part of experienced forensic psychiatrists as to proper legal standard).

141. On how many of these decisions are pretextual, *see* Perlin, *Pretexts*, *supra* note 85; Perlin, *Morality*, *supra* note 85; *see generally infra* chapter 8 C.

142. Kronsky & Cutler, *The Battered Woman Syndrome: A Matter of Common Sense?* 2 FORENS. REPS. 173 (1989).

143. *See e.g.*, GROUP FOR THE ADVANCEMENT OF PSYCHIATRY, CRIMINAL RESPONSIBILITY AND PSYCHIATRIC TESTIMONY, Report # 26 (May, 1954), at 1 ("It is

2. OCS and the Insanity Defense

I propose that this reliance on OCS is one of the keys to an understanding of why and how our insanity defense jurisprudence has developed. Not only is it "prereflexive" and "self-evident,"[144] it is susceptible to precisely the type of idiosyncratic, reactive decision making that has traditionally typified insanity defense legislation and litigation.[145] It also ignores our rich, cultural, heterogenic fabric that makes futile any attempt at establishing a unitary level of "OCS" to govern decision making in an area where we have traditionally been willing to base substantive criminal law doctrine on medieval conceptions of sin, redemption and religiosity.[146] Paradoxically, the insanity defense is necessary precisely *because* it rebuts "common-sense everyday inferences about the meaning of conduct."[147] In the words of the Group for Advancement of Psychiatry, "The problem involves more than common sense."[148]

Extensive reliance on OCS infects all players in the drama. Careful research studies have thus found that judges, attorneys, legislators and mental health professionals all inappropriately employ irrelevant, stereotypical negative information in coming to conclusions on the related question of the potential future dangerousness of a mentally disabled criminal defendant.[149] What we *call* "common

---

abundantly clear that not all individuals are accountable—even the *M'Naghten* rules accept this—and that the problem involves more than 'common sense'") (*GAP Report*).

144. Sherwin, *supra* note 82, at 737. *Cf.* Sendor, *Crime as Communication: An Interpretative Theory of the Insanity Defense and the Mental Elements of Crime*, 74 GEO. L.J. 1371, 1406 n. 142 (1986) (*citing* sources rejecting suggestions that responsibility be assessed in light of "intrapsychic forces [and neurochemical reactions").

145. *See* Jones v. United States, 463 U.S. 354, 365 n. 14 (1983) (*quoting* Overholser v. O'Beirne, 302 F. 2d 852, 861 (D.C. Cir. 1961)), discussed *supra* at chapter 4 E 2 d.

146. *See* Gusfield, *supra* note 127, at 55-56.

147. Sendor, *supra* note 144, at 1372.

148. GAP REPORT, *supra* note 143, at 1. See also, Saks, *Judicial Attention to the Way the World Works*, 75 IOWA L. REV. 1011, 1015 n. 19 (1990) ("While much common sense is no doubt correct, other parts of the body of common sense knowledge are found, when finally put to a serious test, to be plain wrong").

149. Jackson, *supra* note 90, at 125-26; Perlin, *supra* note 62, at 397-98 n. 170; *see also,* Tversky & Kahneman I, *supra* note 31, at 18 (those with extensive training in statistics similarly inappropriately rely on heuristics in making probability assessments); Kahneman & Tversky, *supra* note 37, as reprinted in D. Kahneman, *supra* note 26, at 34-35 (sophisticated psychologists equally susceptible to

sense" is frequently nothing more than sanism: the irrational thought processes, founded on stereotype, that are at the roots of our incoherent insanity defense jurisprudence.[150]

This becomes even more important in the Burger-Rehnquist era. The public's perception that Warren Court decisions prevented the police from stopping crime led to an impairment of public confidence in the court; the Burger Court's rhetoric (although not always its decisions) reflected this impaired public confidence.[151] Justice White's concurring opinion in *Illinois v. Gates*,[152] expressing his fears that excluding reliable evidence of guilt where the police acted in good faith might weaken community confidence in the criminal justice system's integrity,[153] underscores the importance of the "instrumentalist perspective:" "the most important consideration is how the process appears to the community."[154] These perceptions help explain the further pretextual basis of insanity defense law.[155]

In short, unwitting reliance on OCS is a hidden animator of criminal justice decision making, whether the decision maker is a judge, a juror, a legislator or an expert witness. Because insanity defense judgments are shrouded in myth, weighed down by symbol, and arise frequently from unconscious and unarticulated motivations, it is especially important that we acknowledge OCS's power if we are to truly understand the operation of the defense.

---

representativeness heuristic). *See e.g.* Application of Miller, 73 Misc. 2d 690, 342 N.Y.S. 2d 315, 330 (Cty. Ct. 1972):

> If the science of psychiatry may, along with other sciences, properly depend upon empirical data, then may not this court also appropriately apply its own experience in similar cases...? In addition, may it not on the basis of plain common sense and in the absence of any more specific tools employ the past as one of the factors of predictability?

150. *See* Perlin, *supra* note 62; Perlin & Dorfman, *Sanism, Social Science, and the Development of Mental Disability Law Jurisprudence*, 11 Behav. Sci. & L. 47 (1993); *see infra* chapter 8 B.
151. Arenella, *supra* note 88, at 191-92.
152. 462 U.S. 213 (1983).
153. *Id.* at 246, 257-58 (White, J., concurring).
154. Arenella, *supra* note 88, at 202. Thus, the exclusionary rule may have a "delegitimatizing effect,...because it confirms the public's impression of a system that is all too willing to protect the victimizer instead of the victim." *Id.* at 238. *Compare* Alschuler, *supra* note 30.
155. *See* Perlin, *Pretexts, supra* note 85; Perlin, *Morality, supra* note 85; *see generally infra* chapter 8 C.

3. Jurisprudential Approaches: OCS and Deviance

In an effort to explore the jurisprudential factors which help shape the way that OCS and the instrumentalist perspective work in concert in insanity defense decision making, I will turn to the jurisprudential work of Professors Van Zandt and Sadurski. While neither scholar has examined the subject under consideration in this paper, the parallels should be obvious and their metaphoric content is especially appropriate.

The process of "coming to grips with the world" is known as "typification,"[156] the "characterizing [of] a current experience as an occurrence of a familiar type of experience."[157] Drawing on our "core of accumulated experience," our understanding of deviance "is based on the more visible types that are classified and brought to [us] every day."[158] When pressed to explain the *fact* of deviation, the layman will probably "redirect the question by talking about the *type of person* the deviant is thought to be: brutal, immature, irresponsible, vicious, inconsiderate, degenerate."[159]

---

156. Van Zandt, *supra* note 48, at 913 (*citing* Cicourel, *Interpretive Procedures and Normative Rules in the Negotiation of Status and Role*, in COGNITIVE SOCIOLOGY 11, 35 (1972)).

157. Van Zandt, *supra* note 48, at 914. Van Zandt's illustration exemplified typification of the mentally disabled (*Id.* (footnotes omitted)):

> [If] I am approached on a public street by an individual who appears disheveled and who is babbling incomprehensible sentences, I am likely to categorize that experience as one involving a mentally disturbed person whose condition is explainable by the presence of mental 'disease.' I may not know what 'disease' he has or what his long-term prognosis might be. It is sufficient for my practical purposes that I am able to understand this experience in that way, predict from that understanding this person's short-term behavior, and adjust my behavior accordingly. Although this process of typification is more noticeable in unusual situations, it is essential to everyday life. Routine and habit are the stuff that makes the world turn; without them, we would be forced to start from scratch on each occasion.

158. Van Zandt, *supra* note 48, at 915 n. 109, *citing* A. SCHULTZ, THE PHENOMENOLOGY OF THE SOCIAL WORLD 77, 80-82 (G. Walsh & F. Lehnert trans. 1982), and *id.* at 915 n. 112, *citing* Cohen, *Introduction*, in IMAGES OF DEVIANCE 9, 10 (S. Cohen ed. 1971). On the importance of visual images in juror and judicial assessment of insanity defenses, *see supra* V C 2-3.

159. Van Zandt, *supra* note 48, at 915 n. 112, *citing* Cohen, *supra* note 158 (emphasis in Van Zandt). This process of typification similarly affects juror decision making: the construction of the jurors' "story" depends significantly on jurors' OCS understanding of the way people behave in a given situation. Van Zandt, *supra* note 48, at 916 n. 115, *citing* Pennington & Hastie, *Evidence Evaluation in Complex Decision Making*, 51 J. PERS. & SOC. PSYCHOLOGY 242, 247 (1986).

To some extent, this is all a self-fulfilling prophecy: as long as we have faith in our stereotypes, we continue to treat others in ways "that actually elicit from them behaviors that support those stereotypes."[160] It is precisely this sort of stereotype that exemplifies sanist mythology. Thus, an important sanist myth is:

> Most mentally ill individuals are dangerous and frightening. They are invariably more dangerous than non-mentally ill persons, and such dangerousness is easily and accurately identified by experts. At best, persons with mental disabilities are simple and content, like children. Either *parens patriae* or police power supply a rationale for the institutionalization of all such individuals.[161]

This "world knowledge" is inherently expansive: the more problems such stocks of knowledge (or "formative contexts") solve, "the firmer is the individual's acceptance of it." We also seek to vindicate our OCS ideas so that they will be accurate "for all foreseeable practical purposes."[162] This type of thought processing leads to the "attribution" heuristic:[163] where new experiences do not "fit neatly" into our pre-existing database, we will "engage in complex elaborations" prior to relinquishing our theories. Consequently, "simple, rational argumentation will be unavailing to change them."[164] Typification, for instance, can lead therapists to "slot" their patients into categories and to then prescribe similar regimens for all fitting into such a slot.[165]

These OCS formulations differ radically from theories constructed by philosophers and scientists: the latter, generally seeking a broader perspective, and searching for a "high degree of systematicity and consistency" within a theoretical structure, will generally base their views on "a fuller information set than that employed by individuals facing practical problems." By contrast, the ordinary individual's orientation toward particular issues will often "trump" concerns for consistency.[166] This often leads to selective use of social science

---

160. Van Zandt, *supra* note 48, at 926 n. 158, *quoting* Snyder, *When Belief Creates Reality*, 18 ADVANCES IN EXP. SOC. PSYCHOLOGY 247, 296 (1984).
161. *See* Perlin, *supra* note 62, at 394 (footnotes omitted).
162. Van Zandt, *supra* note 48, at 917-18.
163. *See supra* text accompanying notes 56-62.
164. Van Zandt, *supra* note 48, at 918, 921-22. *See generally*, Snyder, *supra* note 41, at 248; D. HEISE, UNDERSTANDING EVENTS 8 (1979).
165. Perlin, *supra* note 93, at 125.
166. Van Zandt, *supra* note 48, at 919-20. For a striking example of the way OCS "trumps" social science, *see* Woolhandler, *Rethinking the Judicial Reception of*

data in judicial decision making: "Judges often select certain proffered data that adheres to their pre-existing social and political attitudes, and use both heuristic reasoning and false OCS in rationalizing such decisions."[167]

Legal rules thus operate against a background of commonsense
understanding about the world that constitutes the formative context
as a stock of knowledge. There are four main strands of the relationship between law and OCS: (1) legal rules may be formulations
derived from the decision maker's commonsense theories of the
world, (2) a lawmaker may choose a rule based on his estimation of
the consistency of that rule with his or her world view, (3) most legal
rules are uncontested (society either agrees with the governing principles or is indifferent to them), but where rules do deviate from OCS,
they fail to be supported, and (4) in spite of the general consensus
between OCS and legal rule- making, the "coercive force of law" is
still important for two reasons: (a) "to deter faulty judgments about
the proper course of action," and (b) "to provide resources for the
negotiation of practical problems."[168]

Where law attempts to alter the public's commonsense theories
("to raise the costs of nonadherence so that individuals will alter their
pictures of the world and comply"), the tension may be a coercive
one. For instance, the Civil Rights Act of 1964 "imposed a new idea
of race relations on a recalcitrant population."[169] While it is not clear
that such coercive laws actually altered individuals' OCS theories, it
may be that they are nonetheless effective "simply because they make

---

Legislative Facts, 41 VAND. L. REV. 111, 121 (1988) (discussing Supreme
Court's decision in McCleskey v. Kemp, 481 U.S. 279 (1987)).

167. Perlin & Dorfman, supra note 150, at 53 (footnote omitted); see generally infra
chapter 8 D.

168. Van Zandt, supra note 48, at 933-36. A legislator's evaluation of the potential
effectiveness of a new sanction will thus be based in large part on "his or her
own understanding of what motivates individual behavior." Id. at 934. See also,
id. at 937 (state's power is further needed to "catch or deter the socially
incompetent"—those "unable or unwilling to accept the ideas about the world
shared by substantial numbers of individuals"—and to "correct" actions taken
by individuals who belong to subcultures "whose understanding of the world
departs in important relevant respects" from the general view).

169. Id. at 938. Other laws dissonant with OCS may be "designed to 'correct'
'inaccurate' commonsense ideas held by some segment of the population." Id.
In this category, Van Zandt includes pollution control and mandatory motorcycle helmet statutes. On the relationship between Professor Van Zandt's insights
and the laws of "tensile strength" and "hydraulic pressure" in this context, see
infra chapter 8 A.

noncompliance unacceptably costly."[170] Official discrimination may still be inhibited despite virulent prejudice.[171] As Professor Sheri Lynn Johnson has argued, "Where discrimination is not legally or socially approved, social scientists predict it will be practiced only when it is possible to do so covertly and indirectly. On the other hand, discrimination may be engaged in without the presence of prejudiced attitudes when it will lead to social approval."[172]

4. OCS and "Conventional Morality"

In considering the relationship between the standards of judicial lawmaking and "dominant, conventional morality,"[173] there are two distinct dimensions to OCS: the OCS employed by courts in deciding the legal status of a particular practice (e.g., the decriminalization of homosexuality or abortion, the constitutionality of capital punishment) and the OCS used in cases where there is less doubt as to legal status but where public morality must "give moral content to the standards by which the practice is legally assessed" (e.g., whether or not a publication is obscene).[174]

It is the first grouping—where there are "yes-or-no" divisions of public opinion and no "general average of community thinking and feeling" can be discerned in "hotly disputed situations"—which poses the more difficult questions when examined through an OCS filter. Search for consensus is made all the more difficult where many members of the community express no view on the underlying subject matter, others hold views that are "clearly mutually inconsistent," and yet others express one set of attitudes in considering concrete policies and another incongruent set while responding more abstractly.[175]

---

170. Van Zandt, *supra* note 48, at 939.
171. Perlin, *supra* note 62, at 381.
172. Johnson, *Black Innocence and the White Jury*, 83 MICH. L. REV. 1611, 1650 (1985).
173. Sadurski, *Conventional Morality and Judicial Standards*, 73 VA. L. REV. 339, 341 (1987). On the question of a "community tolerance threshold" in insanity defense cases, *see supra* chapter 4 D 4.
174. Sadurski, *supra* note 173, at 351-54. For a broader reading of Sadurski's jurisprudential views, *see* Sadurski, *The Right, the Good, and the Jurisprude*, 7 LAW & PHIL. 35 (1988).
175. Sadurski, *supra* note 173, at 355-58. *See* L. FREE & H. CANTRIL, THE POLITICAL BELIEFS OF AMERICANS: A STUDY OF PUBLIC OPINION 36-37 (1968); B. HENNESSY, PUBLIC OPINION 345 (1965).

Faced with this muddy landscape, judges' ascertainments of a conventional morality occupy a broad range of positions between two extremes: the representation of their own moral standards as community morality, and "radical skepticism as to the possibility of stating what conventional morality is."[176] Located on a continuum between these end points are the seemingly-intermediate positions articulated in *Furman v. Georgia*[177] by Justice Marshall (rejecting results of public opinion polls based on responses of people not "fully informed" as to the death penalty's purposes),[178] and by Justice Brennan (relying on "actual social practice and public opinion" to support his argument).[179]

Both the Brennan and Marshall positions reveal "the basic dilemma facing a judge who wants to use [the] argument [of appealing to conventional morality to condemn the death penalty] in a morally pluralistic society: either the conventional morality must be concocted in such a way that it is merely a proxy for the judge's own

---

176. Sadurski, *supra* note 173, at 360. The paradigm expression of the first position is Justice Stewart's famous "I-know-it-when-I-see-it" definition of obscenity in his concurring opinion in Jacobellis v. Ohio, 378 U.S. 184, 197 (1964) (Stewart, J., concurring). The second position might be characterized as "I can't fathom how others see it." *See id.* at 361, *quoting and discussing In re* Lolita, 1961 N.Z.L.R. 542, 549 (C.A.) (Gresson, P., dissenting)).

177. 408 U.S. 238 (1972). Sadurski rejects both Marshall's and Brennan's positions as well. Sadurski, *supra* note 173, at 360-62.

178. *Furman*, 408 U.S. at 361 (Marshall, J., concurring). This may be characterized as the "they'd know it if they really saw it" argument. *See* Sadurski, *supra* note 173, at 363, characterizing as "pretextual" Marshall's subsequent dissent in Gregg v. Georgia, 428 U.S. 153, 232 (1976), that, if Americans "were better informed, they would consider [the death penalty] shocking, unjust, and unacceptable." *But see,* Vidmar & Dittenhoffer, *Informed Public Opinion and Death Penalty Attitudes*, 23 CANAD. J. CRIMINOL. 43, 52 (1981) ("on the whole, if the public were informed, opinion polls would show more people opposed to capital punishment than favor it"); *see also,* Doob & Roberts, *supra* note 23, at 277 (public's attitudes toward judicial sentencing are shaped not by reality that takes place in courts but by mass media; "policy makers should not interpret the public's apparent desire for harsher penalties at face value; they should understand this widespread perception of leniency is founded upon incomplete and frequently inaccurate news accounts"); *see generally,* Fattah, *Perceptions of Violence, Concerns About Crime, Fear of Victimization, and Attitudes to the Death Penalty*, 21 CANAD. J. CRIMINOL. 22 (1979); Rankin, *Changing Attitudes Toward Capital Punishment*, 58 SOC'L FORCES 194 (1979).

179. *Furman*, 408 U.S. at 295-300 (Brennan, J., concurring). Sadurski, who criticizes Brennan for his "nonchalant" use of data, Sadurski, *supra* note 173, at 364, characterizes this as a "half empty, but not half full" type of argument. *Id.* at 365.

opinions, or it will fail to support the argument, because there is an important segment of the general public that is directly opposed to the views propounded by the trial judge." To resolve this dilemma, courts thus developed "laundering devices" as a means by which to "filter the actual, divergent moral opinions of the community through the sieve of rationality."[180]

Ultimately Sadurski turns to moral philosophy for a solution. Drawing extensively on the writings of Michael Walzer,[181] who argues that questions of justice should be answered by the detection of "shared understandings,"[182] he concludes that any theory[183] must explicitly admit and reconcile two "usually concealed" facts: "first, that judicial decisions are, and should be seen as, part of the broader process of societal decision making about morally controversial matters, and second, that in this process judges make their own substantive choices, the responsibility for which they must not, and cannot, abdicate."[184]

---

180. *Id.* at 364, 366.
181. *See e.g.*, Walzer, *Philosophical Democracy*, 9 POL. THEORY 379 (1981); M. WALZER, SPHERES OF JUSTICE (1983).
182. *See* M. WALZER, *supra* note 181, at 29. Sadurski characterizes these as "decisions about the values of distinct social goods that have already been made by people in the course of their common life." Sadurski, *supra* note 173, at 386.
183. Sadurski's preferred approach is as follows: "[W]hat is important is that [a judge] does not begin his search for morally valid rules in a vacuum when he runs out of precise legal rules as conveyed by legal texts or by the precedent: he can make an appeal to actual social facts that carry a particular moral opinion. From this, in a process of 'reflective equilibrium,' he will reconstruct a more general principle. He will be in effect saying to his community, even though he knows well that not all the people in the community share this view: 'If you accept this particular moral view, then you must also, on pain of self-contradiction, accept this more general principle.' From this general principle he will descend to the particularities of his case: 'If you have accepted this general principle, then you must agree with this particular decision which applies it to a specific matter.'" *Id.* at 396-97.
184. *Id.* at 397.

5. OCS and Judicial "Cognitive Dissonance"

These works illuminate as well as any efforts to date the cognitive dissonance[185] between OCS and what we now "know"[186] about mental illness, the interplay between mental illness and criminal behavior, and about the disposition of cases in which defendants plead (both successfully and unsuccessfully) the insanity defense.

a. Attribution theory. Any OCS "portrait" must rely on the basic fundamentals of attribution theory. At virtually all intellectual costs, we will strain to fit new experiences into our preexisting theories of the world.[187] Thus, almost autonomically, we reject much of the rich empirical insanity defense database that has developed in the past decade, simply because it does not fit our picture of "world knowledge."[188] This is especially pernicious where so much of our OCS insanity defense "data" is anecdotal and heuristic,[189] and, consequently, where insanity defense decisionmaking is so animated by the "vividness effect," our picture of "reality" will inevitably be distorted.[190]

---

185. *See* Van Zandt, *supra* note 48, at 920 n. 133, *discussing* L. FESTINGER, A THEORY OF COGNITIVE DISSONANCE (1957); *see* Perlin, *Morality, supra* note 85, at 139; Winick, *Harnessing the Power of the Bet: Wagering with the Government as a Mechanism for Social and Individual Change*, 45 U. MIAMI L. REV. 737, 763 (1991). Cognitive dissonance is the tendency of individuals to reinterpret information or experience that conflicts with their internally accepted or publicly stated beliefs in order to avoid the unpleasant personal state that such inconsistencies produce. *Id.*

186. *Cf.* Sherwin, *supra* note 82, at 737.

187. Van Zandt, *supra* note 48, at 918. *See also*, Vidmar, *Retributive and Utilitarian Motives and Other Correlates of Canadian Attitudes Toward the Death Penalty*, 15 CANAD. PSYCHOL. 337 (1974); Vidmar & Dittenhoffer, *supra* note 178. *See generally*, "Angle Broadcast," *supra* note 73.

Empirical research supports the thesis that attribution theory is applied to clinical judgments in attempts to perceive the dangerousness and treatability of offenders. *See* Quincey & Cyr, *Perceived Dangerousness and Treatability of Offenders: The Effects of Internal Versus External Attributions of Crime Causality*, 1 J. INTERPERS. VIOL. 458 (1986); Jackson, *supra* note 88; Jackson, *supra* note 89.

188. Van Zandt, *supra* note 48, at 916 n. 115, *quoting* Pennington & Hastie, *supra* note 159. *See e.g.*, Russell, *The Causal Dimension Scale: A Measure of How Individuals Perceive Causes*, 42 J. PERS. & SOC'L PSYCHOLOGY 1137 .

189. *See supra* chapter 6 C 2.

190. *See* Rosenhan, *supra* note 27. *Compare e.g.*, Hall, *Science, Common Sense, and Criminal Law Reform*, 49 IOWA L. REV. 1044, 1051 (1964) (insanity defense decision making "depends mostly on ordinary experience").

Communications theory leads us to the same conclusion. "Para-messages" are peripheral data "relating to and/or emanating from the source, the message, and the context of the communication that can directly or indirectly determine persuasive effects" that may be the "primary vehicle of the information that determines persuasive responses."[191] In issue-centered communications, "affirmation of the actuality of the motivational conditions must result from the communication itself" through "message credibility," an unconscious judgment deriving from the paramessage of the communication.[192] The heuristics of the insanity defense reflect, to the public at large and to legal decisionmakers, a potent "message credibility," deriving from the communication's "paramessage."[193] The "peripheral data"—the accumulated centuries of myth, the vividness of the "outrageous" case, the sources of the outrage itself—all help to inform an "unconscious judgment" that appears to comport with ordinary common sense, but which, at base, gravely distorts the underlying scientific, empirical, philosophical and moral realities.

Similarly, legislative change is driven by the legislator's "own understanding of what motivates individual behavior."[194] If that understanding is seriously in error, it exposes the frequent legislative call for "scientific studies of social problems" to be frequently little more than a sham.[195] Where such studies conflict with the legislators' OCS, they will simply be ignored, especially where they bring disorder to an areas where the process of typification ordinarily would drastically reduce the "complexity of reality."[196]

---

191. Rosenthal, *The Concept of the Paramessage in Persuasive Communication*, 58 Q.J. SPEECH 15, 16 (1972).
192. *Id.* at 23. See also, *id.*: "[T]he only perception that is inherently believable is a sense experience, and in issue-centered communications, such perceptions of the phenomena that provide the persuasive motivation are rare."
193. *See* Sendor, *supra* note 144.
194. Van Zandt, *supra* note 48, at 934.
195. *Id.; see e.g.,* Pasewark & Pantle, *Insanity Plea: Legislator's View,* 136 AM. J. PSYCHIATRY 222-23 (1979) (in response to survey, one state's legislators estimated that, during a specified time period, 4400 defendants pled insanity and that 1500 were found NGRI; in reality, only 102 defendants asserted the defense, and only one was successful); *see supra* chapter 3 B 1 b (1).
196. Van Zandt, *supra* note 48, at 914. See e.g., Vidmar & Dittenhoffer, *supra* note 178, at 53 ("the persons most resistant to the effects of information are those who favor capital punishment most strongly"), and *see* sources cited *supra* note 178.

b. A twilight zone: OCS and individual jury verdicts. Although the public is disinterested in most legal rules,[197] "when a legal rule does deviate from commonsense understandings, it fails to gain support."[198] Much insanity defense decision making—the Hinckley verdict is the perfect example—reflects such deviation from OCS. It is within this twilight zone that consensus breaks down, and that public outrage (at the apparent dissonance between the law and OCS) is greatest. It is within this dissonance that the roots of judicial pretextuality in insanity defense cases may be found.[199]

If it is true that legal rules that deviate from common understanding may not be employed if the costs of ignoring them are not high,[200] then the episodic nature of the insanity furor is better understood: because the insanity defense is employed so rarely, it may be generally ignored. It is only when the public is confronted with the defense's "reality" (that in some cases, it exculpates those whom we feel "ought" to be punished), that its putative costs become apparent.[201]

The recent empirical work of Professor Norman Finkel and his colleagues illuminates this point. In an important series of manuscripts and papers, Finkel demonstrates the power of OCS in insanity

---

197. Van Zandt, *supra* note 48, at 935. Professor Monaghan, in his discussion of *stare decisis*, asks "Why, for example, is it proper to overrule National League of Cities [v. Usery, 426 U.S. 833 (1976), overruled by San Antonio Metropol. Trans. Auth. v. Garcia, 469 U.S. 528 (1985)], Kentucky v. Dennison, [65 U.S. 66 (1861), overruled by Puerto Rico v. Branstad, 483 U.S. 219 (1987)], and General Motors Corp. v. Washington, [377 U.S. 436 (1964), overruled by Tyler Pipe Indus. v. Wash. St. Dep't of Revenue, 483 U.S. 232 (1987)], but not Roe [v. Wade, 410 U.S. 113 (1973)]?" Monaghan, *Stare Decisis and Constitutional Adjudication*, 88 COLUM. L. REV. 723, 747 (1988). Intuitively, there is far greater public interest in *Roe* (abortion) than in *National League* (application of Tenth Amendment to federal wage statutes), *Dennison* (scope of federal courts' authority under extradition clause of constitution), or *Washington* (applicability of commerce clause to business and occupation tax providing certain manufacturers' exemptions).
198. Van Zandt, *supra* note 48, at 936. "Obvious examples" suggested by Van Zandt include the death penalty, abortion, and the prohibition on marijuana use. *Id.* n. 199.
199. *See* Perlin, *Morality*, *supra* note 199; Perlin, *Pretexts*, *supra* note 85; *see generally infra* chapter 8 C.
200. Van Zandt, *supra* note 85, at 939 n. 201, *discussing* Ellickson, *Of Coase and Cattle: Dispute Resolution Among Neighbors in Shasta County*, 38 STAN. L. REV. 623, 672-73 (1986).
201. On the relationship between these behaviors and the "tensile strength" of the law, *see infra* chapter 8 A.

decision making in individual cases. Recognizing that the commonsense perspective of jurors "remains a minor chord at best" in the
shaping of insanity defense law,[202] he points out that "commonsensi-
cal"-sounding insanity defense reformulations such as those suggested by Stephen Morse and Michael Moore "still lack a sound
empirical base."[203]

Ever since the "wild beast" test, insanity developments have
reflected "jurors' own *intuitive, commonsense* understanding of what
is sane and what is insane." It is "this common sense understanding
that has been consistently overlooked in the long running legal debate that has surrounded insanity."[204] The choice of a substantive test
(or the articulation of any test at all) thus made little difference in
mock jurors' determinations, as evidence showed that jurors interpreted instructions "to fit with their *common sense, intuitive* understanding of insanity."[205] The fact that the wording of tests made little
difference did not support the inference that juror decisionmaking
was random. Rather, different jurors contextualize (i.e., frame) specific cases differently, jurors construe cases differently, and differences in case disposition are frequently a reflection of "an underlying
perspectival problem—a disagreement in seeing or construing:"

> [I]nsanity, as jurors understand and construe it, is a multi-dimensional,
> complex construct, or, in the vernacular of the construct theorists, is a
> superordinate construct. The essence of insanity is not the same thing as
> any of its correlated attributes, which may or may not be manifest in a
> particular defendant. Thus, a person can be judged "insane" whether or
> not they are manifesting clear or distorted perception, clear or distorted
> thinking, or control or lack of control of their actions; the latter three—
> perception, thinking, and volitional control—are attributes, lower level
> constructs—and not the essence of insanity. Furthermore, I argue that a
> sound and coherent insanity test—one that specifies the essence of insanity,

---

202. N. FINKEL, *supra* note 120, at 10; on the role of juries generally, *see infra* text
    accompanying notes 204-10.
203. N. FINKEL, *supra* note 120, at 13 (emphasis in original). On the influence of
    Moore and Morse, *see supra* chapter 3 B 4.
204. Finkel, *Malingering and Misconstruing Jurors' Insanity Verdicts: A Rebuttal*, 1
    FORENS. REPS. 97, 100 (1988) (emphasis in original). He notes elsewhere: "A
    legal test that does not adequately capture the essence of insanity as understood
    by ordinary citizens invites disregarding or reconstruing." Finkel & Handel,
    How Jurors Construe Insanity, 13 LAW & HUM. BEHAV. 41 (1989).
205. Finkel, *supra* note 204, at 106-07 (emphasis in original). *See generally*, N.
    FINKEL, *supra* note 120, at 157-76 (summarizing research).

and accords with our legal, psychological, and common sense notions of insanity—has not yet been developed, but certainly ought to.[206]

This construct may result in some verdicts that "raise eyebrows and questions," as "dispositive sentiments" (as to where the defendant might wind up after the verdict) come into play, as do "jurors' sentiments, sympathies and antipathies for the defendant and victim." Thus, as part of their OCS approach, some jurors will weigh the victim's actions and character along with the defendant's in their "delicate calculus."[207]

Finkel is ambivalent about his findings. He applauds this juror use of OCS as a "necessary addition to the mix," and calls for a new test that "harmonizes legal, psychological, and common sense perspectives."[208] Yet, he also points out and appears somewhat disquieted by the fact that jurors tend to shift their determinative constructs from case to case. This creates another problem. Any new empirically-derived common law insanity test might meet the same fate as other legal tests: "it might work well for one case but not the next, when what we want is an insanity test that works from case to case."

On reexamination, at least two hidden variable factors appear to significantly animate juror decisionmaking here: the readiness of jurors to use a third alternative verdict (such as GBMI) when the verdict options are graded rather than dichotomous, and the presence of a "time/action" variable (some jurors assess a defendant culpability at other times as well as at the moment of the criminal

---

206. Finkel, *supra* note 204, at 109-11 (emphasis deleted). The test cases used by Finkel included defendants who were (1) epileptic, (2) chronic alcoholics, (3) paranoid-schizophrenic, and (4) suffering from a traumatic stress-induced disorder (a battered spouse case). *Id.* at 109. *See also id.* at 112 (while jurors who find a defendant NGRI may construe the case as "fitting" into an "insane person" image, those who find him guilty may construe it as "fitting" into a "normal criminal" image).

207. *Id.*; *see also*, N. FINKEL, *supra* note 120, at 178 ("the law's constructs fail to match well with the relevant and determinative constructs of jurors"). This seems to offer some important empirical support to Professor Wexler's "offense-victim" approach, *see generally*, Wexler, *supra* note 11, at 20-21 (recommending retention of the insanity defense except in those cases where its availability would likely be viewed "as going against the grain of community tolerance and the community sense of justice"), that jurors do, to some extent, "try the victim" in certain insanity defense cases.

208. N. Finkel, "De Jure and De Facto Insanity Tests," (paper delivered at the annual convention of the American Psychological Association, Atlanta, GA, August 1988), at 20.

act).[209] Juror use of these variables is neither "inexplicable nor eccentric;" rather, it reflects an additional "common sense cluster" to the mix which would make a test upon which it is based "likely to harmonize with existing legal and psychological tenets, rather than to nullify them."[210] Such juror processes highlight the dominance of OCS in insanity defense decision making and underscore its further importance to our inquiry.

c. Other dissonances.   The conflict between the insanity defense and conventional community morality leads to other jurisprudential dissonances. Thus, because the insanity defense appears to fly in the face of society's informed OCS, it is received with the same sort of hostility that greeted civil rights laws in the south twenty-five years ago: it is seen as "the [coercive] imposition of an alien ideology by one [social] group on another."[211] While many of the scholars and philosophers who write about the insanity defense note this hostility, few see the hostility as the inevitable outgrowth of the tension between the seemingly coercive legal rules and the public's OCS.[212]

Majoritarian legal theory raises the troubling question of whose community standards are at play. Sadurski generally rejects Michael Perry's implicit argument that the Supreme Court can recognize, in

---

209. Finkel, *supra* note 76, at 115-18 (emphasis in original). "For example, in the epilepsy case, a significant number of jurors focus on an earlier time, when the defendant, on her own, without consulting her doctor, chose to stop taking her medication, and then chose to go to a party and had an alcoholic drink. These preceding moments of time, when fateful decisions were made—decisions that perhaps had significant effects on the defendant's capacity, mental condition, and actions at the moment of the act—were evaluated by many of the mock jurors." N. Finkel, "De Facto Departures From Insanity Instructions: Toward the Remaking of Criminal Law," unpublished manuscript at 24. The epilepsy case is based on People v. Grant, 71 Ill. 2d 551, 377 N.E. 2d 4 (1978).

There is support for this position in other studies as well. *See e.g.*, White, *supra* note 64, at 125 n. 11 (key variables in attempts to establish insanity defense is whether defendant had "previously sought help for his illness").

210. N. Finkel, *supra* note 208, manuscript at 20.

211. Van Zandt, *supra* note 48, at 938. On the link between society's attitudes toward the mentally disabled and toward racial, religious and sexual minorities, *see* Fleming, *Shrinks vs. Shysters: The Latest Battle for Control of the Mentally Ill*, 6 LAW & HUM. BEHAV. 355, 356 . On the relationship of this insight to sanism, *see* Perlin, *supra* note 62; Perlin & Dorfman, *supra* note 150; *see generally infra* chapter 8 B.

212. *See* Rodgers & Hanson, *The Rule of Law and Legal Efficacy: Private Values Versus General Standards*, 27 W. POL. Q. 387, 393 (1974) ("the individual's attachment to a general standard seems to be a symbolic orientation that has little or no relation to specific legal disputes").

part, its own standards "as a proxy for community standards," but seems cautiously to endorse partially Judge Frank's position that courts should be guided "by the attitudes of our ethical leaders."[213] He finds Frank's position ultimately wanting, however, because of the apparent "indeterminacy of conventional morality," as demonstrated by a comparison of the public positions of Jesse Jackson, Jerry Falwell and John Rawls.[214]

This raises, but fails to fully address, a collateral issue: in assuming that the indeterminacy question can be answered, are judges and other lawmakers in a position to either calculate or reflect "the attitudes of our ethical leaders?"[215] Certainly, little of the accumulated database of insanity defense jurisprudence suggests that many judges can articulate such "ethical leadership."[216] It is probably not coincidental that judicial OCS and public OCS appear to be in substantial harmony on this issue. Here, Sadurski asks yet another question, the answer to which may finally illuminate the entire role of OCS in insanity defense jurisprudence:

> A political philosopher (or, for our purposes, a judge) must do more than register actual moral opinions, but at the same time he must stop short of stipulating his own views from "outside." How deeply is he allowed to dive in order to ascertain these "deeper" understandings, in order to

---

213. Sadurski, *supra* note 173, at 372-73, discussing Perry, *Substantive Due Process Revisited: Reflections on (and Beyond) Recent Cases*, 71 Nw. U. L. Rev. 417 ((1976), and Repouille v. United States, 165 F. 2d 152, 154 (2 Cir. 1947) (Frank, J., dissenting). Sadurski also appears to substantially approve of Ronald Dworkin's criteria for a "moral position" (that one's reactions must pass through an analytical test that would remove prejudice, irrational emotions, rationalizations, and "parroting," and would also insure "sincerity and consistency of a 'moral position'"). Sadurski, *supra* note 173, at 369-70, discussing R. Dworkin, Taking Rights Seriously 248-53 (1977).

214. Sadurski, *supra* note 173, at 373. Observe Professors Rodgers and Hanson, *supra* note 212, at 393: "[W]hat we have found is that the individual's attachment to a general standard seems to be a symbolic orientation that has little or no relation to specific legal disputes." On the way that judges often give normative weight to allegedly neutral language in their decisions, *see* Hiers, *Normative and Ostensibly Norm-Neutral Conventions in Contemporary Judicial Discourse*, 14 Leg. Stud. Forum 107 (1990).

215. This may be nothing more than a complicated way of asking: are judges simply at a sufficiently advanced stage of moral development—*compare infra* chapter 7 D 4-5—to be able to sort out their OCS from that of society?

216. Judge Bazelon is the clearest example of a judge who has exerted such leadership. *See e.g.*, Wald, *Disembodied Voices: An Appellate Judge's Response*, 66 Tex. L. Rev. 623, 627 (1988) (characterizing Bazelon as one of our "greatest appellate judges"). On other "nonsanist judges," *see* Perlin, *supra* note 62, at 403-4.

reconcile the competing requirements of consistency in a moral system and of respect for actual people who hold divergent views? Will they still recognize these "deeper" opinions and understandings as their own?[217]

We frequently refuse to "go deeper" when we unconsciously fear what we may learn at a deeper level of exploration. A court's embrace of OCS serves as an effective brake so as to prohibit the judge from "diving" into his or her own unconscious so as to "reconcile the competing requirements of consistency in a moral system." How ironic it is that the paradigmatic OCS insanity defense opinions—those of Justice Francis and Chief Justice Weintraub in *State v. Sikora*[218] and *State v. Lucas*[219]—consciously articulate a position that refuses to "go deeper" and explore the psychodynamic roots of unconscious motivations. Such willful blindness[220]—utterly reflective of the public's uninformed and distorted OCS—has served to shape insanity defense jurisprudence.

Here, the "wrong verdict" phenomenon[221] is especially pernicious. The aberrant Hinckley verdict threatens to overwhelm the system, not simply because it is seen as "wrong," but because of the reasons why it is so seen. The public employs a toxic combination of OCS and a broad array of heuristic reasoning devices—predominantly, the vividness effect, representativeness, and attribution theory, along with typification—so as to create a kind of systemic cognitive sensory overload beyond the criminal justice system's limits of "tensile strength."

6. OCS and Jury Behavior

a. Jury research. A significant amount of effort has already been expended on questions involving the unique role of juries in insanity defense cases in making their "normative interpretation[s] of the

---

217. Sadurski, *supra* note 173, at 388.
218. 44 N.J. 453, 210 A. 2d 193 (1965), and *id.*, 210 A. 2d at 204 (Weintraub, C.J., concurring).
219. 30 N.J. 37, 152 A. 2d 50, 74 (1959) (Weintraub, C.J., concurring).
220. *See* Finer, Gates, Leon, *and the Compromise of Adjudicative Fairness (Part II): Of Aggressive Majoritarianism, Willful Deafness, and the New Exception to the Exclusionary Rule*, 34 Cleve. St. L. Rev. 199, 205 (1986) (criticizing current Supreme Court for its "willful refusal to listen" to party against whom it is ruling in criminal procedure cases).
221. *See supra* chapter 6 B.

defendant's conduct."[222] Do jurors understand the technical language of substantive insanity defense tests, or do they merely attempt to "do justice" by applying their own "test?" Do jurors attempt to apply the law to the facts in such cases (as they presumably do in alibi, self-defense, and identification cases), or does their decisionmaking rest on an entirely different set of variables? To what extent are jurors' "crime control" or "due process" orientations significant in their determination of insanity defense cases? If jurors do, in fact, misapply the relevant law, are we (as a society) terribly upset about this development? To what extent have the obscurity and mystification that has traditionally enveloped the jury decision process contributed to the underlying confusion?

While the research is neither complete nor unanimous, certain conclusions may be reached. While jurors are generally *hostile* to the insanity defense,[223] they are *receptive* to it in those rare instances when they can empathize with the *defendant*; thus, mothers accused of killing their small children, police officers, and individuals about whom jurors can say "there but for the grace of God go I" are disproportionately acquitted by reason of insanity.[224] These cases of seemingly-paradoxical sympathy may reflect the reality that *some* insanity defense jury verdicts should more appropriately be "read" as a version of jury nullification.

(1) Jury nullification. Jury nullification is a jury's unreviewable power to acquit in disregard of the applicable law.[225] In those juris-

---

222. Sendor, *supra* note 144, at 1403. *See id.* at 1402-3: "[T]he jury's interpretation is informed, guided, and limited by the official definition of the alleged crime established by legislation or common law, the indictment or other charging document, evidence, rules of evidence, jury instructions, and attorneys' arguments. The important point here, however, is that the criminal law regards the jury's interpretation as the authoritative interpretation of the relevant meaning of a defendant's conduct. It is for the jury to interpret the defendant's behavior to determine whether he showed disrespect."

223. *See e.g.*, Hans & Slater, *supra* note 121.

224. *See supra* chapter 4 D 2-3.

225. *See e.g.*, Hornig v. District of Columbia, 254 U.S. 135, 138 (1920) (jury has "power to bring in a verdict in the teeth of both law and fact"); *see generally*, United States v. Moylan, 417 F. 2d 1002, 1005-06 (D.C.Cir. 1969), *cert. den.*, 397 U.S. 910 (1970) (prosecution for interference with operation of Selective Service System). *See also* Note, *The Insanity Defense: Effects of an Abolition Unsupported By a Moral Consensus*, 9 AM. J. L. & MED. 471, 492 n. 108 & 493 n.111 (1984) (*citing* sources); *see generally*, Horowitz, *Jury Nullification: The Impact of Judicial Instructions, Arguments, and Challenges on Jury Decision Making*, 12 LAW & HUM. BEHAV. 439 (1988).

dictions where courts accept its legitimacy,[226] the nullification power leaves with the jury the responsibility of deciding whether "special factors present in the particular case compel the conclusion that the defendant's conduct was not blameworthy."[227] Jury nullification is especially likely to occur when the substantive law fails to incorporate "strong moral impulses such as those traditionally encompassed by the insanity defense."[228]

The "very essence of the jury's function [in] its role as spokesman for the community conscience" in determining blameworthiness is thus vindicated, and our understanding of community values and "standards of blameworthiness" is informed.[229] Under this theory, the use of the nullification device mirrors *all* jury decision making as "a reflection of the morality of the community and the standards of behavior it espouses."[230] As the New Jersey Supreme Court has stated:

> The responsibility of the jury in the domain of factual findings, and ultimate guilt or innocence, is so pronounced and preeminent that we accept inconsistent verdicts that accrue to the benefit of a defendant... Indeed, a jury has the prerogative of returning a verdict of innocence in the

---

226. For sharply conflicting views, *see* State v. Ragland, 105 N.J. 189, 519 A. 2d 1361 (1987), and *id.*, 519 A. 2d at 1374-78 (Handler, J., concurring in part & dissenting in part).

   See Arenella, *supra* note 88, at 215: "Indeed, juries may nullify the law because their function extends beyond simply applying legal norms to the facts. They may negate the substantive criminal law's clear application to a particular defendant in cases in which they believe applying the legal standard would be unjust."

   But see, Note, *Chance, Freedom, and Criminal Liability*, 87 COLUM. L. REV. 125, 132 (1987) ("unprincipled deference to community sensibilities is rarely a satisfying solution to apparent conceptual incoherences"). The same author suggests that the fear of jury nullification may have been the real reason for the exception to the equal grading made for capital crimes and first degree felonies in the Model Penal Code, *id.* at 131 n. 34, characterizing these exceptions as "grudging bows to community sentiment." *Id.*

227. United States v. Dougherty, 473 F. 2d 1113, 1140 n. 5 (D.C. Cir. 1972) (Bazelon, J., dissenting) (Vietnam war protest case; defendants entered offices of Dow Chemical without permission, and spilled containers of blood).

228. Note, *supra* note 225, at 492.

229. *Dougherty*, 473 F. 2d at 1142 (Bazelon, J., dissenting). *See also*, Williams v. Florida, 399 U.S. 78, 100 (1970) ("the essential feature of a jury obviously lies in...community participation and shared responsibility that results from the group's determination of guilt or innocence").

230. Singer, *The Resurgence of Mens Rea: I—Provocation, Emotional Disturbance, and the Model Penal Code*, 27 B.C. L. REV. 243, 322 (1986).

face of overwhelming evidence of guilt. It may also refuse to return a verdict in spite of the adequacy of the evidence...This is indicative of a belief that the jury in a criminal prosecution serves as the conscience of the community and the embodiment of the common sense and feelings reflective of society as a whole...[231]

While nullification is usually discussed in what are popularly considered "political cases,"[232] it has clearly also been a historic element in insanity defense decision making as well. The defense, thus, was comfortably accepted by juries in cases of defendants who did not exhibit florid psychiatric symptomatology where jurors were especially sympathetic to the circumstances of the underlying crime.[233] Jurors have often resolved sanity cases "with reference to [their] own understanding of community concepts of blameworthiness."[234]

In discussing juror response to an infanticide case, Justice Cardozo simply stated, "No jury would be likely to find a defendant responsible in such a case, *whatever a Judge might tell them.*"[235] Similarly, William A. White told of insanity acquittals in cases involving the murder of the man who seduced the defendant's daughter, and

---

231. State v. Ingenito, 87 N.J. 204, 432 A. 2d 913, 916 (1981) (citations omitted).

232. *See e.g.*, Dougherty, *supra*; Moylan, *supra*. On the potential role of jury nullification in the Bernhard Goetz verdict, *see* Johnson, *Jury's Power Comes Into Play In Goetz Trial*, N.Y. Times (Apr. 5, 1987), at 6.

233. *See* Comment, *Recognition of the Honor Defense Under the Insanity Plea*, 43 YALE L.J. 809, 813 (1934) (use of insanity defense where husband finds wife *en flagrante delit* generally accepted by jurors, but criticized for its potential "to confuse an already distorted legal concept"). *But see* Ireland, *Insanity and the Unwritten Law*, 32 AM. J. LEG. HIST. 157, 172 (1988)(more recent research suggests, however, that there was "impressive evidence" of insanity in many of the so-called "honor defense" cases)

234. Eule, *The Presumption of Sanity: Bursting the Bubble*, 25 U.C.L.A. L.REV. 637, 661 (1978); *see also* W. WHITE, INSANITY AND THE CRIMINAL LAW 91 (1923) (Da Capo ed. 1981) ("the community, through the medium of its selected agent, the jury...projects its own feelings upon the accused, so that from this point of view responsibility stands for something which exist in the minds of the jury rather than in that of the defendant").

235. People v. Schmidt, 216 N.Y. 324, 110 N.E. 945, 949 (1915) (emphasis added). Professor Horowitz's research demonstrates that, when judges *tell* jurors that a nullification verdict is permissible, that information "clearly affects" criminal trial verdicts, with jurors moving "in the direction of mercy." Horowitz, *supra* note 225, at 450. On juror response to infanticide pleas in general, *see* Steadman & Braff, *Defendants Not Guilty By Reason of Insanity*, in MENTALLY DISABLED OFFENDERS: PERSPECTIVES IN LAW AND PSYCHOLOGY 109 (J. Monahan & H. Steadman eds. 1983).

of a man who broke his long-term promise to marry his mistress (by whom he had fathered several children); in both instances, "the written law offend[ed] the public conscience, or the public standard of justice," and the jury disregarded it "out of its collective sense of justice."[236] More recent scholarship reveals a similar pattern.[237]

While this has not been the subject of abundant scholarship,[238] several commentators have focused upon nullification as a "swing factor" in the debate on the substantive limits of the insanity defense. Thus, it has been suggested that the jury's potential use of the device in marginal cases counsels in support of the abandonment of the ALI test's volitional prong.[239] As there is no "objectifiable basis" for such

---

236. W. WHITE, *supra* note 234, at 100-1. White is clear: except in such nullification cases, he had "*never* known a criminal to escape conviction on the plea of 'insanity' where the evidence did not warrant such a verdict." *Id.* at 3 (emphasis added).

237. *See* Packer, *Homicide and the Insanity Defense: A Comparison of Sane and Insane Murderers*, 5 BEHAV. SCI. & L. 25, 34 (1987) (defendant killed "extremely abusive father;" *judge* entered NGRI verdict because defendant "did not qualify for any other exculpatory verdict"); Glantz, *Withholding and Withdrawing Treatment: The Role of the Criminal Law*, 15 LAW, MED., & HEALTH CARE 231, 232-34 (1987-88) (juries acquitted defendant on insanity grounds in six of nineteen reported "mercy killing" cases); *see* N. FINKEL, *supra* note 120, at 176 (where jurors "appear to depart from the law and instructions," they may be invoking their power of "legitimate interposition," *quoting* Kadish & Kadish, *The Institutionalization of Conflict: Jury Acquittals*, in LAW, JUSTICE AND THE INDIVIDUAL IN SOCIETY: PSYCHOLOGICAL AND LEGAL ISSUES 308, 316 (J. Tapp & F. Levine eds. 1977).

238. *But see e.g.*, A. GOLDSTEIN, THE INSANITY DEFENSE 62-63 (1967); *see also*, Gobert, *In Search of the Impartial Jury*, 79 J. CRIM. L. & CRIMINOL. 269, 304 (1988) ("In specific cases, nullification allows the jury to express its view of the moral blameworthiness of the defendant").

239. Bonnie, *Morality, Equality, and Expertise: Renegotiating the Relationship Between Psychiatry and Law*, 12 BULL. AM. ACAD. PSYCHIATRY & L. 5, 17 (1984). However, there is now significant empirical doubt as to the accuracy of the ABA's position that "'morally correct' results are likely to be achieved more often under a narrow test which does not include a volitional criterion." Keilitz, *Researching and Reforming the Insanity Defense*, 39 RUTGERS L. REV. 289, 297 (1987), quoting AMERICAN BAR ASSOCIATION, STANDING COMMITTEE ON ASSOCIATION STANDARDS FOR CRIMINAL JUSTICE, PROPOSED CRIMINAL JUSTICE MENTAL HEALTH STANDARDS 329 (1984) and noting that the ABA's position was based on "unverified observations by psychiatrists." *See* Silver & Spodak, *Dissection of the Prongs of ALI: Retrospective Assessment of Criminal Responsibility by the Psychiatric Staff of the Clifton T. Perkins Hospital Center*, 11 BULL. AM. ACAD. PSYCHIATRY & L. 383, 390 (1983) (contemporaneous empirical research has shown some evidence that *this* "truncation" of the insanity defense "may systematically exclude...that class of psychotic patients [patients with manic disorders] whose illness is clearest in symptomatology, most likely biologic in

an inquiry, volitional insanity defense litigation thus "degenerates into individualized moral guesses." If the factfinder is "otherwise sympathetic to the defendant, the possibility arises that the claim will be accepted in morally inappropriate cases," thus raising the "discernible risk of moral mistake at the margins."[240]

Yet, this view further acknowledges that, in the case of "legally unrecognized claims of 'situational excuse'" (the interfamilial murder; the mercy killing), the insanity defense functions as a "safety valve—and an instrument for nullification." Such aberrational cases may illustrate an inevitable feature of any government by rules; "some safety valve will be found to nullify the law when it pinches too tightly. If not the insanity defense, some other way will be found."[241]

One of the defense's most implacable opponents, Dr. Abraham Halpern, former president of the American Academy of Psychiatry and Law, has similarly drawn on the nullification doctrine to support the creation of a "justly acquitted" doctrine to "uncloset the conscience of the jury...a defendant is not criminally responsible if, in the circumstances surrounding his unlawful act, his mental or emotional processes or behavioral controls were functioning in such a manner that he should be justly acquitted."[242]

Such a doctrine refers to the functioning of mental processes without a showing of "disease," eschews the notion of a mental state at the "precise time of the act," and allows the factfinder to take into account the "entire gamut of relevant factors influencing the defendant in the matter of the commission of the act." This would thus allow the expert witness to "really talk 'unfettered by arbitrary legal formulae,'" and would allow the jury "'to confront the causes of criminal conduct in a way that might teach us all something about human behavior.'"[243]

---

origin, most eminently treatable, and potentially most disruptive in penal detention").

240. Bonnie, *supra* note 239, at 17. *But see* Rogers, *Assessment of Criminal Responsibility: Empirical Advances and Unanswered Questions*, 15 J. PSYCHIATRY & L. 73, 78 (1987), characterizing this position, on basis of available empirical evidence, as "an intellectual charade played for the benefit of an uninformed public"); Silver & Spodak, *supra* note 239, at 390; English, *supra* note 4, at 40-41 (supporting Silver and Spodak's findings).

241. Bonnie, *supra* note 239, at 18.

242. Halpern, *Uncloseting the Conscience of the Jury—A Justly Acquitted Doctrine*, 52 PSYCHIAT. Q. 144, 147, 154-55 (1980).

243. *Id.* at 153-55, *quoting*, in part, United States v. Brawner, 471 F. 2d 969, 1031,

Dr. Halpern distinguishes his formulation from Judge Bazelon's "justly responsible" test (suggested in his concurrence in *United States v. Brawner*) that a defendant is not responsible if, at the time of his unlawful conduct, his mental or emotional processes or behavioral controls were impaired to such an extent that he cannot be held "justly responsible" for his act.[244] First, the "justly responsible" doctrine would require proof of some sort of "mental disease or defect" or "impairment of mental processes with its inescapable medical implications."[245] Also, a narrow construction of "at the time of the act or conduct" would, in Halpern's view, "confine the analysis of the mental state of the defendant to an unrealistically brief time frame."[246] Finally, automatic confinement would still follow on the heels of Bazelon's alternative.[247]

More recently, Dr. Halpern has endorsed the views of William Carnahan that a diminished capacity test would solve the underlying problems: the defendant would be convicted of a lesser included criminal offense not requiring either an intentional or a knowing mental state, and the "ensuing 'clutchability' would enable the sentencing court to 'take the present mental condition of the offender

---

1034 (D.C. Cir. 1972) (Bazelon, J., concurring), and Douglas, *The* Durham *Rule: A Meeting Ground for Lawyers and Psychiatrists*, 41 IOWA L. REV. 485, 489 (1956). Halpern qualifies this by limiting its application to "at least some cases of ordinarily law-abiding and honest persons." Halpern, *supra* note 242, at 155. *But see*, Bonnie, *supra* note 239, at 18 (expressing some concern over this formulation, cautioning that a principle of situational excuse must be structured "to frame the moral inquiry without opening the door to wholesale individualization of the standards of criminal liability"). Professor Finkel's empirical mock jury research shows no significant differences between jurors given *some* legal instructions and those given no specific instructions at all. Finkel & Handel, *Jurors and Insanity: Do Test Instructions Instruct?* 1 FORENS. REP. 65, 75 (1988).

244. 471 F. 2d at 1032 (Bazelon, J. concurring).
245. Halpern, *supra* note 242, at 152.
246. *Id.*
247. *Id* at 153. For earlier alternatives of the "justly responsible" test, *see id.* at 148-50, discussing the REPORT OF THE ROYAL COMMISSION ON CAPITAL PUNISHMENT (1953) and the position of the minority dissenters of the American Law Institute at the time of drafting §4.01 of the Model Penal Code, that a defendant shall be found NGRI if his mental impairment were so substantial that he could not be held "justly responsible." *See* MODEL PENAL CODE §4.01, alternative (a) to §4.01(1) (Tent. Draft No. 4 1955), discussed in Hermann & Sor, *Convicting or Confining? Alternative Directions in Insanity Defense Reform: Guilty But Mentally Ill Versus New Rules for Release of Insanity Acquittees*, 1983 B.Y.U. L. REV. 499, 524-25.

into account in determining an appropriate disposition, namely, conditional discharge, probation or penal confinement.'"[248]

Finally, Halpern has explicitly revealed his expectations of political compassion in cases involving mentally disabled offenders:

> In almost thirty years of psychiatric practice, I have never seen a deserving case of acquittal by reason of insanity that could not have been dealt with in a more humane and compassionate manner *by other means available* to the jury and sentencing judge.[249]

While these analyses are provocative and illuminating,[250] some fairly serious underlying substantive issues remain.[251] First, I am considerably less sanguine than is Dr. Halpern about the track record of judges and jurors in exhibiting "humane and compassionate" behavior toward the individuals in question. The record before us reflects irrational brutality, prejudice, hostility and hatred toward insanity pleaders.[252] Although Dr. Halpern has demonstrated *his* support for the "rational and humane handling of mentally ill of-

---

248. Halpern, *The Insanity Verdict, the Psychopath, and Post-Acquittal Confinement*, 63 PSYCHIAT. Q. 209, 236 (1992) (Halpern I), *quoting*, in part, Carnahan, *Changing the Insanity Defense*, in THE INSANITY DEFENSE IN NEW YORK—A REPORT TO GOVERNOR HUGH L. CAREY 131, 141 (1978); *see also*, Halpern, *The Insanity Verdict, the Psychopath, and Post-Acquittal Confinement*, 24 PAC. L.J. 1125 (1993) (Halpern II); *see also*, Halpern, *The Politics of the Insanity Defense*, 14 AM. J. FORENS. PSYCHIATRY 3 (1993). On the meaning of "clutchable" in this context, *see e.g..* J. FEINBERG, DOING AND DESERVING 265-68 (1970); H.L.A. HART, PUNISHMENT AND RESPONSIBILITY 205 (1968) (persons who break the criminal law, whether or not seriously mentally ill, should remain in state's "clutches").

249. Halpern, *supra* note 242, at 168 (emphasis added).

250. As a retentionist, I find Dr. Halpern's formulation especially appealing, but only as an *alternative*—in what Professor Bonnie calls "situational excuse cases"—to a "standard" insanity defense, *not* as a replacement.

251. *See also*, Note, *supra* note 225, at 493, raising two objections to reliance on nullification: (1) since it provides no "vehicle" for the introduction of expert testimony, the jury may not recognize defendant's incapacity' (2) the jury may be unaware of its prerogative to acquit. *Cf. Ragland*, 519 A. 2d at 1374-78 (Handler, J., concurring in part & dissenting in part).

252. Ironically, Prof. Norval Morris, one of the most respected academic foes of the insanity defense, *see supra* chapter 3 C, has criticized Professor Richard Bonnie for the latter's reliance on the "community's moral intuitions" in *retaining* the defense. States Morris, "The history of the insanity defense is that the community thinks it is a mechanism for getting people off; that it is characterized historically by leniency, fraud, and all sorts of complexities." Bonnie & Morris, *Debate: Should the Insanity Defense Be Abolished?* 1 J. L. & HEALTH 113, 127 (1986-87) (remarks of Prof. Morris).

fenders,"[253] there is no evidence before us that suggests that fact-finders and sentencers in these cases share Dr. Halpern's sense of humanity, or that—putting aside the few exceptions discussed previously[254]—a nullification-type verdict is a realistic likelihood.

Courts purportedly rely on voir dire to "screen out prospective jurors who [cannot] consider an insanity defense due to their prejudices or biases against it,"[255] but the caselaw reflects a steady pattern of cases in which jurors' expressions of sanist attitudes do not result in their being removed for cause,[256] as well as cases where judges refuse to even ask exploratory questions about such bias[257] or allow jurors with obvious biases to be empaneled,[258] or where counsel fails to inquire into possible bias against the insanity defense.[259]

The "other means available" that Halpern refers to presumably include the judicial power to suspend sentence and/or to recommend speedy parole. Yet, these powers have been severely truncated following the adoption of determinate sentencing guidelines in the federal system and in many states.[260]

Next, reliance on the diminished capacity defense is also problematic. Instrumentally, the doctrine has been routinely criticized for its alleged difficulty and arbitrariness in application, leading to "uneven or inequitable outcomes,"[261] and has lost much of the judicial

---

253. Halpern I, *supra* note 248, at 236; Halpern II, *supra* note 248, at 1162 n. 175. *See also*, Halpern, *The Insanity Defense in the 21st Century*, 35 INT'L J. OFF. THER. & CRIMINOL. 188, 188 (1991) (criticizing indeterminate confinement of insanity acquittees); Halpern, "Abolition of the Insanity Defense in Australia" (keynote address to annual meeting of Australian & New Zealand Association of Psychiatry, Psychology and Law, Melbourne, 1989), manuscript at 1 (abolition would enable state "to develop a rational system of providing mental health treatment services for mentally ill offenders").

254. *See supra* chapter 4 D 2-3.

255. State v. Moore, 122 N.J. 420, 585 A. 2d 864, 881 (1991); *see also*, Collingwood v. State, 594 A. 2d 502 (Del. 1991); People v. Stack, 112 Ill. 2d 301, 493 N.E. 2d 339 (1986).

256. *See e.g.*, People v. Seuffer, 144 Ill. 2d 482, 582 N.E. 2d 71, 79 (1991) (defense "overused"); State v. Duckworth, 496 So. 2d 624, 635 (La. App. 1986) (defendant would be responsible for his acts if he "wanted to do them").

257. *See e.g.*, People v. Pitts, 104 Ill. App. 3d 451, 432 N.E. 2d 1062 .

258. *See e.g.*, State v. Pierce, 109 N.M. 596, 788 PO. 2d 352, 354 (1990) (no error where juror who had testified that "he could see the devil in [defendant]," and stated, "I saw in her witchcraft" was empaneled).

259. Wade v. Vasquez, 752 F. Supp. 931 (C.D. Cal. 1990).

260. *See supra* chapter 4 E 2 e.

261. Weiner, *Mental Disability and Criminal Law*, in S. BRAKEL, J. PARRY & B. WEINER, THE MENTALLY DISABLED AND THE LAW 693, 711 (3d ed. 1985);

and academic support that it once claimed.[262] More importantly, normatively, the substitution of diminished capacity for the insanity defense would not solve many of the core problems identified earlier: jurors will still be suspicious of feigned mental status defenses; judges will still "punish" (via enhanced sentences) defendants for raising unsuccessful mental status defenses; our ambivalence about psychiatric testimony, psychiatrists and the psychiatric method will continue to color our decision making; we will still employ heuristic reasoning and false OCS in deciding cases (in accordance with pre-existing *schemas*); sanist thinking and pretextual judicial decisions will still dominate insanity defense jurisprudence.

Also, jurors' tendencies to ignore medical evidence and legal tests may equally demonstrate the sort of freakish inconsistency that led to the Supreme Court's decision in *Furman v. Georgia*[263] that administration of the death penalty constituted cruel and unusual punishment, and may reflect nothing less than "jury vigilantism."[264] The suggestion that jurors must simply determine whether the discrepancy between the defendant's mental capacity and that of a "normal" individual is sufficient to negate responsibility similarly "ignores the dangers of arbitrary and discriminatory judgments inherent in decisional discretion."[265] As Professor Ingber has noted, reliance on jurors' "common sense" "provides no criteria for evaluation, no limits or direction to aid in avoidance of the abuses of discretion. At most it constitutes an after-the-fact rationalization for judgments already reached. The jury is allowed to focus on the lowest level of generality —that of the specific actor—and the process

---

Comment, *A Punishment Rationale for Diminished Capacity*, 18 UCLA L. REV. 561, 567-72 (1977).

262. Weiner, *supra* note 255, at 711; Morse, *Undiminished Confusion in Diminished Capacity*, 75 J. CRIM. L. & CRIMINOL. 1 (1984). *See generally*, 3 M. L. PERLIN, MENTAL DISABILITY LAW: CIVIL AND CRIMINAL, §15.08, at 303-6 (1989).

263. 408 U.S. 238, 306, 310 (1972) (Stewart, J., concurring) ("The Eighth and Fourteenth Amendments cannot tolerate the infliction of a sentence of death under legal systems that permit this unique penalty to be so wantonly and so freakishly imposed").

264. Spring, *The Insanity Defense in a Public Needs Perspective*, 4 DET. COLL. L. REV. 603, 610 (1979).

265. Ingber, *Ideological Boundaries of Criminal Responsibility* (review of H. FINGARETTE & A. HASSE, MENTAL DISABILITIES AND CRIMINAL RESPONSIBILITY (1979) 27 U.C.L.A. L. REV. 816, 831 (1980). The author notes that this "unstructured moral inquiry" was *precisely* the sort of role rejected in *Brawner*. *Id*. at 832 n. 90.

is consequently subject to the vicissitudes inherent in the emotionality and drama of a trial. The vagaries of common sense determinations are made apparent by the virtual impossibility of a conceiving a situation in which a jury's determination of rationality would be overturned on appeal."[266]

Critics also may lose sight of an important underlying psychodynamic issue that bears repeating: in their role as "conscience of the community," jurors will continue to make judgments based on their "ordinary common sense" vision of "rough justice"[267] as to who "*ought* to be punished."[268] The insanity defense has developed in large part in response to "outrageous" verdicts that shock the community's conscience—*vide* the post-Hinckley shrinkage and the public's endorsement of the wild beast test.[269] Jury verdicts here may reflect nothing more than community values that are the irrational product of majoritarian prejudices and bigotry.[270] Nullification becomes an issue only in that minute handful of cases where the jury's empathy lies with the defendant because of the defendant's *persona*, his or her role as social "victim," or because—in the circumstances of the offense (e.g., a mercy killing) —we "trust" jurors to "do the right thing."[271]

Here is the irony: if it were not for the ultra-rigid limitations on the *substantive* test (because of the fear of "wrong verdicts"),[272] the entire nullification debate would probably never have arisen in this context. It is only because the insanity defense has been "overshrunk" (in response to the jury's articulation of an OCS-based community

---

266. *Id.* at 831-32. On the perils of "OCS," *see supra* chapter 6 D 2-4.
267. Singer, *supra* note 230, at 322.
268. Eule, *supra* note 234, at 661 (emphasis added).
269. *See* Roberts, Golding & Fincham, *supra* note 123, at 226; *see supra* chapter 3 A 1 a (2).
270. Gobert, *supra* note 238, at 305. *See generally*, Perlin, *State Constitutions and Statutes as Sources of Rights for the Mentally Disabled: The Last Frontier?* 20 Loy. L.A. L. Rev. 1249, 1258 (1987) (on ways that Supreme Court decisions involving the mentally disabled reinforce majoritarian values).
271. *Cf.* Pea v. United States, 397 F. 2d 627, 638 (D.C. Cir. 1967) (Burger, J., dissenting on rehearing) ("This case is but another manifestation in this court of a tendency—happily not widespread in appellate courts—to follow the Jerome Frank syndrome—a school of thought which profoundly mistrusts juries, and prefers fact finding by one judge whose conclusions can more readily be upset by appellate judges") (footnote omitted) (referring to J. Frank, Courts on Trial 108-45 (1949)).
272. *See*, in this context, Professor Bonnie's concern of "moral mistakes" inherent in potential volitional prong acquittals. Bonnie, *supra* note 239, at 17.

conscience), that nullification needs be employed as a compensatory device in those rare cases where the community's conscience rebels at a guilty verdict.[273] Until we understand why *this* is (and why the community's conscience is as *it* is), reliance on nullification (in any form) will simply be a temporal palliative.

(2) Jury research and psychodynamic conclusions. Until very recently, there has been little serious interest in whether the choice of a substantive defense test makes an actual, empirical difference.[274] Common wisdom had been that the test employed really *does not* matter in "real life," since an artful expert witness can shape his or her testimony to fit any test,[275] especially where the defendant is "clearly psychotic."[276] More recent research involving mock jurors helps illuminate some of these intuitive conclusions.[277]

---

273. *Cf.* A. GOLDSTEIN, *supra* note 238 at 90 ("The real problem has been to find a [substantive] formula that keeps the [responsibility] exemption closely attuned to what the public can accept"). *See* Note, *In Search of Madness in the Sixth Amendment*, 15 COLUM. HUM. RTS. L. REV. 131, 154 (1983) ("It takes only one well-publicized event—such as John Hinckley's attempted assassination of President Reagan—to whip up a fervent distaste for this time- honored right").

274. On what else makes a difference, *see* J. ROBITSCHER, PURSUIT OF AGREEMENT: PSYCHIATRY AND THE LAW 66 (1966): "Economic factors, the tensions prevailing in society, the extent of knowledge, the understanding in society of psychiatric concepts, the concepts of what society is trying to accomplish—all these are more important than the wording of a 'test.'...But whoever makes the [insanity] determination is acted on by the forces of the world in which he lives. Any 'test' in time is shaped to the mood of that time."

275. As previously discussed, there is some evidence that limiting the ALI test might, paradoxically, *increases* psychiatric participation in criminal trials. Silver & Spodak, *supra* note 237, at 389; *see also id.* at 390:

The proposed truncation of the ALI test may systematically exclude from a successful plea of insanity that class of psychotic patients whose illness is clearest in symptomatology, most likely biologic in origin, most eminently treatable, and potentially most disruptive in penal detention.

276. Bromberg & Cleckley, *The Medico-Legal Dilemma: A Suggested Solution*, 42 J. CRIM. L., CRIMINOL. & POL. SCI. 729, 731 (1952).

277. A new "generation" of empirical inquiry into *jurors'* perspectives on the insanity defense is now resulting in data on the jurors' "intuitive understanding of mental disease, responsibility, culpability, punishment and treatment prior to deliberating with fellow jurors." *See e.g.,* N. FINKEL, *supra* note 120; Finkel, *supra* note 76; Finkel & Handel, *supra* note 204; Finkel & Handel, *supra* note 243; *see also,* Ogloff et al., *Empirical Research Regarding the Insanity Defense: How Much Do We Really Know?* in LAW AND PSYCHOLOGY: THE BROADENING OF THE DISCIPLINE 171 (J. Ogloff ed. 1992). On the connection between attribution theory and jury behavior, *see* N. FINKEL, *supra* note 120, at 168.

This research shows that jurors who are given no instructions decide cases similarly to jurors who are instructed on the law, and, when such mock jurors are given varied instructions, "no one specific text instruction produces discriminably different verdicts than any other."[278] These findings remain constant even where the Insanity Defense Reform Act (a *reduced* version of M'Naghten) is added as an alternative: test instructions "did not produce significantly different verdict patterns."[279] Although jurors did focus on other "logical, general factors" (e.g., defendant's intent to harm, expert testimony, defendant's history of mental illness, defendant's remorse), legal criteria were not seen as particularly important.[280] Professor James Ogloff has thus concluded that jurors do not distinguish between insanity defense standards in determining whether or not a defendant is NGRI.[281]

In their study of insanity defense verdicts in California before and after that state changed from an ALI test to a restrictive M'Naghten test, Dr. Henry Steadman and his colleagues found no change in the volume of insanity pleas, their success rate, the characteristics of those who pled insanity or those who were acquitted, or the length of confinement of those few defendants who had been found NGRI.[282]

---

278. Finkel & Handel, *supra* note 243, at 75. Note the authors dryly: "This outcome is certainly not what judges, jurists, psychological experts, and legislators had in mind." *Accord*, Pasewark, Randolph & Bieber, *Insanity Plea: Statutory Language and Trial Proceedings*, 12 J. PSYCHIATRY & L. 399 (1984) (no difference found regarding rate and success of insanity plea or disposition of insanity acquittal cases in jurisdiction which employed M'Naghten, the Model Penal Code rule with a bifurcated trial, and the Model Penal Code rule with a single-phase trial sequentially over six year period).

Finkel's findings hold in a series of comparisons: whether jurors are given the "wild beast" test or M'Naghten; the "wild beast" test or M'Naghten-plus-irresistible impulse; or the "wild beast" test, M'Naghten, ALI, or *Durham*. N. FINKEL, *supra* note 120, at 59-60. On the other hand, when jurors are offered the "diminished responsibility" alternative or the GBMI alternative, those verdict choice are used selectively, discriminately, and more appropriately. See N. Finkel & K. Duff, "The Insanity Defense: Giving Jurors a Third Option," (unpublished manuscript, 1988); Poulson, *Mock Juror Attribution of Criminal Responsibility: Effects of Race and the Guilty But Mentally Ill (GBMI) Verdict Option*, 30 J. APPL. SOC'L PSYCHOLOGY 1596 (1990).

279. Finkel, *The Insanity Defense Reform Act of 1984: Much Ado About Nothing*, 7 BEHAV. SCI. & L. 403 (1989).

280. Ogloff, *supra* note 277, at 198.

281. *Id.* at 203.

282. H. STEADMAN, REFORMING, *supra* note 19, at 12-13.

Notwithstanding this fairly clear empirical picture, however, the choice of test remains important for other normative and instrumental reasons.[283] The *process* by which the insanity defense has shrunk reflects widespread public and judicial dissatisfaction with the defense; it is thus likely that the narrower "reform" tests help create an *atmosphere* in which insanity defenses are contemplated even more rarely in the future. Also, as the *substance* of the new federal IDRA is even narrower than the *M'Naghten* test, it is likely that jury instructions on the Insanity Defense Reform Act will be even narrower.

This is especially important given the new interest in novel/"syndrome" cases[284] that are prototypic of the sort that appeared to animate the cries for reform:[285] non-"crazy" looking defendants; the presence of "planful" behavior; the potential presence of "political" issues; suspicious, "soft" expert testimony.[286] In Klofas and Yandrasits' study of juror behavior in a GBMI case, they reported on jurors' responses to their question of the case's probable disposition if GBMI were *not* a verdict option:

---

283. Professor Finkel emphatically does *not* draw nihilistic conclusions from his data. He concludes that "jurors' own *intuitive, common sense* understanding of what is sane and what is insane [is] finally determinative." Finkel, *supra* note 204, at 100 (citation omitted; emphasis in original).

284. One of the rare judicial mentions of heuristics in the insanity defense literature occurs in such a novel case. *See* United States v. Torniero, 735 F. 2d 725, 733 (2d Cir. 1984), *quoting*, with approval, *American Psychiatric Association Statement on the Insanity Defense*, 140 AM. J. PSYCHIATRY 681 (1983): "Persons with antisocial personality disorders (such as compulsive gambling) should, at least for heuristic reasons, be held accountable for their behavior." *Compare* Kuczka, *Insanity Plea a Gamble in Bettor's Case*, Chi. Trib. (Aug. 9, 1992), at 1 (*quoting* criminal justice professor Henry Lesieur, "Addiction is not perceived by the courts, or the American people, as an excuse for crime") (full text available on NEXIS).

285. *See* Resnick, *Perceptions of Psychiatric Testimony: A Historical Perspective on the Hysterical Invective*, 14 BULL. AM. ACAD. PSYCHIATRY & L. 203, 208 (1986); *see also*, Note, *The Syndrome Syndrome: Problems Concerning the Admissibility of Expert Testimony on Psychological Profiles*, 37 U. FLA. L. REV. 1035, 1045-46 (1985) (discussing impact of judges' "personal perceptions regarding the substance of syndromes" on determination of admissibility of expert testimony). On the impact of judicial preconceptions on insanity defense decision making, *see infra* chapter 8 B-D.

286. Golding & Roesch, *The Assessment of Criminal Responsibility: A Historical Approach to a Current Controversy*, in HANDBOOK OF FORENSIC PSYCHOLOGY 395, 400 (I. Weiner & A. Hess eds. 1987) (planfulness will rule out exculpation in "strict interpretation" jurisdictions).

[A]ll of the jurors believed that he would have been found guilty...[A] juror stated it...directly:

> "I would imagine they would have found him guilty. There might have been a couple that would have had a little problem with it, from a religious standpoint....However, you go back through the Bible, and it says "an eye for an eye, a tooth for a tooth." He took someone else's life, so." [287]

There is even some evidence in cases involving idiosyncratic *physiological* expert testimony that suggests that the choice of test *has* traditionally made a difference.[288] Also, some other available more recent "real life" empirical studies *do* seem to indicate that the choice of test *may* be more significant than has been traditionally believed.[289]

On the other hand, it appears fairly clear that jurors exhibit a "startlingly low comprehension" of the court's charge,[290] *especially* in insanity defense cases.[291] In reporting their study of the responses of 229 college psychology and sociology students (a sample which, intuitively, is better educated than any typical jury cross-section)[292] to

---

287. Klofas & Yandrasits, *"Guilty But Mentally Ill" and the Jury Trial,* 24 Crim. L. Bull. 424, 441 (1988) (case study of actual GBMI verdict, see *supra* note 265)
288. *See* Note, *Epilepsy and the Alternatives for a Criminal Defense,* 27 Case W. Res. L. Rev. 771, 790 (1977). *Cf.* Finkel & Handel, *supra* note 204, at 18 (in mock case involving epilepsy defense, jurors focused primarily on "nonculpable acts" (72.4%), "could not control impulses and actions" (48.1%), and "no evil motive" (45.5%) as factors supporting their verdict choices). *See also,* N. Finkel, *supra* note 210, manuscript at 24 (in assessing culpability of insanity defendant in epilepsy case, a significant number of jurors focused upon "an earlier time, when the defendant on her own, without consulting her doctor, chose to stop taking her medication and then chose to go to a party and had an alcoholic drink").
289. *See* Keilitz, *supra* note 239, at 298-303 (reviewing five studies on the effects of statutory changes on the success of the insanity defense).
290. Arens, Granfield & Susman, *Jurors, Jury Charges, and Insanity,* 14 Cath. U. L. Rev. 1, 25 (1965). *See generally,* Tanford & Tanford, *supra* note 7; Steele & Thornburg, *supra* note 117, at 83-87. Some of the blame for juror lack of comprehension may be laid at the feet of the trial judges who, in one post-*Durham* District of Columbia study, improperly avoided the "product" language demanded by that case, and whose charges, instead "still reflected an overwhelming number of symbols suggestive of the cognitive [M'Naghten] formulation." Arens & Susman, *supra* note 120, at 33.
291. *See also,* Eule, *supra* note 234, at 661 n.121 (jury studies "consistently reveal that the accuracy rate in recalling an insanity formulation is the lowest of any material heard during a trial"), citing James, *Status and Competence of Jurors,* 65 Am. J. Soc. 563, 565 (1959).
292. *See e.g.,* Field & Barnett, *Simulated Jury Trials: Students vs. 'Real' People as Jurors,* 104 J. Soc'l. Psychology 287-93 (1978) (students more lenient in

mock jury instructions, researchers found that in seventy-five percent of trials, during deliberations, only one-third of the jurors could recall the judge's charge with "significant accuracy," that "comprehension will not be significantly increased regardless of the quality of the jury," and that, most shockingly, the jurors deliberated under the "operative presumption of the defendant's guilt."[293] A more recent study of real jurors revealed an understanding of fewer than half of the instructions given at trial.[294] Unless jurors clearly understand judicial charges (reflections of legislative formulations of substantive insanity defense tests), "they cannot return verdicts which give effect to the will of the people."[295]

Hidden beneath the surface in these studies is a crucial psychodynamic issue: the significance of those underlying psychological and personality traits of jurors that animate their decision making. This is especially important in light of Professor Finkel's findings that lay perspectives of "intuitive, common sense understanding of insanity, responsibility, culpability, punishment, and treatment" are critical

---

setting sentences for defendants in mock trials); *see also,* Jackson, *supra* note 90, at 118 (lawyers—demonstrably a better educated group than either a "true" jury or a "college sophomore" sample—are prone to show same heuristic biases as lay people in making similar judgments based on same information).

293. Arens, Granfield & Susman, *supra* note 293, at 22-26; *see also,* Arens & Susman, *supra* note 120, at 17 (study of 30 jury charges suggests "not only needless complexity of verbiage but explicit failure to communicate the notion of the acceptability of non-psychotic mental illnesses as a valid basis for insanity acquittals in clear and compelling language"). *Id.* at 26. This disturbed the researchers "far more...than the morass of ignorance respecting mental disease and defect" shown by the mock jurors. *Id.*

294. Reifman, Gusick & Ellsworth, *Real Jurors' Understanding of the Law in Real Cases,* 16 LAW & HUM. BEHAV. 539 (1992).

295. Strawn & Buchanan, *Jury Confusion: A Threat to Justice,* 59 JUDICATURE 478, 483 (1976). *See also,* Charrow & Charrow, *Making Legal Language Understandable: A Psycholinguistic Study of Jury Instructions,* 79 COLUM. L. REV. 1306, 1359 (1979) ("The inability of jurors to comprehend the charge adequately has obvious implications concerning the soundness of the jury system: if many jurors do not properly understand the laws that they are required to use in reaching their verdicts, it is possible that many verdicts are reached either without regard to the law or by using improper law..."); Elwork, Sales & Alfini, *Juridic Decisions: In Ignorance of the Law or in Light of It?* 1 LAW & HUM. BEHAV. 163, 178 (1977) (unless situation corrected, "juries will continue to reach decisions arbitrarily, and countless litigants will be denied their constitutional right to a fair trial"); Steele & Thornburg, *supra* note 117, at 99 (studies show juror comprehension of pattern instructions "to be so low as to be dysfunctional"), and *id.* at 109 (juror comprehension of charges "pitifully low"); *see generally,* V. HANS & N. VIDMAR, *supra* note 12, at 193-94.

to jury decision making here.[296] As jurors have significantly different ethnic, class and educational backgrounds than do medical and academic experts,[297] they may be "less tolerant of and more impassioned by deviance."[298] Such fear of jurors' expected "excessive responses to deviant behavior" has led scholars to fear "virtually unlimited jury discretion," and to caution against the "facade of jury neutrality."[299]

---

296. N. FINKEL, *supra* note 120, at 164-67.

297. On the impact of presumption instructions on juror deliberation in insanity cases, *see* Note, *The Improper Use of Presumptions in Recent Criminal Law Adjudication*, 38 STAN. L. REV. 423, 450 (1986), concluding that the "authority" with which the presumption instruction is communicated can sufficiently reorient the jurors' decision making processes in a way that "seriously challenges the jury's obligation to act as the 'conscience of the community' and to draw upon ordinary common sense in making its decisions."

   Other studies have demonstrated that jurors' pre-existing beliefs regarding racial and gender characteristics affected their determinations of guilt and innocence most strongly in cases where evidence was equivocal. *See* Fraher, *Adjudicative Facts, Non-Evidentiary Facts, and Permissible Jury Background Information*, 62 IND. L.J. 333, 339 (1987), discussing Ugwuegbu, *Racial and Evidential Factors in Juror Attribution of Legal Responsibility*, 15 J. EXPERIMENTAL SOC. PSYCHOLOGY 133 (1979). On jurors' responses to novel scientific evidence, *see* Note, *The Frye Doctrine and Relevancy Approach Controversy: An Empirical Evaluation*, 74 GEO. L.J. 1769 (1986), and *see id.* at 1783-85 (discussing the interplay between heuristic reasoning devices and juror response to expert testimony in cases where jurors feel well informed).

298. Ingber, *supra* note 265, at 835. Professor Ingber here relied, *inter alia*, on the epochal study of American anti-semitism in the 1940s, THE AUTHORITARIAN PERSONALITY. *Id.* at 835 n. 109. On the way that race, gender and physical attractiveness can generally prejudice jurors' assessments, *see* MacCoun, *The Emergence of Extralegal Bias During Jury Deliberation*, 17 CRIM. JUST. & BEHAV. 303 (1990); Dane & Wrightsman, *Effects of Defendants' and Victims' Characteristics on Jury Verdicts*, in THE PSYCHOLOGY OF THE COURTROOM 83 (N. Kerr & R. Bray eds. 1982).

299. Ingber, *supra* note 265, at 836 & *id.* n. 110. For Ingber's views on the critical issue of the role of crime in animating jurors' "passionate" response to deviance, *see id.* at 842-48. On the significance of jurors' views on the attractiveness of the victim and the character of the criminal as a determinant in their decision making, *see* Landy & Aronson, *supra* note 65.

   On the impact of jurors' perceptions on their "reading" of expert testimony, *see* Tanton, *Jury Preconceptions and Their Effect on Expert Testimony*, 24 J. FORENS. SCI. 681, 690 (1979) (most jurors "have a remarkably precise, albeit inaccurate, visual preconception of the forensic scientist in the courtroom"). *See also*, Rosenthal, *Nature of Jury Response to the Expert Witness*, 28 J. FORENS. SCI. 528 (1983) (jurors swayed by the "*secondary* content emanating from the witnesses as sources, from peripheral aspects of the message itself, and from the environment of the trial"—the expert's "paramessage"); Rosenthal, *supra* note 191; *see generally*, Saks & Wissler, *Legal and Psychological Bases of Expert Testimony: Surveys of the Law of Jurors*, 2 BEHAV. SCI. & L. 435 (1984); Note, *supra* note 297.

There is some case law support for this position in other criminal procedure areas. In *Jackson v. Denno*,[300] a voluntariness of confession case, the Supreme Court found that a jury may be "ill-suited to do justice to a defendant's full constitutional entitlement,"[301] an example of due process "trumping" OCS. More recent Supreme Court decisions show significant backsliding from this position,[302] yet the *Jackson* court's concern is still important. There are certain due process values that are not intuitively endorsed by lay persons on an OCS basis, a reality exacerbated by the frequent employment of heuristics in the way we weigh such cases.[303]

Thus, Professor Sherwin has questioned the basis for assuming that a court has superior expertise to a jury in determining the voluntariness of a putatively-coerced confession.[304] This skepticism must be considered on two additional levels. First, we need to consider whether judges are—or, at least, are *expected* to be—at a higher stage of "moral development" than other individuals.[305] Second, an objective consideration of the factual underpinnings of early confessions cases reflects the accuracy of the *Jackson* court's position; thus, at the time of *Brown v. Mississippi*,[306] the fact that police officers brutalized an indigent "and ignorant" black defendant,[307] might have been—under OCS principles—perfectly appropriate to white Mississippi jurors, but *not* so to a majority of Supreme Court justices, who demonstrably have a different set of "intuitions" than such jurors,

---

300. 378 U.S. 368 (1964).
301. Sherwin, *supra* note 82, at 763. The database that helped support this conclusion included Brown v. Mississippi, 297 U.S. 278, 281-83 (1936) (detailing whipping and torture of defendant; jury had accepted confession as not coerced), and Blackburn v. Alabama, 361 U.S. 199, 200-03 (1960) (mentally disabled defendant interrogated for at least eight hours of sustained questioning; jury had accepted confession as not coerced).
302. *See e.g.*, McCleskey v. Kemp, 481 U.S. 279 (1987), discussed *supra* chapter 3, note 244, and *infra* chapter 8, text accompanying notes 159-60. *See generally*, Woolhandler, *supra* note 166, at 121 (court ignores social science data that appears to "trump" OCS); Perlin & Dorfman, *supra* note 150, at 52-54.
303. *See e.g.*, Alschuler, *supra* note 30, at 347-48.
304. Sherwin, *supra* note 82, at 764.
305. *Cf.* Monaghan, *supra* note 197, at 749 (discussing John Hart Ely's characterization of certain "elite groups" (including judges) as "the reasoning class." *See id.* n. 153, citing J. ELY, DEMOCRACY AND DISTRUST 59 n. ** (1980).
306. 297 U.S. 278 (1936).
307. *Id.* at 281.

based, in some part, on their different "ethnic, class and educational backgrounds."[308]

Other empirical research corroborates these concerns. Jurors more concerned with crime control values are more likely to reject insanity pleas while those who take due process concerns more seriously are more likely to return an NGRI verdict.[309] Conviction proneness may also be revealed by an individual's attitude toward the legitimacy of the insanity defense.[310] These findings may help explain why female jurors appear to respond more favorably to mental disability defenses, as some evidence indicates that women may be more concerned with due process and men with controlling crime.[311]

Society also desires jurors to make "moral and practical judgments" as well as purely factual ones. Jurors regularly go beyond the simple application of the law to the facts, in cases involving such doctrines as justification or duress. "Society does not want jurors to be automatons; it wants them to make the unavoidable moral judgments involved in applying disputed facts to necessarily imprecise legal doctrines."[312] This analysis appears to be equally applicable to cases involving mental capacity issues.

---

308. Ingber, *supra* note 265, at 835.
309. Ellsworth et al., *The Death Qualified Jury and the Defense of the Insanity*, 8 LAW & HUM. BEHAV. 81 (1984).
310. Bronson, *On the Conviction Proneness and Representativeness of the Death-Qualified Jury: An Empirical Study of Colorado Veniremen*, 42 U. COLO. L. REV. 1, 7 n. 32 (1970). In response to the statement, "The plea of insanity is a loophole allowing too many guilty men to go free," responses broke down in the following manner as to the respondents' conviction proneness (CP) and innocent proneness (IP) on death penalty attitudes:

	CP	IP
Strongly favor	82	8
Favor	238	42
Oppose	147	45
Strongly oppose	40	26

   Id. at 8 n.34. *See also*, White, *supra* note 64, at 125, discussing Ellsworth, *supra* note 309, at 90 (death-qualified subjects more likely to see insanity defense as "a ruse and an impediment" to conviction).
311. White, *The Mental Illness Defense in the Capital Penalty Hearing*, 5 BEHAV. SCI. & L. 411, 418 (1987). *But see*, Ford, *supra* note 28, at 17-18 (discussing studies finding women *more* conviction-prone than men); *compare* Faulstich, *Effects Upon Social Perceptions of the Insanity Plea*, 55 PSYCHOLOG. REP. 183 (1984) (female jurors more likely to find defendant not responsible, but only where evidence of psychiatric history available).
312. Goldberg, *The Reluctant Embrace: Law and Science in America*, 75 GEO. L.J. 1341, 1348 (1987).

Finally, lawyers have always accepted as a "given" the mysticism inherent in the jury system, and how little we really know about what goes on in real (as opposed to simulated) jury deliberations.[313] Discussing squarely the impact of this mystification on the trial of insanity defense cases, Professor Grant Morris and his colleagues thus concluded:

> We simultaneously deify and degrade jurors. We entrust them with the awesome responsibility of deciding a defendant's guilt or innocence. We attribute to them the superhuman quality of being able to ignore their own backgrounds and to approach the trial tabula rasa. We assume that they are able to understand and apply the most complex legal formulae—ones that philosophers and lawyers have debated for centuries. Nevertheless, we camouflage jurors' importance to the criminal trial, telling them that they are merely factfinders and the judge will decide the defendant's disposition....
>
> Is society served by its continued tolerance of the mystique surrounding real juror deliberations? We think not. Efforts to investigate these obscure rites should be encouraged and expanded.[314]

This notion of "camouflage" is an important one for our purposes. So much of our insanity defense jurisprudence serves as a camouflage for hidden feelings, drives and desires, for what is truly socially neurotic decision making. Our shrouding juror deliberations with this "mystique" simply keeps us one further step away from understanding the psychodynamic processes at work in insanity defense cases.

b. Conclusion. In short, a wide variety of research on jury behavior reveals the pervasive use of both OCS and heuristic reasoning in all aspects of insanity defense decision making, in the "typical" case and the rare nullification case alike. Until we are willing to unshroud the jury's articulation of *its* view of the community's conscience and to carefully identify the cognitive "potholes" into which heuristic thinking frequently leads jurors in their decision making, we will continue to fruitlessly "grind our wheels" over the precise terminology of

---

313. *See e.g.*, Tanford & Tanford, *supra* note 7, at 759-71 (on jury behavior). *But see*, Reifman, Gusick & Ellsworth, *supra* note 294 (discussing research involving "real" jurors).

314. Morris et al., *Whither Thou Goest? An Inquiry Into Jurors' Perceptions of the Consequences of a Successful Insanity Defense*, 14 SAN DIEGO L. REV. 1058, 1078 (1977).

substantive insanity defense tests, as we remain blind to the underlying psychological motivations that truly *matter* in insanity defense cases.

7

Authoritarianism and the Insanity Defense

A. Introduction

I have, to this point, sought to demonstrate the power of the symbolic values that underlie the superficialities that dominate legislative and popular press characterizations of the insanity defense, to "unpack" the myths that perpetuate the defense's incoherence, and to show that the survival of these myths can best be understood by studying both the power of heuristic reasoning and the flawed use of "ordinary common sense" (OCS) in explaining the aberrant mental processes that lead a few individuals into committing otherwise-seemingly-inexplicable acts of random violence.

An examination of these processes is a necessary predicate for an understanding of the psychodynamic underpinnings of the insanity defense debate, but it is not a sufficient explanation for jurisprudential developments. To come to a more complete understanding of why, really, the Hinckley acquittal galvanized all players in the American political arena so as to result in the erasure of a century and a half of study and comprehension of the complexities of psychological behavior,[1] and why, at the end of the twentieth century, a landslide

---

1. *See supra* chapter 2 A 2 c, discussing the Insanity Defense Reform Act of 1984 (IDRA), 18 U.S.C. §20 (1988), and state legislative responses to the Hinckley acquittal. *See generally*, Callahan, Meyer & Steadman, *Insanity Defense Reform*

majority of our population expresses approval of the "wild beast" test of criminal responsibility discarded soon after its articulation in 1724,[2] we must ask a deeper and more troubling question: is there anything about our national character that has led to this state of affairs?

In order to understand these phenomena, I believe that we must examine the construct of the authoritarian personality to help illuminate the basic issues. I conclude that it is only through an understanding of the profoundly authoritarian bent of our national political character that we can make sense of our insanity jurisprudence.[3] Until we come to grips with our national failures of spirit in this sphere, we are doomed to perpetuate the time-and-energy draining charade that we have been enacting since March 30, 1982—the day that John W. Hinckley, Jr. shot Ronald Reagan. This will also help explain why we fall prey so easily to sanist thinking, why we engage in pretextual decisionmaking, and why we weigh social science evidence teleologically in insanity defense cases.[4]

This section will proceed in this manner. First, I will consider Reagan's role as victim in the context of the way the public has traditionally treated attacks on certain authority figures. Then, I will consider authoritarian personality theory, and the role of authoritarianism in American life, in the contexts of politics, the media, public opinion, and attitudes towards mental disability and the mentally ill, and then consider the body of research that has attempted to "read" our capital punishment jurisprudence through this filter. I will then

---

in the United States—Post-Hinckley, 11 MENT. & PHYS. DIS. L. REP. 54, 55 (1987) (full survey of state developments); H. STEADMAN ET AL., REFORMING THE INSANITY DEFENSE: AN EVALUATION OF PRE-AND POST-HINCKLEY REFORMS (1993) (H. STEADMAN, REFORMING) (comprehensive analysis of impact of changes in eight states); Wexler, *Redefining the Insanity Problem*, 53 GEO. WASH. L. REV. 528, 529-30 (1985) (role of Hinckley acquittal in shaping positions of relevant professional interest groups).

2.   Roberts, Golding & Fincham, *Implicit Theories of Criminal Responsibility: Decision Making and the Insanity Defense*, 11 LAW & HUM. BEHAV. 207, 226 (1987). The "wild beast" test, articulated in Rex v. Arnold, 16 How. St. Tr. 695 (1724), *reprinted in* 16 COMPLETE COLLECTION OF STATE TRIALS 695 (T.B. Howell ed. 1812), is discussed in this context *supra* chapter 3 A 1 a (2); *see* Quen, *Anglo-American Criminal Insanity*, 2 BULL. AM. ACAD. PSYCHIATRY & L. 115, 116 (1973) (*Arnold* the first "historically significant" insanity defense trial).

3.   In a subsequent work, I hope to explore the way that the atrophied level of development of our moral and psychological character contributes to this dilemma.

4.   *See generally infra* chapter 8 B-D.

look at the way that this authoritarianism has affected our insanity defense policies. I conclude that, in order to understand why the social meta-myths and the use of heuristics and OCS inform our jurisprudence the way that they do, we must focus on authoritarian personality theory.

B. Reagan as Hinckley's Victim/ Hinckley as Reagan's Victim

It is impossible to consider the psychodynamic formation of insanity defense jurisprudence in 1989 without acknowledging the significance of John Hinckley's choice of foil in his attempts to seek redemption in the eyes of Jodie Foster.[5] Not merely did Hinckley attempt to kill a President; his target was a President onto whom a significant percentage of the public had projected[6] the image of both father and king.[7] While we cannot simply "read" insanity defense history as the history of "public figure" cases,[8] there can be no minimizing the significance of Ronald-Reagan-as-victim in the wake of Hinckley's assassination attempt.

Inevitably, when a famous person is attacked, there is great public outcry to abolish or limit the insanity defense. Similarly, cases used as vehicles by which courts have "liberalized" the insanity

---

5. Some legal scholars, of course, contend that it is impossible to ever separate legal and political discourse. *See* Kelman, *Interpretive Construction in the Substantive Criminal Law*, 33 STAN. L. REV. 591, 591-92 n. 2 (1981).

6. Projection is the attribution of one's own ideas, feelings, or attitudes to other people or to objects, especially the externalization of blame, guilt or responsibility as a means of safeguarding self-esteem and avoiding self-censure, and as a defense against anxiety. *See e.g.*, C. BRENNER, AN ELEMENTARY TEXTBOOK OF PSYCHOANALYSIS 101 (1955); J. PAGE, PSYCHOPATHOLOGY: THE SCIENCE OF UNDERSTANDING DEVIANCE 13 (1971).

7. R. Rogers, "Assessment of Criminal Responsibility: Empirical Advances and Unanswered Questions" (paper presented at national conference of the American Psychological Association, Aug. 1985), at 6, characterizing Hinckley's offense as attempted "regicide." *See generally*, Fairbairn, *The Effect of the King's Death Upon Patients in Analysis*, 17 INT'L J. PSYCHOANALYSIS 278 (1936); *see also*, Rothstein, *Presidential Assassination Syndrome, I & II*, 11 ARCH. GEN'L PSYCHIATRY 245 (1964), and 15 ARCH. GEN'L PSYCHIATRY 260 (1966).

8. *See e.g.*, Smith, *Criminal Insanity: From a Historical Point of View*, 11 BULL. AM. ACAD. PSYCHIATRY & L. 27, 33 (1983) ("there is a very real danger with a 'famous case' approach in assuming that the procedure and outcome of specific cases circumscribes the process of historical change").

defense have involved unknowns.[9] Only in *Jones v. United States*[10]— a case involving an attempted shoplifting—was such an unknown case a vehicle for limiting the use of the insanity defense; in that case, however, a strong argument an be made for the proposition that the Supreme Court was implicitly using *Jones* "as a vehicle for an explicit social agenda: the diminution of the insanity defense in the wake of the Hinckley acquittal."[11]

Indeed, in a law review article urging insanity defense limitation, former U.S. Attorney General William French Smith observed: "Since the cases in which the defense is presented tend to receive intense public scrutiny, they have the capacity to influence far beyond their numbers the citizen's perceptions—and ultimately the citizen's acceptance—of the rationality, fairness and efficiency of the criminal justice process."[12] Smith, of course, overstated the issue. The public is totally unaware of most insanity defense cases (frequently involving indigents charged with petty crimes about whom there is no important psychiatric disagreement as to diagnosis or responsibility).[13] It is in precisely those rarest of cases where there is an "outside event" (e.g., famous defendant; sensationally-committed violent crime; sharp disagreement between prominent forensic witnesses) that the public's skepticism is triggered.[14] I will thus examine how the Hinckley attack "fits" in the context of other "political" insanity defense trials to consider how these trials have helped shape public perceptions, and how these perceptions have altered the insanity defense jurisprudence.

---

9. *E.g.*, Durham v. United States, 214 F. 2d 862 (D.C. Cir. 1954); United States v. Brawner, 471 F. 2d 969 (D.C. Cir. 1972) (overruling *Durham*); *see supra* chapter 3 A 1 c (2) & (3).
10. 463 U.S. 354 (1983); *see supra* chapter 4 E 2 d.
11. Perlin, *The Supreme Court, the Mentally Disabled Criminal Defendant, and Symbolic Values: Random Decisions, Hidden Rationales, or "Doctrinal Abyss?"* 29 ARIZ. L. REV. 1, 81 (1987); *see also generally*, Wexler, *supra* note 1.
12. Smith, *Limiting the Insanity Defense: A Rational Approach to Irrational Crimes*, 47 MO. L. REV. 605, 606 (1982).
13. *See e.g.*, L. CAPLAN, THE INSANITY DEFENSE AND THE TRIAL OF JOHN W. HINCKLEY, JR. 49-58 (1983) (discussing developments in obscure insanity defense case with unknown defendant being tried at same time as Hinckley).
14. On the significance of the publicity about the underlying crime on the final judicial outcome in insanity defense cases, *see e.g.*, Rogers, Wasyliw & Cavanaugh, *Evaluating Insanity: A Study of Construct Validity*, 8 LAW & HUM. BEHAV. 293, 296 n. 2 (1984).

1. Attacks on Authority Figures[15]

M'Naghten was clearly not the first "political case" involving the controversial use of an insanity defense. The trials of James Hadfield (attempted assassination of King George III), John Bellingham (successful assassination of British Prime Minister Perceval), and Edward Oxford (attempted assassination of Queen Victoria) all preceded M'Naghten, and all had significant political aspects.[16] The significance of a "scandalous" trial for subsequent insanity defense pleaders was apparent many years ago to Lord Coleridge, who stated, "Judges swing to and fro like pendulums in their charges to juries, and if a man is tried, after some scandalous acquittal, he gets no fair justice."[17]

Even by the time of M'Naghten, one of the major themes animating the development of insanity defense jurisprudence was already in place: the shaping of both the substantive insanity defense test and the appropriate procedural insanity defense rules within the context of a "political trial." While this phenomenon has been fre-

---

15. I am consciously bypassing the question of whether "political insanity defense" cases should also be read as political cases. Moran has argued, for instance, that M'Naghten's actions were the result of what, today, would be characterized as a "paid political hit." R. Moran, Knowing Right From Wrong: The Insanity Defense of Daniel McNaughtan 38, 87-90, Appendix E (1981) (*but see e.g.*, Rollin, *Crime and Mental Disorder: Daniel McNaughton, A Case in Point*, 50 Medico-Legal J. 102 (1982) (sharply criticizing Moran's views), and sources cited *id.* n. 38). For an analysis of John Hinckley's "politics," *see* L. Caplan, supra note 13, at 35 (Hinckley had toyed with membership in the National Socialist Party (the American Nazis), and characterized himself as an "all-out anti-Semite and white racialist"). Professor Christenson has argued that a survey of trials involving political/public figure victims in cases in which defendants have raised the insanity defense reveals "the ubiquity of a political agenda." R. Christenson, "From Hadfield to Hinckley: The Insanity Plea in Politically-Related Trials," (paper delivered at the 1983 Academy of Criminal Justice Sciences' Annual Meeting, March 22, 1983), at 45.
16. *See generally*, R. Christenson, *supra* note 15; R. Christenson, Political Trials: Gordian Knots in the Law 86-104 (1986); Sadoff, *Insanity: Evaluation of a Medicolegal Concept*, 9 Transactions & Studies Coll. Phys. Philadelphia 237 (1987). Hadfield's trial is discussed extensively from this perspective in Moran, *The Origin of Insanity as a Special Verdict: The Trial for Treason of James Hadfield*, 19 Law & Soc'y Rev. 487 (1985), and *see id.* at 509-10 (contrasting lack of public outcry with "considerable judicial concern" following Hadfield's unsuccessful attempt).
17. *See The Criminal Responsibility of the Alleged Insane*, 1 Camb. L.J. 302, 313 (1923), *quoting* R. v. Pearsall.

quently noted, its significance in the development of insanity defense law has yet to be fully appreciated.[18]

Almost every major change in the law of the insanity defense since the development of the "wild beast" test came in a politically-charged trial: James Hadfield shot at King George III (and missed); John Bellingham assassinated Prime Minister Perceval; Edward Oxford shot at Queen Victoria (and missed);[19] Daniel M'Naghten assassinated Prime Minister Peel's secretary (thinking he was Peel). Whether or not Richard Moran's thesis—that M'Naghten had been paid to assassinate Peel,[20] and that his trial demonstrated "how the insanity verdict can be used effectively to detain and discredit political offenders"[21]—is accepted as a political construct, it is clear that the insanity defense debate has been played out in the battlefield of the politically-charged trial.[22]

The saga of Queen Victoria's outrage at the M'Naghten acquittal (shared by the public as reflecting an irrational legal system which could "acquit" a defendant whom "everyone knew" was guilty) has

---

18. *See* Milner, *What's Old and New About the Insanity Plea*, 67 JUDICATURE 499, 501 (1984), *quoting* testimony of Sander Gilman, before the National Commission on the Insanity Defense ("The United States has this tradition in media coverage that attempts to [assassinate] the President turn out to be the way the generation defines madness").

19. According to Nigel Walker, this was one of three assassination attempts of George III's life "by lunatics." Walker, *1883 And All That*, 1966 CRIM. L. REV. 17, 18. According to Walker, Queen Victoria was shot at on six occasions between 1840 and 1882 (and on a seventh was assaulted with a cane); virtually all her assailants appeared to be seriously mentally impaired. *Id.* at 18-19. *See also*, R. SMITH, TRIAL BY MEDICINE: INSANITY AND RESPONSIBILITY IN VICTORIAN TRIALS 28 (1981) ("Most of these attacks were outrageous rather than dangerous").

20. R. MORAN, *supra* note 15, at 38, 87-90. *Compare* Quen, *An Historical View of the M'Naghten Trial*, 42 BULL. HIST. MED. 43, 46 (1968) (M'Naghten's symptoms indicate he was suffering from paranoid schizophrenia).

21. R. MORAN, *supra* note 15, at 115. *But see*, Quen, *Book Review*, 58 BULL. HIST. MED. 266, 268 (1984) (criticizing Moran's historiography, methodology, and use of source materials, and concluding, "This book cannot be recommended to scholars of the history of medicine or of criminal insanity"). *Compare* Mills, *Book Review*, 11 BULL. AM. ACAD. PSYCHIATRY & L. 91, 92 (1983) (characterizing book as "provocative," and, "despite its shortcomings," a "useful and interesting work").

22. *See* Quen, *supra* note 20, at 49 (M'Naghten's act took place against a backdrop of "violence and profound political unrest"). Similarly, Christenson suggests that the referendum decision of California voters to reject the diminished capacity defense came "largely in reaction to the [Dan] White verdict." R. Christenson, *supra* note 15, at 94.

been frequently told.[23] Similarly, after Guiteau's insanity defense was rejected (in the course of the "most celebrated American insanity trial of the nineteenth century" in which thirty-six medical experts testified),[24] and the defendant was executed for the murder of President Garfield,[25] the issues of criminal responsibility, the propriety of forensic testimony, and the systemic implications of broadened definitions of psychological motivation were hotly debated,[26] leading to the frequently-repeated recommendation that "neutral" court-appointed forensic experts be used in such cases.[27]

Finally, the impact of the attempted assassination of President Reagan—characterized by one of the country's leading forensic psychiatrists as the M'Naghten case of the twentieth century[28]—on the ongoing insanity defense debate is apparent.[29] There should be no

---

23. See e.g., Diamond, *Criminal Responsibility of the Mentally Ill*, 14 STAN. L. REV. 59, 66 (1961) ("Within a few months the public furor over the [M'Naghten] verdict led to a parliamentary investigation and the judges retreated under political pressure back to the medieval formula..."); Diamond, *Isaac Ray and the Trial of Daniel M'Naghten*, 112 AM. J. PSYCHIATRY 651 (1956) (Diamond II). See also, Walker, *supra* note 19, at 17 (discussing Henry VIII's introduction into Parliament of a bill allowing for the execution of lunatics found to have committed high treason, a bill ordered drafted by the King "when the law seemed likely to protect Lady Rocheford, who had been party to Katherine Howard's infidelities with Thomas Culpepper").

24. R. Christenson, *supra* note 15, at 91.

25. See generally, C. ROSENBERG, THE TRIAL OF THE ASSASSIN GUITEAU: PSYCHIATRY AND LAW IN THE GILDED AGE (1968); see also, R. CHRISTENSON, *supra* note 16, at 91-92; R. Christenson, *supra* note 15, at 26-30. The relationship between Guiteau and Hinckley is discussed in Bulmash, *The Irony of the Insanity Defense: A Theory of Relativity*, 10 J. PSYCHIATRY & L. 285 (1982). Garfield was not the first American President to be the subject of an assassination attempt in a case which involved an insanity plea. See Zonana, *The First Presidential Assassination Attempt*, 12 BULL. AM. ACAD. PSYCHIATRY & L. 309 (1984) (discussing Richard Lawrence's successful use of the plea to a misdemeanor charge following his attempted assassination of President Andrew Jackson).

26. Bulmash, *supra* note 26, at 286-87.

27. Resnick, *Perceptions of Psychiatric Testimony: An Historical Perspective on the Hysterical Invective*, 14 BULL. AM. ACAD. PSYCHIATRY & L. 203, 215 (1986). Dr. Bernard Diamond has argued (persuasively, to my mind) that such "neutrality " is mythic. See Diamond, *The Psychiatrist as Advocate*, 1 J. PSYCHIATRY & L. 5 (1973); Diamond, *The Fallacy of the Impartial Expert*, 3 ARCH. CRIM. PSYCHODYNAMICS 221 (1959); see generally, Perlin, *Power Imbalances in Therapeutic and Forensic Relationships*, 9 BEHAV. SCI. & L. 111 (1991).

28. Sadoff, *supra* note 16, at 246.

29. See Callahan, Meyer & Steadman, *supra* note 1, for a full jurisdiction-by-jurisdiction examination of the national changes in both the procedural and substantive insanity defense in the years following the Hinckley shooting.

surprise about the "river of fury"[30] and outpouring of outrage that quickly followed Hinckley's acquittal.[31]

What is it about cases such as these involving "public figure" defendants that disproportionately alters the insanity defense debate, and what is it about the Hinckley trial—involving an attack on one of the most popular Presidents in history—that distorted the debate even more significantly? While it may appear intuitively obvious that any attack on any authority figure will result in immediate public revulsion, it is necessary to consider additional factors in attempting to formulate a response.

In such cases, it is more likely that the public simply refuses to believe that the assassination attempt can truly be the result of mental illness.[32] The public knows more about such cases, of course, because of the intense amount of publicity they receive in the news media, publicity which brings with it an inevitably distorting effect.[33] Asks Professor Christenson, "[W]hat is society to do when the hydraulic pressure of public opinion and events surrounding an attempted assassination...forces these hard cases into court?"[34]

Also, since any decision by a defendant to plead insanity results in public fear/revulsion/skepticism/anger, fueling the fire of never-

---

30. Perlin, *The Things We Do For Love: John Hinckley's Trial and the Future of the Insanity Defense in the Federal Courts* (review of L. CAPLAN, *supra* note 13), 30 N.Y.L. SCH. L. REV. 859, 860 (1985).

31. *See supra* chapter 2 A 2 a. *Compare* State v. Jasuilewicz, 205 N.J. Super. 58, 501 A. 2d 583, 587-89 (App. Div. 1985) (error for trial judge to fail to voir dire jurors on way that Hinckley verdict might potentially taint factually-unrelated insanity trial); Smith v. State, 703 S.W. 2d 641, 644 n. 2 (Tex. Cr. App. 1985) (such questioning should have been conducted of individual jurors rather than of entire venire panel); *but see*, State v. Rogers, 1984 WL 7811 (Ohio App. 1984), at **13-14 (no error where court denied defense motion to suspend trial because of publicity in Hinckley case).

32. Diamond II, *supra* note 23, at 655.

33. Thus, the uproar in the British press following the *M'Naghten* verdict appears nearly identical to the post- Hinckley furor. *See e.g.*, R. MORAN, *supra* note 15, at 19-21, recounting editorial positions of *London Times* (verdict reflected physicians invading traditional province of judiciary); the *London Standard* ("monomaniacs [are] just objects of punishment, because...monomania is itself the effect of a long indulgence in depraved habits or action;" "mad doctors" were permitted to "dictate the law"); the *Illustrated London News* (those who "passively" indulge themselves in socialism and infidelity and thus willingly undergo a process of "mental intoxication" cannot claim to be without "legal or moral responsibility"), and the *Weekly Chronicle* ("[is it] a better policy to have a Queen, or a Premier, shot at occasionally, or to dispose of the parties likely to take this course, before their disorders breaks out into overt acts[?]")

34. R. Christenson, *supra* note 15, at 46. *See generally infra* chapter 8 A.

dormant myths, it should be apparent that these sentiments will be heightened where the putative victim is such a public figure. After the verdict was entered in M'Naghten's case, an enraged Queen Victoria wrote to Robert Peel:

> The law may be perfect, but how is it that whenever a case for its application arises, it proves to be of no avail? We have seen the trials of Oxford and MacNaughtan conducted by the ablest lawyers of the day— Lord Denman, Chief Justice Tindal, and Sir Wm Follett,—and they allow and advise the Jury to pronounce the verdict of Not Guilty on account of Insanity,—*whilst everybody is morally convinced that both malefactors are perfectly conscious and aware of what they did!* It appears from this, that the force of law is entirely put into the Judge's hands, and that it depends merely upon his charge whether the law is to be applied or not. Could not the Legislature lay down the rule...which Chief Justice Mansfield did in the case of Bellingham; and why could not the Judges be bound to interpret the law in this and no other sense in their charges to the Juries?[35]

Here society's deep-seated and rarely-articulated ambivalence about punishment, its projection of unacceptable hostile impulses onto an insanity-pleading defendant, and its unconscious fears of its own impulses[36] exaggerate its response to a "political" case, where, intuitively, the likelihood of reasoned discourse will be lessened.[37] Thus, when the insanity defense is raised in a sensational/political case where "public feeling runs high against the accused,...the more vociferously may the public, by a subconscious inability to identify itself with the

---

35. *See* R. MORAN, *supra* note 15, at 21 (emphasis added) (*quoting* letter of March 12, 1843 [Royal Archives A14/8], from Queen to Sir Robert Peel). There is some evidence that royal intercession in such cases preceded M'Naghten by three centuries. *See* Walker, *supra* note 19, at 17 (discussing King Henry VIII's role in the trial of Thomas Culpeper, and his introduction of legislation in Parliament "which had the effect of ratifying the execution of lunaticks who had been found to have committed high treason").

36. *See e.g.*, Schoenfeld, *Law and Unconscious Motivation*, 8 HOWARD L.J. 15, 17 (1962) ("it is no surprise to learn that the apprehension and punishment of criminals helps direct the unconscious aggressive tendencies of policemen and prison officials into socially useful channels") (footnote omitted); *see generally supra* chapter 2 C.

37. *Cf.* Grissom, *True and False Experts*, 34 AM. J. INSAN. 1, 4 (1878): "There are those as we shall see, who would fain restore the good old days. It was but a hundred and twenty years ago, when Christendom witnessed the tortures of Robert Francois Damiens, who in a maniacal paroxysm, wounded Louis XV. The merciful law burned his hand, tore his flesh with red-hot pincers, poured melted lead and sulphur into the wounds, and tore him apart with four horses, after many efforts, amid the jokes of the pitiful insane wretch."

offender, demand that 'justice be done,' or otherwise express its desire for a Roman holiday."[38]

Finally, because political trials are inherently hard cases, there is an extra level of distortion where "the jury is sometimes too frightened of the hard case, and the judge of the bad law, [reflecting] the eternal conflict between law in the abstract and the justice of the case."[39] Also, in part because of attention focused upon political trials, the "outlier" problems—battles of the experts; high-priced lawyers; sharply-conflicting testimony—appear (inaccurately) to reflect the norm.

Beyond these factors, however, it is necessary to explore further the particular and peculiar role of President Reagan—and his unconscious importance to much of the American public—in attempting to understand why an assassination attempt on his life mobilized the public in a way that abortive attempts on, for instance, President Ford's life did not.[40] Only through this inquiry will the subsequent legislative developments come into clearer focus.

2. Symbolism and Politics

There is little question that the image that the shooting evoked— an irrational "Oedipal crime,"[41] victimizing a royal leader of unsurpassed popularity—played an important role in shaping the future direction of insanity defense law. The public's "astonishing" overreaction[42] to the Hinckley acquittal must thus be evaluated in light of the interplay between public opinion and social policy, the way that institutions such as the media and respected national political and legal figures distorted reality in their depictions of the insanity defense in the post-*Hinckley* legislative hearings, the unique *persona* of Ronald Reagan, and the symbolic role he filled in the early days of his Presidency. It is necessary to examine each of these factors in an effort to more fully understand all of the forces at play here, in the

---

38. Overholser, *The Place of Psychiatry in Criminal Law*, 16 B.U. L. REV. 322, 328 (1936).

39. P. DEVLIN, TRIAL BY JURY 124 (1966). *See* Quen, *supra* note 20, at 50 (judicial redefinition in *M'Naghten* played out "under the national stress of the time").

40. *See e.g.*, G. FORD, A TIME TO HEAL 308-12 (1979).

41. *See supra* chapter 2, text accompanying note 111; chapter 4 text accompanying note 71.

42. Kaufman, *Should Florida Follow the Federal Insanity Defense?* 15 FLA. ST. U. L. REV. 793, 836 (1987).

specific context of politics' part in the creation of an insanity defense jurisprudence.

a. Symbolism and social policy. Symbolism is particularly rich in the complicated arena of law and psychiatry.[43] Affirmation of a norm (*e.g.*, that mental illness is not exculpatory unless the defendant is "really crazy") is both public and political. It symbolizes a "gesture of public affirmation" that both prevents recognition of the norm violator's existence by the public and "quiets and comforts" those whose interests and sentiments it embodies, and also "directs the major institutions of the society to its support."[44] Simultaneously, the designation of behavior as violating public norms "confers status and honor on those groups with conventional cultures and derogates those whose cultures are considered deviant."[45] Such circumstances can give rise to "disinterested indignation"—"hostility directed against a norm violator despite the absence of direct or personal damage to the norm upholder and designator."[46]

Changes in public opinion are important causes of political policy changes.[47] This becomes problematic when opinion is manipulated through "lies or deception;"[48] the means by which public opinion has become a proximate cause of policy changes in insanity defense jurisprudence has greatly been through the functional equivalent of "lies or deception:" unconscious or conscious distortion and fact manipulation by otherwise-respected political leaders,[49] and

---

43. *See e.g.*, Edelman, *Law and Psychiatry as Political Symbolism*, 3 INT'L J. L. & PSYCHIATRY 235 (1980); *see generally*, M. EDELMAN, THE SYMBOLIC USES OF POLITICS (1964).

44. Gusfield, *On Legislating Morals: The Symbolic Process of Designating Deviance*, 56 CALIF. L. REV. 54, 58 (1968); *see also*, M. EDELMAN, *supra* note 43, ch. 2 (discussing "political quiescence").

45. Gusfield, *supra* note 44, at 59.

46. *Id.* at 54. Here, the norm upholder's "righteous hostility" leads him to define the deviant as "immoral." *Id.* Self-evidently, the number of individuals who suffer "direct or personal damage" as a result of a successful insanity defense plea is minimal; the number who so suffer because of improper insanity defense pleas is too small to count. *See supra* chapter 3 B 1 b (1).

47. Page & Shapiro, *Effects of Public Opinion on Policy*, 77 AM. POLI. SCI. REV. 175, 188-89 (1983).

48. *Id.* at 189.

49. *See e.g.*, Mickenberg, *A Pleasant Surprise: The Guilty but Mentally Ill Verdict Has Succeeded on Its Own Right and Successfully Preserved the Traditional Role of the Insanity Defense*, 55 U. CIN. L. REV. 943, 955 (1987) (discussing testimony of U.S. Attorney Rudolph Guiliani before the National Commission on the Insanity Defense); *see supra* chapter 2 A 2 b (3).

sloppy reporting by the press.[50] Post-Hinckley insanity defense limitations "fit" precisely into this general pattern.[51]

b. Political and press distortions. The shaping of public opinion becomes especially important in this context, where "outbursts of hostility" have created an environment in which the legislator "who obtains a tactical advantage is the one who is willing to introduce the most 'absolute' bills with the most drastic sanctioning requirements."[52] Indeed, legislative fear of public outcry when an infamous insanity acquittee is released has been focused upon as one of the animating forces in the development of this area of the law.[53]

On a less abstract level, it is easy to see why the insanity defense has become such a popular target for prosecutors and legislators.[54] In the early 1970s, the Nixon White House's abolition efforts were patently political;[55] if, as appeared likely, its motivation in seeking abolition was to raise conviction rates by "stripping from unbalanced defendants" the opportunity to proffer an insanity defense, such a

---

50. *See* Mickenberg, *supra* note 49, at 946-47 n. 14; Perlin, *On "Sanism,"* 46 SMU L. REV. 373, 373 n. 1 (1992). In a subsequent work, I will explore the role of the media in the shaping of sanist attitudes toward mentally disabled persons, and the impact of those attitudes on insanity defense policies. On the way that the media shapes criminal justice attitudes, *see e.g.,* Humphries, *Serious Crime, News Coverage and Ideology: A Content Analysis of Crime Coverage in a Metropolitan paper,* 27 CRIME & DELINQ. 191 (1981); Gorelick, *"Join Our War:" The Construction of Ideology in a Newspaper Crimefighting Campaign,* 35 CRIME & DELINQ. 421 (1989); Cavendar, *"Scared Straight:" Ideology and the Media,* 9 J. CRIM. JUST. 431 (1981); Fishman, *Crime Waves as Ideology,* 26 SOC. PROBS. 531 (1978); Gordon & Heath, *The News Business, Crime, and Fear,* in REACTIONS TO CRIME (D. Lewis ed. 1981).
51. Hans & Slater, *"Plain Crazy:" Lay Definitions of Legal Insanity,* 7 INT'L J. L. & PSYCHIATRY 105, 113 (1984).
52. Lasswell, *What Psychiatrists and Political Scientists Can Learn From One Another,* 1 PSYCHIATRY 30 (1938).
53. Kirschner, *Constitutional Standards for Release of the Civilly Committed and Not Guilty By Reason of Insanity,* 20 ARIZ. L. REV. 223, 276 (1978), and *see id.* at n. 380.
54. As to which legislators are most susceptible to this position, *see e.g.,* McGarrell & Flanagan, *Measuring and Explaining Legislator Crime Control Ideology,* 24 J. RES. CRIME & DELINQ. 102, 115 (1987) (white, nonurban, Republican legislators most likely to reflect conservative crime and justice ideology); *compare* Mickenberg, *supra* note 49, at 970 ("For many years, right-wing politicians have viewed the insanity defense as symbolic of many of their grievances against the criminal justice system").
55. *See e.g.,* Titus, *Criminal Law Revision in Oregon: A New Game Plan?* 51 ORE. L. REV. 553-556 (1972).

motive was accurately labeled "odious."[56] While the Reagan-inspired attempts at abolition flowed more closely from an idiosyncratic and sensational case, the positions of Attorney Generals Smith and Meese seemed to have been cut from the same cloth as Nixon's.[57]

c. The Reagan persona. No discussion of the post-Hinckley furor can be complete without some consideration of the specific identity of the victim.[58] It is probably not coincidental that some of Reagan's popularity stems from his style of discourse-by-heuristics.[59] The insanity defense "debate" is an anecdotal, emotion-arousing heuristic one,[60] a style which President Reagan has perfected.[61]

In the context of this inquiry, it is revealing to consider Reagan's anecdotal response to the difficult question of the propriety of lethal injection as the means of inflicting capital punishment.[62] According to Zimring and Hawkins:

> The origins of the American revival of lethal injection are obscure. As early as 1973, then-Governor Reagan of California endorsed the concept with characteristic optimism:

> "Being a former farmer and horse raiser, I know what it's like to try to eliminate an injured horse by shooting him. Now you call the veterinarian and the vet gives it a shot and the horse goes to sleep—that's it. I myself have wondered if maybe this isn't part of our problem [with capital punishment], if maybe we should review and see if there aren't even more humane methods now—the simple shot or tranquilizer."

---

56. Platt, *The Proposal to Abolish the Federal Insanity Defense: A Critique*, 10 CAL. WEST. L. REV. 449, 470 (1974).
57. *See supra* chapter 3 C.
58. For a psychoanalytic reading of Reagan's popularity, *see generally*, L. DeMAUSE, REAGAN'S AMERICA (1984).
59. *See supra* chapter 6 C 1-2.
60. Saks & Kidd, *Human Information Processing and Adjudication: Trial by Heuristics*, 15 LAW & SOC'Y REV. 123, 137 (1980-81), discussing Nesbitt & Temoshok, *Is There an "External" Cognitive Style?* 33 J. PERSONAL. & SOC'L PSYCHOLOGY 36 (1976).
61. *See supra* chapter 6, note 73. On the simplifying heuristic of attribution theory, *see supra* chapter 6 C 1; *see also,* Rosenthal, *The Concept of the Paramessage in Persuasive Communication*, 58 Q.J. SPEECH 15, 20 (1972) ("[W]hen the personality becomes the focal point of reaction, the issue control of the message ceases to be motivational and the persuasive effect is governed by the impact of the source data"); *see generally*, Tiefenbrun, *Legal Semiotics*, 5 CARDOZO ARTS & ENTERTAINMENT J. 89 (1986).
62. *See e.g.*, Heckler v. Chaney, 470 U.S. 821 (1985) (FDA decision to not take certain action regarding drugs used for lethal injections held not subject to review under the Administrative Procedure Act).

Two aspects of Governor Reagan's account deserve comment. First, the analogy he draws neglects a distinction between animal euthanasia and human injection that we regard as decisive: The horse doesn't know the injection is scheduled; the prisoner does.... Yet the Reagan excerpt, without any supplement, constitutes the essence of the case for lethal injections in the legislative chambers of several states. It is not so much a summary as the totality of the argument for lethal injections.[63]

It is this sort of reliance on heuristics which allowed the distorted and inaccurate public response to the Hinckley acquittal to pass with virtually no comment.[64]

We must also consider the roots of President Reagan's political philosophy. Reagan spoke, clearly, persuasively, and eloquently to what, in the late 1960s and early 1970s was called "the silent majority:"

By the late 1960s, many Middle Americans-to-be were becoming discontent with the quite dramatic changes in the political culture. They objected to the cultural and political concerns of the civil rights, antiwar and women's movements and were resentful of the attention those movements garnered. Their animosity to these movements was couched in antistatism and anti-elitism—as well as racism, national chauvinism, moralistic indignation and anti-feminism—because they, understandably, saw the Great Society and the liberal decisions of the Warren Court as aligned with these dissident political movements and cultural tendencies. Liberal culture, liberal policies, and the liberal electoral coalition were all implicated as sources of their resentment. The manner in which racial, gender, and generational changes were politically articulated divided the liberal voting bloc and marginalized those who had been celebrated in the earlier American dream.[65]

The public's perception of Reagan's personality similarly bore out Geoffrey Gorer's thesis that, due to our "insatiable" demands for

---

63. F. ZIMRING & G. HAWKINS, CAPITAL PUNISHMENT AND THE AMERICAN AGENDA 110 (1987), *quoting* in part, Schwarzchild, *Homicide By Injection*, N.Y. Times, Dec. 23, 1982, at A15.
64. *See e.g.*, Gantz, *The Diffusion of News About the Attempted Reagan Assassination*, 33 J. COMMUNIC. 56 (Winter 1983) *see also*, Mickenberg, *supra* note 49, at 970-72 (discussing "[f]alse impressions of the frequent success of the insanity defense" that have been fostered by political propaganda, citing statements by Senators, Congressmen, Attorney General Smith, and Justice Department officials).
65. Hunter, *The Role of Liberal Political Culture in the Construction of Middle America*, 42 U. MIAMI L. REV. 93, 108 (1987).

the signs of friendship and love, if all else is equal, our votes will go to the candidate who "most adequately demonstrates friendly interest."[66]

d. Reagan's role in the early 1980s. President Reagan had taken office at a time when seventy-five percent of Americans believed that "the United States had gone off on the wrong track," sixty percent that we needed a leader who would "bend the rules a bit," and fifty percent that it might be necessary to use force to restore "the American Way of Life;"[67] such poll results reflected feelings of "disintegration and growing rage [that] were not really rational,"[68] a rage that was specifically focused on an allegedly "wildly 'out of control' crime wave," and that was reflected in a series of popular press articles characterized by "extraordinarily frightening imagery."[69] A memo written by Assistant White House Chief of Staff Richard Darman as part of the 1984 re-election campaign strategy illustrates the point:

> Paint Ronald Reagan as the personification of all that is right with or heroized by America. Leave Mondale in a position where an attack on Reagan is tantamount to America's idealized image of itself—where a vote against Reagan is, in some subliminal sense, a vote against mythic "AMERICA."[70]

There is some measure of dissonance here between perception and reality.[71] In reality, at the time that President Reagan was inaugu-

---

66. G. Gorer, The American People: A Study on National Character 133-34 (1948). On how different branches of the media portrayed these aspects of Reagan's persona in significantly different ways, *see* Paletz & Guthrie, *The Three Faces of Ronald Reagan*, 37 J. Communic. 7 (Autumn 1987).

67. L. deMause, *supra* note 58, at 2.

68. *Id.* at 5. *Compare* Cullen, Clark & Wozniak, *Explaining the Get Tough Movement: Can the Public Be Blamed?* 49 Fed. Probation 16, 22 (June 1985) (discussing "dilemma between whether elected officials should seek to be servants of the public's will or moral entrepreneurs who attempt to shape what citizens think").

69. L. DeMause, *supra* note 58, at 11.

70. S. Ducat, Taken In: American Gullibility and the Reagan Mythos 95 (1988), *quoting* P. Erickson, Reagan Speaks: The Making of an American Myth 100 (1985).

71. On these perceptions in general in the criminal justice process, *see e.g.*, Fattah, *Perceptions of Violence, Concern About Crime, Fear of Victimization and Attitudes to the Death Penalty*, 21 Canad. J. Criminol. 22 (1979); Cohen & Doob, *Public Attitudes to Plea Bargaining*, 32 Crim. L.Q. 85 (1989-90); Flanagan, McGarrell & Brown, *Public Perceptions of the Criminal Courts: The Role of Demographic and Related Attitudinal Variables*, 22 J. Res. Crime & Delinq. 66 (1985); Miller, Rossi & Simpson, *Felony Punishments: A Factorial*

rated, studies by the National Council on Crime and Delinquency showed slight decreases in the incidence of and arrests for major crimes, leading to that council's conclusion that "crime waves are created by the human imagination."[72]

Also, rigorous evidence suggests that "the public 'will'...is much more complex and tolerant than politicians acknowledge,"[73] and that legislative response sometimes outstripped public preference.[74] Nonetheless, the political fervor that accompanied Reagan's election was driven by an explicit crime control ideology, and Reagan stood as a symbol for a host of "get tough" crime positions.[75]

When Reagan's shooting is juxtaposed with the apocalyptic, conservative and fundamentalist politics that served as the hallmark of his campaign and his first term, and the traditional role of Presidents as "father figures," the depth of the public's outrage should not be surprising.[76] The dominant political discourse at the time of the

---

Survey of Perceived Justice in Criminal Sentencing, 82 J. CRIM. L. & CRIMINOL. 396 (1991).

72. L. DE MAUSE, *supra* note 58, at 11, *quoting* N.Y. Post, Feb. 6, 1981, at 1. On the way voters perceive the candidate they support to be closer to their own level of authoritarianism than the candidate they oppose, *see* Levy, *Perceptions of Leader Authoritarianism*, 4 ACAD. PSYCHOL. BULL. 431 (1982).

73. Cullen, Clark & Wozniak, *supra* note 68, at 22, *citing* D. DUFFEE, EXPLAINING CRIMINAL JUSTICE: COMMUNITY THEORY AND CRIMINAL JUSTICE REFORM 120-22 (1980).

74. Thomson & Raqgona, *Popular Moderation Versus Governmental Authoritarianism: An Interactionist View of Public Sentiment Toward Criminal Sanctions*, 33 CRIME & DELINQ. 337 (1987); *see also*, Skovron, Scott & Cullen, *The Death Penalty for Juveniles: An Assessment of Public Support*, 35 CRIME & DELINQ. 546 (1986); Hamm, *Legislator Ideology and Capital Punishment: The Special Case for Indiana Juveniles*, 6 JUST. Q. 219 (1989).

75. *See* Caringella-MacDonald, *State Crises and the Crackdown on Crime Under Reagan*, 14 CONTEMP. CRISES 91 (1990); on the ascendancy of an "explicit crime control ideology," *see* Pillsbury, *Understanding Penal Reform: The Dynamic of Change*, 80 J. CRIM. L. & CRIMINOL. 726, 751-52 (1989).

76. *See e.g.*, G. WILLS, REAGAN'S AMERICA: INNOCENTS AT HOME (1987); THE REAGAN LEGACY (S. Blumenthal & T. Edsall eds. 1988); Pierard, *Protestant Support for the Political Right in Wiemar Germany and Post-Watergate America: Some Comparative Observations*, 24 J. CHURCH & STATE 245 (1982).

On reactions to Presidential deaths, *see e.g.*, de Grazia, *A Note on the Psychological Position of the Chief Executive*, 8 PSYCHIATRY 267, 268 (1945) (study of reactions to President Roosevelt's death revealed all subjects made explicit linkages of the President with the father figure; on an unconscious level, however, president may personify the "imago" of the "original sexless mother," the figure that "omnipotently satisfied all needs"); *see generally*, Kirschner, *Some Reactions of Patients in Psychotherapy to the Death of the President*, 5 PSYCHO-ANALYTIC REV. 125 (1964); Kirschner, *The Death of a President: Reactions of*

shooting reflected a philosophy significantly cognitively dissonant from any theory of criminal justice that appears to give great weight to unconscious, intangible, invisible factors in the determination of criminal responsibility.[77]

The public's desire to punish, "creating the illusion that the world is fair," nurtures emotions of vengeance, thus furthering "social solidarity," and protecting "against the terrifying anxiety that the forces of good might not triumph against the forces of evil after all."[78] This desire is further exacerbated by our subjective perceptions of risk and fear of crime.[79] These punitive desires serve as a near-perfect (albeit anachronistic) summary of the Reaganite criminal justice position; it should be no wonder that the sight of Hinckley "getting away with it" caused such a public uproar.[80]

Psychoanalytic Patients, 51 PSYCHOANALYTIC REV. 125, 126-27 (1964) (identification of death of President Kennedy with symbolic loss of father figure would seem "axiomatic").

77. *See e.g.*, Romanucci-Ross & Tancredi, *Psychiatry, the Law and Cultural Determinants of Behavior*, 9 INT'L J. L. & PSYCHIATRY 265, 291 (1986) (discussing "inevitabl[e]" effect of conservative philosophy on psychiatric intervention, given the way psychiatry is "inextricably tied to the values of a culture"); Kalven, *Insanity and the Criminal Law—A Critique of* Durham v. United States, 22 U. CHI. L. REV. 317, 321 (1955) (analogizing basis of *M'Naghten* rules to traditional child- rearing practices, and arguing that our process of "guilt- fastening" and infliction of punishment is "a continuation of our child-rearing system into adult life on a community scale of social interaction").

78. Diamond, *From* Durham *to* Brawner: *A Futile Journey*, 1973 WASH. U. L.Q. 109, 110. Note that Professor Diamond refers to these as "theological notions." *Id.* On the theological roots of Reagan's politics, *see* Wicker, *Pushing a Christian Republic*, 97 L.A. Daily J. (Sept. 12, 1984), at 4, *quoting* Reagan ("Politics and morality are inseparable. And as morality's foundation is religion...we need religion as a guide"). Wicker characterized this statement as "poppycock," and reflecting "as clear a statement this president can make of his belief that if you aren't religious you will have no 'sense of moral obligation' in your private or public life." *Id.* On our societal desire to punish, *see supra* chapter 2 C.

79. *See e.g.*, Donnelly, *Individual and Neighborhood Influences on Fear of Crime*, 22 SOCIOLOG. FOCUS 69 (1988); LaGrange, Ferraro & Supancic, *Perceived Risk and Fear of Crime: Role of Social and Physical Incivilities*, 29 J. RES. CRIME & DELINQ. 311 (1992).

80. Punishment also is seen as furthering the "mythology of justice, [by] creating the illusion that the world is fair," and as furthering social solidarity by protecting against "the terrifying anxiety that the forces of good might not triumph against the forces of evil after all." Diamond, *supra* note 78, at 110. As Professor Sendor has pointed out, "punishment expresses to other members of the community its self-image as a society that places great value on the preservation of designated interests." Sendor, *Crime as Communication: An Interpretive Theory of the Insanity Defense and the Mental Elements of Crime*, 74 GEO. L.J. 1371, 1428-29 n. 208 (1986).

This brings two other issues into sharper focus. First, there is an important parallel to the Guiteau trial: the Reagan Administration's use of the Hinckley attack as a springboard for the abolition of the insanity defense reflects an approach virtually identical to the parallel attacks on the concept of "moral insanity"[81] which followed the Guiteau trial, which, according to Dr. Philip Resnick, "dealt a death blow to moral insanity as an accepted diagnosis in the United States."[82] The chief psychiatric consultant to the prosecutor, John P. Gray, the superintendent of a New York state hospital and editor of the *American Journal of Insanity*,[83] criticized the impact that "moral insanity"—if accepted as a legitimate psychiatric diagnostic category—would have on religious beliefs, moral standards and legal practices.[84]

Second, because of Reagan's popularity and his unique role in American politics, Hinckley's attack could fairly well be characterized as attempted regicide. Dr. Richard Rogers has suggested (facetiously, by his own terms) that, perhaps, a solution would be "to exclude from the insanity defense the crime of regicide and its modern equivalents."[85] It is the regicidal nature of the assassination attempt that must be factored into any effort to fully understand its significance.

C. The Roots of "Willful Deafness:" The Insanity Defense as Victim

The characterization of the Hinckley assassination attempt as "regicidal" can lead to another question: "So what?" Why were the shootings' regicidal aspects so important? What roots of our American character did they expose? *Why* does this question—perennially—reveal the "raw nerve at the cutting edge of law and psychia-

---

81. *See supra* chapter 2, text accompanying notes 152-59.
82. Resnick, *supra* note 27, at 207-08; *see also*, Quen, *Isaac Ray and the Development of American Psychiatry and the Law*, in 6 PSYCHIATRIC CLINICS OF N. AMER. 527, 534 (R. Sadoff ed. 1983) (Guiteau trial used as vehicle through which to discredit concept of moral insanity).
83. Quen, *supra* note 82, at 534.
84. Dain & Carlson, *Moral Insanity in the United States, 1835-1866*, 117 AM. J. PSYCHIATRY 795, 797 (1980).
85. R. Rogers, *supra* note 7, at 6. On our possible unconscious ambivalence about such regicide, see generally, L. DEMAUSE, *supra* note 58; Schmidt, *A Differential Poison Index From the Gallup Poll*, 10 J. PSYCHOHIST. 523 (1983).

try"?[86] As we have seen, it is impossible to understand, rationalize, or predict future developments in insanity defense jurisprudence through simple reliance on scientific innovation, understanding of either empirical data or principles of moral philosophy, or analysis of legal doctrine. It is thus necessary to turn to other disciplines in an effort to bring some measure of coherence to the underlying issues.

As a society, and as a legal system, we exhibit nothing less than willful deafness in our approach to insanity defense decisionmaking.[87] That approach reflects a rejection of psychodynamic principles —the role of the unconscious in animating behavior and the irrationality of most such behavior, the mythology of pure "free will," the gradations of mental disability and the integration of personality characteristics[88]—which have been basic elements of virtually every attempt to understand motivations, drives, instincts and actions since prior to the M'Naghten case. This willful deafness is condoned (or encouraged) by the courts, by elected officials, and by media representations in spite of staggering scientific and statistical proofs to the contrary.[89]

While we may say that some of this dissonance stems from a distrust of psychiatrists, a rejection of the concept of mental illness, a characterization of the insanity defense as a "loophole" through which the "obviously guilty" can escape punishment, a suspicion of "clever lawyers," the need for concreteness in evaluating disability claims, the fear of feigning, and the continued reliance on distorted stereotypes of "crazy" and "normal" appearances and behavior,[90] the persistence of these myths do not fully explain the problem at hand.[91]

---

86. Perlin, *supra* note 30, at 863.
87. *See* Finer, Gates, Leon, *and the Compromise of Adjudicative Fairness (Part II): Of Aggressive Majoritarianism, Willful Deafness, and the New Exception to the Exclusionary Rule*, 34 CLEVE. ST. L. REV. 199, 205 (1986).
88. *See generally*, Watson, *Some Psychological Aspects of the Trial Judge's Decision Making*, 39 MERCER L. REV. 937, 938 n. 6 (1988).
89. *See generally infra* chapter 8 C; *see* Perlin, *Morality and Pretextuality,Psychiatry and Law: Of "Ordinary Common Sense," Heuristic Reasoning, and Cognitive Dissonance*, 19 BULL. AM. ACAD. PSYCHIATRY & L. 131 (1991); Perlin, *Pretexts and Mental Disability Law: The Case of Competency*, 47 U. MIAMI L. REV. (1993) (in press).
90. *See e.g.*, E. BERGLER & A. MEERLOO, JUSTICE AND INJUSTICE 144 (1963) (stumbling blocks in developing legal system that appeals to our "sense of justice" include "(1) widespread and timebound popular misconceptions; (2) blind prejudices based on inner fear; (3) fallacies of judgment based on 'probabilities;' (4) panic reactions").
91. *See e.g.*, Roberts, Golding & Fincham, *supra* note 2, at 211-12; Hans, *An*

While the myths' longevity can be understood through the filters of heuristics and false OCS, that understanding still leaves us one step short of our goal: why do we rely on these reasoning devices, and why are we willing to embrace them in spite of any and all rational evidence to the contrary?

Over twenty years ago, Professor Abraham Goldstein pointed out that public attitudes toward crime and mental illness "inevitably limit the impact of any legal rule."[92] Is this simply another characterization of the "tensile strength"/hydraulic pressure phenomenon,[93] or is it something more?[94] Is there something truly unique about the interplay between crime and mental illness that has created a situation in which we concede that the legal system is powerless to overcome private prejudice?[95] If there is, how can we explain it?

Finally, can we answer this question without turning—once more—to the fact-specific context of insanity defense "law reform" of the 1980s: the attempted assassination of Ronald Reagan? Again, Professor Goldstein explicitly has characterized the insanity test as an "ordering principle of a process of decision which uses a 'political' solution to advance subtle social agendas.[96] I conclude that it is utter blindness to attempt to structure an explanation for legislative and judicial developments in this area without conscious and overt consideration of the role of Hinckley's choice-of-victim.

Many of the myths which traditionally animated our decision-making in other aspects of the law were, indeed, mythic, and have

---

Analysis of Public Attitudes Toward the Insanity Defense, 24 CRIMINOL. 393, 394-95 (1986); Hans & Slater, *supra* note 51, at 111.

92. A. GOLDSTEIN, THE INSANITY DEFENSE 95 (1967).
93. *See generally infra* chapter 8 A.
94. *Cf.* Van Zandt, *Common Sense Reasoning: Social Change and the Law,* 81 Nw. U. L. REV. 894, 938 (1987) (discussing the way the Civil Rights Act of 1964 "imposed a new idea of race relations on a recalcitrant population"); *see* M. Perlin, "The ADA and Mentally Disabled Persons: Can Sanist Attitudes Be Undone?" paper presented at Disability Rights Conference, Hofstra Law School, November 1992, manuscript at 11-12 (if Americans with Disabilities Act is "to make any true headway in restructuring the way that mentally disabled citizens are dealt with by society,…it must provide a means by which to deal frontally with…sanist attitudes").
95. *Cf.* City of Cleburne v. Cleburne Living Center, 473 U.S. 432, 448 (1985), quoting Palmore v. Sidoti, 466 U.S. 429, 432-34 (1984) ("Private biases may be outside the reach of the law, but the law cannot, directly or indirectly, give them effect"), discussed in this context in 2 M. L. PERLIN, MENTAL DISABILITY LAW: CIVIL AND CRIMINAL §7.22, at 664 (1989).
96. A. GOLDSTEIN, *supra* note 92, at 91.

subsequently altered our perceptions and our expectations in conformity with the "corrected" information.[97] Yet, insanity defense decisionmaking remains prisoner of our collective refusal to confront the "house of cards" upon which so many of the myths (and metamyths) are built.

This may be because, in our attempts to rationally explain away these myths (by highlighting empirical data, scientific advances, and the logic of philosophic reasoning), we have paid scant attention to the importance of personality theory in insanity defense jurisprudence. By examining this school of thought, focusing especially on what is termed "authoritarian personality theory"[98]—and by integrating its teachings into the current investigation—we may better understand why insanity defense jurisprudence continues to develop as it has, with little likelihood of expected significant change.

D. Personality Theory: A Brief Overview[99]

1. Introduction

Personality is the "dynamic organization within the individual of those psychosocial systems that determine his unique adjustments to his environment,"[100] and personality theory revolves around the motives for an individual's behavior and behavior systems.[101] A person

---

97. See Van Zandt, *supra* note 94, at 938 (citing pollution control and mandatory motorcycle helmet statutes as two examples of laws dissonant with OCS that may be "designed to 'correct' 'inaccurate' common sense ideas held by some segment of the population").

98. See generally *infra* chapter 7 D 2.

99. For an excellent survey, *see* F. ALEXANDER & S. SELEZNICK, THE HISTORY OF PSYCHIATRY 297-309 (1966).

100. G. ALLPORT, PERSONALITY: A PSYCHOLOGICAL INTERPRETATION 48 (1937). Allport's theories are discussed in depth in L. BISCHOF, INTERPRETING PERSONALITY THEORIES 285-330 (2d ed. 1970).

101. *Id.* at 5-6; *see also generally*, C. HALL & G. LINDZEY, THEORIES OF PERSONALITY (1957). For earlier overviews, *see e.g.*, G. ALLPORT, *supra* note 393; E.G. BORING, A HISTORY OF EXPERIMENTAL PSYCHOLOGY (2d ed. 1950); MacKinnon, *The Structure of Personality*, in PERSONALITY AND THE BEHAVIOR DISORDERS 3 (J. Hunt ed. 1944); MacKinnon & Maslow, *Personality*, in 2 ANNUAL REVIEW OF PSYCHOLOGY 113 (C. Stone & D. Taylor 1951); G. MURPHY, HISTORICAL INTRODUCTION TO MODERN PSYCHOLOGY (1949).

Researchers have cataloged at least a dozen separate schools of theory (embodying at least seventy-one separate principles), L. Bischof, *supra*, at 619-20, emphasizing disparate criteria, including heredity and instincts; the developmental process from infancy to old age; and idiographic (individual)

is viewed as a product of his inherited and constitutional makeup in "continuous transaction with potent persons and forces in his life experience," and personality is viewed as an "open system," continuously and varyingly responsive to "input" and "feedback" from outside itself, "especially responsive at points of high need in emotionally invested roles."[102] In responding to events, an individual's actions are shaped by his perceptions as well as by "other ego qualities (such as intelligence, judgment, impulse control, defenses), superego and ego ideal, the maturity of his object relationships, and the strength and quality of his aggressive drive."[103]

Theorists such as Talcott Parsons have suggested that personality development is, in part, a result of an individual's interactions with external social systems, including "the religious grounding of the institutionalized values of a society," science, ideology, "political organization and its relation to phenomena of authority, power, coercion, and...the use of force," "the institutionalization of economic production," and religious organizations.[104] According to Parsons, the main structure of an individual's personality is "built up through the processes of social interaction," developing through "the internalization of social objects and of the normative patterns governing the child's interactions in social situations."[105] In their classic study of personality and social institutions, Hans Gerth and C. Wright Mills thus construed "person" as being composed "of the

---

versus nomothetic (discovering general rules of behavior) approaches. *Id.* at 620-21. For a comparison of important personality theories, *see e.g.*, C. HALL & G. LINDZEY, *supra*, at 538-58.

102. Perlman, *The Problem-Solving Model in Social Casework*, in THEORIES OF SOCIAL CASEWORK 129, 142-43 (R.W. Roberts & R.H. Nee eds. 1970). *See e.g.*, West, *Law, Rights, and Other Totemic Illusions: Legal Liberalism and Freud's Theory of the Rule of Law*, 134 U. PA. L. REV. 817, 837-38 (1986) ("Each individual inherits the contents of his parent's superego so that the value system and laws of each generation are handed down to all members of society through their families"), and *id.* at 838 n. 87, *quoting* ROAZEN, FREUD: POLITICAL AND SOCIAL THOUGHT 189 (1968) ("Society acts through the family; in each individual family, custom gets internalized into each new member of the family").

103. Hollis, *The Psychosocial Approach to the Practice of Casework*, in THEORIES OF SOCIAL CASEWORK, *supra* note 102, at 33, 59.

104. Parsons, *Mental Illness and "Spiritual Malaise:" The Role of the Psychiatrist and of the Minister of Religion*, in SOCIAL STRUCTURE AND PERSONALITY 292, 296-97 (T. Parsons ed. 1964) (reprinted from THE MINISTRY AND MENTAL HEALTH (H. Hoffman ed. 1960)).

105. *Id.* at 300.

specific roles which [man] enacts and of the effects of enacting these roles upon his self."[106]

Such roles must be viewed within a sociocultural construct.[107] Pioneering anthropologists have concluded that the "molding influences" of the culture into which one is born determine "in great measure" which aspects of an individual's personality will be reinforced and which suppressed.[108] In his review of the literature on culture and personality, and their impact on psychopathology,[109] Professor Page thus concluded:

> 1. The role of culture in shaping personality (and in producing personality types especially vulnerable to particular mental disorders) does not exclude the significance of genetic factors...

> 2....[T]he molding influence of the culture is pervasive, consistent, and continuous throughout the life of the individual...

> 3. The success of culture (or heredity) in creating uniform or standard human personalities is limited...

> 4. The fact that certain cultures...accepted as normal some attitudes and traits that would be suggestive of psychopathology in our culture... points to the unreliability of "symptoms" as cross-cultural indicators of psychopathology.[110]

The relationship between personality and social structure is a clear one.

If we accept the theoretical validity of the sociocultural construct, we must then acknowledge the idiosyncratic means through

---

106. H. GERTH & C.W. MILLS, CHARACTER AND SOCIAL STRUCTURE: THE PSYCHOLOGY OF SOCIAL INSTITUTIONS 14 (1953).

107. See generally, Scheff, A Sociological Theory of Mental Disorders, in APPROACHES TO PSYCHOPATHOLOGY 250 (J.D. Page ed. 1966); T. SCHEFF, BEING MENTALLY ILL: A SOCIOLOGICAL THEORY (1966).

108. J. PAGE, PSYCHOPATHOLOGY: THE SCIENCE OF UNDERSTANDING DEVIANCE 157 (1971); see generally, R. BENEDICT, PATTERNS OF CULTURE (1934); M. MEAD, SEX AND TEMPERAMENT IN PRIMITIVE CULTURES (1935).

109. See e.g., J.W. EATON & R.J. WEIL, CULTURE AND MENTAL DISORDERS: A COMPARATIVE STUDY OF THE HUTTERITES AND OTHER POPULATIONS (1955); see generally, MAGIC, FAITH AND HEALING (A. Kiev ed. 1964); A. KIEV, TRANSCULTURAL PSYCHIATRY (1972); C. LÉVI-STRAUSS, STRUCTURAL ANTHROPOLOGY (1963); C. GEERTZ, LOCAL KNOWLEDGE: FURTHER ESSAYS IN INTERPRETIVE ANTHROPOLOGY (1983).

110. J.D. PAGE, supra note 108, at 159-60. On the importance of trans-cultural inquiry in classification of mental disorders, see 1 M.L. PERLIN, supra note 95, §2.05.

which American culture affects personality development.[111] Whether there is a discrete, measurable entity known as "the American character" remains in dispute.[112] Nonetheless, it is difficult to ignore—or deny—Erik Erikson's conclusion that our path of child, personality and family development[113] remains "distinctly culture-bound."[114] Any inquiry into the typology of the authoritarian personality must thus be seen in the specific context of contemporaneous American culture.

2. Authoritarian Personality Theory

Sociologists, political scientists and psychologists have developed a theoretical construct to describe individuals who reflect an "authoritarian personality."[115] Responding to the hypothesis that

111. Cf. H. MAIER, THREE THEORIES OF CHILD DEVELOPMENT: THE CONTRIBU-TIONS OF ERIK H. ERIKSON, JEAN PIAGET, AND ROBERT B. SEARS, AND THEIR APPPLICATIONS 27 (1969) ("A mature, healthy personality may be summarized as individual happiness combined with responsible citizenship") (emphasis in original) (discussing works of Erikson including E. ERIKSON, CHILDHOOD AND SOCIETY (2d rev. ed. 1963), and Erikson, Studies in the Interpretation of Play—Part I: Clinical Observations of Play Disruption in Young Children, 22 GENET. PSYCHOLOG. MONOGR. 557 (1940)).

112. Compare A. deTOQUEVILLE, DEMOCRACY IN AMERICA (1961 rep.); R. REEVES, AN AMERICAN JOURNEY (1982); J. HENRY, CULTURE AGAINST MAN (Vintage ed. 1965).

113. See e.g., FAMILY THERAPY: THEORY AND PRACTICE (P. Guerin ed. 1976); M. BOWEN, FAMILY THERAPY IN CLINICAL PRACTICE (1978); J. HALEY & L. HOFF-MAN, TECHNIQUES OF FAMILY THERAPY (1967). On the importance of family development theory in the formulation of legal strategies aimed at curbing child sexual abuse, see Weisberg, The "Discovery" of Sexual Abuse: Experts' Role in Legal Policy Formulation, 18 U.C. DAVIS L. REV. 1, 39-41 (1984).

114. H. MAIER, supra note 111. at 73. See id. at 73-78 (enumerating peculiarly American cultural influences on personality development), discussing, inter alia, E. ERIKSON, supra note 111; Erikson, The California Loyalty Oath, 14 PSYCHIA-TRY 244 (1951); Erikson, On the Sense of Inner Identity, in CONFERENCE ON HEALTH AND HUMAN RELATIONS 124 (1953)).

115. The classic work is T. ADORNO, E. FRENKEL-BRUNSWICK, D. LEVISON & R. SANFORD, THE AUTHORITARIAN PERSONALITY (1950) (AP) (subsequent pagina-tion cites will be to the 1982 abridged and revised edition). AP has generated the most widely used typology of political personality available. See generally, Lerner, A Bibliographical Note, in F. GREENSTEIN, PERSONALITY & POLITICS: PROBLEMS OF EVIDENCE, INFERENCE, AND CONCEPTUALIZATION 154, 167-178 (Norton ed. 1975). While it has been critiqued vigorously, see e.g., STUDIES IN THE SCOPE AND METHOD OF "THE AUTHORITARIAN PERSONALITY" (R. Christie & M. Jahoda eds. 1954); Smith, Review of The Authoritarian Personality, 45 J. ABNORMAL & SOCIAL PSYCHOLOGY 775 (1950), and while important methodo-logical errors have been uncovered, see e.g., F. GREENSTEIN, supra, at 100-2,

"the political, economic, and social convictions of an individual often form a broad and coherent pattern, as if bound together by a 'mentality' or 'spirit,' and that this pattern is an expression of deep-lying trends in his personality,"[116] T.W. Adorno and his colleagues first conceived of the authoritarian personality to characterize an individual whose behavior was marked by a bundle of personality traits:

> dominance of subordinates; deference toward superiors; sensitivity to power relationships; need to perceive the world in a highly structured fashion; excessive use of stereotypes; and adherence to whatever values are conventional in one's setting.[117]

An authoritarian personality-type[118] is intolerant of ambiguity and is made uncomfortable by disorder.[119] In response to complex and subtle phenomena, he imposes his own "tight categories" upon them, thus making "more than the usual use of stereotypes."[120] Perhaps more subtly, he is "preoccupied with virility," tending toward "exaggerated assertion of strength and toughness,"[121] and is fre-

---

114-16, AP remains a valuable construct for explaining both the roots of political psychology and the significance of personality on political beliefs. On the relationship between the authoritarian personality and sanism (*see infra* chapter 8 B), *see* Perlin, *supra* note 50, at 377 n. 19.

116. AP, *supra* note 115, at 1

117. F. GREENSTEIN, PERSONALITY & POLITICS: PROBLEMS OF EVIDENCE, INFERENCE AND CONCEPTUALIZATION 104 (Norton ed. 1975). *See also, e.g.*, J. KIRSCHT & R. DILLEHAY, DIMENSIONS OF AUTHORITARIANISM: A REVIEW OF RESEARCH AND THEORY 35-69 (1967); R. NISBET, PREJUDICES: A PHILOSOPHICAL DICTIONARY 8-23 ()1982).

118. Later researchers have described two theories of authoritarian personalities: the "ego-defensive" theory (the authoritarian personality covers his feelings of personal weakness with a "facade of toughness," through a combination of the ego defenses of repression and reaction formation which leave his emotional capacities stunted), and the "cognitive" theory (the authoritarian personality's behavior patterns stem from the learning of a reality prevalent in one's individual subculture). Greenstein, *Personality and Political Socialization: The Theories of Authoritarian and Democratic Character*, 361 ANNALS 81, 88-89 (1965). Subsequent research is compatible with both or either underlying theory. *See id.* at 89 n. 24, *citing* A. CAMPBELL ET AL., THE AMERICAN VOTER 512-15 (1960); Pettigrew, *Personality and Sociocultural Factors in Intergroup Attitudes: A Cross-National Comparison*, 2 J. CONFLICT RESOLUTION 29 (March 1958).

119. *See e.g*, Frenkel-Brunswick, *Intolerance of Ambiguity as an Emotional and Perceptual Personality Variable*, 18 J. PERSONALITY 108 (1949); Greenstein, *supra* note 118, at 86.

120. Greenstein, *supra* note 118, at 86; *See generally*, Perlin, *supra* note 50, at 377 n. 18.

121. Greenstein, *supra* note 118, at 87. On the relationship between "hypermasculinity, the authoritarian personality, and homophobia, *see* Kimmel, *Issues for*

quently unable to be introspective (to acknowledge his own feelings and fantasies).[122] He demands obedience to rules and insists on conformity, and is willing to rely on coercion and punishment to enforce that obedience.[123]

Authoritarians have difficulty in accepting impulses they consider deviant—"fear, weakness, sex and aggression."[124] It is thus no surprise that authoritarians are particularly intolerant of psychodynamic explanations of human behavior,[125] nor that a major study of attitudes about mental illness concluded that, "in a community climate characterized by an authoritarian social-political structure, we can expect to find authoritarian and socially restrictive attitudes toward the mentally ill."[126]

Authoritarian traits are frequently exhibited by individuals characterized as "rigid, racist, anti-Semitic, sexually repressed, [and] politically conservative...who will accept the word of an authority figure over that of a lesser person."[127] Attitudes toward crime control, due process and legal punishment are also positively linked to authoritarianism,[128] and legal verdicts reflect juror authoritarianism in assessments of defendants' guilt.[129] Some arrest decisions similarly

---

Men in the 1990s, 46 U. MIAMI L. REV. 671, 681 (1992).

122. *Id.* Compare Tanay, *Psychodynamic Differentiations of Homicide*, 6 BULL. AM. ACAD. PSYCHIATRY & L. 364, 365-66 (1978) (ego-dystonic murderers—whose homicides occur "against the conscious wishes of the perpetrator"—reflect characteristics of an "agressiphobic personality," including rigidity, moralism, and being "highly conflicted about their own aggressive strivings").

123. Henderson, *Authoritarianism and the Rule of Law*, 66 IND. L.J. 379, 382 (1991).

124. Delgado, *Campus Antiracism Rules: Constitutional Narratives in Collision*, 85 Nw. U. L. REV. 343, 372 (1991), discussing work of Gordon Allport, *see supra* note 100.

125. S. DUCAT, *supra* note 70, at 64 n. *.

126. Levine, *A Cross-National Study of Attitudes Toward Mental Illness*, 80 J. ABNORMAL PSYCHOLOGY 111, 111 (1972).

127. McConahay et al., *The Uses of Social Science in Trials with Political and Racial Overtones: The Trial of Joan Little*, 41 LAW & CONTEMP. PROBS. 205, 217 (1977). *But see*, Broderick, *Why the Peremptory Challenge Should be Abolished*, 65 TEMP. L. REV. 309, 312 (1992) (criticizing this characterization—when used as a tool in jury selection—as contrary to the "legal and political structure of a pluralistic democracy").

128. Schumacher, "Measuring Attitudes Toward Crime Control" (paper presented at the American Psychological Association annual conference, August 1991, San Francisco, CA); Vidmar & Miller, *Socialpsychological Processes Underlying Attitudes Toward Legal Punishment*, 14 LAW & SOC'Y REV. 565 (1980).

129. Narby, Cutler & Moran, "A Meta-analysis of the Association Between Authoritarianism and Jurors' Perceptions of Defendant Culpability" (paper presented at the American Psychological Association annual conference, August 1991, San

reflect authoritarianism.[130] It has been suggested that civil procedure rules imposing more stringent pleading requirements in certain federal actions stems from judicial "hostility to the assertion of civil rights against authority figures."[131] Finally, institutions—such as the traditional American prison system of the 1920s–1950s—can be characterized by authoritarian traits as well.[132]

3. Authoritarianism and Public Opinion

One of the recurrent themes in insanity defense literature is the peculiar role of public opinion in shaping judicial policy.[133] The Hinckley trial loosed a torrent of public criticism, rarely equalled in contemporaneous trials:

> Separate streams of public opinion—outrage over the courts' perceived "softness on crime;" outrage over a jurisprudential system that could even allow a defendant who shot the President in cold blood (on national television) to plead "not guilty" (by *any* reason); outrage at a jurisprudential system that countenanced obfuscatory and confusing testimony by competing teams of psychiatrists as to the proper characterization of a defendant's mental illness; in short, the outrage over the "abuse" of the insanity defense—became a river of fury after the NGRI verdict was announced.[134]

Francisco, CA); Weir & Wrightsman, *The Determinants of Mock Jurors' Verdicts in a Rape Case*, 20 J. APPL. SOC'L PSYCHOLOGY 901 (1990); Mitchell & Byrne, *The Defendant's Dilemma: Effects of Jurors' Attitudes and Authoritarianism on Judicial Decisions*, 25 J. PERSONAL. & SOC'L PSYCHOLOGY 123 (1973).

130. Wortley, *The Human Factor in the Decision to Arrest*, 13 POLICE STUDIES 26 (1990).

131. Rotolo v. Borough of Chareleroi, 532 F. 2d 920, 924 (3d Cir. 1976) (Gibbons, J., concurring & dissenting).

132. Willens, *Structure, Content, and the Exigencies of War: American Prison Law After Twenty-Five Years, 1962-1987*, 37 AM. U. L. REV. 41, 69-70 (1987). On the role of authoritarian decisionmaking in a "boot camp"-type of correctional setting, *see* Morash & Rucker, *A Critical Look at the Idea of Boot Camp as a Correctional Reform*, 36 CRIME & DELINQ. 204 (1990).

133. *See e.g.*, Herman, *The Insanity Defense in Fact and Fiction: On Norval Morris's* MADNESS AND THE CRIMINAL LAW, 1985 AM. BAR. FOUND. RES. J. 385, 392 ("Morris's argument against the insanity defense relies in part on a sense that *decent* community reaction favors abolition. As is generally true, community reaction colors the discussion of the defense without being subjected to close evaluation") (emphasis added).

134. Perlin, *supra* note 30, at 859 (footnote omitted) (emphasis in original). On perceptions of judicial leniency in general, *see* Stalans & Diamond, *Formation*

In considering the impact of public opinion on the shaping of insanity defense jurisprudence, it is necessary to consider the impact of two important public opinion "shapers:" the media and (purportedly) responsible governmental officials.[135] Here, the record is stark: the public's distorted view of the insanity defense and its impacts can directly be traceable to misinformation (the perpetuation of the myths and meta-myths discussed extensively earlier) disseminated by both media and official sources.[136]

Researchers have demonstrated that the public's gross overestimation of both the frequency and the success rate of the insanity defense plea is substantially derived from media publicity accorded to certain notorious criminal cases, virtually none of which involved defendants actually found NGRI.[137] Although the extent to which mass media representations distorted the prevalence and symptomatology of mental illness was first articulated over thirty years ago by J. D. Nunnally,[138] it was not until Steadman and Cocozza's study was published in 1978 that the earlier media critique was further generalized to encompass the criminally insane.[139]

This distortion was exacerbated further after the Hinckley trial. The media's interest in the defense—responding to the "river of fury" unleashed in the verdict's aftermath—helped to legitimatize long-standing movements to abolish or shrink the defense.[140] In the trial's

---

and Change in Lay Evaluations of Criminal Sentencing: Misperception and Discontent, 14 LAW & HUM. BEHAV. 199 (1990).

135. On the interplay of the media and the legal process, see e.g., Editorial, The Media and the Law, 26 CRIM. L. Q. 145 (1984); Harper, When Your Case Hits the Front Page, 70 A.B.A. J. 78 (1984); Shaw, Media Coverage of the Courts: Improving But Still Not Adequate, 65 JUDICATURE 18 (June-July 1981).

136. On the special responsibility upon the media to articulate and debunk criminal justice myths, see Shaw, supra note 135, at 24. On the role of the media as an outlet for the expression of retributive tendencies, see Vidmar & Miller, Socialpsychological Processes Underlying Attitudes Toward Legal Punishment, 14 LAW & SOC'Y REV. 565, 595-96 (1980), discussing THE MANUFACTURE OF NEWS (S. Cohen & J. Young eds. 1973).

137. In their classic study, Henry Steadman and Joseph Cocozza asked respondents to list criminally insane persons. Although forty-two percent named at least one individual in response to this inquiry, none of the persons listed had actually been found NGRI. Steadman & Cocozza, Selective Reporting and the Public's Misconceptions of the Criminally Insane, 41 PUB. OPIN. Q. 523, 528 (1978).

138. J. NUNNALLY, POPULAR CONCEPTIONS OF MENTAL HEALTH (1961); see also, T. SCHEFF, BEING MENTALLY ILL: A SOCIOLOGICAL THEORY (1966).

139. Steadman & Cocozza, supra note 137, at 532.

140. Arenella, Reflections on Current Proposals to Abolish or Reform the Insanity Defense, 8 AM. J., L. & MED. 271, 272 (1982).

wake, the National Commission on the Insanity Defense specified that the public's perceptions were largely formed by "selective news reporting," patiently rebutting each of the myths which had been perpetuated, in part, by media mis-coverage.[141]

In addition, insanity defense myths have been perpetuated by the nation's political leaders' appeal to "emotionality and impulsive change."[142] Officials of both the Nixon and Reagan Administrations regularly used the insanity defense as the whipping boy for a host of unrelated criminal justice and social problems. Using heuristic reasoning and appealing to alleged "ordinary common sense," they panted a false picture of the insanity defense, its role in the criminal justice system, and its impact on public safety.[143]

Shaped in significant part by these distortions, public opinion has a significant "real world" impact on insanity defense jurisprudence.[144] Professor Susan Herman has noted this phenomenon and argued that, while public opinion may be an appropriate determinant for some insanity defense decision making,[145] it is inappropriate for other aspects: if the public wished to abandon moral blameworthiness (and to substitute factual guilt) as an underpinning for criminal liability, then "the defenders of the insanity defense would be in trouble."[146]

Such an articulation of public opinion would mimic the public's view of such topics as preventive detention and the exclusionary rule, Professor Herman further argued, noting the irony that "the same public that does not seem to mind the inaccuracy of predictions of dangerousness when preventive detention is at issue finds our inability to predict intolerable when the release of a defendant found NGRI is involved."[147]

---

141. *See* Wexler, *supra* note 1, at 537, discussing NATIONAL MENTAL HEALTH ASS'N, MYTHS AND REALITIES: A REPORT OF THE NATIONAL COMMISSION ON THE INSANITY DEFENSE 14-23 (1983).

142. Lagrone & Combs, *Alternatives to the Insanity Defense*, 12 J. PSYCHIATRY & L. 93, 96 (1984).

143. *See supra* chapter 3 C.

144. *But see*, Hall, *The Insanity Defense: Thumbs Down to Wexler's "Offense-Victim" Limitation*, 27 ARIZ. L. REV. 329-30 (1985) (questioning whether public opinion is an appropriate measuring device for continued use of the insanity defense).

145. Herman, *supra* note 133, at 398.

146. *Id.* at 397.

147. *Id.* at 398.

This irony reflects our social ambivalence about the use of psychiatry as a tool of social control: where inaccurate predictions support lengthier detentions, they are privileged; where they may lead to the earlier release of an individual who has the potential of committing a subsequent violent act, they are seen as intolerable.[148] The constant here is our desire for a settled social order. The uncertainty that would result from contrary use of psychiatric expertise is rejected, in part, perhaps, because it is dissonant with the authoritarian intolerance of ambiguity.[149]

4. Authoritarianism and the Death Penalty

a. Introduction. Professor Herman's linkage of insanity defense jurisprudence to criminal procedure developments in other areas is an intriguing one. I wish to take her premise one step further and reinvestigate the link between insanity defense jurisprudence and death penalty jurisprudence through the filter of authoritarian personality theory.[150] Here, the true importance of personality theory should reveal itself—as an insanity defense jurisprudence animator and as a rich source for future study and investigations by scholars and decision makers in this area.

b. The relationship between the insanity defense and death penalty decision making. For centuries, the two symbols of the insanity defense and the death penalty "have been linked—symbolically and empirically—in a dance of death."[151] It was—and still remains—common wisdom that the insanity defense developed as a procedural shield to thwart the use of the death penalty sanction.[152] While *this*

---

148. *See supra* chapter 4, text accompanying note 8, discussing J. LA FOND & M. DURHAM, BACK TO THE ASYLUM: THE FUTURE OF MENTAL HEALTH LAW AND POLICY 156 (1992) in this context.

149. On the way that the opportunity to exercise authority influences some individuals to accept low-paying jobs as "gatekeepers" in psychiatric emergency facilities, *see* Tolbert, *Decision Making in Psychiatric Emergencies: A Phenomenological Analysis of Gatekeeping,* 17 J. COMMUN. PSYCHOLOGY 471 (1989)

150. For my earlier thoughts, *see* Perlin, *The Supreme Court, the Mentally Disabled Criminal Defendant, Psychiatric Testimony in Death Penalty Cases, and the Power of Symbolism: Dulling the Ake in Barefoot's Achilles Heel,* 3 N.Y. L. SCH. HUM. RTS. ANN. 91 (1985).

151. *Id.* at 91-92 (footnotes omitted).

152. *Id.* at 92-93, 95-96 nn. 26-30. This myth has been repeated by some of the most respected opponents of the insanity defense. *See supra* chapter 3, text accompanying notes 280-83, discussing work of Professor Norval Morris.

myth has had remarkable staying power,[153] its inaccuracy does not obscure the connection—in the mind of scholars and the general public alike—between the two.[154]

What is worthy of significant further attention is the psychodynamic relationship between insanity defense jurisprudence and death penalty jurisprudence: what does an individual's position as to one tell us about his or her likely sentiments about the other? What sort of a link—overt or covert—is there between the underlying philosophies? Is there a "type" that is, grossly, "pro-insanity defense" and "anti-death penalty" and a contrasting "type" that is "anti-insanity defense" and "pro-death penalty?" If there is, what do we know about each type? What sort of personality type comes to these positions? Most important, what kinds of predictions can we make about future insanity defense jurisprudential developments as a result of what we learn about these types?

Empirically, we know that death penalty attitudes are symptomatic of a more general cluster of social/political attitudes, and that death penalty opponents and supporters consistently differ in their views on a broad spectrum of criminal justice and procedure issues.[155] Professors Ellsworth and Fitzgerald have thus found that

---

153. *See e.g.*, A. MATTHEWS, MENTAL DISABILITY AND THE CRIMINAL LAW 23 n. 4 (1970) (private communication from Dr. Karl Menninger (Dec. 9, 1969)); A. GOLDSTEIN, *supra* note 92, at 24; L. RADZINOWICZ, IDEOLOGY AND CRIME 112 (1965); Morris, *The Criminal Responsibility of the Mentally Ill*, 33 SYR. L. REV. 477, 504-5 (1982).

154. First, historically, the insanity defense has not proven to be an impenetrable bulwark to prevent execution of the insane. Second, while the insanity defense may have developed as a tactical plea to prevent executions, its use in non-capital cases was well documented as early as the nineteenth century; today its use clearly permeates all levels of the criminal law from capital cases to misdemeanors. Third, capital punishment simply has not disappeared. If anything, it is probably a stronger force in American society than it has been in thirty years. In short, the insanity defense has never been a death-only plea, and as reports of the death penalty's demise appear greatly exaggerated, it is likely that that reason, at least, can no longer be used as a predictor of the demise of the insanity defense.

Perlin, *supra* note 150, at 96-97 (footnotes omitted).

155. Fitzgerald & Ellsworth, *Due Process vs. Crime Control: Death Qualification and Jury Attitudes*, 8 LAW & HUM. BEHAV. 31, 33 (1984); *see generally e.g.*, Tyler & Weber, *Support for the Death Penalty: Instrumental Response to Crime or Symbolic Attitude*, 17 LAW & SOC'Y REV. 121 (1982). On authoritarian attitudes and the significance of public executions, *see* Blum, *Public Executions: Understanding the "Cruel and Unusual Punishments" Clause*, 19 HAST. CONST'L L.Q. 413 (1992). On attitudes of *inmates* toward capital punishment, *see* Stevens, *Research Note: The Death Sentence and Inmate Attitudes*, 38 CRIME & DELINQ. 272 (1992).

jurors excluded from death penalty trials[156] are "more concerned with the maintenance of the fundamental due process guarantees of the Constitution, less punitive, and less mistrustful of the defense,"[157] and that individuals' death penalty attitudes are "an important indicator of a whole cluster of attitudes about crime control and due process." [158]

Psychologically, we have also known that certain authoritarian personality characteristics—conservatism, rigidity, punitiveness, excessive moralism, an inability to understand or tolerate deviance, and hostility toward low status individuals (the socially inferior, the uneducated, the racial or religious minority)—also characterize individuals more prone to favoring capital punishment.[159] As Professor Jurow discovered in a simulated study, "The more a subject is in favor of capital punishment, the more likely he is to be politically conservative, authoritarian, and punitive in assigning penalties upon conviction."[160] Moral punitiveness, in brief, is part of the authoritarianism syndrome.[161]

---

156. *See* Witherspoon v. Illinois, 391 U.S. 510 (1968) (setting out process for determining if potential jurors should be excluded from death penalty trials because of their adamant opposition to the death penalty). *Witherspoon* was somewhat blurred in Wainwright v. Witt, 469 U.S. 412 (1985) (jurors can be excluded for cause if their death penalty views would "prevent or substantially impair" their ability to apply the law and judge a case impartially).

157. Fitzgerald & Ellsworth, *supra* note 155, at 46-48. *See also*, Neapolitan, *Support For and Opposition to Capital Punishment: Some Associated Social-Psychological Factors*, 10 CRIM. JUST. & BEHAV. 195 (1983) (death penalty opponents "have greater respect for human life, greater opposition to interpersonal violence, greater respect for the law, and more sympathy for the victims of murder than either retentionists who support capital punishment because they believe it deters murder and those who would support it even if it did not").

158. Fitzgerald & Ellsworth, *supra* note 155, at 46.

159. Jurow, *New Data on the Effect of a "Death Qualified" Jury on the Guilt Determination Process*, 84 HARV. L. REV. 567, 570-571 (1971); Oberer, *Does Disqualification of Jurors for Scruples Against Capital Punishment Constitute Denial of Fair Trial on Issue of Guilt?* 39 TEX. L. REV. 545, 565 n. 87 (1961).

160. Jurow, *supra* note 159, at 588. *See also*, Tyler & Weber, *supra* note 155, at 26 (citing studies showing that death penalty support is related to authoritarianism, dogmatism, and/or conservatism); Ellsworth et al., *Death Penalty Attitudes and Conviction Processes: The Translation of Attitudes into Verdicts*, 8 LAW & HUM. BEHAV. 95 (1984) (death-qualified jurors expressed less regret about erroneous convictions). *But see*, Elliott & Robinson, *Death Penalty Attitudes and the Tendency to Convict or Acquit: Some Data*, 15 LAW & HUM. BEHAV. 389 (1991) (questioning existence of correlation between attitudes and jury behavior).

161. Vidmar & Miller, *supra* note 136, at 591. While Adorno's construct of authoritarianism, *see* AP, *supra* note 115, and *see supra* text accompanying notes

These findings reflect the earlier studies of the authoritarian personality. Drawing on this literature, Virginia Boehm has thus speculated that the authoritarian person "might well enjoy the opportunities for punishment provided by service on a jury," where the meting out of harsh punishment is done with the "blessing given by external authority"—the prosecutor as representative of "the majesty of the state."[162] Similarly, Professor Rokeach and a colleague reanalyzed pertinent research data[163] to conclude that potential jurors favoring the death penalty as the sole punishment in capital cases (i.e., those who would not consider life imprisonment as an alternative penalty) were "significantly more dogmatic" than other juror groups.[164] In short, authoritarianism has been found to be positively correlated with both conviction-proneness and pro-death penalty attitudes.[165]

It is also necessary to consider the unique and important role of

---

115-29, as a pathological syndrome and while his methodology have been criticized on a variety of grounds, *see supra* note 115, there has been no disputing the findings that "high" and "low" authoritarians consistently reflect different attitudes toward punishment. Vidmar & Miller, *supra* note 136, at 591-92 n.6.

162. Boehm, *Mr. Prejudice, Miss Sympathy, and the Authoritarian Personality: An Application of Psychological Measuring Techniques to the Problem of Jury Bias*, 1968 WIS. L. REV. 734, 738.

163. *See* Comment, Witherspoon—*Will the Due Process Clause Further Regulate the Imposition of the Death Penalty?* 7 DUQ. L. REV. 414 (1969) (data failed to support allegation raised unsuccessfully in *Witherspoon* that pro- death potential jurors reflected highly authoritarian, dogmatic personalities).

164. Rokeach & McClellan, *Dogmatism and the Death Penalty: Interpretation of the Duquesne Poll Data*, 8 DUQ. L. REV. 125, 129 (1969-70). *See also*, Goldberg, *Toward Expansion of Witherspoon: Capital Scruples, Jury Bias, and Use of Psychological Data To Raise Presumptions in the Law*, 8 HARV. CIV. RTS.-CIV. LIBS. J. 53 (1970).

165. Ford, *The Role of Extralegal Factors in Jury Verdicts*, 11 JUST. SYS. J. 16, 20 (1986). *See generally*, Berg & Vidmar, *Authoritarianism and Recall of Evidence About Criminal Behavior*, 9 J. RES. PERSONALITY 147 (1975); Bray & Noble, *Authoritarianism and Decisions in Mock Juries: Evidence of Jury Bias and Group Polarization*, 36 SOCIAL PSYCHOLOGY 1424 (1978); Moran & Comfort, *Scientific Jury Selection: Sex as a Moderator of Demographic and Personality Predictors of Impaneled Felony Juror Behavior*, 43 J. PERS. & SOCIAL PSYCHOLOGY 1052 (1982); Cowan, Thompson & Ellsworth, *The Effects of Death Qualification on Jurors' Predisposition to Convict and on the Quality of Deliberation*, 8 LAW & HUM. BEHAV. 53 (1984); Sigh & Jayewardene, *Conservatism and Tough Mindedness as Determinants of the Attitudes Toward Capital Punishment*, 20 CAN. J. CRIMINOL. 191 (1978); Vidmar, *Retributive and Utilitarian Motives and Other Correlates of Canadian Attitudes Toward the Death Penalty*, 15 CAN. PSYCHOLOGIST 337 (1974).

public opinion in the formulation of a death penalty jurisprudence.[166] This role stems, in large part, from the Supreme Court's Eighth Amendment jurisprudence, reflecting "public opinion [as] enlightened by a human justice,"[167] and "the evolving standards of decency that mark the progress of a maturing society."[168] With this backdrop, the Court's 1972 decisions in *Furman v. Georgia*[169] striking down the death penalty as violative of the Eighth Amendment's "cruel and unusual punishment" ban[170] have been scrutinized in an attempt to determine "where the public stands on the issue of capital punishment, whether opinion polls are valid indicators of public sentiment about capital punishment, and the extent to which enlightened public opinion determines contemporary standards of decency."[171] Specifically, investigators have attempted to respond to Justice Marshall's hypothesis: (1) the public is ill-informed about capital punishment, (2) if it were informed it would tend to reject the death penalty, but (3) to the extent that retribution provides the basis of death penalty support, information would have no effect on public opinion.[172]

In their landmark studies of public attitudes toward capital punishment, Professors Vidmar and Ellsworth thus concluded that merely noting general levels of support for or against capital punishment is an insufficient data base to be used in determining what the public "really wants" or whether those wants "are based on constitu-

---

166. *See generally*, Vidmar & Ellsworth, *Public Opinion and the Death Penalty*, 26 STAN. L. REV. 1245 (1974). *See also*, White, *The Role of the Social Sciences in Determining the Constitutionality of Capital Punishment*, 13 DUQ. L. REV. 279 (1974).

167. Weems v. United States, 217 U.S. 349, 378 (1910).

168. Trop v. Dulles, 356 U.S. 86, 101 (1958).

169. 408 U.S. 238 (1972).

170. *But see* Gregg v. Georgia, 428 U.S. 153 (1976) (upholding post-*Furman* statutes).

171. Vidmar & Ellsworth, *supra* note 166, at 1246. *Compare e.g.*, *Furman*, 408 U.S. at 329, 362 (Marshall, J., concurring) (American citizens are grossly uninformed about the death penalty; if they were adequately informed about its purposes and liabilities, a majority would finds it morally unacceptable), to *id.* at 382, 384-385 (Burger, C.J., dissenting) (public opinion polls show support for legislative enactments reviving the death penalty). *See generally*, Kohlberg & Elfenbein, *The Developments of Moral Judgments Concerning Capital Punishment*, 45 AM. J. ORTHOPSYCHIATRY 614 (1975) (discussing how attitudes towards penal practices serve as a benchmark of the "developing moral standards" of American civilization).

172. *Furman*, 408 U.S. at 362-64. *See* Sarat & Vidmar, *Public Opinion, the Death Penalty, and the Eighth Amendment: Testing the Marshall Hypothesis*, 1976 WIS. L. REV. 171, 196.

tionally acceptable standards of morality."[173] Thus, if death penalty jurisprudence should take into account only "informed" public opinion,[174] and it is found (1) that some significant support for the death penalty stems from motives "inconsistent with contemporary legislative and judicial goals,"[175] and (2) that the public is "largely ignorant" about capital punishment,[176] then the question is squarely put: can "imperfect" public opinion fairly animate death penalty jurisprudence?[177]

In his recent study of death penalty attitudes, criminologist Robert Bohm has identified three sources of such attitudes: (1) the family;[178] (2) moral crusaders, politicians and law enforcement officials, and (3) developing moral standards.[179] Each of these sources helps explain the symbolic values of a pro-death penalty position.[180]

Perhaps in part due to these symbolic values, death penalty attitudes are often impervious to change. More recent studies have thus demonstrated that education has little impact on most death

---

173. Vidmar & Ellsworth, *supra* note 166, at 1247.

174. *Furman*, 408 U.S. at 362 (Marshall, J., concurring).

175. Vidmar & Ellsworth, *supra* note 166, at 1267: "[S]upporters of capital punishment...are more likely than opponents to endorse attitude statements supporting prejudice and discrimination, violence as a means for achieving social goals, and restrictions on civil liberties. Eight or nine percent of the population are even willing to endorse the position that all robbers or muggers should be executed..." *Id.* (footnotes omitted).

176. *Id.* at 1268, discussing Gold, *A Psychiatric Review of Capital Punishment*, 6 J. FORENS. SCI. 465 (1961). *See also*, Ellsworth & Ross, *Public Opinion and Capital Punishment: A Close Examination of the Views of Abolitionists and Retentionists*, 29 CRIME & DELINQ. 116 (1983); Sarat & Vidmar, *supra* note 172.

177. *Compare* Thomas, *Eighth Amendment Challenges to the Death Penalty: The Reverse of Public Opinion*, 30 VAND. L. REV. 1005, 1016 (1977) ("the important issues cannot be resolved through speculation, examination of legislative enactments, or evaluation of public opinion poll data that focus narrowly on the relatively simple determination of the proportion of the public that favors some kind of death penalty"); *see also*, Neapolitan, *supra* note 157, at 205-6.

178. *See also*, Tyler & Weber, *supra* note 155, at 41-42 (citing literature supporting position that death penalty views are shaped in childhood).

179. Bohm, *American Death Penalty Attitudes: A Critical Examination of Recent Evidence*, 14 CRIM. JUST. & BEHAV. 380, 391 (1987).

180. *Cf.* Bailey & Peterson, *Police Killings and Capital Punishment: The Post-Furman Period*, 25 CRIMINOL. 1 (1987) (return to capital punishment following *Gregg* has had no systematic impact on police homicides). *See also*, T. SELLIN, THE PENALTY OF DEATH (1980); Bailey, *Capital Punishment and Lethal Assaults Against Police*, 19 CRIMINOL. 608 (1982) (accord).

penalty attitudes.[181] Also, those who favor the death penalty are most resistant to learning new information about it.[182] Finally, of those who, upon being presented with new evidence, *do* alter their beliefs in a pro-death penalty position, a significant number "maintain [their] opposition [to abolition] by supporting it with another argument in which the dissonance demanding alteration of beliefs does not exist."[183]

Thus, the political strategy by which politicians typically "exacerbate and channel legitimate public concern about crime into public support for capital punishment"[184] is a symbolic strategy for conservatives "to shield them[selves] from any charges of 'liberalism' directed against them."[185] Further, since public support for the death penalty appears to be based largely on reasons (or the results of reasons) provided by politicians and law enforcement officers,[186] death penalty support is thus promoted "as a symbol of support for law enforcement in general."[187]

Finally, if Kohlberg and Elfenbein were correct in arguing that components of death penalty attitudes are determined by "developing moral standards,"[188] then the "radical decline in support for

---

181. Bohm, Clark & Aveni. *The Influence of Knowledge on Reasons for Death Penalty Opinions: An Experimental Test*, 7 Just. Q. 175 (1990); Bohm, Clark & Aveni, *Knowledge and Death Penalty Opinions: A Test of the Marshall Hypotheses*, 28 J. Res. Crime & Delinq. 360 (1991).

182. Vidmar & Dittenhoffer, *Informed Public Opinion and Death Penalty Attitudes*, 23 Can. J. Criminol. 43 (1981).

183. Jayewardene & Singh, *Public Opinion Polls on the Death Penalty*, 44 Psycholog. Reps. 1191, 1194 (1979); Singh & Jayewardene, *Philosophical Consistency in Public Attitudes on Crime and Justice*, 11 Aust. & N.Z. J. Criminol. 182, 183 (1978).

184. Amsterdam, *Capital Punishment*, in The Death Penalty in America 346, 353 (H.A. Bedau ed. 3d ed. 1982).

185. Bohm, *supra* note 179, at 392.

186. Thomas & Foster, *A Sociological Perspective on Public Support For Capital Punishment*, 45 Am. J. Orthopsychiatry 641 1975); *see also*, Thomas, *supra* note 177.

187. Bohm, *supra* note 179, at 393.

188. Kohlberg's work can be seen as an extension of the writings of Jean Piaget. *See e.g.*, B. Inhelder & J. Piaget, The Growth of Logical Thinking From Childhood to Adolescence (A. Parsons & S. Milgram trans. 1958); J. Piaget, The Moral Judgment of the Child (1948). Piaget first suggested that children cannot maturely understand concepts such as justice or morality until the age of about fifteen, and that, in social groups where there is a deficiency in educational opportunity or other similar social interactions, children never achieve the level of abstract thinking that otherwise develops between the ages of 12 and 15. *See*

capital punishment"[189] that they saw in 1975 (after *Furman* and before *Gregg*) should have continued to accelerate rather than reverse.[190] This reversal of attitudes led Bohm to speculate that either (1) Kohlberg and Elfenbein relied on faulty theory, (2) they were wrong in assessing American society's moral evolution, or (3) the American public is regressing in its moral development.[191]

Whichever conclusion is correct, it appears likely that Kohlberg and Elfenbein seriously underestimated the importance of symbolism in the development of death penalty attitudes.[192] For instance, while deterrence is generally offered as a major rationalization in support of a constitutional death penalty,[193] it has been clear for a dozen years that a large proportion of capital punishment proponents would continue to support it even if it were proven that it had no deterrent value.[194] One empirical survey revealed that sixty percent of tested subjects displayed no change in their attitudes after they were ex-

---

e.g., J. PIAGET, PSYCHOLOGY AND EPISTEMOLOGY 49-62 (1971); *see generally,* J.H. FLAVEL, THE DEVELOPMENTAL PSYCHOLOGY OF JEAN PIAGET (1963).

Interestingly, Piaget and other developmental psychologists have been relied upon in a psychoanalytically-oriented analysis of the substantive *M'Naghten* rules:

Taken together, the results of this psychological research reveal that to grasp effectively, rather than merely to verbalize, the difference between right and wrong described in the *M'Naghten* test, an individual must have reached a specified level of psychological development. This finding becomes of the utmost importance when we realize that a substantial proportion of the criminal accused have never reached this stage of mental development. Thus, under the allegedly conservative *M'Naghten* rule, a large number of those criminally accused could plead not guilty by reason of insanity if knowledge of right and wrong were defined in light of recent psychological discoveries.

Gray, *The Insanity Defense: Historical Development and Contemporary Relevance,* 10 AM. CRIM. L. REV. 559, 575 (1972).

189. Kohlberg & Elfenbein, *supra* note 175, at 637-38.
190. The trend toward acceleration was discernable by 1976. *See* Sarat & Vidmar, *supra* note 168, at 175.
191. Bohm, *supra* note 179, at 394.
192. *See e.g.,* Tyler & Weber, *supra* note 155, at 40-41 (support of the death penalty reflects a "symbolic perspective" of citizens' basic values).*Compare* Henderson, *supra* note 123, at 449 (individuals who score highly on Kohlberg's and Carol Gilligan's moral development scales exhibit anti-authoritarian tendencies).
193. *See e.g.,* Spaziano v. Florida, 468 U.S. 447, 461 (1984); Gregg v. Georgia, 488 U.S. 153, 184-87 (1986); Collins v. Francis, 728 F, 2d 1322, 1339-40 (11th Cir. 1984).
194. Sarat & Vidmar, *supra* note 172, at 176, discussing results reported in Vidmar & Ellsworth, *supra* note 166, at 1251-52 and 1256-62, and in Vidmar, *supra* note 165.

posed to a significant amount of information about the death penalty (focusing substantially on its utilitarian aspects).[195] Moreover, recent research suggests that individuals resist learning new information about the death penalty when it contradicts their prior views;[196] in the words of Professors Ellsworth and Ross, "[P]eople are not enlightened: They are ignorant, and they seem unconcerned about their ignorance."[197]

Thus, Professors Sarat and Vidmar have concluded that Justice Marshall's three-part hypothesis—that additional empirical information would not have a significant impact on that portion of the pro-death penalty public that adheres to a retributionist position—was substantially supported by the data,[198] while, in another study, Ellsworth and Ross found that, in spite of opinions to the contrary expressed by judges and by legislators, such information was "of little relevance in assessing the evidentiary basis for the public's opinions."[199]

What conclusions can be drawn from this evidence? Tyler and Weber suggest that the influence of crime-control concerns is, in reality, a small one in the development of pro-death penalty attitudes, and that citizens' policy preferences concerning the use of the death

---

195. Sarat & Vidmar, *supra* note 172, at 192. The information disseminated to participants is reproduced at *id.*, Appendix (198-206). *See also*, Ellsworth & Ross, *supra* note 176, at 147 (two-thirds of those who supported death penalty indicated they would continue to support it even if it had no deterrent value beyond that provided by life imprisonment; 48 percent would continue to factor it even if it were proven to be no deterrent at all), and Tyler & Weber, *supra* note 155, at 42 (justifications offered in support of death penalty positions are "rationalizations").

196. *Id.* at 41, discussing Lord, Ross & Lepper, *Biased Assimilation and Attitude Polarization: The Effects of Prior Theories on Subsequently Considered Evidence*, 37 J. PERSONALITY & SOCIAL PSYCHOLOGY 2098 (1979); *see supra* chapter 6 C.

197. Ellsworth & Ross, *supra* note 176, at 167; *see also*, Vidmar & Dittenhoffer, *supra* note 182, at 53 (independent finding consistent with those of Sarat & Vidmar, *supra* note 172, although falling short of statistical significance). Thus, in response to a survey questionnaire, the only questions answered correctly by a substantial majority of a population sample (of which one-fifth had some postgraduate education) involved "simple, well-publicized facts" (there are many people on death row; poor people are more likely to be sentenced to death than rich people); responses to questions requiring specific knowledge of history, economic facts, social science research or current death penalty practices "strongly supported" a hypothesis of "general ignorance." Ellsworth & Ross, *supra* note 176, at 144.

198. Sarat & Vidmar, *supra* note 172, at 196.

199. Ellsworth & Ross, *supra* note 176, at 148-49; *see also id.* at 162.

penalty "are a reflection of their basic values, not a result of their specific concern about crime."[200]

Just as studies have shown that positions on school busing, the Vietnam War, national health insurance and unemployment compensation policies, and voting preferences are animated by general political-social attitudes (as reflected in the subject's conservatism) and not by such factors as one's personal experience with the busing process, or personal involvement in a war, so do such "basic political-social values" exert predominant influence over one's attitude toward the death penalty.[201]

Ellsworth and Ross also endorse the symbolic perspective: it is the idea of the death penalty rather than its application that elicits strong public support.[202] The public's attitudes are expressive rather than instrumental, and are "tightly bound up with deeply-held convictions concerning the proper organization of society."[203] Retentionists thus see the death penalty as having "enormous symbolic value as an expression of a no-nonsense stand in the war on crime."[204]

5. Authoritarianism and the Insanity Defense

How then does what we have learned about the linkage between authoritarianism and the death penalty affect insanity defense jurisprudence? Do the rigidity and conventionality and the need for definiteness that characterize the authoritarian personality[205] and help shape their death views similarly help explain their insanity defense views?

Professor Lynn Henderson offers an important insight:

---

200. Tyler & Weber, *supra* note 155, at 40, 43.
201. *Id.*, discussing, *inter alia*, Sears et al., *Self-Interest vs. Symbolic Politics in Policy Attitudes and Presidential Voting*, 74 Am. Poli. Sci. Rev. 670 (1980); Kinder & Sears, *Prejudice and Politics: Symbolic Racism Versus Racial Threats to the Good Life*, 40 J. Personality & Social Psychology 414 (1981); Lau, Brown & Sears, *Self-Interest and Civilians' Attitudes Toward the Vietnam War*, 42 Pub. Opin. Q. 464 (1978).
202. Ellsworth & Ross, *supra* note 176, at 138.
203. *Id.* at 165, discussing Sears & Kinder, *The Good Life, White Racism, and the Los Angeles Voter*, in Los Angeles: Viability and Prospects for Metropolitan Leadership 51 (W.Z. Hirsch ed. 1971) (discussing suburban racism).
204. Ellsworth & Ross, *supra* note 172, at 158.
205. *See* Karon, *Kicking Our Gift Horse in the Mouth—Arbitration and Arbitrators' Bias: Its Sources, Symptoms, and Solution*, 7 Ohio St. J. Disp. Res. 315, 325-26 (1992) (arguing that these views lead authoritarian personalities to use ethnic minorities as "targets for racial bias").

It may be that when we are most threatened with death anxiety we seek authority and are vulnerable to authoritarianism. The more chaos threatens us, the more rigid we may become.[206]

We have known for some time that conviction proneness in death penalty cases is revealed in many ways by an individual's attitudes towards the legitimacy of the insanity defense,[207] and towards the perception whether the defense is "a loophole allowing too many guilty men to go free."[208] Upon reviewing the literature, Professor Ellsworth and her colleagues have thus labeled the finding that death penalty and insanity defense attitudes are related as a "robust one."[209] Perhaps research that reveals that a pro-death penalty attitude is correlated with a high level of "resentment of outgroups" helps further explain this link; after all, what group is *more* of an "outgroup" than insanity defense pleaders?[210]

Thus, it has been found that jurors permitted to sit on capital cases are more likely to convict insane defendants than would jurors representing the full spectrum of attitudes toward the death penalty, that "a crime control ideology has underlain objections to the insanity defense at least since M'Naghten's time," and that pro-death jurors are much more likely than anti-death jurors "to regard the insanity defense as a ruse and as an impediment to the conviction of criminals."[211] In short, the process of death-qualification for jurors "undermines one of the most important defenses available to the mentally ill: the insanity defense."[212] When confronted with the state-

---

206. Henderson, *supra* note 123, at 388.
207. Bronson, *On the Conviction Proneness and Representativeness of the Death-Qualified Jury: An Empirical Study of Colorado Veniremen*, 42 U. COLO. L. REV. 1, 7, n. 32 (1970), discussing H. KALVEN & H. ZEISEL, THE AMERICAN JURY 330 (1966) (such response may reveal willingness to violate the law to convict "bad men;" lack of regard for a legitimate legal defense, or an unsympathetic posture on the scope of moral or criminal responsibility).
208. Bronson, *supra* note 207, at 8 n. 34. *See supra* chapter 6, n. 310.
209. Ellsworth et al., *supra* note 160, at 83. *Compare* People v. Williams, 201 Ill. App. 3d 207, 558 N.E. 2d 1258, 1268 (1990) (rejecting defendant's argument based on the article by Ellsworth and her colleagues that excusing jurors opposed to the death penalty resulted in a jury "organized to convict [the defendant] because of its opposition to the insanity defense").
210. *See* Kelley & Braithwaite, *Public Opinion and the Death Penalty in Australia*, 7 JUST. Q. 529, 529-30 (1990).
211. Ellsworth et al., *supra* note 160, at 83, 90, 92. On the specific attitudes of victims, see Erez, *Victim Participation in Sentencing: Rhetoric and Reality*, 18 J. CRIM. J. 19 (1990).
212. Ellsworth et al., *supra* note 160, at 92. At least one court has recognized the

ment, "The plea of insanity is a loophole allowing too many guilty people to go free," over half of the death-qualified respondents agreed, as compared to only slightly more than a quarter of death-excludable participants in the sample.[213]

Professor Ellsworth and her colleagues have pinpointed the enmity of pro-death jurors:

> [O]ur results also indicate that the pro-death penalty jurors' refusal to accept the insanity defense clearly reflects their mistrust of the concept of a mental disorder as an excusing condition....[W]here the defense of insanity was based on a physical disease or defect, there was no difference between the death-qualified and excludable jurors. The distinction in the minds of the jurors is striking. In part it may reflect the public's generally greater hostility towards the mentally ill than towards people with other types of disease or handicap, including mental retardation,[214] but, in part it probably also reflects a particular resentment against the idea of a purely mental problem as an excuse for unacceptable behavior. To a person who believes strongly in crime control, who believes that people must be made to pay for their irresponsible behavior, it must be particularly galling to see one form of irresponsibility excused by another. A physical disorder may be seen as external to the person, creating a sort of necessity or duress, but a purely mental disorder may be seen as simply another manifestation of a weak or corrupted character.[215]

In simulated studies, mock jurors offer three primary reasons for rejecting insanity defenses: "mental illness is no excuse; [the defendant] might have fooled the psychiatrist; [the defendant] should have sought help for his problems."[216]

---

significance of this insight. *See* People v. Stack, 112 Ill. 2d 301, 497 N.E. 2d 339, 344-45 (1986) ("Just as the State is allowed to probe the venire for jurors who would not follow the law of capital punishment, the defendant should be able to identify and challenge those prospective jurors who would refuse to follow the statutory law of the insanity defense").

213. Fitzgerald & Ellsworth, *Due Process vs. Crime Control: Death Qualifications and Jury Attitudes*, 8 Law & Hum. Behav. 31, 45 (1984).

214. Tringo, *The Hierarchy of Preference Toward Disability Groups*, 4 J. Special Ed. 295 (1970); *see generally*, M. Perlin, *supra* note 94.

215. Ellsworth et al., *supra* note 160, at 90. *See also*, White, *The Mental Illness Defense in the Capital Penalty Hearing*, 5 Behav. Sci. & L. 411, 417 (1987) (insanity defense more likely to succeed when supported with "objective" evidence of psychopathology). On the roots of these views, *see* Perlin, *supra* note 50; Perlin & Dorfman, *Sanism, Social Science, and the Development of Mental Disability Law Jurisprudence*, 11 Behav. Sci. & L. 47 (1993).

216. White, *Juror Decision Making in the Capital Penalty Trial: An Analysis of Crimes and Defense Strategies*, 11 Law & Hum. Behav. 113, 125 (1987).

These findings are consistent with other research demonstrating that jurors with unfavorable attitudes toward psychiatry appear to have "a more basic approach to the relationship between crime and punishment."[217] In short, the research confirms the "enduring pattern of public animosity to the insanity plea."[218]

There is a clear "fit" between the retribution-driven punitive response favored by authoritarians[219] and the authoritarian's resentment of the insanity defense and his general hostility toward psychiatry.[220] This should not be surprising, given authoritarians' propensity to endorse punishment as an end in itself;[221] by its very nature, the insanity defense allows certain mentally impaired criminal defendants—frequently perceived as morally deviant—to escape punishment.[222] Similarly, eighty-two percent of surveyed death penalty retentionists endorsed the proposition that a capital punishment advantage is that it "makes it impossible for convicted murdered to

---

Conversely, Professor White found that an insanity defense had a greater chance of success where defense counsel could establish (1) that the defendant had not "fooled" the examining psychiatrist, and (2) he had previously sought help for his illness. *Id.* n. 11, and *see* raw data reported *id.* at 124. In his study, White found that mock jurors identified a defendant's mental illness both as a reason for giving a life sentence (e.g., 13 respondents indicated "defendant is mentally ill; cannot be held completely responsible for his actions") and for choosing the death penalty (e.g., eight stated "mental illness is no excuse;" seven "defendant is not crazy; could have fooled a psychiatrist." and six "defendant did not seek help for his problems"). *Id.*, Tables 5-6.

217. Arafat & McCahery, *The Insanity Defense and the Juror*, 22 DRAKE L. REV. 538, 549 (1973).

218. Hans, *An Analysis of Public Attitudes Toward the Insanity Defense*, 24 CRIMINOL. 393, 394 (1986).

219. *See e.g.*, Vidmar & Miller, *supra* note 136, at 591.

220. *Compare* Brancale, *More on M'Naghten: A Psychiatrist's View*, 65 DICKINSON L. REV. 277, 279 (1961) (discussing death penalty cases): "Let us not delude ourselves that we have accorded the defendant a fair consideration through due process of law and have weighed the moral and psychologic issues involved. We are seeking the extermination of a dangerous person and we are seeking revenge."

221. Vidmar & Miller, *supra* note 136, at 591.

222. *See e.g.*, Rappeport, *The Insanity Plea Scapegoating the Mentally Ill—Much Ado About Nothing?* 24 S. TEX. L.J. 686, 690 (1983) ("The insanity plea offers an opportunity to soften some of the harshness of our criminal justice system..."); Hans & Slater, *supra* note 51, at 203 (public opinion polls have consistently shown a majority of Americans believe insanity defense a "loophole that allows too many guilty people to go free"); White, *supra* note 209, at 418 (jurors who are primarily concerned with efficient crime control are likely to reject insanity plea, while those primarily concerned with due process more likely to accept plea).

later go free on account of some legal technicality."[223] When we factor in additional research revealing that legislators who attribute crime to "free will" support capital punishment more strongly than do those who attribute it to social factors,[224] another piece of the puzzle is filled in. Believers in free will are often precisely those who reject mental disability as a causal explanation for criminal behavior;[225] this rejection may well stem from the same behavioral and cognitive sources as do the related death penalty attitudes.

Authoritarians hold harshly punitive attitudes toward those who do not comply with the law,[226] and "condemn, reject and punish people who violate conventional values."[227] The insanity defense by its own terms "exculpates" those who do not comply with criminal statutes, and, frequently, this noncompliance is exhibited in nonconventional ways. We should not be surprised that the authoritarians' distrust of "difference" is especially marked in their dealings with insanity defense issues.

As with the death penalty, it is clear that much public opinion about the insanity defense is "imperfect" and uninformed. If a substantial percentage of the public takes the position that even the "truly insane" should be punished for criminal behavior, the extent to which this opposition rests on false premises must be carefully considered.[228]

Insanity defense decision making is—to an important extent—"irrational." Similarly, death penalty decision making reflects an "emotionally based attitude," albeit one tempered "by a sense of social desirability."[229] As Ellsworth and Ross explain, death penalty

---

223. Ellsworth & Ross, *supra* note 176, at 156.

224. Hamm, *supra* note 73, at 220; Cullen et al., *Attribution, Salience, and Attitudes Toward Criminal Sanctioning*, 12 Crim. Just. & Behav. 305 (1985).

225. *See supra* chapter 5, text accompanying notes 146-48, discussing the free will/ determinism dichotomy in insanity defense jurisprudence, in the context of State v. Sikora, 44 N.J. 453, 210 A. 2d 193 (1965), and State v. Lucas, 30 N.J. 37, 152 A. 2d 50, 76 (1959) (Weintraub, C.J., concurring).

226. Henderson, *supra* note 123, at 394.

227. AP, *supra* note 115, at 157.

228. Hans, *supra* note 218, at 411. *See also e.g.*, Bird, *The Role of Law in an Instant Society: Implications for Law and Psychology*, 39 Am. Psychologist 158 (1984) (cautioning against unquestioning acceptance of public opinion in legal rule development).

229. Ellsworth & Ross, *supra* note 176, at 152. *See also id.* at 163 (death penalty attitudes are basically emotional, and beliefs are determined by these attitudes).

attitudes—formed by outrage[230]—are "emotionally powerful and immediate, and [the public's] rational explanations are derivations from, rather than sources of, these attitudes."[231]

Further, insanity defense attitudes—like death penalty attitudes—are laden with symbolism. They are "almost wholly abstract, ideological, and symbolic in nature, with essentially no personal relevance to the individual."[232] These abstracted attitudes are expressed not only by lay people but by experts as well. Professors Homant and Kennedy have thus demonstrated that expert witnesses' previously-articulated general attitudes toward the insanity defense would significantly govern their determination as to insanity in an individual hypothetical case.[233]

Just as studies have shown that the death penalty's symbolic values result in change-resistant attitudes (even in the face of disconfirming evidence),[234] similar symbolic content in insanity defense attitudes should lead us to expect "that providing accurate information about the use of the insanity plea will have only a minimal impact overall."[235]

The insanity defense is the authoritarian's worst-case disaster fantasy. It explicitly states that certain individuals can "break the rules;" what is worse, the rule breakers are definitionally deviant: they are individuals *not* "like us," outgroup members whose very essence appears to be a rejection of the conformity values most prized by the authoritarian personality. To the authoritarian, the insanity defense condones—indeed, *rewards*—the deviant for flaunting the law, and the defense refuses to force such an individual to take

---

230. *See id.* at 155-156 (80 percent of retentionists reported feeling "outraged" by a murderer getting less than a death sentence).

231. *Id.* at 155.

232. *Id.* at 164, *quoting* Sears & Kinder, *supra* note 203.

233. Homant & Kennedy, *Determinants in Expert Witnesses' Opinions in Insanity Defense Cases*, in Courts and Criminal Justice: Emerging Issues 57, 73-74 (L. Talerico ed. 1985) ("attitude toward the insanity defense in general was a powerful predictor of how subjects judged [a] particular case..."); *see also infra* chapter 9.

234. *See e.g.*, Ellsworth & Ross, *supra* note 176; Tyler & Weber, *supra* note 155.

235. Hans, *supra* note 218, at 408. Professor Hans added that accurate information would likely "primarily affect those whose attitudes are not strongly held." *Id.* Compare Jeffrey & Pasewark, *Altering Opinions About the Insanity Plea*, 11 J. Psychiatry & L. 29, 39 (1983) (speculating that the dissemination of accurate data about insanity defense use "might help dispel myths, increase understanding, and ultimately allow for a more rational appraisal of its function in the criminal justice system").

responsibility for his actions. The insanity defense thwarts the administration of punishment and does so with judicial sanction.

This perhaps helps explain why we adhere to insanity defense myths in spite of the overwhelming weight of contrary empirical evidence; psychologically, the dissonance that would be caused by acknowledging the mythic basis of our insanity defense beliefs is more than our social psyche can bear. It may also explain why we adhere to the use of heuristic cognitive devices in evaluation information about the insanity defense, and why we refuse to concede that our common sense may simply not be a sufficient explanation for the complex problems under discussion.

In the following chapter, I will explore these questions from other perspectives. After looking for an explanation for why the legal system is so poorly equipped to deal with the dissonances caused by the insanity defense,[236] I will explain how the bundle of attitudes and behaviors that I have been discussing —heuristic thinking, false OCS, authoritarianism, adherence to myths—can best be explained by what I call sanism.[237] I will then show how court decisions in this area are frequently pretextual, and how, in order to support pretextuality in decision making, judges are teleological in their use of social science evidence.[238] I will then look at these questions through the filter of "therapeutic jurisprudence," in an effort to determine if the insights of that discipline can bring a measure of coherence to the key doctrinal questions.[239] Finally, I will offer my recommendations as to how we can restructure our insanity defense jurisprudence and the way we think about the insanity defense.[240]

---

236. *See generally infra* chapter 8 A.
237. *See generally infra* chapter 8 B.
238. *See generally infra* chapter 8 C & D.
239. *See generally infra* chapter 8 E.
240. *See generally infra* chapter 9 B.

8

New Jurisprudential Explanations

A. Is This Too Much for Our System to Bear?
Of Hydraulic Pressure and Tensile Strength

1. Introduction

According to Professor Ernest Roberts, every legal principle can hold only so much "emotional or political freight," an amount he defines as its "tensile strength." When a principle is pushed beyond its strength through litigation or legislation, "it will simply fall a-part."[1] Warning of the disproportionate impact that great cases may make, Justice Holmes recognized that such cases—involving an "immediate, overwhelming interest which appeals to feelings and distorts the judgment"—exercise a sort of "hydraulic pressure...before which

---

1. Fentiman, *"Guilty But Mentally Ill:" The Real Verdict Is Guilty*, 12 B.C. L. Rev. 601, 611 n. 63 (1985) (*quoting* Roberts). *Compare* Sinclair, *The Use of Evolution Theory in Law*, 64 Det. C.L. Rev. 451, 469-70 (1987) ("it would seem that social systems are capable of absorbing a considerable amount of stress before they precipitate a need for a change. Legislatures seem to act only when such needs become, or appear to become, comparatively urgent"); Smolla, *Rethinking First Amendment Assumptions About Racist and Sexist Speech*, 47 Wash. & Lee L. Rev. 171, 176 (1990) ("Patterns of thought often are forged by the hydraulic pressure of events").

even well settled principles of law will bend."[2] If this hydraulic pressure raises arousal to "dysfunctionally high levels," the "limits of boundless rationality"[3] and of logic[4] may be exceeded; these pressures can imperil any decision making entity, including the Supreme Court.[5] As a result, the principle of psychological reactance controls our behavior; that is, once an individual believes he has a specific freedom, "any force on the individual that makes it more difficult...to exercise the freedom constitutes a threat to it."[6] Social influences—such as legal doctrines that are dissonant with "ordinary common sense"—that appear to limit our exercise of a freedom (in this case, to punish the "factually guilty") are internalized as a social and/or psychological threat.[7]

These insights are universal. They were at the core of Justice Douglas's dissent in the search and seizure case of *Terry v. Ohio*[8] and of Chief Justice Burger's opinion in the separation of powers case of

---

2.   Northern Sec. Co. v. United States, 193 U.S. 197, 400 (1904). This concept has since been regularly applied to other areas in which "hard cases" dominate. *See e.g.,* Payne v. Tennessee, 111 S. Ct. 2597, 2631 (1991) (Stevens, J., dissenting) (introduction into evidence of Victim Impact Statement in capital punishment case not violative of the Eighth Amendment); Skinner v. Railway Labor Executives' Ass'n, 489 U.S. 602, 654 (1989) (Marshall, J., dissenting) (drug testing reasonable under Fourth Amendment); Federenko v. United States, 449 U.S. 490, 538 (1981) (Stevens, J., dissenting) (denaturalization of former concentration camp guard proper).

      The State Justice Institute of the National Center for State Courts now funds a Managing Notorious Cases Project to provide a forum in which defendants can discuss the handling of high profile, high publicity cases. *See Notorious Cases: Judges' Forum,* 18 NCSC REPORT 1 (Feb. 1991).

3.   Perlin, *Morality and Pretextuality, Psychiatry and Law: Of "Ordinary Common Sense," Heuristic Reasoning, and Cognitive Dissonance,* 19 BULL. AM. ACAD. PSYCHIATRY & L. 131, 140 (1991), *quoting,* in part, Wexler, *Redefining the Insanity Problem,* 53 GEO. WASH. L. REV. 528, 537 (1985), *quoting* Weick, *Small Wins: Redefining the Scale of Social Problems,* 39 AM. PSYCHOLOGIST 40, 48 (1984).

4.   *See* Business Ass'n of University City v. Landrieu, 660 F. 2d 867, 878 (3d Cir. 1981) (low income housing case).

5.   *See* Barnhizer, *Prophets, Priests and Power Brokers: Three Fundamental Roles of Judges and Legal Scholars in America,* 50 U. PITT. L. REV. 127, 167 (1989).

6.   S. BREHM & J. BREHM, PSYCHOLOGICAL REACTANCE: A THEORY OF FREEDOM AND CONTROL 30-31 (1981); *see generally,* Perlin, *supra* note 3, at 138-39.

7.   S. BREHM & J. BREHM, *supra* note 6, at 30-31.

8.   392 U.S. 1, 39 (1968) (Douglas, J., dissenting) ("There have been powerful hydraulic pressures throughout our history that bear heavily on the Court to water down constitutional guarantees and give the police the upper hand. That hydraulic pressure has probably never been greater than it is today").

INS v. Chadha.[9] They apply to jurors, to members of the public, to legislators, to trial judges, and to members of the Supreme Court.[10]

2. Construing the Principles

These principles of hydraulic pressure and tensile strength "play out" in insanity defense jurisprudence in several discrete ways.[11] First, they appear most graphically in the insanity defense debate that I have discussed throughout this book. More broadly, they reflect the tension felt when citizens no longer feel that they can rely on the criminal justice system for protection.[12] State-sanctioned punishment serves as a safety-valve to ensure that individuals do not resort to private vengeance;[13] when the public feels that the insanity defense impeded justice from "being done" (whether or not these feelings are empirically "correct"), the system's tensile strength will be severely tested. The combination of our reliance on the negative vivid anecdote (the heart of the heuristic style), our prereflective and self-referential reliance on *faux* "ordinary common sense" in dealing with complex social, moral and philosophical questions, and our authoritarian cognitive rejection of ambiguity all only serve to make this test a more difficult one.

To the general public, it is irrelevant that the "circus" atmosphere of the Hinckley trial was a statistically insignificant occurrence, that there is no dispute as to the question of responsibility in over

---

9.   462 U.S. 919, 951 (1983) ("The hydraulic pressure inherent within each of the separate Branches to exceed the outer limits of its power, even to accomplish desirable objectives, must be resisted"). *See also,* Mistretta v. United States, 488 U.S. 361, 382 (1989) (upholding constitutionality of federal sentencing guidelines) (*quoting Chadha*).

10. *Compare* Haney, *The Fourteenth Amendment and Symbolic Legality: Let Them Eat Due Process,* 15 LAW & HUM. BEHAV. 183, 201 (1991) ("In managing the nation's symbolic legality, the Supreme Court struggles with the difficult balance of rendering decisions that appear fair but do not go too far in their redistributional or restructuring effect").

11. *See generally,* Durham, *The Impact of Deinstitutionalization on the Current Treatment of the Mentally Ill,* 12 INT'L J. L. & PSYCHIATRY 117, 129 (1989) (suggesting that the mental health system and the criminal justice system may work together in a "hydraulic" manner so that change in one segment of one system may change an aspect of the other system).

12. *See* Rychlak, *Society's Right to Punish: A Further Exploration of the Denunciation Theory of Punishment,* 65 TULANE L. REV. 299, 319-20 (1990).

13. *See supra* chapter 2 C.

eighty percent of all cases in which insanity is raised,[14] or that, in simulated studies, the use of instructions required by the Insanity Defense Reform Act do not produce statistically significant verdict patterns than result from the use of other substantive insanity tests.[15] These underlying perceptions will *remain* irrelevant until decision-makers begin to openly discuss the impact that the public's misconceptions have on insanity policy development, the concessions by Congress and forensic hospital administrations that policy will be set in accordance with myth, and the pretextuality of some of the suggested solutions (*e.g.*, the belief that the GBMI verdict provides treatment and offers a humane sentencing alternative, or the belief that the elimination of the volitional prong of the insanity defense will lessen the likelihood of a "moral mistake").[16]

Next, consider the psychological motivations that animate juror decision making. Although the Hinckley prosecution's attempts to minimize the defendant's mental illness by suggesting that his emotional problems were "largely his fault"[17] may have backfired, other information in our juror data base suggests that these motivations are extraordinarily important and puzzlingly underconsidered. We now know that evidence of "planfulness" will "trump" evidence of mental illness, that defendants who acknowledge their mental illness prior to the criminal event will have their insanity defense considered more favorably than a defendant who never sought prior treatment, that some defendants do better at the death penalty stage if they suppress potentially mitigating mental status evidence, and that jurors' social and moral attitudes about the insanity defense are far stronger predictors of verdicts than are factual variables in cases or substantive differences in insanity tests.[18] Yet, we pay no attention to this data in our policy formulation,[19] perhaps because the "immediate interest"

---

14. *See* Doherty, *Misconceptions About Mentally Ill Patients*, 146 AM. J. PSYCHIA-TRY 131 (1989) (letter to the editor).
15. *See* Finkel, *The Insanity Defense Reform Act of 1984: Much Ado About Nothing*, 7 BEHAV. SCI. & L. 403 (1989).
16. *See supra* chapter 5, text accompanying note 55.
17. *See* Balkin, *The Rhetoric of Responsibility*, 76 VA. L. REV. 197, 238 (1990).
18. *See supra* chapter 6 D 5-6.
19. *See e.g.*, English, *The Light Between Twilight and Dusk: Federal Criminal Law and the Volitional Insanity Defense*, 40 HASTINGS L.J. 1, 47-48 (1988) (discussing Congress's failure to consider empirical research of Drs. Richard Rogers and Stephen Golding in post-*Hinckley* insanity defense debate).

of a case like Hinckley's generates such hydraulic pressure that the criminal justice system's tensile strength is endangered.

Finally, besides wilfully blinding ourselves to empirical realities about insanity defense pleas and trials, we blind ourselves to what happens to mentally disabled criminal defendants *after* trial if we let this hydraulic pressure dominate our jurisprudence. Initially, we must recall that a significant portion of that jurisprudence—the substantive tests and procedural safeguards that accompany the post-acquittal commitment process, and the creation of the GBMI verdict— flows directly from our concern that "too many defendants are 'getting off' without adequate punishment."[20] This concern leads to decisions such as *Jones v. United States*[21] that allow for far less stringent standards of proof at the post-acquittal stage than in involuntary civil commitment cases, and that allow for post-NGRI commitments that last for longer terms than the maximum sentence for the underlying crime.[22] It also leads to a body of caselaw (in GBMI cases) that allows for punishment without treatment in spite of jury verdicts that specifically incorporate the fact of the defendant's mental illness.[23]

We also blind ourselves to other insanity decision making outcomes. Thus, the first consideration of Utah's *mens rea* insanity defense suggested that the defense served a "ritual function whereby lawyers can move clients from the legal system to the mental health system."[24] After Montana "abolished" its insanity defense by retaining solely a *mens rea* exception,[25] researchers found that most indictees who might have attempted an insanity defense under pre-abolition legislation were, instead, found incompetent to stand trial, and were thus committed indefinitely to the same units in the same forensic facilities in which they would have been housed had they been acquitted by reason of insanity; while "[t]he insanity statutes were

---

20. Ellis, *The Consequences of the Insanity Defense: Proposals to Reform Post-Acquittal Commitment Laws*, 35 CATH. U. L. REV. 961, 963 (1986).
21. 463 U.S. 354 (1983).
22. *See supra* chapter 4 E 2 d.
23. *See supra* chapter 3 A 1 c (4).
24. Heinbecker, *Two Years' Experience Under Utah's* Mens Rea *Insanity Law*, 14 BULL. AM. ACAD. PSYCHIATRY & L. 185, 190 (1986). On the pretextual nature of such decision making, *see generally infra* chapter 8 C.
25. *See e.g.*, Bender, *After Abolition: the Present State of the Insanity Defense in Montana*, 45 MONT. L. REV. 133 (1984); *see supra* chapter 2 A 2 d.

reformed, the detention system was not."[26]

This "abolition" thus resulted in little more than the paper transfer of certain severely mentally disabled criminal defendants from one status to another.[27] Perhaps the abolition decision assuaged legislators and the general public to such an extent that the actual treatment and disposition of the defendants in question simply became irrelevant. What is most revealing is that the findings of the Montana researchers appear to have had almost no impact on subsequent insanity defense litigation in other states where the defense was abolished or significantly truncated.[28]

3. Conclusion

The furor over the Hinckley insanity acquittal, the subsequent legal debate, the eventual dismantling of the federal insanity defense and the massive retooling of the insanity defense in the states all demonstrate that we cannot understand and learn from the extreme dissonance caused by such a verdict in such a case with such a victim. We repeat banal myths, we take refuge in pre-reflective and heuristic thinking, and we ignore scientific, behavioral and empirical studies that could—and should—illuminate the underlying issues. We do this because our "limits of boundless rationality"[29] have been exceeded, and because, to do otherwise, would threaten the core values of our society's "culture of punishment."

---

26. Steadman, Callahan, Robbins & Morrisey, *Maintenance of an Insanity Defense Under Montana's "Abolition" of the Insanity Defense*, 146 AM. J. PSYCHIATRY 357, 359 (1989).
27. On the interplay between an incompetency to stand trial finding and a defendant's ability to enter an NGRI plea, *see* 3 M.L. PERLIN, MENTAL DISABILITY LAW: CIVIL AND CRIMINAL (1989), §14.21A, at 118 (1992 pocket part).
28. An April 1, 1993 WESTLAW search reveals no citations to this research by Steadman and his colleagues in *any* litigated case.
29. *See supra* note 3.

B. Why Do We Feel the Way We Do?
The Meaning of Sanism

1. Introduction[30]

"Sanism" is an irrational prejudice of the same quality and character as other irrational prejudices that cause (and are reflected in) prevailing social attitudes of racism, sexism, homophobia and ethnic bigotry.[31] It infects our jurisprudence, our lawyering practices,[32] and our interpersonal discourse.[33] Sanism is largely invisible and largely socially acceptable. It is based upon stereotype, myth, superstition and deindividualization, and is sustained and perpetuated by our use of false "ordinary common sense" and heuristic reasoning in an unconscious response to events both in everyday life and in the legal process.[34]

---

30. The material *infra* text accompanying notes 31-52 is generally adapted from Perlin, *On "Sanism,"* 46 S.M.U. L. REV. 373, 374-76, 400-4 (1992), and Perlin & Dorfman, *Sanism, Social Science, and the Development of Mental Disability Law Jurisprudence*, 11 BEHAV. SCI. & L. 47, 51-52 (1993).

31. The classic study is G. ALLPORT, THE NATURE OF PREJUDICE (1955). On the way that other groups are similarly targeted, *see* Perlin, *supra* note 30, at 384 n. 78. On the negative attributions made in a related context about physically unattractive individuals in the criminal justice system by judges and by jurors, *see* Wertleib, *Individuals With Disabilities in the Criminal Justice System: A Review of the Literature*, 18 CRIM. JUST. & BEHAV. 332, 333 (1991); MacCoun, *The Emergence of Extralegal Bias During Jury Deliberation*, 17 CRIM. JUST. & BEHAV. 303, 311 (1990). On the relationship between homophobia and bias toward mentally disabled individuals, *see* Mison, *Homophobia in Manslaughter: The Homosexual Advance as Insufficient Provocation*, 80 CALIF. L. REV. 133, 157 (1992).

32. The phrase "sanism" was, to the best of my knowledge, coined by Dr. Morton Birnbaum. *See* Birnbaum, *The Right to Treatment: Some Comments on its Development*, in MEDICAL, MORAL AND LEGAL ISSUES IN HEALTH CARE 97, 106-7 (F. Ayd ed. 1974); Koe v. Califano, 573 F. 2d 761, 764 n. 12 (2d Cir. 1978).

33. *See e.g.*, Parry, *1987 in Review*, 12 MENT. & PHYS. DIS. L. REP. 2, 2 (1988) ("1987 was the year in which underlying negative feelings and prejudice toward mentally disabled persons could again be registered in polite society without condemnation").

34. *See supra* chapter 6 D. For a rare example of a court consciously seeking to avoid stereotypical thinking in a related context, *see* People v. McAlpin, 53 Cal. 3d 1289, 283 Cal. Rptr. 382, 812 P. 2d 563, 570-71 (1991) (rejecting OCS notion of a "typical" profile of a child molester).

2. Sanist Courts

Judges are not immune from sanism. "[E]mbedded in the cultural presuppositions that engulf us all,"[35] they express discomfort with social science[36] (or any other system that may appear to challenge law's hegemony over society) and skepticism about new thinking; this discomfort and skepticism allows them to take deeper refuge in heuristic thinking that perpetuates the myths and stereotypes of sanism.

Judges reflect and project the conventional morality of the community, and judicial decisions in all areas of civil and criminal mental disability law continue to reflect and perpetuate sanist stereotypes.[37] Their language demonstrates bias against mentally disabled individuals[38] and contempt for the mental health professions.[39] At least one court has, without citation to any authority, found that it is less likely that medical patients will "fabricate descriptions of their complaints"

---

35. D'Amato, *Harmful Speech and the Culture of Indeterminacy*, 32 WM. & MARY L. REV. 329, 332 (1991).
36. *See generally*, Perlin & Dorfman, *supra* note 30; *see generally infra* chapter 8 D.
37. Compare Mohr, *The Trinational Debate over Insanity and the Law in the 19th Century: Harris's Contribution* (book review of R. HARRIS, MURDERS AND MADNESS: MEDICINE, LAW, AND SOCIETY IN THE "FIN DE SIÈCLE" (1989), 16 LAW & SOC'L INQUIRY 635, 640 (1991) (historically, judges construed criminal responsibility cases in manner that allowed the to "reassert what they took to be the bedrock virtues of their society"). On the authoritarian roots of the judicial use of stereotypes, *see* Henderson, *Authoritarianism and the Rule of Law*, 66 IND. L.J. 379, 383 (1991). On the relationship between authoritarianism and sanism, *see* Perlin, *supra* note 30, at 377 n. 19.
38. *See e.g.*, Corn v. Zant, 708 F. 2d 549, 569 (11th Cir. 1983), *reh. den.*, 714 F. 2d 159 (11th Cir. 1983), *cert. den.*, 467 U.S. 1220 (1984) (defendant referred to as a "lunatic"); Sinclair v. Wainwright, 814 F. 2d 1516, 1522 (11th Cir., 1987), *quoting* Shuler v. Wainwright, 491 F. 2d 213 (5th Cir. 1974) (using "lunatic"); Brown v. People, 8 Ill. 2d 540, 134 N.E. 2d 760, 762 (1956) (judge asked defendant, "You are not crazy at this time, are you?"); Pyle v. Boles, 250 F. Supp. 285, 289 (N.D. W. Va. 1966) (trial judge accused habeas petitioner of "being crazy"); *but cf.* State v. Penner, 772 P. 2d 819 (Kan. 1989) (unpublished disposition), at *3 (witnesses admonished *not* to refer to defendant as "crazy" or "nuts"). Compare Addkison v. State, 608 So. 2d 304, 308 (Miss. 1992) (defendant's own expert witness characterized defendant as "high end imbecile").
39. *See e.g.*, Commonwealth v. Musolino, 320 Pa. Super. 425, 467 A. 2d 605 (1983) (reversible error for trial judge to refer to expert witnesses as "headshrinkers"); *compare* State v. Percy, 146 Vt. 475, 507 A. 2d 955, 956 (1986), *app'l after remand*, 156 Vt. 468, 595 A. 2d 248 (1990), *cert. den.*, 112 S. Ct. 344 (1991) (conviction reversed where prosecutor, in closing argument, referred to expert testimony as "psycho-babble").

than will "psychological patients."[40] Another court has likened psychiatric predictivity of future dangerousness to predictions made by an oncologist as to consequences of an untreated and metastasized malignancy,[41] in spite of the overwhelming weight of clinical and behavioral literature that concludes that psychiatrists are far more often incorrect in predicting dangerousness than they are accurate.[42]

Courts often appear *impatient* with mentally disabled litigants, ascribing their problems in the legal process to weak character or poor resolve. Thus, a popular sanist myth is that "Mentally disabled individuals simply don't try hard enough. They give in too easily to their basest instincts, and do not exercise appropriate self-restraint."[43] A trial judge who responded to a National Center for State Courts survey indicated that, in his mind, defendants who were incompetent to stand trial could have understood and communicated with counsel and the court "if they [had] only wanted."[44] While

---

40. People v. LaLone, 432 Mich. 103, 437 N.W. 2d 611, 613 (1989), *reh. den.* (1989).
41. *In re* Melton, 597 A. 2d 892, 898 (D.C. 1991).
42. *See e.g.*, J. MONAHAN, THE CLINICAL PREDICTION OF VIOLENT BEHAVIOR (1981); Monahan, *Risk Assessment of Violence Among the Mentally Disordered: Generating Useful Knowledge*, 11 INT'L J. L. & PSYCHIATRY 249 (1989); Monahan, *Mental Disorder and Violent Behavior: Perceptions and Evidence*, 47 AM. PSYCHOLOGIST 511 (1992); Slobogin, *Dangerousness and Expertise*, 133 U. PA. L. REV. 97 (1984). *See supra* chapter 4 C 3.
43. *See e.g.*, Balkin, *The Rhetoric of Responsibility*, 76 VA. L. REV. 197, 238 (1990) (Hinckley prosecutor suggested to jurors, "if Hinckley had emotional problems, they were largely his own fault"); State v. Duckworth, 496 So. 2d 624, 635 (La. App. 1986) (juror who felt defendant would be responsible for actions as long as he "wanted to do them" not excused for cause) (no error). *Compare* Noe v. Florida, 586 So. 2d 371, 374-79 (Fla. Dist. App. 1991), *reh. den.* (1991) (reversible error where trial judge failed to grant defendant's challenge to jurors who indicated "philosophical problems" with the insanity defense). On the way society traditionally denigrated mentally disabled persons because of their perceived "refusal [or inability] to work," *see* Midelfort, *Madness and Civilization in Early Modern Europe: A Reappraisal of Michel Foucault*, in AFTER THE REFORMATION: ESSAYS IN HONOR OF J. H. HEXTER 247, 251 (B. Malament ed. 1980).
44. K. Gould, I. Keilitz & J.R. Martin, "Criminal Defendants With Trial Disabilities: The Theory and Practice of Competency Assistance" (unpublished manuscript), at 68; *see also*, Lamb, *Deinstitutionalization and the Homeless Mentally Ill*, 35 HOSP. & COMMUN. PSYCHIATRY 899, 943 (1984) (society tends to "morally disapprove of [mentally disabled] persons who 'give in' to their dependency needs"). *Compare* Matter of Commitment of Tarpley, 581 N.E. 2d 1251 (Ind. 1991), *reh. den.* (1992) (error to hold defendant in contempt of court for failing to take medication as required by outpatient commitment).

Justice Holmes' infamous and florid language in *Buck v. Bell*[45] is rarely repeated,[46] judicial decisions in all areas of mental disability law continue to reflect and perpetuate sanist stereotypes.

Thus, individuals incompetent for one purpose are presumed incompetent for all other purposes, and judges question whether it is even possible to distinguish between different kinds of incompetencies.[47] If a person subject to civil commitment refuses to take medication—a constitutional right in most jurisdictions—that refusal is often seen as a presumptive indicator of dangerousness and need for institutionalization.[48] Adherence to involuntary civil commitment statutory criteria is subverted because of fears that strict construction of those laws would lead inexorably to homelessness.[49] The minimal-

---

45. "Three generations of imbeciles are enough." 274 U.S. 200, 207 (1927). For contemporaneous reevaluations of this opinion, the factual record in *Buck*, and Justice Holmes' personal view, *see e.g.*, Gould, *Carrie Buck's Daughter*. 2 Const'l Commentary 331 (1985); Lombardo, *Three Generations, No Imbeciles: New Light on* Buck v. Bell, 60 N.Y.U. L. Rev. 31 (1985); Dudziak, *Oliver Wendell Holmes as a Eugenic Reformer: Rhetoric in the Writing of Constitutional Law*, 71 Iowa L. Rev. 833 (1986); Comment, *We Have Met the Imbeciles and They Are Us: The Courts and Citizens With Mental Retardation*, 65 Neb. L. Rev. 768 (1986).

46. *But see* Robertson, *Letter to the Editor*, 11 Dev. in Mental Health Law 4 (Jan-June 1991) (sitting trial judge's endorsement of Holmes' *dictum*).

47. *See e.g.*, United States v. Charters, 863 F. 2d 302, 310 (4th Cir. 1988) (en banc), *cert. den.*, 494 U.S. 1016 (1990); Perlin, *Are Courts Competent to Decide Competency Questions? Stripping the Facade from* United States v. Charters, 38 U. Kan. L. Rev. 957, 87-88 (1990); Wexler, *Grave Disability and Family Therapy: The Therapeutic Potential of Civil Libertarian Commitment Codes*, reprinted in Therapeutic Jurisprudence: The Law as a Therapeutic Agent 165, 170 (D. Wexler ed. 1990) (Therapeutic Jurisprudence) (discussing courts' historic improper equation of serious mental illness with "incompetence, grave disability and committability"); *see generally*, T. Grisso, Evaluating Competencies: Forensic Assessments and Instruments 273 (1986).

48. *In re* Melas, 371 N.W. 2d 653, 655 (Min. Ct. App. 1985); Matter of J.B., 705 P. 2d 598, 602 (Mont. 1985); 1 M.L. Perlin, *supra* note 27, §3.45, at 341 n. 741, and *id.* at 72-73 (1992 pocket part). *Compare* Durham & La Fond, *A Search for the Missing Premise of Involuntary Therapeutic Commitment: Effective Treatment of the Mentally Ill*, 40 Rutgers L. Rev. 303 (1988), reprinted in Therapeutic Jurisprudence, *supra* note 45, at 133, 154 (literature review suggests that anywhere from 21-79 percent of patients studied who were treated with drugs may do no better than those given placebos).

49. *See* Perlin, *Competency, Deinstitutionalization, and Homelessness: A Story of Marginalization*, 28 Hous. L. Rev. 63, 116-17 n. 308 (1991), discussing *In re* Melton, 565 A. 2d 635, 649 (D.C. 1989) (Schwelb, J., dissenting), *hearing granted & opinion vacated*, 581 A. 2d 788 (D.C. 1990), *superseded on rehearing*, 597 A. 2d 892 (D.C. 1991).

ist "substantial professional judgment" test[50] is endorsed in a wide variety of institutional cases so that only the most arbitrary and baseless decision making can be successfully challenged.[51] Even when non-sanist court decisions reject sanist myths and stereotypes, the enforcement of such decisions is frequently only sporadic.[52]

3. Sanism and the Insanity Defense

Insanity defense decision making is often irrational. It rejects empiricism, science, psychology and philosophy, and substitutes myth, stereotype, bias and distortion. It resists educational correction, demands punishment regardless of responsibility, and reifies medievalist concepts based on fixed and absolute notions of good and evil and of right and wrong. In short, our insanity defense jurisprudence is the jurisprudence of sanism.[53]

This irrationality is, on occasion, recognized by courts and by litigants. In reversing a conviction in a case where the trial judge refused to ask prospective jurors if they could fairly judge an insanity case, the Illinois Supreme Court specifically found:

---

50. *See* Youngberg v. Romeo, 457 U.S. 307, 323 (1982).
51. *See Charters*, 863 F. 2d at 313, critiqued sharply in Perlin, *supra* note 47, at 935. For a comprehensive critique of the *Youngberg* standard, *see* Stefan, *Leaving Civil Rights to the Experts: From Deference to Abdication Under the Professional Judgment Standard*, 102 YALE L.J. 639 (1992).
52. *See e.g.*, Perlin, *Fatal Assumption: A Critical Evaluation of the Role of Counsel in Mental Disability Cases*, 16 LAW & HUM. BEHAV. 47-48 (1992), discussing lack of implementation of Jackson v. Indiana, 406 U.S. 715 (1972), applying due process clause to post-incompetency to stand trial commitment proceedings; *see also*, Winick, *Restructuring Competency to Stand Trial*, 32 U.C.L.A. L. REV. 921, 940-41 (1985).
53. Media errors compound the problem. A *USA Today* article about the Jeffrey Dahmer case stated inaccurately that the ALI Test was operative in all federal courts. *See* Howlett, *The Dahmer Debate // Sanity Trial Raises Social-Legal Questions*, USA Today, Feb. 10, 1992, at 3A (full text available on NEXIS). Of course, that test was legislatively repealed nearly a decade ago in the Insanity Defense Reform Act of 1984, *see* 18 U.S.C. §20, legislatively overruling United States v. Brawner, 471 F. 2d 969 (D.C. Cir. 1972); *see generally supra* chapter 2 A 2 c. At the time of the Hinckley trial, the *New York Times* incorrectly stated that the *then*-operative insanity defense was the *Durham* test. Roberts, *High U.S. Officials Express Outrage, Asking For New Law and Insanity Plea*, N.Y. Times, June 23, 1982, at B6, col. 3 (full text available on NEXIS). *That* test had been judicially overruled a decade prior to the publication of *that* article. *See Brawner*, 471 F. 2d at 981, overruling Durham v. United States, 214 F. 2d 862 (D.C. Cir. 1954); *see generally supra* chapter 3 A 1 c (3).

Although the insanity defense upon which the defendant relied is a well-recognized legal defense, it remains a subject of intense controversy, [and one] "which is known to be subject to bias or prejudice."[54]

Also, a California appellate court has retroactively applied an earlier judicial decision that a defendant must be advised that his post-insanity acquittal may exceed the maximum possible term of imprisonment for the underlying crime.[55] On the other hand, the New Jersey Supreme Court affirmed a trial judge's rejection of a defendant's application for a non-jury trial on a murder charge where his insanity defense was based upon "abnormal homosexual fantasies."[56] In its decision, the court stressed "the importance of maintaining the public's confidence in our criminal justice system," and described the jury system as "the best vehicle for attaining justice."[57]

Like the rest of the criminal trial process, the insanity defense process is riddled by sanist stereotypes and myths.[58] Examples include the following:

- •reliance on a fixed vision of popular, concrete, visual images of "craziness"[59]

---

54. People v. Stack, 112 Ill. 2d 301, 493 N.E. 2d 339, 344 (1986), *quoting*, in part, People v. Bowel, 111 Ill. 2d 58, 488 N.E. 2d 995 (1986).

55. People v. Minor, 227 Cal. App. 3d 37, 277 Cal. Rptr. 615, 616 (1991).

56. State v. Dunne, 124 N.J. 303, 590 A. 2d 1144 (1991). The trial judge had ruled that "this is the kind of case that it is appropriate to have the community decide," adding that proposed voir dire questions could sufficiently screen out prejudiced venire members. *Id.* at 1146.

57. *Id.* at 1152. It concluded on this point: "We surrender to no clamor when we protect trial by jury; we simply accept the wisdom of the ages and benefit from the experience of thousands of judges over hundreds of years who continue to marvel at the consistent soundness of jury verdicts." *Id.*

58. Other decisions are pretextual, and based on phantasmic reasoning. *See generally infra* chapter 8 C. In one case, turning on whether a defendant had the requisite specific intent to attempt to rob a bank, the trial court refused to allow the county jail psychiatrist to testify that he had been prescribing antipsychotic medication for the defendant for a specific time period, reasoning that such testimony might "be interfering with the treatment of [other] prisoners in jails because [other] prisoners might ask for drugs to create the impression they need more drugs." United States v. Still, 857 F. 2d 671, 672 (9th Cir. 1988). Nothing in the case suggests that there was ever *any* evidence that spoke remotely to this issue; nonetheless, the Ninth Circuit affirmed as "not manifestly erroneous." *Id.* See Perlin, *supra* note 3, at 135 (discussing *Still* as an example of judicial pretextuality).

59. *See e.g.*, Wainwright v. Greenfield, 474 U.S. 284, 297 (1986) (Rehnquist, J., concurring); State v. Clayton, 656 S.W. 2d 344, 350-51 (Tenn. 1983). Similar standards are employed in civil cases. *See e.g.*, St. Louis S.W. Ry. Co. v. Pennington, 261 Ark. 650, 553 S.W. 2d 436, 448 (1977) (recovery for mental

- an obsessive fear of feigned mental states[60]
- a presumed absolute linkage between mental illness and dangerousness[61]
- sanctioning of the death penalty in the case of mentally retarded defendants, some defendants who are "substantially mentally impaired," or defendants who have been found guilty but mentally ill (GBMI)[62]
- the incessant confusion and conflation of substantive mental status tests[63]
- imposing a "clear and convincing" burden on the defendant to prove insanity, thus allowing for conviction even where it is "more likely than not" that the defendant was not responsible[64]
- the determination that an insanity acquittee's need for medication renders him not "fully recovered" so as to be eligible for outpatient care or conditional release[65]

---

anguish of adult survivors of wrongful death victims allowed where survivors demonstrated that suffered "more than the normal grief"). See *supra* chapter 5 C 3.

60. See e.g., Lynch v. Overholser, 369 U.S. 705, 715 (1962); United States v. Brown, 478 F. 2d 606, 611 (D.C. Cir. 1973), as discussed in Margulies, The *"Pandemonium Between the Mad and the Bad:" Procedures for the Commitment and Release of Insanity Acquittees After* Jones v. United States, 36 RUTGERS L. REV. 793, 806-07 n. 85 (1984). See *supra* chapter 5 C 1. *Compare* Strickland v. Francis, 738 F. 2d 1542 (11th Cir. 1984) (jailer's lay testimony that defendant was feigning symptoms was not a sufficient basis upon which to disregard uncontradicted that defendant was incompetent to stand trial).

61. See *e,g,* Jones v. United States, 463 U.S. 354, 365 (1983); Overholser v. O'Beirne, 302 F. 2d 852, 861 (D.C. Cir. 1961). See *supra* chapter 4 E 2 d.

62. Penry v. Lynaugh, 492 U.S. 302 (1989) (mental retardation); Commonwealth v. Faulkner, 528 Pa. 57, 595 A. 2d 28, 38 (1991) (substantial mental impairment); Harris v. State, 499 N.E. 2d 723 (Ind. 1986) (GBMI); *see also,* People v. Crews, 122 Ill. 2d 266, 522 N.E. 2d 1167 (1988) (permissible to sentence GBMI defendant to post-life expectancy term). *Compare* Ford v. Wainwright, 477 U.S. 399 (1986) (barring execution of the currently insane). On the question of whether mentally retarded individuals' lessened capacity for moral development prohibit their execution, *see Penry*, 492 U.S. at 345 (Brennan, J., concurring in part & dissenting in part). See *supra* chapter 4 E 2 f (3).

63. See e.g., Buttrum v. Black, 721 F. Supp. 1268, 1295 (N.D. Ga. 1989), *aff'd*, 908 F. 2d 695 (11th Cir. 1990); Covey v. State, 504 S.W. 2d 387, 392-93 (Tenn. Cr. App. 1973). See *generally*, R. ROESCH & S. GOLDING, COMPETENCY TO STAND TRIAL 15-17 (1980); Perlin, *Pretexts and Mental Disability Law: The Case of Competency*, 47 U. MIAMI L. REV. (1993) (in press), manuscript at 96-99.

64. See e.g., State v. Zmich, 160 Ariz. 108, 770 P. 2d 776 (1989); *see supra* chapter 3, note 126.

65. People v. DeAnda, 114 Cal. App. 3d 480, 170 Cal. Rptr. 830, 832-33 (1980), discussed in Wexler, *Inappropriate Patient Confinement and Appropriate State*

•the refusal in insanity cases of providing jury instructions that NGRI defendants face long-term post-acquittal commitment[66]

•the regularity of sanist appeals by prosecutors in insanity defense summations, arguing that insanity defenses are easily faked, that insanity acquittees are often immediately released, and that expert witnesses are readily duped[67]

•the characterization of the allocation of treatment resources for GBMI defendants as "not...helpful" or a "waste."[68]

Justice Thomas's dissents in *Riggins v. Nevada*[69] and *Foucha v. Louisiana*[70] are "textbook [examples] of sanist behavior."[71] As I have already discussed,[72] his opinions reify the full range of sanist myths, rely irrationally on behavioral stereotypes, and employ distorted heuristic cognitive devices. As much as anything else, they reflect all that is wrong in insanity defense jurisprudence.

Advocacy, 45 Law & Contemp. Probs. 193 (Spring 1982), reprinted in Therapeutic Jurisprudence, *supra* note 47, at 347, 350-51.

66. State v. Neely, 819 P. 2d 249, 256 (N.M. 1991); United States v. Shannon, 981 2d 759 (5th. Cir. 1993). *See also*, Mitchell v. Commonwealth, 781 S.W. 2d 510 (Ky. 1989), *reh. den.* (1990), discussed *supra* chapter 3, text accompanying notes 106-07 (no instructions need be given as to consequences of GBMI verdict). *Compare* Commonwealth v. Mutina, 36 Mass. 810, 323 N.E. 2d 294, 300-2 (1975): "[W]e believe it is best to entrust juror with a knowledge of the consequences of a verdict of not guilty by reason of insanity. If jurors can be entrusted with responsibility for a defendant's life and liberty in cases such as this, they are entitled to know what protection they and their fellow citizens will have if they conscientiously apply the evidence and arrive at a verdict of not guilty by reason of insanity—a verdict which necessarily requires the chilling determination that the defendant is an insane killer not legally responsible for his acts. The instant case represents a classic example of the injustice which may occur when such information is withheld from the jury..." On the split in the courts on this issue, *see* 3 M.L. Perlin, *supra* note 27, §15.16 at 336-39.

67. *See e.g.*, People v. Aliwoli, 1992 WL 329070 (Ill. App. 1992), at *3; People v. Camden, 219 Ill. App. 3d 124, 578 N.E. 2d 1211, 1223 (1991), *reh. den.* (1991).

68. Robinson v. Solem, 432 N.W. 2d 246, 249 (S.D. 1988).

69. 112 S. Ct. 1810, 1822 (1992) (insanity-pleading defendant's fair trial rights violated by administration of antipsychotic medication during pendency of trial); *see supra* chapter 4 E 2 f (2); 2 M.L. Perlin, *supra* note 27, §5.65A (1992 pocket part).

70. 112 S. Ct. 1780, 1797 (1992) (state law providing for the continued detention of non-mentally ill insanity acquittee unconstitutional); *see supra* 3 M.L. Perlin, *supra* note 27, §15.25A (1992 pocket part).

71. Perlin & Dorfman, *supra* note 30, at 60; *see also* M. Perlin, "Law as a Therapeutic and Anti- Therapeutic Agent," paper presented at the Massachusetts Department of Mental Health's Division of Forensic Mental health's annual conference, May 1992 (Auburn, MA).

72. *See supra* chapter 4 E 2 e (2); chapter 4 E 2 f (2).

This analysis is not entirely pessimistic. For instance, in his concurrence in a recent case holding that an appeal from an involuntary civil commitment order was not mooted solely by the individual's release from hospitalization, Florida Supreme Court Judge Gerald Kogan revealed his understanding of the role of sanism in mental disability law: "The law itself is beginning a process of rooting out acts of irrational prejudice based on mental disability, just as the law in the 1960s began eliminating the irrational bigotry posed by racism."[73]

Other, more well-known opinions have been written in the same voice. Some nonsanist opinions such as Judge Johnson's *Wyatt v. Stickney*[74] decisions are firmly rooted in a rights/empowerment model;[75] others like Justice Blackmun's dissent in *Barefoot v. Estelle*,[76] Justice Stevens' partial dissent in *Washington v. Harper*,[77] Justice Kennedy's concurrence in *Riggins*,[78] or the New Jersey Supreme Court's opinion in *State v. Krol*[79] specifically rebut sanist myths. Others such as Justice Stevens' dissent in *Pennhurst State School & Hospital v. Halderman II*,[80] Justices Stevens' and Marshall's separate opinions in *City of Cleburne v. Cleburne Living Center*,[81] and Judge Kaufman's use of a "Gulag archipelago" metaphor in a Second Circuit case involving a mentally disabled prisoner[82] express eloquent outrage at institutional conditions that flow inevitably from a sanist

---

73. Godwin v. State, 593 So. 2d 211, 215 (Fla. 1992) (Kogan, J., concurring in part & dissenting in part).
74. 325 F. Supp. 781 (M.D. Ala. 1971), 334 F. Supp. 1341 (M.D.Ala.), 344 F. Supp. 373 (M.D. Ala.), 344 F. Supp. 387 (M.D. Ala. 1972) (subsequent citations omitted) (articulating constitutional right to treatment).
75. *See generally*, M. MINOW, MAKING ALL THE DIFFERENCE: INCLUSION, EXCLUSION, AND AMERICAN LAW 131-45 (1990).
76. 463 U.S. 880, 916 (1983). *See supra* chapter 4 E 2 f (1); *see generally*, 3 M.L. PERLIN, *supra* note 27, §§17.13-17.14.
77. 494 U.S. 210, 236 (1990) (limiting right of convicted prisoners to refuse psychotropic medication). *See generally*, 2 M.L. PERLIN, *supra* note 27, §5.64A.
78. 112 S. Ct. at 1817; *see supra* chapter 4, text accompanying notes 384-87.
79. 68 N.J. 236, 344 A. 2d 289 (1975) (applying broad due process protections to post-insanity acquittal commitment process). *See supra* chapter 4 E 2 d.
80. 465 U.S. 89, 126 (1984) (limiting, on Eleventh Amendment grounds, right of civil rights plaintiffs to sue state defendants on pendant state claims). *See* 2 M.L. PERLIN, *supra* note 27, §§7.15-7.17, at 627-45.
81. 473 U.S. 432, 452 (1985) (Stevens, J., concurring), and *id.* at 455 (Marshall, J., concurring in part & dissenting in part) (equal protection challenge to municipal ordinance excluding group homes). *See* 2 M.L. PERLIN, *supra* note 27, §7.22, at 657-71.
82. United States *ex rel.* Schuster v. Vincent, 524 F. 2d 153, 154 (2d Cir. 1975).

society; yet others express true empathy and understanding about the plight of the institutionalized mentally disabled.[83] A handful of judges—David Bazelon is the finest example—spent their careers rooting out sanist myths and stereotypes, and raising the legal system's consciousness about sanism's impact on all of society;[84] other judges in lesser known cases have also shown real sensitivity to the underlying issues.[85]

These examples, however, are clearly the minority. Sanism regularly and relentlessly infects the courts in the same ways that it infects the public discourse. It synthesizes all of the irrational thinking about the insanity defense, and helps create an environment in which groundless myths can shape the jurisprudence. As much as any other factor, it explains why we feel the way we do about "these people." As I will discuss next, it also provides a basis for courts to engage in pretextual reasoning in deciding insanity defense cases.

---

83. *See e.g.*, Rennie v. Klein, 476 F. Supp. 1294, 1309 (D.N.J. 1979): "Medicine has not yet found a cure for the terrible pain of mental illness. The law cannot assist in this endeavor. But the Constitution can and does prevent those who have suffered so much at the hands of nature from being subjected to further suffering at the hands of man."

84. *See e.g.*, Wald, *Disembodied Voices—An Appellate Judge's Response*, 66 Tex. L. Rev. 623, 627 (1988) (Bazelon one of the "greatest appellate judges;" Wales, *The Rise, the Fall, and the Resurrection of the Medical Model*, 63 Geo. L.J. 87 (1974) (Judge Bazelon "invited the world of mental health professionals and criminologists into his courtroom" to "extend his courtroom back to the world"). *See generally, e.g.*, Bazelon, *Institutionalization, Deinstitutionalization, and the Adversary Process*, 75 Colum., L. Rev. 897 (1975); Bazelon, *Veils, Values and Social Responsibility*, 37 Am. Psychologist 115 (1982). On the way that Judge Bazelon's opinions reflected his "sensitivity to pain and suffering," *see All Things Considered* (Nat'l Publ. Radio transcript) (Feb. 20, 1993), *quoting* Daniel Schorr (full text available on NEXIS).

85. *See e.g.*, S.H. v. Edwards, 860 F. 2d 1045, 1053 (11 Cir. 1989) (Clark, J., dissenting), *cert. den.*, 491 U.S. 905 (1989), *vacated*, 880 F. 2d 1203 (11th Cir. 1989), *on rehearing*, 886 F. 2d 1292 (11th Cir. 1989); Godwin v. State, 593 So. 2d 211, 215 (Fla. 1992) (Kogan, J., concurring in part & dissenting in part), discussed *supra* text accompanying note 73; Commonwealth v. Mutina, 36 Mass. 810, 323 N.E. 2d 294, 300-02 (1975), discussed *supra* note 66.

C. How Do We Rationalize What We Do? The Role of Pretextuality

1. Introduction[86]

The entire relationship between the legal process and mentally disabled litigants is pretextual. By "pretextual," I mean simply that courts accept (either implicitly or explicitly) testimonial dishonesty and engage in similarly dishonest (frequently meretricious) decision making,[87] specifically where witnesses, especially *expert* witnesses, show a "high propensity to purposely distort their testimony in order to achieve desired ends."[88] This pretextuality is poisonous; it infects all players, breeds cynicism and disrespect for the law, demeans participants, and reinforces shoddy lawyering, blasé judging, and, at times, perjurious and/or corrupt testifying. The reality is well known to frequent consumers of judicial services in this area: to mental health advocates and other public defender/legal aid/legal service lawyers assigned to represent patients and mentally disabled criminal defendants, to prosecutors and state attorneys assigned to represent hospitals, to judges who regularly hear such cases, to expert and lay witnesses, and, most importantly, to the mentally disabled person who is the subject of the litigation in question.

The pretexts of the forensic mental health system are reflected both in the testimony of forensic experts and in the decisions of legislators and fact-finders.[89] Experts frequently testify in accordance

---

86. The material *infra* accompanying notes 86-120 is generally adapted from Perlin, *supra* note 63, manuscript at 1-26.

87. *See* Perlin, *supra* note 3, at 133.

88. Sevilla, *The Exclusionary Rule and Police Perjury*, 11 SAN DIEGO L. REV. 839, 840 (1974). *Compare* Butterfoss, *Solving the Pretext Puzzle: The Importance of Ulterior Motives and Fabrications in the Supreme Court's Fourth Amendment Pretext Doctrine*, 79 KY. L. J. 1 n. 1 (1990-91) (defining "pretexts" to include situations where "the government offers a justification for activity that, if the motivation of the [police] officer is not considered, would be a legally sufficient justification for the activity" as well as those activities for which the preferred justification is "legally insufficient").

89. *See e.g.*, Streicher v. Prescott, 663 F. Supp. 335, 343 (D.D.C. 1987) (although District of Columbia Code contained provision that patient could invoke to seek periodic review of commitment or independent psychiatric evaluation, in 22 years since passage of relevant statute, not a single patient exercised rights to statutory review).

with their own self-referential concepts of "morality"[90] and openly subvert statutory and caselaw criteria that, for instance, impose rigorous behavioral standards as predicates for commitment[91] or articulate functional standards as prerequisites for an incompetency to stand trial finding.[92] Often this testimony is further warped by a heuristic bias. Expert witnesses—like the rest of us—succumb to the meretricious allure of simplifying cognitive devices in their thinking, and employ such heuristic gambits as the vividness effect or attribution theory in their testimony.[93]

This testimony is then weighed and evaluated by sanist fact-finders.[94] Judges and jurors, whether consciously or unconsciously, frequently rely on reductionist, prejudice-driven stereotypes in their decisionmaking, thus subordinating statutory and caselaw standards as well as the legitimate interests of the mentally disabled persons who are the subjects of the litigation. Judges' predispositions to employ the same sorts of heuristics as do expert witnesses further contaminate the process.[95]

Thus, Professor Michael Saks reports on comments made by a Massachusetts trial judge (sitting on an involuntary civil commitment docket) to Saks's students after they observed a day of hearings:

---

90. *See e.g.*, Spohn & Horney, *"The Law's the Law, But Fair Is Fair:" Rape Shield Laws and Officials' Assessments of Sexual History Evidence*, 29 CRIMINOL. 137, 139 (1991) (a legal reform that contradicts deeply held beliefs may result either in open defiance of the law or in a surreptitious attempt to modify the law); *compare* H.R. UVILLER, TEMPERED ZEAL 116-18 (1988) (police sanction perjury in cases where Supreme Court has imposed constitutional rules that do not comport with officers' "own idea of fair play"), and *see* Maclin, *Seeing the Constitution from the Backseat of a Police Squad Car* (book review of H.R. UVILLER, *supra*) 70 B.U. L. REV. 543, 580-82 (1990) (criticizing view).
91. *See e.g.*, Perlin, *supra* note 3, at 135-36.
92. *See e.g.*, People v. Doan, 141 Mich. App. 209, 366 N.W. 2d 593, 598 (1985), *app'l den.* (1985) (expert testified that defendant was "out in left field" and went "bananas").
93. *See supra* chapter 6 C 3; *see generally*, Saks & Kidd, *Human Information Processing and Adjudication: Trial by Heuristics*, 15 LAW & SOC'Y REV. 123 (1980-81); Bersoff, *Judicial Deference to Nonlegal Decisionmakers: Imposing Simplistic Solutions on Problems of Cognitive Complexity in Mental Disability Law*, 46 SMU L. REV. 329 (1992).
94. *See generally*, Perlin, *supra* note 30; Perlin & Dorfman, *supra* note 30; *see supra* chapter 8 B.
95. *See generally*, Perlin, *supra* note 47.

I guess you noticed that some of these people were fit subjects for commitment under the statute. But, after all, I am a human being. I care about what is best for these people, and I have to do what I think is right.[96]

As Saks explained, "this judge in effect abolished the state's commitment laws, substituted his own, and produced the result he wanted notwithstanding the democratic and legal processes that existed to control these decisions."[97]

This combination of heuristic, "moral" experts and sanist courts helps define a system in which (1) dishonest testimony (sometimes overtly perjurious, but more frequently, simply sloppy and/or "morally righteous") is regularly (and unthinkingly) accepted, (2) statutory and caselaw standards are regularly subverted, and (3) unsurmountable barriers are raised to insure that the allegedly "therapeutically correct" social end is met, and that the worst-case-disaster-fantasy—the false negative—is avoided.

2. Explaining Pretextuality

Pretextuality fulfills certain social purposes. The "dropsy" phenomenon in search and seizure law is an excellent example.[98] A recent important empirical study has shown that 86 percent of judges, public defenders and prosecutors questioned (including 77 *percent* of judges) believe that police officers fabricate evidence in case

---

96. Saks, *Expert Witnesses, Nonexpert Witnesses, and Nonwitness Experts*, 14 LAW & HUM. BEHAV. 291, 293 (1990).

97. *Id.*

98. In the prototypical dropsy case, a police officer testifies that a criminal defendant dropped certain contraband and admitted to its ownership (thus "saving" a warrantless search from Fourth Amendment proscriptions). Testimony in such cases is frequently fabricated, a reality acknowledged by all participants in the criminal justice system. *See e.g.*, Sevilla, *supra* note 88, at 839-40; Alschuler, *"Close Enough for Government Work:" The Exclusionary Rule After Leon*, 1984 S. CT. REV. 309, 347-49; Garbus, *Police Perjury: An Interview With Martin Garbus*, 8 CRIM. L. BULL. 363, 365 (1972); Grano, *A Dilemma for Defense Counsel*: Spinella-Harris *Search Warrants and the Possibility of Police Perjury*, 1971 U. ILL. L.F. 405, 408-09; Kittel, *Police Perjury: Criminal Defense Attorneys' Perspectives* 11 AM. J. CRIM. JUST. 11 (1986); Barker, *An Empirical Study of Police Deviance Other than Corruption*, 6 J. POL. SCI. & ADMIN. 264 (1978); Jenkins, *The Lobster Shift: One Night in the Nation's Busiest Court*, 72 A.B.A. J. 56 (1986); Barker & Carter, *"Fluffing Up the Evidence and Covering Your Ass:" Some Conceptual Notes on Police Lying*, 11 DEVIANT BEHAVIOR 61 (1990); Park, *A Subject Matter Approach to Hearsay Reform*, 86 MICH. L. REV. 51, 95-96 n. 185 (1987).

reports at least "some of the time," and that 92 percent (including *91 percent* of judges) believe that police officers lie in court to avoid suppression of evidence at least "some of the time."[99] Pretextuality here serves an important police purpose (the conviction of factually guilty defendants) and is condoned as a "necessary evil" required to solve "the basic problems of police work."[100] Because the goal is perceived to be both legitimate (putting criminals in jail and preventing future crime) and necessary (as a means of mediating against "improper" liberal rules of law imposed by the Supreme Court),[101] "deviant lies" are condoned. There is frequently also an explicitly *moral* justification for these actions: police officers feel that, because of their unique experiences with criminals, they "know" the factual guilt or innocence of those subject to arrest, and they can therefore appropriately shape their testimony to serve a greater social good.[102] The courts are compliant "partners in crime." A recent empirical study suggests that criminal court judges refuse to follow the law and suppress evidence in large part due to their "personal sense of 'justice;'" a state's attorney pointed out, "When judges apply the exclusionary rule, *they feel they are doing something wrong.*"[103]

3. Pretexts and Mental Disability Cases

Pretextuality concerns extend far beyond the question of police lies. The pretextual devices that I have discussed—condonation of perjured testimony, distorted readings of trial testimony, subordination of statistically significant social science data, and enactment of prophylactic civil rights laws that have absolutely no "real world" impact—similarly dominate the mental disability law landscape, usu-

---

99. Orfield, *Deterrence, Perjury, and the Heater Factor: An Exclusionary Rule in the Chicago Criminal Courts*, 63 U. COLO. L. REV. 75, 100, 107 (1992).
100. *See* Barker & Carter, *supra* note 98, at 62-66.
101. *See* Younger, *The Perjury Routine*, THE NATION (May 8, 1967), at 596, as quoted in People v. McMurty, 64 Misc. 2d 63, 314 N.Y.S. 2d 194, 196 (Sup. Ct. 1970).
102. Manning, *Lying, Secrecy and Social Control*, in POLICING: A VIEW FROM THE STREET 238 (P.K. Manning & J. Van Maaness eds. 1978).
103. Orfield, *supra* note 99, at 121 (emphasis added). *See also*, Orfield, *The Exclusionary Rule in Chicago*, 19 SEARCH & SEIZ. L. REP. 81 (1992). On the relationship between this sort of pretextuality and authoritarianism, *see* Henderson, *Authoritarianism and the Rule of Law*, 66 IND. L.J. 379, 404-05 (1991), discussing Cover, *The Supreme Court, 1982 Term—Foreword:* Nomos *and* Narrative, 97 HARV. L. REV. 4 (1983).

ally flowing from the same motives that inspire similar behavior by courts and legislatures in other cases.[104]

Again, a few unrelated examples should illustrate my point. Although the District of Columbia Code contains a provision that patients can invoke seeking either periodic review of their commitment or an independent psychiatric evaluation, in the first twenty-two years following the law's passage, not a single patient exercised his right to statutory review.[105] In a case that turned on the question of whether a defendant had the requisite specific intent to attempt a bank robbery, a federal district court judge refused to allow a county jail psychiatrist to testify that he had been prescribing antipsychotic medications for the defendant for a particular purpose and a particular length of time, reasoning that such testimony "might be interfering with the treatment of [other] prisoners in jails because [they] might ask for more drugs to create the impression they need more drugs." This decision was affirmed by the Ninth Circuit as "not manifestly erroneous," even though there was *no* evidence *anywhere* in the case that spoke to this issue.[106] Also, and more globally, it is assumed that vigorous, independent, advocacy-focused counsel is now made available to all mentally disabled litigants, in spite of an empirical reality that is—in almost every jurisdiction—totally to the contrary.[107]

---

104. *Compare* Eastman, *Metaphor and Madness, Law and Liberty*, 40 DePaul L. Rev. 281, 347 (1991): "The premise is as follows: since all the nonpatient participants think an adversarial commitment process is meaningless, they respond in nonadversarial ways, rendering the process meaningless; therefore the process is meaningless. The patent circularity of the premise should end the discussion..."

105. Streicher v. Prescott, 663 F. Supp. 335, 343 (D.D.C. 1987), discussed *supra* note 89. *Compare* In Interest of C.W., 453 N.W. 2d 806, 809 (N. Dak. 1990) (rejecting patient's argument that discharge hearings were "rare occurrences"). On the significance of *Streicher, see* Kanter, *Abandoned But Not Forgotten: The Illegal Confinement of Elderly People in State Psychiatric Institutions*, 19 NYU Rev. L. & Soc'l Change 273, 304-07 (1991-92).

106. United States v. Still, 857 F. 2d 671, 672 (9th Cir. 1988), *cert. den.*, 489 U.S. 1060 (1989).

107. *See* Perlin, *Fatal Assumption: A Critical Evaluation of the Role of Counsel in Mental Disability Cases*, 16 Law & Hum. Behav. 39, 40, 49, 54 (1992). *Compare In re* Micah S., 198 Cal. App. 3d 557, 243 Cal. Rptr. 756, 760 (1988), *rev. den.* (1988) (Brauer, J., concurring) ("As in other areas where counsel is furnished at public expense, *every petition*, however meritorious, is vigorously challenged. 'Cherchez l'avocat' is the battle cry of every appellate lawyer today") (parental rights termination case), *to* Andalman & Chambers, *Effective Counsel for Persons Facing Civil Commitment: A Survey, a Polemic, and a Proposal*, 45

Police officers perjure themselves in dropsy cases "to ensure that criminals do not get off on 'technicalities,'"[108] and trial judges condone such behavior so as to "mediate the draconian effect of imposed-from-above constitutional decisions"[109] such as *Mapp v. Ohio.*[110] Similarly, expert witnesses in civil commitment cases seek to impose their own self-referential concept of "morality" to insure that patients who "really need treatment" are not released;[111] this testimony is accepted in light of trial judges' own "instrumental, functional, normative and philosophical" dissatisfaction[112] with decisions such as *O'Connor v. Donaldson,*[113] *Jackson v. Indiana*[114] and *Lessard v. Schmidt.*[115] Just as judges—including former Chief Justice Burger—have expressed incredulity at the thought that police testi-

---

MISS. L.J. 43, 72 (1974) (counsel was so inadequate in sample studied that patients' chances for release from hospital were enhanced if no lawyer was present); Dix, *Acute Psychiatric Hospitalization of the Mentally Ill in the Metropolis: An Empirical Study,* 1968 WASH. U. L.Q. 485, 540 (only 2 of 1700 contested cases resulted in patient's release); *see generally,* Perlin & Sadoff, *Ethical Issues in the Representation of Individuals in the Commitment Process,* 45 LAW & CONTEMP. PROBS. 161 (Summer 1982); 2 M.L. PERLIN, *supra* note 27, §8.11, at 783-86.

108. Barker & Carter, *supra* note 98, at 69. On the ways that police officers engage in "rule bending" in the questioning of criminal suspects, *see* Sanders & Bridges, *Access to Legal Advice and Police Malpractice,* 1990 CRIM L.REV. 494, 498-99.

109. Perlin, *supra* note 3, at 134. *See also* Orfield, *supra* note 96, at 121 (judges refuse to suppress evidence because of (1) their personal "sense of justice," (2) the fear of adverse publicity, and (3) the fear that such a decision might lead to re-election difficulties). For a rare candid judicial articulation of this position, *see* Rogers v. State, 332 So. 2d 165, 167 (Ala. Crim. App. 1976), *cert.den.,* 332 So. 2d 168 (Ala. 1976) (*quoting* trial judge, "In Alabama we had sensible [criminal procedure] rules until the damn Supreme Court went crazy").

110. E.g., on the pretextual ways that judges developed alternative sentencing mechanisms to avoid compliance with Michigan's mandatory gun control law, *see* Loftin, Heumann & McDowall, *Mandatory Sentencing and Firearms Violence: Evaluating an Alternative to Gun Control,* 17 LAW & SOC'Y REV. 287 (1983). On the pretextual ways that judges have developed to disobey legislative mandates to jail drunk drivers, *see* Ross & Foley, *Judicial Disobedience of the Mandate to Imprison Drunk Drivers,* 21 LAW & SOC'Y REV. 315 (1987).

111. *See* McCormick, *Involuntary Commitment in Ontario: Some Barriers to the Provision of Proper Care,* 124 CAN. MED. ASS'N J. 715, 717 (1981).

112. Perlin, *supra* note 3, at 134.

113. 422 U.S. 563 (1975) (right to liberty).

114. 406 U.S. 715 (1972) (application of due process clause to commitments following incompetency to stand trial findings).

115. 349 F. Supp. 1078 (E.D. Wis. 1972) (application of substantive and procedural due process clauses to involuntary civil commitment process) (subsequent footnotes omitted).

mony in dropsy cases requires special scrutiny,[116] so do they express astonishment at the assertion that expert testimony in involuntary civil commitment cases may be factually inaccurate.[117]

In addition, courts fantasize about *feared* pretextuality in cases where anecdotal myths prevail or where unconscious values predominate.[118] Thus, a sheriff's lay opinion that a potentially incompetent to stand trial defendant learned how to feign mental illness by nature of his having had the opportunity to speak to (presumably wily and sophisticated) state prisoners during his pre-trial incarceration was seen as more persuasive than the uncontradicted clinical testimony that the defendant was schizophrenic, mentally retarded, and suffering from acute pathological intoxication.[119] Empirically-grounded evidence has had no significant impact on fact-finders in such cases.

In short, mental disability law is a textbook example of pretextuality in the law.[120] This pretextuality is reflected both *consciously*

---

116. Bush v. United States, 375 F. 2d 602, 604 (D.C. Cir. 1967) ("It would be a dismal reflection on society to say that when the guardians of its security are called to testify in court under oath, their testimony must be viewed with suspicion"). *Compare* Orfield, *supra* note 99; People v. McMurty, 64 Misc. 2d 63, 314 N.Y.S. 2d 194, 197 (Crim. Ct. 1970) (Younger, J.) (disagreeing with Burger's point of view). *McMurty* is discussed in Comment, *Police Perjury in Narcotics "Dropsy" Cases: A New Credibility Gap*, 60 GEO. L. J. 507 (1971).

117. *See e.g., In re* Melton, 597 A. 2d 892, 902-03 (D.C. 1991) (asking "Where else would the doctor go for such information?" in response to patient's argument that his it was violation of the hearsay rules for witness to base his medical conclusion on *factual* information given him by the patient's relatives); on the application of the hearsay rules to the involuntary civil commitment process in general, *see* 1 M.L. PERLIN, *supra* note 27, §3.31, at 291-96. *See also* United States v. Charters, 863 F. 2d 302, 310 (4th Cir. 1988) (*en banc*), *cert. den.*, 494 U.S. 1016 (1990), criticized in Perlin, *supra* note 47. On the way that opinion testimony by psychiatrists is "routinely and unquestioningly accepted" at involuntary civil commitment hearings, *see* Hammond, *Predictions of Dangerousness in Texas: Psychotherapists' Conflicting Duties, Their Potential Liability, and Possible Solutions*, 12 ST. MARY'S L.J. 141, 150 n. 71 (1980).

It is rare for an appellate court to even ponder the degree to which mental disability law proceedings are designed to elicit or suppress "the truth." For two thoughtful and conflicting visions, *compare* Matter of the Commitment of Edward S., 118 N.J. 118, 570 A. 2d 917, 933-35 (1990), to *id.* at 937-39 (Handler, J., concurring) (statutory mandate requiring that involuntary civil commitment hearings be held *in camera* inapplicable to cases involving insanity acquittees).

118. *See* Perlin, *supra* note 3, at 134.

119. State v. Willard, 292 N.C. 567, 234 S.E. 2d 587, 591-93 (1977).

120. Pretexts also riddle the incompetency to stand trial process. *See* Perlin, *supra* note 63, at 48-59. For one illustrative example, *see* Siegel & Elwork, *Treating*

(in the reception and privileging of "moral" testimony that flaunts legislative criteria) and *unconsciously* (in the use of heuristic devices in decision making, and in the application of sanist attitudes toward such decisions).[121] It is in insanity defense cases that this pretextuality is often the most striking.

4. Pretexts and the Insanity Defense

Pretextual decision making riddles the entire insanity defense decision making process; it pervades decisions by forensic hospital administrators, police officers, expert witnesses and judges.

Hospital decision making is a good example. As I have already noted, an NIMH Task Force convened in the wake of the Hinckley acquittal underscored this in its final report: "From the perspective of the Hospital, *in controversial cases such as Hinckley*, the U.S. Attorney's Office can be counted upon to oppose *any* conditional release recommendation."[122] As John Parry has explained, "hospitals have been pressured by public outrage to bend over backwards to make sure that no insanity acquittee is released too soon, *even* if such pressure is contrary to the intent and spirit of being found not guilty by reason of insanity."[123]

Expert witnesses are similarly pretextual. In one case, a testifying doctor conceded that he may have "hedged" in earlier testimony (as to whether an insanity acquittee could be released) "because he did not want to be criticized should [the defendant] be released and then commit a criminal act."[124] Law enforcement officials frequently act in similar ways. Thus, at the same time that Attorney General William French Smith told Congress that the insanity defense allows *so many persons* to commit crimes of violence, one of his top aides candidly told a federal judicial conference that the number of insan-

---

 Incompetency to Stand Trial, 14 LAW & HUM. BEHAV. 57, 58 (1990) (mental health professionals assessing incompetency to stand trial equate it to serious mental disability in spite of courts' uniform rejection of that test).

121. *See generally*, Perlin, *supra* note 63, at 27-74.

122. *Final Report of the National Institute of Mental Health (NIMH) Ad Hoc Forensic Advisory Panel*, 12 MENT. & PHYS. DIS. L. REP. 77, 96 (1988) (emphasis added); *see supra* chapter 3, text accompanying note 303.

123. Parry, *The Civil-Criminal Dichotomy in Insanity Commitment and Release Proceedings: Hinckley and Other Matters*, 11 MENT. & PHYS. DIS. L. REP. 218, 223 (1987).

124. Francois v. Henderson, 850 F. 2d 231, 234 (5th Cir. 1988).

ity defense cases was, statistically, "probably insignificant."[125] In addition, police officers act pretextually in cases involving potential insanity defendants. In analyzing police decisions as to which defendants should be arrested and which should be hospitalized, researchers found that police often "invoked a form of insanity defense," governed by their perceptions of the actor's "degree of intentionality" and responsibility.[126]

Most importantly, all aspects of the judicial decision making process embody pretextuality. To a significant extent, the fear that defendants will "fake" the insanity defense to escape punishment continues to paralyze the legal system in spite of an impressive array of empirical evidence that reveals (1) the minuscule number of such cases, (2) the ease with which trained clinicians are usually able to "catch" malingering in such cases, (3) the inverse greater likelihood that defendants—even at grave peril to their lives—will more likely try to convince examiners that they're "not crazy," (4) the high risk in pleading the insanity defense (leading to statistically significant greater prison terms meted out to *unsuccessful* insanity pleaders), and (5) the far greater time that most successful insanity pleaders (a minute universe to begin with) remain in maximum security facilities than they would have served had they been convicted on the underlying criminal indictment.[127]

Thus, some judges simply ignore appellate decisions that they perceive might make it more likely for defendants to be found NGRI.[128] Elsewhere, decision after decision—in obscure and famous cases—reveals appellate affirmances of conviction in insanity defense

---

125. Perlin, *supra* note 3, at 134, *quoting, inter alia*, Mickenberg, *A Pleasant Surprise: The Guilty But Mentally Ill Verdict Has Succeeded On Its Own Right and Successfully Preserved the Traditional Role of the Insanity Defense*, 55 U. Cin. L. Rev. 943, 980 (1987), and *Proceedings of the Forty-Sixth Judicial Conference of the District of Columbia Circuit*, 111 F.R.D. 91, 225 (1985).

126. Rogers, *Policing Mental Disorder: Controversies, Myths, and Realities*, 24 Soc'l Pol. & Admin. 226, 231 (1990); *see also*, Menzies, *Psychiatrists in Blue: Police Apprehension of Mental Disorder and Dangerousness*, 25 Criminol. 429 (1987); Teplin & Pruett, *Police as Streetcorner Psychiatrists: Managing the Mentally Ill*, 15 Int'l J. L. & Psychiatry 139, 154-55 (1992).

127. *See supra* chapter 3 B 1 b (1).

128. Ogloff et al., *Empirical Research Regarding the Insanity Defense: How Much Do We Really Know?* in Law and Psychology: Broadening the Discipline 171, 187-88 (J. Ogloff ed. 1992) (following the *Durham* decision [*see supra* chapter 3 A 1 c (2)], District of Columbia trial judges continued to substantially charge juries in language of *M'Naghten* decision).

cases (or affirmances of trial court decisions to not charge jurors on the insanity defense) despite overwhelming expert testimony as to defendants' profound mental disability and lack of responsibility,[129] or despite equally profound legal errors in jury charge.[130] In one case, a jury conviction was affirmed where the state's insanity rebuttal was based on evidence that the defendant "could have gained knowledge of psychological testing" while a college student, and thus consequently "could lie and might have been faking."[131] In *Jones v. United States*, the Supreme Court justified its upholding of a post-insanity acquittal commitment scheme on the grounds that the commission of an attempted misdemeanor (shoplifting) provided "concrete evidence" of the individual's continuing dangerousness.[132] Again, Justice Thomas's dissents in *Riggins* and in *Foucha* are animated by pretextual reasoning.[133]

---

129. *See e.g.*, Commonwealth v. Hildreth, 30 Mass. App. 963, 572 N.E. 2d 18 (1991) (evidence insufficient to support insanity instruction) (defendant had contemporaneously made multiple suicide attempts, was diagnosed with bipolar disorder, and had bragged about nonexistent communications with individuals such as Donald Trump); State v. Jarrett, 218 Conn. 766, 591 A. 2d 1225, 1228-29 (1991) (conviction affirmed; uncontradicted expert testimony introduced that defendant suffered from delusional beliefs about "astroplaning," reincarnation and life on other planets); Ellis v. State, 570 So. 2d 744 (Ala. Crim. App.. 1990), *reh. den.* (1990), *cert. den.* (1990) (conviction affirmed; uncontradicted expert testimony that defendant was not responsible; state produced no contrary expert testimony); People v. Beehn, 205 Ill. App. 3d 533, 563 N.E. 2d 1207 (1990) (same); DePasquale v. State, 803 P. 2d 218 (Nev. 1990), *reh. den.* 1991) (conviction affirmed despite defendant's psychiatric history that included pulling his own eye from its socket); State v. Stacy, 601 S.W. 2d 696, 700 (Tenn. 1980) (Henry, J., dissenting) (conviction affirmed; dissenters charge that majority opinion operationally returns state to "wild beast" test [*see supra* chapter 3 A 1 a (2)]; expert testimony gave "thundering support" to defendant's insanity plea)
130. *See* State v. Chavez, 143 Ariz. 281, 693 P. 2d 936 (App. 1984) (omission of first prong of *M'Naghten* test from judge's charge harmless error).
131. State v. Mercer, 625 P. 2d 44, 50 (Mont. 1981).
132. 463 U.S. 354, 364-65 (1983); *see supra* chapter 4 E 2 d. *See* Appel, *The Constitutionality of Automatic Commitment Procedures Applied to Persons Found Not Guilty By Reason of Insanity*: Jones v. United States, 21 HOUS. L. REV. 421, 440 (1984) (*Jones* decision based on "subterfuge of a statutory presumption").
133. Thus, in dissenting from the reversal of Riggins' conviction on the grounds that the administration of antipsychotic medication may have violated the defendant's right to a fair trial, *see supra* chapter 4 E 2 f (2). Thomas suggested that, under the majority's language, a criminal conviction might be reversed in cases involving "penicillin or aspirin." *Riggins*, 112 S. Ct. at 1826. This argument is, to be charitable, bizarre; *nowhere* in the history of right to refuse litigation—civil or criminal—is this position seriously raised. *See* Perlin & Dorfman, *supra* note

On some occasions, judges recognize when their brethren are being pretextual. In *Geschwendt v. Ryan*, where defendant's sole defense was insanity, the Third Circuit, sitting *en banc*, upheld a habeas corpus denial in a Pennsylvania multiple murder case where the trial judge had not charged the jury that they could specifically find the defendant NGRI. In a tortured opinion for a seven-judge majority, Judge Morton Greenberg reasoned that, although the jurors were not informed of the insanity option, they had been told that they could find the defendant guilty of third-degree murder if they found that the defendant had a diminished mental capacity.[134] Since the defendant was convicted of first-degree murder, Judge Greenberg concluded, "We think that it would be irrational to believe, if the jury would have found Geschwendt [NGRI] if given that explicit choice, the same jury would reject a third degree murder verdict."[135]

In an impassioned opinion (on behalf of himself and three others), Judge Aldisert dissented. After noting that the Pennsylvania Supreme Court had explicitly rejected the argument that a third-degree murder instruction was "fundamentally similar" to an insanity instruction,[136] Aldisert turned to the pretextual nature of the majority's decision:

> I had always thought there was a difference between being found guilty and being acquitted. I thought that this was a basic principle taught in junior high school civics classes. I am, therefore, somewhat distressed that the majority are not willing to extend the same right to be found not guilty by reason of insanity that the U.S. District Court for the District of Columbia accorded John Hinckley, Jr., who, after attempting to assassinate then President Ronald Reagan in 1981, successfully interposed this defense.

> The right to be committed to a mental institution, rather than imprisoned in a penitentiary, also was the critical issue in the plea entered this year in the internationally publicized case of Jeffrey L. Dahmer, who admitted strangling and dismembering 17 young males. He was permitted under Wisconsin law to plead not guilty of murder by reason of mental disease or defect, which constitutes an admission as to the elements of the substantive offense, except for the mental state, and raises a defense of

---

30, at 58, and *id*. n. 77.

134. 967 F. 2d 877, 885-86 (3d Cir. 1992), *cert. den.*, 113 S. Ct. 472 (1992).

135. *Id.* at 887.

136. *Id.* at 894-95, discussing Commonwealth v. Reilly, 519 Pa. 550, 549 A. 2d 503, 510-11 (1988).

insanity. Dahmer thus was entitled to a fair determination of his mental capacity, notwithstanding the extreme brutality of his crimes.

I am melancholy that this court, long recognized as a shining acropolis of constitutional law protection, now stands in the shade. In the shade of a federal district court in our nation's capital and a state trial court in Wisconsin.

There is a fundamental difference between being found guilty of an offense and being acquitted, albeit by reason of insanity. Every member of this court knows this. And irrespective of the reprehensible acts committed in this case, we are a reviewing court of judges; we are not an ingathering or collection of the laity, untrained in the law. As judges we must rise above the passions of the streets, above superstition or popularity or opprobrium. In the words of Justice Felix Frankfurter, we are committed to the "institutionalized medium of reason, [and] that's all we have standing between us and the tyranny of mere will and the cruelty of unbridled, unprincipled, undisciplined feeling."[137]

Sometimes mental disability pretexts become intertwined with other pretexts. Thus, it has been held that the defendant's decision to raise the insanity defense opened the door to prosecutorial cross-examination about his membership in the Black Muslim religion and his attitudes toward police authority.[138] On the other hand, a conviction was reversed where the court found that the prosecutor's *sanist* attitudes (striking a venire member employed in the mental health field because he allegedly believed that "someone who works in mental health would be more liberal than conservative") were a pretext for an impermissible *racially*-based challenge.[139]

Yet another layer of pretext involves the quality of counsel provided to mentally disabled criminal defendants at insanity defense proceedings. Counsel has traditionally been found to be "grossly inadequate" on behalf of all mentally disabled individuals, and *especially* substandard in cases involving mentally disabled criminal defendants.[140] This inadequacy is especially troubling because of the

---

137. *Id.* at 869-87 (footnotes omitted).
138. People v. Aliwoli, 238 Ill. App. 3d 602, 606 N.E. 2d 347, 354 (1992) (expert was asked whether he was aware that, in the 1960s, the Black Muslim newspaper, *Muhammad Speaks*, referred to police officers as "pigs").
139. House v. State, 1993 WL 48244 (Fla. Dist. App. 1993), at *1.
140. Perlin, *supra* note 52, at 43; Perlin, *supra* note 30, at 405. *See generally*, Uphoff, *The Role of the Criminal Defense Lawyer in Representing the Mentally Impaired Criminal Defendant: Zealous Advocate or Officer of the Court?* 1988 Wis. L. Rev. 65.

false assumption that adequate counsel is generally available for such persons.[141] Thus, a conviction was reversed on the grounds of counsel's failure to have a competency evaluation done on his client prior to trial; when the defendant had asked for an adjournment to "get some help," counsel had opposed the request with this reasoning:

> [t]his is a lady who has never faced stress. She always tries to run from it. I don't think it's going to—this may sound harsh—I think making her stand trial might be good for her. It's going to be very difficult because I know she will interrupt, and everyone knows she's going to have trouble. But if she stands trial and gets through it, I think it will benefit her...[142]

This inadequacy has been further heightened in the aftermath of the Supreme Court's "sterile and perfunctory" adequacy standard established in *Strickland v. Washington*.[143] Most courts adhere to a minimalist reading of *Strickland*, and the Supreme Court has countenanced this reading, even in death penalty cases.[144] Although, occasionally, a conviction is reversed based on inadequacy of counsel in failing to raise an insanity defense,[145] courts' refusal to acknowledge the frequently substandard job done by counsel in this most demanding area of the law is simply pretextual. In reporting on the way that trial judges basically ignored the dictates of the *Durham* decision in charging juries in the District of Columbia after 1954, Professor James Ogloff and his colleagues thus note, "[I]t is troubling that the defendants' lawyers apparently did not understand the differences between *M'Naghten* and *Durham* sufficiently to appeal their clients' cases based on the incorrect instructions the judges had given the juries."[146]

---

141. *See generally,* Perlin, *supra* note 52; *compare* Seidman, Brown *and* Miranda, 80 CALIF. L. REV. 673 (1992) (decisions such as *Brown* and *Miranda* provide "false sense of closure and resolution" about contradictions in democratic society).

142. People v. Harris, 185 Mich. App. 100, 450 N.W. 2d 239, 241-42 (1990).

143. Perlin, *supra* note 52, at 53. In *Strickland*, 466 U.S. 668, 687-88 (1984), the court found there to be no constitutional violation if counsel provided "reasonably effective assistance" to be measured objectively by "prevailing professional norms."

144. *See e.g.,* 2 M.L. PERLIN, *supra* note 27, §8.30, at 845 n. 617 (citing cases); Alvord v. Wainwright, 469 U.S. 956 (1984) (Marshall, J., dissenting from denial of grant of *certiorari*), discussed in 2 M.L. PERLIN, *supra* note 27, §8.30, at 848 n. 637; *see also,* O'Dell v. Thompson, 112 S. Ct. 618 (1991) (statement by Blackmun, J., respecting denial of *certiorari*).

145. *See e.g.,* People v. Jones, Mich. Lawyers Weekly (Aug. 31, 1992) (full text available on NEXIS).

146. Ogloff et al., *supra* note 128, at 188.

In short, pretextuality dominates insanity defense decisionmaking. Again, Judge Aldisert's dissent in *Geschwendt* eloquently explains its roots:

> In a case such as this, where it is difficult to muster any sympathy for the petitioner, the task of determining whether the state trial court protected his constitutional rights taxes the accountability, if not the very integrity, of the federal judicial system in its obligation to implement the Great Writ....
>
> As we measure the contours of the Constitution, federal judges are keenly aware that we do not engage in a popularity contest. We must disregard public opinion on a given issue or in a given case. As ultimate guardians of the Constitution, our role is to insure that society, when prosecuting those who breach its rules of conduct, does not breach its own rules of procedure. Our task in federal collateral review of state convictions, therefore, is not to inquire whether the habeas petitioner has violated rules of social conduct, but only whether society, in this case the Commonwealth of Pennsylvania, has respected the rules it has established to guarantee fair trials.[147]

The inability of judges to do just this—disregard public opinion and inquire into whether defendants have had fair trials—is both the root and the cause of pretextuality in insanity defense jurisprudence.

D. Why Do Courts Decide Cases the Way They Do? The Power of Teleology and the Curious Role of Social Science

1. The Role of Social Science Data

Judge David Bazelon has written revealingly of his "passionate ambivalence" about the behavioral sciences, an ambivalence reflected in his desire to "open the courthouse doors" to psychologists and other mental health experts but to "never hand over the keys."[148] In order to understand the depths of Judge Bazelon's ambivalence, it is

---

147. *Geschwendt*, 967 F. 2d at 892 (Aldisert, J., dissenting).
148. Bazelon, *Veils, Values, and Social Responsibility*, 37 AM. PSYCHOLOGIST 115 (1982) (Bazelon I). *See also*, on the question of the jurisprudential implications of what non-scientists can contribute to the scientific community, Bazelon, *Coping With Technology Through the Legal Process*, 62 CORNELL L. REV. 817 (1977) (Bazelon II).

necessary to consider the history of the tension in the relationship between social science and the law.[149]

The Supreme Court's relationship with social science data can be traced to Justice Marshall's opinion in *Gibbons v. Ogden,* asserting that "all America understands and has traditionally understood the word commerce to comprehend navigation," but citing no data and demanding "on faith" acceptance of his expertise on the state of public opinion, and his ability to "measure" the public's views.[150] While Louis Brandeis's brief in *Muller v. Oregon* is generally seen as the Court's initial confrontation with social science data,[151] *Gibbons* is the true forerunner. Since Marshall's time, "progress in utilization of social science data by the Supreme Court has not kept pace, even remotely, with the progress in social science skills for gathering and interpreting such data."[152]

2. The Psychodynamics of Judicial Suspicion

Courts remain profoundly suspicious of much social science evidence.[153] The roots of this suspicion most likely stem from multiple causes. Like the judicial process, social science is normative and value-driven.[154] Also, judges' pre-existing social values and views

---

149. *See* Rosenblum, *Affinity and Tension in Relationships Between Social Science and Law,* 33 St.L. U. L.J. 1 (1988) ("Nonperceptions, misperceptions, and dissonance between law and social science are anything but new in the annals of professional relationships").

150. 22 U.S. (9 Wheat.) 1, 190 (1824); *see* Rosenblum, *A Place for Social Science Along the Judiciary's Constitutional Law Frontier,* 66 Nw. U. L. Rev. 455, 456-57 (1971); Rosenblum, *supra* note 149, at 1-2 n. 1.

151. 208 U.S. 412 (1908); *see generally,* Collins & Friesen, *Looking Back on* Muller v. Oregon, 69 A.B.A. J. 294 (1983).

152. Rosenblum, *supra* note 150, at 457. *See also id.* at 479 (calling for the application of social science to judicial decisionmaking "when the courts themselves formulate or invoke propositions or norms conditioned upon knowledge within the competence of the social sciences").

153. *See generally,* McCleskey, *supra.* For an earlier view in an insanity defense case, *see* People v. Nash, 52 Cal. 2d 36, 338 P. 2d 416, 424 (1959) ("There is danger in judicial changes of long-established rules of law when such changes proceed from a court's assumption that it can recognize what has become a fact of social science"). On a similar legislative misuse of social science data in an unrelated context, *see* Mullenix, *The Counter-Reformation in Procedural Justice,* 77 Minn. L. Rev. 375, 396-407 (1992).

154. *See* Woolhandler, *Rethinking the Judicial Reception of Legislative Facts,* 41 Vand. L. Rev. 111, 119 (1988); Berk, *The Role of Subjectivity in Criminal Justice Classification and Prediction Methods,* 7 Crim. Just. Eth. 35 (1988).

taint their perceptions of the probative value of social science data.[155] Judges may view social science as a "threat, a competitor for the judge's historical role as society's primary intellectual broker."[156] In addition, we fear that social science may introduce "complexities that shake the judge's confidence in imposed solutions."[157] Finally, judges' recognition that their failure to possess a "general framework for determining the content of [social] policy...generates a sense of discomfort," as the attendant lack of clarity "permits policy to be used as a kind of *deus ex machina,* whose sudden appearance produces the desired result."[158] The Supreme Court's treatment of the statistical data in *McCleskey v. Kemp*[159] can be read to show "the fate of legislative facts that seek to undermine legal and personal assumptions that discrimination is not an important causative factor in the disproportionate racial effects of the death penalty."[160]

Courts thus respond negatively to social science data even to the extent of suggesting there is something faintly supernatural or fictive at its basis[161] because such evidence is dissonant with the judges' "read" of their own prereflective OCS.[162] Just as Chief Justice

---

155. Woolhandler, *supra* note 154, at 120; *see also id.* at 118 n. 47 (statistical showing in *McCleskey* was "outweighed by majoritarian preferences for retribution and assumed deterrence, and the need for discretion in the administering of the criminal justice system").

156. Kerr, *Social Science and the U.S. Supreme Court,* in THE IMPACT OF SOCIAL PSYCHOLOGY ON PROCEDURAL JUSTICE 56, 71 (M. Kaplan ed. 1986), citing P. ROSEN, THE SUPREME COURT AND SOCIAL SCIENCE (1972).

157. Woolhandler, *supra* note 154, at 125 n. 84, *quoting* D. HOROWITZ, THE COURTS AN SOCIAL POLICY 284 (1977) Social science is thus relied upon by advocates in their efforts to persuade the court only as a "last resort." Kerr, *supra* note 156, at 66, *citing* Haney, *Psychology and Legal Change: On the Limits of a Factual Jurisprudence,* 4 LAW & HUM. BEHAV. 147 (1980).

158. Rubin, *The Practice and Discourse of Legal Scholarship,* 86 MICH. L. REV. 1835, 1889 (1988). *See also,* Kerr, *supra* note 168, at 64 (courts only use social science in opinions to bolster a pre-existing favored position).

159. 481 U.S. 279 (1987); *see supra* chapter 3, note 244.

160. Woolhandler, *supra* note 155, at 121 (footnote omitted) (emphasis added). *See also,* Appelbaum, *The Empirical Jurisprudence of the United States Supreme Court,* 13 AM. J. L. & MED. 335,344, 347 (1987) (on the way the *McCleskey* court heuristically erred in its statistical analyses). Appelbaum speculates that the *McCleskey* court feared that acceptance of the data offered by the defendant might have led to other "'unexplained discrepancies' in sentencing patterns that might require restructuring the entire sentencing process." *Id.* at 345. On the pretextuality of such reasoning, *see* Perlin, *supra* note 3, at 133-34.

161. Ballew v. Georgia, 435 U.S. 223, 246 (1978) (Powell, J., concurring) (criticizing reliance on "numerology" of statistical studies).

162. *See supra* chapter 6 D.

Rehnquist has sketched out his vision of "abnormal" mental behavior in *Wainwright v. Greenfield*[163] and *Ake v. Oklahoma*,[164] and as he has trivialized scientific discourse on jury bias cases,[165] so do he and his colleagues continue similarly to debase social science research and data.[166] Thus, in *Jones v. United States*, the court rejected petitioner's argument that available research "fail[ed] to support the predictive value of prior dangerous acts," by simply responding, "We do not agree with the suggestion that Congress' power to legislate in this area depends on the research conducted by the psychiatric community."[167] In response to the further argument that it was unreasonable for Congress to determine that an insanity acquittal "supports an inference of continuing mental illness," it merely concluded, without citation or reference, "It comports with common sense to conclude that someone whose mental illness was sufficient to lead him to commit a criminal act is likely to remain ill and in need of treatment."[168]

3. The Selective Use of Social Science[169]

The skepticism toward statistical data and evidence about the behavioral sciences appears to stem directly from the belief that such

---

163. 474 U.S. 284 (1986). *See supra* chapter 5, text accompanying notes 125-29.
164. 470 U.S. 68 (1985). *See infra* chapter 9, text accompanying notes 71-73.
165. *See e.g.*, Lockhart v. McCree, 476 U.S. 160, 166-68 (1986) ("death qualification" of jury does not violate constitutional right to impartial trial). *See* Tanford & Tanford, *Better Trials Through Science: A Defense of Psychologist-Lawyer Collaboration*, 66 N.C. L. REV. 741, 774 n. 224 (1988) (Rehnquist's opinion "an excellent example of how lay persons tend to reject scientific knowledge in favor of folklore and traditional ignorance"); Kerr, *supra* note 156, at 63 (Rehnquist relied on social science less frequently than any other justices in study sample).
166. The same attitude infects the lower courts as well. *See* Kennedy, McCleskey v. Kemp: *Race, Capital Punishment, and the Supreme Court*, 101 HARV. L. REV. 1388, 1400 n. 45 (1988), discussing remand trial court opinion in McCleskey: "[Racial disparities found in Baldus study were produced by] arbitrarily structured little rinky-dink regressions that accounted for only a few variables....They prove nothing other than the truth of the adage that anything may be proved by statistics." McCleskey v. Kemp, No. C87-1517A. at 12 (N.D. Ga. Dec. 23, 1987) (order granting relief to petitioner on other grounds).
167. 463 U.S. 354, 364-65 n.13 (1983).
168. *Id.* at 366. Jones had been charged with attempted petit larceny (shoplifting). *Id.* at 359. On the pretextual nature of this decision, *see supra* chapter 8 C.
169. The material *infra* accompanying notes 170-88 is adapted from Perlin & Dorfman, *supra* note 30, at 52-54.

data are not "empirical" in the same way that "true" sciences are and therefore are not trustworthy.[170] Social science data is seen as overly subjective and as falsifiable, and as being subject to researcher bias.[171]

As I have already indicated, courts often see social science as a threat. Judges may be especially threatened by social science when it is presented to a jury, as such presentation may appear to undermine "judicial control" of trial proceedings.[172] Courts' general dislike of social science is reflected in self-articulated claims that judges are unable to understand the data and are thus unable to apply it properly to a particular case.[173] Courts tend to be shamefully poor in the application of such data;[174] their track record has been "dreadful."[175] It is not at all clear, though, why courts should have such difficulty here when judges regularly decide complex cases in a wide array of social and scientific contexts.[176]

Again, this dislike and distrust of social science data has led courts to be teleological in their use of this evidence.[177] Social science

---

170. See e.g., Faigman, *To Have and Have Not: Assessing the Value of Social Science to the Law as Science and Policy*, 38 EMORY L.J. 1005, 1010 (1989).
171. *Id.* at 1016, 1026.
172. Lindman, *Sources of Judicial Distrust of Social Science Evidence: A Comparison of Social Science Jurisprudence*, 64 IND. L.J. 755, 755 (1989); Loftus & Monahan, *Trial By Data: Psychological Research as Legal Evidence*, 35 AM. PSYCHOLOGIST 270, 270-71 (1980).
173. See e.g., Perlin, *supra* note 47, at 986-93, discussing decision in United States v. Charters, 863 F. 2d 302 (4th Cir. 1988) (en banc), *cert. den.*, 494 U.S. 1016 (1990) (limiting right of pretrial detainees to refuse medication). The *Charters* court rejected as incredulous the possibility that a court could make a meaningful distinction between competency to stand trial and competency to engage in medication decision making: "[Such a distinction] must certainly be of such subtlety and complexity as to tax perception by the most skilled medical or psychiatric professionals...To suppose that it is a distinction that can be fairly discerned and applied even by the most skilled judge on the basis of an adversarial fact-finding proceeding taxes credulity." *Charters*, 863 F. 2d at 310.
174. Melton, *Bringing Psychology to the Legal System: Opportunities, Obstacles, and Efficacy*, 42 AM. PSYCHOLOGIST 488 (1987).
175. Sperlich, *Trial By Jury: It May Have a Future*, in SUPREME COURT REVIEW 191, 208 (P. Kurland & G. Casper eds. 1979); Grofman, *The Slippery Slope: Jury Size and Jury Verdict Requirements—Legal and Social Science Approaches*, 2 LAW & POL'Y Q. 285, 300 (1980).
176. See e.g., Monahan & Walker, *Social Authority: Obtaining, Evaluating and Establishing Social Science in Law*, 134 U. PA. L. REV. 477, 511 n. 119 (1986) ("Anyone who can comprehend the Federal Tort Claims Act can learn what standard deviation and statistical significance mean").
177. Cases such as *Jones* may simply reveal that the Supreme Court's use of social

literature and studies that enable courts to meet predetermined sanist ends are often privileged while data that would require judges to question such ends are frequently rejected.[178] Several scholars have argued that individual justices employ an outcome-determinative approach, "uncritically" accepting social science data bolstering opinions when they are in the majority, but "debunk[ing]" it when they are in the minority.[179] Judges often select certain proffered data that adhere to their pre-existing social and political attitudes, and use both heuristic reasoning and false OCS in rationalizing such decisions.[180] As attribution theory teaches, when the import of a body of data is contrary to a justice's otherwise-articulated or deeply-held views, the tendency to discount such data "must at times be difficult to resist."[181] Thus, members of the court bypass substantial bodies of data and substitute "from wisps of inconclusive data their own findings of substantiality."[182] The less that research supports decisionmakers' pre-existing policy positions, the less likely that it will be influential.[183]

Involuntary commitment decisionmaking illustrates this discontinuity. Opinions in such cases frequently rest on normative and instrumental societal judgments about patient behavior.[184] Social sci-

---

science data is only teleological. *See* Appelbaum, *supra* note 160, at 341, discussing Perlin, *The Supreme Court, the Mentally Disabled Criminal Defendant, and Symbolic Values: Random Decisions, Hidden Rationales, or "Doctrinal Abyss?"* 29 ARIZ. L. REV. 1, 71 (1987).

178. Appelbaum, *supra* note 160 at 341; Tanford, *The Limits of a Scientific Jurisprudence: The Supreme Court and Psychology*, 66 IND. L.J. 137, 144-50 (1990); Faigman, *"Normative Constitutional Fact- Finding:" Exploring the Empirical Component of Constitutional Interpretation*, 139 U. PA. L. REV. 541, 581 (1991).

179. Kerr, *supra* note 156, at 58, *quoting* P. ROSEN, *supra* note 156, at 90 ("When the court wished to uphold social welfare measures, it generally accepted the validity of facts contained in Brandeis briefs...[b]ut whenever it chose to reject such legislation, the court found extralegal data spurious and unconvincing").

180. On the courts' heuristic use of social science data, see Perlin, *supra* note 63, at 74-77.

181. Appelbaum, *supra* note 160, at 347.

182. Rosenblum, *supra* note 150, at 15.

183. *See e.g.*, Tanford, *Law Reform by Courts, Legislatures and Commissions Following Empirical Research on Jury Instructions*, 25 LAW & SOC'Y REV. 155 (1991).

184. *See e.g.*, B.A.A. v. Chief Medical Officer, University of Iowa Hospitals, 421 N.W. 2d 118 (Iowa 1988), *citing* Bezanson, *Involuntary Treatment of the Mentally Ill in Iowa: The 1975 Legislation*, 61 IOWA L. REV. 262, 262-63 (1975) ("the decision to commit ... in large part depends on how far society is willing to tolerate 'deviant' behavior"); BEN BURSTEN, BEYOND PSYCHIATRIC EXPERTISE

ence data is used pretextually in such cases to rationalize otherwise baseless judicial decisions.[185]

Courts thus will take the literature out of context,[186] misconstrue the data or evidence being offered,[187] read such data selectively,[188] and/or inconsistently.[189] Other times, courts choose to flatly reject[190] this data or ignore its existence.[191] In other circumstances, courts simply "rewrite" factual records so as to avoid having to deal with social science data that is cognitively dissonant with their OCS.[192] Even when courts do acknowledge the existence and possible validity of studies that take a position contrary to their decisions, this acknowledgement is frequently little more than mere "lip service."[193]

---

167 (1984) (any decision as to whether behavior is product of mental illness is a "matter of social policy"). On the frequently-pretextual basis of involuntary civil commitment decisions (supported by allegedly "moral" values), *see* Perlin, *supra* note 63, at 34-48; *see also,* Perlin, *Reading the Supreme Court's Tea Leaves: Predicting Judicial Behavior in Civil and Criminal Right to Refuse Treatment Cases,* 12 AM. J. FORENS. PSYCHIATRY 37 (1991).

185. *See supra* chapter 8 C.

186. Faigman, *supra* note 178, at 577.

187. *Id.* at 581.

188. Katz, *Majoritarian Morality and Parental Rights,* 52 ALB. L. REV. 405, 461 (1988) (on courts' reading of impact of parents' homosexuality in custody decisions); Tanford, *supra* note 178, at 153-54; *see e.g.,* Holbrook v. Flynn, 475 U.S. 560, 571 n. 4 (1986) (defendant's right to fair trial not denied where uniformed state troopers sat in front of spectator section in courtroom; court rejected contrary empirical study, and based decision on its own "experience and common sense").

189. *See e.g.,* Hafemeister & Melton, *The Impact of Social Science Research on the Judiciary,* in REFORMING THE LAW: IMPACT OF CHILD DEVELOPMENT RESEARCH 27 (G. Melton ed. 1987).

190. *See e.g., Barefoot,* 463 U.S. at 897-902.

191. Faigman, *supra* note 178, at 581; *see e.g.,* Watkins v. Sanders, 449 U.S. 341 (1981) (refusal of courts to acknowledge social science research on ways that jurors evaluate and misevaluate eyewitness testimony).

192. The classic example is Chief Justice Burger's opinion for the court in Parham v. J.R., 442 U.S. 584, 605-10 (1979) (approving more relaxed involuntary civil commitment procedures for juveniles than for adults). *See e.g.,* Perry & Melton, *Precedential Value of Judicial Notice of Social Facts:* Parham *as an Example,* 22 J. FAM. L. 633, 645 (1984): "The *Parham* case is an example of the Supreme Court's taking advantage of the free rein on social facts to promulgate a dozen or so of its own by employing one tentacle of the judicial notice doctrine. The Court's opinion is filled with social facts of questionable veracity, accompanied by the authority to propel these facts into subsequent case law and, therefore, a spiral of less than rational legal policy making."

193. *See e.g.,* Washington v. Harper, 494 U.S. 210, 229-30 (1990) (prisoners retain limited liberty interest in right to refuse forcible administration of antipsychotic medications), in which the majority acknowledges, and emphasizes in response

4. Social Science and the Insanity Defense

While scholars have recently considered critically the impact of social science data on child custody decision making and in death penalty cases,[194] little attention has been paid in general to the specific methodological problems afoot in insanity defense decisionmaking.[195] The law's suspicion of the psychological sciences is well documented.[196] Also, the issues before the courts in insanity defense cases raise such troubling issues for decisionmakers that the courts' inherent suspicion of the social sciences will be further heightened.[197] In related contexts, for example, Professor Sperlich has noted that opposition to the use of social science has explicitly masked political agendas in areas such as public education funding and jury trial outcomes.[198]

Thus, historically, one of the earliest criticisms of the law's "willful indifference to the question of the application of psychology" was "destroyed" by Dean Wigmore in a responsive article that argued that psychology had nothing to offer to the law.[199] As decisions as to

---

to the dissent, the harmful, and perhaps fatal, side-effects of the drugs. The court also stressed the "deference that is owed to medical professionals...who possess...the requisite knowledge and expertise to determine whether the drugs should be used." *Id.* at 230 n. 12. *Compare id.* at 247-49 (Stevens, J., concurring in part & dissenting in part) (suggesting that the majority's side effects acknowledgement is largely illusory). *But compare* Riggins v. Nevada, 112 U.S. 1810 (1992) discussed *supra* chapter 4 E 2 f (2).

194. *See* Appelbaum, *supra* note 160 (critiquing Barefoot v. Estelle, 463 U.S. 880 (1983), and McCleskey v. Kemp, 481 U.S. 279 (1987), and charging, *id.* at 341, that the Supreme Court acts with "blatant wrongheadedness" in dealing with empirical data in such cases.

195. A related exception is the literature which has developed in the wake of the Supreme Court's decision in *Barefoot* on the ability of psychiatrists to accurately predict future dangerousness. *See* 3 M.L. PERLIN, *supra* note 27, §17.14, at 536-40, and *id.* n. 308, at 213-14 (1992 pocket part).

196. *See e.g.*, Tanford & Tanford, *Better Trials Through Science: A Defense of Psychologist-Lawyer Collaboration*, 66 N.C. L. REV. 741, 742-46 (1988).

197. *See supra* chapter 4 B-D.

198. *See e.g.*, Sperlich, *Social Science Evidence and the Courts: Reaching Beyond the Adversary Process*, 63 JUDICATURE 280, 282 n. 9 (1980) (noting that Senator Moynihan's opposition to such use was grounded on his unhappiness with restrictions on public funding of public eduction and that Amitai Etzioni's opposition was based on his fear that such use would increase jury acquittals, discussing Moynihan, *Social Science and the Courts*, 54 PUB. INTEREST 12 (Winter 1979), and Etzioni, *Creating an Imbalance*, 10 TRIAL 28 (Nov.-Dec. 1974)).

199. *See* Wigmore, *The Psychology of Testimony*, 3 ILL. L. REV. 399 (1909), responding to H. MUENSTENBERG, ON THE WITNESS STAND (1908). *See* Tanford

sanity clearly do "contain social judgments,"[200] legal decision makers have been overtly reluctant to cede decision making autonomy in this area to social scientists; the roots of Judge Bazelon's non-xenophobic fear[201] of handing the "keys to the courthouse" to the social scientists become clear.

Although social scientists have now begun to examine the ways in which insanity judgments are reached,[202] there still has been little attention paid to the way courts are willing (or unwilling) to look at social science research in insanity defense cases.[203] While Judge Bazelon's advice to psychologists—"Unveil your values. Unveil our values. In combining those two tasks, you will be setting an enviable standard of social responsibility"[204]—has not yet been heeded, his recommendations remain sound ones.

This lack of interest should not surprise us. Traditionally, social science has played less of a role in the establishment of legal policy in areas "dominated by clear ideological division" or "political debate."[205] The more that social science contradicts "sentiments essential to other legal institutions," the less likely it will influence legal policy.[206]

& Tanford, *supra* note 196, at 744 n.8.

200. Wesson, *Historical Truth, Narrative Truth, and Expert Testimony*, 60 WASH. L. REV. 331, 333 (1985). *See also*, Bazelon I, *supra* note 148, at 116 (legal and policy questions "multidimensional," involving "scientific, moral, and social judgments"); *see generally*, Perlin, *Power Imbalances in Therapeutic and Forensic Relationships*, 9 BEHAV. SCI. & L. 111 (1991).

201. *See* Wales, *The Rise, the Fall, and the Resurrection of the Medical Model*, 63 GEO. L.J. 63, 87 (1974) (Judge Bazelon "invited the world of mental health professionals and criminologists into his courtroom and...extended his courtroom back into the world").

202. *See e.g.*, Ogloff, *A Comparison of Insanity Defense Standards on Juror Decision Making*, 15 LAW & HUM. BEHAV. 309 (1991); Finkel, *The Insanity Defense: A Comparison of Verdict Schemas*, 15 LAW & HUM. BEHAV. 533 (1991).

203. On juror perceptions of expert testimony, *see* Saks & Wissler, *Legal and Psychological Bases of Expert Testimony: Surveys of the Laws of Jurors*, 2 BEHAV. SCI. & L. 435 (1984). *But see*, Keilitz, *Researching and Reforming the Insanity Defense*, 39 RUTGERS L. REV. 289, 291-92 (1987) ("The aim of this article is to encourage scholars and practitioners in law and mental health to look more often to social science research to determine the effect of the insanity defense").

204. Bazelon I, *supra* note 148, at 120-21 (emphasis deleted).

205. Tanford, *Thinking About Elephants: Admonitions, Empirical Research and Legal Policy*, 60 UMKC L. REV. 645, 648 (1992), *citing, inter alia*, Melton, *Bringing Psychology Into the Legal System: Opportunities, Obstacles, and Efficacy*, 42 AM. PSYCHOLOGIST 488, 491 (1987).

206. Tanford, *supra* note 205, at 648, *citing, inter alia*, Tanford, *supra* note 178, at

By way of example, the Supreme Court's parsimonious approach to social science evidence in death penalty cases stems from its pre-existing policy position (and leads to "foregone conclusions" in such cases).[207] In the same way, judges' pre-existing positions in insanity defense cases—positions formed by sanism, supported by pretextuality, and defended through heuristic reasoning—lead to similarly "foregone conclusions." Decisions such as the majority opinion in *Jones v. United States*[208] and the dissents in *Riggins v. Nevada*[209] and *Foucha v. Louisiana*[210] are perfect examples of teleology in insanity defense decision making.

E. Conclusion

I believe that much of the incoherence of insanity defense jurisprudence can be explained by the phenomena I have discussed in this chapter. Stereotyped thinking leads to sanist behavior. Sanist decisions are rationalized by pretextuality on the part of judges, legislators and lawyers, and are buttressed by the teleological use of social science evidence and empirical data. This combination of sanism and pretextuality "fits" with traditional ways of thinking about (and acting toward) mentally disabled persons; it reifies centuries of myths and superstitions, and is consonant with both the way we use heuristic cognitive devices and our own *faux*, non-reflective "ordinary common sense."

In the final chapter of this book, I will search for answers to this dilemma. In doing so, I will first discuss the insanity defense in the context of therapeutic jurisprudence, and then conclude with some behavioral recommendations for all participants in the insanity defense system.

153-54.
207. Ellsworth, *Unpleasant Facts: The Supreme Court's Response to Empirical Research on Capital Punishment,* in CHALLENGING CAPITAL PUNISHMENT: *Legal and Social Science Approaches* 177, 208 (K. Haas & J. Inciardi eds. 1988), and *see generally id.* at 206-08.
208. 463 U.S. 354 (1983).
209. 112 S. Ct. 1810 (1992).
210. 112 S. Ct. 1780 (1992).

(How) Can We Make the Incoherent Coherent?

A. Introduction

I began this book by stating that our insanity defense jurisprudence was incoherent and that this incoherence mattered. I have sought to demonstrate the depth of that incoherence, the roots of the incoherence, and the way that our biases, prejudices and cognitive distortions perpetuate the incoherence. In this final chapter, I will first assess recent developments in the field of therapeutic jurisprudence, in an effort to determine what insights can be brought to bear on this inquiry. After that, I will offer some proscriptions and prescriptions that, I believe, will help lead us to a reconstructed insanity defense jurisprudence.

B. The Promise of Therapeutic Jurisprudence

1. Introduction[1]

"Therapeutic jurisprudence" studies the role of the law as a

---

1.   The material *infra* notes 2-9 is generally adapted from Perlin & Dorfman, *Sanism, Social Science, and the Development of Mental Disability Law Jurisprudence*, 11 BEHAV. SCI. & L. 47, 63-64 (1993).

therapeutic agent.[2] This perspective recognizes that substantive rules, legal procedures and lawyers' roles may have either therapeutic or antitherapeutic consequences, and questions whether such rules, procedures and roles can or should be reshaped so as to enhance their therapeutic potential, while not subordinating due process principles.[3]

While an impressive body of literature has been produced,[4] there has not yet been a systematic investigation into the reasons *why* some courts decide cases "therapeutically" and others "anti-therapeutically." I believe that the answer can be found, in significant part, in sanism. Sanism is such a dominant psychological force that it (1) distorts "rational" decision making, (2) encourages (albeit on at least a partially-unconscious level) pretextuality *and* teleology, and (3) prevents decision makers from intelligently and coherently focusing on questions that are meaningful to therapeutic jurisprudential inquiries.[5]

The types of sanist decisions that I have already discussed operate in an ostensibly *a*therapeutic world; although some decisions may be, in fact, therapeutic and others may be, in fact, antitherapeutic,[6]

---

2. *See* THERAPEUTIC JURISPRUDENCE: THE LAW AS A THERAPEUTIC AGENT (D. Wexler ed. 1990) (THERAPEUTIC JURISPRUDENCE); ESSAYS IN THERAPEUTIC JURISPRUDENCE (D. Wexler & B. Winick eds. 1991); Wexler, *Putting Mental Health Into Mental Health Law: Therapeutic Jurisprudence*, 16 LAW & HUM. BEHAV. 27 (1992) (Wexler, *Putting*); Wexler & Winick, *Therapeutic Jurisprudence and Criminal Justice Mental Health Issues*, 16 MENT. & PHYS. DIS. L. RPTR. 225 (1992) (Wexler & Winick, *Criminal Justice*); Wexler, *Therapeutic Jurisprudence and Changing Conceptions of Legal Scholarship*, 11 BEHAV. SCI. & L. 17 (1993) (Wexler, *Changing*); Wexler & Winick, *Therapeutic Jurisprudence as a New Approach to Mental Health Law Policy Analysis and Research*, 45 U. MIAMI L. REV. 979 (1991) (Wexler & Winick, *New Approach*); Klotz et al., *Cognitive Restructuring Through Law: A Therapeutic Jurisprudence Approach to Sex Offenders at the Plea Process*, 15 U. PUGET SOUND L. REV. 529 (1992).
3. Wexler, *Health Care Compliance Principles and the Insanity Acquittee Conditional Release Process*, in ESSAYS, *supra* note 2, at 199, 199-200 n. 5; *see generally*, Wexler, *Putting*, *supra* note 2.
4. *See* Wexler & Winick, *New Approach*, *supra* note 2, at 981 n. 9.
5. *See* M. Perlin, "Law as a Therapeutic and Antitherapeutic Agent," paper presented at the Massachusetts Department of Mental Health's Division of Forensic Mental Health's annual conference, Auburn, MA (May 1992) (suggesting that influence of sanism must be considered in therapeutic jurisprudence investigations); Perlin, *What Is Therapeutic Jurisprudence?* 10 N.Y.L. SCH. J. HUM. RTS. (1993) (in press).
6. E.g., I believe that the decision in State v. Krol, 68 N.J. 236, 344 A. 2d 289 (expanding procedural due process protection rights at the post-insanity acquit-

these outcomes seem to arise almost in spite of themselves.[7] In short, we cannot make any lasting progress in "putting mental health into mental health law"[8] until we confront the system's sanist biases and the ways that these sanist biases blunt our ability to intelligently weigh and assess social science data in the creation of a mental disability law jurisprudence.

2. Therapeutic Jurisprudence and the Insanity Defense

Application of therapeutic jurisprudence principles to the insanity defense reveals many "pressure points" that bear on any jurisprudential reconstruction. In order to make our insanity defense system coherent, we need to weigh the therapeutic potential of the different policy choices that are presented at each of these points. If we do this, we may uncover a strategy that will enable us to combat the sanism and pretextuality that currently drives the insanity defense system. At the same time, this strategy should serve as an effective counterweight to the teleological ways that courts have traditionally weighed social science evidence in insanity defense cases.[9]

a. Is a non-responsibility verdict therapeutic? Given the "rivers of ink, mountains of printers' lead [and] forests of paper" that have been spilled over every aspect of the insanity defense,[10] it is astonishing that

---

tal commitment hearing) is therapeutic and the decision in Jones v. United States, 463 U.S. 354 (1983) (restricting such rights) is anti-therapeutic. *See supra* chapter 4 E 2 d.

7. *See e.g.*, discussions in Wexler & Winick, *New Approach, supra* note 2, at 990-92 (right to refuse treatment), 992-97 (treatment of incompetent death row inmates), and 997-1001 (treatment of incompetency to stand trial); Wexler & Winick, *Criminal Justice, supra* note 2, at 229-30 (sex offender guilty pleas); *see also*, Perlin, Tarasoff *and the Dilemma of the Dangerous Patient: New Directions for the 1990's*, 16 LAW & PSYCHOL. REV. 29, 54-62 (1992) (duty to protect in tort law); Perlin, *Reading the Supreme Court's Tea Leaves: Predicting Judicial Behavior in Civil and Criminal Right to Refuse Treatment Cases*, 12 AM. J. FORENS. PSYCHIATRY 37, 54 (1991) (Perlin, *Tea Leaves*) (right to refuse treatment); Perlin, *Hospitalized Patients and the Right to Sexual Interaction: Beyond the Last Frontier?* 21 NYU REV. L. & SOC'L CHANGE (1993) (in press) (right of institutionalized patients to sexual autonomy); *see generally*, 1 M.L. PERLIN, MENTAL DISABILITY LAW: CIVIL AND CRIMINAL (1989), §1.05A, at 5-8, and sources cited (1992 pocket part).

8. *See* Wexler, *Putting, supra* note 2.

9. *See* Wexler, *Insanity Issues After Hinckley: Time for a Change*, 35 CONTEMP. PSYCHOL. 1068, 1069 (1990) (explicitly calling for therapeutic jurisprudence inquiries into insanity defense cases).

10. *See* Morris, *Psychiatry and the Dangerous Criminal*, 41 S. CAL. L. REV. 514,

this question has been so rarely asked (and even more rarely answered). Insanity defense adherents often couch their support with reference to our traditional disapproval of punishment without responsibility.[11] Opponents (mostly) raise fraudulent arguments about the ways that the insanity defense contributes to crime waves and allows "factually guilty" persons to evade punishment; other opponents construct principled arguments that look to other aspects of the criminal justice system to mediate against the punishment of mentally disabled criminal defendants.[12] Rarely are therapeutic jurisprudence issues raised anywhere in the debate.

There are, though, some exceptions. One undercurrent of the abolition movement is an insinuation of volition on the part of insanity defense pleaders: that certain defendants "indulge" in certain behaviors to "make themselves" not responsible. Thus, a popular sanist myth is:

> Mentally disabled individuals simply don't try hard enough. They give in too easily to their basest instincts, and do not exercise appropriate self-restraint.[13]

These arguments, of course, are never buttressed by any empirical support. Prosecutors or jurors make assertions as if they were "givens," and rebuttals are rarely offered. Sanism underlies these

---

516 (1968).

11. *See e.g.*, United States v. Lyons, 739 F. 2d 994, 995 (5th Cir. 1984) (Rubin, J., dissenting) (insanity defense reflects "fundamental moral principles of our criminal law" and rests on "assumptions that are older than our Republic"); Bonnie & Slobogin, *The Role of Mental Health Professionals in the Criminal Process: The Case for Informed Speculation*, 66 VA. L. REV. 427, 448 (1980) (insanity defense rests on "beliefs about human rationality, deterrability and free will"); Livermore & Meehl, *The Virtues of M'Naghten*, 51 MINN. L. REV. 789, 797 (1967) (insanity defense is bulwark of law's "moorings of condemnation for moral failure").

12. *Compare e.g.*, *The Insanity Defense Hearings Before the Senate Comm. on the Judiciary*, 97th Cong., 2d Sess. 27 (1982) (comments of then-Attorney General William French Smith) (insanity defense is major stumbling block in the restoration of the "effectiveness of Federal law enforcement," and "tilts the balance between the forces of law and the forces of lawlessness"), *to supra* chapter 6 D 6 a (1) (discussing work of Dr. Abraham Halpern).

13. Perlin, *On "Sanism,"* 46 SMU L. REV. 373, 396 (1992). *See e.g.*, State v. Duckworth, 496 So. 2d 624, 635 (La. App. 1986) (juror who felt defendant would be responsible for actions as long as he "wanted to do them" not excused for cause) (no error); Balkin, *The Rhetoric of Responsibility*, 76 VA. L. REV. 197, 238 (1990) (Hinckley prosecutor suggested to jurors "if Hinckley had emotional problems, they were largely his own fault").

allegations, and, as currently formulated, they can be dismissed out of hand in any therapeutic jurisprudence analysis.[14]

There are other approaches, however, that might illuminate the underlying issues. Labeling theory, for example, might appear to lend support to a finding that the insanity defense is antitherapeutic.[15] Labeling theory is the study of the process by which a label is, correctly or incorrectly, placed on a particular individual, as well as society's perception of and reaction to that label (and to the labeled person), and the labeled person's eventual fulfillment of society's expectations concerning that label.[16] Labels are more readily accepted by the community if a high-ranking person does the initial characterization.[17]

Labeling theorists believe that the potential negative consequences of stigmatizing offenders outweigh any benefits. Specifically, they argue that, by labeling an offender "deviant," the state may produce "secondary deviance," or other antisocial acts that are a result of the labeling.[18] On the other hand, critics of labeling theory have responded that no empirical data prove that secondary deviance is, in fact, a result of the labeling.[19] These critics also see positive outcomes as flowing from labeling, such as isolation, incapacitation and general deterrence, and, perhaps, "channeling [the labeled individual] toward appropriate rehabilitative services (specific deterrence and

---

14. If empirical support were to be offered in support of any of these propositions, it would, of course, be appropriate to re-evaluate them in that context.

15. *But compare* Weisberg, *Criminal Law, Criminology, and the Small World of Legal Scholarship*, 63 U. Colo. L. Rev. 521, 527 (1992) ("The history of American sociological criminology has yielded largely a plethora of schemes—from deviance theory to strain theory to control theory to labeling theory to subcultural differential association to reintegrative shaming theories—that almost all criminal law scholars ignore out of a predisposed disdain for the intellectual power of sociology").

16. Lynn, *Unconstitutional Inhibitions: "Political Propaganda" and the Foreign Agents Registration Act*, 33 N.Y.L. Sch. L. Rev. 345, 368 n.153 (1988), *citing, inter alia*, F. Cullen, Toward a Paradigm of Labelling Theory 30 (1978).

17. Lynn, *supra* note 16, at 368, *citing* E. Rubington & M. Weinberg, Deviance, the Interactionist Perspective 6 (4th ed. 1981).

18. Massaro, *Shame, Culture, and American Criminal Law*, 89 Mich. L. Rev. 1880, 1919 (1991), discussing, *inter alia*, R. Trojanowicz & M. Morash, Juvenile Delinquency: Concepts and Control 59-61 (4th ed. 1987); Gove, *The Labelling Perspective: An Overview*, in The Labeling of Deviance 9 (W. Gove ed., 2d ed. 1980).

19. Massaro, *supra* note 18, at 1920, *citing, inter alia*, Gove, *supra* note 18, at 13-15 (collecting empirical work).

rehabilitation)."[20]

Labels accompany stereotypes. These labels stigmatize, assign negative associations to an outsider, "complicate any effort to resist the designation implied by difference,"[21] and allow the labeler to fail to imagine the perspective of the outsider.[22] Labels are especially pernicious, for they frequently lead labeled individuals to internalize negative expectations and social practices that majoritarian society identifies as characteristically endemic to the labeled group.[23] From these labels, "categorizations assume a life of their own."[24] In turn, any act that fails to follow standards set by a dominant group becomes a deviation.[25]

Labeling must be considered through the special filter of mental disability. There is, for example, a growing body of psychological research that the stigma attached to the label of mental illness can affect a person's self-perception and interpersonal relations, as well as the response of society in general.[26] Society's attitudes toward the

---

20. Massaro, *supra* note 18 at 1920, *citing* Gove, *supra* note 18, at 18.

21. Minow, *1984 Forward: Justice Engendered*, 101 HARV. L. REV. 10, 38 (1987); S. GILMAN, DIFFERENCE AND PATHOLOGY: STEREOTYPES OF SEXUALITY, RACE AND MADNESS 12, 18-35 (1985).

22. Minow, *supra* note 21, at 51 n. 201. *See generally*, *Final Report: Task Force on Stigma and Discrimination* (NY State Office of Mental Health, Mar. 6, 1990), at 1-2.

23. Note, *Teaching Inequality: The Problem of Public School Tracking*, 102 HARV. L. REV. 1318, 1333 (1989); Glassner, *Labeling Theory*, in *The Sociology of Deviance* 71 (M. Rosenberg, R. Stebbins & A. Turowitz eds. 1982); L. TEMPEY, AMERICAN DELINQUENCY: ITS MEANING AND CONSTRUCTION 341-68 (1978); *see generally*, Weithorn, *Mental Hospitalization of Troublesome Youth: An Analysis of Skyrocketing Admission Rates*, 40 STAN. L. REV. 773, 805-07, 820-26 (1988); Sweet, *Deinstitutionalization of Status Offenders: In Perspective*, 18 PEPPERDINE L. REV. 389 (1991).

24. Delgado et al., *Fairness and Formality: Minimizing the Role of Prejudice in Alternative Dispute Resolution*, 1985 WIS. L. REV. 1359, 1381: "What enables people to reject members of other races is the supportive (unconscious and automatic) bias elicited by categorization," *quoting* Larsen, *Social Categorization and Attitude Change*, 111 J. SOC'L PSYCHOLOGY 113, 114 (1980).

25. Chester, *Perceived Relative Deprivation as a Cause of Property Crime*, 22 CRIME & DELINQ. 17, 22 (1976), as quoted in Wilson, *Urban Homesteading: A Compromise Between Squatters and the Law*, 35 N.Y.L. SCH. L. REV. 709, 714-15 n. 38 (1990).

26. Splane, *Tort Liability of the Mentally Ill in Negligence Actions*, 93 YALE L.J. 153, 167 n. 75 (1983), *citing, inter alia*, Farina et al., *Mental Illness and the Impact of Believing Others Know About It*, 77 J. ABNORMAL PSYCHOLOGY 1 (1971) (believing others to be aware of their status as mentally ill caused persons

mentally ill have a demonstrable effect on how patients see themselves and how adequately they adjust, and the public is more tolerant of deviance when it is not described by a mental disability label.[27]

What impact should this have on the insanity defense? The
phrase "insanity acquittee" is clearly a pejorative label. Does that
labeling affect the individual's self-perception?[28] If he were, instead,
labeled "criminal," would that be a better or worse alternative? What
other negative attributions does society make about such a person?
Would society still make these attributions if there were no insanity
defense? Do insanity acquittees act in certain ways to conform their
behavior to public perceptions?

Several scholars have discussed the question of whether defendants could be denied the use of the insanity defense if they were
found to have been "culpable" in causing the conditions that led to
the use of the defense.[29] On the other hand, as Professor Wexler has
pointed out, a schizophrenic patient who fails to take antipsychotic
medication may not be culpable if his impaired mental state led to
that refusal.[30] In such an instance, Professor Finkel argues, "When we

---

to feel less appreciated, appear more tense, and to find performance tasks more
difficult); Farina, Holland & Ring, *Role of Stigma and Set in Interpersonal
Interaction*, 71 J. ABNORMAL PSYCHOLOGY 421 (1966) (mentally ill persons
described as less desirable as friends and neighbors than criminals).

27. Johannsen, *Attitudes Toward Mental Patients: A Review of Empirical Research*,
53 MENTAL HYGIENE 218, 222-23 (1969); Sarbin & Mancuso, *Failure of a
Moral Enterprise: Attitudes of the Public Toward Mental Illness*, 35 J. CONSULT.
& CLIN. PSYCHOLOGY 159, 159 (1970).

28. On the impact of sex offender labeling, *see* Walsh, *Twice Labeled: The Effect of
Psychiatric Labels on the Sentencing of Sex Offenders*, 37 SOC'L PROBS. 375,
385-86 (1990) (both probation officers and judges "are consistently and pow-
erfully influenced" by labels).

29. *See e.g.*, Wexler, *Inducing Therapeutic Compliance through the Criminal Law*,
in ESSAYS, *supra* note 3, at 187, 196, *quoting, inter alia*, Robinson, *Causing the
Conditions of One's Own Defense: A Study of the Limits of Theory in Criminal
Law Doctrine*, 71 VA. L. REV. 1, 23-25 (1985); *see e.g.*, WASH. REV. CODE ANN.
§10.77.010 (7) (1990) ("No condition of the mind proximately induced by the
voluntary act of a person charged with crime shall constitute 'insanity'"); *see
also, e.g.*, Slodov, *Criminal Responsibility and the Noncompliant Psychiatric
Offender: Risking Madness*, 40 CASE W. RES. L. REV. 271 (1989); Tiffany, *The
Drunk, the Insane, and the Criminal Courts: Deciding What to Make of
Self-Induced Insanity*, 69 WASH. U. L.Q. 221 (1991).

30. Wexler, *supra* note 29, at 195; *see generally*, Slodov, *supra* note 28. This issue
is addressed, albeit elliptically, in People v. Smith, 124 Ill. App. 3d 805, 465 N.E.
2d 101, 103 (1984) (antipsychotic medication had been prescribed for defendant
which he took only one time; "One week later, the defendant fatally stabbed the
victim in the instant case").

recognize...that we are in danger of coming apart at the psychic seams, so to speak...then we should get ourselves help;...the alternative course, to do nothing, is unacceptable and inexcusable..."[31]

Taking a slightly different tack, Robert Fein claims that the insanity defense encourages NGRI acquittees to absolve themselves of responsibility for their actions and retards their treatment progress.[32] His thesis is this: for the NGRI verdict to work, insanity acquittees must "accept emotional responsibility for actions committed during periods of gross mental disorder;" operationally, the fact of acquittal serves to retard the acceptance of this responsibility.[33]

He gives several examples to illustrate his thesis (drawn from his experiences at Bridgewater State Hospital in Massachusetts). In one case, a patient to whom he refers as H.B. stated, "The judge said I was not guilty; I shouldn't be here. I am no longer sick." The same patient complained further that it was "unfair" that he was institutionalized since he had not committed a crime. In addition, the patient refused to participate in psychotherapy and "was granted his wish to stop taking his medicine."[34] A second insanity acquittee (A.L.), when asked by the judge at his recommitment hearing to describe how he felt about having injured his victims, replied, "The judge said I was not guilty. I'm sorry I did it but I think I've done enough time...I haven't gotten in any fights here."[35]

According to Fein, the fact that the insanity defense implies "that violent behavior is caused by 'illness' and is not committed by persons with thoughts and feelings...appears to decrease the possibility that mentally disordered persons will be able to utilize treatment services," and that the NGRI verdict thus "may work against the

---

Other questions are raised if an individual asserts a constitutional right to refuse medication, see Perlin, *Tea Leaves, supra* note 7, and then commits a criminal act, or if he commits a criminal act while under the influence of a prescribed antipsychotic drug, see People v. Caulley, 197 Mich. App. 177, 494 N.W. 2d 853 (1992) (reversing conviction; defendant could establish viable insanity defense if he could demonstrate that the "involuntary use," via medical prescription, of drugs created a state of mind equivalent to insanity).

31. N. FINKEL, INSANITY ON TRIAL 288 (1988). This argument assumes a fact not necessarily in evidence: that such "help" is available to all individuals who might seek it.

32. Fein, *How the Insanity Acquittal Retards Treatment*, in THERAPEUTIC JURISPRUDENCE, *supra* note 2, at 49.

33. *Id.* at 52.

34. *Id.* at 53.

35. *Id.* at 54.

needs of the defendants labeled by the courts as 'sick.'"[36] The verdict, he concludes, "provides a convenient way for the offender to avoid thinking about his violent behavior and its meaning."[37]

Fein's arguments are provocative, but, to my mind, fail to prove his point.[38] First, H.B.'s perceptions of the verdict are simply wrong; a finding of NGRI does not mean that a defendant is "no longer sick" or that he "shouldn't be in the hospital." On the other hand, this misunderstanding may be an indicia of the degree of severity of his illness; he may be *so* seriously mentally disabled that he cannot frame the type of thought process that would lead him to understand the limits of his responsibility. Second, his refusal to participate in psychotherapy and his decision to exercise his right to refuse the involuntary imposition of medication may raise therapeutic jurisprudence questions about the right to refuse treatment[39] but not about the underlying substantive insanity verdict.[40]

On the other hand, H.B.'s complaint that it was "unfair" not to know when he would be discharged may raise a serious issue but not necessarily one that goes to Fein's central thesis. This uncertainty *may* be antitherapeutic. However, if it is, it would seem to call into question post-commitment retention schemes such as the one upheld by the Supreme Court in *Jones v. United States*[41] under which a defendant can be held in a forensic hospital beyond the maximum

---

36. *Id.* at 58.
37. *Id.* at 55.
38. First, both of his NGRI examples are exceptional cases. H.B. was a former police officer and marine whose victim was a bar bouncer who had attacked the defendant a year prior to the murder that led to his insanity acquittal. *Id.* at 52-53. As I have discussed, such verdicts are disproportionately entered in cases where law enforcement officials are defendants; the additional fact that the victim was a non- stranger/former aggressor might make the verdict even more understandable. *See supra* chapter 4 D 4. A.L., a quiet, withdrawn man who attacked several strangers (leaving one permanently disfigured), was visited daily in the forensic hospital by his family who referred to the series of attacks as "Al's accident." Fein, *supra* note 31, at 54. Certainly, this constant exculpatory "support" by his family could have served as a powerful incentive leading him to deny responsibility for his actions.
39. *See e.g.*, Perlin, *Tea Leaves, supra* note 7; Winick, *Competency to Consent to Treatment: The distinction Between Assent and Objection*, in ESSAYS, *supra* note 2, at 41.
40. There has also been virtually no litigation on the question of a "right to refuse psychotherapy," and what little has been attempted has been unsuccessful. *See* 2 M.L. PERLIN, *supra* note 7, §5.56, at 398-99 (discussing United States v. Stine, 675 F. 2d 69, 71-72 (3d Cir. 1982)).
41. 463 U.S. 354 (1983).

term to which he could have been sentenced had he been convicted of the underlying crime. This does not challenge the therapeutic potential of the insanity defense, but of a commitment system that insures lengthier stays in hospitals for insanity acquittees.

What about Fein's conclusions? Does failure to assign responsibility lessen an insanity acquittee's initiative to get better? Does this question imply some quantum of blame; that the patient could get better "if he really wanted to?"[42] Is there any responsibility on institutional staff here? Should they be held accountable to try to deal with the type of behavior exhibited in the H.B. and A.L. cases?

What about his conclusion that the verdict implies that violent behavior is "caused" by mental illness? This use of causation sounds like the *Durham* product test,[43] a formulation that was abandoned in the District of Columbia in 1972. Neither the *M'Naghten* nor the ALI tests are couched in causal language; to make this link here is to set up an ultimate straw man.

Also, the implication that the insanity verdict suggests that the behavior in question is not that of individuals with "thoughts and feelings" falls wide of the mark. The insanity defense is usually pled only by people with the most disordered thoughts; when the verdict is successful, it is often the reflection of jurors' conclusions that the underlying crime was a response to the power of those strong thoughts.

In short, although I find Fein's piece thoughtful, I do not believe that it makes the case that the insanity defense is anti-therapeutic. It appears that no one in the facility ever explained to the two acquittees the actual meaning of the jury's verdict nor, apparently, did anyone ever counsel A.L.'s family that their reinforcement of his denial was most likely antitherapeutic.[44] He provides no evidence that his criticism would be valid if such explanations had been offered. It is not the fact of the nonresponsibility verdict that is antitherapeutic, but the way that the verdict is processed by the defendant after the insanity acquittal. It would seem that some measure of

---

42. *See supra* chapter 8, note 43, discussing State v. Duckworth, 496 So. 2d 624, 635 (La. App. 1986), and Balkin, *supra* note 13, at 238.
43. *See supra* chapter 3 A 1 c (2).
44. Of course, if the individuals' mental states were so impaired that they could not understand the meaning of the insanity acquittal, it is unlikely that *any* explanation would have been therapeutic or antitherapeutic.

cognitive restructuring as to the defense's meaning[45] and its likely consequences for the defendant would eliminate almost all of Fein's criticisms.

What about the other side? May a non-responsibility defense be "therapeutic?" I believe that it may be. The standard explanation as to why the defense is therapeutic is articulated best by Judge Bazelon: "By declaring a small number not responsible, we emphasize the responsibility of all others who commit crimes."[46] In other words, the existence of the insanity defense gives coherence to the entire fabric of criminal sentencing. We punish responsible defendants for a variety of reasons: to incapacitate them, to deter others, to educate others, (perhaps) to rehabilitate them.[47] By punishing non-responsible defendants, we diminish all the rationales for punishment of the others whom we believe to be responsible for their crimes.

However, this argument may simply be a retrospective rationalization and not a therapeutic justification at all. It may be that we allow the insanity defense to survive precisely because so few criminal defendants come within its scope.[48] This allows us to isolate those few without endangering the overall administration of the criminal justice system.[49] This may also explain why Judge Bazelon's consideration of "rotten social background" as potentially providing a basis for an insanity defense (on the theory that it significantly impaired the defendant's ability to exercise free choice)[50] never attracted more positive public support.[51] Recognition and/or acceptance of this position would imperil the legal system's "tensile strength,"[52] by calling into question literally thousands of criminal convictions entered each

---

45. *Compare* Klotz et al., *supra* note 2.
46. D. BAZELON, QUESTIONING AUTHORITY: JUSTICE AND CRIMINAL LAW 2 (1988).
47. *See supra* chapter 2 C.
48. *See supra* chapter 3 B 1 b (1).
49. This may actually be s *sanist* justification for the insanity defense, since it enables us to say that these few defendants are so sufficiently not "like us" that we can treat them safely as an outgroup. Not coincidentally, such individuals are often treated in facilities in areas at a significant distance from major population centers.
50. United States v. Alexander, 471 F. 2d 923, 957-65 (D.C. Cir. 1972) (Bazelon, J., concurring in part & dissenting in part).
51. For a sampling of the academic debate, *see e.g.,* Bazelon, *The Morality of the Criminal Law,* 49 S. CAL. L. REV. 385 (1976); Morse, *The Twilight of Welfare Criminology: A Reply to Judge Bazelon,* 49 S. CAL. L. REV. 1247 (1976); Delgado, *"Rotten Social Background:" Should the Criminal Law Recognize a Defense of Severe Environmental Deprivation?* 3 LAW & INEQUAL. 9 (1985).
52. *See supra* chapter 8 A.

year. In other words, this argument in support of the insanity defense is an important instrumental one, but may not normatively provide a therapeutic basis for the defense.

On the other hand, the insanity defense system recognizes that certain individuals—because of mental disability—are to be diverted from the criminal justice system.[53] If such defendants receive constitutionally meaningful treatment in psychiatric hospitals, then this diversion will be therapeutic.[54] More importantly, if these defendants are spared prison—where mentally disabled prisoners are often institutionalized in facilities bereft of even minimal mental health services, and are often treated more harshly than other inmates[55]—then there may be an additional therapeutic impact.[56] If, in a prison

---

53. *Compare* Halpern, *The Insanity Defense in the 21st Century*, 35 INT'L J. OFFENDER THER. & COMPAR. CRIMINOL. 188, 188 (1991) (arguing that insanity defense draws resources of forensic hospitals "while individuals with clear-cut psychiatric illnesses...are left to deteriorate in prison without a modicum of therapy"). On the recent increase in the number of mentally ill pre-trial jail detainees, *see* Palermo, Gumz & Liska, *Mental Illness and Criminal Behavior Revisited*, 36 INT'L J. OFFENDER THER. & COMPAR. CRIMINOL. 53 (1992).

54. In the "pecking order" of prisoners, the mentally ill have always been plagued by an exceptionally low status. *See* Halleck, *The Criminal's Problem With Psychiatry*, in READINGS IN LAW AND PSYCHIATRY 51 (R. Allen et al. eds. 1975).

55. *See e.g.*, Tillery v. Owens, 907 F. 2d 418, 424-25 (3d Cir. 1990) (mentally ill inmates often double-celled with inmates in administrative custody, a practice characterized by an expert witness as "putting the chickens in the fox's lair"); Baskin, Sommers & Steadman, *Assessing the Impact of Psychiatric Impairment on Prison Violence*, 19 J. CRIM. JUST. 271, 272 (1991) (psychiatrically impaired inmates more likely to be victimized by other prisoners due to displays of bizarre or inappropriate behavior). On the multiple roots of homicide defendants' post-detention psychotic reactions, *see* Arboleda-Florez, *Post-Homicide Psychotic Reaction*, 25 INT'L J. OFFENDER THER. & COMPAR. CRIMINOL. 47 (1981). On the relationship between prison violence and mental illness, *see* Baskin, Sommers & Steadman, *supra*.

    Proponents of abolishing involuntary civil commitment have conceded that this might result in more mentally disabled persons being imprisoned. *See* C. WARREN, THE COURT OF LAST RESORT: MENTAL ILLNESS AND THE LAW 100-1 (1982) (section written by Stephen J. Morse). Responds Andrew Scull: "While Morse may not balk at the prospect of sending the mentally ill to prison, a...system of justice built around the concept of criminal responsibility almost certainly will." Scull, *The Theory and Practice of Civil Commitment*, 82 MICH. L. REV. 793, 803 (1984).

56. On the way that progressive conditional release of NGRI acquittees is therapeutically beneficial, *see* McGreevey, Steadman, Dvoskin & Dollard, *New York State's System of Managing Insanity Acquittees in the Community*, 42 HOSP. & COMMUN. PSYCHIATRY 512 (1991). On the other side of this coin, if severely mentally disabled persons are diverted from prisons, it may serve to make those facilities safer for non-mentally disabled prisoners as well.

context, we are likely to cognitively resolve the "logical dissonance of classifying mad/bad persons as bad persons,"[57] then the separation of severely mentally disabled individuals from the prison population will have yet an extra therapeutic outcome.[58]

A therapeutic jurisprudence analysis also underscores the banality and vacuity of the guilty but mentally ill (GBMI) plea.[59] Jurors are deceived into entering the GBMI verdict as a compromise, either as a means of expressing their position that the defendant's mental illness should be seen as somehow contributory to his criminal behavior, or as an aspiration that the defendant receive treatment while serving his sentence. The statistics reveal that this hope is an illusion; GBMI defendants receive no treatment, and are subject to life-plus sentences (or the death penalty). Further, the reality that the GBMI verdict is nothing more than a label is hidden from jurors who are denied information by the court as to the verdict's operational meaning.

I suggest that this analysis is a starting point for a more comprehensive investigation of the question posed. As I will argue in my concluding section, unless scholars and insanity defense decision makers confront the importance of this inquiry, our endless tinkering with the procedural and substantive contours of the defense will have little ultimate meaning.

b. Does the substantive standard matter?[60] The much-ballyhooed Insanity Defense Reform Act eliminated the volitional prong from the

---

57. Hayman, *Beyond* Penry: *The Remedial Use of the Mentally Retarded Label in Death Penalty Sentencing,* 59 UMKC L. REV. 17, 47 n. 161 (1990) (quoting H. TOCH & K. ADAMS, THE DISTURBED VIOLENT OFFENDER 18-19 (1989)),

58. *See generally,* H. TOCH & K. ADAMS, COPING: MALADAPTATION IN PRISONS (1989); H. TOCH, MOSAIC OF DESPAIR: HUMAN BREAKDOWN IN PRISON (rev. ed. 1992). On the other hand, if adequate treatment is not offered in forensic mental health facilities, the ensuing institutionalization in such environments may also be antitherapeutic.

59. *See supra* chapter 3 A 1 c (4).

60. For the purposes of this section, I will assume that the choice of standard has at least a symbolic value. *See e.g.,* Homant & Kennedy, *Subjective Factors in Clinicians' Judgments of Insanity: Comparison of a Hypothetical Case and an Actual Case,* 18 PROF'L PSYCHOL.: RES. & PRAC. 439, 455 (1987): "[I]nsanity defense trials...will continue to play an important symbolic role. They will underline the fact that reasons for criminal behavior are indeed important, and that a principled and effective response to offenders must follow from an understanding of the individuals."

At the least, the choice of standard conveys a paramessage, *see supra* chapter 6, text at notes 191-92, to jurors as to the legislature's feelings about the role of the insanity defense in a criminal justice system. This is an area that has seen

insanity defense in federal courts because of the fear that this was not "measurable" (as cognition presumably was), and that this reduction would lead to an elimination of verdicts that had been termed "moral mistakes."[61] Yet, the best available empirical studies suggest that volition may be accurately measurable, in some instances even more accurately than cognition.[62]

This same evidence offers an important therapeutic jurisprudence insight. The very individuals who meet the volitional standard (but not the cognitive test) may be exactly those individuals who would be the most problematic prison inmates and whose mental disabilities might be most treatable in a controlled forensic hospital setting.[63] Here, it appears that our political cant and rhetoric has blunted any efforts to inform ourselves of the therapeutic potential of substantive insanity formulations less restrictive than the *M'Naghten* test.

c. Do procedural rules matter? The allocation of proof to the state or the defendant may be a critical decision in the formulation of an insanity defense standard.[64] The placement of the burden on the defendant (especially where it involves a clear and convincing quantum of evidence) will make it more likely that insanity defenses offered by severely mentally disabled criminal defendants will be rejected.[65] This, in turn, may increase the number of imprisoned seriously mentally disabled prisoners, an outcome that is self-evidently anti-

---

significant empirical inquiry. *See supra* chapter 6 D 5 b, and chapter 6 D 6 a, discussing, *inter alia*, the work of Professor Norman Finkel and his colleagues.

61. *See supra* chapter 5, text at note 55.
62. *See* Silver & Spodak, *Dissection of the Prongs of ALI: Retrospective Assessment of Criminal Responsibility by the Psychiatric Staff of the Clifton T. Perkins Hospital Center*, 11 BULL. AM. ACAD. PSYCHIATRY & L. 383, 390 (1983) (contemporaneous empirical research has shown some evidence that the elimination of this prong from the insanity defense "may systematically exclude...that class of psychotic patients [patients with manic disorders] whose illness is clearest in symptomatology, must likely biologic in origin, most eminently treatable, and potentially most disruptive in penal detention"); *see also*, Rogers, *Assessment of Criminal Responsibility: Empirical Advances and Unanswered Questions*, 15 J. PSYCHIATRY & L. 73, 78 (1987) (arguments that volitional non-responsibility cannot be measuredare "an intellectual charade played for the benefit of an uninformed public"). *See supra* chapter 6, note 239.
63. *See* Silver & Spodak, *supra* note 62.
64. *See supra* chapter 3 A 2.
65. For a pointed case example, *see* State v. Zmich, 160 Ariz. 108, 770 P.2d 776 (1989), discussed *supra* chapter 3, note 123.

therapeutic for the unsuccessful insanity pleaders and may also be potentially hazardous for prison staff and other prisoners.[66]

Other procedural issues call out for further study as well. Courts are hopelessly split on informing insanity jurors about the meaning of the insanity verdict, and about whether or not counsel can comment on such verdict outcomes in summations.[67] If we learn that jurors are misinformed about the ultimate outcome of a successful insanity plea [68] and that jurors may over-convict "legitimate" insanity defendants (because of a false fear that they will be quickly released from all custodial restraints, a fear often exacerbated by inflammatory prosecutorial summations),[69] then decisions that deprive them of this empirical information (and allow for the dissemination of inaccurate information) are antitherapeutic.[70]

In *Ake v. Oklahoma*, the Supreme Court ruled that, if a criminal defendant were to make an "ex parte threshold showing...that his sanity was likely to be a significant factor in his defense," the state must assure him access to a "competent psychiatrist...[to] assist in the evaluation, preparation, and presentation of the defense."[71] Most post-*Ake* decisions have read that holding tepidly,[72] and defendants are frequently deprived of adequate expert assistance.[73] Again, in

---

66. By saying this, I am *not* suggesting that mentally disabled criminal defendants are, as a class, more dangerous than other criminal defendants. I am arguing rather that the placement of such individuals into a general prison population (supervised by a prison staff that may have no training or experience in the identification and/or treatment of such disabilities) may create hazardous and harmful conditions for all involved.

67. *See generally*, 3 M.L. PERLIN, *supra* note 7, §15.16, at 336-39 (categorizing cases).

68. *See e.g.*, Price v. State, 274 Ind. 479, 412 N.E. 2d 783, 788 (1980) (De Bruler, J., concurring in result) (explaining that, as a result of his "success," the insanity acquittee "is placed on a separate track towards confinement under the auspices of attendants and doctors rather than on a track toward confinement under the auspices of guards and wardens").

69. *See supra* chapter 3 B 1 b (1).

70. For perhaps the most incomprehensible decision dealing with judicial instructions, *see supra* chapter 7, text accompanying notes 133-35, discussing Geschwendt v. Ryan, 967 F. 2d 877 (3d Cir. 1992) (en banc), and *id.* at 891 (Aldisert, J., dissenting).

71. 470 U.S. 68, 82-83 (1985).

72. *See* 3 M.L. PERLIN, *supra* note 7, §17.17, at 549-53, and *id.*, n. 404.1 at 215-26 (1992 pocket part) (listing cases).

73. *See e.g.*, Brown v. State, 743 P. 2d 133 (Okla. Crim. App. 1987); State v. Bearthes, 329 N.C. 149, 405 S.E. 2d 170 (1991); Henderson v. Dugger, 925 F. 2d 1309 (9th Cir. 1991). *But see*, De Freece v. State,—S.W. 2d —, 1993 WL 44429 (Tex. Cr. App. 1993) (*Ake* requires more than a disinterested witness;

those few cases where insanity is contested, this may lead to legitimately non-responsible defendants being improperly convicted.

In *Barefoot v. Estelle*, the Supreme Court approved of expert testimony on future dangerousness, even where the expert testimony had not examined the defendant in question.[74] This uniformly-criticized decision[75] "flies in the face of...relevant scientific literature,...is inconsistent with the development of evidence law doctrine, and... makes a mockery of earlier Supreme Court decisions cautioning that *extra* reliability is needed in capital cases."[76] Again, it heightens the likelihood of inappropriate convictions in insanity cases—an anti-therapeutic outcome.

This leads to another set of inquiries. What impact do examiners' pre-existing political attitudes have on insanity case dispositions? A body of research literature has developed that demonstrates that various sorts of political biases affect mental health professionals' judgments of insanity in particular cases,[77] and that the primary predictor of an expert witness's view on a particular case is his pre-existing feelings about the defense.[78] Other research shows that most expert witnesses do not know the actual substantive insanity standard used in their jurisdiction.[79] If improper or inaccurate verdicts in insanity cases are entered because of these biases or lack of knowledge, this would clearly also affect any therapeutic effect that the defense might have.

---

expert must be able to assist in developing favorable testimony, supply bases on which to cross-examine state's expert and, if necessary, testify on behalf of the defendant).

74. 463 U.S. 880 (1983); *see supra* chapter 4 E 2 f (1).
75. *See* 3 M.L. PERLIN, *supra* note 7, §17.14, at 536-40; *see e.g.,* Risinger, Denbeaux & Saks, *Exorcism of Ignorance as a Proxy for Rational Knowledge: The Lessons of Handwriting Identification "Expertise,"* 137 U. PA. L. REV. 731, 780-81 n. 215 (1989) ("We have yet to find a single word of praise for, or in defense of, *Barefoot* in the literature of either science or law").
76. Perlin, *The Supreme Court, the Mentally Disabled Criminal Defendant, Psychiatric Testimony in Death Penalty Cases, and the Power of Symbolism: Dulling the* Ake *in* Barefoot's *Achilles Heel,* 3 N.Y.L. SCH. HUM. RTS. ANN. 91, 111 (1985) (emphasis in original).
77. *See e.g.,* Homant et al., *Ideology as a Determinant of Views on the Insanity Defense,* 14 J. CRIM. JUST. 37, 57 (1986).
78. Homant & Kennedy, *Judgment of Legal Insanity as a Function of Attitude Toward the Insanity Defense,* 8 INT'L J. L. & PSYCHIATRY 67 (1986).
79. Rogers & Turner, *Understanding of Insanity: A National Survey of Forensic Psychologists and Psychiatrists,* 7 HEALTH L. CANADA 71 (1987).

*d. Should post-acquittal commitment procedures track the tradi-
tional involuntary civil commitment model, or is a separate, more
restrictive means of determining commitment appropriate?*   Few
contrasts in insanity defense jurisprudence are more stark than the
difference between post-acquittal commitments in states that follow
the model of the New Jersey Supreme Court in *State v. Krol*[80] and
those that adhere to the system found to be constitutional by the
United States Supreme Court in *Jones v. United States.*[81] *Krol* finds
the distinction between criminal and civil commitment a meaningless
one; *Jones,* on the other hand, sees the prior commission of a criminal
act (even a *de minimis* one) as a sufficient predicate for an entirely
different set of procedural and substantive rules.

Self-evidently, the *Krol* system should lead to fewer defendants
being institutionalized and to shorter terms of confinement; the *Jones*
scheme should have just the opposite result. Is it therapeutic for
defendants to be released from custody more quickly, or is it more
therapeutic for insanity pleaders to be institutionalized for longer
periods of time (longer, perhaps, than had they been sentenced to the
maximum for the underlying crime)?[82]

In addition, the *Krol/Jones* split has a symbolic value that may
also mask therapeutic content. If we say (as did the *Krol* court) that
there is no difference between criminal and civil commitment, then
we are minimizing the criminal component of the insanity defense
finding, and maximizing the mental disability component. On the
other hand, if we say that a defendant's original criminal act (no
matter how minor) colors all subsequent aspects of the criminal
process, then we are saying that *any* involvement in that process
serves as a "trump" over any other individual facet of the case. The
resolution of this symbolic split is likely to be longer terms of post-acquittal hospitalization in *Jones* jurisdictions and shorter in *Krol* jurisdictions. Again, therapeutic jurisprudence questions are raised by
this inquiry.

In a careful analysis of the collateral issue of how the release
hearing should be structured, Professor Wexler has examined the

---

80. 68 N.J. 236, 344 A. 2d 289 (1975); *see supra* chapter 4 E 2 d.
81. 463 U.S. 354 (1983); *see supra* chapter 4 E 2 d.
82. Michael Jones, the appellant in the Supreme Court case, had been arrested and
    charged with attempted petit larceny in 1975, was still institutionalized at the
    time of the Supreme Court decision in 1983, and remains institutionalized today.

work of Donald Meichenbaum and Dennis Turk[83] that was written
to help medical professionals increase patient treatment adherence.[84]
Meichenbaum and Turk's research led them to conclude that such
adherence is likely to be increased when a patient is given choice and
participation in the selection of treatment alternatives and goals.[85]

Placing this work in the context of the release hearing, Wexler
looks for ways that courts might employ these compliance principles
to increase a patient's adherence behavior once released.[86] Such strategies as the use of behavioral contracts, the creation of procedures
that track plea bargain approval hearings,[87] and the involvement of
the acquittee in the hearing itself ("to test the patient's understanding
of the regimen and to insure that the patient agrees with it and had
input into its design")[88] would assure a greater level of patient compliance. Under this model, "the court is itself an HCP [health care
professional]," and Wexler recommends behaviors to the judge to
enhance patient adherence.[89]

Importantly, Wexler acknowledges that courts may resist these
behaviors for many of the same reasons that health care professionals
may resist, among them that the procedures are complicated, en-
hancement strategies are a "frill," the strategies will not work with
the population in question.[90] Notwithstanding these potential (and
likely) complaints, Wexler concludes that this approach is one that
deserves experimental implementation. "[L]ike it or not," he concludes, it is probable that "the behavior of courts play a critical role
in the adherence behavior of conditionally released insanity acquittees."[91] The simple recognition by courts that their decisions and

---

83. D. MEICHENBAUM & D. TURK, FACILITATING TREATMENT ADHERENCE: A
    PRACTITIONER'S GUIDEBOOK (1987) (FACILITATING).
84. Wexler, *supra* note 3, at 199.
85. Winick, *Harnessing the Power of the Bet: Wagering with the Government as a
    Mechanism for Social and Individual Change*, in ESSAYS, *supra* note 2, at 245
    n. 93, citing FACILITATING, *supra* note 83, at 157, 159, 175.
86. Wexler, *supra* note 3, at 209.
87. *See* FED. R. CRIM. PROC. 11.
88. Wexler, *supra* note 3, at 210.
89. *Id.* at 212. *See also id.*: "For instance, the judge can make sure to introduce
    himself or herself to the patient, can be attentive, can avoid using legal or medical
    jargon, can allow the patient to tell his or her story without undue interruption,
    can make sure the patient understands the precise treatment regimen, and can
    even sit at the same level and at the same conference table as the patient—perhaps
    in a mental health facility conference room rather than in a courtroom."
90. *Id.* at 217.
91. *Id.* at 218.

actions have a therapeutic or anti-therapeutic consequence should be a critical factor in this sort of decision making.[92]

Wexler's arguments here are compelling ones, and offer a blue-print for scholars and other insanity defense decision makers. As of yet, there has been little reaction to his suggestions among other legal scholars.[93] On the other hand, as the face of mental disability law scholarship changes,[94] we can hope that researchers turn their attention to this important question.

e. Once institutionalized, how are insanity acquittees to be treated?
Little academic attention has been paid to the question of the institutional treatment rights of insanity acquittees. Although a smattering of caselaw finds that both the right to treatment and the right to refuse treatment apply,[95] there has been little systemic consideration of this question since Anne Singer and June German's groundbreaking analysis in 1976.[96]

On the question of a right to refuse treatment, several questions are raised from a therapeutic jurisprudence perspective. If refusal of treatment serves autonomy values (by allowing institutionalized patients to make individual health care decisions that they could freely make in the community), is it therapeutic to expand this right for this population? On the other hand, if refusal of medication leads to more florid symptomatology (and an exacerbation of delusions and hallucinations), is that antitherapeutic *in se*? If drugs merely mask symptoms, resulting in damaging neurological side-effects? Now that Justice Kennedy has taken a bold and expansive pro-refusal position

---

92. *Id.* at 218 n. 147, *citing* Wexler & Schopp, *Therapeutic Jurisprudence: A New Approach to Mental Health Law*, in HANDBOOK OF PSYCHOLOGY AND LAW (D. Kagehiro & W. Laufer eds.) (in press).

93. The only citation to the article is in Wexler & Winick, *Therapeutic Jurisprudence as a New Approach to Mental Health Law Policy Analysis and Research*, 45 U. MIAMI L. REV. 979, 981 (1991).

94. *See* Wexler, *Changing, supra* note 2; M. Perlin & D. Dorfman, "The Invisible Renaissance of Mental Disability Law Scholarship: A Case Study in Subordination" (manuscript in progress).

95. *See supra*; *see* Perlin, *Tea Leaves, supra* note 7.

96. German & Singer, *Punishing the Not Guilty: Hospitalization of Persons Found Not Guilty By Reason of Insanity*, 29 RUTGERS L. REV. 1011, 1017-35 (1976). A recent case has expanded the right of access to a law library and to legal research materials—previously held to apply to prisoners, pretrial detainees and persons committed following a finding of incompetency to stand trial—to patients institutionalized after an NGRI verdict. *See* Hatch v. Yamauchi, 809 F. Supp. 59 (E.D. Ark. 1992).

in his autonomy-privileging concurrence in *Riggins v. Nevada*,[97] can we expect that further attention will be paid to this issue? Until rigorous therapeutic jurisprudence analyses are applied here, arguments as to whether insanity acquittees should have the same rights, fewer rights, or more rights than civil patients in these areas will likely remain unresolved.

f. How should insanity acquittees be monitored in community settings? The paradox here should be self-evident. Insanity acquittees are the most despised group of individuals in society. Most commentators agree that one of the reasons our insanity defense jurisprudence is so repressive is to make it as difficult as possible for insanity acquittees to ever reenter society;[98] the thought that such individuals are ever to be released fills much of the public with dread and/or consternation.[99] On the other hand, most research studies show that individuals who are subject to gradual lessening of restraints are better reintegrated into the community upon release.[100] Some sort of monitoring appears to be appropriate, but little attention has been paid in the legal literature to this question from a therapeutic jurisprudence perspective.[101]

g. Other therapeutic jurisprudence issues. In addition to these questions, there remains a menu of other issues that need to be considered from a therapeutic jurisprudence perspective: the procedural due process requirements needed at the recommitment process,[102] the right

---

97. 112 S. Ct. 1810, 1817 (1992); *see supra* chapter 4 E 2 f (2).

98. *See supra* chapter 4 E 2 d.

99. *See e.g.*, Ellis, *The Consequences of the Insanity Defense: Proposals to Reform Post- Acquittal Commitment Laws*, 35 CATH.U. L. REV. 961, 962 (1986) ("the public's concern is less with whether blame properly can be assigned to a particular defendant than with determining when he will get out").

100. *See e.g.*, McGreevey, Steadman, Dvoskin & Dollard, *supra* note 56; Wexler, *supra* note 3, at 213-14.

101. For a parallel inquiry, *see* Renaud, R. v. Fuller: *Time to Brush Aside the Rule Prohibiting Therapeutic Remands?* 35 CRIM. L. Q. 91 (1992) (Part I), and *id.*, 35 CRIM. L. Q. 156 (1993) (Part II).

102. On the procedural due process protections required in civil cases following a conditional release, *see* 1 M.L. PERLIN, *supra* note 7, §3.54 at 363-68. The case law that has developed around conditional release generally calls for procedural due process protections much like those at initial involuntary civil commitment hearings. As of yet, there has been virtually no case law dealing with this specific question as it applies to the population of insanity acquittees.

Some questions that must be addressed here include the following: Is a hearing with full procedural due process protections therapeutically valuable for

of defendants to refuse to enter an insanity plea,[103] the impact of a failed insanity plea on a subsequent sentence,[104] the impact of a successful plea on other legal statutes,[105] and the systemic ways that counsel is assigned to potential insanity pleaders[106] are all questions that can and should be considered in therapeutic jurisprudence analyses.

3. Conclusion

As I have sought to demonstrate, the therapeutic jurisprudence inquiry is a critical one to the future development of the insanity defense. I believe that, if we are to make any headway as a society in eliminating the sanism that affects all of mental disability jurisprudence (but that especially contaminates insanity defense law), we must carefully consider each of these therapeutic jurisprudence questions.

---

individuals facing recommitment? Or, is the possibility that such protections might result in fewer recommitments antitherapeutic? Does the Supreme Court's decision in Foucha v. Louisiana, 112 S. Ct. 1780 (1992) (declaring unconstitutional a state law that provided for the continued insanity commitment of an NGRI acquittee who was no longer mentally ill) apply in this context?

103. *See generally*, 3 M.L. PERLIN, *supra* note 7, §15.34, at 384-88.

104. Statistics seem to indicate that defendants who are unsuccessful in their NGRI pleas are frequently given lengthier sentences than like defendants who do not raise a non-responsibility defense. *See supra* chapter 3 B 1 b (1). If we assume that a significant percentage of these defendants are mentally ill, this finding suggests that the plea is even a riskier gambit than has generally been thought.

105. *See e.g.*, Salton, *Mental Capacity and Liability Insurance Clauses: The Effect of Insanity Upon Intent*, 78 CALIF. L. REV. 1027 (1990). When a defendant is found NGRI, there are potential effects on other legal interactions. Can an NGRI defendant be prosecuted for "criminal" acts that take place in forensic hospitals or other mental institutions? Can he be disciplined for violating institutional rules? Can he be civilly liable for his tortious acts? *Compare* Koehler v. State, 830 S.W. 2d 665 (Tex. App. 1992), *rev. den.* (1992) (determination of incompetence to manage one's own affairs not a prima facie showing of incompetency to stand trial).

106. Counsel made available to mentally disabled criminal defendants is often substandard. *See* Perlin, *Fatal Assumption: A Critical Evaluation of the Role of Counsel in Mental Disability Cases*, 16 LAW & HUM. BEHAV. 39 (1992). Lawyers representing such persons often ignore potential mental status defenses, or, in some cases, contradictorily, seek to have the insanity defense imposed on their client over his objection. Such lawyers often succumb to sanist stereotypes and are compliant co-conspirators in pretextual court decisions. *See* Perlin, *supra* note 13, at 404-6.

C. Toward a Reconstruction of Insanity Defense Jurisprudence

1. Introduction

I recognize that there is a certain measure of *hubris* (if not to say folly) in attempting to articulate a new vision of insanity defense jurisprudence. Our current vision reflects attitudes and biases that stem from medieval concepts of mental illness, evil, and punishment. Much of the public remains wed to notions of criminal responsibility that were seen as dated by the middle of the eighteenth century. The hopes and aspirations articulated in the 1950s and 1960s by judges such as David Bazelon were dashed on the rocks of the public's response to John Hinckley's insanity acquittal, and were dealt a mortal blow by Congress and the state legislatures in their hysterical response to that verdict. We appear doomed to repeat a neverending cycle of overreaction.

Nonetheless, I offer these suggestions. I must begin with the rueful recognition that our societal track record is not one to inspire much optimism. On the other hand, as Dr. Henry Steadman and his colleagues have pointed out, there has been an impressionistically-measurable change in press and media attitudes in the *framing* of insanity defense questions.[107]

Thus, while I am not entirely optimistic about the future of this enterprise, I am offering a series of what I will call *behavioral* suggestions for insanity defense policymakers, scholars and other citizens. I do this since I believe that, if there is to be any meaningful insanity defense reform, it is critical that each of us begin the process of changing the way that we behave when confronted with the insanity defense and insanity defense pleaders.

I believe that such behavioral changes are an absolutely essential precondition to certain needed legal reforms. As should be clear to the reader from earlier chapters, I believe, for instance, that the Insanity Defense Reform Act of 1984 was nothing more than a pandering charade, and that Congress should abandon its return to this restrictive form of the *M'Naghten* test. The combination of this cognitive-only test, coupled with the Act's placement of the burden of

---

107. *See* H. STEADMAN ET AL., REFORMING THE INSANITY DEFENSE: AN EVALUATION OF PRE-AND POST-HINCKLEY REFORMS (1993) (in press), manuscript at 258-59.

proof on defendants (by more than the preponderance standard), leads, I believe, to an increase in the number of severely mentally disabled criminal defendants who will be incarcerated inappropriately in penal facilities.

I believe that the guilty but mentally ill verdict is nothing more than a meretricious sham, and should be abandoned. I believe that decisions such as *Barefoot v. Estelle*[108] and *Jones v. United States*[109] are cynical, outcome-determinative and cruel, and expose the worst side of this Supreme Court.[110] I believe that we must identify and expose courts' refusals to take seriously prosecutorial misconduct in insanity defense summations (that hint at likely speedy releases of defendants if insanity acquittals are entered), to make a serious effort at ferreting out prejudice in the *voir dire* process, and to inform jurors of the true consequences of a successful insanity plea. Litigants need to articulate careful arguments designed to reverse the trends reflected in these cases.

I believe that decisions such as *State v. Krol*[111] should serve as models for other jurisdictions when they are confronted with similar questions, and that state courts should, on state constitutional grounds,[112] reject the Supreme Court's decision in *Jones*. Similarly, I believe that decisions such as *Ake v. Oklahoma*[113] should be interpreted expansively, and that lower courts should study closely the decisions in *Riggins v. Nevada*[114] in attempting to restructure the fair trial rights of insanity pleaders seeking to refuse the imposition of antipsychotic medication at trial.

Yet, I believe that, even if *all* of these reforms were to be judicially and/or legislatively mandated, the incoherence of our insanity defense jurisprudence would continue. I say this because I believe that none of these legal questions focuses on the single most important inquiry that I tried to identify in my introductory chapter: why

---

108. 463 U.S. 880 (1983).
109. 463 U.S. 354 (1983).
110. *See generally* Perlin, *The Supreme Court, the Mentally Disabled Criminal Defendant, and Symbolic Values: Random Decisions, Hidden Rationales, or "Doctrinal Abyss?"* 29 ARIZ. L. REV. 1 (1987).
111. 68 N.J. 236, 344 A. 2d 289 (1975).
112. *See* Perlin, *State Constitutions and Statutes as Sources of Rights for the Mentally Disabled: The Last Frontier?* 20 LOYOLA L.A. L. REV. 1249 (1987).
113. 470 U.S. 68 (1985).
114. 112 S. Ct. 1810 (1992).

do we feel the way we do about these people?[115]

The answer to that question is to be found in the way that centuries of myths have led to sanist thoughts and practices on the part of all insanity defense decisionmakers. This sanism—abetted by heuristic reasoning and reliance on a false, alleged "ordinary common sense" and further contaminated by our authoritarian spirit—leads to pretextual judicial decisions supported by teleological reasoning. I thus conclude that it is only through behavioral change that there can be any meaningful amelioration of this jurisprudential incoherence.

2. Behavioral Recommendations

First, we must discuss the underlying issues openly. We must openly discuss sanism, identify it, and explain its pernicious impact on *all* aspects of the legal system.[116] System decision makers must regularly engage in a series of "sanism checks" to ensure—to the greatest extent possible—a continuing conscious and self-reflective evaluation of their decisions to best avoid sanism's power. As part of this strategy, we must educate judges and legislators and other policy makers as to the roots of sanism, the malignancy of stereotypes and the need to empathically consider alternative perspectives.

Sanism infects all aspects of the insanity defense process: legislators, judges, jurors, and counsel, as well as the media that report on insanity defense cases. Each and every one of these participants bears some culpability in our current state of affairs, and all must bear the burden of eradicating sanist thought and behavior.

At the same time, courts employ pretextuality as a "cover" for sanist-driven decision making. Judges must acknowledge the pretextual basis of much of the case law in this area and consciously seek to eliminate it from future decision making.

Second, it is essential that the issues discussed here be added to the research agendas of social scientists, behaviorists and legal schol-

---

115. *See supra* chapter 1, text following note 25.
116. *See* Perlin, *supra* note 13, at 407: "[We must] bear witness to sanist acts—by colleagues, other professionals, other legal system 'players,' and the public at large—and should cause us to speak up—at the faculty lunch table, on the train, at the bait and tackle shop, wherever—when sanist stereotypes are employed."

ars.[117] One example should suffice: researchers have determined that over forty percent of all sanity evaluations could be done in community settings; yet, all legislative and judicial "reforms" are geared to guarantee that more restrictive controls are placed on insanity pleaders at all stages of the process.[118] Researchers must carefully examine case law and statutes to determine the extent to which social science is being teleologically used for sanist ends in insanity defense decisionmaking. They must also study the empirical database that rebuts the empirical and behavioral sanist myths, and must confront this discontinuity in their writings. In addition, researchers must enter the public arena, and share their research findings with legislators, the media and the public.[119]

These inquiries will help illuminate the ultimate impact of sanism on this area of the law, aid lawmakers and other policymakers in understanding the ways that social science data are manipulated to serve sanist ends, and assist in the formulation of both normative and instrumental strategies that can be used to rebut sanism in insanity defense decisions.

Third, we must find ways to attitudinally educate counsel for mentally disabled criminal defendants so that representation becomes more than the hollow shell it all too frequently is.[120] We must restructure the provision of counsel to insure that mentally disabled individuals are no longer represented by, in Judge Bazelon's famous phrase, "walking violations of the Sixth Amendment."[121]

---

117. *See* Perlin & Dorfman, *supra* note 1, at 64. For a parallel example, *see* Mackay, *The Decline of Disability in Relation to the Trial*, 1991 CRIM. L. REV. 87 (urging incompetency to stand trial reform based upon empirical research findings).

118. *See* Schutte et al., *Incompetency and Insanity: Feasibility of Community Evaluation and Treatment*, 24 COMMUN. MENT. HEALTH J. 143 (1988).

119. *See e.g.*, Rogers, *Missed Opportunities: Politics, Research and Public Policy*, 35 INT'L J. OFFENDER THER. & COMPAR. CRIMINOL. 279, 281 (1991): "Just as government officials ignore research, researchers too often ignore opportunities to affect public policy. I rarely see criminologists or mental health professionals testify before the City Council when ordinances concerning crime are being considered. One rarely sees articles by researchers in the popular press where they could affect public opinion and ultimately public policy....The media only occasionally picks up tidbits to report [from scholarly journals in which researchers report their findings], and then may do so in overly simplified or sensationalized manner."

120. The same prescription applies to counsel for state psychiatric facilities. *See e.g.*, Wexler, *Inappropriate Patient Confinement and Appropriate State Advocacy*, in THERAPEUTIC JURISPRUDENCE, *supra* note 2, at 347.

121. Bazelon, *The Defective Assistance of Counsel*, 42 U. CINN. L. REV. 1, 2 (1973).

Fourth, we must create a new scholarship agenda that critically examines the questions I have raised here.[122] This agenda could, by way of example, explore the wider potential application of Martha Minow's social relations approach to insanity defense jurisprudence.

Professor Minow argues that there is a basic connectedness between individuals, that social relations theory "casts doubt on the notion that difference is located solely in the person who is different," and that attributions of difference should be sustained "only if they do not express or confirm the distribution of power in ways that harm the less powerful and benefit the more powerful."[123] A judicial strategy could adopt the social relations approach, for example, "to explore the social meanings that exclusion and isolation carry in a community."[124] If mental disability law scholars were to take Professor Minow's insights and apply them to a wide array of jurisprudential issues—including the insanity defense—this new scholarship agenda might creatively alter the predictable path of developments in this area of the law.

Fifth, system decision makers should study the steps recently outlined by John Monahan and Laurens Walker for courts to adhere to when addressing questions concerning human behavior.[125] They should then assess the potential impact on developments in insanity defense law if these steps were to be followed, as well as the extent to which adherence to these proposals could minimize teleological decision making. If courts genuinely did follow these recommendations—and, for instance, began to "evaluate...available research by determining whether the research has survived the critical review of

---

122. *See* M. Perlin & D. Dorfman, *supra* note 94; Wexler, *Changing, supra* note 2.

123. M. MINOW, MAKING ALL THE DIFFERENCE: INCLUSION, EXCLUSION, AND AMERICAN LAW 111-12 (1990). I recommend the consideration of Professor Minow's work in this context in Perlin, *supra* note 13, at 407.

124. *Id.* at 113.

125. *See* Monahan & Walker, *Judicial Use of Social Science Research*, 15 LAW & HUM. BEHAV. 571, 582-84 (1991). These steps include: (1) determining whether the law governing the case raises an issue that may make social science research relevant; (2) determining whether this empirical issue "bears on an assumption underlying a choice of a legal rule that has general applicability, a factual dispute pertaining only to the parties before the court, or a mixture of the two in which general empirical information provides a context for determining a specific fact;" and (3) in the case of issues involving underlying rules of general applicability or in the case of issues relating to a general context to be applied specifically to the parties in the case before it, looking at and evaluating any relevant research regarding the issue at hand, including determination of whether the research has survived critical scholarly review. *Id.* at 582-83.

the scientific community, has used valid research methods,...and is supported by a body of related research"[126]—the "reasoning" in decisions such as *Barefoot v. Estelle* and *Jones v. United States* is certainly less likely to be repeated in future litigation.

Sixth, we need to consider carefully the burden of heuristic thinking. Judges, like the rest of us, use simplifying cognitive heuristic devices in their thinking. Biased assimilation processes, for instance, lead to the survival and perseverance of a pre-existing set of beliefs even in light of "the total discrediting of the evidence that first gave rise to such beliefs."[127] These processes include a propensity to remember the strengths of confirming evidence but not the weakness of disconfirming evidence, and may cause an individual to "judge confirming evidence as relevant and reliable but disconfirming evidence as irrelevant and unreliable...while scrutinizing [such] evidence hypercritically."[128] Recent scholarly literature has begun to carefully assess the impact of heuristics on Supreme Court decisionmaking;[129] we need to apply this same thinking more comprehensively so as to similarly assess the behavior of expert witnesses, counsel, mental health professionals and jurors.

Seventh, we must rigorously apply therapeutic jurisprudence principles to each aspect of the insanity defense.[130] We need to take what we learn from therapeutic jurisprudence to strip away sanist behavior, pretextual reasoning and teleological decision making from the insanity defense process. This would enable us to confront the pretextual use of social science data in an open and meaningful way.

Eighth, we need to integrate insanity defense insights into all aspects of mental disability law. Mental disability is no longer—if it ever was—an obscure subspecialty of legal practice and study. Each of its multiple strands forces us to make hard social policy choices about troubling social issues—psychiatry and social control, the use of institutions, informed consent, personal autonomy, the relationship between public perception and social reality, the many levels of

---

126. *Id.* at 583.

127. Lord, Ross & Lepper, *Biased Assimilation and Attitude Polarization: The Effects of Prior Theories on Subsequently Considered Evidence*, 37 J. PERSONALITY & SOC'L PSYCHOLOGY 2098, 2108 (1979).

128. *Id.* at 2099.

129. *See e.g.*, Bersoff, *Judicial Deference to Nonlegal Decisionmakers: Imposing Simplistic Solutions on Problems of Cognitive Complexity in Mental Disability Law*, 46 SMU L. REV. 329 (1992).

130. *See supra* chapter 9 B.

"competency," the role of free will in the criminal law system, the limits of confidentiality, the protection duty of mental health professionals, the role of power in forensic evaluations. These are all difficult and complex questions that are not susceptible to easy, formulistic answers. When sanist thinking distorts the judicial process, the resulting doctrinal incoherence should not be a surprise.[131]

D. Conclusion

It is impossible to understand the current state of insanity defense jurisprudence without reflecting on the links between mental illness and sin, criminal law and theology, and the impact of medievalism on our conscious and unconscious social attitudes.[132] Despite the development of dynamic psychology and psychiatry, we have regularly rejected psychodynamic explanations for behavior because such explanations were cognitively dissonant with our need to punish:[133] we choose to reinterpret information and experience that conflicts with our internally accepted beliefs to avoid the unpleasant state that such inconsistency produces.[134] As a result, our jurisprudence has developed out of consciousness.

The development of the insanity defense has tracked the tension between psychodynamics and punishment, and reflects our most profound ambivalence about both. On one hand, we are especially punitive toward the mentally disabled, "the most despised and feared group in society;"[135] on the other, we recognize that in some narrow and carefully circumscribed circumstances, exculpation is—and historically has been—proper and necessary. This ambivalence infects a host of criminal justice polici issues that involve mentally dysabled criminal defendants beyond insanity defense decision making: issues of expert testimony, mental disability as a mitigating (or aggravating) factor at sentencing and in death penalty cases, and the creation of a "compromise" GBMI verdict.

---

131. Perlin & Dorfman, *supra* note 1, at 65-66.
132. *See supra* chapter 2 B.
133. *See supra* chapter 2 C.
134. *See* Perlin, *Morality and Pretextuality, Psychiatry and Law: Of "Ordinary Common Sense," Heuristic Reasoning, and Cognitive Dissonance*, 19 BULL. AM. ACAD. PSYCHIATRY & L. 131, 139 (1991), and *id.* at 148 n. 129 (citing sources).
135. Scott, Zonana & Getz, *Monitoring Insanity Acquittees: Connecticut's Psychiatric Review Board*, 41 HOSP. & COMMUN. PSYCHIATRY 980, 982 (1989).

The post-Hinckley debate revealed the fragility of our insanity defense policies, and demonstrated that there was simply not enough "tensile strength" in the criminal justice system to withstand the public's dysfunctionally heightened arousal[136] that followed the jury verdict. In spite of doctrinal changes and judicial glosses, the public remains wed to the "wild beast" test of 1724,[137] a reflection of how we *truly* feel about "those people." It should be no surprise that, when Congress chose to replace the ALI/Model Penal Code insanity test with a stricter version of *M'Naghten*, that decision was seen as a victory by insanity defense supporters.[138]

These dissonances, tensions and ambivalences—again, rooted in medieval thought—continue to control the public's psyche. They reflect the extent of the gap between academic discourse and social values, and the "deeply rooted moral and religious tension" that surrounds responsibility decision making.[139] They lead to sanism, to pretextuality and to teleological decision making. They seek confirmation in "ordinary common sense" and in the use of heuristic cognitive devices. Ours is a culture of punishment, a culture that grows out of our authoritarian spirit. Only when we acknowledge these psychic and physical realities, can we expect to make sense of the underlying jurisprudence.

---

136. Wexler, *Redefining the Insanity Problem*, 53 GEO. WASH. L. REV. 528, 537 (1985), *quoting* Weick, *Small Wins: Redefining the Scale of Social Problems*, 39 AM. PSYCHOLOGIST 40, 48 (1984).
137. Roberts, Golding & Fincham, *Implicit Theories of Criminal Responsibility Decision Making and the Insanity Defense*, 11 LAW & HUM. BEHAV. 207, 226 (1987).
138. *See* Milner, *What's Old and New About the Insanity Plea*, 67 JUDICATURE 499, 505 (1984).
139. Golding, *Mental Health Professionals and the Courts: The Ethics of Expertise*, 13 INT'L J. L. & PSYCHIATRY 281, 287 (1990).

Index

Abolitionist movement (against the insanity defense), 25, 133–43
expansion to other "excusing" criminal law defenses, 266–68
Hinckley verdict "fit" and, 138–42, 264
impact on number of defendants pleading NGRI, 141–42
"lemon squeezer" exception, 134
Nixon Administration position, 133–35, 342
Reagan Administration position, 140
Acquittees, insanity, monitoring of, 436
Ake v. Oklahoma, 244–45, 409, 431, 439
ALI/MPC (American Law Institute/Model Penal Code) test, 8, 426
adopted in *U.S. v. Brawner*, 87, 88, 152
discarded by Insanity Defense Reform Act (IDRA), 25
Assessment tools, use of in insanity defense test formulation, 117–20
Attribution
heuristic, 275, 298
negative, about insanity acquittees, 423
theory, 126, 303–4,
and "wrong verdict" phenomenon, 310
Authoritarianism, generally, 331–75
and public opinion, 357–60

and the death penalty, 360–69
attitudes, sources of, 365
relationship between insanity defense and death penalty decision making, 360–69
role of public opinion in formulation of death penalty jurisprudence, 364
and the insanity defense, 369–75
"Reagan-as-victim," 333–48
attacks on authority figures, 335–40
"public figures" and news media distortion, 338–39
symbolism and politics, 340–48
political and press distortions, 342–43
Reagan's role in the early 1980s, 345–48
symbolism and social policy, 341–42
the Reagan persona, 343–45
personality theory, 351–54
authoritarian personality theory, 354–57
death penalty, authoritarianism and, 360–69
attitudes, sources of, 365
relationship between insanity defense and death penalty decision making, 360–69
role of public opinion in formulation of death penalty jurisprudence, 364
insanity defense, authoritarian-

ism and, 369–75
public opinion, authoritarianism
    and, 357–60
media and, 358
Authoritarian personality traits, 355–
    57
Authority figures, attacks on, 335–39
    Hinckley compared with
        M'Naghten, 19–20
    M'Naghten, 335–37
    Reagan assassination attempt as
        twentieth century M'Naghten
        case, 337

Barefoot v. Estelle, 210–12, 391, 432,
    439, 443
"Battles of the experts," insanity de-
    fense trials as, 112, 147, 230
    myth, 112–13
Bazelon, David, 8, 85, 88, 91, 95,
    315–16, 392, 406, 414, 427,
    438, 441
"Beat the rap," insanity defense as em-
    ployed to, 16, 29, 198, 223, 232
    myth, 113–14
Behavioral changes
    as essential precondition to certain
        needed legal reforms, 438–40
    recommendations for reconstruc-
        tion of insanity defense juris-
        prudence, 440–44
Blackmun, Harry, 200, 293, 391
Brawner, U.S. v., 87, 89–91, 152, 315
    and adoption of ALI/MPC test, 87
    compared with M'Naghten, 90
    discarding of Durham "product
        test," 89
Brennan, William, 200, 301
Burden of proof
    allocation of, therapeutic jurispru-
        dence analysis, 430–31
    sanism and, 389
Burger, Warren, 151, 199, 296, 378,
    398

Cognitive dissonance, 65
    and conflicting views of psychiatry,
        214
    and inaccuracy of forensic testi-

mony, 173
Durham as cognitively dissonant
    from moral feelings of commu-
    nity, 87
judicial "OCS" and, 303–10
    in Riggins v. Nevada, 261
use of social science data and,
    412
Colorado v. Connolly, 146, 242, 261
"Community tolerance threshold,"
    182–86
Counsel, attitudinal education of, as
    recommendation for reconstruc-
    tion of insanity defense jurispru-
    dence, 441
Coy v. Iowa, 292–93
Crime, psychiatry and, 161–62
"Culture of punishment," 59–69, 382
    and rejection of psychodynamic
        principles in criminal decision
        making, 59–61

Dahmer, Jeffrey L., 137, 183–84, 273,
    403
Dangerousness (future), predictivity
    of, 165–70, 385
    false negatives, 165, 176, 271
    false positives, 165, 168
        due to representativeness heuris-
            tic, 271
Death penalty
    attitudes
        sources of, 365
        symbolism, importance of in de-
            velopment of, 367
    authoritarianism and, 360–69
        relationship between insanity de-
            fense and death penalty deci-
            sion making, 360–69
        role of public opinion in formula-
            tion of death penalty juris-
            prudence, 364
    cases, Supreme Court approach to
        social science evidence in, 414–
        15
    decision making, similarity to insan-
        ity defense decision making,
        372–74
    mental disability and, 210–26

execution of the "insane," 220–24
expert testimony and future
    dangerousness, 210–212
medicating defendants prior to
    execution, 224–26
mental disability as mitigating
    factor to jurors, 213–20
sanism and, 389
"Defendant doesn't 'look crazy' "
    (myth), 236, 252–58
sanism and, 388
Diagnosis, ambivalence of, 162–65
"Dropsy" phenomenon as example of
    pretextuality, 395–96, 398
Durham v. U.S., 18–19, 85–89, 95,
    405, 426
and rejection of *M'Naghten* and "ir-
    resistible impulse" tests, 87–88
"product test" discarded in
    Brawner, 89

Ellsworth, Phoebe, 364–65, 368–71,
    373–74
Empathy
    ambivalence of, 174–77
    explained, 174
    outlier defendants, 192
Empirical data
    and insanity defense myths, 105–
        16, 236
    "deconstructing" eight empirical
        myths, 107–14
Empiricism, alternative view on in in-
    sanity defense test formulation,
    114–16
Estelle v. Smith, 255–57
Expert witnesses
    heuristics, 283–87
    jury demand for firm conclusions
        by, 145, 162
    pretextuality and, 393–95, 400
    testimony and future dangerous-
        ness, 210–12
    trials as "battles of," 112, 147, 230
Externalities, role of in insanity de-
    fense test formulation, 100–32
    assessment tools, use of, 117–20
    explained, 100
    empirical data

and insanity defense myths, 105–
    16, 236
    "deconstructing" eight empiri-
        cal myths, 107–14
    empiricism, alternative view on,
        114–16
    moral philosophy, 102–03, 128–
        32, 278
    as solution to dilemma of "OCS"
        and "conventional moral-
        ity," 302
    scientific evidence, significance of,
        120–28
    diagnostic tools, 123
    DSM–III, 122–23
    models of mental illness, 121–25

Faking or feigning insanity by defen-
    dants
    and "differentness" between mental
        and physical illness, 249–50
    empirical studies and malingering ,
        239–41
    sanity, feigning of, 240–41
    fear of, 66–67, 134, 170
    forensic psychiatrists, testimony
        of, and, 246–47
    judicial pretextuality and, 401
    sanism and, 389
    unpacking the myth, 110–12,
        236–47
    raising of false or spurious claims
    cases resulting in insanity acquit-
        tal, 238
    to fend off execution, 223, 237
    risks of, 240
    Thomas, Justice and, 203–4, 205,
        246
Federal sentencing guidelines, mental
    disability and, 207–9, 318
Ford v. Wainwright, 245
Forensic mental health system, pre-
    texts of, 393–95
Forensic psychiatrists, testimony of,
    and fear of faking, 246–47
Forensic psychiatry, public's negative
    view of, 259–60
Foucha v. Louisiana, 145–46, 202–6,
    219, 245, 390, 402, 415

Freud, Sigmund, 44–49
Furman v. Georgia, 319, 364, 367

GBMI (guilty but mentally ill) verdict,
    27–28, 91–95, 380–81, 439
  criticisms of, 93–95
  readiness of jurors to use, 307
  therapeutic jurisprudence analysis,
    429
Giuliani, Rudolph W.
  insanity defense reform testimony,
    21–24

Halpern, Abraham, 315–18
  "justly acquitted" doctrine, 315
Heuristics, 10, 115, 128, 134, 440
  and recommendations for recon-
    struction of insanity defense ju-
    risprudence, 443
  as behavioral roots of insanity de-
    fense decision making, 269–87
  expert witnesses and clinicians and,
    283–87
  explained, 269–70
  heuristic decision making, 115
  heuristic fallacies and reliance on
    OCS, connection between,
    280–82
  "Reagan-as-victim" due to, 278–82
  simplifying heuristics, generally,
    271–78
    adjustment and anchoring, 274
    and social science data, selective
      use of by courts, 411
    attribution theory, 275
      and "wrong verdict" phenome-
        non, 310
    availability, 272–73
      susceptibility of mental health
        professionals to, 283–84
    hindsight illusion, 277
    illusory correlation, 273–74
      susceptibility of mental health
        professionals to, 283–84
    insensitivity to sample size, 271
    overconfidence in judgments, 274
    particularistic proofs, myth of,
      275
    representativeness, 271

and "wrong verdict" phenomenon, 310
susceptibility of mental health
  professionals to, 283–84
underincorporation of statistical information, 274
validity, illusion of, 272
"trial by heuristics," 270
"vividness effect," 269–70, 303
  and Hinckley acquittal, 279–80
  and "wrong verdict" phenome-
    non, 310
Hinckley, John W., 6, 13, 14–24, 35,
    95, 150, 158–60, 248, 262, 333–
    34, 338, 342, 347–48, 350, 358,
    379–81, 400, 403, 438
  as compared with *M'Naghten* case,
    19–20
  Congressional response to acquittal
    of, 17–24, 194, 279–80
  jury verdict as deviation from
    "OCS," 305, 310
  verdict's "fit" with insanity defense
    abolitionist movement, 138–
    42, 264, 319
  "vividness effect," Hinckley acquit-
    tal and, 279–80
Hostility, judicial, 179, 253,
  to assertion of civil rights against
    authority figures, 357
"Hydraulic pressure" and "tensile
  strength"
  effects on insanity defense jurispru-
    dence, 379–82
  explained, 377–79

IDRA
  see Insanity Defense Reform Act
Incarceration, effect on offenders suffering from mental illness, 68–69
Incoherence of insanity defense jurisprudence, 1–3, 12, 417
Insanity defense generally
  abolitionist movement, 133–39
    Hinckley case and, 138–39
    impact on number of defendants
      pleading NGRI, 141–42
  and death penalty decision making,
    relationship between, 360–69

arguments for reform/elimination, 17–18
as employed to "beat the rap," 16, 29, 198, 223, 232
myth, 113–14
as "loophole," 229, 257–58, 370–71
as "perfect scapegoat" for perceived inexplicability of criminal justice system, 70
as "safety valve" to nullify the law, 314
as symbol, 30–36
as victim of "willful deafness," 348–51
authoritarianism and, 369–75
decision making
similarities to death penalty decision making, 372–74
social science, teleological use of in, 116, 406–15
doctrine, development of, 73–100
fault and, 139
"lemon squeezer" exception, 134, 137
jurisprudence
"hydraulic pressure," effects of on, 379–82
incoherence of, 1–3, 12, 417
recommendations for reconstruction of, 438–45
behavioral changes as essential precondition, 438–40
behavioral recommendations, 440–44
"tensile strength," effects of on, 379–82
mens rea exception, 66, 137, 140–41, 381
"moral mistake," avoidance of, 2, 242, 380
myths
"deconstructing," 107–14
OCS and, 295–96
roots of, 229–65
"OCS" and, 295–96
pretexts and, 400–6
procedural changes in insanity defense cases as result of IDRA, 96–100
rejection by jury due to heinousness of defendant's act, 254
substantive tests, 73–100
confusion and conflation of, and sanism, 389
trials as "battles of the experts," 112, 147, 230
Insanity defense substantive tests, 73–100
M'Naghten, 15, 21, 28, 78–84, 95, 405, 426, 430, 438
criticism of, 81–83
defense of, 83–84
IDRA (Insanity Defense Reform Act) as more restrictive version, 25
stated, 80
Post–M'Naghten
Brawner, 87, 89–91, 95
ALI/MPC test adopted in, 87
compared with M'Naghten, 90
Durham ("product test"), 18–19, 85–89, 95, 405, 426
GBMI (guilty but mentally ill) verdict, 27–28, 91–95, 380–81, 439
IDRA (Insanity Defense Reform Act), 20, 25–26, 95–100, 429–30, 438
"irresistible impulse" exception to M'Naghten, 84
Pre–M'Naghten, 73–78
"good and evil," 74
"right and wrong," 76–77
"wild beast," 6, 30, 75, 105, 257, 290, 306, 319, 336
volitional element of
abolished by IDRA, 26
in Brawner, 89
Insanity Defense Reform Act (IDRA), 20, 25–26, 95–100, 159–60, 429–30, 438–39
abolition of ALI/MPC volitional prong, 26
and procedural changes in insanity defense cases, 96–100
as insanity defense reform compromise, 25

Justice Department position on, 281

Jackson v. Indiana, 202, 398
Jones v. U.S., 199–201, 203, 206, 381, 402, 409, 415, 425, 433, 439, 443
　implicit use by Supreme Court to diminish insanity defense, 334
Judicial teleology, 12
　and courts' ambivalence about role of psychiatry in adjudicative process, 145–47
Jurek v. Texas, 210
Jury behavior
　appearance of defendant and, 253–54
　authoritarianism, 356
　demand for firm conclusions by expert witnesses, 145, 162
　effect of frustration due to lack of empathy, 175–76
　expression of sanist attitudes, 317
　"hard" data, effect of, on, 153–57
　in death penalty cases involving mitigating mental disability testimony, 215–21
　"OCS" ("ordinary common sense") and, 310–29, 380
　　and diminished capacity defense, substitution of, 318
　　and individual jury verdicts, 305–7
　　jurors' reliance on, 152–53
Jury instructions, sanism and, 390
Jury nullification, 310–20
　and feigned insanity, 247
　explained, 311–12
　Halpern, Abraham, 315–18
　　"justly acquitted" doctrine, 315
Jury research, 310–29
　and psychodynamic conclusions, 320–29
　　choice of substantive insanity defense test, 321–23
　　comprehension of court's charge, 324–27
　on jury nullification, 310–20
"Justly acquitted" doctrine, 315
　distinguished from "justly responsi-

ble" test in *Brawner* concurrence, 315

Krol, State v., 198–99, 391, 433, 439

Labeling theory, 421–23
　and stigmatization of mentally ill offenders, 422–23
"Lemon squeezer" exception to insanity defense, 134, 137

M'Naghten test for insanity, 15, 21, 28, 78–84, 405, 426, 430
　criticism of, 81–83
　defense of, 83–84
　Insanity Defense Reform Act (IDRA) as more restrictive version, 25
Marshall, Thurgood, 199, 301, 364, 368
McNally, Josee, 235–36, 251, 255
Media
　depictions of mental illness by, 172–73, 252
　news, and cases involving "public figures," 338–39
Medievalism, and mental illness, 38–41
Mens rea, 21, 64, 66
　exception to insanity defense, 66, 137, 140–41, 381
Mental illness
　as (improperly) exculpatory excuse (myth), 258–61
　death penalty, mental disability and, 210–26
　media depictions of, 172–73, 252
　medievalism and, 38–41
　perceived invisibility of, 152
　sanism, and linkage between dangerousness and, 389
　stigmatization of mentally ill offenders, 422–23
Mental health professionals, susceptibility to heuristics, 283–87
Meta–myths
　explained, 7
Moore, Michael, 129–132, 306
"Moral insanity," 42–44

"Moral mistake," formulation of insanity defense to avoid, 2, 242, 380

Moral philosophy, 102–3, 128–32, 278
as solution to dilemma of "OCS" and "conventional morality," 302

Morris, Norval, 64, 135–36

Morse, Stephen, 129–32, 136, 181–82, 306

Myths, insanity defense
as informed by sensational cases pp?
"deconstructing" the myths, 107–14
"defendant doesn't 'look crazy,' " 236, 252–58
empirical data and, 9–10, 105–16
in "real life" (Josee McNally case), 235–36, 251, 255
mass media and, 136
"OCS" and, 295–96
persistence of, 229–34
public resistance to change, 230
reasons for, 232–33
political figures and, 136
roots of, 229–65
social, 10
unpacking the, 236–61
"defendant doesn't 'look crazy,' " 236, 252–58
fear of faking, 236–47
forensic psychiatrists, testimony of, 246–47
mental illness as (improperly) exculpatory excuse, 258–61
mental illness is "different," 247–51

NGRI (not guilty by reason of insanity) verdict, 21
community tolerance threshold and, 182–86
impact of abolitionist movement on number of defendants pleading NGRI, 141–42
jury research and psychodynamic conclusions, 321–22, 327
myths, 109–10

public opinion and, 357–60
therapeutic jurisprudence analysis, 424–27
treatment of persons found, 198–207, 381

Nixon, Richard M.
insanity defense abolition attempts, 133–35, 342

Nonsanist opinions, 391–92

"OCS" ("ordinary common sense"), generally, 287–329
and "conventional morality," 300–2
moral philosophy as a solution to dilemma of, 302
and deviance, 297–99
and individual jury verdicts, 305–7
and insanity defense, 295–96
"instrumentalist perspective," importance of, 296–97
and judicial "cognitive dissonance," 303–10
attribution theory, 303–4
and "wrong verdict" phenomenon, 310
and jury behavior, 310–29
and diminished capacity defense, substitution of, 318
and individual jury verdicts, 305–7
and other dissonances, 308–10
and social science data, selective use of by courts, 411–12
as sanism, 296
as unconscious animator of legal decision making, 287–94, 440
connection between heuristic fallacies and reliance on, 280–82
Hinckley verdict as deviation from, 305, 310
jurors' reliance on, 152–53
jury research, 310–29
and psychodynamic conclusions, 320–29
jury nullification, 310–20
relationship between law and, 298–99

Penry v. Lynaugh, 223–24

Perry v. Louisiana, 224–27
"Planful" behavior, 30
    and rejection of insanity defense
        claims, 380
    by fact finders, 215
    by jurors, 245, 255
"Pretextuality," 393–406
    and insanity defense abolitionist
        movement, 142
    and mental disability cases, 396–
        400
    and quality of counsel, 404–5
    and recommendations for recon-
        struction of insanity defense ju-
        risprudence, 440
    and social science data, selective
        use of by courts, 411–12
    and the insanity defense, 400–6
    courts and, 194–95
        feared pretextuality, 399
    "dropsy" phenomenon as example,
        395–96, 398
    expert witnesses and, 393–95, 400
    explained, 11, 393–94
        social purposes of, 395–96
    judicial, in insanity defense cases,
        306, 401–4, 440
    therapeutic jurisprudence, use of, to
        combat, 419
Procedure
    importance of, in development of
        substantive insanity defense
        doctrine, 96–100
    therapeutic jurisprudence analysis,
        430–31
Psychiatric method, the law's ambiva-
    lence about, 161–70
    crime, psychiatry and, 161–62
    dangerousness, predictivity of fu-
        ture, 165–70, 385
    diagnosis, ambivalence of, 162–65
Psychiatrists
    as wizards or charlatans, 155–61
    court distrust of, 246
    forensic, testimony of, and fear of
        faking, 246–47
Psychiatry
    as "soft," "exculpatory," and "con-
        fusing," 147–51

as "unseeable" and "imprecise,"
    151–55
the law's ambivalence about, 144–
    61
Psychiatry and psychology, develop-
    ment of, generally, 37–49
    and forensic psychiatry, public's
        negative view of, 259–60
    dynamic, 41–49
        Freud, Sigmund, 44–49
        "moral insanity," 42–44
    pre–dynamic, 37–41
        medievalism, 38–41
    symbolic role of in the determina-
        tion of insanity defense cases,
        32–33
Psychodynamic principles
    as tempering societal need for pun-
        ishment, 64
    in criminal decision making, rejec-
        tion of, 59–61
    specific rejection of in insanity de-
        fense decision making, 171–86
    "community tolerance thresh-
        old," 182–86
    empathy, ambivalence of, 174–77
    sympathy, paradox of, 178–82
Psychodynamic principles, the law
    and, 143–227
    psychiatric method, the law's am-
        bivalence about, 161–70
    crime, psychiatry and, 161–62
    diagnosis, ambivalence of, 162–
        65
    dangerousness, predictivity of,
        165–70
    psychiatrists as wizards or charla-
        tans, 155–61
    psychiatry
        as "soft," "exculpatory," and
            "confusing," 147–51
        as "unseeable" and "imprecise,"
            151–55
        the law's ambivalence about,
            144–61
Punishing the mentally ill, the law's
    ambivalence about, 187–226
    death penalty, mental disability
        and, 210–26

execution of the "insane," 220–24

expert testimony and future dangerousness, 210–12

medicating defendants prior to execution, 224–26

mental disability as mitigating factor to jurors, 213–20

federal sentencing guidelines, mental disability and, 207–9

insanity defense, role of in, 192–94

NGRI, treatment of persons found, 198–207

psychiatry, role of in the legal process, 194–98

the "right" to punish the mentally disabled, 188–92

Punishment, role of in development of insanity defense jurisprudence, 49–69

as ritual, 55–57

as socially-sanctioned "safety valve," 57–58, 62, 379

"culture of," 59–69, 382

and rejection of psychodynamic principles in criminal decision making, 59–61

major aims of, 51–53

psychodynamic principles as tempering societal need for punishment, 64

social role of, 51–55

Reagan, Ronald, 50, 149, 331–32, 350

and role of presidents as "father figures," 346

as symbol for "get-tough-on-crime" positions, 346

"-as-victim," 278–82, 333–48

attacks on authority figures, 335–40

symbolism and politics, 340–48

political and press distortions, 342–43

Reagan's role in the early 1980s, 345–48

symbolism and social policy, 341–42

the Reagan persona, 343–45

heuristics, reliance on, 343–44

Reagan Administration position on abolition of insanity defense, 140

Recommendations for reconstruction of insanity defense jurisprudence, 440–45

Rehnquist, William, 186, 194, 203, 222–23, 233, 255–57, 261, 292, 296, 408–9

and "OCS," 287–89

as "buying into" faking/feigning meta-myth, 244–45

Riggins v. Nevada, 216–20, 390, 391, 402, 415, 435, 438

Right to refuse treatment, therapeutic jurisprudence analysis, 435–36

Sanism, 139, 385–86

and recommendations for reconstruction of insanity defense jurisprudence, 440–41

and the insanity defense, 387–92

"common sense" as, 296

explained, 11, 183, 296

judicial decision making and, 201, 440

nonsanist opinions, 391–92

stereotypes and myths, 276, 297–98, 385, 388–90

therapeutic jurisprudence, use of, to combat, 419

Sanity, feigning, 240–41

Scalia, Antonin, 213, 245, 292–93

Scientific evidence, significance of in insanity defense test formulation, 120–28

diagnostic tools, 123

DSM–III, 122–23

models of mental illness, 121–25

Social science

and teleology, 116, 406–15

and the insanity defense, 413–15

data and the law, relationship between, 406–7

evidence in death penalty cases, Supreme Court approach to, 414–15

selective use of, 409–12

heuristic devices, use of, 411
suspicion, judicial, psychodynamics
    of, 407–9
Steadman, Henry, 98, 111, 116, 141–
    42, 179–81, 280, 322, 438
    and Joseph Cocozza, 358
Stereotypes
    and attribution theory, 275–76
    and labeling theory, 421–23
    and sanism, 296, 297–98
    excessive use of by authoritarian
        personality, 355
Stigmatization of mentally ill offend-
    ers, 422–23
Strickland v. Washington, 405
"Substantial professional judgment"
    test, 387
Suspicion, judicial, psychodynamics
    of, 407–9
Sympathy
    and juror responses to individual
        defendants, 178
    and press coverage of famous ath-
        letes, 182
    jury nullification and, 312
    paradox of, 178–82

Teleology
    and recommendations for recon-
        struction of insanity defense ju-
        risprudence, 441, 442
    and use of social science data by in-
        sanity defense decision makers,
        116, 406–15
    judicial, 12, 440
        and courts' ambivalence about
            role of psychiatry in adjudi-
            cative process, 145–47
        therapeutic jurisprudence
            strategy as counterweight
            to, 419
"Tensile strength" and "hydraulic
    pressure"
    effects on insanity defense jurispru-
        dence, 379–82
    explained, 377–79
Therapeutic jurisprudence
    and recommendations for recon-

struction of insanity defense
    jurisprudence, 443
and the insanity defense, 419–37
    monitoring of insanity acquittees
        in community settings, 436
    non–responsibility verdicts, 419–
        29
        GBMI verdicts, 429
        labeling theory, 421–23
            and stigmatization of men-
                tally ill offenders, 422–
                23
        NGRI verdicts, 424–28
    post–acquittal procedures, 433–
        35
    procedural rules, 430–32
        burden of proof, 430
        other procedural issues, 431–
            32
    substantive standard, 429–30
    treatment of institutionalized de-
        fendants, 428–29, 435–36
explained, 12, 417–19
other issues for consideration, 436–
    37
use of
    as counterweight to courts' teleol-
        ogy, 419
    to combat sanism and pretextual-
        ity, 419
Wexler, David, 26, 183–85, 423,
    433–35
Thomas, Clarence
    dissent in Foucha v. Louisiana, 145–
        46, 203–5, 245, 390, 402
    dissent in Riggins v. Nevada, 217–
        18, 390, 402
Typification, 298, 304
    and "wrong verdict" phenomenon,
        310

"Vividness effect," 269–70, 303
    and Hinckley acquittal, 279–80
    and "wrong verdict" phenomenon,
        310
Volitional element of insanity test, 89–
    91
    abolition of ALI/MPC test by

IDRA, 26
adoption of ALI/MPC test in *U.S. v. Brawner*, 87

Wainwright v. Greenfield, 256, 408
"Walkthroughs," explained, 4
Washington v. Harper, 225, 391
Wexler, David, 26, 183–85, 423, 433–35
"Why do we feel the way we do about these people?" 3, 439–40
sanism, 383–92
"Wild beast"
characterization of mentally ill as, 177, 188, 192

test for insanity, 6, 30, 75, 105, 257, 290, 306, 319, 336
"Willful blindness," 6, 309, 381
"Willful deafness," insanity defense as victim of, 348–51
"Wrong verdicts," significance of, 264–68, 310
as compared to unpopular verdicts based on other "excusing" criminal law defenses, 266–68
fear of, 320
IDRA as means to reduce number of "mistaken" verdicts, 97–98